CU00693148

The Mercat Anth
of
Early Scottish Literature

THE MERCAT ANTHOLOGY OF EARLY SCOTTISH LITERATURE 1375-1707

Edited by

R.D.S. Jack and P.A.T. Rozendaal

First published in 1997 by Mercat Press
This revised edition published in 2000 by Mercat Press
This short run edition first published in 2008 by John Donald

ISBN-13: 978 1 906566 00 5

The publisher acknowledges subsidy from the Scottish Arts Council, and an award from the Deric Bolton Poetry Trust, towards the publication of this volume

Typeset in Goudy Old Style by Servis Filmsetting Ltd., Manchester
Printed and bound in Great Britain by Bell & Bain Ltd., Glasgow

Contents

Appendix

CRITICAL INTRODUCTION
Where Stands Scottish Literature Now?

Forthi I seye, as I seyde er, by sighte of thise textes
Whan alle tresors arn tried, Truthe is the beste.
(Therefore I say, as I have said before, from the sense of these texts, when all treasures are tried out, Truth is the best.)

William Langland, *Piers Plowman* I,134-5

Anthologies, by their very nature, are influential in determining the way readers look at a subject. If one looks at the Medieval and Renaissance periods in Scottish Literature through the lens of either *The Oxford Book of Scottish Verse* (1966) or *The Poetry of Scotland: Gaelic, Scots and English* (1995) it is clear from the choices within them that the earliest writers from Barbour until Lindsay are highly valued; that the period from 1560 until the Union of the Crowns causes problems, and that the seventeenth century is not well regarded at all.[1] Strangely, however, the Renaissance poets who suffer in this way are not deemed markedly inferior to English writers in literary anthologies covering the broader range of British literature within that period. *The New Oxford Book of Seventeenth Century Verse* (Fowler, 1991) grants forty-four pages to Scottish poets in direct chronological competition with the 'Golden Age' of Shakespeare, Jonson, Donne and Milton.[2] The writers concerned—James VI, Drummond, Ayton and Alexander—are allotted two pages in the MacQueen/Scott anthology, none at all in Watson. This essay seeks to explore the reasons behind this strange situation. It seeks to redefine the accepted canon and suggest an alternative way of approaching Scottish literary history.

That a major oddity exists is indisputable. In which other European literature do the words 'The Renaissance' refer to early twentieth century literature (MacDiarmid and Muir) rather than the advent of humanism? The implied loss of the first Renaissance along with the assumed bleakness of the seventeenth century allows serious study to overleap, chronologically, the Union of the Crowns in 1603 and the Union of the Parliaments in 1707. Serious literary study of 'Scottishness', on these terms, may begin without undue attention being paid to writing within the crucial period when national identity was sacrificed. Further, a national literature which chooses to excise about a century and a half of its own history sends out a clear message to critics in other countries that they need not trouble themselves with the Scottish contribution during the Renaissance, and that only the ballad is worth contemplating.

This is not all. The situation, in Alice's terms, becomes 'curiouser and curiouser' when one compares evaluative assessments of the period in modern 'Scottish' and 'British' anthologies. Most anthologists and literary historians who adopt the former perspective quietly acquiesce in the view of T. F. Henderson as adopted in his *Scottish Vernacular Literature: A History*. In the Renaissance section of that study, published in 1900, Henderson made an exception of Alexander Scott (fl. 1550) and Alexander Montgomerie (fl. 1580) but excluded all others on grounds of linguistic treachery (i.e.

1. *The Oxford Book of Scottish Verse*, edited by John MacQueen and Tom Scott (Oxford, 1966) provides a fuller Renaissance selection than *The Poetry of Scotland: Scots, English and Gaelic*, edited by Roderick Watson (Edinburgh, 1995).
2. *The New Oxford Book of Seventeenth Century Verse*, edited by Alastair Fowler (Oxford, 1991).

anglicisation). First amongst Henderson's 'traitors' stands James VI: 'Scottish vernacular prose as well as poetry virtually terminates with James VI'.[3] But John Knox vies with him for the post of major anti-hero in an account which places linguistic treachery at the centre of the argument and whose evaluations are undisguisedly nationalistic. Henderson's thesis—that the successors of the late and great medieval makars abandoned Middle Scots for English, intentionally and treacherously—remains, to-day, a keystone of critical belief for most students. Scholars within the later periods do not trust so naively. But this is an age of specialism and it is a convenient mythology which relieves one, both qualitatively and patriotically, of the need to cover the mass of creative and critical endeavour in the field adjacent to one's own.

Henderson's views were to be echoed in the 1930s and 1940s by a much more powerful voice, that of Hugh MacDiarmid. Coming from an overtly anglophobic position and finding himself without a subtle national language, it is unsurprising that he should view Henderson's thesis sympathetically. In *Lucky Poet* (1936), he echoed the broad conclusions of that source: an alliance of 'philistinism' in 'the Scottish Kirk' with cultural treachery at court had indeed combined to initiate a time of shame, beginning in the 1560s and accelerating towards full-scale realisation in 1603:

> At that time, Scottish culture was still vigorously but hopelessly without direction and becoming increasingly divorced from the real national situation. Owing to the difficulty of initiating what ought to have been the task before the age in Scotland as it was elsewhere in Europe—namely the evolution of renaissance literature in the vernacular, incorporating the lessons learned from the Humanists...the literature becomes royalist and episcopalian as well as circumscribed in outlook.[4]

In fact, James VI in his rhetorical treatise, *The Reulis and Cautelis* of 1584, had done all of these things. But the Scottish Text Society edition of that work did not appear until 1948 and Henderson, on whom MacDiarmid often relied, had dismissed the *Reulis* as 'trite' without discussing their content.

The fact that his opinions were corroborated by Edwin Muir is of supreme importance. Not only was Muir the other major voice of the later Scottish Renaissance—he and MacDiarmid disagreed on practically everything except this! When, in *Scott and Scotland*, Muir also lamented the loss of a 'homogenous language', he approached the ensuing authorial dilemma from a psychological and post-Romantic perspective, defining it as follows: 'Reduced to its simplest terms, this linguistic division means that Scotsmen feel in one language and think in another.'[5] His remedy—to opt for 'English'—was diametrically opposed to MacDiarmid's search for a form of Synthetic Scots. Inescapably, however, they were agreed on the nature of the illness and, as it happened, on its causes and time of origin. They also agreed with Henderson in blaming Calvinism, a movement which had proved itself 'adverse both to the production of poetry, and poetry itself' (pp. 18, 24-5); in dating the origins of the perceived linguistic decline in the 1560s and 1570s and in finding Scott and Montgomerie to be talented exceptions:

> Since some time in the sixteenth century, Scottish Literature has been a literature without a language. Middle Scots survived Sir David Lindsay for a while in the lyrics of Alexander Scott and Montgomery. But a little later, Drummond of

3. T. F. Henderson, *Scottish Vernacular Literature: A History* (London, 1900; Edinburgh 1910) p. 333.
4. Hugh MacDiarmid, *Lucky Poet* (London, 1936) p. 206.
5. Edwin Muir, *Scott and Scotland* (London, 1936; reprinted Edinburgh, 1971) p. 22.

Hawthornden was already writing in pure English. (p. 18)

With the name Drummond of Hawthornden, the third villain of the Scottish literary paradigm enters the scene. Highly valued by his English contemporaries, Drayton and Ben Jonson, Drummond's status as a talented poet is supported in a British, seventeenth-century context by Alastair Fowler. No fewer than twenty-seven poems by Drummond are cited in his anthology.[6] Tom Scott and Rory Watson are committed by their own defined remit to include English works. Yet Scott, who edits that part of the *Oxford Book of Scottish Verse*, opts for a single sonnet; Watson ignores Drummond entirely.

Strange though this may seem, the uniformity in negativity on the Scottish side of the equation is as daunting as it is impressive. Scott and Watson, in choosing to fill the gap left by seventeenth century literature with the entire ballad selection regardless of date, tacitly adhere to another perjorative judgment, advanced by Henderson and seconded by the MacDiarmid-Muir alliance. During the Renaissance in Scotland, it is claimed, an uninspired, élitist court not only paid homage to a foreign muse, they also scorned popular music and art. These achieved their highest quality in the ballad, being primarily associated with the 'harpers and violers...of the Borders' (Muir p. 163). Throughout the seventeenth century, therefore, the folk alone maintained Scottish culture until it was, as marvellously as belatedly, re-discovered in the eighteenth by that patriot among poets or poet among patriots, Robert Burns.

Neither MacDiarmid nor Muir had much effect on the academic curriculum in the late 1950s and early 1960s, when I was a student. The Great (English) Tradition of Leavis determined the canon and, within it, Scottish writers were marginalized. However, a number of benevolent influences were coming together which would transform that picture. John MacQueen at Edinburgh, Tom Crawford and Matthew MacDiarmid at Aberdeen and Alexander Scott at Glasgow began to raise the academic profile of Scottish writing. Crucially, in America, Ross Roy founded *Studies in Scottish Literature*, the first academic journal to suggest that this was a legitimate area of research.

I did not feel that the Leavisite tradition was, in itself, a bad route to follow. I was introduced to poetry and prose which moved and impressed me greatly. In retrospect, however, I came to see that its sins of omission had given me an unhealthy disregard for all those Scottish authors I had never even read. If they were not 'set', they must in some sense be flawed. Such is the subtle power of the academic canon. For those of us who shared this feeling, Kurt Wittig's alternative path, as described in *The Scottish Tradition in Literature*, proved appealing. One patterned arrangement of texts governed by predetermined English criteria was to be answered in kind by another, essentially Scottish, one. 'In Scotland, a different set of traditions has created a society which in many respects (though not all) is very different from that which exists in England.'[7] These were to be isolated: 'In expounding these values I have picked out the ones which seem to me specifically Scottish and have largely ignored the rest.' (p. 4) Self-evidently, this paradigm would not favour those periods which aligned themselves closely with either English language or poets. The Renaissance in particular would find it more difficult to establish its credentials under Wittig than Leavis.

While this was theoretically true, those of us who specialized in that period were as free to open up new territory as anyone else. A spirit of optimism and discovery dominated

6. Fowler, *Seventeenth Century Verse*, pp. 202-23. Drayton is also granted 22 pages. This compares favourably with the 31 pages granted to Donne and Jonson. On this rough evaluative equation, Ayton ranks with Davenant and Waller.

7. Kurt Wittig, *The Scottish Tradition in Literature* (Edinburgh and London, 1958) p. 3.

the entire range of Scottish Literature as studied in the late 1960s and 1970s. However anglicised the Scottish Renaissance might have appeared to Wittig, his principles acted as a catalyst rather than defining in delimitation what was distinctively 'Scottish' and what was not. As a result Helena Shire's *Song, Dance and Poetry at the Court of King James VI*[8] spearheaded an impressive series of critical books, editions and anthologies centred on the very authors proscribed by Muir and MacDiarmid. Indeed, it is not too much to claim that the Castalians of the late sixteenth century and the Scoto-Britanes of the seventeenth were re-discovered by a paradigm which, taken at face value, ought to have buried them.

In the 1980s and 1990s, much of this optimism has disappeared so far as Medieval and Renaissance Scottish literature is concerned. One need only reflect on the comparative publishing situation. In the 1970s four editions of James I's *Kingis Quair* existed; now there are none. The fact that this anthology will be the only one available for students who wish to gain an overview of three centuries of achievement is, for me, a source of sadness.[9] A deal of the blame, however, rests with those of us who specialize within the field. As one who has published in a variety of periods, I have the strong sense that there is a growing communication gap especially between pre- and post-1707 scholarship. The critical bias of the earlier group remains (even in this theoretical age) staunchly biographical and historicist.[10] This conservatism has meant that attempts to influence the broader discipline from within the literature of nationhood have been rare, leaving more ambitious accounts to those whose interests lie in the eighteenth century or later. I find the recent studies by Robert Crawford and Cairns Craig powerful and convincing but both concentrate rigorously on the post-1707 period.[11] My own views may, in this sense, be regarded as complementary. The degree to which they are also revisionary remains to be explored.

These trends take place at a time when a novel premise has entered Scottish education. Early literature, I am frequently told, is either too difficult or too irrelevant for students. In my own University, the first year Scottish Literature course allots forty-five weeks to the Enlightenment until present day period, much of which is already taught in schools. The supposedly more difficult sixty per cent of the chronological range is introduced in five weeks, via the Dunbar and Henryson selections in the MacQueen-Scott anthology. True, the synchronic and interdisciplinary biasses in literature generally have followed a similar course. But while more established literary traditions can turn these innovations to their advantage, the newer area of Scottish literary studies has had more difficulty in adapting to them. In practical pedagogical terms, they have played their part in re-opening a gap within the perceived history of Scottish Literature, which had been closing twenty years ago.

The Reformation and Renaissance periods, which had in the 1960s and 1970s made their own modest claim for a place in the curriculum, are again excluded. The

8. Helena Shire, *Song, Dance and Poetry at the Court of King James VI* (Cambridge, 1969)

9. The first and earliest volume of *Scottish Literature: An Anthology*, edited by David McCordick (Frankfurt am Main, 1996) appeared while this work was in preparation. Its coverage of the Renaissance is closely in line with our own but its methodology and proposed audience are markedly different.

10. There is some excuse for this. Alastair Fowler has recently noted that the early stage of work in that period gives 'the old-fashioned bed-rock scholarship' of the contributors a power which it would not have elsewhere. Review of *The Renaissance in Scotland*, edited by A.A. MacDonald et al (Leiden, 1994), *The Library*, 1996.

11. They define their remit honestly. Robert Crawford in *Devolving Scottish Literature* (Oxford, 1992) posits a loop structure from the eighteenth century to the present day; Craig in *Out of History* (Edinburgh, 1996) makes the same chronological delimitation. (The appearance more recently of Marshall Walker's *Scottish Literature Since 1707*, London 1996, continues this trend.)

idea of a continuous literary history has little or no support. Rather, we are in danger of following, critically, Barbour's 'Romantic' method, as exemplified in the first excerpt in this anthology. He mythologized the past, purifying the image of Robert the Bruce and blackening that of Edward I, so that his patriotic appeal in the present might be more affectively effective. But he did so self-consciously, carefully and under artistic licence. Can we when purifying Dunbar, blackening Drummond but effectively ignoring them both to concentrate on the political agenda of the present make the same apology? And can we be excused if, in the laudable name of interdisciplinarity, we produce students who are happiest when the textual evidence can be related to the criteria of other disciplines but who find the specifically literary aspects of analysis beyond them?

From 'Scots Alone' to a 'Variety of Voices'

What are the problems inherent in Wittig's evaluative model? In particular, why does it tend to produce a broken line in literary history and set author-heroes against author-villains? First, it measures contrastively against another, larger literary tradition—'different from...England'. Secondly, it does so in terms of 'traditions' and 'values'. Wittig's first criterion narrows the range over which examination may take place. His second permits a list of non-literary entrance preferences to be accumulated. A simplifed list of these would certainly include:

Writing in Scots	(The language of the Scot)
Writing unpretentiously	(The down-to-earth Scot)
Writing on Scottish themes	(The patriot Scot)
Writing from a democratic viewpoint	(The democratic Scot)

Inevitably, this makes it more difficult for some authors—for example, those who write manneristically in English on universal themes from a right wing viewpoint—to enter the introductory curriculum. Textual choice will be influenced as well—Muriel Spark is almost always represented by her 'Edinburgh' novel, *The Prime of Miss Jean Brodie*; Walter Scott by *Waverley* rather than *Quentin Durward* or *Ivanhoe*. Translated into English terms, this is analogous to preferring *Henry IV* to *Othello* because it is Italian or *Macbeth* because it is Scottish.

This helps to account for the thinner line of acceptable texts—they have to satisfy not only the test of quality within the discipline itself—they must all be acceptably 'Scottish'. Early literature is particularly vulnerable to this approach on three grounds. As Barthes notes, the logic of this sort of pattern or paradigm is first of all to dehistoricize, secondly to polarize and thirdly to do so retrospectively. 'In passing from history to nature, myth acts economically; it abolishes the complexity of human acts, it gives them the simplicity of essences, it does away with dialectics, with any going back beyond what is immediately visible.'[12] Therefore, when 'differentiated Scottish values' are applied, they tend to produce the simplifed antitheses of 'treacherous James VI' against 'patriotic Burns' noted above.

Whatever may be said for or against the Leavisite Great Tradition, it was inexorably founded on evaluative criteria determined within the literary discipline. This view was shared by the medieval makars. When Barbour and Henryson seek to define the unique brand of 'truth' which separates their art from history or theology, they are still aware of attacks on it as 'triviality' or 'lies':

12. Roland Barthes, *Mythologies* (London, 1984) p. 143.

Tharfor I wald fayne set my will,
—Giff my wyt mycht suffice thartill—
To put in wryt a suthfast story.
(§ 1: *Bruce*, 11-15)

Thocht fenyeit fabils of ald poetre
Be not al grunded upn truth, yit than,
Thair polite termes of sweit rhetore
Richt pleasand ar unto the eir of man...
(§ 14: *Morall Fabillis*, I, 1-4)

As we shall see, the early and later makars follow Aristotle, Aquinas and Dante in mounting a specialized defence for their art based on the powers of 'imagination' and 'analogy'.

To-day, there are different views on which of these approaches should recommend itself. In the context of this argument, I am only concerned to note that a tradition which seeks to draw modern concepts of interdisciplinarity into the original selection process works against the views held by the writers it seeks to judge. After all, why was verse so much preferred to prose; why were both prose and verse called 'poesy' in the Renaissance period and why is Urquhart's prose *Jewel* so self-consciously 'poetic' in its use of images and language if there was no belief at that time in a clearly defined world of artifice, with its own distinct rules? Verse marks it off, while 'labouring' to acquire its skills is consistently demanded from the author.[13]

In adopting a diachronic approach, I shall only advance the most widely shared views on literature and aesthetics as supported by the makars themselves. This will avoid the pitfall of creating my own eclectic patterning of the evidence in areas where sources disagree. The argument begins with the clash on language between modern poets and their predecessors, for it is this variance, above all, which sets up the evaluative opposition between the supposedly patriotic, golden age of Middle Scots against the treacherous, 'pure English' of the Renaissance.

The fact that the evaluative *literary* league table as presented by Henderson and maintained by most critics to-day is a fairly exact reflection of the perceived health-in-distinctiveness of the 'Scottis' tongue is not wholly accidental. In order, it reads:

1) The Middle Scots Makars (1480-1520)
2) The Early Makars (1375-1480)
3) The Later Makars (1520-1560)
4) Marian and Castalian Poets (1560-1603)
5) The Scoto-Britanes (1603-1700)

If one assumes that the 'pre-requisite of an autonomous literature is a homogenous language' (Muir, p. 19) then the creation of a national tradition and evaluation within it will reflect that tenet. Nor is it an unusual idea. To-day, minority groups often rally behind a linguistic banner—French for the French-Canadians; Basque for the Basques. Whether the same may be assumed in the case of Scotland the Nation, centuries ago, is another question.

Was 'Scottis' the accepted, homogenous literary language of Scotland in earlier times? Once the historical dimension to that question is opened up and one looks at

13. See § 14 Henryson, 'Prologue' to *Moral Fables* st. 2; § 15; Douglas, *Eneados*, Prologue Bk 1, 109-10.

origins, it becomes clear that the answer is 'No'. The dialect known as 'Scottis' has no claim to be the original national tongue. In fact, if there were any politico-linguistic 'treachery', it was that which resulted in 'Scottis' gaining dominance over the native Gaelic. At the end of the thirteenth century Malcolm Canmore and David I had intentionally 'driven Gaelic back to (virtually) the present highland line'.[14] Scots originated as Northumbrian English and only grew later into proud distinctiveness, because of the positive sociolinguistic forces inherent in nationhood.

Unsurprisingly, therefore, lowland Scottish writers from the fourteenth century until the seventeenth almost always claim to be composing in 'Inglis' and seek their poetic origins south of the border. Dunbar eulogises his master, Chaucer, in *The Goldyn Targe*, posing the rhetorical question 'Was thou noucht of oure *Inglisch* all the lycht,/ Surmounting eviry tong terrestriall,/ Alls fer as Mayes morow dois mydnycht?' (§ 7 st. 29: 7-8) Only in two instances do the writers of that time call their language 'Scottis'. The limitations of the nationalist claims made in this way by Gavin Douglas and James VI will be discussed later.

The loss of the 'nationalist' prop to the icon of the 'homogenous national literary language' inevitably makes the easy identification between anglicization and treachery untenable. It also reminds the critic that the ideals of a past age may not coincide with those held to-day. If one relates these findings specifically to the three supposed villains of Scottish culture, it confirms the sophistry on which their supposed guilt is constructed. Knox and the Calvinists are accused of writing in English; James VI is accused of anglicisation because he was a patron of an English Bible which bears his name. Those who advance these complaints are engaged in a perfectly proper quest for national identity. They should, however, remember that the aims and ideals of others may differ.

Knox and James are on a different, theological quest directed at opening the hidden Latin Word of God to the widest possible reading audience. Where, if at all, does one find contemporary anger at this form of anglicization? Initially, it might appear that David Lindsay voices it. In the *Satyre* one character does voice patriotic anger at a Bible in English:

Quhat buik is that, harlot, into thy hand?
Out, walloway, this is the New Testament
In Englisch toung, and printit in England!
Herisie, herisie! Fire, fire, incontinent!
(I, 1152-4)

But that character is a Vice, Flattery. He is at once corrected by the voice of Divine Truth:

Forsuith, my freind, ye have ane wrang judgement,
For in this Buik thair is na heresie,
Bot our Christs word, baith dulce and redolent
Ane springing well of sinceir veritie.
(I, 1155-8)

The Bible referred to is the 1561 Geneva Bible which, by a Scottish law of 1579, had to be possessed by every householder whose income exceeded three hundred merks.

14. Janet M. Templeton, 'Scots: An Outline History', in *Occasional Papers* (Association for Scottish Literary Studies), ed. by A J Aitken, II, 1973, 4-11.

If this evidence reminds us that free choice between a Scots or an English version of any book did not exist in the days of early printing houses, it also moves the argument into the second iconic area—that of the 'homogenous' language. Printing was done in Edinburgh but London was the main centre of production. This caused the sort of anglicisation which can be observed by comparing the two openings of Montgomerie's *Cherrie and the Slae* in § 16. Montgomerie's earlier 'Scots' version (Waldegrave) is nonetheless more anglicized than the Middle Scots of Dunbar. The later version—printed after his death—may not give evidence of the *poet*'s changed practice but of printing house policy in London.

The problems of evidence in this area are many. I raise them because the paradigm behind traditionalist criticism interprets the idea of linguistic 'homogeneity' in a strange way. It simplifies the contrastive search by viewing the languages of the past as if they moved abruptly from one extreme and fixed state to another at the behest of poets and dramatists—so 'Middle Scots' becomes the 'pure English' of Drummond after the Union of the Crowns because the late 'makars' chose to anglicise. In fact, languages are themselves in a constant state of gradual flux under the influence of much broader sociolinguistic pressures. The Reformation and the invention of printing would have been strong enough catalysts on their own without the prospect of Union. As Jespersen notes, 'It is self-evident that, where we have previously divided states combining under a single government, the chances of a common language being evolved are so much the better. The court, the government have occasion for a language which will carry its message to all the inhabitants.'[15] When the prospect of a Union centred in London beckons, therefore, anglicisation may result from the social change itself. When the distinctive tongue of the smaller nation (in this case) 'Scots' is itself a dialect of 'Inglis' and has dubious patriotic roots, anglicisation cannot simply be viewed as treachery. Yet on that premise the 'Tradition' is based and the excision of the Renaissance founded.

It is tempting but sophistic to avoid the effort of research as Muir does. 'The reasons for this disintegration of the language of Scottish literature are controversial and I have no space to enter into them here' (p. 18). The logical sidestep permits him an easy return to the static and polarized model which presents the fewest challenges to his own case. It also brings that case out of actuality into the realm of myth.

James VI and the poets who went south with him after the Union of the Crowns did not betray a homogenous nationalist language when anglicising their work. Nor did they anglicise from one linguistic extreme ('pure' Scots) to another ('pure' English). Middle Scots at the end of the fifteenth century was already closer to English than it was when the century began. At the other 'pole', the English into which James VI amended his own writings still contained Scotticisms according to Charles I.[16] Robert Ayton's manuscripts provide the best example of this process as they exist in earlier and later states and do contain some authorial revisions.[17]

Revising those poems for publication shortly before his death in 1638, Ayton confirms the essentially pragmatic, non-nationalist view of language development as argued in this essay. But he also notes that Scottish poets are accustomed to using different voices when composing, thus challenging the idea of linguistic homogeneity from another angle. Sir John Ayton notes that he included 'old Scots peeces, w[hi]ch were done in his younger dayes. The lattin ones were publisht...in the *Delitiae Poetarum Scotorum*

15. Oscar Jespersen, *Mankind, Nation and Individual from a Linguistic Point of View* (Bloomington, Ind., 1946).
16. See *The Poems of James VI of Scotland*, edited by James Craigie, 2 vols. (STS: Edinburgh, 1958) II, xli.
17. Matthew P. McDiarmid, 'Some Versions of Poems by Sir Robert Aytoun and Sir William Alexander', *Notes and Queries*, 4 (1957) 32-5.

in his owne tyme.' The passing of time introduces a third, more anglicised group because 'the style of all vulgar Languages changes every age.'[18]

A comparison between poems existing in both the earlier Edinburgh manuscript, dated prior to the Union, and the post-Union London MS, reveals thorough but not wholesale anglicisation. In the 'Scottish' Edinburgh MS of 'Will thow, remorsless fair', the Scots form 'mycht' (l. 15) and the English 'might' (l. 13) exist as acceptable alternative forms within two lines of each other. In the 'English' Manuscript, Ayton follows James VI's practice of retaining Scots forms where they have special force or are not easily replaced by an English equivalent.[19] For example, in 'Ane Dyor', 'since syne' (l. 23) and 'Stygian stankes' (l. 53) emerge from the Edinburgh MS's 'sen syne' and 'stygeoun stankes'. Each involves only partial anglicisation. This maintains the alliterative power of the text, in obedience to James's earlier advice that patriotic Castalians should 'let all (their) verse be literall als far furth as may be' (§ 22 *Reulis* Chap. 3).

Ayton's assumption that any Scottish author may move easily from Scots-English to Anglo-Scots and to Latin constitutes another attack on the idea of the homogenous language, but it does so with specific reference to their understanding of literature's position among the branches of knowledge. All early writers defined their discipline rhetorically—that is, as a branch of persuasive oratory. Within this scheme, linguistic variety rather than homogeneity was the key to success. That earlier Scottish writers saw and evaluated their work in this way is easily proved. Henryson obeys the 'polite termes of sweit rhetore' (§ 14 st. 1); Douglas wishes to match Vergil's 'sawys in sic eloquens...so inventive of rethorick flowris sweit' (§ 15 ll. 69-70); the rules and warnings to be observed and avoided in James's treatise of that name are those of Rhetoric. Rhetorical adaptability-in-variety was more important for them than safeguarding one dialect with dubious claims for patriotic primacy. Indeed Gavin Douglas, James VI and Sir Thomas Urquhart argue explicitly that linguistic internationalism—in the sense of drawing coinages from other tongues—is the only way in which a vernacular may eventually surpass the subtlety of Latin.

Scottish Literary History: Seeking Continuity

In seeking first of all to distinguish Scottish Literature broadly from English Literature through rhetorical differentiations within the discipline rather than values outside it, I am not returning to an antiquated pattern, irrelevant to modern thought. The word 'rhetoric' covers practically all the headings of practical criticism, other than meaning. Diction, imagery, figures of speech, form and the proposed 'ends' of effective persuasion all come within its remit, as does the decorous relation of style to topic. The 'rhetorical' school education, which turned Robert Burns, on his own evidence, into an expert on 'how' to compose in the mid-eighteenth century,[20] had much in common with the educational philosophy of Scottish schools in the 1950s and early 1960s.

18. *The Poems of Robert Ayton*, edited by Charles B Gullans (Edinburgh, 1963) p. 261. The reference to the *Delitiae* of 1637 suggests the date; Ayton died in 1638 and, perhaps because of this, the proposed volume did not appear.

19. James's narrative poem, *The Lepanto*, shows how early anglicizing procedures in relation to the printed word began. Even for the 1591 edition from Waldegrave's Edinburgh printing house, the king made substantial changes to his manuscript version (Bodley 165). Comparison also reveals the king's loyalty to his own rules in retaining the sounds of Scots when no English equivalent is available. This applies in the lower stylistic range and to alliterative formulae especially. In the London print, the Archangel Gabriel imitates a Scots wind, which 'From hilles can hurle *ore heugh*', gaining 'speed *aneugh*' to clinch a Scots rhyme.

20. *The Letters of Robert Burns*, ed. G. Ross Roy, 2nd edn. (Oxford, 1985) 2 vols. I, 135 (no. 125: To Dr John Moore).

Language and Literature are examined together in the Scottish examinations rather than inhabiting different curricular areas as in England. The logic behind this is the Medieval one of 'making'. Until one knows how word-buildings are constructed, there is little point in looking at texts, simple or elaborate. Within this 'how', resides the unique qualities and qualifications of the imaginative discipline. 'What' is said is relevant but it is not quidditative. The literary laurel goes to the best craftsman in his creative uniqueness, not to the writer with whose sentiments one happens to agree, as William Alexander argues in *Anacrisis*.[21]

Nor am I suggesting that early writers were opposed to interdisciplinarity. As the interlinking patterns of the Seven Liberal Arts demonstrate, the *end* of imaginative persuasion was interdisciplinary in its fullest sense. The findings of the literary discipline were vitally related to and enriched other areas of knowledge, including sociology and politics. Aesthetic thought in the Medieval and Renaissance periods was itself comprehensive and pragmatic. Dante, following Aristotle's argument from causality, defined that end as 'removing those living in this life from a state of misery and bringing them to a state of happiness.'[22] That is—literature fed into all knowledge on an open and intertwining pattern. But it could only do so with dignity, once its claim for uniqueness had been established. Aristotle did not begin his *Poetics* by launching into the rules of that art—he began by lamenting its lack of an identity and a name—'The form of art which uses language alone...has up to the present been without a name.'[23]

He then highlighted those qualities which made that art unique and gave it different rules. It did not deny truth on the literal level because it was not primarily concerned with 'is' but with 'might be'; it sought neither the simple truth of 'was' like the historian nor 'ought' like the philosopher. Instead, by embracing imagination as its chosen faculty of the soul, it sought out 'universal truths' in the manner of the latter but tested them through a fuller, more fanciful remit than the former. From Barbour's presentation of Robert I as a 'family hero' constructed out of his grandfather's biography as well as his own (§ 1), by way of the Morals to Henryson's *Fabillis* with their repeated directions that the audience imagine a supposed case ('may weill be applicate' etc. § 4) to James VI's repetitive emphasis on 'Inventioun' as 'ane of the cheif vertewis in a Poete' (§ 22), that vision unites the literature of the Scottish nation before the Union of the Parliaments.

But surely it also unites the literature of any Western European nation within that period? True, but there are ways in which the Scottish interpretation of Scholastic and Humanist thought recognizably differs from English. As a starting point, let us look at the position of Henderson's 'terminator' of vernacular Scots.

James VI opens his *Reulis* with an apology. He excuses the work for being 'late' and 'thin', a doubly negative judgment shared by traditionalist critics, when comparing Scottish Literature with English Literature throughout the period. The truth of this is undeniable. But two more positive contrasts emerge from the same literary evidence. First, James's treatise gives evidence of his great *learning*. To compose a work of this sort while still in one's teens is quite remarkable. Secondly, that treatise gives notice of his intention to lead the Scottish Renaissance as patron of a *professional* group of poets. Early Scottish Literature is, on an English model, comparatively late, but its writers are

21. § 23. 'I condemn their opinions, who, as they would include all perfection in one, do prefer someone with whom they sympathize, or whom they have most practised, to all others...I like the phrase, stile, method and discreet carriage of Virgil; the vigour and variety of invention in Ovid; the deep judgement and grave sentences of Horace and Juvenal...'

22. Dante, 'Epistle to Can Grande'.

23. Aristotle, *Poetics*, Chap. 1.

almost all academic in the strict sense of that term. From Barbour to Urquhart, they are practically all degree holders or expensively educated noblemen.[24] The paid post of 'laureate' or chief poet is held by the 'maister poetis' Alexander Scott and Montgomerie before any equivalent post was thought of south of the border. The first literary difference resulting from this is their trained, critical and more analytic response to the freer European models they inherit.

This produces a more analytic and self-consciously erudite kind of art than that practised in England, making clear but ambitious demands on its audience. In the Prologue to his *Fabillis*, Henryson's emphasis on 'labour' and 'diligence' (sts. 2, 3) echoes the view of rhetorical handbooks that the best art is also the most demanding. Scotland's erudite writers held on to this view for much longer than their English counterparts. How, then, does this view of authorship influence the traditional negative judgements in narrowness and tardiness?

I am not challenging the evidence. When, for example, we consider Scottish writing before Henryson in relation to its English counterpart, it is correct to note comparative modal thinness (Where are the modes other than Romance? Where is the movement towards prose?). It is correct to note chronological lateness (Where is Scottish literature at the time of Langland and Chaucer?). I am concerned with the causes producing these symptoms. I am also suggesting that we are not comparing like with like. The academic basis of Scottish writing suggests that it should first of all be related to the ideals of the rhetorical text-books which its authors had studied. From these, three major guidelines emanate.

(i) Poetry is prioritised because it is more difficult and artificial than prose.

(ii) Imaginative oratory is thought of as embracing the lyrical, narrative and dramatic voices. These are counterpointed on the analogy of music.

(iii) Texts at their most demanding contain all themes potentially within the one structure.

To follow each of these lines through Scottish Medieval and Renaissance literature is, in fact, a simple task because the writers themselves are anxious to explain their craftsmanship in precisely those terms.[25] What follows is only a brief résumé of the wealth of evidence available.

Verses and Voices: One tends not to question one's own most basic assumptions. When a modern critic finds a lot of poetry, little prose and scarcely any drama, he is thinking against a twentieth century background of genres, printed evidence and a predominantly prose-dominated culture. When he or she finds prose romances developing in England but Scotland retaining verse alone (or even, in the case of *Golagros and Gawane*, returning a later prose version to its origins in verse) it is easy to assume that the innovatory movement must hold the high ground. The contrary case could be argued—that Scottish 'makars' remained true to the more difficult forms of craftsmanship.

After all, in the Middle Ages and early Renaissance, writers composed with aurality

24. There are very few exceptions to this rule. The University affiliations of the early makars are as follows: Barbour (Paris); Henryson (?Glasgow; a European University); Dunbar (?St Andrews); Douglas (Glasgow). The Castalians were described as one of the most 'learned' groups in Europe, while Drummond (Edinburgh), Ayton (St Andrews), Alexander (Glasgow) and Urquhart (Aberdeen) continued the erudite line. The Neo-Latin poets, led by Buchanan (St Andrews, Aberdeen, Bourges) were, by definition, well schooled. Add the private education of James I, Mary and James VI and the European tours conducted by the few (e.g. Montgomerie) for whom no evidence of University allegiance is extant.

25. In teaching, I find it easier to explain rhetorical theory using Scottish writers as an example for the same reasons.

and oratory in mind. Sir Philip Sidney, it has been noted, could still refer to all literature (including prose) as 'poesie'. For the trained mind, literature began with imagination and aimed at maximising the distance between normal speech and art. Scotland holds on to that preference throughout the later Renaissance and Restoration periods as the critical views of Alexander confirm. In the *Anacrisis*, Alexander accepts that prose Romances exist. Indeed he is proud of his own contribution to Sidney's *Arcadia*.[26] But his method of analysis retains the older rhetorical priorities. Xenophon he finds worthy of praise because he has shown 'with what grace and spirit a poem might be delivered in prose'. That is—all imaginative writing is poetic. Verse and prose are two means of achieving poetry, with the touchstone of difficulty-in-artifice granting priority to the former. It is no coincidence, therefore, that arguably the greatest verse-poet (Dunbar) and prose-poet (Urquhart) specialize in such 'poetic' virtuosity. Dunbar's 'Hale, sterne superne' celebrates the Virgin Mary appropriately by adopting the most demanding of rhyme schemes and skilfully counterpointing the themes and motifs surrounding Mary. That hymn and the parodically self-conscious high-style of *The Jewel* may seem overly manneristic or even eccentric to those who are looking for couthy Scots. They are, nonetheless, the logical zenith in complexity of the literary theory which sustained the more overt and self-consciously Rhetorical tradition in Scotland until the late Victorian period at least. David Masson's writings show that the Professor of Rhetoric and Belles Lettres at Edinburgh University still placed Dickens above other prose writers *because* he was more poetic than his rivals. In the early years of the twentieth century, his student, J. M. Barrie, is still capable of writing of a 'descent' from verse to prose.[27]

The maintained preference for poetry over prose in Early Scots is accompanied by another critically self-conscious retention of an older categorisation—that of voices. In the early days when aurality ruled, the division of writing into narrative, dramatic and lyrical voices was natural. With recitation and a listening audience in mind, the early makars were adept at stylistically signing a move from one voice to another. Lyrical setpieces, such as the song of the birds in st. 34 of the *Kingis Quair* or the orisoun to Mary in Holland's *Buke of the Howlat* (ll. 716ff), were frequently favoured. The difference, in comparison to an English model, lies in the tenacious retention and development of this interlacing model by later writers. A comparison between Henryson's *Testament of Cresseid* and Chaucer's *Troilus and Criseyde* reveals the Scottish schoolmaster using the most up-to-date critical vocabulary, when justifying his 'new' version of her later years:

> Quha wait gif all that Chauceir wrait was trew?
> Nor I wait nocht gif this narratioun
> Be authoreist or fenyeit of the new
> Be sum poeit throw his inventioun,
> Maid to report the lamentatioun
> And wofull end of this lustie Creisseid,
> And quhat distres scho thoillit, and quhat deid.
> (§ 6 st. 10)

Henryson's invention is not, however, limited to 'excusing' the heroine. Instead of following Chaucer's literary methods he chooses to judge her within a consciously

26. The short linking passage needed to join the 'Old' *Arcadia* to the 'New' was written by Alexander.
27. See my discussion of Masson and the continuity of the Scottish Rhetorical tradition in *The Road to the Never Land: A Reassessment of J. M. Barrie's Dramatic Art* (Aberdeen, 1991) pp. 121-3. Masson, *British Novelists and their Styles*, p. 2: 'The novel, at its highest, is a prose epic'.

patterned and moralised poem-pattern. Within this, clear changes from narrative to dramatic and lyrical voices helpfully guide the audience as to how the material is being organized.

The three lyrical complaints of Cresseid are separated from each other by narrative and dramatic portions, but one 'hears' the same voice returning. If one follows this counterpointing pattern and compares shared 'voice' sections, important echoes and variations emerge. These are not confined to the lyric sections but the lyrical highlights may be used as an obvious example of the method. Cresseid's first two soliloquies are complaints. In the first, she blames her fate 'Upon Venus and Cupide angerly' (st. 18); in the second a greater awareness of the effects of her conduct is balanced by an even wider divine attribution of guilt to all 'Our craibit goddis' (st. 51). In the third lament, she not only accepts moral responsibility ('Sa elevait I was in wantones', st. 77) but modulates her voice into the tones of penitence and righteous amend-making. The exemplary purpose of the poem is, therefore, underlined by the rhetorical principle of repetition and variation.

This careful signing of meaning through form translates exactly a basic tenet of rhetorical theory. The image of the poet-builder ('makar') as interpreted by Hugh of St Victor implies that the author-architect must first plan the entire structure of his word-building according to a design suited to the needs of the consumer. Only once that has been done may the author as artisan lay out the first brick-words in the line of his text. In terms of 'difficulty' Geoffrey of Vinsauf advised good writers to leave it to beginners to organize their tales in the simple 'natural order' (from start to finish). Advanced craftsmen would, like Henryson, plan according to one of the many 'artificial orderings' available, perhaps beginning in the middle or coming full circle, depending on its suitability for their chosen theme.

As Scottish poets also prided themselves on having a wide linguistic range, it was an obvious move to build on this significant linking of form and meaning by using stylistic as well as vocal variety to highlight the key movements within the chosen design. Dunbar's *Goldyn Targe* (§ 6) and *Tretis of the Twa Mariit Wemen and the Wedo* (§ 7) counterpoint the line of the tale against circular and overlapping structures respectively. They also sign changes, tonal and thematic, by moving from one style to another. In the *Tretis*, for example, the Latinate high style and narrative voice of the opening suggests that these ladies, 'all full of flurist fairheid', are noble in character. Later, there is a change to the dramatic voice and the middle style, whose pragmatism and verbal ambiguity make the audience wonder whether they have been tricked—'Think ye it nocht ane blist band that bindis so fast?' Finally, the low style lyricism of the first wife's diatribe—'I have ane wallidrag, ane worme, ane auld wobat carle...'—confirms that we have literally been 'made' to read the signs wrongly. This is no idyll of love but a bitter satire, dressed up to look like an idyll. Language, as all else in medieval literature, is significant. A skilled makar may use the signs to confirm or to subvert our anticipations.

That the decorous linking of style and theme was a major tenet for Scottish writers throughout the Medieval and Renaissance periods is confirmed by the comments and practice of the writers themselves. Douglas notes the difficulties in *Eneados* I, Prologue ll. 67-78; 105-124. James VI in his *Reulis* outlines the essentials of the method:

> Ye man lykewayis tak heid, that ye waill your wordis according to the purpose.
>
> Gif your purpose be of love, to use commoun language, with some passionate wordis.

> Gif your purpose be of tragicall materis, to use lamentable wordis, with some heich, as ravischt in admiratioun.
>
> (§ 22 Chap. 3)

James's most obedient apprentice, Stewart of Baldynneis, obeys these rules to the letter throughout his analytically conceived[28] abridgement of Ariosto's *Orlando Furioso*. In Canto 11 (§ 17) he moves from the pastoral high style of 'Reverent Ovid' (C. 11: 11) to the 'tumbling' vein, recommended by James for low topics and states of mind, when describing Roland's madness. He even explicitly comments on the decorous necessity of so doing: 'this bailfull bittir blast,/ Quhilk dois my style renverse in disaray' (C. 11: 29-30). At the start of the next Canto, he will announce the reversal of the process, 'I change my sang, quhilk soundit sad befoir,/ From dolent dyt to joyfull verse againe' (C. 12: 5-6). In the poems as a whole, he ranges through all styles from the dignified Ciceronean rhythms of the high style to the alliterative, staccato tones of the lowest; Latin borrowings vie with French and Dutch as he rings the changes on a vast variety of rhetorical figures (e.g. underwriting) and tropes (e.g. impossibility topos).

Themes and Thoroughness: The close linking of style to theme is a leitmotiv which is even more firmly forged in the Renaissance by James VI in the *Reulis*. His account of decorum is unusual in carrying that essentially stylistic system into the area of argument—that is from rhetoric to dialectics. A poet should think not only of high, middle and low styles but of noble, ordinary and mean ways of advancing an argument:

> This is lykewayis neidfull to be usit in sentences, als weill as in wordis.
>
> (§ 22 Chap. 3)

Those who find the work of the makars modally or thematically narrow must, therefore, be sure that they are reading the signs correctly.

The Early Scots period (§ 1-3) will illustrate the issues clearly. Those who regret the domination of that period by the Romance mode are looking only at the story-line and modal surface. As 'makars', Barbour and his contemporaries may have moved artlessly from one voice to another but they were every bit as well-versed as their successors in signing theme through structure. The story-line cannot be divorced from the moral patterning and the shared journey motif in *Bruce*, *Quair* or *Rauf*. In seeking guidance on what these poems are about, therefore, one looks first at their 'signing' form. If one does this, it becomes clear that practically all of the early Scottish Romances—*Golagros* and *The Buke of the Howlat* as well as those represented in the Anthology—counterpoint the natural line of the story against artificial arrangements of the material. Usually the latter traces a circular structure. *The Bruce*'s ordered national journey opens and closes with a pilgrimage (Bks. I and XX),[29] James's personal quest from Venus to Minerva to Fortune begins and ends 'Heigh in the hevynnis figure circulere' (sts. 1 and 196), while *Rauf's* parallel hospitality scenes offered in cottage and castle are framed by the alpha and omega of 'harbery', St Julian and the deeds of temporal mercy used by Christ as his test for entry into heaven in Matthew 24. 33-46 (st. 5 and st. 75). This complex form—line, pattern and circle—was advocated for tales which embraced not only a particular tale but its moral sense as understood within God's mysteriously benign purpose. These are not only Romances—they comprehend, within the one potential structure, as many themes as they have voices to proclaim them. The particular story of Bruce's

28. See § 17 C 5, 1-22.

29. Books I and XX even have the same number of lines—630.

victory over the English or James's victory over self is also an exploration of everyone's dark journey through the moral tests of life in search of the ineffable light beyond death.

Henryson's re-workings of Chaucer's 'Nun's Priest's Tale' and *Troilus and Criseyde*, with their more overt transitions from tale to moral, particular to conceptual, take this principle of analytic thoroughness into the Middle Scots period. In the Renaissance, this highly self-conscious, if reactive poetics continues. In part, it is reflected in a reluctance to abandon the allegoric method; in part, it is mirrored in a preference for non-allegoric modes which lend themselves to the clear transmission of ideas. Montgomerie's *Cherrie and the Slae* (§ 16) is an example of the first; the Scottish Sonnet (§ 18) and the Pastoral (§ 19) of the second.

Montgomerie's allegory makes some concessions to a new age. Composed for court performance, it maintains the light tones and dancing rhythms which C. S. Lewis detected behind all Castalian verse.[30] Nonetheless, the idea of establishing a central theme at the literal level (cherrie/aspiration v. slae/contentment) and then moving it through romantic, political, philosophical and spiritual forms of examination is as clear in this work as in James's *Quair*.

Once more, critical theory justifies poetic practice. As the highest mysteries are conceived through the image of the harmony of the spheres, so the text which contains within itself the largest number of potential interpretations mirrors most closely in words the divine intention of the Word and the interrelations of the Book of Nature. Henry of Ghent's model as set up for the theologian was swiftly adapted to 'the allegory of the poets':

> The appropriate mode for this branch of knowledge is not that all the individual things relating to it should be treated separately...but that disparate themes and tenets should be contained in one and the same discourse, tailored to suit different individual needs and abilities.
>
> (*Summa Quaestiones* XIV. i. vii.)

Thus, while each listener will interpret differently, each will draw sense at the level to which their capacities delimit their needs.

On the advice of James VI, the earlier Scottish sonnet form during the 1580s and early 1590s preferred a wide range of themes to the more conventional love emphasis practised later and discussed above. If this meant, at one pole, more moral and religious sonnets than were common south of the border, it implied at the opposite pole more bawdy sonnets, such as Stewart's hostess sonnets, the convivial sonnets of Montgomerie or the wittily obscene sonnets of Ayton (§ 18). Before and after the Union of the Crowns, Scotland's major sonnet sequences continue this bias. They are clearly structured, analytically conceived and comprehend the idea of love in its broadest sense. The methodology may differ—Fowler's *Tarantula of Love* traces the lover's ascent, rung by rung, up the Ficinean ladder of love from lust to charity; Drummond's series of sequences celebrate, in turn, the lady in life, in death, as idea of beauty and as image of God; William Alexander in *Aurora* wrestles with the philosophy behind Petrarchism while Alexander Craig offers seven mistresses each representing one element of the passion, from Lais the courtesan at one extreme to Idea as the type of platonic love at the other.

Pastoral poetry is another mode with an obvious appeal for learned, professional poets. It provided a perfect vehicle for a self-conscious poetics, concerned with the

30. C. S. Lewis, *The Allegory of Love* (Oxford, 1936) p. 259.

exploration of themes through a variety of voices. The first element is highlighted by Harold Bloom, when he comments that the great pastoral elegies are as much if not more concerned with 'their composers' creative anxieties' as with grief.[31] Literary theory and practice walk hand in hand through the pastoral grove. Like the sonnet it is a form ideally suited to argue its themes thoroughly from one extreme to another. In another sense, it provides the major Renaissance analogue for the 'open' Romance form, as practised in early Scots. The brevity of the sonnet form implies that different poems or sequences are needed to provide exhaustive coverage of a topic in the manner defined by James. The thematic definition of love, from its lowest manifestation in lust, through the various possibilities of human passion to its implications moral and divine, is as easily comprehended within the Renaissance pastoral as in Medieval allegoresis. That is because the image of the shepherd lends itself to the kind of analogous transference so dear to early poetics.

As such, it recommends itself to the learned Scottish tradition with its desire to embrace thematic and tonal extremes. In § 19, the divine shepherd (Christ) and the shepherd priest lie behind *Teares on the Death of Moeliades*. Less idealised transferences, with the shepherd as a type of bucolic simplicity or rustic lewdness, produce the comic pathos of Henryson's *Robene and Makyne* or the bawdy wordplay of Ayton's 'The Shiphird Thirsis'. As early as Theocritus's *Idylls* with their 'constant juxtaposition of high and low throughout',[32] Pastoral had established the interplay of extreme voices as one of its major defining conventions. In this way it also naturally harmonized with the biasses of the Scottish multi-vocal tradition.

This mode, which allows many worlds to meet and produced Shakespeare's *Tempest* as well as Milton's *Lycidas*, therefore becomes a favoured vehicle for the Scottish Renaissance. Yet it is exiled from the traditional Scottish canon on two erroneous suppositions. Its use, decorously, of English is confused with linguistic disloyalty and it is simplistically equated with its idealistic and rarified strain alone.

Does this not make early Scottish literature in all its periods too challenging to be either enjoyable or widely comprehensible? The danger is present but care is taken to avoid it. Although Scottish authors range deeply and widely, they usually delimit and explain the area within which they are working. Henryson extracts one line from the broader narrative canvas of Chaucer. 'Of his [Troilus'] distres me neidis nocht reheirs' so only 'the wofull end of this lustie Creisseid' needs tracing *and* moral evaluation, 'I sall excuse, als far furth as I may'. The morals in his *Fabillis* may move from actual to potential with great freedom but the precise symbolisation and specific area of hidden meaning selected are usually explained—'To our purpose, this cok may we call/Nyse proud men, void and vaneglorious'.

In the Renaissance, Stewart of Baldynneis follows exactly the same procedures. Faced with Ariosto's loosely constructed and busy epic, he sets about controlling the material analytically:

> The historie all interlest I find
> With syndrie sayings of so great delyt,
> That singlie, most I from the rest out spind,
> As the unskilful prentes imperfyt
> Quho fyns the gould frie from the laton quyt.
> (§ 17 C. 5, 9-13)

31. Harold Bloom, *The Anxiety of Influence* (Oxford, 1973) p. 151.
32. Judith Haber, *Pastoral and the Poetics of Self-Contradiction* (Cambridge, 1994) p. 14.

This is not an unrelievedly humble modesty topos, as the reference to refining alchemically anticipates. Stewart may simplify and 'abridge' by focussing only on the major hero and heroine, he also claims that his work is gold refined from the common metal of Ariosto by adding a serious moral and religious conclusion to the Italian's epic. While this meets the higher extremes of thorough analysis, he also extends the bawdy episodes surrounding the lustful hermit's attempts to rape Angelica.

More particularly, Stewart's *Roland*, like Henryson's *Testament*, originates from a critical decision to simplify a complex tale ('mak my passage plaine', Invocation l. 4) and ends with the decision to add spiritual correction for one character. In Stewart's case, it is the hero, Roland, whose 'maladie' is 'mended' (12.84); in Henryson's it is Cresseid. Within a circular poem pattern whose invocation both anticipates Roland's final madness and 'signs' his holy death, the adventures of hero and heroine are discussed alternately, setting up a parallel structure which invites comparison and contrast. Even Henryson's desire to interpret Cresseid's love allegorically as the battle between reason and passion recurs as a leitmotiv in Stewart's poem—'quhair luife dois reule no resone may refraine' (4.1).

I am not suggesting that Henryson is a source; I am suggesting that Stewart follows in the same learned, professional and critically self-conscious tradition. Many of the shared poetic features result inevitably from that perspective. Stewart's six introductions to the *Roland*, each of which praises his would-be patron and proves his learned skills by denying them, are an extreme plea for the patronage which Henryson passes over lightly. But the hundred years which separate them cannot disguise the school to which both belong.

This view of early Scottish Literature finds its distinctive voice in comparison to English precisely in the antitheses of the canonical values used by the traditionalists to test it. Not in linguistic homogeneity but in vocal variety; not in couthiness but in greater erudition; not in simplicity but in controlled complexity; not in naturalism but in a different approach to artifice do the makars make their claim to be different. Using Scots alone, couthiness and the language of the market to discover 'difference' is not, therefore, just misleading. It is perverse.

Discovering a Dramatic Voice: From this viewpoint, it becomes clear that the definition of drama has to be re-considered. If one thinks of the 'dramatic voice' within a general poetics of performance rather than looking solely for theatres and playscripts, a wider range of dramatic evidence is uncovered. Of course, a new perspective, however well authorized, will not magically convert weakness into strength. At the same time, an approach which opens the full linguistic and topical range in obedience to the views of the writers themselves, may offer a more sympathetic account and discover 'national distinctivenesses' in areas excised by modern expectations.

Does the literary way lead into a more optimistic view of the impoverished realm of Scottish drama, apparently inhabited by Lindsay's *Satyre* alone? Certainly, it avoids the English (in this case atypical) contrastive bias of the paradigm. Nowhere else in Europe, with the possible exception of Spain, did the popular theatre of the Renaissance enjoy so spectacular a revival as in England. Elsewhere, one would be looking at a humbler and broader range of dramatic evidence more in line with Scottish practice.

As Scottish rhetorical theory maintained the ideal of poetry-in-performance within a view of art centred on 'modes' and 'voices', it is also misleading to think in clear-cut generic categories. What look to us like verses to be read were often sung or recited. Montgomerie's *Cherrie and the Slae* was probably sung with one or many voices. The flyting between *Montgomerie and Polwart* was certainly performed.

As verse remains the superior means for the makar on the twin grounds of greater artifice and greater difficulty, the divisions between poem and play are blurred in another way. David Lindsay's *Ane Satyre of the Thrie Estaitis* and the anonymous farce, *Philotus*, are clearly intended for enactment. Yet, both are set out stanzaically and use overt rhetorical changes from high-style to low-style stanzas to sign dramatic or thematic developments. Both have commentators and lengthy narrative sections; both interweave song and dance. Indeed *Philotus* opens with three stanzas which could well be a love lyric while Lindsay's Diligence, when advising the audience about what is to come, states:

> Thairfoir, till all our rymes be rung
> And our mistonit sangis be sung,
> Lat everie man keip weill ane toung
> And everie woman tway.
> (§ 12 *Satyre* I: 70-77)

These polyphonic and intertwining structures, being based ultimately on the mysterious harmony of the spheres, were regarded as one of the highest and most demanding types of art. The Scottish men of letters, learnedly aware of that fact, again cherished them more self-consciously and held on to them longer than in England.

The analytic structuring of Scottish verse forms is every bit as striking in *Ane Satyre* and *Philotus* as in poems where narrative or lyrical voices dominate. The first Act of the *Satyre* cures the poisoned head of the realm while the second advances to the body; questions of kingship lead into the satire of the three estates proper. *Philotus* follows a different but equally controlled scheme of dramatic development. Based on classical conventions, it traces the four major movements which commentators distinguished when analysing Plautus or Terence. As Evanthius differentiates protasis ('the first act and the beginning of the play proper') from epitasis ('the forward progression of the turmoils'); catastrophe ('the reversal of affair') from the discovery ('cheerful outcome'), so the anonymous Scottish author in turn sets age against youth; uses disguise and trickery to complicate matters; allows true intentions and identities to be revealed and finally permits young love to triumph.[33]

A decorous search for the Scottish dramatic 'voice' rather than dramatic playscripts serves to broaden one's modal anticipations when searching for evidence. Think not only of Shakespeare and the Globe theatre but of private stages, of pageant plays and interludes such as Montgomerie's *Navigation*. Think of open air performances, on hill or in church, where preachers—perhaps the most popular actors of their day—acted out the bitter theological and political dramas of the Reformation period. Think of translations from European pastoral drama, such as Ayton's from Guarini's *Il Pastor Fido*. Above all, think of George Buchanan. In Neo-Latin verse drama, Scotland led Europe.

Royal entrances and celebrations were devised and written by Fowler, by James himself and by Drummond (§ 19 *Forth Feasting*). William Alexander's description of his Senecan Tragedies as 'Tragicall Poemes' does not, of itself, consign them to the category of 'drames du fauteuil'. One would expect such a description even for enacted pieces at that time within that critical context. It is the lack of theatrical evidence and their stolidly reflective texture which might lead a critic to that conclusion. Consider the tenacity of the folk drama traditions of Robin Hood and other figures of the green

33. See Marvin T. Herrick, *Comic Theory in the Sixteenth Century* (Urbana, 1950) p. 59.

world, which scholars have found in legal and court records.[34] Cross to the lyric and contemplate James's demand that the Scottish sonnet be adapted for purposes of 'argument' or return to the intense debates between Dunbar's widow and the two wives, described (like *Philotus*) as a *Tretis*. Think rather of the dramatic voice in prose and there is the witty, fictive debate form of Maitland's *Pretended Conference*. Finally, pass to Urquhart's Admirable Crichton, master of all voices as lyrical lover, gifted story-teller and inspired actor/debater.

Urquhart is the proper end of this linguistic journey in another sense. In the period of Cromwell and the Restoration, he claims for himself verbally (through his Universal Language) and stylistically (through the poetic-dramatic-narrative amalgam of *The Jewel*) the status of the rhetorical alchemist, who synthesizes quintessentially all the rhetorical virtues I have claimed for Scotland's distinctively learned, professional poetics. And he does so thematically in a plea for attention to be paid to Scotland's distinctive excellences. Lists of heroes in diverse fields give way to mysterious fusion once more, this time within the perfect 'figure' of Crichton, who excels in all instantaneously. To see the modest aims of Barbour in the late fourteenth century continuing through three centuries and culminating with the extravagant virtuosity of Urquhart is not, I think, an unhelpful or misleading way of viewing the unique rhetorical route traced by the makars.

Broadening the Field

(i) Allegorically: Now that a distinctive rhetorical identity has been forged for the makars on their own terms, it is possible to look more closely at the ways in which this affects their understanding of what constitutes the proper language of literature. Once linguistic variety has replaced linguistic homogeneity as the principle behind their thinking and any idea of anglicisation as treachery been removed, the field for consideration will broaden. Within that field, as re-defined, the comparative literary picture in relation to English will be further developed and the broader nationalist or patriotic distinctions re-contextualized.

The three remaining canonical tests as listed on p. xi are all unreliable. The idea of 'writing unpretentiously' is an entirely inappropriate criterion for testing literary quality in an age when all imaginative writing used 'vocabula artis' (poetic diction). One does not write spontaneously but follows rules which will make 'your wordis *appeare* to have cum out willingly and by nature' (§ 22 James: *Reulis*, Ch. 3). The canonical tests of writing from a democratic viewpoint and seeking political themes make no allowance for the hierarchical model of the world and its values as accepted in the Middle Ages ('At the top of this hierarchical and interlaced structure stand the good life and God rather than politics and humane concerns'[35]). These were still present in the Renaissance—'In the late sixteenth and the early seventeenth centuries the traditional Tudor idea of order continued to explain social reality, albeit less convincingly as the years passed.'[36]

The procedure of one set of premises beng applied to judge another may be simply exemplified. None of the makars would have disagreed with Henryson's claim that the

34. Hamish Henderson, 'The Ballad and Popular Tradition to 1660' in *The History of Scottish Literature*, 4 vols. general editor R. Cairns Craig (Aberdeen, 1989) Volume I: *Origins to 1603*, edited by R.D.S. Jack, p. 273; John J. McGavin, 'Robert III's "Rough Music": Charivari and Diplomacy in a Medieval Scottish Court', *Scottish Historical Review*, LXXIV, 1995, 144-58.
35. Alastair Fowler, *A History of English Literature* (London, 1987) p. 29.
36. Stephen L. Collins, *From Divine Cosmos to Sovereign State* (Oxford, 1989) p. 15.

narrative, fictive line of their stories was a means of conveying ideas. The latter (allegorical) part of this 'prolixitee off doubilnesse' (§ 3 *Kingis Quair*, st. 18: 1-2) is the all-important kernel within 'the nuttis schell' (§ 14 Prologue, *Morall Fabillis*, st. 3). Wittig, programmed to look at the story-line for 'Scottish values' opens Henryson's *Testament* and defines the wintry spring setting as a distinctively Scottish, geographic trait. In fact, the narrator has made it perfectly clear that he is not weather-forecasting. The spring he describes *must*, under the rules of rhetoric, resemble winter as a sign that the poem's theme is one of disorder at all levels—'Ane doolie sessoun to ane cairfull dyte/Suld correspond and be equivalent' (§ 5 *Testament* st. 1: 1).

The extended category of Allegory describes the various levels of reference served by imaginative writing. Its comprehensive model contains the single line of nationalist concern but at the lowest (tropological) level of priority. Of equal potential relevance but higher status within the metaphysical view of that period stand spiritual concerns (allegory)[37] and ontological issues (anagogy). In short, this is a world which prioritises the divine mysteries. To look *only* for political concerns is to seek for one subordinate line within its interlinked patternings.

Even within the relevant (tropological) area, a clear distinction was made between moral theory and practice—between absolute virtues ('charity') and their contingent existence in a fallen world ('kinds of loving'). The key concepts for the traditionalist critics—patriotism or freedom—are defined at the contingent level of practical ethics. Many critics extricate one line from Barbour's intricate discussion of political liberty (§ 1 *Bruce*, ll. 219-77). 'A! fredome is a noble thing!' (l. 225) is not an anticipation of the democratic intellect. It is defined contingently via its opposite 'thraldome' ('Thus contrar thingis evirmar/ Discoveringis of the tothir ar', ll. 241-242; see ll. 219-42). The hierarchical context which exacerbates this tension between ideal and actual is accepted throughout by narrator and heroes. Bruce leads Douglas and they lead the nobles, who lead the people within the tiered division of labour system which mirrors God's perfect, if inscrutable, plan. When Barbour presents the insoluble problem of the serf, whose low status allows him no real freedom in this world (ll. 243-74), the narrator's ideal is not the destruction of that order but the perfect society in which each individual loves his brother. It is the shadow of that world which Barbour invokes when making all the 'folk' of Scotland (l. 19) the patriotic heroes of the wars of liberty *under* Bruce and Douglas (ll. 13-33, 'stalwart folk'—'of thaim') before showing the impossibility of the ideal working in the case of a serf. Fortunately, such mysteries are not his major concern and so he passes the problem of resolving them to 'clerkis' (l. 219) and 'thaim...off mar renoun' (260). This is hardly surprising: the gap between divine commands and fallen practice is one of the most recurrent themes in the literature of Barbour's time.

The single line of canonical criteria, therefore, fails to contextualise its search properly. The interlocking mode of thought, encouraged by early Rhetoric and Metaphysics, is demonstrated throughout the rhetorical theory represented in this anthology. When James thinks of a 'Scottish' Renaissance, for example, his view of the national language is not one of 'Scots alone' but as a different twig differing from but closest to its nearest neighbour (English) on the tree of languages, whose diverse branches split from the divine root at Babel. This image, drawn most immediately from Du Bellay, results in his defining the one in relation to the other—'English, quhilk is lykest to our language, yit we differ from thame in sindrie reulis of Poesie' (§ 22 Preface).

37. Confusingly, the same word—'allegory'—is used to mean the entire method of using overt text to present covert meanings *and* to define the area of spirituality within that method.

(ii) Adding 'English', Latin and Manneristic Scots: The traditional search for Scottish themes in ordinary, unpretentious language is also conducted with little or no sense of the rules governing composition at that time. Ironically, decorum and the many voices suggest that it is in the higher, anglicized levels of style that we should be looking for serious treatment of national issues. The very language which seems unpatriotic to naturalist anticipations is the rhetorical sign that a writer values his native land. Drummond, who did not go south to England and wrote a history of Scotland, has many poignant and powerfully patriotic works, including *Teares on the Death of Moeliades* and *Forth Feasting*. Urquhart's inventive, high style English prose is used to celebrate Scottish heroism through the ages. It is, however, extremely difficult for a Scottish Renaissance author to weave a way past the various swinging balls of the modern sociologically contrastive canon. If either of these writers happens to pass the inappropriate 'English sounds treacherous' test, their Royalist and Unionist leanings mean that, almost certainly, they will be laid low by the 'radical and democratic' challenge.

It may also be noted that these examples come after the dissolution of the Castalian band. This is because the king as monarch-patron specifically discouraged his Castalians from writing in the vernacular about political concerns. In the *Reulis*, he is quite specific. 'Materis of commoun weill...are to grave materis for a Poet to mell in' (Ch.7). His mother had suffered badly at the hands of poets and poetasters (§ 11 'The Lamentatioun of Lady Scotland'). James had been warned by his tutors to prevent this recurring. He fared badly in the ballad[38] but the more influential printed evidence had been royally censored in advance. Ironically, vernacular silence on political themes is itself a sign of patriotic obedience.

To seek evidence of patriotism in the Latin poetry of the period is, therefore, both advisable and advised. It is suggested by James's comment and confirmed by his analysis of decorum—Latin being another possible 'voice' and still the most subtle language of all. A later critic who ignores the Latin evidence when assessing Scottish literature in the sixteenth and seventeenth centuries, also turns a blind eye to the interlinked and inclusive linguistic arguments of his predecessors. He will miss the crucial fact that a nation which prided itself on its learning and humanism then possessed the leading Latin poet in Europe, George Buchanan ('Poeta sui saeculi facile princeps'—'Easily the leading poet of his age/century').

Indeed, the wealth of Latin poetry and prose composed in Scotland at that time, itself constitutes an important literary distinctiveness, as the wealth and vastness of the *Delitiae Poetarum Scotorum* suggests (§ 24). The Neo-Latin evidence also directly contradicts the assumption that the Scots felt insecure linguistically or politically at the Union of the Crowns. A superior paternalism towards the English is expressed over and over again as the following lines from Patrick Adamson indicate:

> Ergo tot monitis Angli caelestibus acti,
> Deposuere iras animis, ac regia passim
> Dona parent[39]

(Accordingly, the English—driven by so many divine warnings—have laid aside anger from their minds and are all preparing regal gifts...)

Thomas Craigie (§ 24) visualizes James as Apollo, source of light 'patriae lux unica,' coming south to enlighten Elizabethan darkness. Indeed, quite possibly, the Scots went south *too* confidently. Had they thought more realistically of the implications of

38. Henderson, p. 277.
39. *Delitiae Poetarum Scotorum*, edited by Arthur Johnston, 2 vols (Amsterdam, 1637) I, 13.

absorption into a larger court, they might have fared better. Certainly, it did not take Alexander Craig long to realize the error of their ways. He returned from London to his Scottish estates with some alacrity but not before composing his 'Scotlands Teares' (1604):

What art thou Scotland then? no Monarchie allace,
A oligarchie desolate, with straying onkow face,
A maymed bodie now but shaip, some monstrous thing,
A reconfused chaos now, a countrey, but a King.

(iii) Re-discovering a Scottish Voice.

a) The Sonnet: If one excludes English and Anglo-Scots writing on 'nationalist' grounds; Latin and Late Middle Scots mannerism for reasons of 'undemocratic pretentiousness' or whatever; makes no allowances for changed definitions of nation and patriotism across the years and searches in the story-line alone, it is self-evident that not much of the 'highest' Renaissance writing will remain to be discussed. But the truly amazing thing is, that even when a mode is directed towards the paradigmatic ideals as expressed, it can also be ignored.

How else can the position of the Scottish sonnet before the Union of the Crowns be regarded? Anthological evidence repetitively points to two works in the mode at that time—one by Barclay of Ladyland and one by Mark Alexander Boyd. Neither of these authors is known to have composed any other vernacular sonnets. Yet James's *Reulis* had suggested that this form make itself different from English sonneteering in a number of ways, as part a of self-conscious movement aimed at nationalistic differentiation. That is: the same motivation as that favoured by the traditionalists, for once, underlies cultural thinking. The sonnet is a major sign of that programme. In the Scottish sonnet, a wider range of topics is to be attempted. Love, being so conventional within the form, will become one among many. Like all other subjects, it may be subjected to argument and discussion, because the form of the sonnet lends itself to 'argumentis...quhair sindrie sentences and change of purposis are requyrit' within a movement designed to accentuate the rougher sounds of Scots. James paved the way for direct, personal sonnets which are certainly both 'couthy' and 'unpretentious'.

The selection of sonnets by Montgomerie, Stewart and Fowler in § 18 will show how obediently and how well the king's guidelines were put into practice. There are more than three hundred Castalian sonnets. The vast majority of these set themselves thematically but also linguistically and formally against English practice. The distinctive interlacing rhyme-scheme—ABABBCBCCDCDEE—was 'invented' and adopted by the Scottish poets before Spenser. It is used in over 80% of Castalian sonnets. In choosing to imitate French sources in preference to Italian ones at this time, the courtier-poets not only proclaimed their independence from English Petrarchism but continued the 'auld alliance' witnessed in the critical sources and vocabulary of the *Reulis* themselves. James's treatise has Du Bellay's *Deffense de la Langue Françoyse* as its prime source and a critical vocabulary based on Scots coinages from the French—'literall' for alliterative; 'sectioun' instead of 'caesura'. If the nationalist paradigm can be unaware of the first instance in which its own methodology flourished, then it must surely be even further out of sympathetic touch with the Renaissance than has so far been supposed.

(b) Translation: Although James's *Reulis* emphasized the need for inventiveness, he also encouraged translation. Matthiessen notes that this mode of writing was in itself regarded as a patriotic pursuit.[40] As the sea-goer claimed new territory for his

40. F. O. Matthiessen, *Translation: An Elizabethan Art* (Cambridge, Mass., 1931) p.3.

monarch, so the translator 'colonized' texts when turning them into his native tongue. Coinage implied an expansive, outward-looking view of language. One made one's native tongue more versatile through the various decorous levels from plain to aureate by borrowing widely from other languages. When Gavin Douglas, in his *Eneados*—the first major Scottish translation—unusually refers to his language as 'Scottis' (VI Prologue, 118) rather than 'Inglis', the argument is proper and specific to the mode he is currently following. It is possible to make the bishop appear to conform with two of the major traditionalist tests, if one dislocates from its context his desire to write in Scots, 'braid and plane' (I Prologue, 111). However, Douglas at once makes a necessary concession 'Nor yit sa clene all sudron I refuss, Bot sum word I pronunce as nyghtbouris doys.' (I Prologue, 113-4). The greater subtlety of Latin and the range of Virgil's 'hye wisdome and maist profund engyne' (V Prologue, 28) make it necessary for Douglas to range 'craftily' over all styles and voices from plain to aureate in order to 'kepe the sentens'.

That the polymathic poets of the Scottish Renaissance should have found translation a particularly suitable medium for their patriotism is unsurprising. William Fowler in the late sixteenth century confirms Douglas's careful, erudite practice. In the Preface to his version of Petrarch's *Trionfi*, he records that he has consulted all available 'French and Inglish traductionis'. As Douglas had attacked the amateur approach of Caxton, so Fowler finds these attempts horribly inaccurate ('not onelie traduced bot evin as it war magled and in everie member miserablie maimed...'). He offers to produce more than two hundred parallel passages as evidence to doubters.[41]

Behind all this characteristic thoroughness and erudition, there stands, yet again, the supposed terminator and traitor—James VI. An English Castalian, Thomas Hudson, records in the Introduction to his version of Du Bartas' *Judith*, that the king had 'assigned' that 'agreable subject' to him during a discussion on translation.[42] Stewart's *Roland Furious* (§ 17) as well as the sections devoted to Sonnet (§ 18) and Pastoral (§ 19) do no more than suggest how far this form of nationalist expression dominated the period from 1580 until the 1650s. James himself translated Du Bartas' *Uranie* and part of his *Seconde Sepmaine*; lyrically he imitated Saint Gelais and Desportes. He was determined that the source-biasses of his Renaissance should reflect the most powerful political alliance of that time. As Scotland and France were joined in covert alliance against England, so the Castalians were encouraged to imitate French authors but be wary of English ones.[43] In the mid-seventeenth century Urquhart's inspired, exuberant prose translation of Rabelais would provide a fitting successor to Douglas's poetic *Eneados*.

But Drummond of Hawthornden, the third of the supposed canonical villains, has a strong claim to lead this kind of nationalistic endeavour. His imaginative subtlety and vast erudition covered a wider linguistic range than that attempted by any other poet in the translation-conscious Renaissance. The most basic list of his European sources would include Petrarch, Marino, Bembo, Tasso, Guarini, Guevera, Granada, Du Bellay, Du Bartas, De Tyard, Spenser, Daniel, Sidney, Fowler and Alexander. And this is to discount his translations from classical Latin and the Scottish Neo-Latinists.

Is it possible or desirable in the face of all this evidence to sustain, for the Scottish Renaissance, the twin beliefs that all writing in English is not 'Scottish' and all courtly writing so poor and pretentious that it is not 'Literature'? This double-barrelled use of

41. *The Works of William Fowler*, edited by H.W. Meikle et al. 3 vols (STS: Edinburgh and London, 1914, 1934, 1940) I, 16.

42. Thomas Hudson, *The Historie of Judith*, edited by James Craigie (STS: Edinburgh, 1941) p.4. Shire, pp. 71-5 gives a full account of the Hudson brothers' position within James's court.

43. There were, of course, exceptions. Constable came to the Edinburgh court and was warmly welcomed.

the term 'Scottish Literature' certainly needs careful justification as it relinquishes any claim on an organically developing literary history in order to prioritize an authentic or essentialist tradition, which needs no boosting at this time anyway. Moreover, as Sarah Dunnigan rightly asks, 'Why should Scottish Literature alone maintain a critical prejudice against "artificial" poetry which participates in a wholly European manneristic love of the ornate and difficult?'[44] If Shakespeare, Jonson or Donne were only valued when they embraced the plain style, wrote from a left-wing viewpoint or mirrored the ballad's simplicity in directness, they would not fare much better than Montgomerie or Drummond.

Bridging the Gap: From a Disjunctive to a Continuous Literary History

I have argued for two major revisions in the critical definition of Scottishness within the period prior to 1707. First, I have contended that the writers from Barbour until 1707 take pride in the possession of a polymathic linguistic inheritance rather than a homogenous language called 'Scots'. Secondly, I have tried to show that this viewpoint is conducted within and justified by the rules of rhetoric and that nationalistic intent of any sort can only be interpreted through an understanding of that artificial code. Consequently, I have also replaced the exclusive, generalized and extreme logic of the paradigm with the comprehensive, specific and gradualistic mode of argument, then held to be proper for aesthetic discussions. To conclude the case, I shall look at the way in which these changes may influence our understanding of literature after 1707.

The first key question is 'How do those who claim to be re-introducing Scots view their contribution?' How did Allan Ramsay, the initiator of what is now called 'The Vernacular Revival' view his linguistic inheritance? Clearly, he is aware of increased anglicisation and a loss of cultural direction. The latter half of the seventeenth century *did* witness a form of linguistic narrowing. English began to dominate in both verse and prose. This trend threatened the quality and the distinctiveness of Scottish writing. But Ramsay could not revive '*the*' vernacular of 'Scottis' because Scots had so far never enjoyed that homogenous and patriotic status. Rather, he revived the Scottish element within the array of voices from Latinate English through English and Anglo-Scots to thick Scots—a range which had been the distinctive, decorous base of Scottish writing from Barbour onwards.

Both his creative practice and his critical reactions confirm this. Ramsay begins by writing English verse in the manner of the English neoclassicals but he recognizably differs from them. That difference can be related to the similarity in difference—Scots against English—of the Scottish writers in the late sixteenth and early seventeenth centuries. (Professor Lyall and others have urged specialists in this area to use the word 'baroque' to sign the difference.) Ramsay's drama, *The Gentle Shepherd*, also derives directly from British interest in the pastoral form. This has Scottish precedents in the work of Drummond (§ 19) and, more particularly, in Ayton's versions of Guarini and the 'commedia erudita' tradition (§ 19). Conscious of the strong Latin voice and the Horatian rhetorical tradition of Buchanan, Ramsay also has versions of the classics, the best known of which is Horace, *Eclogues* I, Ode VI.

If this were not the case, Ramsay should surely have turned down the offer to join the Easy Club—Scottish bastion of the literati. Instead, he argued that he could not be confined to the one pen-name offered to members. Being the inheritor of the Scottish

44. Sarah M. Dunnigan, *Glasgow University M. Phil in Scottish Literature, Teaching Guide*, 'Scottish Poetry in the Early Seventeenth Century', p. 1.

'voice' of the Scottish Makars as well as the 'voice' of English Neoclassicism, he asked to be called both 'Gavin Douglas' (for the one) and Isaac Bickerstaff (for the other). He did not deny the 'Inglis' tradition; he assumed it was also his by right and practice.

The case of Robert Burns, most of whose writing belongs to the 1780s, is rather different. In those eighty years, the literary situation had altered. Moreover, Burns seems intent on presenting himself as an early Romantic. Over and over again, he claims to be the poet of the heart and of easy inspiration. 'I rhyme for fun', I am the 'hero of these artless strains, a lowly bard' celebrating the 'heart abune them a''. He also claims to be opposed to learning and rhetorical artifice:

> In days when mankind were but callans,
> At Grammar, Logic, an' sic talents,
> They took nae pains their speech to balance,
> Or rules to gie,
> But spak their thoughts in plain, braid lallans,
> Like you or me.
>
> ('Epistle to Davie', p. 75)[45]

And, near the end of the anarchist cantata, *The Jolly Beggars*, he makes his bard figure reject learned and mannerized verse by discarding its mythological source for more immediate liquid stimulation:

> I never drank the Muses' stank
> Castalia's burn an' a' that,
> But there it streams an' richly reams
> My Helicon I ca' that.
>
> (p. 167)

The specific example he uses to represent learned and mannerized verse happens to be the signature tune of James VI's courtly poetic Renaissance of the 1580s; the Castalian fountain, which he brings down to earth as a 'burn', happens to be the name of the group led by that King as Maecenas and patron.

But Burns is a dramatic poet, capable of changing his own voice at will. Another of his songs opens as follows:

> O were I on Parnassus hill;
> Or had o' Helicon my fill;
> That I might catch poetic skill,
> To sing how dear I love thee.
>
> ('O were I on Parnassus Hill', p. 337)

Burns here praises the very type of inspiration damned by the bard in *The Jolly Beggars*. The imaginative power of containing multitudes, claimed by MacDiarmid, belongs also to Burns. The craft of the neoclassicals, the rhetoric he was taught so assiduously by Murdoch and overtly prides himself on in the 'letter to Dr John Moore', is as important a line in his verse as the romantic.[46]

The authorial perspective and the idea of dramatic voices remind us that the bard who speaks these lines is only one created voice among many in that anarchic cantata.

45. All Burns citations follow *Burns, Poems and Songs*, ed. James Kinsley (Oxford, 1969).
46. See n. 20.

If one then looks at verse forms, a curious fact emerges. The Heliconian stanza, derided by Burns's character, is the one used by the Castalian 'maister poete', Alexander Montgomerie in his major allegoric poem, *The Cherrie and the Slae* (§ 16):

About a bank with balmie bewes,
Where nightingals their nots renews
With gallant goldspinks gay,
The mavise, mirle and Progne proud,
The lintwhite, lark and laverock loud,
Saluted mirthful May:
When Philomel had sweetly sung,
To Progne she deplored
How Tereus cut out her tongue
And falsely her deflorde;
Which storie, so sorie,
To shew ashamd she seemde,
To heare her, so neare her,
I doubted if I dream'd.
(§ 16 st. 1)

Which stanza form does the narrator use to begin *The Jolly Beggars*?

When lyart leaves bestrow the yird,
Or wavering like the Bauckie-bird,
Bedim cauld Boreas' blast;
When hailstanes drive wi' bitter skyte,
And infant Frost begin to bite,
In hoary cranreuch drest;
Ae night at e'en a merry core
O' randie, gangrel bodies,
In Poosie-Nansie's held the splore,
To drink their orra dudies:
Wi' quaffing, and laughing,
They ranted an' they sang;
Wi' jumping an' thumping,
The vera girdle rang.
(p. 157)

This signature tune of the Castalians, with its intricate fourteen line form, is rejected as too contrived and learned by the Bard-persona only after Burns has himself has used it to introduce *The Jolly Beggars* in its entirety. A variation of the same stanza directly follows the Bard's own song in which he has, literally, consigned all conscious artifice down the 'Stank':

So sung the BARD—and Nansie's waws
Shook with a thunder of applause
    Re-echo'd from each mouth!
They toom'd their pocks, they pawn'd their duds,
They scarcely left to coor their fuds
    To quench their lowan drouth:

Then owre again the jovial thrang
The Poet did request
To lowse his PACK an' wale a sang
A BALLAD o' the best.
He, rising, rejoicing,
Between his TWA DEBORAHS,
Looks round him an' found them
Impatient for the Chorus.
(p. 168)

Rhetorically, as Burns the avid reader of Pope and Shenstone would know, this is a witty form of the modesty topos as also practised by the early makars. This 'rule' advises the artist to claim no knowledge of the crafts of writing but in such a way that his more learned listeners understand that the opposite is the case. The practice of appearing to write spontaneously, while obeying rules, is specifically urged by Douglas and by James in their rhetorical theory. If one then returns to the 'Epistle to William Simpson', one is less surprised to note that even this plea for freedom from authorities exists in a mode imitating the Horatian Epistle, whose verse form encourages precisely that 'balancing of speech', which the literal sense denies.

Is this too sophisticated a view of the 'people's bard'? Such a question can best be resolved by examining the Ayrshire poet's approach to language and style. This is, self-evidently, based on the principles of decorum and many voices. Otherwise, why would he praise Dame Scotland in *The Vision*, using the archaisms and composed words of the latinate high style?

Her *Mantle* large, of greenish hue,
My gazing wonder chiefly drew;
Deep lights and shades, bold-mingling, threw
A lustre grand;
And seem'd to my astonish'd view,
A well-known Land.

Or reserve his thickest Scots for farcical vituperations directed against lower class harridans?

Auld baudrans by the ingle sits,
An wi' her loof her face a washin;
But Willie's wife is nae sae trig,
She dights her grunzie wi' a hushian:
Her waly nieves like midden-creels,
Her feet wad fyle the Logan-water;
Sic a wife as Willie's wife,
I wad na gie a button for her.

This is the decorous practice of Douglas in the *Eneados*, a poem which Burns knew, as the quotation at the head of *Tam o' Shanter* reveals.[47] Burns's other styles may briefly be noted. The Middle Style is Anglo-Scots, the norm for his work. Middle High is a purer English. As with the Makars, these transitions may 'sign' seriously or comically;

47. ' "Of Brownis and of Bogillis full is this buke." Gawin Douglas.'

set up expectations which are fulfilled or subverted in the manner of *Holy Willie's Prayer*.

As the contents of § 24 confirm, all of these different voices were still practised at the end of the seventeenth century. This polymathic inheritance was of long standing, especially in the Celtic areas of the Lowlands (after all, George Buchanan's native language was Gaelic) and in the Highlands where three written languages—Gaelic, Scots/English and Latin—were all practised.[48] In the early seventeenth century, the Western Isles were drawn into trilingual parity by a Statute demanding that 'everie gentilman or yeaman' send their eldest son or daughter to 'scuillis on the Lawland', there to learn 'sufficientlie to speik, reid, and wryte Inglisch.'[49]

Why, then, do scholars, who have intelligently traced the same Scots, Latinate and English voices and the same popular modes (eclogues, elegies, odes and epodes) for Ramsay and Fergusson as I have traced in the seventeenth century for Ayton, dismiss two of them hurriedly as 'derivative *English* verse?'[50] Perhaps if you are listening for one authentic tone, you will not hear others, authentic or not.

'Why is Scottish Literature Standing Still?'

> Now is Perkin and thise pilgrimes to the plow faren.
> To erie this half-acre, holpen hym manye.
>
> [Now Perkin and these pilgrims set themselves to the plough. Many folk helped him to turn over the soil in this half-acre of land.]
>
> William Langland, *Piers Plowman* VI.105-6

In the quotation from *Piers Plowman* which heads the opening section of this essay, Lady Truth descends from on high to tell the dreamer that she is the end of his quest. As this revelation comes in the first book of the poem, one might have thought his journey was over before it had begun. But Truth as an absolute goal may be easily stated by its own embodiment. Viewed from the different perspectives on the field full of folk, it will be an ever-elusive subject and object. Translated into the textual terms of the Anthology, this implies that the value of the collection as a whole will be much easier to accept and define than the particular pleasures and profits which each of us uniquely derives from it.

What right have I, in that case, to write a critical introduction? The second quotation, offered above, provides one answer. When the pilgrims find themselves unable to find Truth in the conventional way, Piers ('Perkyn') the Ploughman, as one who has laboured long in the field, offers an alternative approach. He does not prescribe nor ask the others to change their viewpoint. But he does question the value of moving forward on a geographic journey, when neither the way nor the end is clear. In asking them to work with him on his field, he does not propose a cessation of labour nor does he over-ride their own perceived position in the scheme of things. But he does invite them to re-think their positions as seen from his small plot of land.

I cannot think of a more exact analogy for the spirit in which I offer my own attempt at guidance. I have had the privilege of labouring in the field of Scottish Literature for over thirty years. Within that period, the subject has made rapid strides forward. I

48. John Bannerman, 'Literacy in the Highlands,' in *The Renaissance and Reformation in Scotland: Essays in Honour of Gordon Donaldson*, edited by Ian B. Cowan and Duncan Shaw (Edinburgh, 1982), pp. 214-35 (214).

49. Statutes of Iona, 1609. Cited by Bannerman, op. cit. , p.215; see also Introduction § 24.

50. *Poems by Allan Ramsay and Robert Fergusson*, edited by A. M. Kinghorn and A. Law (Edinburgh and London, 1974) p. xix.

simply believe that the linear 'Tradition' model, like the linear journey model of the physical pilgrimage, no longer serves.

I have also published in all periods from medieval to modern. That breadth of endeavour has given me a genuine regard for the skill with which different kinds of ploughing are conducted within this small domain. So why should I—even in Piers' humble spirit—claim the right to demand a pause on my terms? And what terms does a literal Jack-of-all-trades have, anyway? Although I have visited other fields, I claim tenancy of the half-acre with no name. This essay has in large part been a demand that the existence of a Renaissance plot be acknowledged. But why should the viewpoint of the apparently least significant area of all warrant the same right to be heard on its own terms as the Enlightenment or the Twentieth Century? I shall sum up the major reasons, using the medieval mode of argument—first negative, then positive.

The Negative Way: Paradoxically, it is precisely the severity of the judgment on the period which makes it a good evaluative viewing-point. It is always advantageous to test at its most vulnerable point any system which claims comprehensive descriptive power. If the years 1585-1700 are practically obliterated within a literary history based on contrastive nationalist values, then that is where any potential weaknesses of the method will most obviously reveal themselves. If they do not, then it would appear that an entire nation has been struck down by the longest and most infectious writers' block ever recorded!

If one compares the qualitative measures applied to Renaissance writing in Scotland with the ideals these writers proposed for themselves, very little common ground can be traced. They did not claim one language nationalistically, but many rhetorically. They did not write within a democracy, but a hierarchy. They did not believe that all literature was political, but placed politics within a wider frame of relevance under divinity. Whether in so doing they embodied 'Truth', is something which only those who talk directly to Lady Truth within her raised tower can assess. That it was their own 'truthful' view is, empirically, the case. To evaluate them on criteria which they did not share will be, by definition, a barren task.

Only those who find no problem with this will be equally at ease with a synchronic method, whose 'hero'—'villain' oversimplifications can, as we have seen, set James VI in 1585 in exact antithesis against Robert Burns in 1785 as if this were an even comparative plane. Those who are not so much at ease will have been unsurprised to discover that practically none of the polarized extremes on which the neat contrast is established withstands close scrutiny. In addition to the examples already given, the supposed opposition between Burns, lover of music, the folk and conviviality as against James, silent and apart in his scholarly cell, also falls down on every particular. True, they were very different men and poets, writing in very different political climates. But James, no less than Burns, initiated his national Renaissance by calling attention to the importance of music in all its diversity. Musical rhythm or 'flowing', simple and complex, is the starting point for James's *Reulis*—'For then they observit not flowing'.[51] One need only listen to the settings of Montgomerie's 'Adeu, O desie of delyt' or 'In throu the windoes of myn ees' to see the effect of his patronage in a court where scholarship enriched song, dance and play.[52]

51. This remark in the Prologue to the *Reulis* is expanded on and explained at length in Chapter 2, e.g. 'To knaw and discerne thir kynde of wordis from utheris, youre eare man be the onely judge, as of all the uther parts of flowing, the verie tuichestane quhairof is musique.'

52. See *Musica Scotica, II: Sixteenth-century Scots songs for voice and lute*, edited and arranged by Kenneth Elliott (Glasgow, 1996); Shire, *Song, Dance and Poetry*.

If this contrasted or 'negative' vision from the field of 'making' explains why traditional literary historians so often look in the wrong places for surprising things, it does not clarify why they sometimes reject even those delimited kinds of literature which they claim to esteem. This is because, while both groups share an interdisciplinary definition of literature's place, only the makars begin by defining those qualities which separate literature from other disciplines. Once these have been established as the root of the argument, it may properly branch out into a consideration of other kinds of knowledge. By way of contrast, the various canonical 'tests' of the Scottish Tradition place literary quality ('how well one writes') beside criteria drawn from sociology, politics and a nationalist reading of history ('what one writes about'). As this is an unprioritized system, 'good' writing may, at least potentially, be rejected or 'bad' preserved on grounds of political or social correctness as viewed from another age.

How else can one assess the following? Throughout the seventeenth century, a simpler, more direct form of lyric co-exists with the exuberant mannerism of Drummond.

> Some loves a woman for her wit,
> Some beauty does admire,
> Some loves a handsome leg or foot,
> Some upwards does aspire;
> Some loves a mistress nice and coy,
> Some freedom does approve;
> Some like their persons to enjoy,
> Some for platonick love.
> (§ 24C, The Election)

This minor, but nonetheless pronounced, strain can be traced by looking through the later lyrical sections of the anthology. In part, it derives from the influence of the English metaphysicals. But it also builds on a particularly Scottish movement with a strong democratic bias, a desire for simplicity and a hatred of excessive artifice.

What is this source, which would appear to be a god-sent anticipation of all the essentialist demands of the tradition? It is the origin of verses in this manner:

> For I, a wyfe with sempill lyfe,
> Dois wyn my meit ilk day,
> For small availl, ay selling caill,
> The best fassoun I may.
> (§ 11.10)

or in this:

> The sisters gray, befoir this day,
> Did crune within thair cloister,
> They feit ane freir, thair keyis to beir,
> The feind ressave the foster.
> (§ 11.11)

This is, of course, the voice of Calvinism, uttered within the popular broadside tradition.

When everything that the traditionalists desire does appear at the surface of the text within a nationally distinctive movement, they still bury it in a blanket denial of quality and content. I am not suggesting that early Calvinist verse attains a consistently high standard. Equally, however, there are many fine practitioners who adapt well to the spare demands of Calvinist art. Their place in literary history has been sensitively traced by workers within the Renaissance field—notably A.A. MacDonald. To admit their influence on the Scoto-Britanes is crucial. Instead, curiously passionate outbursts damn them and all their kind. It is indeed difficult to see how a 'villainous' age can make any claim on its own behalf, when work which manages to be not English nor Latin nor mannerist nor pretentious nor courtly, can still fall. Why? Perhaps Alexander has the answer in his *Anacrisis*, when he pities nationalist critics ('affectioned patriots') for only valuing those views, which can 'be digested and converted to their own use' (§ 23.1).

The Positive Way: Three questions are relevant in deciding whether this journey has only called attention to deficiencies or may—more positively—contribute to a remedy. They are: What has valuably been discovered? Does it offer a way forward? Is it to be heeded 'more than' or 'along with' the other voices of discontent issuing from the post-1707 period? Each may be assessed via the analogy of Piers on his field.

First, Piers' pilgrimage is based on experience. In the same way, the radical review I am proposing is firmly based on the voices of writers from Barbour to 1707. That is—not only do they establish the origins of our discipline, they cover more than half its chronological span and the entirety of our history as a nation. Piers in his own voice is properly apologetic—as the inheritor of a greater authority he speaks out confidently. With the same confidence, I do not offer the following as an opinion but as proven fact—Scottish vernacular literature is not founded on a homogenous language, known as Scottis, it originates with a variety of voices, which the learned and professional 'makars' of that country welcomed and built upon. The Scottish rhetorical tradition which emerges from this is recognizably different from its English counterpart in many ways. More critically self-conscious, more analytic, often more thorough in its treatment of themes, it is also more conservative and reactive, re-interpreting older categories and aesthetic values rather than casting them aside.

Second, Piers found a way in which all labourers could join together—each in his or her own station—within the field of labour. He achieved that by limiting himself to the contingent within a broad and comprehensive model. The literary criticism of the makars defines this 'trivial' discipline of ours at the specific and contingent level. Alexander, when he argues in *Anacrisis* that each text warrants special consideration on its own terms, speaks with a representative voice, his views having been anticipated by Barbour, Henryson, Douglas and James VI. This essentially rhetorical or craft-based approach to writing in all its forms has been maintained, as earlier noted, in Scotland's educational system from Barbour's days until the twentieth century.[53] Literature, on this model, is the most artificial and highly imaginative branch of word-building. Each of its texts justifies itself through that artifice as practised effectively and affectively in unique works. Different modes set up different tests of craftsmanship. Thus, fantasy may be a proper criterion for epic, in Alexander's eyes, but tragedy ought to have a base in history. One author will excel in one way, another impress on different grounds, one will find his major relevance politically, another theologically, another amorously. 'There is none singular in all, and yet all are singular in some things' (§ 23).

In the present state of our discipline, it would be naive to expect the various groups of theoretically divided critics to share this vision of 'making'. I hope, however, that we

53. See pp. xv-xvi.

may soon return to the openness within the dialectical field proposed by Piers. Those who believe that '*All* literature is politics', or that 'The *only* relevance the subject-ideas of a poem have is to themselves' use an exclusive and condescending rhetoric, which would have seemed very odd in earlier days. That any work could be interpreted politically, the makars would have agreed; that political relevance should always be the optimally relevant meaning transmitted, would have been a sin against that freedom in imaginative potential, which defined the poet in his uniqueness. That no language transmitted perfectly, they knew; that this trapped it within its own codes, they strongly disputed, as Urquhart's plans for a Universal Language reveal.

Third, Piers re-defined the quest for Truth in a manner which he believed to be the most appropriate for these people at this stage. Not everyone joined. While I hope that my appeal to Scottish Literature's polymathic origins may be a fruitful starting point for enquiry, I do begin from the belief that the study of imaginative literature is a valuable pursuit. Scottish literature's defensive return to social values brings it easily into harmony with another group of critics, so far unmentioned. Some new historicists and followers of cultural studies associate literature with élitism. As their own discipline has become an instrument for oppression, they tend to depreciate it, seeking redemption at the hands of sociologists and politicians.

The rhetorical foundation of the new way, as noted earlier, does not close off other disciplines. The whole point of the Liberal Arts concept is to link different kinds of knowledge. But Barbour's Prologue to the *Bruce*, Henryson's Prologue to his *Morall Fabillis*, Douglas's Prologue to the *Eneados*, James's *Reulis*, Alexander's *Anacrisis* and Urquhart's *Jewel*, are all explanations of the unique contribution made by the imaginative artist and a reiteration of those skills which he or she has, skilfully, mastered.

Finally, Piers offered his new model for one stage and one time. For the same reasons, he rejected the easy model of the linear journey, with all the conventional rules which had accumulated around it. To establish a tradition is exactly like that. It claims to create a uniqueness in diversity by imposing one pattern, unchanging, throughout time. My own model is also at base drawn from the study of early Scottish Literature. It has been structured to account for that period so as to make its voice heard at this stage in the evolution of the discipline as a whole. It does challenge the value of linguistic premises and canonical methods which are either inaccurate or inapposite to the literature of that period. It does so with the aim of replacing the broken-line view of Scottish literary history with an alternative model.

Indeed, if one substitutes for the linear neatness of a 'tradition' the analogy of medieval music, the difference will at once become clear and Scottish Literature may be freed to move forward. All voices within the medieval motet harmonized with the tenor but were mutually discordant. In the same way, all viewpoints may be welcomed into a mature national literature on their own terms, only when the governing harmony of the discipline's unique role and function has been established. On this analogy, I am convinced that Scotland's particular music opens with many voices not one. The reactive, critically self-conscious poetics and the thoroughness of thematic range which the medieval makars practised, mirrored their learning and professionalism. As such, they dominate the opening medieval movement. Within the part of the score as studied in this essay, it seems to me that these unique rhetorical cadences can still be detected through the variations of the Renaissance and Eighteenth Century passages. I even suspect that they may remain to-day, but would not regard that as either a necessary conclusion or within my scope to determine.

In urging his followers to plough their own half acre before moving forward, Piers asked them to look inwards and consider how far they were responsible for their own situation. What concerns those of us who plough the half acre called Scottish Literature? We complain that critics in other fields label us parochial or think our area too small to worry about. We lament an inadequate language and the lack of a continuous literary history. Yet it is our own decision to delimit ourselves within a tradition and to assume an unnecessarily narrow view of our linguistic inheritance. The time has surely come to forsake insecurities over '**Scottish**'-ness and open up that field unapologetically to the accepted methods of interpreting '**literature**', especially when subjection to the niceties of critical analysis restores linguistic virtuosity and literary continuity. It is only necessary to cease assuming that materialist, literal and rationalist values can be used validly to assess the work of those who prioritise mystery, allegory and the imagination.

RDSJ

TEXTUAL INTRODUCTION
Principles of Selection

Recently, a number of specialised anthologies covering areas of the field have gone out of print. These include Priscilla Bawcutt and Felicity Riddy's *Longer Scotttish Poems* and R.D.S. Jack's *A choice of Scottish Verse 1560-1600* and *Scottish Prose 1550-1700*. The need for a new literary Anthology, with full apparatus, is intensified by the equally discouraging situation faced by those wishing to set individual authors. The reliable texts, which formerly existed at a price within the student range, have for the most part, either disappeared, or given way to expensive alternatives.

All editorial decisions have been guided by two principles: firstly, to offer the student a rich variety of texts representative of good writing within their period and mode; secondly, to ensure that the texts are presented in as intellectually and pragmatically accessible a form as is consistent with academic integrity and the limitations of the printed page.

Challenged by the usual selection problems, we decided to seek breadth modally and chronologically. This means that the dramatic and narrative voices are represented as thoroughly as the lyrical, throughout the period of Scottish National Literature—that is, until the Union of the Parliaments in 1707.

However, breadth and depth cannot be attained economically without narrowing the focus elsewhere. The wide-ranging definition of imaginative persuasion espoused in *Scottish Prose 1550-1700* has, therefore, been sacrificed in favour of a specifically 'literary' selection. We are concerned that current interdisciplinary and thematic biasses within the discipline may serve the later (i.e. post-1707) periods well, but run counter to the priorities set by the 'makars' for their own art. Students of literature seem more comfortable when discussing 'what' a work is or ought to be saying, than if required to return to an earlier vision, which asks 'how' imaginative persuasion specifically works.

These issues are addressed in three ways. (i) Four essays on Scottish Rhetorical Theory (§ 14, 15, 22, 23) have been included to provide contemporary contextualisation. (ii) The appendix (§ 24) ranges more widely, in order to provide a reliable view of the major strands of composition inherited by Ramsay, Fergusson and Burns. Here, areas such as the Ballad and Latin Literature, which have been excluded elsewhere, enter our remit. (iii) The Critical Introduction seeks an alternative, rhetorically based answer to the traditional 'peaks' and 'troughs' view of Scottish Literary History.

Editorial Principles

Each text is preceded by a Sectional Introduction, containing brief biographical and historical information on authors.

With the exception of § 11B IX-X and § 24E, all texts—manuscript or print—have been freshly edited, either from a single Copy Text or from a considered collation of texts. Editorial comments within the Notes are introduced by the letters 'ED'.

While the considerable diversity of spelling (particularly within the earlier texts) has been retained, some modernisation has been effected in the normalisation of initial *ff* to *f* and in the substitution of *y* for ȝ (yogh). Modern distinctions are made between *i* and *j* (*Iames* > *James*; *ioy* > *joy*) and between *u* and *v* (*reproue* > *reprove*; *vpward* > *upward*). The letter *w*, often used indiscriminately with *v* and *u*, has been normalised as follows: where *w* = *u* (*Bwnnock* > *Bunnock*; *wther* > *uther*), where *w* = consonantal *v* (*trawaill* > *travaill*; *wawis* > *wavis*), where *u* = consonantal *w* (*suerd* > *swerd*; *tua* > *twa*).

Capitalisation is editorial. Punctuation is also editorial and, particularly within the earlier texts, reflects the rhythms of the reading voice. Editorially therefore, in texts written to be read aloud, with pauses left to the discretion of the orator, we have not inserted words lacking manuscript authority, simply to produce metrical regularity (see *The Kingis Quair*, st. 8, n. 9).

In later printed texts we have tried to keep punctuation alterations to a minimum. There are however exceptions. In the extract from *The Jewel*, consistant with our aim of encouraging textual accessibility, we have added and altered punctuation, as well as inserting paragraphs in this thinly punctuated and convoluted text.

Glosses: The glossing procedure is also governed by the principle of accessibility. The prime aim is to convey the sense accurately. On occasions this may imply a departure from the strict grammatical sense although such instances have been kept to a minimum. Translations which express the sense freely are preceded by 'i.e.' When a phrase, line or lines of text are too complex to be explained within the glossing they are translated and/or explained within the Notes.

Glosses for verse are placed to the side of the text; glosses for prose are situated at the foot of the relevant page. The glossed word or phrase is indicated by '°'. As the following quotation from Henryson's 'The Cok and the Fox' illustrates, a semi-colon marks off the next gloss within the line; alternative senses of the same word are separated by '/'.

'And ouerheillit° with typis figurall'° *covered over/adorned; symbols*

Capital letters are the only punctuation transferred from text to gloss. We have exercised our editorial judgement in relation to the reiteration (as memorial aid or because of variant meanings due to context change) of glosses within a given text.

Notes, placed at the foot of the page of verse texts or at the end of prose texts, cover editorial and glossing issues. A thorough noting and glossing policy has been pursued in line with our wish to balance sensitive transcription of individual texts with scholastic integrity, and in the hope that it is helpful to provide a full range of guidance options—which can be side-stepped within each reader's individual quest.

Language

(i) Linguistic. This provides brief guidelines on Early and Middle Scots.

i and *y* are used interchangeably: *sine/syne*; *nicht/nycht*.

quh corresponds to English *wh*—as in *quha* (who); *quhat* (what).

Metathesis of *r* is not uncommon: *crudis* for *curdis*; *brist* for *birst* etc.

The plural form *is/ys* (sometimes treated as a separate unstressed syllable—'And nevir to uther *craftis* clame') is generally pronounced as *s*—'Pansches, *puddingis* of Jok and Jame'. ('To the Merchantis of Edinburgh', st. 5.4; st. 4.4) The alternative *es* form of the plural is shown in 'Pansches'.

Present participles of verbs end in *and*: *stinkand* = stinking; *lachand* = laughing.

The past participles of strong verbs end in *yn/in*: *writtyn*; *bundin*.

The past participles of weak verbs end in *t/yt/it*: *polist; offendit.*

The ending of present indicative verbs in the 2nd and 3rd person singular is *ys/is*. However, if the subject of the verb is a plural noun or if the subject is the personal pronoun not immediately preceding the verb, then the ending *ys/is*. can occur with other persons. For example: *I weip and sichis; we kiss and cossis; as clerkis sayis.*

Periphrastic forms of the past tense—*gan lyte; did waver*—are not uncommon; the particularly Scottish construction (*can* + infinitive, where *can* is a form of *gan*) may be confusing. Example:

> '[ane paddock]...
> Put up hir heid and on the bank can clym
> Quhilk be nature could douk and gaylie swym.'
> ('The Paddock and the Mous' st. 2.2-4)

(ii) Faux Amis: A non-comprehensive list of word forms in Scots, which may occasionally suggest an obvious equivalent in English, yet mean something different.

air	early
bald	bold fellow
be	by
belyve	quickly
burde	maiden
but	without, outside
careful	anxious
cleine	pure
fast	firmly, forcibly
fell	cruel
gif	if
hard	heard
he/hie	haste
incontinent	immediately
let (n)	delay
let (v)	hinder, neglect
liking	happiness
list	wish, choose
luffly	loveable
lustie	agreeable, delightful
man	must
meit	suitable
myschieff	misfortune, evil fate
or	before
our	over
quhil	until
ressave	receive
rid	advise
sad	serious, solemn
s[c]hed	parted
sely	simple, feeble, poor, innocent

serve	deserve
stout	brave
than	then
the	you
then	than
till	to, for
uncouth	unknown
wait	know
walk	wake, waken
wantoun	high spirited, unbridled,wild
wants	lacks
win	gain, earn
wise	manner, fashion
without	outside

Acknowledgements

For financial support, we are grateful to The Binks Trust; The Deric Bolton Poetry Trust; The Scottish Arts Council; The Carnegie Trust for the Universities of Scotland and The Pilgrim Trust. For moral support we are inexpressibly grateful to our long suffering families. We also thank the many colleagues who willingly answered the endless number of questions engendered by a work of this nature. In particular, John and Winifred MacQueen advised on the Latin translations and Notes; Sarah M. Dunnigan aided us on the Renaissance lyric and on the Bibliography; William Gillies counselled us carefully and patiently on the Gaelic selections, while Graham Runnalls counterchecked the French editions. Substantial assistance was also tendered by Jamie Reid Baxter, David Donachie, Janet Foggie, John McGavin, Kevin McGinley, Roy Pinkerton, Chris Robinson, Donna Rodger and Catriona Scott. The 1996-97, 'Scottish Literature 1470-1700' Honours Class are also thanked for their interest and enthusiastic reponse. To the Council of the Scottish Text Society, the Editors of *The Dictionary of the Older Scottish Tongue* and the staff of all the libraries which held relevant manuscripts and early printed books, we wish to record our thanks for granting consultation rights with such good will. Inevitably, the work of earlier scholars has enriched the book. In particular, we profited from the scholarship of Priscilla Bawcutt and Felicity Riddy's *Longer Scottish Poems 1375-1650* and Roderick Lyall's edition of Lindsay's *Ane Satyre of the Thrie Estaitis*. Our own textual journey has been a long, humbling but hopefully profitable one.

Dedication

This book is dedicated to George Elder Davie

SECTION A: EARLY SCOTS

§ 1 John Barbour (c.1320–1395): *The Bruce.*

John Barbour probably came from the south west of Scotland—Ayrshire or Dumfries—but the first extant records concerning his life place him, in May 1355, as Precentor of Dunkeld Cathedral. In order to prepare himself for a career within the legal and administrative division of the church, he studied at the University of Paris and on his return was rewarded with rapid promotion. By 1357, Barbour had become Archdeacon of Aberdeen. He was, therefore, a prominent figure during the latter part of David II's reign. But it was Robert II who drew him into the immediate court circle in order to take advantage of his talents as cleric, historian and poet.

The Bruce *is the earliest surviving Scots poem of any length. Barbour worked on it during the 1370s and it comprises 20 books. Centred on Robert I, it traces the Scottish Wars of Independence in the early fourteenth century from their origins through Bannockburn to the Irish Wars and the death, not only of Bruce, but of his major ally, James Douglas. The proclaimed political purpose is to remind the weak nobles in the reign of the second Robert of the courage-in-patriotism of their predecessors under the first Robert. The poem may well have been performed in front of this audience at the royal command.*

Text: *Barbour's major literary strengths lie in his powerful, yet simple, narrative style. In the chosen extract (Book I), passages of this kind mingle with a more serious critical introduction to the author's intentions. The first verse paragraph (1–36) gives a valuable account of the persuasive methods employed by a fourteenth century bard, whose works—even when written down—were designed to be recited or sung. The retrospective look at earlier Scottish history (37–444) dramatically contextualises Bruce's task within the long battles over succession to the crown of Scotland. Despite the surface simplicity, a good deal of thought has gone into the 'romantic' presentation of the war—its heroes and villains. The notes, while discussing broader issues, including the form of the work as a whole, provide historical background and trace the way in which the conventions of Epic and Chanson de Geste intertwine with those of Romance (445–630). In this final section, the major contestants are introduced, the battle lines are drawn and the extended struggle for national freedom begins.*

Context: *Books II–IV trace the early defeats suffered by Bruce and his followers, culminating with the death of Edward I of England. Books V-X cover the successful campaign through a series of phases—guerilla tactics, trick victories, the gaining of castles. Books XI–XIII are devoted to the crucial victory over Edward II and the full English army at Bannockburn. Books XIV–XIX are primarily concerned with Edward Bruce's campaigns in Ireland, but they also enact the need to be constantly vigilant at home if English attempts to regain feudal supremacy are to be countered. Book XX brings peace, the holy death of Bruce and Douglas's crusade—carrying his monarch's heart. It also sites a second 'golden age' within Barbour's own time under Robert II.*

The Bruce: Book One

Storys to rede° ar delitabill° — *read (aloud); delightful*
Suppos that° thai be nocht bot fabill;° — *Even if; only fiction*
Than° suld storys that suthfast° wer — *Then; truthful*
—And° thai war said on gud maner°— — *If; well recited*

Have doubill plesance° in heryng.[1] *pleasure*
The first plesance is the carpyng,° *reading aloud*
And the tothir° the suthfastnes *second*
That schawys the thing rycht as it wes;
And suth thyngis that ar likand° *enjoyable*
Tyll° mannys heryng ar plesand. *To*
Tharfor I wald fayne set my will
—Giff° my wyt° mycht suffice thartill°— *If; ability; thereto*
To put in wryt° a suthfast story *write down*
That it lest ay° furth in memory[2] *may endure for ever*
Swa that na tyme of lenth it let
Na ger it haly be foryet.[3]
For aulde storys that men redys
Representis to thaim the dedys
Of stalwart folk that lyvyt ar,° *who lived before*
Rycht as thai than in presence war;[4]
And certis thai suld weill have prys,° *honour*
That in thar tyme war wycht° and wys,° *strong; wise*
And led thar lyf in gret travaill,° *hardship*
And oft in hard stour° off bataill *conflict*
Wan gret price off chevalry,° *chivalric renown*
And war voydyt off cowardy° *devoid of cowardice*
(As wes King Robert off Scotland,[5]
That hardy° wes off hart and hand, *bold*
And gud Schyr James off Douglas,[6]
That in his tyme sa worthy was,
That off hys price and hys bounte° *goodness*
In fer landis° renownyt wes he) *far-off lands*
Off thaim[7] I thynk° this buk to ma.° *intend; make*
Now God gyf grace that I may swa° *so (in such a way)*
Tret° it and bring it till endyng, *Handle*
That I say nocht bot suthfast° thing. *truthful*

Quhen Alexander the king wes deid[8]
That Scotland haid to steyr° and leid, *guide*
The land sex yer and mayr, perfay° *in faith*

1. ED. Copy Text: Edinburgh MS. The fact that the poem is to be read aloud is heavily stressed in the opening section. Until printing was established, written compositions were recited from the few manuscripts available.
2. Memorial techniques result from the aurality noted above. Poetry was regarded as a branch of persuasive oratory as Barbour's introduction confirms.
3. ll. 15–16. 'So that the length of time passing may not obscure it nor cause it wholly to be forgotten'.
4. 'Just as they [i.e. the stalwart folk of earlier days] then appeared...' In this case, the weak nobles at Robert II's court in the mid 1370s are being imaginatively returned to the patriotic example set by their predecessors at the turn of the fourteenth century.
5. Robert Bruce, the major hero of Barbour's Romance, was a claimant for the Scottish throne from 1304. He reigned as Robert I until 1329.
6. Sir James Douglas (d. 1330). He plays a major role in the Romance. If you are trying to persuade a group of nobles to change their ways, it is wise to keep a noble at the centre of the action. (See n. 4.)
7. 'Thaim' refers to the 'stalwart folk' of l. 19. Bruce and Douglas are merely outstanding leaders within a national movement.
8. Barbour returns to the unexpected death of King Alexander III. His fall from his horse at Kinghorn in 1286 began the uncertainty over the succession to the Scottish throne.

Lay desolat eftyr hys day;° *i.e. reign*
Till that the barnage° at the last *barons (in assembly)*
Assemblyt thaim and fayndyt fast° *tried hard*
To cheys a king thar land to ster,° *to guide their land*
That off awncestry cummyn wer° *Who might be descended by ancestry*
Of kingis that aucht that reawte° *had royal blood*
And mayst had rycht thair king to be.
Bot envy, that is sa feloune,° *cruel/wicked*
Maid amang thaim gret discencioun;° *disagreement*
For sum wald haif the Balleoll king[9]
For he wes cummyn off the offspryng
Off hir that eldest systir was;
And othir sum nyt° all that cas° *denied; argument*
And said that he thair king suld be
That war in alsner degre° *as near degree (of kinship)*
And cummyn war of the neist° male *nearest*
And in branch collaterale.° *related by descent*
Thai said, successioun of kyngrik° *inheritance of a kingdom*
Was nocht to lawer feys[10] lik,° *not similar to lower fiefs*
For thar° mycht succed na female *there (in those cases)*
Quhill° foundyn mycht be ony male *So long as*
That were in lyne evyn° descendand. *in direct line*
Thai bar all othir wayis on hand,° *stated it was quite otherwise*
For than the neyst cummyn off the seid°— *seed (i.e. to be born)*
Man *or* woman—suld succeid.
Be this resoun that part thocht hale° *that faction all agreed*
That the Lord off Anandyrdale,
Robert the Bruys, Erle off Carryk,[11]
Aucht to succeid to the kynryk.
The barownys° thus war at discord, *barons*
That on na maner mycht accord;° *could concur*
Till at the last thai all concordyt° *agreed*
That all thar spek° suld be recordyt° *discussion; reported*
Till Schyr Edward of Yngland King,[12]
And he suld swer° that, but fenyeyng,° *swear; without deceit*
He suld that arbytre° disclar° *arbitration; pronounce*
—Off thir twa that I tauld of ar°— *before*
Quhilk° suld succeid to sic a hycht° *Which one; high position*
And lat him ryng° that had the rycht.° *reign; right*
This ordynance° thaim thocht the best, *arrangement*
For at that tyme wes pes and rest
Betwyx° Scotland and Ingland bath,° *Between; both*

9. When the Maid of Norway died in 1290, John Balliol claimed the throne through his mother Devorguilla (ll. 51–2).

10. Fiefs = estates surrendered on death to a feudal superior.

11. This competition for the succession precedes the time of Robert I by two generations. With examples in Anglo Norman Romance as his authority, Barbour 'confuses' three generations of the Bruces to create a 'family hero'.

12. Edward I, King of England (1272–1307), known as 'the hammer of the Scots'. He also was a competitor for the Scottish crown in opposition to all three Bruces.

And thai couth nocht persave° the skaith° *foresee; evil*
That towart thaim wes apperand;° *brewing*
For that at° the King off England *For because*
Held swylk° freyndschip and cumpany *such*
To thar king that wes swa worthy,° *who was so noble*
Thai trowyt° that he, as gud nychtbur° *believed; neighbour*
And as freyndsome compositur,° *friendly arbiter*
Wald have jugyt in lawte;° *according to law*
Bot othir wayis all yeid the gle.° *went the game*
A, blynd folk, full off all foly!
Haid ye umbethocht yow enkrely° *you reflected carefully*
Quhat perell to yow mycht apper,
Ye had nocht wrocht° on that maner. *would not have acted*
Haid ye tane keip how at,° that king *taken account of the way in which*
Alwayis, forowtyn sojournyng,° *without stopping*
Travayllyt for to wyn senyory[13]
And throw° his mycht till° occupy *through; to*
Landis that war till him marcheand,° *bordering upon*
As Walis° was and als° Ireland, *Wales; also*
That he put to swylk thrillage,° *such thraldom/servitude*
That thai that war off hey parage° *noble lineage*
Suld ryn on fute as rebaldaill.[14]
Quhen he wald our folk assaill,° *go to battle against*
Durst nane of Walis in bataill ride;°[15] *ride on horseback*
Na yet, fra evyn° fell, abyd *after evening*
Castell or wallyt toune within,
That he ne suld lyff and lymmys tyne.° *lose*
Into swilk thrillage[16] thaim held he,
That° he ourcome throw his powste,° *Whom; power*
Ye mycht se° he suld occupy *You might guess*
Throw slycht,° that he ne mycht throw maistri.° *guile; power*
Had ye tane kep° quhat was thrillage *taken account of*
And had consideryt his usage,° *custom*
That gryppyt° ay but gayne-gevyng,° *seized; without restoring*
Ye suld (forowtyn his demyng)° *without his judging*
Haiff chosyn yow a king that mycht
Have haldyn weyle° the land in rycht.° *governed well; justice*
Walys° ensample mycht have bene *Wales*
To yow, had ye it forow sene.° *seen beforehand/kept in mind*
And wys men sayis he is happy
That, be othir, will him chasty,°[17] *improve himself*
For unfayr° thingis may fall perfay° *unfortunate; in truth*
Als weill to-morn as yisterday.
Bot ye traistyt in lawte

13. 'Laboured [or journeyed] to gain feudal control.'
14. 'Had to fight horseless as if they were mere menials.'
15. ll. 104–5. When the Scots, under Wallace at Falkirk and under Bruce at Bannockburn, fought the Welsh, they were infantrymen within the English army.
16. Serfdom, through the example of Wales (l. 119), is a focus in the poem before freedom. See n. 23.
17. ll. 121–2. Proverbial, 'Wise men learn by other men's mistakes, fools by their own'.

As sympile folk but mawyte,°	*without malice*
And wyst nocht quhat suld eftir tyd.°	*happen*
For in this warld that is sa wyde	
Is nane determynat,° that sall	*fated*
Knaw thingis that ar to fall;°	*are about to happen*
Bot° God, that is off maist poweste,°	*Only; most powerful of all*
Reservyt till° His majeste,	*Has reserved for*
For to knaw in His prescience°	*foreknowledge*
Of alkyn tyme the movence.°[18]	*mutation*
On this maner assentyt° war	*agreed*
The barownis, as I said yow ar;°	*before*
And throuch thar aller hale assent°	*full assent of them all*
Messingeris till hym thai sent,	
That was than in the Haly Land,°	*Holy Land*
On Saracenys warrayand.°[19]	*making war*
And fra he wyst° quhat charge thai had,	*the moment he knew*
He buskyt hym° but mar abad°	*hastened; more delay*
And left purpos° that he had tane°	*abandoned the cause; undertaken*
And till Ingland agayne is gane;	
And syne° till Scotland word send he	*afterwards*
That thai suld mak ane assemble,°	*form an assembly*
And he in hy° suld cum to do	*haste*
In all thing as thai wrayt° him to.	*wrote (asking)*
But he thocht weile, throuch° thar debat,°	*by means of; wrangling*
That he suld slely° fynd the gate,°	*cunningly; way*
How that he all the senyowry°	*sovereignty*
Throw his gret mycht suld occupy.	
And to Robert the Bruyss said he: [20]	
'Gyf yow will hald in cheyff of° me	*tenure from*
For evirmar, and thine ofspryng,	
I sall do swa° yow sall be king.'	*work so that*
'Schyr,' said he, 'sa God me save,	
The kynryk yarn° I nocht to have.	*yearn*
Bot—gyff it fall of rycht to me	
And gyff God will that it sa be—	
I sall als frely in all thing	
Hald it as it afferis to king,°	*is appropriate to kingship*
Or as myn eldris forouth° me	*forefathers before*
Held it in freyast reawte.'°	*most free/noblest regality*
The tothir wreyth him° and swar°	*grew angry; swore*
That he suld have it nevir mar	
And turnyt him in wreth away.	
Bot Schir Jhon the Balleoll, perfay,	

18. Though God alone is entirely free because He knows all in advance, the more man uses his knowledge to anticipate events, the less he will be bound by fate.
19. This visit to the Holy Land is introduced against the evidence of history to provide a neat contrast between the first book and the last (Book 20).
20. Fordun, Barbour's major source, notes that this is the 'senior' Bruce (i.e. Robert I's grandfather). Barbour again encourages his audience to equate grandfather and grandson.

Assentyt till him° in all his will— *i.e. to Edward*
Quharthrouch° fell, eftir, mekill° ill. *Whereby; much*
He° was king bot a litill quhile *i.e. Balliol*
And, throuch gret sutelte and gyle° *guile*
(For litill enchesone° or nane) *reason*
He was arestyt syne° and tane, *then arrested*
And degradyt° syne wes he *stripped*
Off honour and of dignite.° *rank*
Quhethir it wes throuch wrang or rycht,
God wat° it, that is maist off mycht. *knows*

Quhen Schir Edward, the mychty king,
Had on this wys done his likyng
Off Jhone the Balleoll—that swa sone° *so soon*
Was all defawtyt° and undone— *found wanting*
To Scotland went he than in hy,° *haste*
And all the land gan occupy,° *occupied*
Sa hale,° that bath castell and toune *So completely*
War intill his possessioune,
Fra Weik anent° Orknay *Wick near to*
To Mullyr-snuk° in Gallaway[21], *Mull-promontory,*
And stuffyt° all with Inglismen.° *crammed; Englishmen*
Schyrreffys° and bailyeys maid he then *Sheriffs*
And alkyn othir officeris° *other officials of every kind*
That, for to govern land afferis,° *appertain to government*
He maid off° Inglis nation; *from within (the)*
That worthyt° than sa ryth fellone° *Who became; so very cruel*
And sa wykkyt and covatous
And sa hawtane° and dispitous° *haughty; contemptuous*
That Scottismen mycht do na thing
That evir mycht pleys to thar liking.
Thar wyvis wald thai oft forly° *rape*
And thar dochtrys dispitusly;° *mercilessly/contemptuously*
And—gyff ony of thaim tharat war wrath—
Thai watyt° hym wele with gret scaith;° *treated; cruelty*
For thai suld fynd sone enchesone° *cause*
To put hym to destruccione
And gyff that ony man thaim by° *in their vicinity*
Had ony thing that wes worthy° *of value*
—As hors or hund or othir thing
That war plesand to thar liking°— *i.e. took their fancy*
With rycht or wrang it have wald thai;
And gyf ony wald thaim withsay,° *oppose*
Thai suld swa do,° that thai suld tyne° *act in such a way; lose*
Othir° land or lyff, or leyff in pyne,° *Either; live in misery*
For thai dempt° thaim eftir thar° will, *judged; i.e. the officers'*
Takand na kep to rycht na skill.[22]

21. I.e. The Mull of Galloway.
22. 'Paying no attention to justice or knowledge.'

A! quhat° thai dempt thaim felonly!° — *how…lawlessly*
For gud knychtis that war worthy,
For litill enchesoune or than nane,
Thai hangyt be the nekbane.

Alas, that folk that evir wes fre[23]
—And in fredome wount for° to be— — *accustomed*
Throw thar gret myschance° and foly — *misfortune*
War tretyt than sa wykkytly
That thar fays° thar jugis war!° — *foes; judges were*
Quhat wrechitnes° may man have mar?° — *misery; more*
A! fredome is a noble thing!
Fredome mays° man to haiff liking,° — *permits; happiness*
Fredome all solace to man giffis,° — *gives*
He levys at es° that frely levys. — *at ease*
A noble hart may haiff nane es,° — *no rest*
Na ellys nocht° that may him ples,° — *Nor anything else; please*
Gif fredome failye, for fre liking° — *free choice*
Is yarnyt our° all othir thing. — *desired above*
Na, he that ay has levyt fre° — *has always lived freely*
May nocht knaw weill the propyrte,° — *(particular) state*
The angyr na° the wrechyt dome,° — *nor; fate*
That is cowplyt to° foule thryldome° — *is coupled with; slavery*
Bot gyff° he had assayit° it. — *Unless; (personally) experienced*
Than, all perquer,[24] he suld it wyt° — *know*
And suld think fredome mar to prys° — *to be more highly valued*
Than all the gold in warld that is!
Thus contrar° thingis evirmar — *contrasting*
Discoveringis of the tothir° ar;[25] — *explanations of the other*
And he that thryll is, has nocht his.° — *has nothing of his own*
All that he has énbandownyt° is — *made subject*
Till° hys lord, quhatevir he be. — *To*
Yeyt,° has he nocht sa mekill fre° — *Yet; so great a freedom*
As° fre wyll to leyve or do° — *As…not to do or to do*
That° at hys hart hym drawis to?° — *Whatever; inclines him to*
Than mays clerkis° questioun — *learned men*
(Quhen thai fall in disputacioun)
That, gyff° man bad his thryll° owcht do — *if; ordered his slave*
And in the samyn tym come him to° — *same time (there) came to him*
His wyff and askyt him hyr det,° — *her due*
Quhethir he his lordis neid suld let° — *neglect*
And pay fryst° that he aucht, and syne° — *first; then*
Do furth° his lordis commandyne;° — *Carry out; command(ment)*
Or leve onpayit° his wyff and do — *unpaid/unrequited*

23. Freedom follows thraldom in the poem and is praised in relation to it—that is, as a contingent, political value rather than an absolute moral one.
24. 'Perquer' from Fr. 'par coeur' and so 'by heart'. Here, it has the sense of 'thoroughly' or 'through heartfelt experience'.
25. The general sense is that opposed causes always have interdependent consequences. This is the topic for the clerkly (scholarly) disputation: l. 250.

Thai° thingis that commaundyt is him to.	*Those*
I leve all the solucioun°	*entire solution (of the case)*
Till thaim that ar off mar renoun.°[26]	*ability*
Bot sen thai mak sic comperyng°	*comparison*
Betwix the dettis° off wedding	*dues*
And lordis bidding till his threll,	
Ye may weile se, thoucht° nane yow tell,	*although*
How hard a thing that threldome is;	
For men may weile se,° that ar wys,°	*well see; who are wise*
That wedding is the hardest band°	*bond*
That ony man may tak on hand,	
And thryldome is weill wer° than deid;°	*much worse; death*
For, quhill° a thryll his lyff may leid,	*as long as*
It merrys° him body and banys,°	*harms; bones*
And dede anoyis° him bot anys.°	*troubles; only once*
Schortly to say is:° nane can tell	*To sum up*
The halle° condicioun of a threll.	*overall*
Thusgat° levyt thai and in sic thrillage°—	*In this way; servitude*
Bath pur° and thai off hey parage°—	*Both poor; of high lineage*
For off the lordis sum thai slew	
And sum thai hangyt and sum thai drew,	
And sum thai put in presoune	
Forowten° caus or enchesoun.°	*Without; reason*
And, amang othir off Dowglas,°	*others of the Douglas family*
Put in presoun Schir Wilyam was,	
That off Douglas was lord and syr;°[27]	*sire*
Off him thai makyt a martyr.	
Fra° thai in presoune him sleuch,°	*From the time that; slew*
Hys land, that is fayr inewch,	
Thai the Lord of Clyffurd gave.[28]	
He had a sone, a litill knave,°	*boy*
That wes than bot° a litill page.	*Who at that time was only*
Bot syne° he wes off gret vaslage,°	*later; valour*
Hys fadyr dede he vengyt° swa	*avenged*
That in Ingland, I undirta,°	*guarantee*
Wes nane off lyve° that hym ne dred,°	*alive; did not dread*
For he sa fele° off harnys° sched,°	*many; brains; split*
That nane that lyvys thaim can tell.°	*can count them up*
Bot wondirly° hard thingis fell°	*wondrously; befell...*
Till him,° or° he till state° wes brocht.	*Him; before; (proper) position*
Thair wes nane aventur that mocht°	*could*

26. This is not a democratic appeal for the removal of serfs. Barbour kept serfs and Robert II was an autocratic ruler. The example shows how two contrasting but divinely authorized bonds may conflict and demand prioritizing.

27. Sir William Douglas, father of Sir James, did fight with Wallace (1296–97), was imprisoned by the English and did die at their hands (1298). But Barbour's attempt to turn his life into a legend is another example of purified history.

28. There is no precise historical support for this assertion but Clifford did command the castle when it was besieged by Douglas in 1307.

Stunay° hys hart na ger him let°	*Daunt; nor make him...*
To do° the thing he wes on set;	*Abandon*
For he thocht ay encrely°	*carefully*
To do his deid° avysily.° [29]	*deed; prudently*
He thocht weill he wes worth na seyle°	*trust*
That mycht of nane anoyis feyle,[30]	
And als for till escheve° gret thingis	*to (be unable to) achieve*
And hard travalys° and barganyngis,°	*undertakings; combats*
That suld ger his price° dowblyt be.	*make his praise*
Quharfor, in all hys lyvetime, he	
Wes in gret payn° and gret travaill	*hardship*
And nevir wald for myscheiff° faill,°	*because of evil fate; give up*
Bot dryve° the thing rycht to the end,	*pursue*
And tak the ure° that God wald send.	*fortune*
Hys name wes James of Douglas; [31]	
And quhen he herd his fadir was	
Put in presoune so fellounly°	*unlawfully/cruelly*
And at° his landis halyly°	*And that; entirely*
War gevyn to the Clyffurd, perfay,	
He wyst nocht quhat to do na say	
For he had na thing for to dispend,°	*money to spend*
Na thar wes nane that evir him kend°	*of his acquaintance*
Wald do sa mekill for him, that he	
Mycht sufficiantly fundyn° be.	*funded*
Than wes he wondir will of wane°	*at a complete loss*
And sodanly, in hart has tane°	*i.e. decided*
That he wald travaile our° the se	*over*
And a quhile in Parys be,	
And dre myscheiff° quhar nane hym kend	*endure misfortune*
Till° God sum succouris° till him send;	*Until; means of aid*
And as he thocht, he did rycht swa.	
And sone to Parys can he ga°	*he went*
And levyt thar full sympylly.°	*very frugally*
Thequethir,° he glaid was and joly	*Nevertheless*
And till swylk thowlesnes he yeid	
As the cours askis off yowtheid; [32]	
And umquhill° into rybbaldaill.°	*sometimes; low company*
And that may mony tyme availl,°	*be of use*
For knawlage off mony statis°	*many conditions of life*
May quhile availye° full mony gatis;°	*sometimes be of use; ways*
As to the gud Erle off Artayis,°	*Artois*
Robert, befell intill his dayis,°[33]	*in his time*

29. The life story of Douglas opens with all the pathos and piety of a Saint's Life.
30. ll. 303–4. 'He deeply believed the man who could not feel injustices to be unworthy of any trust.'
31. See n. 6.
32. 'And gave himself up to the sort of riotous behaviour which time's course expects from youth.' The argument here—supported by Cato and later dramatised by Shakespeare in *Henry IV*—is that a leader may gain experience of all kinds of people through youthful revelry.
33. Robert of Artois, like Douglas, wished to regain his father's lands. To achieve this he feigned madness.

For oft feynyeyng° off rybbaldy°	*pretence; dissipation*
Availyeit him and that gretly.	
And Catone sayis us° in his wryt°	*tells us; writing*
To fenye foly quhile is wyt.°	*sometimes is wisdom*
In Parys ner thre yer dwellyt he;°	*i.e. James Douglas*
And then come tythandis° our° the se	*tidings; (from) over*
That his fadyr wes done to ded.°	*put to death*
Then wes he wa° and will of red,°	*woeful; bewildered*
And thocht that he wald hame agayne	
To luk gyf° he, throw ony payn,°	*see whether; effort*
Mycht wyn agayn his heritage	
And his men out off all thryllage.°	*slavery*
To Sanct Androws° he come in hy,°	*St Andrews; haste*
Quhar the byschop full curtasly	
Resavyt° him and gert him wer°	*Received; had him carry about*
His knyvys, forouth° him to scher;°[34]	*in front of; carve*
And cled° him rycht honorabilly	*dressed*
And gert ordayn° quhar he suld ly.°	*gave orders (as to); lodge*
A weile gret quhile° thar dwellyt he.	*(For) a very long time*
All men lufyt him for his bounte,°	*goodness*
For he wes off full fayr effer°	*conduct*
—Wys, curtais° and deboner,°	*courteous; debonair*
Larg° and luffand° als wes he—	*generous; loving*
And our° all thing luffyt lawte.°[35]	*above; loyalty*
Leawte to luff° is na foly;	*to love loyalty*
Throuch leawte liffis men rychtwisly.°	*righteously*
With A vertu° and leawte [36]	*one virtue only*
A man may yeit° sufficyand° be	*still; sufficient*
And, but° leaute, may nane haiff price°	*without; worth*
Quethir he be wycht° or he be wys;	*strong*
For quhar it failyeys,° na vertu	*is lacking*
May be off price na of valu°	*neither of worth nor value*
To mak a man sa gud that he	
May symply callyt, 'gud man', be.	
He wes in all his dedis° lele,°	*deeds; faithful*
For him dedeynyeit nocht° to dele	*he did not deign*
With trechery na with falset.°	*falsehood*
His hart on hey honour wes set	
And hym contenyt° on sic maner,	*(he) conducted himself*
That all him luffyt that war him ner.	
Bot he wes nocht sa fayr that we	
Suld spek gretly off his beaute.	
In vysage° wes he sumdeill° gray	*countenance; somewhat*
And had blak har°, as Ic hard° say,	*hair; I heard*
Bot off lymmys° he wes weill maid,	*limbs*

34. By permitting Douglas to carve, Bishop Lamberton of St Andrews shows his high regard for his squire.
35. The spirit of loving loyalty, if spread downwards through all the individuals in a nation, may overcome the problems exemplified in the cases of 'Wales' and the serf.
36. ED. The Edinburgh MS has a capital A for emphasis. The line allows metrically for the dramatic pauses of the speaking voice, which highlight the crucial word 'leawte'.

With banys gret° and schuldrys° braid.	*mighty bones; shoulders*
His body wes weyll maid and lenye,°	*lean/supple*
As thai that saw hym said to me.	
Quhen he wes blyth, he wes lufly,°	*loveable*
And meyk and sweyt in cumpany;	
Bot quha in battaill mycht him se°	*(for) whoever saw him*
All othir contenance° had he.	*A wholly different aspect*
And in spek,° wlispyt he sumdeill°—	*speech; he lisped slightly*
Bot that sat° him rycht wondre weill.	*suited*
Till gud Ector of Troy°[37] mycht he	*Hector of Troy*
In mony thingis liknyt° be.	*compared*
Ector had blak har° as he had	*black hair*
And stark lymmys, and rycht weill maid	
And wlispyt alswa as° did he;	*lisped just as*
And wes fullfillyt of leawte°	*filled full of loyalty*
And wes curtais and wys and wycht.	
Bot, off° manheid and mekill mycht,	*But as regards*
Till Ector dar I nane comper°	*compare*
Off all that evir in warldys wer.	
Thequhethir,° in his tyme sa wrocht he°	*Nonetheless; he (Douglas)*
That he suld gretly lowyt° be.	*praised*
He dwellyt thar quhill on a tid,°	*until a time (when)*
The king Edward, with mekill prid°	*pomp*
Come to Strevillyne° with gret mengye°	*Stirling; company*
For till hald thar ane assemble.	
Thiddirwart° went mony baroune.	*Thither*
Byschop Wylyame off Lambyrtoun	
Raid thiddyr als and with him was	
This squyer, James of Douglas.	
The Byschop led him to the king	
And said, 'Schir, heyr I to yow bryng	
This child, that clemys° your man to be	*claims*
And prayis° yow par cheryte,°	*beseeches; in Charity's name*
That ye resave her° his homage	*receive here*
And grantis him his heritage.'	
'Quhat landis clemys he?' said the king.	
'Schyr, giff that it be your liking,	
He clemys the lordschip off Douglas,	
For lord tharof hys fadir was.'	
The king then wrethyt hym encrely°	*grew very angry*
And said: 'Schir Byschop, sekyrly,°	*certainly*
Gyff thow wald kep thi fewte,°	*allegiance*
Thow maid nane sic speking to me!	
Hys fadyr ay wes my fay feloune°	*bitter enemy*
And deyt° tharfor in my presoun,°	*died; prison*
And wes agayne° my majeste.	*against*

37. Douglas is the first Scot to be linked with one of the nine heroes ('Worthies') of Romance. The Matter of Rome was centred on Alexander, Hector and Julius Caesar.

Tharfor hys ayr° I aucht to be. *(William Douglas') heir*
Ga purches° land quharevir he may, *Let him (James Douglas) go and buy*
For tharoff havys he nane° perfay. *owns none*
The Clyffurd sall thaim haiff, for he
Ay lely° has servyt to me.' *Always loyally*
The byschop hard° him swa answer *heard*
And durst than spek till him na mar,
Bot fra his presence went in hy,
For he dred sayr his felouny° *was sorely afraid of his ferocity*
Swa that he na mar spak tharto.
The king did that he com to do
And went till Ingland syn agayn° *then again*
With mony man of mekill mayn.° *strength*

Lordingis,° quha likis for till her,° *My lords; to hear/listen*
The Romanys° now begynnys her,[38] *Romance*
Of men that war in gret distres
And assayit° full gret hardynes° *experienced; hardship*
Or° thai mycht cum till thar entent.° *Before; reach their goal*
Bot syne our Lord sic grace thaim sent
That thai syne throw thar gret valour
Come till gret hycht° and till honour— *eminence*
Magre° thar fayis everilkane,° *In spite of; every one*
That war sa fele,° that ane till ane° *many; for every one (of us)*
Off thaim thai war weill a thowsand—
Bot, quhar God helpys, quhat may withstand!
Bot, and° we say the suthfastnes,° *if; tell the truth*
Thai war sum tyme erar may° then les; *rather more*
Bot God—that maist is of all mycht—
Preservyt thaim in His forsycht,° *prescience*
To veng° the harme and the contrer°[39] *avenge; persecution*
At that° fele° folk and pautener° *Which; numerous; cruel*
Dyd till sympill folk and worthy,
That° couth nocht help thaim self; forthi,° *Who; therefore,*
Thai war lik to the Machabeys°[40] *Maccabees*
That, as men in the Bibill seys,
Throw thar gret worschip and valour
Fawcht into mony stalwart stour° *combat*
For to delyvir thar countre
Fra folk that, throw iniquite,° *by evil means*
Held thaim and thairis in thrillage.

38. ll. 445–6 are a bardic formula. As ll. 1–444 have explained the rhetorical aims and historical background, this may be a second call for attention directed at those who only wish to hear a rousing tale. By defining his mode as 'Romance' rather than 'Chronicle', Barbour justifies his occasional historical preference for 'should have been' and 'might have been' over 'actually was'.
39. Barbour, in describing the foresight of God, also imitates it authorially. From the viewpoint of 1370, he reassures his audience in Bk I that Bk XX will end with a Scottish victory.
40. The Maccabees were a 'chosen' Biblical race. By linking the Scottish people with them, Barbour introduces the line of mythic history which traces Scotland's history via a journey from the Holy Land, by way of Spain and Ireland, to their intended homeland. Fordun makes the same comparison.

Thai wrocht swa throw thar vasselage° — *despite their slavery*
That, with few folk,° thai had victory — *with small forces*
Off° mychty kingis, as sayis the story, — *Over*
And delyveryt thar land all fre.
Quharfor thar name suld lowyt° be. — *praised*

Thys lord, the Bruys, I spak of ayr,[41]
Saw all the kynryk° swa forfayr,° — *kingdom; go to ruin*
And swa trowblyt the folk saw he,
That he tharoff had gret pitte.° — *pity*
Bot quhat pite that evir he had,
Na contenance° tharof he maid, — *visible sign*
Till on a tym Schyr Jhone Cumyn,[42]
As thai come ridand fra Strevillyn,° — *Stirling*
Said till him, 'Schir, will ye nocht se
How that governyt is this countre?
Thai sla our folk but enchesoune° — *without cause*
And haldis this land agayne resoune°— — *against (the rule of) reason*
And ye tharoff suld lord be!
And gyff that ye will trow to me,° — *believe me*
Ye sall ger mak tharof king,° — *be made king of it*
And I sall be in your helping,
With-thi° ye giff me all the land — *On the condition that*
That ye haiff now intill your hand.
And gyff that ye will nocht do swa
Na swylk a state° apon yow ta,° — *such a position; take*
All hale° my land sall youris be, — *Entirely*
And lat me ta the state on me
And bring this land out off thryllage;° — *slavery*
For thar is nothir man na page
In all this land than thai sall be
Fayn° to mak thaimselvyn fre.'[43] — *Eager*
The lord the Bruis hard his carping° — *heard what he said*
And wend° he spak bot° suthfast thing; — *thought; only*
And, for it likit till° his will, — *accorded with*
He gave his assent sone° thartill — *soon*
And said, 'Sen ye will it be swa,
I will blythly apon me ta° — *gladly take upon myself*
The state, for I wate° that I have rycht, — *know*
And rycht mays° oft the feble,° wycht.'° — *renders; feeble; strong*

The barownys thus accordyt° ar, — *agreed*
And that ilk° nycht writyn° war — *same; written down*

41. 'This lord, the Bruce, of whom I spoke before.' Barbour explicitly invites his audience to accept his new, 'romantic' biography of Robert I. By substituting the patriotic youth of his grandfather, Robert the Competitor, for Robert I's youthful service to Edward I, the poet obscures historical 'suthfastnes' in order to promote a clearer model of patriotism.
42. John Comyn was a nephew of King John and the main counter-claimant to the throne in the days of Robert the Competitor.
43. Barbour alone makes Comyn propose this agreement.

Thair endenturis,° and aythis maid° *bonds; vows sworn*
To hald° that thai forspokyn haid.° *keep to; had agreed upon*
Bot off all thing, wa worth tresoun!° *down with treason*
For thar is nothir duk ne baroun,
Na erle, na prynce, na king off mycht°— *might*
Thocht he be nevir° sa wys na wycht— *Be he never*
For wyt,° worschip,° price° na renoun, *Through knowledge; valour; praise*
That evir may wauch hym with° tresoune. *guard himself against*
Wes nocht all Troy with tresoune tane,° *captured through treason*
Quhen ten yeris of the wer wes gane?
Then slayn wes mony thowsand
Off thaim withowt, throw strenth of hand,
As Dares in his buk he wrate,[44]
And Dytis° that knew all thar state.° *Dyctes; condition*
Thai mycht nocht haiff beyn tane throw mycht,
But tresoun tuk thaim throw hyr slycht.° *trickery*
And Alexander° the conqueroure, *Alexander the Great*
That conqueryt Babilonyis tour°[45] *Babylon's tower*
And all this warld off lenth and breid° *breadth*
In twelf yer, throw his douchty deid,° *valiant action*
Wes syne destroyit throw pusoune,° *by poison (or treachery)*
In his awyne hows throw gret tresoun;
But, or he deit,° his land delt° he; *before he died; divided*
To se his dede wes gret pite.
Julius Caesar als, that wan° *conquered*
Bretane,° and Fraunce,° as douchty man, *Britain; France*
Afryk,° Arrabe,° Egipt, Surry° *Africa; Arabia; Syria*
And all Europe halyly,
And for his worschip and valour
Off Rome wes fryst maid Emperour,° *made the first Emperor*
Syne—in his Capitole°—wes he, *Capitol*
Throw thaim of his consaill prive,° *privy council*
Slayne with pusoune° rycht to the ded;° *through treachery; death*
And, quhen he saw thar wes na rede,° *nothing to be done*
Hys eyn° with his hand closit he *eyes*
For to dey with mar honeste.° *greater dignity*
Als Arthur,° that throw chevalry *King Arthur*
Maid Bretane° maistres and lady *Brittany*
Of twelf kinrykis° that he wan; *kingdoms*
And alswa° as a noble man *in addition*
He wan throw bataill Fraunce all fre,
And Lucius Yber vencusyt° he *vanquished*
That then of Rome wes Emperour.
Bot yeit, for all his gret valour,
Modreyt° (his systir son)° him slew *Mordred; nephew*

44. Dares of Crete and Dictys of Phrygia are often cited as eye-witness reporters of the Trojan war. Their accounts have not been discovered.

45. Barbour's intention of claiming, for Robert I, a place beside the established nine heroes of Romance starts here. The case of treachery, which Bruce faces, is compared to that of Alexander, Julius Caesar (ll. 529, 537: Matter of Rome) and to Arthur (l. 549: Matter of England).

And gud men als ma then inew°	*more than enough*
Throw tresoune and throw wikkitnes.	
The Broite° beris tharoff wytnes.[46]	*(the story of)* The Brut
Sa fell of this conand-making,°	*This agreement turned out similarly*
For the Cumyn° raid to the King	*(John)* Comyn
Of Ingland and tald all this cas;	
Bot, I trow, nocht all as it was.	
Bot,° the endentur° till him gaf he,	*Anyway; deed*
That soune schawyt the iniquite,	
Quharfor syne° he tholyt ded°—	*afterwards; suffered death*
Than, he couth set tharfor na rede!°	*lead no counter-argument!*
Quhen the king saw the endentur	
He wes angry out of mesur,°	*beyond measure*
And swour that he suld vengeance ta	
Off that Bruys that presumyt swa°	*so presumed*
Aganys him to brawle° or rys°	*strive; rise*
Or to conspyr on sic a wys.°	*in such a way*
And to Schyr Jhon Cumyn said he,	
That he suld, for his leawte,°	*loyalty*
Be rewardyt and that hely.	
And he him thankit humyly.	
Than thocht he to have° the leding	*would have*
Off all Scotland, but ganesaying,°	*without contradiction*
Fra at° the Bruce to dede war brocht.	*Once*
Bot oft failyeis° the fulis thocht,°	*fails; fool's thinking*
And wys mennys etling°	*planning*
Cummys nocht ay to that ending	
That thai think it sall cum to.	
For God wate° weill quhat is to do.	*knew*
Off Hys etlyng° rycht swa it fell	*In accord with His intent*
As I sall eftirwartis tell.	
He° tuk his leve and hame is went,	*He (Comyn)*
And the king a parlyament	
Gert set° thareftir hastely;[47]	*Had (parliament) convened*
And thiddir somownys he in hy	
The barownys of his reawte.°	*realm*
And to the lord the Bruce send he	
Bydding to cum to that gadryng.°	*gathering*
And he, that had na persavyng°	*presentiment*
Off the tresoun, na the falset,°	*deceit*
Raid to the king but langir let,°	*without further delay*
And in Lundon° hym herberyd° he	*London; lodged*
The fyrst day off thar assemble;	
Syn, on the morn,° to court he went.	*following day*
The kyng sat into parleament	

46. Geoffrey of Monmouth's *Historia Regum Britanniae*, which mentions the demand for tribute from King Arthur by the Roman noble, Lucius Yber (l. 554).

47. The parliament and 'seal' are invented. The many failed vows in Book 1 contrast man's deviousness and injustice against God's perfect synthesis of justice and mercy.

And, forouth° hys consaile prive,°	*before; inner council*
The lord the Bruce thar callyt he	
And schawyt hym the endentur.	
He wes in full gret aventur°	*danger*
To tyne his lyff;° bot God of mycht	*Of losing his life*
Preservyt him till hyer hycht,°	*for higher eminence*
That° wald nocht that he swa war dede.	*Who (i.e. God)*
The king betaucht° hym in that steid°	*handed over; place*
The endentur, the seile° to se,	*seal*
And askyt gyff it enselyt he.°	*whether he put his seal to it*
He lukit° the seyle ententily°	*examined; closely*
And answeryt till him humyly°	*humbly*
And sayd, 'How that I sympill be,[48]	
My seyle is nocht all tyme° with me.	*constantly*
Ik have ane othir° it to ber.°	*someone else; carry*
Tharfor, giff that your willis wer,°	*if you were to agree*
Ic ask yow respyt for to se°	*respite to look at*
This lettir,° and tharwith avysit be,°	*document; make myself acquainted*
Till to-morn that ye be set;°	*assembled*
And then, forowten langir let,°	*further delay*
This lettir sall I entyr° heyr	*produce*
Befor all your consaill planer,°	*plenary*
And thartill into boruch draw I°	*I put in pledge against it*
Myn heritage all halily.'°	*My entire inheritance*
The king thocht he wes traist inewch°	*trustworthy enough*
Sen he in bowrch° hys landis drewch,°	*in pledge...held*
And let hym with the lettir passe°	*leave*
Till entyr it, as forspokin° was.[49]	*previously agreed/uttered*

48. 'However simple I [i.e. my life style] may be...'
49. 'forespoken' by both God, the Author of all, and Barbour.

§ 2 ?James I (1396–1437): *The Kingis Quair*

Although, strictly, there is some doubt as to whether James I wrote the 'book' ('quair'), which bears his name and purports to tell his story, the fact remains that, within the fiction, it is his voice which speaks. The relevant part of his biography which occasions the drama of the poem focusses on his youth. Threatened by enemies abroad and treachery from anarchic nobles at home, the king's father, Robert III, put his eleven year old son on a ship at Leith in an attempt to ensure his safety in France, and to safeguard the succession. The vessel was captured and James delivered into English captivity for eighteen years (sts. 22–5). He also records—in an elaborate passage which owes much to Chaucer's 'Knight's Tale'—his meeting with and love for his future queen, Lady Joan Beaufort (sts. 30–67). To this extent the poem is its own history.

Over the years, critics have argued as to why the supposed heroine, Joan, then disappears throughout the long dream sequence. She is next mentioned in st. 181 and never again resumes a central position in the drama. They have also debated whether the work is well-organized or a hotchpotch; an allegory or a romance or a biography, or all three. The notes seek to give guidance and, inevitably, suggest our own views on these matters. A simple guide to the Quair's 'story' and form may well be the most helpful way of initiating readers into the search for their own interpretation.

The Kingis Quair *begins with the regal narrator reading Boethius's* **Consolation of Philosophy.** *Looking back at his experiences, he wishes to tell others what he has learned from them but has difficulty in starting to write (sts. 1–13). He thinks of his life and writing as a difficult boat journey (sts. 14–18), which then merges into the account of his literal sea-journey from Leith into imprisonment and the meeting with Joan. On her departure he is cast into misery again (sts. 19–72). THE DREAM BEGINS and has three sections—in the first (sts. 73–123) James talks with Venus; in the second (sts. 124–151) he is counselled by Minerva and in the third, journeys through an idealized vision of nature to be placed by Fortune on her wheel (sts. 152–172). THE DREAM ENDS and the awakened poet is visited by a turtle dove, bearing a message confirming that his sufferings have been divinely decreed. It is this news which leads him to thank not only Joan, but most of the characters and settings in the poem, as well as his poetic predecessors, Gower and Chaucer (sts. 173–97).*

The Kingis Quair[1]

1

Heigh in the hevynnis figure circulere,°[2] — *circular figure/sign*
The rody° sterres twynklyng as the fyre, — *reddish*
And in Aquary,° Citherea°[3] the clere — *Aquarius; the planet Venus*
Rynsid° hir tressis° like the goldin wyre, — *Rinsed; tresses*
That late tofore° in fair and fresche atyre — *Who shortly before*

1. ED. Copy Text: MS Selden (Arch. B. 24). The narrator assumes the role of King James I and tells his story. In the notes, the autobiographical nature of the poem is accepted but certainty is not possible.
2. Cf. st. 196.7 'Hich in the hevynnis figure circulere'. The poem ends as it began. Circular structures and images, which rhetoricians usually advised for poems with a divine message, characterize the *Quair*.
3. ED. Some editors amend to Cynthia. But Citherea, as the spirit of benign love, looks after the world. This is consistent with the narrator's early concern (sts. 26–39) that he does not share Nature's harmony.

Through Capricorn[4] heved° hir hornis bright.[5] *lifted up*
North northward° approchit the mydnyght; *Ever northward*

2

Quhen as I lay in bed allone waking,
New partit out of slepe° a lyte tofore,° *awakened; a short time before*
Fell me to mynd° of mony diverse thing, *There occurred to me*
Of this and that; can I noght say quharfore,° *why*
Bot slepe for craft° in erth myght I no more. *skill*
For quhich, as tho,° coude I no better wyle,° *at that time; strategy*
But toke a boke, to rede apon a quhile:° *to study for a while*

3

Of quhich the name is clepit° properly *called*
Boece° (eftere him that was the compiloure),° *Boethius; compiler*
Schewing the counsele of philosophye,[6]
Compilit by that noble senatoure
Off Rome, quhilom that was° the warldis floure, *(who) once was*
And from estate,° by Fortune for a quhile *high status*
Forjugit° was to povert° in exile. *Condemned; poverty*

4

And there to here° this worthy lord and clerk° *to hear (in that book); scholar*
His metir° swete, full of moralitee! *versifying*
His flourit° pen, so fair he set awerk *eloquent*
Discryving,° first, of his prosperitee *Describing*
And out of that his infelicitee°— *misfortune*
And than° how he, in his poleyt report,° *then; polished account*
In philosophy can him to confort.° *he gained comfort*

5

For quhich thogh I in purpose at my boke
To borowe a slepe at thilke tyme began,
Or ever I stent, my best was more to loke
Upon the writing of this noble man,[7]
That in himself the full recover wan° *gained full recovery*
Off° his infortune, povert° and distresse, *From; poverty*
And in tham set his verray sekirnesse.° *true stability*

6

And so the vertew° of his youth before *virtue*
Was in his age° the ground° of his delytis. *maturity; foundation*
Fortune the bak him turnyt,° and therfore *turned her back on him*
He makith joye and confort, that he quit° is *free*
Off thir unsekir° warldis appetitis.° *these uncertain; appetites*

4. The cycle of the zodiac is at it most southerly point.
5. Hair arranged in hornlike rolls at each side of the head.
6. Boethius (A.D. 480–524/5) wrote his *Consolation of Philosophy* while, like James, an exile in prison.
7. ll. 1–4. I.e. 'Although my initial purpose at that time was to use my book to help myself to sleep, well before I finished, my best (interest) lay in studying further what this noble man had written.'

And so aworth° he takith his penance,°	*worthily; endures his suffering*
And of his vertew maid it suffisance,[8]	

7

With mony a noble resoun,° as him likit,°	*fine argument; as it pleased him*
Enditing° in his faire Latyne tong,°	*Writing down; Latin tongue*
So full of fruyte and rethorikly pykit,°	*adorned rhetorically*
Quhich to declare my scole° is over yong.°	*scholarship; too immature*
Therefore I lat him pas and, in my tong,°	*in my (own) vernacular*
Procede I will agayn to the sentence°	*theme*
Of my mater° and leve all incidence.°	*material; incidental matter*

8

The long nyght beholding°, as I saide,	*gazing (at the book)*
My eyen° gan to smert for studying;	*eyes*
My buke I schet,° and at my hede it laide,	*shut*
And doune I lay but ony tarying,°	*without any delay*
This matere new in my mynd rolling:°	*turning over*
This is to seyne—how that eche estate,°	*rank*
As Fortune lykith, thame will translate.°[9]	*(she) will alter*

9

For sothe° it is, that on hir tolter quhele,°	*true; unstable wheel*
Every wight° cleverith in his stage,°	*individual; climbs to his set place*
And failyng foting° oft, quhen hir lest rele,°	*footing; it pleases her to whirl*
Sum up, sum doune; is non estate nor age	
Ensured more°—the prynce than the page.	*More secure (than another)*
So uncouthly° hir werdes° sche devidith,°	*strangely; fates; apportions*
Namly° in youth, that seildin ought providith.°	*Namely; seldom foresees anything*

10

Among thir thoughtis rolling to and fro,	
Fell me to mynd of my fortune and ure:°	*luck*
In tender youth how sche was first my fo°	*foe*
And eft° my frende, and how I gat recure°	*afterwards; recovered*
Off my distresse: and all myn aventure°	*all that happened to me*
I gan ourehayle°[10] that langer slepe ne rest	*I reviewed*
Ne myght I nat, so were my wittis wrest.°	*tormented*

11

Forwakit and forwalowit, thus musing,	
Wery, forlyin, I lestnyt sodaynlye.[11]	
And sone I herd the bell to matyns° ryng	*midnight matins*
And up I rase;° no langer wald I lye.	*I got up*

8. Elliptical. 'And out of his virtue gained contentment.' That is—through understanding his moral position Boethius found happiness.
9. ED. The reading voice would pause dramatically after 'lykith'. There is, therefore, no need to add words to the manuscript evidence.
10. Boethius worked through his problems, solving them in Book 5. James begins by remembering a battle which he has already won.
11. ll. 1–2: 'Weary with wakefulness and tossing about while lying in bed, musing in this way, I suddenly pricked up my ears.'

Bot now, how trowe ye,° swich a fantasye° — *would you believe; fancy*
Fell me to mynd, that ay me thoght° the bell — *I kept thinking that*
Said to me, 'Tell on, man, quhat the befell.'° — *what happened to you*

12

Thoght I tho° to myself, 'Quhat may this be? — *then*
This is myn awin ymagynacioune,
It is no lyf° that spekis unto me; — *real person*
It is a bell or that impressioune°[12] — *impression (as on wax)*
Off my thoght causith° this illusioune, — *(which) is causing*
That dooth me think so nycely in this wise.'° — *in this precise manner*
And so befell as I schall you devise.° — *relate*

13

Determynit furth therewith° in myn entent,° — *Thus resolved; intention*
Sen° I thus have ymagynit of this soune,° — *Since; sound*
(And in my tyme more ink and paper spent
To lyte° effect) I tuke conclusioune° — *little; decided*
Sum new thing to write. I set me doune° — *set myself down*
And furthwithall° my pen in hand I tuke — *straightaway*
And maid a croce°[13] and thus begouth° my buke. — *the sign of the cross; began*

14

Though youth, of nature indegest,° — *by nature immature*
Unrypit fruyte with windis variable,
Like is to the bird that fed is on the nest
And can noght flee; of wit° wayke° and unstable, — *innate understanding; weak*
To fortune both and to infortune hable;[14]
Wist thou° thy payne to cum and thy travaille,° — *If you knew; toil*
For sorow and drede wele myght thou wepe and waille!

15

Thus stant° thy confort° in unsekirnesse,° — *is based; solace; uncertainty*
And wantis it that suld° the reule and gye:° — *lacks that which should; guide*
Ryght as° the schip that sailith stereles° — *Just as; rudderless*
Upon the rokkis most to harmes hye,° — *prone to rush to harms*
For lak of it that suld bene hir supplye;° — *aid*
So standis thou here in this warldis rage,° — *fury of this world*
And wantis that suld gyde all thy viage.° — *your entire journey*

16

I mene this by myself, as in partye;° — *partly for myself*
Though Nature gave me suffisance° in youth, — *sufficiency/contentment*
The rypenesse of resoun lakkit I
To governe with my will, so lyte I couth,° — *little I understood*

12. Medieval definitions of the imagination often opposed it to the senses in this way. It works from the inner images of the mind—not from actual sounds and sights.
13. The scribe puts a cross sign in the manuscript. This underlines the Christian context of the poem as he literally 'makes the sign of the cross' before beginning.
14. 'Vulnerable to good and bad fortune alike.'

Quhen stereles to travaile° I begouth,° — *journey; began*
Amang the wavis of this warld to drive°— — *surge forward*
And how the case° anone I will discrive:° — *case (developed); describe*

17

With doutfull° hert, amang the rokkis blake° — *fearful; black*
My feble° bote full fast° to stere and rowe, — *frail; very firmly*
Helples, allone, the wynter nyght° I wake, — *throughout the winter night*
To wayte° the wynd that furthward suld me throwe.° — *Awaiting; propel me*
O empti saile, quhare is the wynd suld blowe
Me to the port,° quhare gynneth° all my game? — *harbour; begins*
Help, Calyope,° and wynd, in Marye° name! — *Calliope (Muse); Virgin Mary*

18

The rokkis clepe° I the prolixitee° — *call; verbosity*
Off doubilnesse,°[15] that doith my wittis pall;° — *duality; appal*
The lak of wynd is the deficultee° — *difficulty*
In enditing° of this lytill trety small;°[16] — *setting down; very brief treatise*
The bote I clepe the mater hole° of all— — *entire substance*
My wit, unto the saile that now I wynd° — *hoist*
To seke connyng,° though I bot lytill fynd. — *knowledge*

19

At my begynnyng, first I clepe° and call — *invoke*
To yow Cleo° and to yow Polymye,° — *Muse of history; Muse of hymning*
With Thesiphone,[17] goddis and sistris all,
In nowmer nine° as bokis specifye; — *number nine (of Muses)*
In this processe my wilsum° wittis gye,° — *wilful; direct*
And with your bryght lanternis wele convoye° — *guide well*
My pen, to write my turment and my joye!

20

In Vere,° that full of vertu° is and gude, — *Spring; regenerative power*
Quhen Nature first begynneth hir enprise,° — *enterprise*
That quhilum° was be° cruell frost and flude° — *formerly; by; flood*
And schouris scharp° opprest in mony wyse, — *bitter showers*
And Synthius° gynneth° to aryse — *Cynthius (Sun); begins*
Heigh° in the est,° amorow° soft and swete, — *High; east; in the morning*
Upward his course to drive in Ariete;°[18] — *Aries*

21

Passit mydday[19] bot foure greis evin° — *by exactly four degrees*
Off lenth and brede° his angel wingis bryght — *breadth*
He° spred upon the ground doune fro the hevin, — *He (the Sun)*

15. The double senses—literal and hidden—of allegory.
16. The allegory of sts. 15–18 shows the ship of James's life facing the 'rokkis blake' (17.1) of apparent bad fortune. This tragic fall parallels Boethius' case. But Boethius—unlike James—*wrote* easily; his difficulty lay in philosophically reconciling his fate with divine benevolence.
17. Tisiphone, one of the three Furies, is a 'sister' to the Muses only through her skill in tragic matters.
18. The sun now starts its movement northwards (cf. n.4).
19. The reference is still to the sun's journey through the zodiac and so towards the sphere of the world. The equator is crossed from south to north.

That for gladnesse and confort of the sight,
And with the tiklyng° of his hete° and light,   *gentle touch; heat*
The tender flouris opnyt thame° and sprad,°   *opened out; spread*
And in thaire nature° thankit him for glad.°   *according to (nature); joy*

22

Noght ferre passit° the state of innocence,   *Not far beyond*
Bot nere about the nowmer of yeris thre[20]
(Were it causit throu hevinly influence
Off goddis will, or othir casualtee,°   *contingency*
Can I noght say), bot out of my contree,°   *country*
By thaire avise° that had of me the cure,°   *advice; care of me*
Be see° to pas, tuke I myn aventure.°[21]   *By sea; I set out on my destiny*

23

Purvait of° all that was us necessarye,   *Provided with*
With wynd at will,° up airly by the morowe,°   *favourable wind; morning*
Streight unto schip, no longere wold we tarye,°   *delay*
The way we tuke—the tyme I tald toforowe°—   *I related previously*
With mony 'Fare wele!' and 'Sanct Johne to borowe!'°   *May St John go with you*
Off falowe° and frende; and thus with one assent°   *companion; accord*
We pullit up saile, and furth oure wayis went.

24

Upon the wavis weltering° to and fro,   *rolling*
So infortunate° was us that fremyt° day,   *inauspicious; hostile*
That maugre playnly quhethir° we wold or no,   *utterly regardless of whether*
With strong hand, by forse,° schortly to say,   *force*
Off inymyis° takin and led away   *By enemies*
We weren all, and broght in thaire contree:°   *country*
Fortune it schupe° none othir wayis to be.   *decreed*

25

Quhare as in strayte ward° and in strong prisoune   *strict confinement*
So ferforth° of my lyf the hevy lyne,°   *henceforth; doleful thread*
Without confort,° in sorowe abandoune,°   *consolation; given over to grief*
The second sistere° lukit hath to twyne°   *(Lachesis); taken care to spin*
Nere by the space of yeris twise nyne,[22]
Till Jupiter his merci list advert,°   *deigned to direct*
And sent confort in relesche° of my smert.°   *relief; suffering*

26

Quhare as in ward° full oft I wold bewaille   *inwardly/in prison (pun)*
My dedely° lyf, full of peyne and penance,   *deathlike*

20. ll. 1–2. The state of innocence lasted until seven. The narrator, therefore, is stating that he was about ten.

21. The literal journey, unusually, *follows* the allegorical account. James was taken to Leith by his father (Robert III), who wished to send him by sea to safety in France. The boat was captured by English pirates off Flamborough Head in March, 1406 (24.5).

22. A just claim. Henry IV rewarded the pirates and kept James a prisoner in England from 1406–24—'yeris twyse nyne'.

Saing right thus: 'Quhat have I gilt,° to faille°	*done wrong; be deprived of*
My fredome in this warld and my plesance,°	*happiness*
Sen every wight° has therof suffisance°	*being; sufficiency*
That I behold, and I, a creature,	
Put from all this? Hard is myn aventure!°	*fate*

27

'The bird, the beste, the fisch eke° in the see,	*also*
They lyve in fredome, everich in his kynd;°	*according to its nature*
And I, a man, and lakkith libertee!—	
Quhat schall I seyne? Quhat resoune may I fynd	
That fortune suld do so?' Thus in my mynd,	
My folk I wold argewe, bot all for noght;	
Was none that myght that on my peynes rought.[23]	

28

Than wold I say: 'Gif God me had devisit°	*ordained*
To lyve my lyf in thraldome° thus and pyne,	*servitude*
Quhat was the cause that He me more comprisit°	*constrained*
Than othir folk to lyve in swich ruyne?°	*ruinous straits*
I suffere allone amang the figuris nyne,°	*nine spheres*
Ane wofull wrecche that to no wight may spede,°	*may be of no use to anyone*
And yit of every lyvis° help hath nede!'	*every living creature*

29

The long dayes and the nyghtis eke	
I wold bewaille my fortune in this wise,	
For quhich, agane° distresse confort to seke,	*against*
My custum was on mornis for to ryse	
Airly as day.° O happy exercise!	*As early as daylight*
By the° come I to joye out of turment!	*Through you*
Bot now, to purpose of my first entent.°	*first/original intention*

30

Bewailing in my chamber thus allone,	
Despeired° of all joye and remedye,	*Having given up hope*
Fortirit of° my thoght and wobegone,	*Worn out with*
Unto the wyndow gan I walk in hye°	*I walked in haste*
To se the warld and the folk that went forby,	
As, for the tyme,° though I of mirthis fude°	*Although then; mirth's food*
Myght have no more, to luke it did me gude.	

31

Now was there maid fast by° the touris° wall	*close to; tower's*
A gardyn faire, and in the corneris set	
Ane herbere° grene with wandis° long and small°	*arbour; palings; closely spaced*
Railit about;° and so with treis set	*Fenced around*

23. ll. 5–7: 'Thus, I would rehearse mental arguments with my followers, but all to no avail; there was no one with power, who took pity on my pains.'

Was all the place, and hawthorn hegis° knet,° *hedges; entwined*
That lyf was none walking there forby
That myght within scarse ony wight aspye.[24]

32

So thik° the bewis° and the leves grene *heavily; boughs*
Beschadit° all the aleyes° that there were; *Shaded; pathways*
And myddis every herbere° myght be sene *plot*
The scharp,° grene, swete jenepere,° *jagged; juniper*
Growing so faire, with branchis here and there,
That, as it semyt to a lyf without,° *someone on the outside*
The bewis spred° the herbere all about.[25] *branches spread*

33

And on the small, grene twistis° sat *twigs*
The lytill swete nyghtingale and song° *sang*
So loud and clere, the ympnis consecrat° *hymns sacred*
Off lufis use,° now° soft, now lowd among, *love's art; at times*
That all the gardyng and the wallis rong° *rang*
Ryght of thaire song. And, on the copill next,° *in the next stanza*
Off thaire swete armony°—lo the text!° *harmony; here are the words*

34

'Worschippe, ye that loveris bene,° this May, *you who are lovers*
For of your blisse the kalendis° are bigonne, *first days*
And sing with us, "Away, winter, away!
Cum, somer, cum, the swete sesoune and sonne!"
Awake, for schame, that have your hevynnis wonne,
And amorously lift up your hedis all!
Thank Lufe° that list you to his merci call.' *Love*

35

Quhen thai this song had song a lytill thrawe° *a little while*
Thai stent° a quhile, and therewith, unaffraid, *stopped*
As I beheld and kest myn eyne alawe,° *cast my eyes down*
From beugh to beugh thay hippit° and thai plaid,° *hopped; played*
And freschly, in thaire birdis kynd,° arraid° *as is the way of birds; displayed*
Thaire fetheris new, and fret thame° in the sonne *preened themselves*
And thankit Lufe that had thaire makis° wonne. *mates*

36

This was the plane ditee° of thaire note,° *plain sense; song*
And therewithall unto myself I thoght,
'Quhat lyf is this, that makis birdis dote?° *act/think foolishly*
Quhat may this be? How cummyth it of ought?
Quhat nedith it to be so dere ybought?° *dearly bought*

24. ll. 6–7: 'That anyone walking past would hardly be able to catch sight of anyone inside.'
25. This harmonious picture of Nature relies heavily on earlier literary models—especially *Le Roman de la Rose* and Chaucer's *Parliament of Fowls*.

It is nothing, trowe I, bot feynit chere,°	*feigned cheerfulness*
And that men list° to counterfeten chere.'	*like*
37	
Eft° wald I think, 'O lord, quhat may this be,	*(Then) again*
That Lufe is of so noble myght and kynde,°	*power and nature*
Lufing his folk? And swich prosperitee,	
Is it of him,° as we in bukis fynd?	*from him (i.e. god of Love)*
May he oure hertes setten° and unbynd?°	*fix; set free*
Hath he upon oure hertis swich maistrye?°	*sovereignty*
Or° all this is bot feynyt fantasye!°	*Otherwise; false imaginings*
38	
'For gif he be of so grete excellence	
That he of every wight hath cure° and charge,	*care*
Quhat have I gilt° to him or doon offense,°	*been guilty of; done offence*
That I am thrall,° and birdis gone at large,°	*a prisoner; go free*
Sen° him to serve he myght set my corage?°	*Since; focus my desire*
And gif he be noght so, than may I seyne,°	*enquire*
Quhat makis folk to jangill° of him in veyne?°	*chatter; nonsensically*
39	
'Can I noght elles fynd,° bot gif that he	*If I can conclude nothing else*
Be lord, and as a god may lyve and regne,	
To bynd and louse° and maken thrallis° free,	*loosen; bondsmen*
Than wold I pray his blisfull grace benigne	
To hable me unto° his service digne,°	*make me fit for; noble*
And evermore for to be one of tho,°	*those*
Him trewly for to serve in wele° and wo.'	*prosperity*
40	
And therewith kest° I doune myn eye ageyne,	*cast*
Quhare as I sawe walking under the tour,	
Full secretly new cummyn° hir to pleyne,°	*newly arrived; disport herself*
The fairest or the freschest yong floure°	*flower*
That ever I sawe, me thoght, before that houre;	
For quhich sodayn abate,° anone astert°	*sudden shock; at once rushed*
The blude of all my body to my herte.[26]	
41	
And though I stude abaisit° tho a lyte,°	*bemused; a short while there*
No wonder was—forquhy° my wittis all	*because*
Were so overcome with plesance and delyte	
—Onely throu latting of° myn eyen fall—	*Just by letting*
That, sudaynly, my hert became hir thrall°	*slave*
For ever,[27] of free wyll,° for of manace°	*of my own free will; menace*
There was no takyn° in hir swete face.	*sign*

26. The poet sees his lady and prays to her in a manner reminiscent of Palamon's first sight of Emily in Chaucer's 'Knight's Tale.'
27. The lady was, indeed, to become his wife and political ally. She is Lady Joan Beaufort (d.1445).

42

And in my hede I drew° ryght hastily, — *I drew my head in*
And eftsones° I lent it forth ageyne — *very soon*
And sawe hir walk, that verray womanly,° — *most womanly of creatures*
With no wight mo bot onely wommen tweyne.° — *except two female companions*
Than gan I studye in myself° and seyne: — *became introspective*
'A, swete, ar ye a warldly creature
Or hevinly thing in liknesse of nature?° — *taking on a natural form*

43

'Or ar ye god Cupidis owin princesse
And cummyn ar to louse me out of band?° — *bondage*
Or ar ye verray Nature° the goddesse — *Nature herself*
That have depaynted° with your hevinly hand — *decorated*
This gardyn full of flouris, as they stand?
Quhat sall I think? Allace, quhat reverence
Sall I minister° to your excellence? — *show in service*

44

'Gif ye a goddesse be, and that ye like° — *wish*
To do me payne, I may it noght astert.° — *escape*
Gif ye be warldly wight that dooth me sike,° — *makes me sigh*
Quhy lest God° mak you so, my derrest hert, — *did God wish to*
To do° a sely° prisoner thus smert° — *cause; poor; hurt*
That lufis yow all,° and wote of noght but wo?° — *utterly; only knows grief*
And therefor, merci, swete,° sen° it is so.' — *dear one; since*

45

Quhen I a lytill thrawe° had maid my moon,° — *little while; complaint*
Bewailling myn infortune and my chance,
Unknawin how or quhat was best to doon,° — *do*
So ferre° I fallying was into lufis dance — *far*
That sodeynly my wit, my contenance,° — *outward appearance*
My hert, my will, my nature and my mynd,
Was changit clene° ryght in anothir kynd.[28] — *totally transformed*

46

Off hir array° the form gif I sall write— — *appearance*
Toward° hir golden haire and rich atyre — *Regarding*
It fretwise couchit was with perllis quhite[29]
And grete balas lemying° as the fyre, — *large rubies glowing*
With mony ane emeraut° and faire saphire; — *emerald*
And on hir hede a chaplet° fresch of hewe, — *garland*
Off plumys partit° rede and quhite and blewe; — *feathers diversely*

47

Full of quaking spangis° bright as gold, — *shimmering spangles*
Forgit of schap° like to the amorettis,° — *Shaped; love-knots*

28. The narrator stylistically emphasizes how completely his vision is transformed by the experience of love.
29. 'It was embroidered with a fretwork of white pearls.'

So new, so fresch, so plesant to behold.
The plumys eke like to the floure jonettis° *flower of the Jonette pear*
And othir of schap like to the floure jonettis°[30] *St John's wort*
And above all this there was, wele I wote,° *know*
Beautee eneuch to mak a world to dote.

48
About hir nek, quhite as the fyre amaille,° *gleaming enamel*
A gudely cheyne of smale orfeverye,° *delicate gold work*
Quhareby° there hang a ruby, without faille,° *From which; fault*
Lyke to ane hert schapin° verily, *shaped*
That as a sperk of lowe° so wantonly *spark of fire*
Semyt birnyng upon hir quhyte throte;
Now gif° there was gude partye,° God it wote! *if ever; good match*

49
And for to walk that fresche Mayes morowe,° *morning*
Ane huke° sche had upon hir, tissew quhite,° *frock; of white cloth*
That gudeliare° had noght bene sene toforowe,° *fairer; before*
As I suppose, and girt° sche was a lyte°— *loosely...girdled*
Thus halflyng louse° for haste; lo swich delyte *half untied*
It was to see hir youth in gudelihede,° *beauty*
That for rudenes° to speke thereof I drede. *forwardness*

50
In hir was youth, beautee with humble aport,° *demeanour*
Bountee, richesse, and wommanly facture° *mien*
(God better wote° than my pen can report). *knows*
Wisedome, largesse,° estate° and connyng° sure *generosity; rank; skill*
In every poynt so guydit hir, mesure° *moderation*
In word, in dede, in schap, in contenance,° *bearing*
That Nature myght no more hir childe avance.° *improve upon her child*

51
Throw quhich anone° I knew and understude *immediately*
Wele, that she was a warldly° creature, *earthly*
On quhom to rest myn eye so mich gude
It did my wofull hert (I yow assure)
That it was to me joye without mesure.° *immeasurable*
And, at the last, my luke unto the hevin
I threwe furthwith, and said thir verses sevin:° *these seven lines*

52
'O Venus clere, of goddis stellifyit,° *metamorphosed into stars*
To quhom I yelde homage and sacrifise,
Fro this day forth your grace be magnifyit,

30. A yellow or white flower. The pun in 47.4,5 is on the name of his lady. Joan Beaufort's name is not explicitly mentioned in the poem. The king follows a courtly love convention by wittily concealing it. 'Jon-ette is', is at once the diminutive form of Joan and the answer to the riddle of her identity—'she is Jon-ette'.

That me resavit have in swich wise,° *have received in such a manner*
To lyve under your law and do servise.
Now help me furth, and for your merci lede
My hert to rest, that deis nere for drede.'° *almost dies for dread*

53

Quhen I with gude entent° this orisoune° *intention; prayer*
Thus endit° had, I stynt a lytill stound;° *ceased; short period*
And eft° myn eye full pitously° adoune *then; piteously*
I kest, behalding unto hir° lytill hound°[31] *i.e. the lady's; lapdog*
That with his bellis playit on the ground.
Than wold I say, and sigh therewith a lyte,
'A, wele were° him that now were in thy plyte!'° *well would it be for; situation*

54

Another quhile, the lytill nyghtingale
That sat apon the twiggis, wold I chide
And say ryght thus: 'Quhare are thy notis smale° *high*
That thou of love has song this morowe° tyde? *morning*
Seis thou noght hire° that sittis the besyde? *her*
For Venus sake, the blisfull goddesse clere,
Sing on againe, and mak my lady chere!° *merry*

55

'And eke I pray, for all the paynes grete
That for the love of Proigne° thy sister dere,[32] *Procne*
Thou sufferit quhilom°—quhen thy brestis wete *once*
Were with the teres of thyne eyen clere
All bludy ronne,° that pitee was to here *running with blood*
The crueltee of that unknyghtly dede,° *unchivalrous deed*
Quhare was fro the° bereft° thy maidenhede°— *from you; robbed; virginity*

56

'Lift up thyne hert and sing with gude entent!
And, in thy notis swete, the tresoun° telle *treachery*
That to thy sister, trewe and innocent,
Was kythit° by hir husband, false and fell;° *shown; cruel*
For quhois gilt, as it is worthy wel,° *very appropriate*
Chide thir° husbandis that ar false, I say, *these*
And bid thame mend,° in the twenty devil way![33] *change for the better*

57

'O lytill wrecche, allace, maist thou noght se
Quho commyth yond?° Is it now tyme to wring?° *over there; lament*
Quhat sory thoght is fallin upon the?
Opyn thy throte! Hastow no lest° to sing? *Have you no wish*

31. An early example of the conceit by which a lover wishes to be his lady's lapdog.
32. According to legend, Procne's husband raped Philomela (62.1) and cut out her tongue. Philomela told the tale in an embroidery. All three were turned into birds, Philomela becoming a nightingale. Gower's version of the tale is followed (see 197.2).
33. Colloquial expression of impatience.

Allace, sen thou of resoun° had felyng,° *rightly; (capacity for) feeling*
Now, swete bird, say ones to me, "Pepe";° *"Peep"*
I dee for wo°—me think thou gynnis slepe!° *I die of grief; (are) falling asleep*

58
'Hastow no mynde of° lufe? Quhare is thy make?° *interest in/memory of; mate*
Or artow seke,° or smyt° with jelousye? *sick; smitten*
Or is sche dede, or hath sche the forsake?° *left you*
Quhat is the cause of thy melancolye,
That thou no more list° maken melodye? *want to*
Sluggart,° for schame! Lo, here thy goldin houre, *Sluggard*
That worth were° hale all° thy lyvis laboure! *would be worth; entirely all*

59
'Gyf thou suld sing wele ever in thy lyve,
Here is, in fay,° the tyme and eke the space.° *in faith; and the place also*
Quhat! Wostow° than sum bird may cum and stryve *Do you suppose*
In song with the, the maistry to purchace?° *to gain mastery over you*
Suld thou then° cesse,° it were grete schame, allace! *because of that; cease/grow silent*
And here, to wyn gree° happily for ever, *victory*
Here is the tyme to syng or ellis never!'

60
I thoght eke° thus: 'Gif° I my handis clap, *also; If*
Or gif I cast,° than will sche flee away; *throw something*
And gif I hald my pes,° than will sche nap;° *peace; fall asleep*
And gif I crye, sche wate noght° quhat I say. *understands nothing of*
Thus, quhat is best, wate I noght,° be this day, *know not at all*
Bot° blawe, wynd blawe, and do° the levis schake, *Except; make*
That sum twig may wag° and mak hir to wake!' *move*

61
With that anone ryght° sche toke up a sang, *right away*
Quhare com anone° mo° birdis and alight.° *at once; more; alighted*
Bot than to here° the mirth was thame amang! *then to hear*
Over that to,° to see the swete sicht *Over and above that*
Off hyr ymage!° My spirit was so light, *image*
Me thoght I flawe° for joye without arest,° *flew/walked on air; restraint*
So were my wittis boundin° all to fest.° *bound; too tightly*

62
And to the notis of Philomene,° *Philomela (n.32)*
Quhilkis sche sang, the ditee° there I maid° *lyrics; composed*
Direct to hir, that was my hertis quene,
Withouten quhom no songis may me glade;° *cheer me*
And to that sanct,° walking in the schade, *saint*
My bedis° thus, with humble hert entere, *(rosary) beads*
Devotly° I said on this manere: *Devoutly*

63
'Quhen sall your merci° rew upon° your man, *mercy; show pity to*
Quhois service is yit uncouth° unto yow, *unknown*

Sen, quhen ye go, there is noght ellis than	
Bot hert, quhere as the body may noght throu,	
Folow thy hevin?[34] Quho suld be glad bot thou,	
That swich a gyde to folow has undertake?°	*undertaken/accepted the task*
Were it throu hell,° the way° thou noght forsake.'	*Even through hell; journey*
64	
And efter this the birdis everichone°	*every one*
Tuke up ane othir sang full loud and clere,	
And with a voce° said: 'Wele is us begone°	*one voice; We have started well*
That with oure makis° are togider here.	*mates*
We proyne° and play without dout° and dangere,	*preen; fear*
All clothit in a soyte° full fresch and newe,	*suit*
In lufis service besy,° glad and trewe.	*busy*
65	
'And ye, fresche May, ay mercifull to bridis,°	*birds/(brides)*
Now welcum ye be, floure of monethis° all;	*months*
For noght onely your grace upon us bydis,°	*abides*
Bot all the warld to witnes this we call,	
That strowit hath° so playnly over all	*You (May) who have strewn*
With new, fresche, swete and tender grene,°	*greenery*
Oure lyf, oure lust,° oure gouvernoure, oure quene!'	*joy*
66	
This was thair song, as semyt me,° full heye,°	*as it seemed to me; very loud*
With full mony uncouth,° swete note and schill;°	*unfamiliar; shrill*
And therewithall that faire° upward hir eye	*fair lady*
Wold cast amang,° as it was° Goddis will,	*direct at times; as if it were*
Quhare I myght se, standing allane full still,	
The faire facture,° that Nature, for maistrye,°	*features; mastery/power*
In hir visage wroght had° full lufingly.	*had fashioned*
67	
And quhen sche walkit had a lytill thrawe°	*short while*
Under the swete, grene bewis bent,°	*overhanging boughs*
Hir faire, fresche face, as quhite as ony snawe,°	*snow*
Sche turnyt° has and furth hir wayis went.	*turned away*
Bot tho° began myn axis° and turment!	*then; anxieties*
To sene hir part° and folowe I na myght!	*To have seen her depart*
Me thoght° the day was turnyt into nyght!	*It seemed to me*
68	
Than said I thus, 'Quhareto° lyve I langer,	*For what purpose*
Wofullest wight and subject unto peyne?	
Of peyne? No. God wote, ya,° for thay no stranger°	*yes; no more harshly*
May wirken ony wight,° I dare wele seyne.°	*affect any man; declare*

34. ll. 3–5 complete the question begun in ll. 1–2. '...Since, when you leave [the garden]—the body being unable to pass through [its walls]—there is no alternative but that my heart follow your heavenliness?'

How may this be, that deth and lyf, bothe tweyne,° *together*
Sall bothe atonis° in a° creature *at once; one*
Togidder° dwell, and turment° thus Nature? *Together; torment*

69

'I may noght ellis done° bot wepe and waile, *I may do nothing else*
Within thir cald° wallis thus ilokin.° *these cold; locked up*
From hennesfurth my rest is my travaile;[35]
My drye thrist° with teris sall I sloken,° *thirst; slake*
And on myself bene all my harmys wrokin.° *sufferings inflicted*
This bute is none,° bot° Venus of hir grace, *This is no remedy; unless*
Wil schape remede,° or do my spirit pace.° *fashion a cure; peace*

70

'As Tantalus I travaile° ay butles° *labour; aimlessly*
That ever ylike hailith° at the well *continually hauls up*
Water to draw with buket botomles
And may noght spede,° quhois penance is an hell.[36] *succeed*
So by myself° this tale I may wele telle° *to myself...aptly apply this tale*
For unto hir that herith noght° I pleyne;° *hears nothing; complain*
Thus, like to him, my travaile is in veyne.'° *in vain*

71

So sore° thus sighit° I with myself allone, *grievously; sighed*
That turnyt° is my strenth in° febilnesse, *turned; into*
My wele in wo, my frendis all in fone,° *foes*
My lyf in deth, my lyght into dirknesse.
My hope in feere, in dout° my sekirnesse,° *doubt; certainty*
Sen sche is gone. And God mote hir convoye,° *may God protect her*
That me may gyde° to turment and to joye! *Who is capable of guiding me*

72

The long day,° thus gan I prye° and poure,° *All day long; I peered; stared*
Till Phebus° endit had his bemes bryght, *(the sun)*
And bad go farewele° every lef° and floure; *told to close up; leaf*
(This is to say, approchen gan the nyght)° *night approached*
And Esperus° his lampis gan to° lyght, *Hesperus/evening star; began to*
Quhen in the wyndow, still as any stone,
I bade° at lenth and, kneling, maid my mone.° *remained; complaint*

73

So lang till even,° for lak of myght and mynd, *evening*
Forwepit and forpleynit° pitously, *Worn out weeping and wailing*
Ourset° so sorow had bothe hert and mynd, *Overwhelmed*
That to the cold stone my hede on wrye° *to one side*

35. Elliptical. This might either be a piece of wit—'From now on my rest is [will be] my unrest' or could convey 'From now on, all that remains to me is misery.'
36. Tantalus did suffer in hell but the bucket punishment was endured by Danaus' daughters for their patricide. The parched Tantalus, in Ovid and Lydgate, was not allowed to drink from the water of a nearby well.

I laid and lent, amaisit verily,° *in a veritable daze*
Half sleping and half swoun,° in swich a wise;[37] *fainting*
And quhat I met, I will you now devise:° *now describe for you*

74

Me thoght,°[38] that thus all sodeynly a lyght *It seemed to me*
In at the wyndow come quhare that I lent,° *was leaning*
Off quhich the chambere wyndow schone full bryght,
And all my body so it hath overwent,° *pervaded*
That of my sicht the vertew° hale iblent,° *capacity to see; was blinded*
And that withall° a voce° unto me saide, *moreover; voice*
'I bring the confort and hele.° Be noght affrayde.'[39] *you comfort and wellbeing*

75

And furth° anone it passit sodeynly° *forth; went suddenly*
Quhere it come in, the ryght way ageyne,
And sone, me thoght, furth at the dure in hye° *in haste out of the door*
I went my weye, nas nothing me ageyne°— *nothing withstood me*
And hastily by bothe the armes tweyne,
I was araisit up° into the aire, *lifted up*
Clippit° in a cloude of cristall clere and faire. *Enveloped*

76

Ascending upward ay fro spere° to spere, *ever upwards from sphere*
Through aire and watere and hote fyre,
Till that I come unto the circle clere
Of Signifere,°[40] quhare faire, bryght and schire° *the zodiac; shining*
The signis° schone and in the glad empire° *signs (of the zodiac); realm*
Of blisfull Venus am caryit° now[41] *carried*
So sodaynly,° almost I wist noght° how![42] *suddenly (that); did not know*

77

Of quhich the place quhen I come there nye
Was all, me thoght, of cristall stonis wroght;° *constructed*
And to the port° I liftit was in hye,° *gate; in haste*
Quhare, sodaynly, as quho sais 'At a thoght!'° *i.e. In a flash*
It opnyt, and I was anon in broght° *at once ushered in*

37. The dream sequence, which lasts until st. 172, begins here. A perturbed mind was one of the reasons adduced for dreams by Macrobius and other commentators.
38. 'Me thoght' = 'Seemed', because the perturbed mind seldom produced reliable dream-messages. James, who will later claim that his vision comes from God, opens fittingly with the language of scepticism.
39. These words and the opening lines of st. 75 echo the angelic reassurances at Christ's nativity to the shepherds and wise men.
40. After ascending from earth, upwards through the other sublunary elements of water, air and fire, he now enters the heavenly spheres.
41. Either Venus has been placed unusually high within her own house of Taurus or, as seems more likely, the dreamer moves first to the highest level and then is lowered to the circle most appropriate to him—in this case, the third sphere of Venus. See Boethius *Consolation*, Bk. 4.6v—'If you desire to see and understand/In purity the mind of God/Your sight must on the highest point of heaven rest.' (Tr. Watts.)
42. Movement into the heavens usually signifies that spiritual teaching will follow.

Within a chamber large, rowm° and faire:° *roomy; elegant*
And there I fand° of peple grete repaire.° *found; a large number gathered*

78

This is to seyne, that present in that place
Me thoght I sawe of every nacioune° *nation*
Loveris, that endit had thaire lyfis space° *span*
In lovis service—mony a mylioune°— *many a million*
Of quhois chancis° maid is mencioune° *fates; mention is made*
In diverse bukis, quho° thame list° to se,° *for those who; want; consult*
And, therefore, here thaire namys lat I be.° *their names I omit*

79

The quhois aventure° and grete labouris *history*
Above thaire hedis writin there I fand;
This is to seyne, martris° and confessouris *martyrs*
Ech in his stage,° and his make° in his hand. *set place; lady/consort*
And therewithall, thir peple sawe I stand,
With mony a solempt° contenance, *solemn*
After° as lufe thame lykit to avance.° *Accordingly; advance*

80

Of gude folkis that faire in lufe befill[43]
There saw I sitt in order by thame one° *on their own*
With hedis hore,° and with thame stude Gude Will *hoary*
To talk and play; and after that anone
Besyde thame and next° there saw I gone° *next (in turn); passing*
Curage° amang the fresche folkis yong, *Desire/Vigour*
And with thame playit° full merily and song.° *played; sang*

81

And in ane othir stage° endlong the wall, *assigned place*
There saw I stand in capis° wyde and lang *capes*
A full grete nowmer;° bot thaire hudis° all *number; hoods*
(Wist I noght quhy) atoure thaire eyen hang;° *hung down over their eyes*
And ay° to thame come Repentance amang *continuously*
And maid thame chere,° degysit° in his wede.° *encouraged; decked out; apparel*
And dounward efter that yit I tuke hede.° *I still directed my attention*

82

Ryght overthwert° the chamber was there drawe *across*
A trevesse° thin and quhite, all of plesance,° *screen; (depicting) pleasure*
The quhich behynd standing, there I sawe
A warld of folk, and by thaire contenance° *expression*
Thaire hertis semyt full of displeasance,° *sorrow*
With billis° in thaire handis, of one assent,° *petitions; with a single purpose*
Unto the Juge thaire playntis to present.[44]

43. 'Some good people for whom love had worked out favourably...'
44. These petitioners, sts. 80–93, derive in part from Lydgate's *Temple of Glas*.

83

And therewithall apperit unto me° — *there came to me*
A voce, and said: 'Tak hede, man and behold
Yond, there° thou seis the hiest stage and gree° — *Yonder where; rank and degree*
Of agit° folk with hedis hore° and olde— — *aged; hoary*
Yone° were the folk that never change wold° — *Those; would alter…*
In lufe,° bot trewly servit him alway, — *…In love (i.e. were faithful)*
In every age,° unto thaire ending day. — *At every stage of life*

84

'For—fro the tyme that thai coud understand
The exercise of lufis craft the cure[45]—
Was none on lyve,° that toke so moch on hand° — *alive; who took on so much*
For lufis sake, nor langer did endure
In lufis service; for, man, I the assure,° — *assure you*
Quhen thay of youth ressavit° had the fill,° — *received; fulness (of years)*
Yit in thaire age thame lakkit no° gude will. — *they were not found wanting in*

85

'Here bene also of swich° as in counsaillis° — *such; counsels*
And all thare dedis were to Venus trewe;
Here bene the princis, faucht° the grete batailis, — *who fought*
In mynd of quhom° ar maid the bukis newe; — *whose memory*
Here bene the poetis that the sciencis knewe,
Throwout the warld, of lufe in thaire swete layes,[46]
Swich as Ovide° and Omere° in thaire dayes. — *Ovid; Homer*[47]

86

'And efter thame, downe in the next stage°— — *level*
There, as thou seis the yong folkis pleye°— — *play*
Lo! thise were they that in thaire myddill age° — *maturity*
Servandis were to lufe, in mony weye,
And diversely happinnit for to deye;° — *in diverse ways chanced to die*
Sum sorowfully, for wanting of thare makis,° — *missing their mates*
And sum in armes, for thaire ladyes sakis.

87

'And othir eke by othir diverse chance,° — *fortune*
As happin folk all day, as ye may se—
Sum for dispaire without recoverance,
Sum for desyre, surmounting thaire degree,° — *aspiring above their rank*
Sum for dispite° and othir inmytee,° — *malice; enmity*
Sum for unkyndenes without a quhy,° — *without rational justification*
Sum for to moch° and sum for jelousye. — *excess (in love)*

45. 'The exercise and care involved in the art of love.'
46. ll. 5–6: 'Here are the poets, who conveyed to the whole world in their sweet songs all the doctrines/techniques of love.'
47. Homer's work was not then known in the original. His reputation for love poetry rests insecurely on later romanticized versions of the Trojan war. Ovid's works *were* read in their original and moralized forms. His reputation as a love poet is well founded.

88

'And efter this, upon yone stage adoune,° — *that place down there*
Tho° that thou seis stond in capis wyde, — *Those*
Yone were quhilum folk of religioune,° — *formerly clerics*
That,° from the warld, thaire governance° did hide — *Who; ruling passion*
And frely° servit lufe on every syde — *freely/outside marriage*
In secrete, with thaire bodyis and thaire gudis.° — *goods*
And lo quhy so° thai hingen doune thaire hudis:° — *therefore; hoods (over their faces)*

89

'For though that thai were hardy at assay° — *courageous when tested*
And did him° service quhilum prively,° — *i.e. Love; sometimes secretly*
Yit to the warldis eye it semyt nay.° — *did not seem thus*
So° was thaire service halfdel cowardy;° — *Thus; partly cowardice*
And—for thay first forsuke him opynly,° — *as they first shunned him in public*
And efter that thereof had repenting[48]—
For schame thaire hudis oure thaire eyne thay hyng.

90

'And seis thou now yone multitude on rawe° — *row*
Standing behynd yone traverse of delyte?
Sum bene of thame that haldin were full lawe,° — *kept in entire subjection*
And take° by frendis, nothing they to wyte,° — *taken away; to blame*
In youth from lufe into the cloistere quite;° — *straight*
And for that cause are cummyn recounsilit,° — *to be reconciled (to Venus)*
On thame to pleyne that so thame had begilit.° — *beguiled*

91

'And othir bene amongis thame also,
That cummyn are to court on Lufe to pleyne,° — *complain against Love*
For he thaire bodyes had bestowit° so, — *bestowed*
Quhare bothe thaire hertes gruchen therageyne;° — *protested against*
For quhich, in all thaire dayes, soth to seyne,° — *truth to tell*
Quhen othir° lyvit in joye and plesance,° — *others; delight*
Thaire lyf was noght bot care and repentance.° — *nothing but misery and regret*

92

'And quhare thaire hertis gevin were and set,
Were coplit with othir that coud noght accord.[49]
Thus were thai wrangit° that° did no forfet°— — *wronged; who; misdeed*
Departing thame that° never wold discord. — *Being driven apart, those who*
Of yong ladies faire and mony lord,
That thus by maistry° were fro thair chose° dryve,° — *by force; choice; driven away*
Full redy were thair playntis there to gyve.'

48. ll. 5–6. 'first...And efter.' The religious lovers seem to have two sources of guilt—towards Love, (because they cannot serve him openly) and to God (for breaking their vow of chastity).
49. ll. 1–2. 'And those whose hearts were pledged and set [elsewhere] were coupled with others with whom no harmony was possible.'

93

And othir° also I sawe compleynyng there	*others*
Upon Fortune and hir grete variance,°	*variability*
That quhere in love so wele they coplit were,	
With thaire swete makis coplit° in plesance,	*dear lovers joined*
So sodeynly maid thaire disseverance,°	*(Fortune) cut them off/killed them*
And tuke thame of this warldis companye°[50]	*out of this world's company*
Withouten cause—there was none othir quhy.°	*reason*

94

And in a chiere of estate° besyde,	*chair of state*
With wingis bright, all plumyt bot° his face,	*plumed except for*
There sawe I sitt the blynd god Cupide,°	*god of love, son of Venus*
With bow in hand, that bent full redy° was;	*ready (to shoot)*
And by him hang thre° arowis in a cas,°	*three; sheath*
Of quhich the hedis grundyn were° full ryght	*tips were ground*
Of diverse metals, forgit° faire and bryght.	*forged*

95

And with the first that hedit° is of gold	*tipped*
He smytis soft, and that has esy cure;°	*an easy cure*
The secund was of silver, mony fold°	*many times*
Wers° than the first and harder aventure;°	*Worse; fortune*
The thrid° of stele is schot without recure.°[51]	*third; recovery*
And on his long yalow lokkis schene°	*bright*
A chaplet° had he, all of levis grene.	*wreath*

96

And in a retrete,° lytill of compas,°	*side-room; small in size*
Depeyntit° all with sighis wonder sad,°	*Decorated; grievously sad*
(Noght swich sighis as hertis doith manace,°	*threaten*
Bot swich as dooth lufaris to be glad)°	*lovers make when happy*
Fond I° Venus upon hir bed, that had	*I discovered*
A mantill cast over hir schuldris quhite.	
Thus clothit was the goddesse of delyte.°	*delight*

97

Stude at the dure Fair Calling,°[52] hir uschere,°	*Kind Welcoming; usher*
That coude his office doon° in connyng wise,°	*discharge his duty; skilful manner*
And Secretee,° hir thrifty chamberere,°	*Secrecy; chambermaid*
That besy° was in tyme° to do servise,	*ready; at the proper time*
And othir mo that I can noght on avise;°	*advise about*
And on hir hede, of rede rosis full swete,	
A chapellet sche had, faire, fresch and mete.°	*becoming*

50. The idea is of the Fates with their shears, cutting short young, happy lives.
51. More usually, as in *Le Roman de la Rose*, the arrows are of gold, silver and lead. The steel arrow of faithfulness comes from another tradition followed by Chaucer in *The House of Fame*.
52. The allegoric personifications are mainly drawn from *Le Roman de la Rose*. Fair Calling, for example, is a literal translation of 'Bel Acueil' in that poem.

98

With quaking hert, astonate of° that sight, *astounded at*
Unnethis° wist I quhat that I suld seyne; *Scarcely*
Bot at the last, febily° as I myght, *feebly*
With my handis,° on bothe my kneis tweyne,° *hands outstretched; two*
There I begouth° my caris to compleyne. *began*
With ane humble and lamentable chere,° *mournful demeanour*
Thus salute I that goddesse, bryght and clere:

99

'Hye° quene of love, sterre° of benevolence,[53] *Exalted; star*
Pitouse princes° and planet merciable,° *pitying princess; merciful*
Appesare° of malice and violence! *Appeaser*
By vertew pure° of your aspectis hable,° *Purely in respect of; enabling*
Unto youre grace lat now ben acceptable
My pure° request, that can no forthir gone° *poor/pure; can go no further*
To seken help—bot unto you allone.

100

'As ye that bene the socoure° and swete well° *succour; well/source*
Of remedye, of carefull° hertes cure *full of care/suffering*
And, in the huge weltering° wavis fell° *rolling; cruel*
Of lufis rage, blisfull havin° and sure;° *haven; secure*
O, anker° and keye° of oure gude aventure, *anchor; quay/key*
Ye have your man with his gude will conquest.
Merci, therefore, and bring his hert to rest!

101

'Ye knaw the cause of all my peynes smert° *pains' hurtfulness*
Bet° than myself, and all myn aventure. *Better*
Ye may convoye° and, as yow list, convert° *direct/protect; change*
The hardest hert that formyt hath Nature.
Sen in your handis all hale° lyith my cure, *entirely*
Have pitee now, O bryght, blisfull goddesse,
Of your pure man° and rew° on his distresse. *poor servant; have pity*

102

'And though I was unto your lawis strange° *estranged from*
(By ignorance and noght by felonye)° *evil-doing*
And that your grace now likit hath° to change *it has now pleased your grace*
My hert, to serven yow perpetualye,
Forgeve° all this and schapith° remedye *Forgive; create*
To saven me of° your benigne grace *(by means) of*
Or do me sterven° furthwith in this place. *make me die*

53. Venus has been depicted as the sensual queen of love but James now addresses her in her higher, Boethian aspect as the spirit of loving charity, which maintains the harmony of the spheres. (See *Consolation* Bk 1.5v; 2.8v; 3.9v). In both roles, she will reply to him.

103

'And, with the stremes of your percyng lyght,
Convoy° my hert that is so wo-begone *Guide*
Ageyne unto that swete, hevinly sight
That I, within the wallis cald as stone,
So swetly saw on morow walk and gone° *arrive and depart*
Law° in the gardyn ryght tofore myn eye. *Down*
Now, merci, quene, and do° me nought to deye!' *cause*

104

Thir wordis said, my spirit in dispaire,
A quhile I stynt° abiding efter° grace. *paused; waiting for*
And therewithall° hir cristall eyen faire *the whole time*
Me kest asyde.° And efter that a space, *Were turned away from me*
Benignely sche turnyt has hir face
Towardis me full plesantly conveide,° *with a very amiable expression*
And unto me ryght in this wise sche seide:

105

'Yong man, the cause of all thyne inward sorowe
Is noght unknawin to my deite,° *deity*
And thy request, bothe now and eke toforowe,° *also earlier*
Quhen thou first maid professioune to me.
Sen of my grace I have inspirit the° *inspired you*
To knawe my lawe, contynew furth; for oft
There as I mynt full sore,° I smyte bot° soft. *aim very grievously; only strike*

106

'Paciently thou tak° thyne aventure.° *accept; fate*
This will my sone, Cupide,° and so will I. *my son Cupid wishes*
He can the stroke;° to me langis° the cure, *He pierced you (arrow); belongs*
Quhen I se tyme; and, therefore, humily° *humbly*
Abyde° and serve and lat Gude Hope the gye.° *Persevere; guide you*
Bot, for I have thy forehede° here present,[54] *forehead/reason*
I will the schewe the more of myn entent.° *my future intention*

107

'This is to say, though it to me pertene° *pertains*
In Lufis lawe the septre to governe,° *wield the sceptre*
That the effectis° of my bemes schene *results*
Has thaire aspectis° by ordynance° eterne *influences; ordinance*
With otheris byndand;° and menes° to discerne, *intertwining; means*
Quhilum in thingis bothe to cum and gone
That langis noght to me to writh allone.[55]

54. Literally 'But, since I have your forehead here in my presence.' However 'forehead' and 'present' also subtly anticipate the change of focus Venus is about to make. The rational element of the brain was held to be at the front of the head and memory at the back. Having talked of emotion in past and future, she will now concentrate on reason and the present.

55. ll. 6–7: 'It does not lie in my power alone to direct any one occasion among things future and past.' Venus delimits her power to James's individual state in present time because the divine plan permits free will to fallen individuals contingently.

108

'As in thyne awin case° now may thou se *in your own case*
Forquhy,° lo, that by otheris influence° *Since; through others' influence*
Thy persone standis noght in libertee;
Quharefore, though I geve the benevolence,° *I grant you good fortune*
It° standis noght yit in myn advertence° *It (= your fate); control*
Till certeyne coursis endit be and ronne,° *have run their course*
Quhill of trew servis° thow have hir° graice iwone. *by faithful service; i.e. the lady's*

109

'And yit, considering the nakitnesse° *impoverished state*
Bothe of thy wit, thy persone and thy myght,° *authority*
It is no mach° of thyne unworthynesse *match*
To hir hie birth, estate° and beautee bryght. *rank*
Als like ye bene as day is to the nyght,
Or sekcloth° is unto fyne cremesye,° *sackcloth; crimson cloth*
Or doken° to the fresche dayesye.° *burdock; daisy*

110

'Unlike the mone is to the sonne schene;° *bright sun*
Eke° Januarye is like unto May; *Equally*
Unlike the cukkow° to the phylomene,° *cuckoo; nightingale*
Thaire tabartis° ar noght bothe maid of one array; *coats*
Unlike the crow is to the papejay;° *parrot*
Unlike in goldsmythis werk a fischis eye° *fish-eye stone*
To prese with perll or maked be° so heye. *be appraised as a pearl or valued*

111

'As I have said, unto me belangith° *belongs*
Specialy° the cure of thy seknesse; *Particularly*
Bot now thy matere° so in balance hangith *business*
That it requerith to thy sekirnesse° *your continued security requires*
The help of othir mo,° that bene goddes° *in addition; gods*
And have in thame the menes and the lore° *knowledge*
In this matere° to schorten with thy sore.° *business; cut short your grief*

112

'And for° thou sall se wele° that I entend° *So that; see clearly; intend*
Unto thy help, thy welefare to preserve,
The streight weye° thy spirit will I send *Directly*
To the goddesse that clepit is Mynerve.° *who is called Minerva*
And se that thou hir hestis° wele conserve° *commands; keep*
For, in this case, sche may be thy supplye° *help*
And put thy hert in rest als wele as I.

113

'Bot, for the way is uncouth unto the,° *unknown to you*
There as hir dwelling is and hir sojurne,° *abode*
I will that Gud Hope servand° to the be, *servant*
Youre alleris° frend to lete the to murn°— *special; to stop you mourning*

Be thy condyt° and gyde till thou returne; *conductor*
And hir besech that sche will, in thy nede,° *(time of) need*
Hir counsele geve to thy welefare and spede.° *success*

114

'And that sche will, as langith° hir office, *pertains to*
Be thy gude lady, help and counseiloure,
And to the schewe hir rype° and gude avise,° *mature; advice*
Throw quhich thou may, be processe and laboure,° *in course of time and by toil*
Atteyne unto that glad and goldyn floure
That thou wald have so fayn° with all thy hart. *dearly*
And, forthirmore, sen thou hir servand art,

115

'Quhen thou descendis doune to ground ageyne,
Say to the men that there bene resident,
How long think thay to stand in my disdeyne,° *to remain in scorn of me*
That in my lawis bene so negligent
From day to day; and list thame noght° repent, *have they no desire to*
Bot breken louse° and walken at thair large?° *break loose; liberty*
Is none that thereof gevis charge?[56]

116

'And for,'° quod sche, 'the angir and the smert *And because*
Off thaire unkyndenesse dooth me constreyne° *constrain*
My femynyne and wofull tender hert,
That than I wepe and to a token pleyne,° *a clear sign*
As of my teris cummyth all this reyne° *rain*
That ye se on the ground so fast ybete° *beating down*
Fro day to day, my turment is so grete.

117

'And quhen I wepe and stynt in othir quhile° *pause at other times*
For pacience that is in womanhede,° *woman's nature*
Than all my wrath and rancoure I exile;
And of my cristall teris that bene schede° *shed*
The hony° flouris growen up and sprede *honey*
That preyen men in thaire flouris wise° *in the way flowers do*
Be trew of lufe and worschip my servise.

118

'And eke, in takin of° this pitouse tale, *as a token of*
Quhen so my teris dropen on the ground,
In thaire nature the lytill birdis smale
Styntith° thaire song and murnyth° for that stound;° *Break off; mourn; period*
And all the lightis in the hevin round

56. 'Gevis charge'—'takes charge of' or 'assumes responsibility for'. Here is the dream-reason for the king's anxiety to tell others what he has learned. Possession of free will, Venus argues, only gives one the right to do as one wishes when it accords with the greater social good and the encompassing divine plan.

Off my grevance have swich compacience° *sympathy*
That, from the ground,° they hiden thair presence. *earth*

119
'And yit, in tokenyng forthir of this thing,
Quhen flouris springis and freschest bene° of hewe *are brightest*
And that the birdis on the twistis° sing, *branches*
At thilke tyme° ay gynnen° folk to renewe *that precise time; begin*
That servis° unto Love, as ay is dewe,° *service; due*
Most commonly has ay his observance° *his (Love's) rites observed*
And of thaire sleuth tofore° have repentance. *earlier slothfulness*

120
'Thus maist thou seyne, that myn effectis grete
(Unto the quhich ye aught and most weye)
—No lyte offense!—to sleuth is forget.[57]
And therefore in this wise to thame seye° *speak*
As I the have bidden,° and conveye *asked*
The mater° all the better tofore said.° *substance; already expressed*
Thus sall on the my charge bene ilaid.° *my charge be laid upon you*

121
'Say on than, quhare is becummyn° for schame *what has become of*
The songis new, the fresch carolis and dance, *carols*
The lusty° lyf, the mony change of game,° *cheery; sport*
The fresche array, the lusty° contenance, *joyful*
The besy awayte,° the hertly° observance *assiduous service; heartfelt*
That quhilum° was amongis thame so ryf?° *once; rife*
Bid thame repent in tyme and mend° thaire lyfe. *amend*

122
'Or I sall, with my fader old Saturne[58]
And with al hale° oure hevinly alliance, *the full complement of*
Oure glad aspectis° from thame writhe and turne, *benevolent aspects*
That all the warld sall waile° thaire governance.° *bewail; manner of governing*
Bid thame betyme° that thai have repentance, *in good time*
And thaire hertis hale° renew my lawe, *wholly*
And I my hand fro beting° sall withdrawe. *from correction*

123
'This is to say—contynew in my servise,
Worschip my law and my name magnifye
That am your hevin and your paradise,
And I your confort here sall multiplye,
And for your meryt° here, perpetualye, *merit*

57. ED. ll. 1–3. A difficult passage. Many editors amend the manuscript but Scots 'is' in its plural form appears to relate to the subject 'effectis'. The sense, without emendation, would be, 'Thus you may understand that my powerful influences (unto which you ought and must pay heed) are—no slight offence!—through slothfulness forgotten.'
58. Saturn was traditionally held to be malevolent towards mankind.

Ressave° I sall your saulis° of my grace, *receive; souls*
To lyve with me as goddis in this place.'[59]

124

With humble thank and all the reverence
That feble wit° and connyng° may atteyne, *weak intelligence; knowledge*
I tuke my leve; and from hir hie° presence *noble*
Gud Hope[60] and I togider, bothe tweyne,
Departit ar. And, schortly for to seyne,
He hath me led by redy° wayis ryght° *accessible; straight*
Unto Minervis° palace, faire and bryght. *Minerva's (goddess of Wisdom)*

125

Quhare as I fand, full redy at the yate,° *gate*
The maister portar,° callit Pacience,° *chief doorkeeper; Patience*
That frely° lete us in unquestionate.° *readily; unquestioned*
And there we sawe the perfyte excellence,
The sad renowne,° the state, the reverence, *solemn renown*
The strenth, the beautee and the ordour digne° *noble*
Off hir court riall,° noble and benigne. *royal*

126

And straught unto the presence sodeynly° *immediately*
Off Dame Minerve, the pacient goddesse,
Gude Hope, my gyde, led me redily;
To quhom, anone, with dredefull humylnesse,° *fearful humility*
Off my cummyng the cause° I gan expresse, *the reason for my coming*
And all the processe hole° unto the end *the entire case*
Off Venus charge, as likit hir to send.° *she was pleased to transmit it*

127

Off quhich ryght thus hir answer was in bref:° *in short*
'My son, I have wele herd and understond° *understood*
Be thy reherse,° the matere of thy gref,° *account; grief*
And thy request to procure° and to fond° *obtain; establish*
Off thy pennance sum confort° at my hond, *consolation*
Be counsele of thy lady Venus clere,
To be with hir thyne help in this matere.

128

'Bot in this case thou sall wele knawe and witt
Thou may thy herte ground° on swich a wise *base your desire*
That thy laboure will be bot lytill quit;° *of little avail*
And thou may set it in othir wise,
That wil be to the grete worschip° and prise.° *honour; praise*
And gif thou durst unto that way enclyne° *i.e. take the latter path*
I will the geve my lore° and disciplyne.° *teaching; code of discipline*

59. The end of Venus' counsel joins pagan heavens with Christian paradise. The terminology echoes the Bible and the argument reconciles merit with grace.
60. In accordance with the techniques of personification allegory, the character Gude Hope enters as a sign that Venus has made the dreamer virtuously hopeful.

129

'Lo, my gude sone,° this is als mich to seyne,°	*son; tantamount to saying*
As—"Gif thy lufe be sett alluterly°	*entirely*
On nyce° lust, thy travail° is in veyne.[61]	*foolish; labour*
And so the end° sall turne of thy folye°	*final outcome; folly*
To payne and repentance." Lo, wate thou quhy?°	*do you know why*
Gif the ne list thy lufe on vertew set,°	*found on virtuous principles*
Vertu sal be the cause of thy forfet.[62]	

130

'Tak Him before° in all thy governance,°	*Place Him first; conduct*
That in His hand the stere° has of you all,	*steering*
And pray unto His hye purveyance°	*high providence*
Thy lufe to gye.° And on Him traist° and call,	*guide; trust*
That° corner-stone and ground° is of the wall	*Who; foundation*
That failis noght;[63] and trust withoutin drede°	*fear*
Unto thy purpose sone° He sall the lede.	*soon*

131

'For lo, the werk° that first is foundit sure	*building*
May better bere a pace° and hyare be	*bear a weight*
Than othirwise, and langere sall endure	
Be monyfald°—this may thy resoune see—	*By many times*
And° stronger to defend° adversitee;	*And (be); oppose*
Grounde thy werk° therfore upon the stone°	*actions; stone/rock*
And thy desire sall forthward with thee gone.°	*advance with you*

132

'Be trewe and meke° and stedfast in thy thoght,	*meek*
And diligent hir merci to procure—	
Noght onely in thy word,° for word is noght,	*in your word alone*
Bot gif° thy werk and all thy besy cure°	*But only if; assiduous care*
Accord thereto, and utrid be mesure°	*are moderately expressed*
The place,° the houre, the maner and the wise,	*At the right place, hour etc.*
Gif° mercy sall admitten thy servise.°	*Only then; accept your service*

133

'"All thing has tyme,"° thus sais Ecclesiaste,[64]	*its allotted time*
"And wele is him that his tyme wel abit."°	*patiently awaits*
Abyde thy tyme for he that can bot haste°	*only hurry*
Can noght of hap,° the wise man it writ;	*Knows nothing of fortune*
And oft gud fortune flourith with gude wit;°	*from virtuous understanding*

61. The first stage in rising from false, temporal love to higher truths. Minerva will only advise if James loves his lady virtuously (cf. 142.2) and unselfishly (cf.142.7).

62. 'Vertu' may refer to the highest virtue of God. We think, however, that there is wordplay involved. The secondary sense of 'vertu' as 'vigour' would indicate that lust without love would be the reason for his loss ('forfet') of lady and soul.

63. The image comes from Psalm 118. 22.

64. The reference is to the sayings of Solomon in Ecclesiastes. Solomon, therefore, is 'the wise man' of l. 4.

Quharefore, gif thou will be wele fortunyt,° *stand well with fortune*
Lat wisedome ay to thy will be junyt.° *joined*

134

'Bot there be mony of so brukill sort° *morally frail a kind*
That feynis° treuth in lufe for a quhile, *feign*
And setten° all thaire wittis and disport° *direct; pleasure*
The sely,° innocent woman to begyle° *innocuous; beguile*
And so to wynne° thair lustis with a wile.° *achieve; by a deception*
Swich feynit treuth is all bot trechorye° *merely treachery*
Under the umbre° of ypocrisye.° *shade; hypocrisy*

135

'For as the foulere quhistlith° in his throte *fowler whistles*
Diversely to counterfete° the brid,° *imitate; bird*
And feynis° mony a swete and strange note *mimics*
That° in the busk° for his desate° is hid, *Who (fowler); bush; deceit*
Till sche be fast lokin° his net amyd; *tightly imprisoned*
Ryght so the fatoure,° the false theif I say, *deceiver*
With swete tresoune oft wynnith thus his pray.° *prey*

136

'Fy on all swich! Fy on thaire doubilnesse!° *double standards*
Fy on thaire lust and bestly° appetite! *beastlike*
Thaire wolfis hertis in lambis liknesse,
Thaire thoughtis blak hid under wordis quhite!
Fy on thaire labour! Fy on thaire delyte,
That feynen outward all to hir honour
And in thaire hert hir worschip° wold devoure! *honour*

137

'So hard it is to trusten now-on-dayes° *nowadays*
The warld—it is so double° and inconstant; *two-faced*
Off quhich the suth° is kid° be mony assayes.° *truth; demonstrated; proofs*
More pitee is for quhich the remanant,° *because those who remain*
That menen wele° and ar noght variant,° *have good intentions; fickle*
For° otheris gilt° ar suspect of untreuth *On account of; guilt*
And hyndrit° oft—and trewely that is reuth.° *hindered; pity*

138

'Bot gif the hert be groundit ferme and stable
In Goddis law, thy purpose to atteyne,[65]
Thy laboure is to me, than, agreable° *pleasing*
And my full help with counsele trew and pleyne
I will the schewe—and this is the certeyne.° *you may be certain of*
Opyn thy hert, therefore, and lat me se
Gif thy remede° be pertynent to me.' *remedy*

65. ll. 1–2: 'But if, in order to attain your purpose, the heart is firmly and stably grounded in God's law…'

139

'Madame,' quod I, 'sen it is your plesance
That I declare the kynd° of my loving *nature*
Trewely and gude withoutin variance:° *virtuously in constancy*
I lufe that floure abufe all othir thing
And wold bene he that to hir worschipping° *to her service*
Myght ought availe°—be Him that starf° on Rude°— *avail himself; died; holy cross*
And nouthir spare for travaile,° lyf nor gude. *stint in labour*

140

'And forthirmore, as touching the nature
Off my lufing, to worschip° or to blame, *honour*
I darre wele say and therein me assure,° *state positively*
For ony gold that ony wight can name° *person might name (a price)*
Nald I be he that° suld of hir gude fame° *I would not be he who; reputation*
Be blamischere° in ony point or wyse, *tarnisher*
For wele nor wo, quhill my lyf may suffise.° *endures*

141

'This is th'effect° trewly of myn entent,° *(caused) effect; intention*
Touching the swete° that smertis me so sore.° *lady; makes me suffer*
Giff this be faute,° I can it noght repent *error*
Allthough my lyf° suld forfaut° be therefore. *life (eternal); forfeit*
Blisfull princes, I can seye you no more;
Bot so desire my wittis dooth compace,° *encompasses*
More joy in erth kepe I noght bot° your grace.' *No joy on earth do I value above...*

142

'Desire,' quod sche, 'I nyl it noght deny,
So thou it ground and set° in Cristin wise; *set (as a jewel)*
And therefore, sone,° opyn thy hert playnly.'° *son; sincerely*
'Madame,' quod I, 'trew, withoutin fantise,° *fantasy*
That day sall I never uprise,° *arise*
For my delyte° to covate ilke plesance,° *my own delight; covet any joy*
That may hir worschip° putten in balance.° *her honour; in jeopardy*

143

'For, oure° all thing, lo, this were° my gladnesse: *above; would be*
To sene the fresche beautee of hir face,
And—gif it myght deserve be processe° *in course of time*
For° my grete lufe and treuth°—to stond in grace, *Because of; faithfulness*
Hir worschip sauf.° Lo, here the blisfull cace *Her honour inviolate*
That I wold ask and thereto attend° *wait for*
For my most joye unto my lyfis end.'

144

'Now wele,' quod sche, 'and sen that it is so,
That in vertew thy lufe is set with treuth,
To helpen the, I will be one of tho° *of those*
From hennesforth, and hertly,° without sleuth,° *sympathetically; delay*

Off thy distresse and excesse° to have reuth,° *extreme condition; pity*
That has thy hert;° I will pray hir full faire *Which grips your heart*
That Fortune be no more thereto contraire.° *opposed to it*

145

'For suth° it is that all ye creaturis *true*
Quhich, under us,° beneth have your dwellyng, *us (= planets)*
Ressaven° diversely your aventuris;° *Receive; fortunes*
Off quhich the cure° and principall melling° *charge; chief involvement*
Apperit is,° withoutin repellyng,° *Is brought; right of rejecting*
Onely to hir° that has the cuttis° two *Before her alone; lots*
In hand, bothe of your wele and of your wo.

146

'And how-so-be that° sum clerkis trete° *no matter if; scholars argue*
That all your chance causit is tofore° *is determined in advance*
Heigh in the hevin, by quhois effectis grete
Ye movit ar to wrething° lesse or more, *vexation*
Quhare in the warld, thus calling that therefore
"Fortune", and so that the diversitee
Off thaire wirking suld cause necessitee;° *should determine your fate*

147

'Bot othir clerkis halden° that the man° *maintain; mankind*
Has in himself the chose and libertee° *choice and freedom (of will)*
To cause his awin fortune, how or quhan
That him best lest,° and no necessitee° *wishes; predestination*
Was in the hevin at his nativitee;° *nativity*
Bot yit the thingis happin in commune° *come together*
Efter purpose, so cleping° thame, "Fortune". *calling*

148

'And, quhare a persone has tofore knawing° *knowledge in advance*
Off it that is to fall purposely,° *providentially*
Lo, Fortune is bot wayke° in swich a thing. *weak*
Thou may wele wit and here ensample° quhy: *here (is) the reason*
To God, that is the first cause onely° *single first cause*
Off every thing, there may no fortune fall.° *turn out by chance*
And quhy? For He foreknawin° is of all.[66] *prescient*

149

'And therefore thus I say to this sentence:° *sum up on this subject*
Fortune is most and strangest° evermore *greatest and strongest*
Quhare leste° foreknawing or intelligence *least*
Is in the man; and, sone,° of wit or lore *my son*
Sen° thou art wayke and feble—lo, therefore, *Since*

66. Like Dame Philosophy in Boethius' *Consolation*, Minerva opposes the narrator's complaint, that there seems to be no order behind, or defence against, the apparently random blows of Fate. God's foreknowing does not predetermine our fate because He sees our past, present and future in one instantaneous present.

The more thou art in dangere and commune° *involved (reliant upon)*
With hir that clerkis clepen° so, "Fortune". *academics call*

150

'Bot for the sake and at the reverence° *in veneration*
Off Venus clere,° as I thee said tofore, *bright*
I have of thy distresse compacience° *compassion*
And, in confort and relesche° of thy sore,° *relief; pain/grief*
The schewit° here myn avise° therefore. *(Have) revealed to you; advice*
Pray Fortune help, for mich unlikly thing° *many an unexpected thing*
Full oft about sche sodeynly dooth bring.° *brings round full circle*

151

'Now, go thy way and have gude mynde upone° *think well*
Quhat I have said in way of thy doctryne.'° *your instruction*
'I sall, madame,' quod I. And ryght anone° *right away*
I tuke my leve als straught° as ony lyne *straight*
Within a beme° that, fro the contree dyvine,° *Inside a ray of light; divine region*
Sche percyng° throw the firmament extendit;° *piercing; extended*
To ground° ageyne my spirit is descendit. *earth*

152

Quhare in a lusty plane°[67] tuke I my way, *joyous plain*
Endlang° a ryver plesant to behold, *Along*
Enbroudin° all with fresche flouris gay, *Embroidered*
Quhare—throu the gravel bryght as ony gold—
The cristall water ran so clere and cold,
That in myn ere maid contynualy
A maner soune,° mellit° with armony;° *kind of sound; mingled; harmony*

153

That° full of lytill fischis by the brym° *That (= river); surface*
Now here, now there, with bakkis blewe as lede° *blue as lead*
Lap° and playit and in a rout can swym° *Jumped; swam in a shoal*
So prattily,° and dressit thame° to sprede *prettily; prepared themselves*
Thaire curall fynnis° as the ruby rede, *coral fins*
That in the sonne on thair scalis° bryght *scales*
As gesserant° ay glitterit in my sight. *Like armour plating*

154

And by this ilke ryversyde alawe
Ane hye way fand I like to bene,[68]
On quhich, on every syde, a long rawe° *line*
Off treis saw I, full of levis grene,
That full of fruyte delitable were to sene,° *delightful to behold*
And also, as it come unto° my mynd, *entered*
Off bestis sawe I mony diverse kynd:

67. He descends into the earthly paradise, whose orderliness foreshadows the benign intention of the creator. See *Consolation* Bk. 1.2v; 2.5v.
68. ll. 1–2: 'And down by this same riverside I found what seemed to be a high-way…'

155

The lyoune king and his fere° lyonesse, — *companion*
The pantere° like unto the smaragdyne,° — *panther; emerald*
The lytill squerell full of besynesse,° — *i.e. ever-active*
The slawe ase,° the druggare beste of pyne,° — *slow ass; drudging beast of toil*
The nyce° ape, the werely porpapyne,° — *foolish; warlike porcupine*
The percyng° lynx, the lufare° unicorne — *sharp-eyed; lover*
That voidis° venym with his evour° horne. — *dispels; ivory*

156

There sawe I dresse him° new out of his hant° — *issue; haunt*
The fery° tiger full of felonye;° — *restless; cruelty*
The dromydare,° the standar oliphant,° — *dromedary; upright elephant*
The wyly fox, the wedowis inemye;° — *widow's enemy*
The clymbare gayte,° the elk for alblastrye,°[69] — *climbing goat; archery*
The herknere° bore, the holsum grey° for hortis,° — *sharp-eared; badger; wounds*
The haire also that oft gooth to the wortis;° — *vegetable patch*

157

The bugill, drawere by° his hornis grete, — *wild ox who draws with*
The martrik sable,° the foynyee° and mony mo; — *sable marten; beach marten*
The chalk-quhite ermyn tippit as the jete,° — *tipped like jet*
The riall hert,° the conyng° and the ro,° — *royal hart; rabbit; roe deer*
The wolf that of the murthir noght says, 'Ho,'° — *never holds from murder*
The lesty bever° and the ravin bare,° — *skilful beaver; ravenous bear*
For chamelot° the camel full of hare, — *For hair-cloth*

158

With mony ane othir beste diverse and strange
That cummyth noght as now unto my mynd.° — *I do not now remember*
But now to purpose—strauncht furth the range° — *straight through the ranks*
I held a way, ourehailing° in my mynd — *rehearsing*
From quhens I come and quhare that I suld fynd
Fortune the goddesse—unto quhom in hye° — *speedily*
Gud Hope, my gyde, has led me sodeynly.

159

And at the last, behalding thus asyde,° — *to one side*
A round place wallit° have I found; — *enclosed by walls*
In myddis quhare,° eftsone,° I have spide — *In the midst of which; quickly*
Fortune the goddesse, hufing° on the ground; — *crouching*
And ryght before hir fete, of compas round,° — *circular in shape*
A quhele,° on quhich—clevering°—I sye — *wheel; clambering*
A multitude of folk before myn eye.

160

And ane surcote° sche werit long that tyde, — *upper garment*
That semyt to me of diverse hewis;° — *shifting colours*

69. The horn of the ox was used in making crossbows—the reference here may suggest a similar use of elk's horn.

Quhilum° thus, quhen sche wald turne asyde, *Occasionally*
Stude this goddesse of Fortune and remewis.°[70] *changes*
A chapelet° with mony fresche anewis° *gold band; bright rings*
Sche had upon hir hed, and with this, hong° *as well as this/from this hung*
A mantill° on hir schuldris large° and long, *mantle; broad*

161

That furrit° was with eremyn full quhite,° *furred; whitest*
Degoutit° with the self° in spottis blake.° *Speckled; same (fur); black*
And quhilum° in hir chiere° thus alyte° *sometimes; expression; briefly*
Louring° sche was—and thus sone it wold slake° *Scowling; cease*
And, sodeynly, a maner smylyng° make *a sort of smiling*
And° sche were glad. At one contenance° *As if; To one expression*
Sche held noght,° bot was ay in variance. *She did not keep*

162

And underneth the quhele° sawe I there *wheel*
Ane ugly pit, depe as ony helle,
That to behald thereon I quoke° for fere.° *quaked; fear*
But o° thing herd I, that quho therein fell *one*
Come no more up agane, tidingis to telle.
Off quhich, astonait of° that ferefull syght, *astonished at*
I ne wist° quhat to done, so was I fricht.° *did not know; frightened*

163

Bot for to se the sudayn weltering° *rolling*
Off that ilk quhele that sloppare° was to hold, *slippery*
It semyt unto my wit a strange thing:
So mony I sawe that than clymben wold
And failit foting,° and to ground were rold.[71] *lost their footing*
And othir eke that sat above on hye
Were overthrawe° in twinklyng of an eye. *overthrown*

164

And on the quhele was lytill void space,
Wele nere ourstraught° fro lawe to hye, *Pretty well crowded*
And they were war° that long sat in place, *wary*
So tolter° quhilum did sche it to wrye.° *jerkily; whirl it round*
There was bot 'Clymbe!' and 'Ryght downward hye!'
And sum were eke that, fallyng, had it sore.
Therefor, to clymbe thaire corage° was no more. *courage*

165

I sawe also that, quhare sum were slungin° *slung*
Be quhirlyng° of the quhele unto the ground, *By the whirling*
Full sudaynly sche hath up ythrungin° *thrust upwards*

70. ED. There is a gap in the manuscript. Norton-Smith suggests 'remewis'.
71. The wheel of Fortune is a cyclical emblem within a circularly constructed poem. First visualised in st. 9, it is usually pictured, as here, upright. Most people fall off its slippery sides or are thrown off at the top. See *Consolation* Bk. 2.1v.

And set thame on agane full sauf and sound.
And ever I sawe a new swarme abound
That thoght to clymbe upward upon the quhele
In stede° of thame that myght no langer rele.°   *place; reel round*

166

And, at the last, in presence of thame all
That stude about, sche clepit° me be name;   *called*
And therewith apon kneis gan I fall°   *I fell*
Full sodaynly hailsing,° abaist° for schame.   *greeting; abashed*
And, smylyng, thus sche said to me in game:°   *playfully*
'Quhat dois thou here? Quho has the hider sent?°   *sent you hither*
Say on anone and tell me thyne entent.

167

'I se wele by thy chere and contenance
There is sum thing that lyis thee on hert.°   *on your heart*
It stant noght° with the as thou wald, perchance?'   *Things are not going*
'Madame,' quod I, 'for° lufe is all the smert,   *because*
That ever I fele, endlang and overthwert,°   *along and across*
Help of your grace me, wofull wrechit wight,°   *wretched creature*
Sen° me to cure ye powere have and myght.'   *Since*

168

'Quhat help,' quod sche, 'wold thou that I ordeyne°   *ordain*
To bringe the unto thy hertis desire?'
'Madame,' quod I, 'bot° that your grace dedeyne°   *only; deign*
Off your grete myght my wittis to enspire,°   *inspire*
To win the well that slokin may° the fyre   *may quench*
In quhich I birn.° A, goddesse fortunate,°   *burn; of fortune*
Help now my game that is in poynt to mate!'°[72]   *on the point of checkmate*

169

'Off mate,' quod sche, 'o verray sely° wrech,   *truly helpless*
I se wele by thy dedely colour pale
Thou art to feble° of thyself to streche°   *too feeble; stretch*
Upon° my quhele, to clymbe or to hale°   *Up on to; hoist (yourself)*
Withoutin help, for thou has fundin stale°   *have been stalemated*
This mony day, withoutin werdis wele,°   *propitious fates*
And wantis now thy veray° hertis hele.°   *faithful; cure*

170

'Wele maistow be a wrechit man ycallit,
That wantis° the confort that suld the glade,°   *lacks; gladden*
And has all thing within thy hert ystallit°   *enclosed*
That may thy youth oppressen° or defade.°   *oppress; dispirit*
Though thy begynnyng hath bene retrograde,°   *backward*

72. The game of life was often compared to chess in medieval verse. James uses the 'checkmate' metaphor to indicate that he sees no way out of his predicament.

Be froward, opposyt, quharetill appert
Now, sall thou turne and luke upon the dert.'[73]

171
And therewithall unto the quhele in hye° — *haste*
Sche hath me led and bad me lere° to clymbe— — *learn*
Upon the quhich I steppit sudaynly.
'Now, hald thy grippis,'° quod sche, 'for thy time,° — *hold tight; your lifespan*
An hour and more it rynnis over prime.°[74] — *runs past prime*
To count the hole, the half is nere away.° — *almost past*
Spend wele, therefore, the remanant of the day.

172
'Ensample,' quod sche, 'tak of this tofore,° — *from this (sight) before you*
That° fro my quhele be rollit° as a ball; — *Those who; rolled off*
For the nature of it° is evermore — *it (= fortune's wheel)*
After ane hicht° to vale° and geve° a fall, — *an upswing; to descend; give/take*
Thus, quhen me likith,° up or doune to fall. — *it pleases me (Fortune)*
Fare wele,' quod sche, and by the ere° me toke° — *ear; seized me*
So ernestly that therewithall° I woke. — *because of that*

173
O besy goste° ay flikering° to and fro, — *active spirit; flickering*
That never art in quiet nor in rest
Till thou cum to that place that thou cam fro,
Quhich is thy first and verray proper nest;° — *own true nest*
From day to day so sore here artow drest° — *treated*
That with thy flesche ay waking art in trouble,
And sleping eke°—of pyne° so hast thou double. — *in sleep too; misery*

174
Towert° myself, all this mene° I to loke. — *In relation to; intend*
Though that my spirit vexit was tofore
In swevenyng,° als sone as ever I woke, — *dreaming*
By twenty fold it was in trouble more,
Bethinking me° with sighing hert and sore — *Pondering*
That nane othir thingis bot dremes had° — *only dreams conveyed…*
Sekernes, my spirit with to glad.° — *…A secure truth to cheer my soul*

175
And therewith sone I dressit me to ryse,° — *prepared to arise*
Fulfilld° of thoght, pyne and adversitee. — *Brimful*
And to myself, I said—in this wise—
'Quhat lyf is this? Quhare hath my spirit be?
A, merci Lord, quhat will ye do with me?

73. ll. 6–7 are problematical and most editors amend. Unamended, the general sense is: 'Be contrary, warlike—to the effect that now you may turn and overtly look upon the target.'
74. Prime is 10 a.m. As 70 was assumed to be a full life span, ten hours out of twenty four suggest an age of 30. James's marriage to Joan was, in fact, being arranged when he was 29.

Is this of my forethoght° impressioune, — *i.e. pre-sleeping thoughts*
Or is it from the hevin a visioune?°[75] — *divine vision*

176
'And gif ye goddis, of your purviance,° — *providence*
Have schewit° this for my reconforting° — *revealed; reassurance*
In relesche° of my furiouse pennance,° — *assuagement; mad suffering*
I yow beseke° full humily° of this thing, — *beseech; humbly*
That of youre grace I myght have more takenyng,° — *(a) further sign*
Gif it sal be, as in my slepe before
Ye schewit have.' And forth, withoutin more,° — *forthwith without more ado*

177
In hye° unto the wyndow gan I walk, — *haste*
Moving within my spirit of this sight,° — *This vision still inspiring me*
Quhare sodeynly a turtur,°[76] quhite as calk,° — *turtle-dove; chalk*
So evinly upon my hand gan lyght° — *alighted*
And unto me sche turnyt hir full ryght
Off quham the chere° in hir birdis aport° — *blitheness; bearing*
Gave me in hert kalendis of confort.° — *new dawnings of comfort*

178
This fair bird ryght in hir bill gan hold
Of red jorofflis° with thair stalkis° grene — *gillyflowers; stems*
A fair branche, quhare writtin was with gold
On every list,° with branchis bryght and schene, — *edge*
In compas fair,° full plesandly to sene,° — *Fair of shape; lovely to behold*
A plane sentence,° quhich (as° I can devise° — *clear message; so far as; describe*
And have in mynd)° said ryght on this wise: — *remember*

179
'AWAK! AWAKE! I BRING, LUFAR,° I BRING — *lover*
THE NEWIS GLAD THAT BLISFULL BENE AND SURE
OF THY CONFORT.[77] NOW, LAUCH AND PLAY AND SYNG,
THAT ART BESID° SO GLAD ANE AVENTUR°— — *close to; outcome*
FOR IN THE HEVYN DECRETIT° IS THE CURE.'°[78] — *decreed; remedy*
And unto me the flouris fair present,° — *having presented*
With wingis spred, hir wayis furth sche went.

180
Quhilk up anon I tuke and, as I gesse,° — *suppose*
Ane hundreth tymes or I forthir went
I have it red° with hertfull glaidnesse; — *read it over*

75. The worry as to whether this is a true or deceptive dream remains.
76. The turtle dove was a sign of married fidelity. After the dream, the poet returns to the early romantic situation (cf. sts. 72–4) armed with knowledge, moral and divine.
77. ll. 2–3: 'The joyous news, which is full of bliss and a sure source of consolation for you.' The dove now also suggests the Holy Spirit descending to James. As to Boethius, spiritual consolation is offered.
78. The fact that the dove appears to James when no longer asleep proves to him that he can rely on having had a true, divinely inspired vision.

And, half with hope and half with dred, it hent° *took away*
And at my beddis hed° with gud entent *bed-head*
I have it fair pynnit up:° and this *pinned up*
First takyne° was of all my help and blisse. *token*

181
The quhich, treuly, efter day be day,
That all my wittis maistrit° had tofore,° *mastered; earlier*
From hennesferth the paynis did away° *put away*
And schortly, so wele Fortune has hir bore° *set herself*
To quikin° treuly day by day my lore,° *To stimulate; learning*
To my larges° that I am cumin agayn *liberty*
To blisse° with hir that is my sovirane.°[79] *Into joy; sovereign*

182
But for als moche as sum micht think or seyne,° *say*
Quhat nedis me apoun so litill evyn° *minor a matter*
To writt all this? I answere thus ageyne,
Quho that from hell war croppin,° onys in hevin *crept out of hell*
Wald efter o[80] thank for joy mak six or sevin!
And every wicht his awin swete or sore° *pleasure or misery*
Has maist in mynde; I can say you no more.

183
Eke,° quho may in this lyfe have more plesance *Further;*
Than cum° to largesse° from thraldom° and peyne, *(he who) comes; freedom; slavery*
And by the mene° of Luffis ordinance, *means*
That has so mony° in his goldin cheyne? *Who holds so many*
Quhich, thus° to wyn his hertis soverayne, *And in this way*
Quho suld me wite to write° tharof, lat se, *blame me for writing*
Now sufficiance° is my felicitee!° *sufficiency; joy*

184
Beseching unto° fair Venus abufe *Interceding with*
For° all my brethir,° that bene in this place *On behalf of; brothers/fellow men*
—This to seyne, that servandis ar to lufe
And of his lady can no thank purchase°— *gain no gratitude*
His pane relesch and sone to stand in grace,
Boith to his worschip° and to his first ese,° *honour; (moment of) ease*
So that° it hir and resoune noght displese; *So long as*

185
And eke for thame that ar nought entrit inne° *have not joined*
The dance of lufe bot thidderwart on way,° *are moving towards it*
In gude tyme and sely° to begynne *innocently*
Thair prentissehed.° And forthirmore I pray *apprenticeship*

79. Both the senses of 'ruler' and 'queen' (in rank) are relevant here.
80. This could mean (i) after one (thanksgiving); (ii) after nothing; (iii) after uttering 'oh!'; (iv) after making the written sign zero. Multiple meanings are often suggested to show the many potential truths available within the divine Word.

For thame that passit bene° the mony affray°	*have left behind them; struggles*
In lufe, and cummyng ar to full plesance,°	*joy*
To graunt thame all, lo, gude perseverance.°	*virtuous perseverence*
186	
And eke I pray for all the hertis dull	
That lyven here in sleuth° and ignorance	*sloth*
And has no curage at the rose to pull,°[81]	*to try and win the rose (= lady)*
Thair lif to mend° and thair saulis° avance	*improve; souls*
With thair swete lore, and bring thame to gude chance.°	*fortune*
And quho that will noght for° this prayer turne,°	*because of; amend*
Quhen thai wald faynest speid° that thai may spurne.°	*most wish to succeed; fail*
187	
To rekyn° of every thing the circumstance	*recount/weigh up*
(As hapnit me quhen lessen gan° my sore)	*began to diminish*
Of my rancoure and wofull chance,°	*miserable lot*
It war to long—I let it be° tharefor.	*pass*
And thus this floure°—I can seye no more—	*flower (= lady)*
So hertly° has unto my help attendit,	*sincerely*
That from the deth° hir man sche has defendit.	*death*
188	
And eke the goddis mercifull wirking,	
For my long pane and trewe service in lufe,	
That has me gevin halely myn asking,°	*granted wholly my petition*
Quhich has my hert for evir sett abufe°	*raised above*
In perfyte joy (that nevir may remufe°	*be removed*
Bot onely deth),° of quhom in laud and prise,°	*Except through death; honour*
With thankfull hert I say richt in this wise:	
189	
Blissit mot be° the goddis all,	*Blessed be*
So fair that glateren° in the firmament;	*glittered*
And blissit be thare myght celestiall	
That have convoyit hale° with one assent	*safely/entirely guided*
My lufe—and to so glade a consequent!°	*outcome*
And thankit be Fortunys exilite°	*exile*
And quhele, that thus so wele has quhirlit me.°	*turned me around*
190	
Thankit mot be and fair lufe befall	
The nychtingale that with so gud entent	
Sang thare of lufe the notis swete and small,°	*high*
Quhair my fair hertis lady was present,	
Hir with to glad or that° sche forthir went.	*To delight her with before…*
And thou, gerafloure,° mot ithankit be	*gillyflower*
All othir flouris for the lufe of the.	

81. An echo of *Le Roman de la Rose*, a French love allegory in which the rose symbolises the beloved lady.

191
And thankit be the faire castell wall
Quhare as I quhilom° lukit furth and lent.° — *once; leant out and looked*
Thankit mot be the Sanctis Marciall° — *Saints with March feast-days*
That me first causit hath this accident.
Thankit mot be the grene bewis° bent — *boughs*
Throu quhom and under, first fortunyt me
My hertis hele and my confort to be.[82]

192
For to the presence swete and delitable
Rycht of this floure that full is of plesance,
By processe° and by menys favorable, — *In due course*
First of the blisfull goddis purveyance
And syne throu long and trew contynuance
Of veray faith in lufe and trew service,
I cum am. And, forthir° in this wise: — *further*

193
Unworthy, lo, bot onely of° hir grace, — *unless uniquely through*
In lufis yok° that esy is and sure, — *yoke of love*
In guerdoun° of all my lufis space,° — *reward; duration of my love*
Sche hath me tak,° hir humble creature. — *accepted*
And thus befell my blisfull aventure
In youth of lufe that now from day to day
Flourith ay newe.° And, yit forthir I say: — *ever anew*

194
Go, litill tretise,° nakit° of eloquence, — *treatise; naked*
Causing simplesse and povertee to wit° — *Revealing simplicity and poverty*
And pray the reder to have pacience
Of thy defaute° and to supporten° it — *With your failings; endure*
Of his gudnesse;° and thy brukilnesse° to knytt, — *(reader's) kindness; jagged edges*
And his tong for to reule and to stere,
That thy defautis helit may bene here.

195
Allace, and gif thou cummyst in the presence
Quhare as of blame faynest thou wald be quite° — *most wish to be free of censure*
To here thy rude° and crukit eloquens,° — *rough; crooked eloquence*
Quho sal be thare to pray for *thy* remyt?° — *remission*
No wicht! Bot geve hir merci° will admytt — *Unless she in her mercy*
The for gud will, that° is thy gyd and stere,° — *(she) who; rudder*
To quhame for me thou pitousely requere.° — *piteously entreat*

196
And thus endith the fatall° influence — *fateful*
Causit from hevyn quhare powar is commytt° — *is delegated*

82. ll. 6–7: 'Through and under whom [the boughs], my heart's cure and future consolation [i.e. Joan] first brought me good fortune.'

Of govirnance, by the magnificence
Of Him that hiest in the hevin sitt.
To Quhame we thank that all oure lyf hath writt,° *written/composed*
Quho couth it red agone syne° mony a yere, *after*
'Hich in the hevynnis figure circulere.'° *circular figure/sign*

197

Unto th' impnis° of my maisteris dere, *hymns*
Gowere° and Chaucere,° that on the steppis satt *Gower; Chaucer*
Of rethorike° quhill thai were lyvand here, *rhetoric*
Superlative as poetis laureate
In moralitee and eloquence ornate,° *stylized persuasive oratory*
I recommend my buk in lynis sevin[83]—
And eke thair saulis unto the blisse of hevin.

83. The final emphasis on the number of lines is not coincidental. Numbers were held to represent mysterious truth directly. Seven, for example, signified the human happiness, which James, according to the *Quair*, has now achieved.

§ 3 Anon (c. 1470): *The Taill of Rauf Coilyear.*

The alliterative Romance form dominated the troubled reigns of James II (1437–60) and James III (1460–88). The deciding factor in choosing **Rauf Coilyear** *to represent the many different branches of that broad type was its comic vitality in contrast to the predominant seriousness of* **The Bruce** *and* **The Kingis Quair**. *The earlier* **Buke of the Howlat** *(c. 1448) by Richard Holland, and* **Golagros and Gawane** *(c. 1470) would have been equally suitable selections. To the same period belongs* **The Wallace** *(1476–8) a martial Romance which remains closer to epic and history and, therefore, invites comparison with* **The Bruce.**

Rauf Coilyear *offers an analytically constructed and predominantly subversive view of the codes of chivalry. It is composed in a complex, alliterative stanza form of the kind originally favoured for Romance topics in the north and midlands of England but now giving way to prose in those areas. It also belongs to the (politically correct in Scottish terms) 'Matter of France', and lays some emphasis on the question of fealty—an issue much more vitally felt and more frequently addressed in Scottish Romance than in its English equivalent.*

As the Notes suggest, the poem is not simply a comic tale. In trying to understand how it treats the question of hospitality, it may be helpful to review the vividly evoked settings—outside and inside—which alternate in the presentation of the tale. On 'rude mure' and 'hie hillis', the major travellers face different tests of courage—personal, chivalric and divine (sts. 1–7; 26–44; 61–73). Protected within cottage and castle (sts. 8–25; 45–60) they meet (as host or as guest) more subtle, but just as testing, challenges of their behaviour.

Yet it would be unwise to become too serious about a poem which was clearly written to evoke laughter. The author's comic skills are perhaps best illustrated when one character's comfortable code of behaviour is invaded by another's. Charlemagne tottering the length of the cottage hall at the receiving end of Rauf's peculiarly physical brand of etiquette control (st. 12), or the porter's open-mouthed bewilderment at meeting a collier with no sense of 'palatial' awe and rather too great a sense of his own rights (st. 48), are among the finest of these.

The Taill of Rauf Coilyear

1

In the cheiftyme° of Charlis,° that chosin chiftane, — *reign; Charlemagne*
Thair fell ane ferlyfull flan° within thay fellis° wyde; — *amazing storm; hills*
Quhair empreouris and erlis and uther mony ane° — *many another*
Turnit° fra Sanct Thomas befoir the Yule tyde.[1] — *Were returning*
Thay past unto Paris, thay proudest in pane° — *most splendidy adorned*
With mony prelatis and princis that was of mekle pryde.
All thay went with the king to his worthy wane° — *dwelling*
Ovir the feildis sa fair thay fure° be his syde. — *journeyed*
All the worthiest° went in the morning — *noblest*
  —Baith dukis and duchepeiris,[2]

1. ED. Copy Text: Lekpreuik Print. After St Thomas's day (21st December) and before the Christmas festivities.
2. The twelve peers (*douzepers*) of Charlemagne.

Barrounis and bacheleiris°— *young knights*
Mony stout° man steiris° *bold; makes his way*
Of° town with the king. *Out of*

2

And as that ryall° raid ovir the rude° mure, *royal person; rough*
Him betyde ane tempest that tyme, hard° I tell. *heard*
The wind blew out of the eist, stiflie° and sture,° *keenly; fiercely*
The drift[3] durandlie draif° in mony deip dell. *rain drove unremittingly*
Sa feirslie fra the firmament, sa fellounlie° it fure, *violently*
Thair micht na folk hald na fute° on the heich fell.° *keep their footing; high hill*
In point° thay war to parische,° thay proudest° men and pure,° *About; perish; most stately; noble*
In thay wickit wedderis° thair wist nane to dwell.° *storms; (where) to shelter*
Amang thay myrk° montanis sa madlie thay mer,° *dark; they became utterly lost*
Be it was pryme° of the day, *the first hour*
Sa wonder hard fure° thay *journeyed*
That ilk ane tuik ane seir° way *separate*
And sperpellit full fer.° *scattered far and wide*

3

Ithand° wedderis of the eist draif on sa fast,° *Continuous; forcefully*
It all to-blaisterit° and blew that° thairin baid.° *scattered; those who; stayed*
Be thay disseverit sindrie,° midmorne was past; *were variously dispersed*
Thair wist° na knicht of the court quhat way the king raid. *knew*
He saw thair was na better° bot God at the last. *no better recourse*
His steid° aganis the storme stalwartlie straid;° *steed; strode*
He cachit fra° the court, sic was his awin cast,° *headed away from; fate*
Quhair nabody was him about, be five mylis braid.° *roughly five miles*
In thay montanis, iwis,° he wox all will,° *truly; became utterly lost*
In wickit wedderis and wicht° *strong*
Amang thay montanis on hicht;° *on high*
Be that it drew to the nicht
The king lykit ill.° *was dismayed*

4

Evill lykand was the king it nichtit him sa lait,
And he na harberie had for his behufe.[4]
Sa come thair ane cant carll° chachand the gait,° *bold rustic; making his way*
With ane capill° and twa creillis cuplit abufe.° *horse; i.e. and two paniers*
The king carpit° to the carll, withoutin debait.° *addressed; ceremony*
'Schir, tell me thy richt name, for the Rude° lufe.'° *holy cross; love (of)*
He sayis, 'Men callis me Rauf Coilyear,° as I weill wait. *The Charcoal Burner*
I leid my life in this land with mekle unrufe,° *trouble*

3. Lekpreuik has 'deip', probably a compositorial anticipation.

4. ll. 1–2: i.e. 'It displeased the king that he was caught out by the approach of night, and that he lacked shelter in his time of need.' 'Harberie' and related words conveying the idea of shelter are a leitmotiv in the poem. To provide lodging for others was the principal test of corporal mercy defined by Christ on the Mount of Olives. See Matthew 25. 31–46.

Baith tyde and time,° in all my travale.°	*All the time; labouring*
Hine° ovir sevin mylis I dwell,	*From here*
And leidis coilis° to sell.	*transport coals*
Sen° thow speiris,° I the tell	*Since; ask*
All the suith hale.'°	*All the facts entirely*

5

'Sa mote I thrife,'[5] said the king, 'I speir for nane ill.°	*ask with no evil intention*
Thow semis ane nobill fallow, thy answer is sa fyne.'	
'Forsuith,' said the coilyear, 'traist quhen thow will,°	*believe what you wish*
For I trow, and it be nocht swa, sum part° salbe thyne.'	*part (of the blame)*
'Mary, God forbid,' said the King, 'that war bot lytill skill!°	*hardly sensible*
Baith myself and my hors is reddy for to tyne.°	*about to perish*
I pray the bring me to sum rest, the wedder is sa schill;°	*piercingly cold*
For I defend° that we fall in ony fechtine°—	*forbid; fighting*
I had mekill mair nait° sum freindschip to find!	*need*
And gif thow can better than I,	
For the name of Sanct July,[6]	
Thow bring me to sum harbery°	*shelter*
And leif° me not behind.'	*leave*

6

'I wait° na worthie harberie° heir neir hand	*know of; refuge*
For to serve sic ane man as me think the°—	*you seem to me*
Nane bot mine awin hous, maist° in this land,°	*largest; part of the land*
Fer furth in the forest, amang the fellis hie.°	*high hills*
With-thy° thow wald be payit of° sic as thow fand,	*Provided; satisfied with*
Forsuith, thow suld be welcum to pas hame with me,	
Or ony uther gude fallow that I heir fand,°	*came across*
Walkand will of his way° (as me think the)	*i.e. lost*
For the wedderis ar sa fell° that fallis on the feild.'	*fierce*
The king was blyth quhair he raid°	*rode*
Of the grant° that he had maid,	*agreement*
Sayand, with hart glaid,	
'Schir, God yow foryeild!'°	*reward*

7

'Na, thank me not ovir airlie,° for dreid that we threip,°	*prematurely; fall out*
For I have servit the yit of lytill thing to ruse;°	*worth praising*
For nouther hes thow had of me fyre, drink, nor meit,	
Nor nane uther eismentis° for travellouris behuse.°	*refreshments; comfort*
Bot micht we bring this harberie this nicht weill to heip,°	*to a satisfactory end*
That we micht with ressoun baith us excuse.°	*justify ourselves*
To-morne, on the morning, quhen thow sall on leip,°	*mount up*
Pryse at the parting how that thow dois.[7]	
For first to lofe° and syne to lak,° Peter,° it is schame!'	*extol; carp; (by St) Peter*

5. Formulaic: literally, 'As I may thrive'—i.e. 'Upon my soul!'
6. St Julian was the patron saint of travellers.
7. Proverb. 'Assess how you have fared [lit. 'do'] when you leave.'

The king said, 'In gude fay,° *faith*
Schir, it is suith that ye say.'
Into sic talk fell thay
Quhill° thay war neir hame. *Until*

8

To the coilyearis hous baith, or thay wald blin°— *i.e. without stopping*
The carll had cunning weill° quhair the gait° lay. *knew well; road*
'Undo the dure belive!° Dame, art thow in? *at once*
Quhy devill makis thow na dule° for this evill day? *do you not lament*
For my gaist° and I baith cheveris with the chin;[8] *guest*
Sa fell° ane wedder feld° I never, be my gude fay!' *cruel; experienced*
The gude wyfe glaid° with the gle° to begin, *bustled about; entertainment*
For durst scho never sit summoundis° that scho hard° him say *disregard orders; heard*
The carll was wantoun of word,° and wox° wonder wraith.° *rough-tongued; grew angry*
All abaisit for blame,° *abashed at the reproof*
To the dure went our dame.
Scho said, 'Schir, ye ar welcome hame,
And your gaist baith.'

9

'Dame, I have deir coft° all this dayis hyre,° *bought dearly; earnings*
In wickit wedderis and weit, walkand full will;° *wandering all over*
Dame, kyith° I am cummin hame and kendill on° ane fyre! *mark well; light*
I trow our gaist be the gait° hes farne° als ill. *on the route; fared*
Ane ryall° rufe-het° fyre war my desyre, *fit for a king; roof-hot*
To fair the better, for his saik, gif we micht win thair till.° *bring it about*
Knap doun capounis° of the best, but° in the byre; *kill capons; out*
Heir is bot hamelie fair,° do belive,° Gill.' *homely fare; look lively*
Twa cant knaifis° of his awin haistelie° he bad: *sturdy servants; urgently*
'The ane of yow my capill ta,° *lead my horse*
The uther his coursour° alswa, *steed*
To the stabill swyith° ye ga!' *quickly*
Than was the king glaid.

10

The coilyear, gudlie in feir,° tuke him be the hand *hospitably*
And put him befoir him,° as ressoun had bene. *let him (king) precede*
Quhen thay come to the dure the king begouth to stand,° *hesitated*
To put the coilyear in befoir maid him to mene.° *intended*
He° said, 'Thow art uncourtes,° that sall I warrand!'[9] *i.e. Rauf; lack manners*
He tyt° the king be the nek, twa part in tene.° *grabbed; in anger*
'Gif thow at bidding suld be boun° or obeysand, *If you ever were biddable*

8. Literally, 'Shivers with the chin', i.e. 'Have chattering teeth.' This phrase is later used by Henryson. See *Testament of Cresseid*, 23.2.
9. Rauf applies the codes of the cottage to the king. The idea of the collier having equal rights in his home to a king in his castle survives in the French proverb, 'Le charbonnier est maître chez soi'.

And gif thow of courtasie° couth, thow hes foryet° it clene. — *courtesy; forgotten*
Now is anis!' said the coilyear. 'Kynd aucht to creip![10]
Sen° ellis thow art unknawin° — *Since; ignorantly disinclined*
To mak me lord of my awin!° — *own (domain)*
Sa mot I thrive, I am thrawin,° — *stubbornly angry*
Begin we to threip!° — *quarrel*

11

Than benwart° thay yeid° quhair brandis° was bricht, — *inside; went; burning logs*
To ane bricht byrnand fyre, as the carll bad.
He callit on Gyliane, his wyfe, thair supper to dicht.° — *prepare*
'Of the best that thair is, help that we had,
****
************************************[11]
Efter ane evill day to have ane mirrie nicht,
For sa troublit with stormis was I never stad.° — *beset*
Of ilk airt° of the eist sa laithly° it laid,° — *compass point; horribly; blew*
Yit was I mekle willar° than — *more off course*
Quhen I met with this man.'
Of sic taillis thay began,
Quhill the supper was graid.° — *laid out*

12

Sone was the supper dicht,° and the fyre bet,° — *ready; built up*
And they had weschin;° iwis, the worthiest was thair. — *washed*
'Tak my wyfe be the hand, in feir,° withoutin let,° — *as partner; delay*
And gang begin the buird,'° said the coilyear. — *And go to the head of the table*
'That war unsemand,° forsuith, and thy self unset'°— — *unseemly; unseated*
The king profferit him to gang,° and maid ane strange fair.° — *let (Rauf) precede; gesture*
'Now is twyse!' said the carll, 'me think thow hes foryet!'[12]
He leit gyrd to° the king, withoutin ony mair,° — *struck; more ado*
And hit him under the eir with his richt hand,
Quhill he stakkerit° thair withall, — *staggered*
Half the bried° of the hall. — *breadth*
He faind never of ane fall
Quhill he the eird fand.[13]

13

He start up stoutly agane—uneis° micht he stand— — *scarcely*
For anger of that outray° that he had thair tane.° — *outrage; endured*
He° callit on Gyliane his wyfe: 'Ga tak him be the hand, — *i.e. Rauf*

10. ' "This is the first (time)!" said the charcoal-burner. "Nature ought to go on all fours." ' The image is designed to counter Charlemagne's pride-in-folly. It has Biblical associations with the punishment of Satan in Eden.
11. ED. There are two lines missing in the text.
12. The device of offering three chances is common in bardic literature and folk tales. Charlemagne only needs to be told twice!
13. 'He never stopped tottering until he hit the ground.'

And gang agane to the buird° quhair ye suld air° have gane.	*table; earlier*
Schir, thow art unskilfull,° and that sall I warrand.°	*ignorant; warrant*
Thow byrd° to have nurtour° aneuch, and thow hes nane.	*ought; breeding*
Thow hes walkit, iwis, in mony wyld land,	
The mair vertew° thow suld have to keip the° fra blame.°	*intelligence; you; censure*
Thow suld be courtes of kynd° and ane cunnand° courtier.	*by nature; wise*
Thocht that I simpill be,	
Do as I bid the!	
The hous is myne, pardie.	
And all that is heir.'	

14

The king said to himself, 'This is ane evill lyfe.°	*i.e. bad state of affairs*
Yit was I never in my lyfe thus gait leird°—	*instructed in this way*
And I have oft tymes bene quhair gude hes bene ryfe°	*abounded*
That° maist couth of courtasie in this Cristin eird!	*Those who*
Is nane sa gude as leif of° and mak na mair stryfe,	*The best course is to desist*
For I am stonischit at this straik° that hes me thus steird.'°	*blow; upset*
In feir° fairlie he foundis° with the gude wyfe	*company; goes*
Quhair the coilyear bad, sa braithlie° he beird.°	*violently; behaved*
Quhen he° had done his° bidding (as him gude thocht)	*(the king); (Rauf's)*
Doun he sat the king neir,	
And maid him glaid and gude cheir,[14]	
And said, 'Ye are welcum heir,	
Be him that me bocht.'°	*bought (i.e. Christ)*

15

Quhen thay war servit and set to° the suppar,	*seated at*
Gyll° and the gentill King Charlis of micht,	*i.e. Rauf's wife*
Syne, on the tother syde sat the coilyear,	
Thus war thay marschellit but mair° and matchit that nicht.	*marshalled without more ado*
Thay brocht breid to the buird and braun° of ane bair°	*brawn; bear*
And the worthyest wyne went upon hicht.°	*i.e. was passed around*
Thay beirnis,° as I wene,° thay had aneuch thair,	*heroes; judge*
Within that burelie bigging° byrnand full bricht.	*noble dwelling*
Syne enteris thair daynteis° on deis° dicht° dayntelie.	*delicacies; dais; prepared*
Within that worthie wane,°	*building*
Forsuith, wantit thay nane.°	*they lacked for nothing*
With blyith cheir,° sayis Gyliane,	*cheerful expression*
'Schir, dois gladlie!'°	*eat, drink and be merry*

16

The carll carpit to the king, cumlie° and cleir,°	*handsome; distinguished*
'Schir, the forestaris, forsuith, of this forest,	
Thay have me all at invy for dreid of the deir![15]	
Thay threip° that I thring doun° of the fattest.	*cavil; bring down*

14. 'And made him happy and treated him in a hospitable manner.'
15. 'They are all envious of me for fear of (my skill in killing) the deer.'

Thay say I sall to Paris, thair to compeir° *appear*
Befoir our cumlie king, in dule to be drest.° *to be painfully dealt with*
Sic manassing° thay me mak,° forsuith, ilk yeir *Such threatening...direct at*
And yit aneuch sall I have for me and ane gest.° *guest*
Thairfoir sic as thow seis, spend on° and not spair!' *eat heartily*
    Thus said gentill° Charlis the Mane° *noble/courteous; Great*
    To the coilyear agane,
    'The king himself hes ben fane° *glad*
        Sum tyme° of sic fair.'° *On occasion; fare*

17

Of caponnis° and cunningis° thay had plentie, *capons; rabbits*
With wyne at thair will and eik vennysoun,° *venison too*
Byrdis bakin in breid,° the best that may be; *Bird-pies*
Thus full freschlie° thay fure into fusioun.° *ever anew; came in abundance*
The carll, with ane cleir voce, carpit on he,° *loudly*
Said, 'Gyll, lat the cop raik° for my bennysoun° *pass round; blessing*
And gar° our gaist° begin and syne° drink thow to me; *have; guest; then*
Sen he is ane stranger, me think it ressoun.'° *appropriate*
Thay drank dreichlie° about, thay wosche° and thay rais.° *deeply; washed; rose*
    The king with ane blyith cheir° *countenance*
    Thankit the coilyeir,
    Syne all the thre into feir° *together*
        To the fyre gais.° *go*

18

Quhen thay had maid thame eis,° the coilyear tald *themselves comfortable*
Mony sindrie° taillis efter suppair. *different*
Ane bricht byrnand fyre was byrnand full bald.° *strongly*
The king held gude countenance and company bair° *was good company*
And ever to his° asking ane answer he yald,° *i.e. Rauf's; (king) gave*
Quhill at the last he began to frane farther mair:° *ask more probingly*
'In faith, freind, I wald wit,° tell gif ye wald, *know*
Quhair is thy maist wynning?'° said the coilyear. *main dwelling place*
'Out of weir,'° said the king, 'I wayndit never to tell.[16] *Assuredly*
    With my lady the quene
    In office maist° have I bene, *highest*
    All thir yeiris fyftene
        In the court for to dwell.'

19

'Quhat kin office° art thow in, quhen thow art at hame, *kind of position*
Gif thow dwellis with the quene, proudest in pane?'° *i.e. noblest of all*
'Ane chyld° of hir chalmer,° schir, be Sanct Jame,[17] *groom; chamber*
And thocht myself it say, maist inwart° of ane. *intimate*
For my dwelling tonicht I dreid me for blame.'° *I fear (her) reproof*

16. 'I had no intention of concealing the information.'
17. St James often appears in 'wandering'/'journeying' poems where the deeds of corporal mercy are tested (see 20.12). His shrine at Compostella was a major focus for pilgrimage.

'Quhat sal I cal the,' said the coilyear, 'quhen thow art hyne gane?'° *gone away*
'Wymond of the Wardrop° is my richt name. *Wardrobe*
Quhairever thow findis me befoir the, thi harberie is tane;° *lodging is guaranteed*
And° thow will cum to the court, this I underta,° *If; undertake*
Thow sall have for thy fewaill° *fuel (i.e. coals)*
For my saik, the better saill° *transaction*
And onwart to° thy travaill° *extra for; labour*
Worth ane laid° or twa.' *load*

20

He said, 'I have na knawledge quhair the court lyis,
And I am wonder wa° to cum quhair I am unkend.' *very reluctant*
'And I sall say thee the suith on ilk syde, iwis,
That thow sall wit weill aneuch or I fra the wend.° *take leave of you*
Baith the king and the quene meitis in Paris
For to hald thair Yule° togidder, for scho is efter send.° *Yule festivities; sent for*
Thair may thow sell, be ressoun, als deir° as thow will prys;° *as dearly; estimate*
And yit I sall help the, gif I ocht° may amend,° *anything; set right*
For I am knawin with officiaris, in cais° thow cum thair. *in the event that*
Have gude thocht on my name
And speir° gif I be at hame, *ask*
For I suppois, be Sanct Jame,
Thow sall the better fair.'° *fare*

21

'Me think it ressoun, be the Rude,° that I do thy rid,° *holy cross; follow your advice*
In cais I cum to the court, and knaw bot the ane.° *only you*
Is nane sa gude as drink and gang to our bed
For, als far as I wait,° the nicht is furth gane.' *can judge*
To ane previe chalmer belive° thay him led, *private chamber at once*
Quhair ane burely° bed was wrocht° in that wane, *fine; prepared*
Closit° with courtingis° and cumlie cled; *Enclosed; curtains*
Of the worthiest wyne wantit° thay nane. *lacked*
The coilyear and his wyfe baith with him thay yeid,° *accompanied him*
To serve him all at° thay mocht, *that*
Till he was in bed brocht.
Mair the king spak nocht
Bot thankit thame thair deid.° *(for) their deeds*

22

Upon the morning airlie,° quhen it was day, *early*
The king buskit him° sone with scant of squyary;° *got ready; few squires*
Wachis° and wardroparis° all war away *Guards; valets*
That war wont for to walkin° mony worthy.° *waken; noblemen*
Ane pauyot° previlie° brocht him his palfray; *lad; secretly*
The king thocht lang of° this lyfe, and lap on in hy.° *grew weary; mounted hastily*
Than callit he on the carll, anent° quhair he lay, *near to*
For to tak his leif, than spak he freindly.
Than walkinnit° thay baith and hard° he was thair. *awakened; heard*
The carll start up sone

And prayit him to abyde none,° *wait till noon*
'Quhill thir wickit wedderis be done
I rid° nocht ye fair.'° *advise; depart*

23

'Sa mot I thrive,' said the king, 'me war laith to byde.° *reluctant to stay*
Is not morne Yule° day, formest° of the yeir? *Christmas; foremost*
Ane man that office suld beir,° be tyme° at this tyde, *is fit to bear; punctually*
He will be found in his fault that wantis,° foroutin weir.[18] *is absent*
I se the firmament fair upon ather syde;
I will returne to the court quhill the wedder is cleir.
Call furth the gude wyfe, lat pay hir° or we ryde *let me repay (her)*
For the worthie harberie that I have fundin heir.'
'Lat be, God forbid,' the coilyear said,
'And thow of Charlis cumpany
—Cheif king of chevalry—
That for ane nichtis harbery
Pay suld be laid!'° *charged*

24

'Yea, sen it is sa that thow will have na pay,
Cum the morne to the court and do my counsall.° *follow my advice*
Deliver the° and bring ane laid, and mak na delay. *Exert yourself*
Thow may not schame with° thy craft, gif thow thrive° sall. *be ashamed of; succeed*
Gif I may help the ocht° to sell, forsuith, I sall assay° *anything; do my best*
And als myself° wald have sum of the fewall.' *I also*
'Peter,' he said, 'I shall preif the morne,° gif I may, *try tomorrow*
To bring coillis° to the court to se gif thay sell sall.' *coals*
'Se that thow let nocht,° I pray the,' said the king. *fail not*
'In faith,' said the coilyear,
'Traist weill, I salbe thair,
For thow will never gif the mair° *commit yourself again*
To mak ane lesing.° *To speak falsely*

25

'Bot tell me now lelely,° quhat is thy richt name? *truthfully*
I will foryet the morne and ony° man me greif.'° *if any; grieves*
'Wymond of the Wardrop, I bid not to lane;° *I'm not trying to hide it*
Tak gude tent to° my name, the court gif thow will preif.' *Heed well*
'That I have said I sall hald, and that I tell the plane;
Quhair ony coilyear may enchaip,° I trow till encheif.'° *trade; expect to succeed*
Quhen he had grantit° him to cum than was the king fane,° *promised (Rauf); pleased*
And withoutin ony mair let° than° he tuke his leif. *delay; then*
Than the coilyear had greit thocht on the cunnand° he had maid *bargain*
Went to the charcoill in hy

18. 'Except in case of war.' In *Gawain and the Green Knight*, only those knights who are engaged in wars or martial challenges are excused the Christmas feast at Camelot.

To mak his chauffray° reddy; *merchandise*
Agane° the morne airly *In preparation for*
He ordanit° him ane laid.° *got together; load*

26

The lyft lemit up° belive and licht was the day, *sky brightened up*
The king had greit knawledge° the countrie to ken.° *well able; to recognize*
Schir Rolland and Oliver[19] come rydand the way,
With thame ane thousand and ma° of fensabill° men *more; armed*
War wanderand all the nicht ovir,° and mony ma than thay. *throughout*
On ilk airt outwart war ordanit sic ten[20]
Gif thay micht heir of the king, or happin° quhair he lay; *come by chance*
To Jesus Christ thay pray that grace thame to len.° *lend*
Als sone as Schir Rolland saw it was the king,
He kneillit doun in the place,
Thankand God ane greit space.° *at great length*
Thair was ane meting of grace° *gracious*
At that gaddering.° *gathering*

27

The gentill knicht Schir Rolland, he kneilit on his kne,
Thankand greit God that mekill was of micht,
Schir Oliver at his hand and bischoppis thre
Withoutin communis° that come, and mony uther knicht. *Not counting common men*
Than to Paris thay pas, all that chevalrie,° *chivalric band*
Betwix none° of the day and Yule nicht. *Between noon*
The gentill Bischop Turpine cummand° thay se *approaching*
With threttie convent° of preistis revest° at ane sicht, *thirty companies; in vestments*
Preichand of prophecie in processioun;
Efter thame, baith fer and neir,
Folkis following in feir,° *together*
Thankand God, with gude cheir,
Thair lord was gane to toun.

28

Quhen thay princis appeirit into Paris
Ilk rew° ryallie with riches thame arrayis. *Each rank*
Thair was digne° service done at Sanct Dyonys,° *worthy; St Denis's*
With mony proud prelat, as the buik° sayis. *i.e. my written authority*
Syne to supper thay went within the palys;
Befoir that mirthfull man menstrallis° playis. *minstrels*
Mony wicht wyfis sone,° worthie and wise, *Many a worthy woman's son*
Was sene at that semblay° ane-and-twentie dayis, *assembly*
With all kin principall° plentie for his plesance. *kinds (of) princely*
Thay callit it the best Yule than

19. Leading knights in Charlemagne's court and heroes of French Romance.
20. The search parties had fanned out in groups of ten.

And maist worthie began,
Sen ever King Charles was man,
Or ever was in France.

29

Than upon the morne airlie quhen the day dew,° *dawned*
The coilyear had greit thocht° quhat he had undertane. *pondered*
He kest° twa creillis° on ane capill with coillis anew, *threw; paniers*
Wandit° thame with widdeis° to wend on° that wane. *Bound; ropes; advance towards*
'Mary, it is not my counsall, bot yone man that ye knew,
To do yow in his gentrise,'[21] said Gyliane.
'Thow gaif him ane outragious blaw° and greit boist blew.° *severe blow; spoke arrogantly*
In faith, thow suld have bocht it deir° and° he had bene allane; *paid dearly for it; if*
For-thy, hald yow° fra the court, for ocht that may be. *Therefore, keep away*
Yone man that thow outrayd° *insulted*
Is not sa simpill as he said;
Thairun my lyfe dar I layd,° *wager*
That sall thow heir and se.'

30

'Yea, Dame, have nane dreid of° my lyfe today. *fear for*
Lat me wirk° as I will, the weird° is mine awin. *do; fate*
I spak not out of ressoun,° the suith gif I sall say, *unreasonably*
To Wymond of the Wardrop, war the suith knawin.
That I have hecht° I sall hald, happin° as it may, *promised; turn out*
Quhidder sa it gang to greif or to gawin.'° *to grief or gain*
He caucht° twa creillis on ane capill and catchit on his way *fixed*
Ovir the daillis sa derf° be the day was dawin, *rugged*
The hie way to Paris, in all that he mocht;
With ane quhip° in his hand, *whip*
Cantlie on catchand,° *Boldly advancing*
To fulfill his cunnand,° *covenant*
To the court socht.° *sought out (the way)*

31

Graith thocht° of the grant° had the gude king, *Ready recall; undertaking*
And callit Schir Rolland him till and gaif commandment—
Ane man he traistit in maist° atour° all uther thing, *trusted most; above*
That° never wald set him on assay° withoutin his assent— *Who; attack*
'Tak thy hors and thy harnes° in the morning, *armour*
For to watche weill the wayis° I wald that thow went. *approach roads*
Gif thow meitis ony leid° lent on the ling,° *person; crossing the moor*
Gar thame boun° to this burgh,° I tell the mine intent; *Direct them; town*
Or gif thow seis ony man cumming furth the way,
Quhat sumever° that he be, *No matter who*

21. ll. 5–6: 'By Mary, I would not counsel you to put yourself in that man's power without (fully) knowing him.'

Bring him haistely to me,
Befoir none° that I him se *noon*
In this hall the day.'° *to-day*

32

Schir Rolland had greit ferly,° and in hart kest° *wonder; pondered*
Quhat that suld betakin° that the king tald, *mean*
Upon solempnit° Yule day quhen ilk man suld rest *solemnized*
That him behovit neidlingis° to watche on the wald,° *he had of necessity; moor*
Quhen his God to serve he suld have him drest.° *prepared himself*
And syne with ane blyith cheir buskit° that bald,° *made ready; bold one*
Out of Paris proudly he preikit° full prest,° *rode; urgently*
Intill his harnes° all haill his hechtis for to hald.° *armour; vows to keep*
He umbekest° the countrie° outwith the toun, *scanned; countryside*
He saw na thing on steir,° *moving*
Nouther fer nor neir,
Bot the feildis in feir,° *adjoining*
Daillis° and doun.° *Dales; hill(s)*

33

He huit° and he hoverit° quhill midmorne and mair, *halted; waited*
Behaldand the hie hillis and passage° sa plane,° *way; clear*
Sa saw he quhair the coilyear come with all his fair,° *load*
With twa creillis on ane capill—thairof was he fane.° *pleased*
He followit to him haistely amang the holtis hair° *frosty woods*
For to bring him to the king at bidding° full bane.° *command; most promptly*
Courtesly° to the knicht kneillit the coilyear *Courteously*
And Schir Rolland himself salust him agane,° *returned the greeting*
Syne bad him leif° his courtasie and boun him° to ga. *put an end to; prepare*
He said, 'Withoutin letting° *delay*
Thow mon to Paris, to the king.
Speid the fast in ane ling° *directly*
Sen I find na ma.'° *no one else*

34

'In faith,' said the coilyear, 'yit was I never sa nyse!°[22] *so precise*
Schir knicht, it is na courtasie commounis° to scorne. *ordinary folk*
Thair is mony better than I cummis oft to Parys
That the king wait not of,° nouther nicht nor morne. *doesn't know of*
For to towsill° me or tit° me, thocht foull be my clais,° *use roughly; drag; clothes*
Or° I be dantit° on sic wyse, my lyfe salbe lorne!'° *Before; intimidated; lost*
'Do way,'° said Schir Rolland, 'me think thow art not wise! *Enough*
I rid° thow at bidding be,° be all that we have sworne, *advise; be obedient*
And call thow it na scorning,° bot do as I the ken,° *mockery; tell you*
Sen thow hes hard mine intent.
It is the kingis commandement,
At this tyme° thow suld have went° *By now; gone*
And° I had met sic ten.'° *Even if; ten such*

22. Rauf insinuates that Rolland is taking the order too literally and ought to discount him. This explains Rolland's riposte at the end of the stanza.

35

'I am bot ane mad° man that thow hes heir met; *simple*
I have na myster° to matche with maisterfull° men, *skill; powerful*
Fairand° ovir the feildis fewell to fet°, *Journeying; to bring fuel*
And oft fylit° my feit in mony foull fen, *fouled*
Gangand° with laidis my governing to get.° *Going along; earn my living*
Thair is mony carll in the countrie thow may nocht ken.
I sall hald° that I have hecht,° bot I be hard set,° *hold (to); vowed; in hard straits*
To Wymond of the Wardrop, I wait full weill quhen.'
'Sa thrive I,' said Rolland, 'it is mine intent
That nouther to Wymond nor Will° *i.e. Tom, Dick or Harry*
Thow sall hald nor hecht till,
Quhill° I have brocht the° to fulfill *Until; you*
The kingis commandment.'

36

The carll beheld to° the knicht as he stude than. *looked closely at*
He bair, gravit in gold and gowlis in grene,° *heraldic red on green*
Glitterand full gaylie quhen glemis began,° *whenever light caught it*
Ane tyger ticht° to ane tre, ane takin° of tene.° *tied; token; wrath*
Trewlie that tenefull° was trimland° than, *angry one; shaking*
Semelie schapin° and schroud° in that scheild schene; *Handsomely formed; couched*
Mekle worschip of weir° worthylie he wan *Many a battle honour*
Befoir, into fechting with mony worthie sene.° *noble men*
His basnet° was bordourit° and burneist° bricht, *helmet; bordered; burnished*
With stanis of beriall deir,° *precious beryl*
Dyamountis° and sapheir,° *Diamonds; sapphires*
Riche rubeis in feir,° *Clusters of rich rubies*
Reulit° full richt.° *Arrayed; fittingly*

37

His plaitis,° properlie picht attour° with precious stanis, *armour; fittingly decorated*
And his pulanis° full prest° of that ilk peir;° *knee armour; ready; quality*
Greit graipis° of gold his greis,° for the nanis,° *bands; greaves; to be sure*
And his cussanis cumlie schynand° full cleir. *thigh-pieces shining nobly*
Bricht braissaris° of steill about his arme banis,° *arm-plates; bones*
Blandit° with beriallis and cristallis cleir,° *Mixed; translucent crystals*
Ticht ovir with thopas and trew lufe atanis,[23]
The teind° of his jewellis to tell° war full teir.° *tenth; relate/count; hard*
His sadill circulit° and set richt sa on ilk syde, *saddle encircled*
His brydill bellisand° and gay, *handsome bridle*
His steid stout on stray;° *bold abroad (formulaic)*
He was the ryallest of array° *most royally adorned*
On ronsy° micht ryde. *horse*

38

Of° that ryall array that Rolland in raid,° *Regarding; rode in*
Rauf rusit in his hart° of that ryall thing. *pondered in his heart*

23. 'Closely interlaced with both topaz and true-love knots.'

'He is the gayest in geir that ever on ground glaid,[24]
Have he grace to the gre° in ilk jornaying.° *grace of victory; any quest*
War he ane manly° man, as he is weill maid,° *(as) valorous…(as) well built*
He was full michtie with magre durst abyde his meting.'[25]
He bad the coilyear in wraith,° swyth, withoutin baid,° *angrily; quickly without delay*
Cast the creillis fra° the capill and gang to the king. *Throw down the paniers from*
'In faith, it war greit schame,' said the coilyear,
'I undertuk thay suld be brocht
This day for ocht that be mocht.° *come what may*
Schir knicht, that word is for nocht° *to no purpose*
That thow carpis° thair. *utter*

39

'Thow huifis° on thir holtis° and haldis me heir *Even if you linger; woods*
Quhill half the haill day may the hicht have.'° *i.e. until noon*
'Be Christ that was cristinnit, and his mother cleir,° *pure/bright*
Thow sall catche to° the court, that sall not *shall go to;*
be to crave.° *a matter for debate*
It micht be preifit prejudice bot gif thow suld compeir[26]
To se quhat granting of grace the king wald the gaif.'° *give you*
'For na gold on this ground° wald I, but weir,° *earthly; for certain*
Be fundin fals° to the king, sa Christ me° save.' *found untrue; i.e. Rauf*
'To gar the cum and be knawin,° as I° am command, *identified/recognized; i.e. Roland*
I wait not quhat his willis be;° *wishes are*
Nor he namit na mair the,° *you in particular*
Nor ane uther man to me,
Bot, quhome that I fand.'° *Only, whomever I found*

40

'Thow fand me fechand° nathing that followit to feid;° *carrying; would lead to enmity*
I war ane fule gif I fled and fand nane affray,° *cause for alarm*
Bot as ane lauchfull° man my laidis° to leid,° *law-abiding; loads; convey*
That leifis° with mekle lawtie° and laubour, in fay. *lives; respect for law*
Be the mother and the maydin° that maid us remeid,° *maiden; brought us a remedy*
And thow mar° me ony mair, cum efter quhat sa may,° *hinder; whatever the outcome*
Thow and I sall dyntis deill° quhill ane of us be deid, *exchange blows*
For the deidis thow hes me done upon this deir day!'
Mekle mervell of that word° had Schir Rolland. *speech/outburst*
He saw na wappinis thair
That the coilyear bair,
Bot ane auld buklair° *ancient buckler*
And ane roustie brand.° *rusty sword*

41

'It is lyke,'° said Schir Rolland and lichtly he leuch,° *likely; laughed*
'That sic ane stubill husband man° wald stryke stoutly.° *stubborn rustic; bravely*

24. 'The most splendidly accoutred man who ever lightly trod the ground;' lit. 'The gayest in gear who ever glided over the ground.' For other alliterative bardic formulae, cf. 'proudest in pane' (1.5); 'ryallest of array' (37.12).
25. 'Anyone who could endure conflict with him [Rolland] would have to be very strong and hostile.'
26. 'Deemed prejudicial to your case, unless you appear.'

Thair is mony toun man° to tuggill° is full teuch,°	*townsmen; wrestle; tough*
Thocht thair brandis° be blak and unburely;°	*swords; inelegant/clumsy*
Oft fair foullis° ar fundin faynt and als freuch.°	*birds; frail also*
I defend° we fecht or fall in that foly;	*forbid (that)*
Lat se how we may dissever° with sobernes aneuch,°	*part; with adequate sobriety*
And catche crabitnes away,° be Christ, counsall I.	*drive away ill humour*
Quhair winnis° that Wymond thow hecht° to meit today?'	*dwells; promised*
'With the quene, tauld he me,	
And thair I undertuke to be	
Into Paris, pardie,°	*by God*
Withoutin delay.'	
42	
'And I am knawin with the quene,'° said Schir Rolland,	*i.e. have the Queen's ear*
'And with mony byrdis° in hir bowre,° be buikis and bellis.°	*ladies; chamber; i.e. truly*
The king is into Paris, that sall I warrand,°	*warrant*
And all his advertance° that in his court dwellis.	*retinue*
Me tharth° have none noy of° myne erand,	*I need; grief about*
For me think thow will be thair, efter as° thow tellis,	*in accordance with what*
Bot gif I fand the forrow now to keip my cunnand.'[27]	
'Schir knicht,' said the coilyear, 'thow trowis me° never ellis,	*believe me*
Bot gif sum suddand let° put it of delay,	*unexpected hindrance*
For that I hecht of my will°	*free will*
And na man threit me thair till,°	*forced me into it*
That I am haldin° to fulfill,	*bound*
And sall do quhill I may!'°	*as long as I am able*
43	
'Yea, sen thow will be thair, thy cunnandis° to new,°	*undertakings; renew*
I neid nane airar° myne erand nor none° of the day.'	*no earlier; than before noon*
'Be thow traist,'° said the coilyear, ' man, as I am trew,	*Believe me*
I will not haist me ane fute faster on the way.	
Bot gif thow raik° out of my renk,° full raith° sall thow rew,	*move; way; very quickly*
Or, be the Rude,° I sall rais° thy ryall array.	*holy cross; slash*
Thocht thy body be braissit° in that bricht hew,°	*tightly enclosed; hue*
Thow salbe fundin als febill,° of thy bone fay.'°	*as weak; good faith (Fr.)*
Schir Rolland said to himself, 'This is bot foly°	*mere folly*
To strive with him ocht mair;°	*any more*
I se weill he will be thair.'	
His leif at° the coilyear	*leave from*
He tuke lufesumly.°	*amiably*
44	
'Be Christ,' said the coilyear, 'that war ane foull scorne°	*vile show of contempt*
That thow suld chaip° bot I the knew, that is sa schynand;[28]	*escape*
For thow seis my weidis° ar auld and all to-worne,°	*clothes; worn-out*

27. 'Only because I intercepted you earlier in keeping with my covenant (to the king).'

28. This line and 43.7 refer to the 'shining' colours refracted by the daylight from the knight's armour. This is also a sign of his higher rank and greater protection.

Thow trowis° nathing thir taillis° that I am telland. *believe; tales*
Bring na beirnis° us by, bot as we war borne,° *warriors; born*
And thir blonkis° that us beiris;° thairto I mak ane band°[29] *steeds; carry; sworn vow*
That I sall meit the heir upon this mure to-morne,
Gif I be haldin in heill,° and thairto my hand, *kept in good health*
Sen that we have na laiser° at this tyme to ta.' *leisure*
In ane thourtour° way *opposite*
Seir gaitis° pas thay, *Different routes*
Baith to Paris, in fay,
Thus partit thay twa.

45

The gentill knicht, Schir Rolland, come rydand full sone,
And left the coilyear to cum, as he had undertane.
And quhen he come to Paris the hie mes° was done;° *high mass; completed*
The king with mony cumly° out of the kirk is gane. *fine people*
Of his harnes in hy° he hynt° withoutin hone,° *armour in haste; took off; delay*
And in ane rob° him arrayit, richest of ane; *robe*
In that worschipfull weid° he went in at none,° *noble garment; midday*
As he was wont, with the wy° that weildit° the wane,° *person; ruled; dwelling-place*
On fute frely° in feir,° formest° of all. *nobly; company; foremost*
Richt weill payit° was the king *pleased (at)/repaid (by)*
Of Schir Rollandis cumming;
To speir of° his tything° *enquire about; news*
Efter him gart call.° *He had him summoned*

46

The king in counsall° him callit, 'Cum hidder, schir knicht, *i.e. to receive his counsel*
Hes thow my bidding done as I the command?'
'In faith,' said Schir Rolland, 'I raid on full richt
To watche wyselie the wayis, that I sall warrand.
Thair wald na douchtie° this day for jornay be dicht°— *bold fellow; prepared for battle*
Fairand ovir the feildis full few thair I fand.
Saif anerly° ane man that semblit in my sicht,° *Save only; came into my view*
Thair was na leid on lyfe lent in this land.'° *i.e. Nobody at all was abroad*
'Quhat kin a fallow° was that ane, schir, I the pray?' *kind of fellow*
'Ane man in husband weid,° *countryman's attire*
Buskit busteously° in breid,° *Hurried energetically; abroad*
Leidand coillis, he yeid° *went*
To Paris the way.'

47

'Quhy hes thow not that husband° brocht, as I the bad? *rustic*
I dreid me,° sa he dantit the,° thow durst not with him deill!' *fear; he daunted you so*
'In faith,' said Schir Rolland, 'gif that he sa had
That war full hard to my hart,° and I ane man in heill.'° *heart (i.e. to bear); full health*
He saw the king was engrevit° and gat furth glaid° *annoyed; left gladly*

29. ll. 5–6: The general sense is: 'If you waive all the chivalric apparatus and accept combat as equals, I will make this promise'.

To se gif the coilyearis lawtie was leill.°	*given word was reliable*
'I suld have maid° him in stour° to be full hard stad°	*forced; combat; tested/pressed*
And° I had wittin° that the carll wald away steill,°	*If; known; slip away*
Bot I trowit not the day that he wald me beget.'°	*deceive*
As he went outwart bayne,°	*readily*
He met ane porter swayne°	*door-keeper fellow*
Cummand raith° him agayne°	*purposefully; towards*
Fast° fra the yet.°	*Directly; gate*

48

'Quhair gangis thow, gedling,° thir gaitis sa gane?'°	*fellow; hastily*
'Be God,' said the grome,° 'ane gift heir I geif!	*servant*
I devise at the yet thair is ane allane	
Bot he be lattin in belive, him lykis not to leif.[30]	
With ane capill and twa creillis cassin on the plane,°	*thrown on to the ground*
To cum to this palice he preissis to prief.'°	*persists in trying*
'Gif thow hes fundin° that freik,° in faith, I am fane.°	*found; fellow; glad*
Lat him in glaidly,° it may not engreif.°	*Welcome him in; harm (you)*
Bot askis he eirnestly efter ony man?'°	*any man in particular*
Than said that gedling on ground,°	*that man (formulaic)*
'Ye, forsuith, in this stound,°	*at this very moment*
Efter ane Wymond	
In all that he can.'	

49

'Pas° agane, porter, and lat him swyith° in,	*Go back; at once*
Amang the proudest in preis,° plesand in pane.°	*throng; dress (i.e. courtiers)*
Say thow art not worthy° to Wymond to win,°	*of fit rank; approach*
Bid him seik him his self° gif thair be sic ane.'	*seek him out on his own*
Agane gangis Schir Rolland quhair gle° suld begin,	*festivity*
And the yaip yeman° to the yet is gane,	*keen yeoman*
Enbraissit the bandis belive or that he wald blin,[31]	
Syne leit the wy at his will wend° in the wane.	*go freely*
'Gang seik him now thyself,' he said upon hicht.°	*loudly*
'My self hes na lasair°	*no leisure time*
Fra thir yettis to fair.'°	*move away*
'Be Christ,' said the coilyear,	
'I set that bot licht!'°	*That's little concern to me*

50

'Gif thow will not seik him, my awin self sall,	
For I have oft tymes swet° in service full fair.	*sweated*
Tak keip to° my capill that na man him call,	*Look after*
Quhill° I cum fra the court,' said the coilyear.	*Until*
'My laid° was I laith to lois,° I leif the° heir all.	*load; sorry to lose; with you*
Se that thow leis thame not, bot yeme° thame full yair!'°	*look after; very carefully*

30. 48. 2–4: Freely translated, these lines mean: 'God, you can have my problem as a gift,' said the fellow. 'There is an individual at the gate, let me tell you, for whom immediate entry is a matter of life or death.'
31. 'Quickly he undid the locks without pausing.'

In that hardy, in hy, he haikit to that hall[32]
For to wit gif° Wymondis wynning° was thair. To *find out whether; dwelling*
He arguit° with the ischar° ofter than anis— *argued; usher*
'Schir, can thow ocht say
Quhair is Wymond the day?° *to-day*
I pray the bring° him gif thow may *extricate*
Out of this wanis.'° *these halls*

51

That the wy° had wittin of Wymond he wend,°[33] *fellow; believed*
Bot to his raifand word° he gave na rewaird.° *raving speech; riposte*
Thair was na man thairin that his name kend;° *knew anyone of that name*
Thay countit not° the coilyear almaist at regaird.° *did not rate; just on sight*
He saw thair was na meiknes° nor mesure° micht mend;° *meekness; moderation; work*
He sped him in spedely and nane of thame he spaird.° *spared*
Thair was na fyve of thay freikis° that micht him furth fend,° *warriors; bar his way*
He socht in sa sadly,° quhill sum of thame he saird,° *intensely; injured*
He thristit in throw thame thraly° with threttis.° *fiercely; threats*
Quhen he come amang thame all,
Yit° was the king in the hall, *Still*
And mony gude man withall
Ungane to the meit.° *Not yet at the feast*

52

Thocht he had socht° sic ane sicht all this sevin yeir, *Had he searched for*
Sa solempnit ane semblie° had he not sene. *Such an august assembly*
The hall was properly apperrellit° and paintit but peir,° *fittingly decorated; peerlessly*
Dyamountis° full dantely° dentit betwene.° *Diamonds; daintily; inlaid*
It was semely set on ilk syde seir,° *different/not matching*
Gowlis° glitterand full gay, glemand in grene,° *Gules; on green (See 36: 2)*
Flowris with flourdelycis formest in feir
With mony flamand ferly ma than fyftyne;
The rufe, reulit about in rewall of reid.[34]
Rois° reulit ryally, *Rose*
Columbyn° and lely;° *Columbine; lily*
Thair was ane hailsum harbery° *generous hospitality*
Into riche steid.° *Within a rich setting*

53

With dosouris° to the duris dicht,° quha sa wald deme,° *hangings; arranged; judge*
With all divers danteis° dicht dantely,° *finery; daintily wrought*
Circulit° with silver, semely to sene;° *Encircled; behold*

32. 'Into that hall, that bold one hastily thrust his way.'
33. ED. Lekpreuik: 'He trowit that the wy...' The line has too many syllables. As 'He trowit' has the same force as 'he wend', this may be a case either of the compositor erroneously adding, or the author failing to delete, the first phrase.
34. ll. 7–9: 'Flowers, among which fleurs de lys were most prominent, with many more than fifteen, which were flaming in a wondrous (ferly) way; the ceiling was set in lines made up of small red circles.' 'Ferly' and 'selcouthly' (53.4) have at once the sense of wonderful (to behold) and strange (causing one to wonder).

Selcouthly, in seinye° was set suttelly	*Wonderfully as an emblem*
Blyth byrdis abufe and bestiall full bene,°	*beasts comfortably disposed*
Fyne foullis in fyrth° and fischis with fry.°	*woodland; (their) young*
The flure, carpit° and cled° and coverit full clene,	*carpeted; overlaid*
Cummand° fra the cornellis° closand quemely°	*Fanning out; corners; fitting tightly*
Bricht bancouris° about browdin° ovir all.	*bench-covers; embroidered*
Greit squechonis° on hicht,	*escutcheons/shields*
Anamalit°[35] and weill dicht,	*Enamelled*
Reulit° at all richt,	*Arranged*
Endlang° the hall.	*The length of*
54	
'Heir is ryaltie,' said Rauf, 'aneuch for the nanis,°	*enough for any occasion*
With all nobilnes anournit° and that is na nay!°	*adorned; undeniable*
Had I of° Wymond ane word, I wald of thir wanis,°	*about; leave these halls*
Fra thir wyis,° iwis, to went on my way;	*Away from these people*
Bot I mon yit° heir mair quhat worthis of° him anis,	*must still; pertains to*
And eirnestly efter him have myne e ay.'°	*keep a constant lookout for him*
He thristit in throw° threttie all atanis,°	*barged through; at one go*
Quhair mony douchtie° of deid° war joynit° that day.	*many a stalwart; deed; gathered*
For° he was unburely° on bak thay him hynt;°	*Because; rough; pushed*
As he gat ben throw°	*won his way through*
He gat mony greit schow,°	*heavy shove*
Bot he was stalwart, I trow,	
And laith° for to stynt.°	*unwilling; give up*
55	
He thristit in throw thame and thraly can thring,°	*obstinately pushed onwards*
Fast to the formest he foundit° in feir;	*He got almost to the very front*
Sone besyde him he gat ane sicht of the nobill king.	
'Yone is Wymond, I wait,° it worthis na weir.°	*know; there can be no doubt*
I ken him weill, thocht he be cled in uther clething,°	*different clothing*
In clais of clene gold kythand yone cleir,°	*showing that (his status) clearly*
* *[36]	
Quhen he harbreit° with me be half as he is heir.	*lodged*
In faith, he is of mair stait° than ever he me tald.	*higher rank*
Allace, that I was hydder wylit,°	*tricked*
I dreid me sair I be begylit.'°	*I greatly fear I've been beguiled*
The king previlie° smylit	*secretly*
Quhen he saw that bald.°	*bold fellow*
56	
Thair was servit in that saill° seigis semelie,°	*hall; handsome knights*
Mony senyeorabill syre° on ilk syde seir;	*Many a noble lord*
With ane cairfull° countenance the coilyear kest his e°	*anxious; eye*
To the cumly° quene, courtes and cleir.°	*lovely; fair*

35. Semi-transparent or opaque mixtures of coloured glass fused directly on to a metal surface.
36. Line missing in text. At this stage in the argument, Rauf is claiming to be able to recognize Charlemagne whatever he wears.

'Dame, of thy glitterand gyde° have I na gle,° — *glittering clothes; pleasure*
Be the gracious God that bocht us sa deir.° — *so dearly*
To ken° kingis courtasie,° the devill come° to me, — *teach; manners; came*
And sa I hope I may say or I chaip heir:° — *before I escape from here*
Might I chaip of this chance° that changes my cheir,° — *mischance; mood*
Thair suld na man be sa wyse
To gar me cum° to Parise — *get me to come (again)*
To luke quhair the king lyis
In faith, this sevin yeir!'

57

Quhen worthie° had weschin° and fra the buirdis° went — *the nobles; washed; tables*
Thay war for-wonderit,° iwis, of thair wyse lord. — *amazed*
The king fell in carping° and tauld his intent; — *began to converse*
To mony gracious grome° he maid his record,° — *attendant; recounted his tale*
How the busteous beirne° met him on the bent° — *rough fellow; moor*
And how the frostis war sa fell and sa strait° ford.° — *so severe; for it (pleonastic)*
Than the coilyear quoke° as he had bene schent,° — *quaked; put to shame*
Quhen he hard the suith say° how he the king schord.° — *truth spoken; threatened*
'Greit God, gif° I war now and thyself withall — *if only*
Upon the mure quhair we met
Baith all suddandly set,° — *suddenly set down (again)*
Or ony knicht that thow may get,
Sa gude in thy hall.'

58

Thir lordis leuch upon loft° and lystinit to the king — *laughed aloud*
How he was ludgeit and led° and set at° sa licht. — *i.e. ordered about; estimated*
Than the curagious knichtis bad have him to hing,° — *counselled that he be hung*
'For he hes servit° that,' thay said, 'be our sicht.'° — *deserved; in our opinion*
'God forbot,'[37] he said, 'my thank war sic thing° — *I should so give thanks*
To him that succourit° my lyfe in sa evill ane nicht. — *succoured (Biblical)*
Him semis ane stalwart man and stout in stryking;° — *giving blows*
That carll for his courtasie salbe maid knicht.° — *made a knight*
I hald the counsall full evill that Cristin man slais,° — *puts to death*
For I had myster° to have ma,° — *need; more*
And not to distroy tha° — *those*
That war worthie to ga
To fecht on° Goddis fais.'° — *against; enemies*

59

Befoir° mony worthie he dubbit° him knicht, — *In front of; dubbed*
Dukis and digne° lordis in that deir hall. — *worthy*
'Schir, se for thyself, thow semis to be wicht,° — *brave*
Tak keip° to this ordour, ane knicht I the call.° — *Pay heed to; pronounce thee*
To mak the manly man,° I mak the of micht;° — *(a) fighting man; powerful*

37. Some editors amend to 'Goddes' or 'Godis' but the genitive form is sometimes dropped, as here, in Northern English dialects.

Ilk yeir thre hundreth pund assigne the I sall,
And als° the nixt vacant,° be° ressonabill richt, *also; vacant office; according to*
That hapnis° in France, quhair sa ever it fall, *occurs*
Forfaitour or fre waird,° that first cummis to hand, *By forfeiture or free-ward*
    I gif the heir heritabilly°— *to you and your heirs*
    Sa° that I heir, quhen I have hy,° *On condition that; am pressed*
    That thow be fundin reddy,° *found ready*
        With birny° and brand.° *coat of mail; sword*

60

'It war my will worthy thy schone° that thow wan° *spurs; won*
And went with thir weryouris,° wythest° in weir;° *warriors; most valiant; war*
Heir ar curagious knichtis, suppois thay the nocht ken° *recognize*
For thy simpill degre° that thow art in heir. *lowly rank*
I beseik God of His grace to make the ane gude man,
And I sall gif the to begin glitterand geir.'° *glittering gear (armour)*
Ane chalmer with armour° the king gart° richt than *armour-room; caused to*
Be taucht° to ane squyar and maid him keipeir, *entrusted*
With clois° armouris of steill for that stout knicht. *tight-fitting*
    Sextie° squyaris of fee,° *Sixty; by feudal law*
    Of his retinew° to be: *retinue*
    That was ane fair cumpany° *company*
        Schir Rauf gat that nicht!

61

Upon the morne airly Schir Rauf wald not rest,
Bot in ryall array he reddyit him° to ryde. *got himself ready*
'For to hald° that I have hecht° I hope it be the best, *hold to; promised*
To yone busteous beirne° that boistit me to byde.° *warrior; detained me with threats*
Amang thir galyart gromis° I am bot ane gest;° *smart knights; outsider*
I will the ganandest gait° to that gay° glyde. *shortest way; fine fellow*
Sall never lord lauch on loft° quhill my lyfe may lest° *laugh aloud; lasts*
That I for liddernes° suld leif,° and levand besyde.° *cowardice; quit; carry on living*
It war ane graceles gude that I war cummin to,
    Gif that the king hard on hicht° *heard it told*
    That he had maid ane carll knicht,° *knight out of a churl*
    Amang thir weryouris wicht,° *those bold warriors*
        And docht nocht to do.° *(Who) did not dare to act*

62

Upon ane rude runsy° he ruschit out of toun, *rough packhorse*
In ane ryall array he rydis full richt,
Evin to the montane he maid him full boun,° *ready to go*
Quhair he had trystit° to meit Schir Rolland the knicht. *agreed*
Derfly° ovir dailis discoverand° the doun° *Stoutly; reconnoitring; hills*
Gif ony douchtie° that day for jornayis° was dicht.° *valiant man; combat(s); ready*
He band° his blonk° to ane busk° on the bent broun,° *tied; horse; bush; brown moor*
Syne baid° be the bair° way to hald that he had hecht, *waited; barren*
Quhill it was neir time of the day that he had thair bene.° *ought to have been there*
    He lukit ane lytill him fra;

He saw cummand in thra° *a violent manner*
The maist° man of all tha° *biggest; those*
That ever he had sene.

63

Ane knicht on ane cameill° come cantly° at hand, *camel; briskly*
With ane curagious countenance and cruell to se.° *look upon*
He semit baldly° to abyde with birny° and with brand,° *boldly; coat of mail; sword*
His blonk was unburely,° braid° and ovir hie.° *ill-proportioned; squat; too big*
Schir Rauf reddyit him sone and come rydand,
And in the rowme of ane renk° in fewtir kest he° *charging distance; he couched his lance*
He semit fer fellonar° than first quhen he° him fand°— *far fiercer; (Rauf); came across*
He foundis throw his forcenes° gif he micht him se.° *tries with all his might; make him out*
He straik the steid with the spurris, he sprent° on the bent!° *sprang forward; plain*
Sa hard ane cours° maid thay *charge*
That baith thair hors deid lay;° *lay dead*
Thair speiris in splenders° away *splinters*
Abufe thair heid sprent.° *flew*

64

Thus was thay for thair forcynes left on fute° baith; *i.e. without their horses*
Thay sture° hors at that straik strikin° deid lay than. *sturdy; struck*
Thir riche restles° renkis ruschit out full raith,° *eager; very angrily*
Cleikit out° twa swordis and togidder° ran, *Drew out; at each other*
Kest thame° with gude will to do uther skaith,° *Set themselves; harm*
Bair on thair basnetis thay beirnis or thay blan.[38]
Haistely hewit° thay togidder,° to leif° thay war laith, *hacked; at each other; leave off*
To tyne° the worschip of weir° that thay air° wan, *lose; battle honour; earlier*
Na° for dout° of vincussing° thay went nocht away. *Nor; fear; being vanquished*
Thus ather uther can assaill,° *each attacked the other*
With swordis of mettaill;
Thay maid ane lang battaill° *fought long*
Ane hour of the day.

65

Thay hard harnest° men thay hewit on in haist, *Those heavily armoured*
Thay worthit hevy with heid° and angerit withall, *heavy in spirit*
Quhill thay had maid thame sa mait° thay failye° almaist, *exhausted; gave way*
Sa laith thay war on ather part to lat thair price fall.° *honour down*
The riche restles men out of the renk° past, *field of battle*
Forwrocht° with thair wapnis and evill rent° withall; *Worn out; badly slashed*
Thair was na girth° on the ground quhill ane gaif the gaist,° *quarter; gave up the ghost*
'Yarne efter yeilding!'° on ilk syde thay call. *Admit you've had enough*
Schir Rauf caucht to cule him° and tak mair of the licht; *took the chance to cool off*
He kest up his veseir° *visor*

38. 'Those warriors bore (the strokes) on their helmets before they stopped (fighting).'

With ane chevalrous cheir,° *demeanour*
Sa saw he cummand full neir
Ane uther kene° knicht. *bold*

66

'Now, be the Rude,'° said Schir Rauf, 'I repreif the,° *holy cross; reproach you*
Thow hes brokin conditioun,° thow hes not done richt! *i.e. terms of agreement*
Thow hecht na bak° heir to bring bot anerly we;° *promised no support; only us*
Thairto I tuik thy hand, as thow was trew knicht.'
On loud° said the Sarazine,° 'I heir the now lie! *Aloud; Saracen*
Befoir the same day° I saw the never with sicht. *Until this very day*
Now sall thow think it richt sone° thow hes met with me, *soon enough*
Gif Mahoun° or Termagant° may mantene my micht.' *Mahomet; a heathen god*
Schir Rauf was blyth of that word and blenkit with his face:° *looked him in the eyes*
'Thow sayis thow art ane Sarazine?
Now thankit be Drichtine,° *God/our Lord*
That ane of us sall never hine° *(go) hence*
Undeid° in this place!' *Alive*

67

Than said the Sarazine to Schir Rauf succudrously,° *arrogantly*
'I have na lyking to lyfe° to lat the with lufe.'° *positive wish; spare you out of love*
He gave ane braid° with his brand° to the beirne by, *blow; sword*
Till the blude of his browis brest out abufe.° *burst out above his brows*
The kene knicht in that steid° stakkerit sturely,° *place; staggered violently*
The lenth of ane rude braid he gart him remufe.[39]
Schir Rauf ruschit up agane, and hit him in hy;
Thay preis furth° properly, thair pithis to prufe.° *press forward; prove their valour*
Ilk ane a schort knyfe braidit° out sone; *pulled*
In stour° stifly° thay stand *combat; stoutly*
With twa knyfis in hand,
With that come Schir Rolland,
As thay had neir done.° *nearly finished*

68

The gentill knicht, Schir Rolland, come rydand ful richt,
And ruschit fra his runsy° and ran thame betwene. *quickly dismounted*
He sayis, 'Thow art ane Sarazine, I se be my sicht,
For to confound° our Cristin men that counteris° sa kene. *destroy; who retaliate*
Tell me thy name tyte,° thow travelland knicht.° *directly; knight errant*
Fy on thy fechting, fell° hes thow bene! *cruel*
Thow art° stout and strang and stalwart in fecht, *(Just as) you are*
Sa is thy fallow,° in faith,° and that is weill sene; *opponent; truly*
In Christ and thow will trow, thow takis nane outray.'° *will be spared any outrage*
'Forsuith,' the Sarazine said,
'Thyself maid me never sa affraid
That I for soverance° wald have praid,° *truce; begged*
Na not sall today.

39. 'He made him back off by roughly a rood's length.' A rood or rod was an ancient measure of length.

69

'Breif° me not with your boist,° bot mak yow baith boun;°	*Address; boastful speech; ready*
Batteris on baldly,° the best, I yow pray.'	*Set to boldly*
'Na,' said Schir Rolland, 'that war na resoun.°	*would not be right*
I trow° in the mekle God, that maist of michtis° may.	*believe; mightiest of deeds*
The tane° is in power to mak the presoun;°	*That one (God); you prisoner*
For that war na vassalage, sum men wald say,[40]	
I rid° that thow hartfully° forsaik thy Mahoun.	*counsel; heartily*
Fy on that foull feind, for fals is thy fay;°	*faith*
Becum Cristin,° schir knicht, and on Christ call!	*Become Christian*
It is my will thow convert	
—This wickit warld is bot ane start°—	*only a beginning*
And have° Him halely° in hart	*receive; wholly*
That Maker is° of all.'	*Who is Creator*

70

'Schir Rolland, I rek nocht of° thy ravingis.	*Take no heed of*
Thow dois bot reverence to° thame that rekkis it nocht.	*ask reverence from*
Thow slane hes oft thyself of my counsingis,°	*cousins (in religion)*
Soudanis° and sib men° that the with schame socht.[41]	*Sultans; kinsmen*
Now thow faindis° to have favour with thy fleichingis,°	*attempt; flattering words*
Now have I ferlie° gif I favour the ocht!	*marvel*
We sall spuilye° yow dispittously° at the nixt springis,	*destroy; mercilessly*
Mak yowr biggingis° full bair°—bodword° have I brocht—	*buildings; (lay) waste; tidings*
Chace Charlis° your king fer out of France.	*Chase Charlemagne*
Fra the Chane° of Tartarie	*Khan*
At° him this message° wald I be,	*To; envoy*
To tell him as I have tauld the,	
Withoutin plesance.'°	*civility*

71

'Tyte° tell my thy name, it servis of nocht,	*At once*
Ye Sarazeins ar succuderus° and self-willit ay.	*arrogant*
Sall never of sa sour° ane brand° ane bricht fyre be brocht!	*green; twig*
The feynd is sa felloun als fer as he may.'°	*cruel to the highest degree*
'Sa thrive I,' said the Sarazine, 'to threip° is my thocht.°	*fight; intention*
Quha waitis° the Cristin with cair, my cusingis° ar thay.	*lies in wait for; cousins*
My name is Magog, in will and I mocht°	*if I could*
To ding° thame doun dourly° that ever war in my way;	*strike; harshly*
For-thy° my warysoun° is full gude at hame quhair I dwel.'	*To that end; wealth*
'In faith,' said Schir Rolland,	
'That is full evill wyn° land,	*evilly won*
To have quhill thow ar levand,	
Sine, at thine end,° hell.'	*at your ending/death*

40. 'As, in the opinion of some, that would be no servitude...'—obedience to the true God, constituting a higher spiritual freedom.
41. 'who sought to put you to shame.'

72

'Wald thow convert the in hy, and cover the of° sin, *save yourself from*
Thow suld have mair profite and mekle pardoun;
Riche douchereis seir° to be sesit in,° *Several rich dukedoms; invested with*
During quhill day dawis that never will gang doun;° *i.e. for ever and a day*
Wed ane worthie to wyfe and weild° hir with win,° *govern; joy*
Ane of the riche° of our realme be that ressoun:° *rich ones; by that right*
The gentill duches,° Dame Jane, that clamis be hir kin° *noble duchess; family*
Angeos° and uther landis, with mony riche toun; *Anjou*
Thus may thow, and thow will wirk the best wise.
    I do the out of dispair;° *free you from despair*
    In all France is nane sa fair
    Als scho is, appeirand air° *heir apparent*
        To twa douchereis.'° *dukedoms*

73

'I rek nocht of° thy riches, Schir Rolland the knicht,' *care nothing for*
Said the rude° Sarazine in ryall array, *bold*
'Thy gold nor thy grassum° set I bot licht. *compensation/bribe*
Bot gif thy God be sa gude, as I heir the say,
I will forsaik Mahoun and tak me to His micht,
Evermair perpetuallie, as He that mair may.° *can do greater things*
Heir, with hart and gude will, my treuth° I the plicht,° *troth; plight*
That I sall lelely leif on° thy Lord ay. *faithfully believe in*
And I beseik Him of grace and askis Him mercy,
    And Christ His sone full schene,
    For I have Cristin men sene
    That in mony angeris° hes bene, *crises*
        Full oft on Him cry.'

74

'I thank God,' said Rolland, 'that word lykis° me, *pleases*
And Christ His sweit sone, That the that grace send.'° *Who sent to you that grace*
Thay swoir on thair swordis swyftlie all thre
And conservit thame° freindis to thair lyfis end, *promised to remain*
Ever in all travell,° to leif and to die. *travail*
Thay knichtis caryit to° the court, as Christ had thame kend.° *proceeded; destined*
The king for thair cumming maid game and gle,° *made merry*
With mony mirthfull man thair mirthis to mend;° *make them happier*
Digne bischoppis that day that douchtie gart bring[42]
    And gave him sacramentis seir,° *various sacraments*
    And callit him Schir Gawteir;
    And sine the duches cleir
        He weddit with ane ring.

75

Than Schir Rauf gat rewaird to keip° his knichtheid; *maintain*
Sic tythingis° come to the king within thay nyne nicht,° *tidings; those nine nights*

42. 'That very day, noble bishops had that valiant man [the Saracen] brought (before them).'

That the Marschell of France was newlingis° deid. *recently*
Richt thair, with the counsall of mony kene knicht,
He thocht him° richt worthie to byde in his steid,° *(Rauf); replace him*
For to weild° that worschip° worthie and wicht. *hold; position of honour*
His wyfe wald he nocht forget, for dout° of Goddis feid;° *fear; wrath*
He send efter that hende° to leif thane° in richt. *gracious lady; from then on*
Syne foundit ane fair place quhair he met the king,
  Ever mair perpetually,
  In the name of Sanct July,° *St Julian*
  That all that wantis harbery° *want/need shelter*
    Suld have gestning.° *hospitality*

SECTION B: MIDDLE SCOTS

§ 4 Robert Henryson (c.1450–c.1505): *Morall Fabillis*

[See also Introductions to § 5 and § 14]

The age in which the first of the great Middle Scots makars lived and wrote was both a time of barbarism and of humanist learning. Henryson was born in the reign of James III, who succeeded to the throne at the age of nine on the violent death of his father, killed by one of his own cannons. Having conspiciously failed to gain control over his nobles, James III was murdered in 1488, after defeat by a group of rebels, who counted his son as one of their number. Yet his reign, and the early years of James IV's regime, were also marked by the reconstruction of churches and by a notable development of the education system through the foundation of grammar schools and universities.

Records suggest much, but confirm little, with regard to the poet himself. He was a schoolmaster (probably headmaster), of the important abbey school in Dunfermline for a period during 1470, when he also held the post of notary public. If he can be identified with the Robert Henryson who gained membership of Glasgow University in 1462, then he held the degrees of Master of Arts and Bachelor of Canon Law—probably from a European university. Certainly, the legal knowledge revealed in his verse is consistent with his holding the latter qualification, while Dunbar would not have called him 'Maister' Robert Henrisoun in **'Timor Mortis Conturbat Me'** *(§ 10. vii—also known as* **'The Lament for the Makaris'**) *had he not believed him to hold a 'Master's' degree. Dunbar's poetic lament confirms that he must have died in or before 1505.*

The Morall Fabillis of Esope the Phrygian *are the collection of poems for which Henryson is most usually remembered. Despite the title, they originate from a variety of sources—some from the Aesopic tradition and Gualterus Anglicus; others from the 'beast epic' popularised in the* **Roman de Renart**. *From the fourteen tales, which, along with the* **'Prologue'**, *constitute the entirety of the collection, we have chosen the first* (**'The Cock and the Jasp'**) *and the last* (**'The Paddock and the Mouse'**) *not only because they are, in this sense, frame tales but because their moralising methods stand in marked contrast. The moralised jasp is given a single significance out of the many possible. It represents knowledge—and, specifically, the duty of academics to bring their knowledge back into the real world. As Henryson is doing just this, it anticipates the broad pedagogic and political function of the entire collection. The fable of 'Paddock and Mouse', on the other hand, is re-translated in a variety of possible allegorical contexts.*

Of the other two tales chosen, **'The Cock and the Fox'** *offers an opportunity of comparing Henryson's version of a fable with that of Chaucer (in the* **'The Nun's Priest's Tale'**). **'The Preaching of the Swallow'** *provides a dramatic image of the chain of signs—words/man/nature—which guide medieval man in his blindness towards an understanding of the mysteriously benevolent plan contained in the Word who is God—'For God is in His power infinite, And mannis saull is febill...Yit nevertheles we may haif knawlegeing Off God almychtie be His creatouris' (sts. 4, 5).*

The Morall Fabillis of Esope the Phrygian[1]

['The Prologue', which immediately precedes 'The Cock and the Jasp', appears as § 14 in the Literary Theory section.]

1. ED. Copy Text for all of the *Morall Fabillis*: Bassandyne.

The Cock and the Jasp° *gemstone/jewel*

1

Ane cok sum° tyme with feddram° fresch and gay, *once (upon a); plumage*
Richt cant° and crous,° albeit he was bot pure,° *bold; jaunty; poor*
Flew furth upon ane dunghill sone be day;° *in early morning*
To get his dennar, set° was al his cure.° *focussed; concern*
Scraipand amang the as° be aventure,° *dust; by chance*
He fand ane jolie jasp° richt precious, *pretty jewel*
Wes castin furth° in sweping of the hous. *thrown out*

2

As damisellis wantoun° and insolent *lax/high-spirited*
That fane wald play and on the streit be sene,
To swoping° of the hous thay tak na tent° *sweeping; care*
Quhat be thairin, swa that° the flure° be clene; *so long as; surface*
Jowellis° ar tint,° as oftymis hes bene sene, *Jewels; lost*
Upon the flure and swopit furth anone;
Peradventure, sa wes the samin° stone. *same/particular*

3

Sa, mervelland upon° the stane, quod he, *wondering at*
'O gentill° Jasp! O riche and nobill thing! *genteel*
Thocht° I the° find, thow ganis not° for me; *Although; you; are not useful*
Thow art ane jowell for ane lord or king.
It wer pietie° thow suld in this mydding° *pity; rubbish heap*
Be buryit thus amang this muke° and mold,° *dirt; soil*
And thow so fair and worth sa mekill° gold. *much*

4

'It is pietie I suld the find, for quhy° *because*
Thy grit vertew° nor yit thy cullour cleir,° *great worth; translucent*
I may nouther° extoll nor magnify; *neither*
And thow to me may mak° bot lytill cheir,° *bring; happiness*
To grit lordis thocht thow be leif° and deir, *precious*
I lufe fer° better thing of les availl,° *far; value*
As draf° or corne to fill my tume intraill.° *husks; empty gut*

5

'I had lever° go skraip° heir with my naillis *rather; scrape*
Amangis this mow° and luke° my lifys fude°— *dust; seek out; food to sustain me*
As draf or corne, small wormis, or snaillis,
Or ony meit wald do my stomok gude—
Than of jaspis ane mekill multitude;
And thow agane,° upon the samin wyis,° *also; in the same way*
May me, as now, for thyne availl° dispyis.° *your purpose; despise*

6

'Thow hes na corne and thairof I had neid;
Thy cullour dois bot° confort to the sicht, *only*

And that is not aneuch° my wame° to feid, *enough; stomach*
For wyfis sayis that lukand werk is licht.[2]
I wald sum meit° have, get it geve I micht,° *food; if I could get hold of it*
For houngrie men may not weill leve on lukis:° *live on appearances*
Had I dry breid, I compt not for na cukis.° *I (would) not count on cakes*

7

'Quhar suld thow mak thy habitatioun?[3]
Quhar suld thow dwell, bot in ane royall tour?° *tower*
Quhar suld thow sit, bot on ane kingis croun
Exalt° in worschip and in grit honour? *Exalted*
Rise, gentill Jasp, of all stanis° the flour,° *gems; flower (i.e. the best)*
Out of this fen,° and pas° quhar thow suld be; *dirt; move on to*
Thow ganis not° for me, nor I for the.' *are not fitting*

8

Levand this jowell law° upon the ground,° *low; ground/foundation of text*
To seik his meit° this cok his wayis went. *food*
Bot quhen or how or quhome be it° wes found, *by whom it (jewel)*
As now I set to hald na argument.[4]
Bot of the inward sentence° and intent° *inner meaning; intention*
Of this fabill, as myne author dois write,
I sall reheirs° in rude and hamelie dite.° *retrace; homely language*

Moralitas° *Moral*

9

This jolie° jasp hes properteis° sevin: *pretty; attributes*
The first, of cullour it is mervelous,° *wondrous*
Part lyke the fyre and part lyke to the hevin;
It makis ane man stark° and victorious; *brave*
Preservis als° fra cacis perrillous;° *also; dangerous situations*
Quha hes° this stane sall have gude hap to speid,° *Whoever possesses; good fortune*
Of fyre nor fallis° him neidis not to dreid.° *accidents; fear*

10

This gentill jasp, richt different of hew,° *colour*
Betakinnis° perfite° prudence and cunning,° *Signifies; perfect; knowledge*
Ornate° with mony deidis of vertew, *Adorned*
Mair excellent than ony eirthly thing,
Quhilk makis men in honour ay° to ring,° *always; reign*
Happie and stark° to haif the victorie *strong*
Of all vicis° and spirituall enemie.° *Over all vices; spiritual foes*

2. Looking on is easy. The phrase, 'lukand werk is licht', was proverbial.
3. Although the cock rejects the jewel, the parallel syntax and high style he uses to address it anticipate its value in another 'setting'. The Moralitas enacts this.
4. 'For the present I do not intend to continue the discussion.' That is— he is leaving the literal level and moving to a moral interpretation.

11

Quha may be hardie, riche and gratious?
Quha can eschew perrell° and aventure?° — *avoid danger;*[5] *risk*
Quha can governe ane realme, cietie or hous[6]
Without science? No man,° I yow assure. — *Nobody*
It is riches° that ever sall indure, — *(spiritual) wealth*
Quhilk maith° nor moist° nor uther rust can freit:° — *maggot; damp; destroy*[7]
To mannis saull, it is eternall meit.

12

This cok, desyrand mair° the sempill corne — *desiring more*
Than ony jasp, may till ane fule be peir,° — *likened*
Quhilk at science° makis bot ane moik° and scorne — *knowledge; mockery*
And na gude can°— als lytill will he leir;° — *knows nothing about good; learn*
His hart wammillis° wyse argumentis to heir, — *spirit is sick/gorge rises*
As dois ane sow to quhome men, for the nanis,° — *indeed*
In hir draf troich° wald saw° the precious stanis.[8] — *feeding trough; set down*

13

Quha is enemie to science and cunning° — *learning and natural wit*
Bot ignorants, that° understandis nocht? — *Except ignorant people who*
Quhilk° is sa nobill, sa precious and sa ding,° — *What; worthy*
That it may with na eirdlie° thing be bocht?° — *temporal; bought*
Weill wer that man, ouer all uther,° that mocht — *above all others*
All his lyfe-dayis in perfite[9] studie wair° — *spend*
To get science, for him neidit na mair.° — *because he required no more*

14

Bot now, allace, this jasp° is tynt and hid; — *(= knowledge as defined)*
We seik it nocht nor preis° it for to find — *strive*
Haif we richis, na better lyfe we bid,° — *ask for*
Of science thocht° the saull be bair and blind. — *although/even if*
Of this mater° to speik I wair bot wind.° — *subject; I only waste my breath*
Thairfore, I ceis and will na forther say.° — *speak no more*
Ga seik the jasp quha° will—for thair it lay.[10] — *whoever*

5. 'Eschew' normally means avoid. Most editors, unusually, translate 'conquer'. But both sides of the question— cowardice as well as bravery— are being contemplated.
6. This division echoes Aristotle's *Politics*.
7. Cf. Matthew 6. 19–20; Luke 12. 33
8. Cf. Matthew 7. 6. 'Neither cast ye your pearls before swine.'
9. 'Perfect', here, has two senses—'only' and 'highest'. The first anticipates the argument of st. 14. The second looks back to st. 12. The highest discipline was Theology and the 'pearl' in Matthew (n. 8) signifies salvation.
10. The last three lines are stylistically simple. They draw in the audience and cross the fact/fiction divide by challenging them with the fictive 'jewel'. Scholars, especially in these materialist days, must leave their ivory tower and become involved in government.

The Cock and the Fox[11]

1

Thocht brutall° beistis be irrationall *(= lacking a rational soul)*
(That is to say, wantand discretioun)° *discrimination*
Yyt ilk ane° in thair kyndis naturall° *each one; species*
Hes mony divers inclinatioun:
The bair busteous,° the wolff, the wylde lyoun, *violent*
The fox fenyeit,° craftie and cawtelows,° *deceitful; tricky*
The dog to bark on nicht and keip° the hows. *guard*

2

Sa different thay ar in properteis,° *characteristics*
Unknawin unto man and infinite
In kynd, havand sa fell° diversiteis, *many*
My cunning° it excedis for to dyte.° *ability; set down*
For thy,° as now I purpose for° to wryte, *Therefore; intend*
Ane cais° I fand, quhilk fell this ather yeir° *example; about a year ago*
Betwix ane foxe and gentill Chantecleir.

3

Ane wedow dwelt in till ane drop° thay° dayis, *village; (in) those*
Quhilk wan hir fude off° spinning on hir rok,° *made her living from; distaff*
And na mair° had, forsuth, as the fabill sayis, *no other (resources)*
Except off hennis scho had ane lytill flok,
And thame to keip° scho had ane jolie cok, *guard/control*
Richt curageous,° that to this wedow ay *bold/lustful*
Devydit[12] nicht and crew befoir the day.

4

Ane lytill° fra this foirsaid wedowis hows, *short distance*
Ane thornie schaw° thair wes off grit defence,° *thicket; protection*
Quhairin ane foxe, craftie and cautelous,° *tricky*
Maid his repair° and daylie residence, *haunt*
Quhilk to this wedow did grit violence
In pyking off pultrie° baith day and nicht, *picking off (her) poultry*
And, na way, be revengit on him scho micht.° *could (be revenged)*

5

This wylie tod,° quhen that the lark couth sing,° *fox; had sung*
Full sair hungrie unto the toun°[13] him drest,° *enclosed yard; directed himself*
Quhair Chantecleir, in to the gray dawing,° *dawn*
Werie for nicht,° wes flowen fra his nest. *(Being awake all) night*
Lowrence° this saw and in his mynd he kest° *i.e. fox; pondered*

11. Compare Chaucer's earlier treatment of this fable in *The Canterbury Tales* ('Nun's Priest's Tale').
12. Refers to Roman guards sounding the trumpet when one watch gave way to another. The general sense of the line is 'His crowing marked off the watches of the night until dawn.'
13. The feudal village stood at the centre of the fields. The yard and thicket become a town in miniature.

The jeperdies,° the wayis° and the wyle, *strategies; devices*
Be quhat menis° he micht this cok begyle. *means*

6

Dissimuland° in to countenance° and cheir,° *Feigning; demeanour; attitude*
On kneis fell and, simuland,° thus he said, *playing a (false) role*
'Gude morne, my maister, gentill Chantecleir!'
With that, the cok start bakwart in ane braid.° *with one leap*
'Schir, be my saull, ye neid not be effraid° *afraid*
Nor yit, for me, to start nor fle abak!° *fly off*
I come bot heir, service to yow to mak.[14]

7

'Wald I not serve to yow,° it wer bot blame°— *serve you/(up); reproof*
As I have done to yowr progenitouris.° *predecessors*
Your father oft fulfillit° hes my wame°[15] *filled full; stomach*
And send me meit fra midding° to the muris:° *midden; moors*
And at his end° I did my besie curis° *death/rear; cures/chores*
To hald his heid and gif him drinkis warme;° *(i.e. boiled him)*
Syne at the last, the sweit swelt° in my arme.' *dear one passed away*

8

'Knew ye my father?' quod the cok and leuch.° *laughed*
'Yea, my fair sone; forsuth,° I held his heid *truly/indeed*
Quhen that he deit° under ane birkin beuch;° *died; birch bough*
Syne, said the Dirigie° quhen that he wes deid. *Office for the Dead*
Betwix us twa how suld thair be ane feid?° *feud*
Quhame suld ye traist bot me, your servitour,° *servant (priest/cook)*
That to your father did sa grit honour?

9

'Quhen I behald your fedderis° fair and gent,° *plumage; becoming*
Your beik,° your breist, your hekill° and your kame°— *beak; hackle; comb*
Schir, be my saull and the blissit sacrament,° *blessed sacrament/Eucharist*
My hart warmys; me think I am at hame.
Yow for to serve, I wald creip° on my wame *creep (humbly/furtively)*
In froist and snaw, in wedder wan° and weit, *gloomy*
And lay my lyart loikkis° under your feit.' *grey locks*

10

This fenyeit foxe, fals and dissimulate,° *dissembling*
Maid to this cok ane cavillatioun:° *sophisticated argument*
'Ye ar, me think, changit° and degenerate° *altered; deteriorated*
Fra your father and his conditioun.° *nature/character*
Off craftie crawing he micht beir the croun,° *bear away the (laurel) crown*

14. Lawrence's speech abounds in double meanings, covering priestly care and cooking. Here, Chauntecleir understands 'to do you service'; the fox means 'serve you up as my meal'.
15. Your father 'provided me with'/'was himself' that meal.

For he wald on his tais stand and craw.
This is na le;° I stude beside and saw.' *lie*

11
With that, the cok, upon his tais hie,° *on tiptoes*
Kest up° his beik° and sang with all his micht.° *Thrust; beak; might*
Quod Schir Lowrence, 'Weill said, sa mot I the!° *so may I thrive*
Ye ar your fatheris sone and air° upricht° *heir; upstanding (pun)*
Bot off his cunning,° yit ye want ane slicht.'° *cleverness; lack one trick*
'Quhat?' quod the cok. 'He wald, and haif na dout,° *be in no doubt*
Baith wink and craw and turne him thryis about.'° *turn around three times*

12
The cok, inflate° with wind and fals vane gloir,° *puffed up; ill-based pride*
That mony puttis unto confusioun,° *ruin*
Traisting to° win ane grit worschip thairfoir, *trusting to/banking on*
Unwarlie° winkand, walkit up and doun *Incautiously/Recklessly*
And syne to chant and craw he maid him boun°— *prepared himself*
And suddandlie, be° he had crawin ane note,° *by the time; one note*
The foxe wes war,° and hint° him be the throte. *alert; seized*

13
Syne to the woid° but tarie° with him hyit,° *woods; without delay; hurried*
Off countermaund° haifand bot lytill dout.° *intervention; fear*
With that, Pertok, Sprutok and Coppok[16] cryit;
The wedow hard° and with ane cry come out. *heard*
Seand the cace,° scho sichit° and gaif ane schout, *situation; sighed*
'How, murther,° reylok!'° with ane hiddeous beir.° *murder; robbery; shout*
'Allace, now lost is gentill° Chantecleir!' *noble*

14
As scho wer woid,° with mony yell and cry, *mad*
Ryvand° hir hair, upon hir breist can beit;° *Tearing; smote (herself)*
Syne, paill off hew,° half in ane extasy,° *colour; delirium*
Fell doun for cair in swoning and in sweit.° *(a fit of) fainting and sweating*
With that, the selie° hennis left thair meit *silly/vulnerable*
And, quhill this wyfe wes lyand thus in swoun,
Fell of° that cace in disputatioun.° *concerning; into debate*

15
'Allace', quod Pertok, makand sair murning,° *mourning grievously*
With° teiris grit° attour° hir cheikis fell.°[17] *As; large; among; coursed*
'Yone wes our drowrie° and our dayis darling,° *beloved; our life's darling*
Our nichtingall and als our orlege bell,° *our alarm clock as well (bathos)*
Our walkryfe watche° us for to warne and tell *vigilant guard*

16. Chaucer does not have this formal debate nor name any of Chauntecleir's paramours. The '-ok' form has diminutive force in Middle Scots.
17. Chaucer and Henryson both use accurate descriptions of the hens for mock heroic effect. Wrinkled skin gives the impression of many cheeks, 'among' which the tears course. Cf. 26.6.

Quhen that Aurora° with hir curcheis° gray — *goddess of dawn; kerchiefs*
Put up° hir heid betwix the nicht and day. — *Raised*

16
'Quha sall our lemman° be? Quha sall us leid? — *lover*
Quhen we ar sad, quha sall unto us sing?
With his sweit bill, he wald brek us° the breid; — *break for us*
In all this warld wes thair ane kynder thing?
In paramouris,° he wald do us plesing,° — *Sexually; give us pleasure*
At his power, as nature list him geif.[18]
Now, efter him° allace, how sall we leif?' — *i.e. after his death*

17
Quod Sprutok than, 'Ceis,° sister, off your sorrow. — *Cease*
Ye be to mad;° for him sic° murning mais.° — *too silly; such; you make*
We sall fair weill, I find° Sanct Johne to borrow;° — *appeal to; as security*
The proverb sayis, "Als gude lufe cummis as gais."° — *arrives as departs*
I will put on my haly-dayis clais° — *festive clothes*
And mak me fresch agane° this jolie May, — *make me alluring for*
Syne° chant this sang, "Wes never wedow sa gay!" — *Then*

18
'He wes angry and held us ay in aw,° — *kept us ever in awe of him*
And woundit with the speir° off jelowsy. — *by the spear*
Off chalmerglew,° Pertok, full weill ye knaw — *bedroom sport*
Waistit° he wes, off nature cauld and dry.[19] — *Enfeebled/Impotent*
Sen he is gone, thairfoir, sister, say I,
Be blyith in baill,° for that is best remeid.° — *cheerful in misery; remedy*
Let quik to quik° and deid ga to the deid.' — *Leave living to the lively*

19
Than Pertok spak, that feinyeit faith befoir,° — *who feigned fidelity earlier*
In lust but lufe,° that set all hir delyte,° — *without (selfless) love; pleasure*
'Sister, ye wait,° off sic° as him ane scoir° — *know; such; a score*
Wald not suffice to slaik° our appetyte! — *slake*
I hecht° yow be my hand,° sen we[20] ar quyte,° — *promise; by my hand; liberated*
Within ane oulk°—for schame and I durst speik°— — *week; if I dare speak shamelessly*
To get ane berne° suld better claw oure breik!'° — *sturdy fellow; caress our rump*

20
Than Coppok, lyke ane curate, spak full crous:° — *smugly*
'Yone wes ane verray° vengeance from the hevin. — *veritable*
He was sa lous° and sa lecherous, — *loose (morally)*
He had,' quod scho, 'kittokis° ma° than sevin! — *wenches; more*
Bot rychteous God, haldand the balandis evin,° — *scales (of justice) level*

18. 'As far as it pleased nature to give him the strength.' See st. 18.
19. Of the four bodily 'humours', the cold and the dry were associated with impotence.
20. ED. Bassandyne reads 'ye'.

Smytis rycht sair,° thocht° He be patient, *painfully; although*
Adulteraris that list° thame not repent. *wish*

21

'Prydefull he wes and joyit off° his sin *revelled in*
And comptit° not for Goddis favour nor feid,° *relied; enmity*
Bot traistit ay to rax° and sa to rin,° *wield power; rule*
Quhill° at the last his sinnis can him leid° *Until; led him*
To schamefull end and to yone suddand deid.° *that sudden death*
Thairfoir, it is the verray hand° off God, *truly the hand*
That causit him be werryit with° the tod!'° *worried by (i.e. grabbed); fox*

22

Quhen this wes said, this wedow fra hir swoun
Start up on fute and on hir kennettis cryde.° *summoned her hunting dogs*
'How, Birkye, Berrie, Bell, Bawsie, Broun,
Rype Schaw, Rin Weil, Curtes, Nuttieclyde!
Togidder all, but grunching,° furth ye glyde!° *grumping; stream forth*
Reskew my nobill cok or° he be slane; *before*
Or ellis, to me, se ye cum never agane!'

23

With that, but baid,° thay braidet° ouer the bent;° *delay; fanned out; open ground*
As fyre off° flint thay ouer the feildis flaw;° *from; flew*
Full wichtlie° thay throw wood and wateris went, *vigorously*
And ceissit not, Schir Lourence quhill thay saw.° *until they caught sight of*
Bot quhen he° saw the raches° cum on raw,° *he (fox); sniffer dogs; in a line*
Unto the cok in mynd°[21] he said, 'God sen° *inwardly; grant*
That I and thow wer fairlie° in my den.' *safely*

24

Than spak the cok, with sum gude spirit inspyrit,° *inspired by some good spirit*
'Do my counsall and I sall warrand the.° *protect you*
Hungrie thow art, and for grit travell° tyrit, *toil*
Richt faint off force° and may not ferther fle:° *strength; flee farther*
Swyith° turne agane° and say that I and ye *Quickly; back*
Freindis ar maid and fellowis for ane yeir.
Than will thay stint°—I stand for° it—and not steir.'° *stop; vouchsafe; stir (further)*

25

This tod, thocht he wes fals and frivolus
And had frawdis,° his querrell° to defend, *guileful stratagems; cause*
Desavit° wes be menis° richt mervelous,° *Deceived; means; wondrous*
For falset failyeis ay° at the latter end. *falsehood always fails*
He start about° and cryit as he wes kend°— *swung round; directed*
With that, the cok, he braid unto a bewch.° *flew off on to a bough*
Now, juge ye all, quhairat Schir Lowrence lewch!° *what Sir Lawrence had to laugh at*

21. He cannot speak aloud without dropping Chauntecleir.

26	
Begylit thus, the tod under the tre	
On kneis fell, and said, 'Gude Chantecleir,	
Cum doun agane and I, but meit or fe,°	*without food or fee*
Salbe your man and servand for ane yeir.'	
'Na, murther,° theif, and revar,° stand on reir!°	*murderer; robber; stand back*
My bludy hekill° and my nek sa bla°	*hackle; blue*
Hes partit° freindschip for ever betwene us twa.	*ended*
27	
'I wes unwyse,° that winkit at thy will,°	*foolish; at your inclination*
Quhairthrow almaist I loissit had my heid.'	
'I wes mair fule,' quod he,° 'coud nocht be still,	*(i.e. fox)*
Bot spake° to put my pray° in to pleid.'°	*spoke aloud; prey; dispute*
'Fair on,° fals theif, God keip me fra thy feid.'°	*Off you go; feuding*
With that the cok ouer the feildis tuke his flicht;	
And in at the wedowis lever°[22] couth he licht.°	*widow's louver; he alighted*

Moralitas

28[23]	
Now worthie folk, suppose° this be ane fabill,°	*given that; fictional tale*
And ouerheillit° with typis figurall,°	*covered over/adorned; symbols*
Yit may ye find ane sentence richt agreabill°	*very advantageous meaning*
Under thir fenyeit° termis textuall.°	*imagined; (of the) literal story*
To our purpose,° this cok weill may we call	*For our purpose(s)*
Nyse,° proud men—woid° and vaneglorious	*Haughty; mad*
Of kin and blude°—quhilk is presumpteous.°	*By family and blood; arrogant*
29	
Fy, puft up pryde, thow is full poysonabill!°	*poisonous*
Quha favoris the, on force, man° haif ane fall!	*necessarily must*
Thy strenth is nocht; thy stule° standis unstabill.	*stool*
Tak witnes of° the feyndis infernall,°	*precedent from; fallen angels*
Quhilk houndit doun wes fra that hevinlie hall°	*dwelling place*
To hellis hole and to that hiddeous hous,	
Because, in pryde, thay wer presumpteous.	
30	
This fenyeit° foxe may weill be figurate°	*imagined; made representative...*
To° flatteraris with plesand wordis quhyte;°	*...Of; white/fair-seeming*
With fals mening and mynd maist toxicate°	*poisonous*
To loif and le,° that settis thair haill delyte.	*praise and lie*
All worthie folk at sic° suld haif despyte,°	*such (people); despise*

22. An early chimney. Turret-like, it stood over the hole in the roof, controlling light and smoke.
23. This stanza neatly sums up the critical methodology of the Prologue. As all benevolently intended writing stemmed from God for man's benefit, many different moral messages might be drawn from the same fiction.

For quhair is thair mair perrellous pestilence°	*subtly dangerous disease*
Nor gif° to learis° haistelie° credence?	*If not to give; liars; hastily*

31

The wickit mynd and° adullatioun,[24]	*combined with*
Of sucker° sweit haifand similitude,°	*sugar; having the semblance of*
Bitter as gall and full of fell° poysoun	*cruel*
To taist it is, quha cleirlie understude.[25]	
For thy,° as now schortlie° to conclude:	*Therefore; briefly*
Thir° twa sinnis, flatterie and vaneglore,	*These*
Ar vennomous: gude folk, fle° thame thairfoir!	*flee from*

The Preaching of the Swallow

1

The hie prudence[26] and wirking mervelous,°	*wondrous working/creation*
The profound wit° off God omnipotent	*knowledge*
Is sa perfyte° and sa ingenious,°	*perfect; subtle*
Excelland far° all mannis jugement;	*By far excelling*
For quhy,° to him all thing is ay present,°[27]	*Because; ever present*
Rycht° as it is or ony tyme sall be,	*Exactly*
Befoir the sicht off° His divinitie.	*From the perspective of*

2

Thairfoir, our saull with sensualitie	
So fetterit° is in presoun corporall,°	*fettered; prison of the body*
We may not cleirlie understand nor se	
God as He is, nor thingis celestiall;	
Our mirk° and deidlie° corps materiale°	*dark; mortal; non-spiritual*
Blindis the spirituall operatioun,	
Lyke as ane man wer bundin° in presoun.	*bound/fettered*

3

In *Metaphisik*, Aristotell[28] sayis,	
That mannis saull° is lyke ane bakkis ee,°	*soul; bat's eye*
Quhilk lurkis still,° als lang as licht off day° is	*lies concealed; daylight*
And in the gloming° cummis furth to fle;°	*twilight/gloaming; fly*
Hir ene° ar waik,° the sone° scho may not se:	*eyes; weak; sun*

24. Adulation is only poisonous when falsely directed.
25. 'It is to the taste of whoever clearly understood.' The line encapsulates the medieval view of self-correcting textual difficulty. Each reader will understand at the level appropriate to his talents and needs.
26. Prudence is one of the cardinal virtues. God's 'high prudence' refers to His ideal government-in-wisdom. His eternal nature (n. 27) implies continual foresight. Cf 20.3.
27. God, existing beyond time, sees the present, past and future of His creatures instantaneously. He can, therefore, foresee without predetermining our actions.
28. Aristotle (348–322 BC) was a Greek philosopher. His *Metaphysics* deals with the first principles of nature and thought, as does Henryson's 'Preiching'. The image of the bat's eye is taken from *Metaphysics* II.i.3.

Sa is our saull with fantasie° opprest, *false impressions*
To knaw the thingis in nature manifest.[29]

4

For God is in His power infinite,
And mannis saull is febill and ouer° small, *too*
Off understanding waik° and unperfite° *weak; imperfect*
To comprehend Him that contenis all;° *contains all*
Nane suld presume be ressoun naturall° *innate reason*
To seirche the secreitis off the Trinitie,
Bot trow fermelie° and lat all ressoun° be. *believe steadfastly; reasoning*

5

Yyt nevertheles, we may haif knawlegeing° *gain understanding*
Off God almychtie be° His creatouris.° *through; creatures*
That He is gude, fair, wyis° and bening,° *wise; benevolent*
Exempill takis be thir jolie° flouris— *these pretty*
Rycht sweit off smell and plesant off colouris,
Sum grene, sum blew, sum purpour,° quhyte and reid, *purple*
Thus distribute° be gift off[30] His Godheid. *distributed*

6

The firmament, payntit° with sternis° cleir, *painted; stars*
From eist to west rolland° in cirkill round, *rolling*
And everilk planet in his proper spheir,° *allotted sphere*
In moving makand° harmonie and sound;[31] *making*
The fyre, the air, the watter and the ground°[32]— *earth*
Till understand, it is aneuch I wis,° *is enough (evidence) certainly*
That God in all His werkis wittie is.° *is wise/purveys wisdom*

7

Luke weill° the fische that swimmis in the se; *Study closely*
Luke weill in eirth all kynd off bestyall;° *animal life*
The foulis° fair, sa forcelie° thay fle,° *birds; strongly; fly*
Scheddand° the air with pennis grit° and small; *Cutting through; large wings*
Syne° luke to man, that He maid last off all, *Then*
Lyke to His image and His similitude:[33]
Be thir° we knaw that God is fair and gude. *From these (authorities)*

8

All creature He made for the behufe° *benefit*
Off man and to his supportatioun° *support*
In to this eirth, baith under and abufe,° *below and above*
In number, wecht° and dew° proportioun; [34] *weight; fitting*

29. The creative intentions of God were held to be mirrored in the order of Nature.
30. As God created the world, we own nothing by right, only by gift.
31. The harmony of the divine spheres was a classical belief, adapted in Christian thought.
32. The four elements of which Nature was then thought to be composed.
33. Genesis 1.26: 'And God said, "Let us make man in our image; after our likeness."'
34. Book of Wisdom 11.21: 'Thou hast ordered all things in measure and number and weight'.

The difference° off tyme and ilk seasoun	*variation*
Concorddand till° our opurtunitie,°[35]	*Corresponding to; convenience*
As daylie, be experience, we may se.	

9

The Somer with his jolie mantill° grene,	*mantle*
With flouris fair furrit° on everilk fent,°	*trimmed (as if with fur); opening*
Quhilk Flora, goddes° off the flouris, quene,	*goddess*
Hes to that lord—as for his seasoun°—lent,°	*i.e. for summer only; loaned*
And Phebus,° with his goldin bemis gent,°	*sun; beautiful*
Hes purfellit° and payntit plesandly,	*adorned*
With heit and moysture stilland° from the sky.	*distilling*

10

Syne Harvest hait,° quhen Ceres,° that goddes,	*hot/sultry Autumn; harvest goddess*
Hir barnis benit° hes with abundance,	*barns filled*
And Bachus, god off wyne, renewit hes	
Hir tume pyipis° in Italie and France,	*Her (Autumn's) empty casks*
With wynis wicht° and liquour off plesance;°	*strong; pleasure-giving*
And *copia temporis*° to fill hir horne,°	*season's plenty; cornucopia*
That never wes full off quheit° nor uther corne.°	*wheat; grain*

11

Syne Wynter wan,° quhen austerne° Eolus—	*gloomy; stern*
God off the wynd—with blastis boreall°	*northern/chilly*
The grene garment off Somer glorious	
Hes all to-rent° and revin° in pecis small.	*ripped to bits; torn*
Than,° flouris fair, faidit with froist, man° fall,	*Then; must*
And birdis blyith° changeis thair noitis° sweit	*merry; notes/tunes*
In styll murning;° neir slane° with snaw and sleit.°	*silent mourning; almost slain; sleet*

12

Thir dalis° deip with dubbis° drounit is;	*These dales; pools*
Baith hill and holt° heillit° with frostis hair;°	*woodland; covered; hoar*
And bewis bene° ar bethit° bair° off blis[36]	*fair boughs; withered; bare*
Be° wickit windis. Off the Winter wair,°	*By; wary (of)*
All wyld beistis, than,° from the bentis° bair	*then/consequently; fields*
Drawis° for dreid° unto thair dennis deip,	*Withdraw; out of fear*
Coucheand° for cauld in coifis° thame to keip.°	*Lying down; caves; preserve*

13

Syne cummis Ver,° quhen winter is away,	*Spring (archaic)*
The secretar° off Somer with his sell,°	*secretary/harbinger; seal*

35. The roll-call of the seasons, which follows, foreshadows mankind's own life-cycle. The chosen order, ending with Spring, emphasizes not death but the promise of re-birth in heaven. If we 'read' these verbal and natural signs well, we may understand the swallow's argument before he preaches.
36. Literally, 'delight'. The teaching emphasis is on nature as sign, however. It is the loss of any sign of eternal delight (heavenly bliss) which Winter lacks but Spring (st. 13) restores. 'Wickit' in l. 4 has the same literal/moral/divine force.

Quhen columbie° up keikis° throw the clay,	*columbine; peeps*
Quhilk fleit wes° befoir with froistes fell.°	*put to flight; cruel*
The mavis° and the merle° beginnis to mell;°	*thrush; blackbird; chatter/sing*
The lark on loft,° with uthir birdis smale,	*on high*
Than drawis furth fra derne° ouer doun and daill.°	*cover; hill and dale*

14

That samin° seasoun, in to ane soft° morning,	*same; balmy*
Rycht blyth° that bitter blastis wer ago,°	*Very glad; over*
Unto the wod,° to se the flouris spring°	*wood; open*
And heir the mavis sing and birdis mo,°	*other*
I passit furth;° syne lukit to and fro	*forth*
To se the soill, that wes richt sessonabill,°	*seasonable*
Sappie° and, to resave° all seidis, abill.°	*Moist; receive; able*

15

Moving thusgait,° grit myrth I tuke in mynd,[37]	*in this way*
Off lauboraris° to se the besines,°	*labourers; activity*
Sum makand dyke° and sum the pleuch can wynd,°	*building a wall; drove the plough*
Sum sawand° seidis fast° frome place to place,	*sowing; vigorously*
The harrowis hoppand° in the saweris trace;°	*hopping; sowers' track*
It wes grit joy to him that luifit° corne	*loved*
To se thame laubour, baith° at evin and morne;	*both*

16

And as I baid° under ane bank full bene,°	*rested; comfortable*
In hart gritlie rejosit off° that sicht,	*cheered by*
Unto ane hedge, under ane hawthorne grene,	
Off small birdis thair come ane ferlie flicht;°	*wondrous flock*
And doun, belyif,° can on the leifis licht°	*at once/suddenly; alighted*
On everilk syde about me quhair I stude;	
Rycht mervellous, ane mekill° multitude!	*great*

17

Amang the quhilks,° ane swallow loud couth cry,°	*Among which; cried*
On that hawthorne, hie in the croip° sittand:	*treetop*
'O, ye birdis on bewis,° heir me by!°	*boughs; gather round and hear me*
Ye sall weill knaw and wyislie understand	
Quhair danger is or perrell appeirand;°	*apparent*
It is grit wisedome to provyde befoir°	*make advance provision*
It to devoyd,° for dreid it hurt yow moir.'	*remove*

18

'Schir Swallow,' quod the lark agane,° and leuch,°	*in reply; laughed*
'Quhat have ye sene that causis yow to dreid?'	
'Se ye yone churll,'° quod scho,° 'beyond yone pleuch,	*that peasant; i.e. swallow*
Fast sawand hemp—lo, se!—and linget° seid?	*flax*
Yone lint will grow in lytill tyme in deid,	

37. 'I took much pleasure into my mind.' That is, he stores the memory in the treasure house of his mind.

And thairoff will yone churll his nettis mak,°	*make his nets*
Under the quhilk he thinkis° us to tak.°	*intends; catch*

19

'Thairfoir, I reid° we pas° quhen he is gone	*counsel; go forth*
At evin,° and with our naillis scharp and small°	*evening; slender*
Out off the eirth scraip we yone seid anone°	*at once*
And eit it up, for giff it growis we sall	
Have cause to weip heirefter, ane° and all.	*one*
Se we remeid° thairfoir furthwith,° *instante*,	*Let us remedy this; at once*
Nam levius laedit quicquid praevidimus ante.[38]	

20

'For clerkis° sayis it is nocht sufficient	*scholars*
To considder that° is befoir thyne ee;°	*what; eye*
Bot prudence is ane inwart argument,[39]	
That garris° ane man provyde befoir and se°	*makes; consider*
Quhat gude, quhat evill, is liklie for to be	
Off everilk thingis at the fynall end,°	*final end (i.e. Day of Judgment)*
And swa fra perrell the better him defend.'	

21

The lark, lauchand, the swallow thus couth scorne,°	*mocked*
And said scho fischit° lang befoir the net—	*fished*
'The barne° is eith° to busk° that is unborne;	*child; easy; clothe*
All growis nocht that in the ground is set;°	*planted*
The nek to stoup° quhen it the straik° sall get	*bow; stroke*
Is sone aneuch;° deith° on the fayest fall!'°	*enough; let death...most fated fall*
Thus scornit thay the swallow ane and all.	

22

Despysing thus hir helthsum document,°	*salutary lesson*
The foulis ferlie° tuke thair flicht anone.	*unexpectedly*
Sum, with ane bir,° thay braidit° ouer the bent,°	*whirring noise; darted; field*
And sum agane ar to the grene wod° gone.	*wood*
Upon the land,° quhair I wes left allone,	*In the open countryside*
I tuke my club° and hamewart couth I carie,°	*staff; I conveyed myself*
Swa ferliand as° I had sene ane farie.°	*As full of wonder as if; marvel*

23

Thus passit furth, quhill° June, that jolie tyde;°	*until; happy time*
And seidis that wer sawin off beforne°	*earlier*
Wer growin hie, that° hairis° mycht thame° hyde,	*so high that; hares; themselves*
And als° the quailye° craikand° in the corne.	*also; corncrake; croaking*
I movit furth betwix midday and morne	
Unto the hedge under the hawthorne grene,	
Quhair I, befoir, the said birdis had sene.	

38. ll. 6–7: 'Instantly, for what we foresee causes us less harm.'
39. An inner sense mirroring rationally God's instantaneous foresight. See ns. 26, 27.

24

And, as I stude, be aventure° and cace° — *fortune; circumstance*
The samin° birdis as I haif said yow air° — *same; told you of before*
(I hoip° because it wes thair hanting place,° — *suppose; meeting place*
Mair off succour° or yit° mair solitair)° — *More secure; else; solitary*
Thay lychtit doun° and, quhen thay lychtit wair,° — *flew down; had landed*
The swallow swyth° put furth ane pietuous pyme,° — *at once; pitiful peep*
Said, 'Wo is him can not bewar° in tyme! — *be wary*

25

'O blind birdis, and full of negligence,
Unmyndfull off your awin prosperitie,
Lift up your sicht and tak gude advertence!° — *good heed*
Luke to the lint that growis° on yone le!° — *grows; yonder meadow*
Yone is the thing I bad,° forsuith, that we, — *advised*
Quhill it wes seid, suld rute furth° off the eird.° — *root out; soil*
Now is it lint; now is it hie on breird.° — *sprouting high*

26

'Go yit quhill it is tender, young and small,° — *thin*
And pull it up; let it na mair incres!° — *develop*
My flesche growis,° my bodie quaikis° all; — *I get goose flesh; quakes*
Thinkand on it, I may not sleip in peis!'
Thay cryit all and bad° the swallow ceis,° — *told...to cease*
And said, 'Yone lint heirefter will do gude,
For linget° is to lytill birdis fude.° — *flax-seed; food*

27

'We think,° quhen that yone lint bollis° ar ryip,° — *intend; pods; ripe*
To mak us feist° and fill us off the seid, — *feast ourselves*
Magre° yone churll, and on it sing and pyip.'° — *In spite of; trill*
'Weill,' quod the swallow, 'freindes, hardilie beid;° — *so be it*
Do as ye will bot certane,° sair° I dreid, — *for sure; sorely*
Heirefter° ye sall find als sour as sweit, — *In the future*
Quhen ye ar speldit° on yone carlis speit.° — *skewered; spit*

28

'The awner° off yone lint, ane fouler° is, — *owner; fowler*
Right cautelous° and full off subteltie;° — *tricky; finesse*
His pray° full sendill tymis° will he mis, — *prey; very seldom*
Bot giff° we birdis all the warrer° be. — *Unless; more wary*
Full mony off our kin° he hes gart de,° — *kind; has killed*
And thocht° it bot ane sport° to spill thair blude; — *believed; just a game*
God keip me fra him, and the halie rude.'° — *holy rood (also)*

29

Thir small birdis, haveand bot lytill thocht
Off perrell° that mycht fall be aventure,° — *danger; chance*
The counsell off the swallow set at nocht,° — *set at nought*
Bot tuke thair flicht and furth togidder fure;° — *set off together*

Sum to the wode,° sum markit to° the mure.° *woods; headed for; moor*
I tuke my staff, quhen this wes said and done,
And walkit hame for it drew neir the none.° *noon approached*

30

The lynt ryipit,° the carll pullit the lyne,° *ripened; gathered the flax*
Rippillit° the bollis° and in beitis° set; *Combed; pods; sheaves*
It steipit° in the burne° and dryit syne° *soaked; stream; then dried it out*
And, with ane bittell,° knokkit it and bet;° *mallet; pounded*
Syne, swingillit it weill, and hekkillit in the flet;[40]
His wyfe it span and twynit° it in to threid, *twisted*
Off quhilk the fowlar nettis maid in deid.° *indeed/(in death)*

31

The Wynter come, the wickit wind can blaw,° *blew*
The woddis grene wer wallowit° with the weit,° *soaked; wetness*
Baith firth° and fell° with froistys wer maid faw,[41] *wood; hill;*
Slonkis° and slaik° maid slidderie° with the sleit; *Dens; valley; slippery*
The foulis fair for falt° thay fell off feit°— *lack of food; could not stand*
On bewis° bair it wes na bute° to byde,° *boughs; remedy; remain*
Bot hyit° unto housis thame to hyde. *hastened*

32

Sum in the barn, sum in the stak° off corne *stack*
Thair lugeing° tuke and maid thair residence. *lodging*
The fowlar saw and grit aithis° hes sworne, *oaths*
Thay suld be tane° trewlie for thair expence;° *caught; costliness*
His nettis hes he set with diligence
And in the snaw he schulit hes ane plane,° *dug out a clear space*
And heillit°it all ouer with calf° agane. *covered; chaff*

33

Thir small birdis, seand the calff, wes glaid;° *glad*
Trowand° it had bene corne, thay lychtit doun, *Believing*
Bot of the nettis na presume° thay had— *anticipation*
Nor of the fowlaris fals° intentioun— *false/deceitful*
To scraip and seik thair meit thay maid thame boun.° *prepared themselves*
The swallow, on ane lytill branche neir by,
Dreiddand for gyle,° thus° loud on thame couth cry: *Fearing trickery; in these* words

34

'In to that calf,° scraip quhill° your naillis bleid— *chaff; scrape until*
Thair is na corne; ye labour all in vane.
Trow ye yone churll for pietie° will yow feid? *out of pity*
Na, na, he hes it heir layit° for ane trane.° *laid out; trap*
Remove,° I reid,° or ellis ye will be slane; *Escape; counsel*
His nettis he hes set full prively,° *secretly*
Reddie to draw;° in tyme be war, for thy!° *draw in; therefore*

40. 'Then scraped it thoroughly with a wooden blade and teased it out with a flax comb in the house.'
41. 'Faw' means 'of different colours'. The loss of 'green' as sign of youth and hope is here highlighted.

35

'Grit fule is he that puttis in dangeir
His lyfe, his honour, for ane thing off nocht.
Grit fule is he that will not glaidlie heir
Counsall in tyme,° quhill it availl him mocht.° — *Timely advice; might*
Grit fule is he that hes na thing in thocht
Bot thing present and efter quhat may fall
Nor off the end hes na memoriall.'[42]

36

Thir small birdis, for hunger famischit neir,° — *almost starving*
Full besie scraipand for to seik thair fude,
The counsall off the swallow wald not heir,° — *did not wish to hear*
Suppois° thair laubour dyd thame lytill gude. — *Even if*
Quhen scho° thair fulische hartis understude — *she (swallow)*
Sa indurate,° up in ane tre scho flew— — *obdurate*
With that, this churll° ouer thame his nettis drew. — *peasant*

37

Allace, it wes grit hart sair° for to se — *heart's grief*
That bludie bowcheour° beit thay birdis doun, — *butcher*
And for till heir, quhen thay wist weill to de,° — *knew well they were to die*
Thair cairfull sang° and lamentatioun. — *miserable song*
Sum with ane staf he straik° to eirth on swoon.° — *clubbed; unconscious*
Of sum the heid he straik,° off sum he brak the crag,° — *cut off; broke the neck*
Sum, half on lyfe,° he stoppit in° his bag. — *half-alive; stuffed into*

38

And, quhen the swallow saw that thay wer deid,
'Lo,' quod scho, 'thus it happinnis mony syis° — *many times*
On thame that will not tak counsall nor reid° — *advice*
Off° prudent men or clerkis that ar wyis. — *From*
This grit perrell° I tauld° thame mair than thryis;° — *danger; (fore)told; three times*
Now ar thay deid—and wo is me thairfoir!'° — *because of it*
Scho tuke hir flicht, bot I hir saw no moir.

Moralitas

39

Lo, worthie folk, Esope,° that nobill clerk,° — *Aesop; scholar/writer*
Ane poet worthie to be lawreate,° — *crowned with laurel*
Quhen that he waikit° from mair autentik° werk, — *had leisure; authoritative*
With uther ma,° this foirsaid fabill wrate,° — *other (fables); wrote*
Quhilk at this tyme may weill be applicate° — *turned/interpreted according*
To gude morall edificatioun,° — *good ethical teaching*
Haifand° ane sentence° according to ressoun.° — *Having; meaning; reason*

42. ll. 5–7: 'He is a great fool, who thinks only of things pertaining to the present and retains no images to remind him of what may befall later or at his latter end.'

40

This carll and bond,° of gentrice spoliate,°	*bondsman; devoid of gentility*
Sawand° this calf thir small birdis to sla°—	*Sowing; slay*
It is the feind,° quhilk fra the angelike° state	*devil; angelic*
Exylit° is, as fals apostata,°	*Exiled; apostate*
Quhilk, day and nycht, weryis not for to ga,°	*untiringly goes forth*
Sawand poysoun and mony° wickit thocht	*many (a)*
In mannis saull,° quhilk Christ full deir hes bocht.°	*soul; has bought at a great price*

41

And quhen the saull,° as seid in to the eird,°	*soul; earth*
Gevis consent unto delectatioun,°	*consent to delightful notions*
The wickit thocht beginnis for to breird°	*burgeon*
In° deidlie sin,° quhilk is dampnatioun;°[43]	*Into; mortal sin; damnation*
Ressoun is blindit with affectioun°	*by emotion*
And carnall lust° growis full grene and gay,	*fleshly lust*
Throw consuetude hantit° from day to day.	*customs practised*

42

Proceding furth be use and consuetude,°	*usage and custom*
The sin ryipis and schame° is set on syde;°	*sense of shame/conscience; aside*
The feynd plettis° his nettis scharp and rude°	*plaits; coarse*
And, under plesance,° previlie° dois hyde;	*pleasure; secretly*
Syne, on the feild he sawis calf° full wyde,°	*chaff; far and wide*
Quhilk is bot tume° and verray° vanitie[44]	*empty; essential/quidditative*
Of fleschlie lust and vaine° prosperitie.	*vain (worldly)*

43

Thir hungrie birdis, wretchis° we may call—	*wretched people*
Ay° scraipand in this warldis vane plesance,°	*Ever; this world's empty delights*
Greddie to gadder gudis temporall,°	*Greedy to gather worldly goods*
Quhilk, as the calf,° ar tume without substance,	*like the chaff*
Lytill of vaill° and full of variance,°	*Of little benefit; ever-changing*
Lyke to the mow° befoir the face of wind	*dust*
Quhiskis° away and makis wretchis blind.	*Whisks (it)*

44

This swallow, quhilk eschaipit is° the snair,	*has escaped*
The halie preichour° weill may signifie,°	*holy preacher; stand for*
Exhortand° folk to walk,° and ay be wair°	*Exhorting; awaken; be wary*
Fra nettis of our wickit enemie,°	*(i.e. the devil)*
Quha sleipis not, bot ever is reddie,	*alert*
Quhen wretchis in this warldis calf dois scraip,	
To draw° his net, that they may not eschaip.°	*draw in; escape*

43. This stanza traces the three Augustinian stages into mortal sin from suggestion through consent to indulging evil thoughts. Habit moves the sinner to evil actions and the death of the spirit.
44. Three divisions of 'ripe' sin match the three stages of 'burgeoning'. Latin 'vanitas' is here associated with the pride and purposelessness of placing your faith in the world, the flesh and the devil.

45

Allace, quhat cair,° quhat weiping is and wo, — *care*
Quhen saull and bodie partit° ar in twane!° — *separated; two*
The bodie to the wormis keitching° go, — *worms' kitchen/grave*
The saull to fyre, to everlestand pane.° — *everlasting pain*
Quhat helpis than this calf,° thir gudis vane,° — *chaff; these worthless goods*
Quhen thow art put in Luceferis° bag — *the devil's*
And brocht to hell, and hangit be the crag?° — *neck*

46

Thir hid° nettis for to persave and se,° — *These hidden; understand and see*
This sarie° calf wyislie to understand, — *vile*
Best is bewar in maist° prosperitie; — *be wary (when) in greatest*
For, in this warld, thair is na thing lestand;° — *abiding*
Is na man wait° how lang his stait° will stand,° — *(who) knows; condition...endure*
His lyfe° will lest° nor how that he sall end — *life...last*
Efter his deith, nor quhidder° he sall wend.° — *whither; go*

47

Pray we, thairfoir, quhill we ar in this lyfe
For four thingis: the first, fra sin remufe;° — *escape from*
The secund is to seis° all weir° and stryfe; — *cease; warfare*
The thrid is perfite cheritie° and lufe; — *charity*
The feird° thing is, and maist for our behufe,° — *fourth; of most benefit to us*
That is—in blis° with angellis to be fallow.° — *bliss; companion(s)*
And thus endis the preiching of the swallow.

The Paddock and the Mouse

1

Upon ane tyme, as Esope culd report,° — *Aesop reported*
Ane lytill mous come till ane rever syde;° — *river bank*
Scho micht not waid, hir schankis° wer sa schort; — *legs*
Scho culd not swym; scho had na hors to ryde;
Off verray force° behovit hir to byde.° — *sheer necessity; she had to stay*
And, to and fra, besyde that revir deip
Scho ran, cryand with mony pietuous peip.° — *(a) pitiful cry*

2

'Help ouer!° Help ouer!' this silie° mous can cry, — *across; wretched/innocent*[45]
'For Goddis lufe...sum bodie°...ouer the brym!'° — *somebody; stream*
With that, ane paddok°[46] in the watter by° — *frog; nearby*
Put up° hir heid and on the bank can clym,° — *raised; climbed up*
Quhilk be nature° culd douk° and gaylie° swym. — *naturally; could dive; blithely*

45. As she is not yet under the power of the frog (body), she may represent the pious/ innocent as well as the pitiful/wretched soul.

46. In the Latin source, 'rana' or 'frog'. Medieval writers did not distinguish between frog and toad. Henryson uses 'taid' twice— see 9.1; 16.7.

With voce full rauk,° scho said on this maneir:°	*very raucous; fashion*
'Gude morne, Schir Mous! Quhat is your erand° heir?'	*business*
3	
'Seis thow', quod scho, 'off corne yone jolie flat°	*fine open field*
Off ryip aitis,° off barlie,° peis and quheit?°	*oats; barley; wheat*
I am hungrie and fane wald be thair at,°	*over there*
Bot I am stoppit be this watter greit;°	*broad river*
And on this syde I get na thing till eit°	*to eat*
Bot hard nuttis, quhilkis with my teith I bore:°	*gnaw through*
Wer I beyond,° my feist wer fer the more.	*i.e. on the other side*
4	
'I have no boit;° heir is no maryner;°	*boat; mariner*
And thocht thair war, I have no fraucht° to pay.'	*ferry-fare*
Quod scho,° 'Sister, lat be your hevie cheir;°	*i.e. frog; gloomy mood*
Do my counsall° and I sall find the way,	*Follow my advice*
Withoutin hors, brig,° boit or yit galay,°	*bridge; even galley*
To bring yow ouer saiflie, be not afeird,°	*afraid*
And not wetand° the campis° off your beird.'	*without wetting; whiskers*
5	
'I haif mervell,'° than quod° the lytill mous,	*I wonder; then said*
'How can thow fleit° without fedder° or fin?	*float; feather*
This rever is sa deip and dangerous,	
Me think that thow suld droun to wed° thairin.	*wade*
Tell me, thairfoir, quhat facultie or gin°	*skill/ingenuity*
Thow hes to bring the ouer this watter wan.'°	*dark*
That to declair, the paddock thus began:	
6	
'With my twa feit,' quod scho, 'lukkin° and braid,°	*webbed; broad*
In steid off airis,° I row the streme full styll;°	*In place of oars; smoothly*
And thocht the brym be perrillous to waid,°	*wade across*
Baith to and fra I swyme at my awin will.	
I may not droun° for quhy° my oppin gill[47]	*cannot drown; because*
Devoidis ay the watter I resaiff:°	*take in*
Thairfoir to droun, forsuith, na dreid° I haif.'	*fear*
7	
The mous beheld unto° hir fronsit° face,	*gazed at; furrowed*
Hir runkillit° cheikis and hir lippis syde,°	*wrinkled; flabby*
Hir hingand° browis and hir voce sa hace,°	*overhanging; hoarse*
Hir loggerand° leggis and hir harsky hyde.°	*loose-jointed; rough skin*
Scho ran abak and on the paddock cryde:	
'Giff I can ony skill° off phisnomy,°[48]	*knowledge; physiognomy*
Thow hes sumpart° off falset° and invy.°	*some signs; falsehood; envy*

47. Adult frogs do not have gills. The detail may have been introduced as a clear sign of the frog's deceitful nature.
48. The art of devising character from the constitution of the body. Stanza 8 expands on the theme.

8	
'For, clerkis° sayis, the inclinatioun°	*scholars; tendency*
Off mannis thocht proceidis commounly°	*usually*
Efter the corporall complexioun°	*bodily constitution*
To gude or evill, as nature will apply: [49]	
Ane thrawart° will, ane thrawin phisnomy.°	*perverse; distorted physiognomy*
The auld proverb is witnes off° this *lorum:*°	*supports; doctrine*
Distortum vultum sequitur distortio morum.'[50]	

9	
'Na,' quod the taid,° 'that proverb is not trew,	*toad (see n. 46)*
For fair thingis oftymis ar fundin faikin;°	*found to be faked*
The blaberyis,° thocht thay be sad off hew,°	*bilberries; hue*
Ar gadderit° up quhen primeros is forsakin;°	*gathered; neglected*
The face may faill to be the hartis takin;°	*heart's token/emblem*
Thairfoir, I find this scripture° in all place:°	*written text; everywhere*
"Thow suld not juge ane man efter his face."°[51]	*according to his looks*

10	
'Thocht I unhailsum° be to luke upon,	*unwholesome*
I have na wyt° quhy suld I lakkit° be.	*insight into; unfavoured*
Wer I als fair as jolie° Absolon,[52]	*handsome*
I am no causer° off that grit beutie;	*creator*
This difference, in forme and qualitie,	
Almychtie God hes causit° Dame Nature	*caused/compelled*
To prent° and set in everilk creature.°	*imprint; every created thing*

11	
'Off sum the face may be full flurischand,°	*flourishing/blooming*
Off silkin° toung and cheir° rycht amorous,°	*silken; aspect; lovable*
With mynd inconstant, fals and variand,°	*capricious*
Full of desait° and menis cautelous.'°	*deceit; tricky habits*
'Let be° thy preiching,' quod the hungrie mous,	*Stop*
'And be quhat craft,° thow gar° me understand,	*by whatever skill; make*
That thow wald gyde me to yone yonder° land.'	*across there*

12	
'Thow wait,'° quod scho, 'ane bodie° that hes neid	*know; individual*
To help thame self suld mony wayis cast.°	*try out*
Thairfoir, ga tak ane doubill twynit threid°	*doubly twined string*
And bind° thy leg to myne with knottis fast:°	*attach; tight*
I sall the leir° to swym—be not agast—	*teach*
Als weill as I.' 'As thow?' than quod the mous.	
'To preif that play,° it wer our° perrillous!	*To test out that game; too*

49. I.e. 'According to the bias of individual natures.' This derives from the theory of different types of personality being determined by the balance of humours.

50. 'Given a distorted face, distorted morals follow.'

51. A common preaching proverb, drawn from Biblical sources—e.g. John 7. 24.

52. The Old Testament Absolon (2 Samuel 14. 25) was famed for beauty. Chaucer's latter-day Absolon in 'The Miller's Tale' is farcically *over*-concerned with his appearance.

13
'Suld I be bund° and fast,° quhar I am fre, *bound; tied*
In hoip off° help? Na, than I schrew° us baith, *Out of a desire for; curse*
For I mycht lois° baith lyfe and libertie! *lose*
Giff it wer swa, quha suld amend the skaith,° *pay the damages (legal)*
Bot gif thow sweir to me the murthour aith:[53]
But° fraud or gyle to bring me ouer this flude,° *Without; torrent*
But hurt or harme?' 'In faith,' quod scho, 'I dude.'° *do (lit. 'did')*

14
Scho goikit up,° and to the hevin can cry:° *gazed up; called out*
'How,° Juppiter, off nature god and king, *Hail*
I mak ane aith trewlie to the,° that I *truly to you*
This lytill mous sall over this watter bring.'
This aith wes maid; the mous, but persaving° *perceiving*
The fals ingyne° of this foull crappald pad,° *intent; evil toady of a frog*
Tuke threid and band° hir leg, as scho hir bad.° *bound; ordered*

15
Than, fute° for fute,[54] thay lap° baith in the brym,° *foot; jumped; stream*
Bot in thair myndis° thay wer rycht different: *intentions*
The mous thocht° na thing bot° to fleit° and swym; *intended; only; keep afloat*
The paddock for to droun° set hir intent. *on drowning (the mouse)*
Quhen thay in midwart off the streme wer went,° *had attained*
With all hir force the paddok preissit° doun, *pressed*
And thocht the mous without mercie to droun.

16
Persavand° this, the mous on hir can cry: *Seeing*
'Tratour to God and manesworne° unto me! *forsworn*
Thow swore the murthour aith richt now that I
But hurt or harme suld ferryit be and fre.'
And quhen scho saw thair wes bot do or de,° *the only option was do or die*
Scho bowtit up° and forsit hir° to swym, *sprang up; tried strenuously*
And preissit° upon the taiddis bak° to clym. *strove; toad's back*

17
The dreid of deith hir strenthis gart incres° *increased*
And forcit° hir° defend with mycht and mane. *compelled (her to); herself*
The mous upwart, the paddok doun can pres;
Quhyle to,° quhyle fra,° quhyle doukit° up agane. *Now one way...other; bobbed*
This selie° mous, this plungit° in grit pane, *innocent; thus plunged*
Gan fecht° als lang as breith wes in hir breist, *Fought*
Till at the last scho cryit for ane preist.

18
Fechtand thusgait, the gled sat on ane twist[55]
And to this wretchit battell tuke gude heid;° *heed*

53. 'Unless you swear to me the oath indemnifying me against any murderous intent on your part.'
54. 'Foot for foot'. A reference to their legs being tied as in a three-legged race.
55. 'As they fought in this way, the kite sat on a bough.'

And with ane wisk,° or owthir° off thame wist, *swoop; before either*
He claucht his cluke betwix° thame in the threid; *closed his claw around*
Syne to the land he flew with thame gude speid,° *speedily*
Fane° off that fang,° pyipand° with mony "Pew!" *Glad; catch; piping*
Syne lowsit thame° and baith, but pietie,° slew. *let them loose; pitilessly*

19

Syne bowellit° thame, that boucheour,° with his bill *disembowelled; butcher*
And bellieflaucht full fettislie thame fled,[56]
Bot all thair flesche wald scant be half ane fill° *satisfying meal*
—And guttis als°—unto that gredie gled. *innards included*
Off thair debait, thus quhen I hard outred,
He tuke his flicht and ouer the feildis flaw.[57]
Giff this be trew, speir ye at thame that saw.° *ask those who saw it*

Moralitas

20

My brother, gif thow will tak advertence,° *warning*
Be this fabill thow may persave and se
It passis far° all kynd of pestilence *It (wicked mind) surpasses*
Ane wickit mynd with wordis fair and sle.° *sly/cunning*
Be war° thairfore with quhome thow fallowis the,° *Be wary; you ally yourself*
For thow wer better beir° of stane the barrow, *to carry*
Or sweitand dig and delf° quhill° thow may dre,° *delve; so long as; endure*
Than to be matchit with° ane wickit marrow.°[58] *coupled to; companion*

21

Ane fals intent under ane fair pretence
Hes causit mony innocent for to de;
Grit folie is to gif ouer sone° credence *too quickly*
To all that speiks fairlie unto the;
Ane silkin toung,° ane hart of crueltie *silken tongue*
Smytis more sore than ony schot of arrow;
Brother, gif thow be wyse, I reid the fle° *advise you to refrain (from)*
To matche the with ane thrawart,° fenyeit° marrow. *perverse; duplicitous*

22

I warne the als, it is grit nekligence
To bind the fast° quhair thow wes frank° and fre: *yourself tightly; liberated*
Fra° thow be bund, thow may mak na defence° *Once; are defenceless*

56. 'And flayed them very neatly, taking the skin whole over their heads.'
57. ll. 5–6: 'When I heard their tale of strife recounted, therefore, he (simply) winged away and flew off over the fields.' The narrator offers two versions and then asks us to check the latter with eye witnesses—'Giff this be trew…'
58. This fable, the last in Henryson's collection, has two morality sections. The first is marked off by its eight line stanza and the 'marrow' refrain. The transition to the second is signed by the bardic formula 'This hald in mynd' (23.1).

To saif thy lyfe nor yit° thy libertie.	*let alone*
This simpill counsall, brother, tak at° me,	*take from*
And it to cun perqueir° se thow not tarrow:°	*learn by heart; delay*
Better but stryfe to leif° allane in le°	*live; tranquillity*
Than to be matchit with ane wickit marrow.	
23	
This hald in mynd;° rycht more I sall the tell,	*Hold this in your memory*
Quhair by° thir beistis may be figurate:°	*In what ways; used as signs*
The paddok, usand° in the flude to dwell,	*accustomed*
In mannis bodie, swymand air° and late	*early*
In to this warld, with cairis implicate:°	*entangled with miseries*
Now hie, now law, quhylis° plungit up, quhylis° doun,	*whiles…whiles*
Ay in perrell,° and reddie for to droun;	*Ever in danger*
24	
Now dolorus, now blyth as bird on breir;°	*briar bush*
Now in fredome, now wardit° in distres;	*imprisoned*
Now haill° and sound, now deid and brocht on beir;°	*whole; carried out on a bier*
Now pure° as Job,[59] now rowand° in riches;	*poor; rolling*
Now gounis° gay, now brats° laid in pres;°	*gowns; torn clothes; cupboard*
Now full as fische, now hungrie as ane hound;	
Now on the quheill,° now wappit° to the ground.	*on (Fortune's) wheel; dashed*
25	
This lytill mous, heir knit° thus be the schyn,°	*tied/joined; shin*
The saull of man betakin may° in deid°—	*may stand for; indeed*
Bundin° and fra the bodie may not twyn,°	*Bound up; separate*
Quhill cruel deith cum brek° of lyfe the threid—	*comes to break*
The quhilk° to droun suld ever stand in dreid°	*Which (= soul); fear*
Of carnall lust be the suggestioun,°	*inclination*
Quhilk drawis° ay the saull and druggis doun.°	*entices; drags down*
26	
The watter is the warld, ay welterand°	*shifting/mutable*
With mony wayis° of tribulatioun,	*voyages*
In quhilk the saull and bodye wer steirrand,°	*battling*
Standand distinyt° in thair opinioun:	*Holding separate*
The spreit° upwart, the body precis° doun;	*spirit; presses*
The saull rycht fane wald be brocht ouer, I wis,°	*know*
Out of this warld into the hevinnis blis.	
27	
The gled is deith, that cummis° suddandlie	*who arrives*
As dois ane theif, and cuttis sone° the battall:	*soon cuts short*
Be vigilant thairfoir and ay reddie,	
For mannis lyfe is brukill° and ay mortall.°	*brittle/frail; subject to death*

59. Old Testament holy man, renowned for his endurance. From riches, he was cast into poverty before being returned to prosperity.

My freind, thairfoir, mak the ane strang castell° — *build yourself a strong castle*
Of gud deidis,° for deith will the assay,° — *good deeds; put you to trial*
Thow wait° not quhen—evin,° morrow° or midday. — *know; evening; morning*

28

Adew, my freind, and gif that ony speiris° — *asks why*
Of this fabill,° sa schortlie° I conclude, — *fable collection; briefly*
Say thow, I left the laif° unto the freiris,° — *rest; friars*
To mak a sample° or similitude.° — *parable; analogy*
Now Christ for us that deit° on the Rude,° — *who died; holy cross*
Of saull and lyfe as thow art Salviour,
Grant us till pas in till ane blissit hour.[60]

60. This means 'Grant that we may pass over [die] at a blessed time'. But the petition can also bear the sense 'travel into a blessed time [eternity]'.

§ 5 Robert Henryson (c.1450-c.1505): *The Testament of Cresseid*

[See also Introductions to § 4 and § 14]

*Henryson's two longer narrative poems—***Orpheus and Eurydice** *and* **The Testament of Cresseid***—link three kinds of authority, being drawn from classical mythology, influenced by the medieval moralising tradition but treated in the neoplatonic manner of early humanism.* **Orpheus***, the earlier of the two, is not included in the Anthology, but is worth reading both for itself and as a guide to the way in which these intertwining traditions may reinforce each other. The classical myth of Orpheus' love for Eurydice is re-told without loss of tragic force, but Henryson uses the allegoric techniques of the medieval moralizing tradition to encourage us to re-view the conflicts enacted in that story in the manner of the neoplatonists. That is—as a shadow of the battle between reason and passion in the soul.*

The Testament*, on Henryson's own evidence, derives from the poet's reading of and critical reaction to Chaucer's* **Troilus and Criseyde***. That poem involves its readers in the sufferings of Cressida in the first three books, only to lose sight of her and concentrate on Troilus in the last two. Seeking to provide an 'invented' conclusion to Cressida's story, Henryson begins after her return to Greece and rejection by her Greek lover Diomede. The narrator imagines her judged by the pagan gods, sentenced to become a leper and (in that state) encountering Troilus again. At each stage of Cressida's tragic journey, she has a soliloquy. Only in the last of these does she blame herself and convert the tones of complaint into the formulation of her last will and testament.*

Like the **Kingis Quair***, the poem has divided critics. Though particular views are legion, one group emphasizes the tragic story-line and welcomes Henryson into the fold of humanism. The other stresses the penitential conclusion and sees him returning Chaucer's subtle text to the categories of medieval self-examination. You might also consider whether the opting for any one 'line' is necessary, when the setting of one perspective against another is integral to the poetic planning. Schoolmaster Henryson is likely to have known that a refining of the questions posed by an issue is more likely to involve students in making the problem their own, than a series of neat answers, which denies it exists.*

The Testament of Cresseid

1	
Ane doolie° sessoun to ane cairfull dyte°	*gloomy; woeful composition*
Suld correspond and be equivalent:°	*be in harmony with*
Richt sa it wes quhen I began to wryte	
This tragedie; the wedder° richt fervent,°	*weather; very sultry*
Quhen Aries, in middis of the Lent,[1]	
Schouris of haill gart° fra the north discend,°	*caused...to fall*
That scantlie° fra the cauld I micht defend.°	*scarcely; protect myself*
2	
Yit, nevertheles, within myne oratur°	*study/oratory*
I stude, quhen Titan° had his bemis° bricht	*i.e. sun; beams*
Withdrawin doun and sylit under cure,°	*concealed under cover*

1. ED. COPY TEXT: Charteris (1593). Astrologically, it is March, when the world was held to have been created. Liturgically, it is Lent.

And fair Venus,° the bewtie of the nicht, *i.e. as planet*
Uprais° and set unto the west full richt *Ascended*
Hir goldin face, in oppositioun
Of god Phebus,° direct discending doun.[2] *i.e. sun*

3

Throw out the glas° hir bemis brast° sa fair, *window; burst*
That I micht se on everie syde me by;
The northin wind had purifyit the air
And sched° the mistie cloudis fra the sky; *dispersed*
The froist freisit; the blastis° bitterly *gales*
Fra Pole Artick° come quhisling° loud and schill° *Pole Star; whistling; shrill*
And causit me remufe° aganis my will. *depart*

4

For I traistit that Venus, luifis quene,° *queen of love*
To quhome sum tyme I hecht° obedience, *a while ago I vowed*
My faidit° hart, of° lufe scho wald mak grene;° *withered; through; cause to blossom*
And therupon,° with humbill reverence, *consequently*
I thocht° to pray hir hie° magnificence; *decided; high/great*
Bot for greit cald, as than,° I lattit° was *as before; prevented*
And in my chalmer° to the fyre can pas.° *chamber; went*

5

Thocht lufe be hait,° yit in ane man of age° *hot; old age*
It kendillis° nocht sa sone as in youtheid,° *ignites/kindles; youth*
Of quhome the blude is flowing in ane rage;° *surging*
And, in the auld, the curage doif° and deid, *desire/ vigour (is) dull*
Of quhilk the fyre outward° is best remeid:° *external (v. emotional); remedy*
To help be phisike°quhair that nature faillit,° *medicine; has failed*
I am expert,° for baith° I have assaillit.° *experienced; both; tried*

6

I mend° the fyre and beikit me about,° *stoke(d) up; warmed myself up*
Than tuik ane drink, my spreitis° to comfort,° *spirits; console/cheer up*
And armit me weill fra° the cauld thairout.° *against; outside*
To cut° the winter nicht° and mak it schort, *divide; night*
I tuik ane quair° and left all uther sport,° *book; diversion(s)*
Writtin be worthie° Chaucer glorious *noble*
Of fair Creisseid and worthie Troylus.[3]

7

And thair I fand, efter that° Diomeid *that once*
Ressavit° had that lady bricht of hew,° *Received/Welcomed; complexion*
How Troilus neir out of wit abraid° *almost went out of his mind*

2. An astrological impossibility prophesying tragic disorder.
3. Chaucer's *Troilus and Criseyde*, to which Henryson here refers, is itself a re-working of a popular classical story. While Chaucer latterly focusses on Troilus and the poem ends with his death, Henryson proposes to concentrate throughout on Cressida.

And weipit soir° with visage paill of hew, *wept sorely*
For quhilk wanhope° his teiris can renew *despair*
Quhill esperance° rejoisit him agane: *Until hopefulness*
Thus, quhyle° in joy he levit, quhyle° in pane: *now...lived, now*

8

Of hir behest° he had greit comforting, *promise*
Traisting° to Troy that scho suld mak retour,° *Trusting; return*
Quhilk he desyrit maist of eirdly thing° *earthly things/temporal values*
For quhy° scho was his only paramour.° *Because; beloved/mistress*
Bot quhen he saw passit baith° day and hour *both passed*
Of hir ganecome,° than sorrow can oppres *(scheduled) return*
His wofull hart in cair° and hevines.° *distress; heaviness/dejection*

9

Of his distres me neidis nocht reheirs° *I need not retell*
For worthie Chauceir in the samin° buik, *same/aforementioned*
In gudelie termis[4] and in joly veirs° *fine verse*
Compylit° hes his cairis, quha will luik.° *Described; (for) all who wish to look*
To brek° my sleip ane uther quair I tuik, *forestall*
In quhilk I fand the fatall destenie° *fated/final destiny*
Of fair Cresseid, that endit wretchitlie.° *who died wretchedly*

10

Quha wait° gif all that Chauceir wrait° was trew? *knows; wrote*
Nor I wait nocht gif this narratioun
Be authoreist° or fenyeit of the new° *authoritative; newly fabricated*
Be sum poeit throw his inventioun,[5]
Maid° to report the lamentatioun° *Formed; lamentation/lamentings*
And wofull end of this lustie° Creisseid, *lusty/beautiful*
And quhat distres scho thoillit,° and quhat deid.° *endured; what (kind of) death*

11

Quhen Diomeid had all his appetyte
And mair,° fulfillit° of this fair ladie, *And more; fulfilled/sated*
Upon ane uther° he set his haill° delyte, *another (woman); entire*
And send to hir ane lybell of repudie° *bill/document of repudiation*
And hir excludit fra his companie.
Than, desolait, scho walkit up and doun,
And—sum men sayis—into the court commoun.° *promiscuity/prostitution*

12

O fair Creisseid, the flour and A per se° *i.e. paragon*
Of Troy and Grece, how was thow fortunait° *destined/fated*
To change in filth all thy feminitie

4. 'Gudelie termis' means 'excellent phrases'. But, as medieval poetry was aimed at improving one's behaviour, it may have the subsidiary force of 'wholesome' (effect) or of 'benevolent' (intention).
5. The first recorded Scots use of the word 'invention' in its literary sense. Henryson chooses to emphasize the inventiveness of any later poetic contribution to a familiar story.

And be with fleschelie lust sa maculait° *defiled/spotted*
And go amang the Greikis air and lait,° *at all times (formulaic)*
Sa giglotlike° takand thy foull plesance!° *wantonly; vile pleasure*
I have pietie° thow suld fall° sic mischance! *pity; undergo*

13

Yit, nevertheles, quhat ever men deme° or say *judge*
In scornefull langage of thy brukkilnes,° *frailty/infidelity*
I sall excuse, als far furth as I may,° *as far as possible*
Thy womanheid,° thy wisdome and fairnes, *womanhood*
The quhilk° Fortoun hes put to sic distres *Which*
As hir pleisit, and nathing° throw the gilt *in no way*
Of the°—throw wickit° langage to be spilt!° *Your (guilt); vilifying; injured*

14

This fair lady, in this wyse° destitute *manner*
Of all comfort and consolatioun,
Richt privelie,° but fellowschip° or refute,° *secretly; company; protector*
Disagysit° passit far out of° the toun *Disguised; beyond*
Ane myle or twa, unto ane mansioun° *mansion*
Beildit full gay,° quhair hir father Calchas *Very finely constructed*
Quhilk than°[6] amang the Greikis dwelland° was. *Who then; living*

15

Quhen he hir saw, the caus° he can inquyre° *reason; he enquired*
Of hir cumming: scho said, siching full soir,° *sighing very painfully*
'Fra° Diomeid had gottin his desyre *Once*
He wox° werie and wald of me no moir.' *grew*
Quod Calchas, 'Douchter, weip thow not thairfoir.
Peraventure,° all cummis° for the best. *Perchance; will come together*
Welcum to me thow art; full deir ane gest!'° *guest*

16

This auld Calchas, efter the law was tho,° *as the law was then*
Wes keiper° of the tempill° as ane preist *guardian; temple*
In quhilk Venus and hir sone Cupido° *son Cupid*
War honourit and his chalmer° was thame neist,° *room; next*
To quhilk° Cresseid, with baill° aneuch in breist, *which (i.e. temple); sorrow*
Usit to pas,° hir prayeris for to say; *Was accustomed to go*
Quhill, at the last,° upon ane solempne day,° *finally; day of solemn rites*

17

As custome was, the pepill° far and neir *people*
Befoir the none° unto the tempill went *noon*
With sacrifice, devoit° in thair maneir;° *devout; in their customary way*
Bot still Cresseid, hevie in hir intent,° *sorrowful in her mind*
Into the kirk° wald not hir self present,° *church; show herself*

6. Calchas, father of Cressida, was a Trojan priest, who prophesied Greek victory. He had earlier been exchanged for a Trojan warrior, leaving Cressida an unwelcome presence in Troy.

For giving of the pepill ony deming° — *inkling*
Of hir expuls° fra Diomeid the king, — *expulsion*

18

Bot past into ane secreit° orature,° — *concealed; small chapel*
Quhair scho micht weip° hir wofull desteny. — *lament*
Behind hir bak scho cloisit fast° the dure° — *firmly; door*
And on hir kneis bair° fell doun in hy;° — *bare; haste*
Upon Venus and Cupide angerly° — *angrily*
Scho cryit out and said on this same wyse,° — *in these very words*
'Allace, that ever I maid yow sacrifice!

19

'Ye gave me anis° ane devine responsaill° — *once; divinely guaranteed reply*
That I suld be the flour of luif in Troy;
Now am I maid ane unworthie outwaill,° — *outcast without honour*
And all in cair translatit° is my joy. — *translated (= transformed)*
Quha sall me gyde? Quha sall me now convoy,° — *escort/protect*
Sen I fra Diomeid and nobill Troylus
Am clene excludit,° as abject° odious? — *utterly banished; outcast*

20

'O fals Cupide, is nane to wyte° bot thow — *blame*
And thy mother, of lufe the blind goddes!
Ye causit me alwayis understand and trow° — *believe*
The seid of lufe° was sawin° in my face, — *Love's seed; implanted*
And ay grew grene throw your supplie° and grace. — *nurturing*
Bot now, allace, that seid with froist is slane
And I fra° luifferis left,° and all forlane!'° — *by…abandoned; forlorn*

21

Quhen this was said, doun in ane extasie,° — *trance*
Ravischit in spreit,° intill ane dreame scho fell — *Ravished in spirit*
And, be apperance, hard°—quhair scho did ly— — *thought she heard*
Cupide the king ringand ane silver bell,
Quhilk men micht heir fra hevin unto hell;
At quhais sound, befoir° Cupide appeiris — *in front of*
The sevin planetis, discending fra thair spheiris;°[7] — *spheres*

22

Quhilk hes power of all thing generabill,° — *capable of being generated*
To reull° and steir,° be thair greit influence, — *rule; steer*
Wedder and wind and coursis variabill.° — *changeable movements/activities*
And, first of all, Saturne gave his sentence,° — *decree/judgement*
Quhilk gave to Cupide litill reverence,° — *respect*
Bot, as ane busteous churle,° on his maneir — *like a rough boor*
Come crabitlie° with auster° luik and cheir.° — *ill-naturedly; austere; bearing*

7. The dream follows the broad tradition of works such as Boccaccio's *Genealogia Deorum* in which the hierarchy of the pagan gods, malevolent and benevolent, is traced from Saturn to the Moon.

23

His face fronsit,° his lyre° was lyke the leid,°	*wrinkled; complexion; leaden*
His teith chatterit and cheverit with the chin,°	*i.e. shivered*
His ene drowpit,° how sonkin° in his heid,	*eyes drooped; deeply sunken*
Out of his nois° the meldrop° fast can rin;°	*nose; mucus; ran*
With lippis bla° and cheikis leine and thin,	*bluish*
The ice schoklis° that fra his hair doun hang°	*icicles; hung*
Was wonder greit° and as ane speir als lang:	*wondrously large*

24

Atouir° his belt his lyart° lokkis lay	*Around; streaked with grey*
Felterit,° unfair,° ouirfret° with froistis hoir;°	*Matted; unlovely; spangled; hoar*
His garmound° and his gyte° full gay° of gray,	*garments; mantle; lovely (ironic)*
His widderit weid° fra him the wind out woir;°	*tattered clothing; billowed out*
Ane busteous° bow within his hand he boir;°	*powerful; bore*
Under his girdill,° ane flasche° of felloun flanis,°	*belt; sheaf; cruel arrows*
Fedderit° with ice and heidit° with hailstanis.	*Feathered; tipped*

25

Than Juppiter, richt fair and amiabill,°	*good natured*
God of the starnis° in the firmament	*stars*
And nureis° to all thing generabill;	*nurse*
Fra his father Saturne far different,	
With burelie° face and browis bricht and brent;°	*handsome; smooth*
Upon his heid ane garland wonder gay	
Of flouris fair, as° it had bene in May.	*as if*

26

His voice was cleir, as cristall wer his ene,	
As goldin wyre sa glitterand was his hair,	
His garmound and his gyte full gay of grene°	*(cf. 24.3)*
With goldin listis gilt° on everie gair;°	*gilded hems; section (of garment)*
Ane burelie brand° about his middill° bair,	*imposing sword; waist*
In his richt hand he had ane groundin speir,°	*sharpened sword*
Of his father the wraith,° fra us, to weir.°	*wrath; ward off*

27

Nixt efter him, come Mars the god of ire,	
Of strife, debait° and all dissensioun,°	*dispute; discord*
To chide and fecht,° als feirs° as ony fyre,	*fight; fierce*
In hard harnes,° hewmound° and habirgeoun,°[8]	*armour; helmet; habergeon*
And on his hanche° ane roustie, fell fachioun,°[9]	*hip; rusty cruel falchion*
And in his hand he had ane roustie sword;	
Wrything° his face with mony angrie word,	*Distorting*

28

Schaikand his sword, befoir Cupide he come,	
With reid° visage, and grislie,° glowrand° ene,	*red; terrible; glowering*

8. Sleeveless coat of armour.
9. A 'falchion' is a sword with a curved blade.

And at his mouth ane bullar° stude of fome,° *bubble; foam*
Lyke to ane bair° quhetting° his tuskis kene;° *boar; whetting; sharp tusks*
Richt tuilyeour-lyke,° but° temperance, in tene° *Like a brawler; without; anger*
Ane horne he blew with mony bosteous brag,° *strident blast*
Quhilk all this warld with weir° hes maid to wag.° *in warfare; caused to shake*

29

Than fair Phebus,° lanterne and lamp of licht, *Sun-god*
Of man and beist, baith frute and flourisching,
Tender nureis° and banischer of nicht,° *nurse/nourisher; night*
And of the warld causing, be his moving
And influence, lyfe in all eirdlie thing;[10]
Without comfort of quhome, of force,° to nocht *of necessity*
Must all ga die, that in this warld is wrocht.° *made*

30

As king royall, he raid° upon his chair,° *rode; chariot*
The quhilk Phaeton° gydit sum tyme unricht;°[11] *son of Phoebus; off course*
The brichtnes of his face, quhen it was bair,° *bare/unclouded*
Nane micht behald for peirsing of° his sicht; *for fear of injuring*
This goldin cart° with fyrie bemis bricht *chariot*
Four yokkit° steidis full different of hew, *yoked*
But bait° or tyring° throw the spheiris drew. *Without halt; wearying*

31

The first was soyr,° with mane als reid as rois,° *sorrel; rose*
Callit Eoye,[12] into the orient;° *east*
The secund steid to name hecht° Ethios, *was called*
Quhitlie° and paill and sum deill ascendent;° *Whitish; rising (astronomical)*
The thrid° Peros, richt hait° and richt fervent; *third; hot*
The feird° was blak[13]—callit Philogie, *fourth*
Quhilk rollis Phebus doun° into the sey.° *downwards; sea*

32

Venus was thair present, that goddes gay—
Hir sonnis querrell° for to defend, and mak *quarrel/case*
Hir awin° complaint—cled° in ane nyce° array, *own; clad; intricate*
The ane half grene, the uther half sabill blak,
With hair as gold, kemmit and sched abak;° *parted backwards*
Bot in hir face semit° greit variance,° *appeared; changeability*
Quhyles° perfyte treuth and quhyles inconstance.° *Sometimes...sometimes inconstancy*

33

Under° smyling scho was dissimulait,° *Under cover of; deceitful*
Provocative with blenkis amorous° *amorous glances*

10. ll. 4–5: 'And through his astrological movement and influence, bringing about life in all earthly things in this (sub-lunar) world...'
11. The youthful Phaeton drove the chariot off course according to legend.
12. The four horses of the sun have different names depending on the source used. Their colours—red, white, reddish orange and black signify the different periods of the day's cycle.
13. ED. The metre allows for the pause of the speaking voice.

And suddanely changit and alterait,°	*altered*
Angrie as ony serpent vennemous,	
Richt pungitive° with wordis odious,°	*stinging; offensive*
Thus variant° scho was; quha list tak keip°—	*changeable; wishes to take note*
With ane eye lauch° and with the uther weip,	*(she) laughs*
34	
In taikning° that all fleschelie paramour,°	*As a sign; bodily love*
Quhilk Venus hes in reull and governance,°	*under rule and control*
Is sum tyme sweit, sum tyme bitter and sour,	
Richt unstabill and full of variance,	
Mingit° with cairfull° joy and fals plesance,°	*Mingled; painful; pleasure*
Now hait,° now cauld, now blyith,° now full of wo,	*hot; joyful*
Now grene as leif,° now widderit° and ago.°	*leaf; withered; departed*
35	
With buik in hand than come Mercurius,[14]	*Mercury*
Richt eloquent and full of rethorie,°	*rhetoric*
With polite termis° and delicious,°	*polished words; delightful*
With pen and ink, to report all reddie;°	*fully prepared*
Setting sangis° and singand merilie;	*Composing songs*
His hude was reid, heklit atouir his croun[15]	
Lyke to ane poeit of the auld fassoun.°	*old kind*
36	
Boxis he bair° with fyne electuairis,°	*bore; honeyed medicines*
And sugerit syropis° for digestioun,	*syrups*
Spycis belangand° to the pothecairis,°	*belonging; apothecaries*
With mony hailsum,° sweit confectioun;°	*wholesome; concoction*
Doctour in phisick,° cled in ane skarlot° goun	*science; rich/red*
And furrit weill,° as sic ane aucht° to be;	*richly adorned with fur; ought*
Honest and gude, and not ane word culd lie.°	*incapable of a lying word*
37	
Nixt, efter him, come lady Cynthia,°	*moon*
The last of all and swiftest° in hir spheir;	*(revolving) fastest*
Of colour blak, buskit°[16] with hornis twa,	*arrayed*
And in the nicht scho listis best° appeir;	*prefers to*
Haw° as the leid,° of colour nathing cleir,	*Livid; lead*
For all hir licht scho borrowis at° hir brother	*from*
Titan,° for of hir self° scho hes nane uther.	*Sun; of her own (nature)*
38	
Hir gyte° was gray and full of spottis blak,	*gown*
And on hir breist ane churle° paintit full evin,°	*rustic fellow; exactly*

14. Mercury was the messenger of the gods and, by extension, renowned for his eloquence.
15. Lit: 'Hackled around his crown'. Hackle = the long feathers on the neck of poultry. 'Croun' could simply mean the crown of the head. But the reference to ancient poets suggests the laurel wreath, worn under (fringed by) an academic hood.
16. The moon was often depicted with the two horns of a crescent attached to her head. Henryson links this with the dressing of women's hair into a horned effect.

Beirand° ane bunche of thornis on his bak,[17] *Carrying*
Quhilk for his thift° micht clim° na nar° the hevin. *theft; climb; no nearer*
Thus, quhen thay gadderit° war, thir goddes sevin, *gathered*
Mercurius thay cheisit° with ane assent *chose*
To be foirspeikar° in the parliament. *speaker/chairman*

39

Quha had bene thair and liken° for to heir *wishing*
His facound° toung and termis exquisite,° *eloquent; precious*
Of rethorik the prettick° he micht leir,° *practice; learn*
In breif sermone° ane pregnant sentence wryte,[18] *In a few words*
Befoir Cupide veiling° his cap alyte,° *doffing; slightly*
Speiris the caus of that vocatioun,° *Asks why they had been convoked*
And he,° anone,° schew° his intentioun. *he (Cupid); at once; revealed*

40

'Lo', quod Cupide, 'quha will blaspheme the name
Of his awin° god, outher in word or deid, *own/tutelary*
To all goddis he dois baith lak and schame,° *sins of omission and commission*
And suld have bitter panis° to his meid.° *punishment; reward*
I say this by yone wretchit Cresseid,
The quhilk,° throw me,° was sum tyme flour of lufe, *Who; because of me*
Me and my mother starklie can reprufe,° *vigorously reproved*

41

'Saying of hir greit infelicitie° *misfortune*
I was the caus, and my mother Venus,
Ane blind goddes hir cald° that micht not se,° *called; who could not see*
With sclander° and defame° injurious. *slander; defamation*
Thus hir leving unclene° and lecherous *her (Cresseid's) impure way of life*
Scho wald returne on° me and my mother, *turn back on/attribute to*
To quhome I schew° my grace abone° all uther. *showed; above*

42

'And sen° ye ar all sevin deificait,° *since; deified*
Participant° of devyne sapience,° *Partaking; divine wisdom*
This greit injure° done to our hie estait° *injury; rank*
Me think with pane° we suld mak recompence;° *punishment; reciprocate*
Was never to goddes° done sic violence: *gods/goddess*
Asweill for yow° as for my self I say,° *on your behalf; speak*
Thairfoir ga help to revenge, I yow pray.'

43

Mercurius to Cupide gave answeir
And said, 'Schir King, my counsall is that ye
Refer yow to the hiest planeit° heir, *highest planet*

17. The man in the moon was shown as a thief, carrying thorns. St. 37 has anticipated one reason for this—the moon steals her light from the sun.
18. 'Write down a pregnant theme'—i.e. one full of different, latent meanings.

And tak to him° the lawest of degre,° — *add to him; lowest in rank*
The pane of Cresseid for to modifie° — *assess (legal)*
As° god Saturne, with him tak Cynthia.' — *For instance*
'I am content,' quod he,° 'to tak thay twa.'° — *he (Cupid); to accept those two*

44

Than thus° proceidit Saturne and the Mone, — *in this way*
Quhen thay the mater rypelie had degest:° — *matter had maturely considered*
For the dispyte° to Cupide scho had done° — *injury...done/contempt...shown*
And to Venus—oppin° and manifest— — *open/overt*
In all hir lyfe with pane° to be opprest° — *suffering; oppressed*
And torment sair° with seiknes incurabill — *sorely tormented*
And to all lovers be abhominabill.° — *odious*

45

This duleful° sentence Saturne tuik on hand° — *dismal; took charge of*
And passit doun, quhair cairfull° Cresseid lay, — *unhappy*
And on hir heid he laid ane frostie wand;° — *rod/staff*
Than, lawfullie,° on this wyse can he say, — *in accord with legal practice*
'Thy greit fairnes and all thy bewtie gay,
Thy wantoun blude and eik thy goldin hair,
Heir I exclude° fra the for evermair. — *banish*

46

'I change thy mirth into melancholy,
Quhilk is the mother of all pensivenes;° — *thoughtfulness*
Thy moisture and thy heit in cald and dry;°[19] — *into the cold and dry*
Thyne insolence, thy play° and wantones° — *amorous sport; wantonness*
To greit diseis;° thy pomp and thy riches — *grave distress*
In mortall neid° and greit penuritie.° — *dire need; poverty/penury*
Thow suffer sall and, as ane beggar, die.'

47

O cruell Saturne, fraward° and angrie, — *harsh/aggressive*
Hard is thy dome° and to malitious.° — *judgment; too malicious*
On fair Cresseid, quhy hes thow na mercie,
Quhilk was sa sweit, gentill° and amorous?° — *genteel; loving*
Withdraw thy sentence and be gracious[20]—
As thow was never; sa schawis through thy deid,
Ane wraikfull° sentence gevin on fair Cresseid. — *vengeful*

48

Than Cynthia, quhen° Saturne past away,° — *after; left*
Out of hir sait° discendit doun belyve° — *throne; quickly*
And red ane bill° on Cresseid, quhair scho lay, — *read out a legal document*

19. The reference is to the four elemental, bodily 'humours', which were believed to determine personality.
20. Theologically, the 'grace' of Christ and the New Testament was opposed to 'justice' and the Old Testament.

Contening° this sentence diffinityve:°	*Containing; final/definitive*
'Fra heit of bodie here I the depryve	
And to thy seiknes sall be na recure°	*remedy/recovery*
Bot in dolour° thy dayis to indure.°	*grieving; live out*
49	
'Thy cristall° ene mingit° with blude I mak,	*crystal/clear; mottled*
Thy voice sa cleir unplesand, hoir° and hace,°	*rough; hoarse*
Thy lustie lyre° ouirspred with spottis blak	*beautiful complexion*
And lumpis haw° appeirand in thy face;	*livid*
Quhair thow cummis, ilk man sall fle the place.	
This° sall thow go begging fra hous to hous	*Thus*
With cop° and clapper° lyke ane lazarous.'°	*cup; leper's rattle; leper*
50	
This doolie° dreame, this uglye visioun	*doleful*
Brocht to ane end, Cresseid fra it awoik	
And all that court and convocatioun°	*assembly*
Vanischit away. Than rais scho up and tuik	
Ane poleist glas° and hir schaddow° culd luik;	*mirror; reflection*
And quhen scho saw hir face sa deformait,°	*deformed*
Gif scho in hart was wa aneuch, God wait.[21]	
51	
Weiping full sair, 'Lo, quhat it is,' quod sche,	
'With fraward° langage for to mufe° and steir°	*perverse; rouse; provoke*
Our craibit° goddis; and sa is sene on me!	*ill-natured*
My blaspheming now have I bocht° full deir;	*paid for*
All eirdlie joy and mirth I set areir.°	*put behind me*
Allace, this day; allace, this wofull tyde	
Quhen I began with my goddis for to chyde!'°	*dispute*
52	
Be° this was said, ane chyld—come fra the hall	*When*
To warn Cresseid the supper was reddy—	
First knokkit at the dure, and syne culd call,°	*called out*
'Madame, your father biddis yow cum in hy:°	*haste*
He hes mervell° sa lang on grouf° ye ly	*is astonished; prone*
And sayis your beedes° bene to lang sum deill;°	*prayers; a good deal too lengthy*
The goddis wait° all your intent full weill.'	*know*
53	
Quod scho, 'Fair chyld, ga to my father deir	
And pray him cum to speik with me anone.'°	*at once*
And sa he did and said, 'Douchter, quhat cheir?'	*how are you*
'Allace!' quod scho, 'Father, my mirth is gone!'	
'How sa?' quod he, and scho can all expone°	*explained everything*

21. 'How deeply woeful in her heart she was, God (alone) knows.'

As° I have tauld°— the vengeance and the wraik° *(Just) as; related; revenge*
For hir trespas,° Cupide on hir culd tak.° *transgression; had taken*

54

He luikit on hir uglye lipper° face, *leprous*
The quhylk° befor was quhite° as lillie flour; *Which; white*
Wringand his handis, oftymes he said, allace,
That he had levit° to se that wofull hour; *lived*
For he knew weill that thair was na succour° *help...*
To° hir seiknes, and that dowblit his pane; *...For*
Thus was thair cair aneuch° betwix thame twane. *(quite) enough distress*

55

Quhen thay togidder murnit° had full lang, *mourned*
Quod Cresseid, 'Father, I wald not be kend.° *do not wish to be recognized*
Thairfoir, in secreit wyse, ye let me gang
To yone hospitall at the tounis end,° *outskirts of the town*
And thidder sum meit° for cheritie me send, *food*
To leif° upon, for all mirth in this eird° *live; earth/world*
Is fra me gane—sic is my wickit weird!'° *cruel fate*

56

Than in ane mantill and ane baver°[22] hat, *beaver*
With cop and clapper, wonder prively,° *secretly*
He opnit ane secreit yet° and out thair at *gate*
Convoyit° hir, that na man suld espy, *Escorted*
Unto ane village half ane myle thairby;
Delyverit hir in at the spittaill hous,° *leper-house*
And daylie sent hir part of° his almous.° *a proportion of; alms*

57

Sum knew hir weill, and sum had na knawledge
Of hir becaus scho was sa deformait,° *deformed*
With bylis° blak ouirspred in hir visage *boils*
And hir fair colour faidit and alterait.
Yit thay presumit, for° hir hie regrait° *because of; noble form of lamenting*
And still° murning, scho was of nobill kin; *continued/quiet*
With better will thairfoir they tuik hir in.

58

The day passit and Phebus went to rest;
The cloudis blak ouerquhelmit° all the sky. *engulfed*
God wait gif Cresseid was ane sorrowfull gest,° *guest*
Seing that uncouth fair° and harbery!° *coarse fare; lodging*
But° meit or drink scho dressit hir° to ly *Without; prepared*
In ane dark corner of the hous allone,
And on this wyse, weiping, scho maid hir mone:° *made her lament (formulaic)*

22. Beaver hats were usually worn by men. Cressida wears one in order to be unrecognized.

The Complaint of Cresseid[23]

59

'O sop[24] of sorrow, sonkin° into cair!°	*sunk/dipped; grief*
O cative° Creisseid, now and ever mair[25]	*wretched*
Gane is thy joy and all thy mirth in eird;°	*(on) earth*
Of all thy blyithnes° now art thou blaiknit bair.°	*joy...stripped clean*
Thair is na salve may saif° or sound° thy sair.°	*cure may relieve; heal; suffering*
Fell° is thy fortoun, wickit° is thy weird.°	*Cruel; wicked; fate*
Thy blys is baneist° and thy baill on breird.°	*banished; misery bursting forth*
Under the eirth, God, gif I gravin wer,°	*if (only) I were buried*
Quhair nane of Grece nor yit of Troy micht heird!°	*hear/learn of it*

60

'Quhair is thy chalmer wantounlie besene°	*luxuriously appointed*
With burely° bed and bankouris browderit bene;°	*fine; finely embroidered seat covers*
Spycis and wyne to thy collatioun,°	*late night refreshment*
The cowpis° all of gold and silver schene,°	*goblets; bright*
Thy sweit meitis° servit in plaittis clene	*dainties*
With saipheron sals° of ane gude sessoun;°	*saffron sauce; flavour*
Thy gay garmentis with mony gudely goun,°	*many (a) handsome gown*
Thy plesand lawn° pinnit with goldin prene?°	*fine linen; pin*
All is areir,° thy greit royall renoun!°	*past; renown*

61

'Quhair is thy garding° with thir greissis° gay	*garden; plants*
And fresche flowris, quhilk the quene Floray°	*Flora (flower goddess)*
Had paintit plesandly in everie pane,°	*part*
Quhair thou was wont full merilye in May	
To walk and tak the dew be° it was day,	*as soon as*
And heir the merle° and mavis° mony ane,	*blackbird; thrush*
With ladyis fair in carrolling° to gane	*dancing and singing carols*
And se the royall rinkis° in thair array,	*warriors*
In garmentis gay garnischit° on everie grane?°	*decorated; in every particular*

62

'Thy greit triumphand fame° and hie honour,	*triumphant renown*
Quhair thou was callit of eirdlye wichtis° flour,	*earthly creatures*
All is decayit,° thy weird° is welterit° so;	*decayed; lot; turned about*
Thy hie estait is turnit in darknes dour;°	*harsh*
This lipper ludge° tak for thy burelie bour,°	*lodging; fine boudoir*
And for thy bed tak now ane bunche of stro,°	*bundle of straw*
For waillit° wyne and meitis thou had tho°	*choice; then*
Tak mowlit° breid, peirrie° and ceder° sour;	*mouldy; perry; cider*
Bot° cop and clapper now is all ago.°	*Except for; gone*

23. The lament is announced by the formula 'scho maid hir mone'. Henryson also changes to a nine-line stanza, conventionally associated with poetic complaints.
24. 'Sop' can mean both 'bread soaked in liquid', and 'the embodiment (of)'. It can, therefore, suggest nourishment physical, moral and divine (bread and wine as the body and blood of Christ).
25. Leprosy was believed to be incurable.

63

'My cleir voice and courtlie carrolling,	
Quhair I was wont with ladyis for to sing,	
Is rawk° as ruik,° full hiddeous, hoir° and hace;°	*raucous; (a) rook; rough; hoarse*
My plesand port,° all utheris precelling,°	*bearing; surpassing*
Of lustines° I was hald° maist conding°—	*youthful beauty; held; worthy*
Now is deformit the figour° of my face;	*appearance*
To luik on it na leid° now lyking hes.	*nobody*
Sowpit° in syte,° I say with sair siching,	*Immersed; sorrow*
Ludgeit amang the lipper leid,° "Allace!"	*leper folk*

64

'O ladyis fair of Troy and Grece, attend°	*pay heed to*
My miserie, quhilk nane may comprehend;	
My frivoll fortoun,° my infelicitie,°	*fickle fate; unhappiness*
My greit mischeif,° quhilk na man can amend!	*sin/misfortune*
Be war in tyme, approchis neir the end; [26]	
And, in your mynd,° ane mirrour mak of me,	*i.e. memory*
As I am now. Peradventure, that ye,	
For all your micht, may cum to that same end	
Or ellis war;° gif ony° war may be!	*worse; any (fate)*

65

'Nocht is your fairnes bot ane faiding flour,	
Nocht is your famous laud° and hie honour	*much praised fame*
Bot wind inflat in° uther mennis eiris,	*puffed into*
Your roising reid° to rotting sall retour; [27]	*rosy red complexion;*
Exempill mak of me in your memour,°	*memory*
Quhilk of sic thingis wofull witnes beiris.°	*offers a lamentable proof*
All welth in eird,° away as wind it weiris;°	*earthly prosperity; fades*
Be war, thairfoir—approchis neir your hour;	
Fortoun is fikkill° quhen scho beginnis and steiris.'° [28]	*fickle; bestirs herself*

66

Thus chydand° with hir drerie destenye,	*quarrelling*
Weiping scho woik° the nicht fra end to end;	*lay awake*
Bot all in vane. Hir dule,° hir cairfull cry	*grief*
Micht not remeid° nor yit hir murning mend.°	*remedy; resolve her lamentation*
Ane lipper lady rais and till hir wend°	*approached*
And said, 'Quhy spurnis° thow aganis the wall[29]	*kick*
To sla° thy self and mend° nathing at all?	*slay; improve*

67

'Sen° thy weiping dowbillis bot° thy wo,	*Since; only serves to double*
I counsall the mak vertew of ane neid;°	*a necessity*

26. 'Be wary at the appropriate time; death is always near.'
27. 'Will return to a state of putrefaction.'
28. The Complaint ends here and the nine-line stanza reverts to seven.
29. The image of someone kicking against a wall is used to alert Cressida to the futility and self-destructiveness of her behaviour.

Go leir° to clap thy clapper to and fro	*learn*
And leif° efter the law of lipper leid.'°	*live; the leper community*
Thair was na buit,° bot furth with thame scho yeid°	*alternative; went*
Fra place to place, quhill cauld and hounger sair	
Compellit hir to be ane rank beggair.°[30]	*out and out beggar*
68	
That samin° tyme, of Troy the garnisoun,°	*same; garrison*
Quhilk had to chiftane° worthie Troylus,	*commander*
Throw jeopardie of weir° had strikken doun	*hazard of war*
Knichtis of Grece in number mervellous.	
With greit tryumphe and laude victorious	
Agane° to Troy richt royallie thay raid°	*Back; rode*
The way quhair Cresseid with the lipper baid.°	*lived with the lepers*
69	
Seing that companie come, all with ane stevin°	*with one voice*
Thay gaif ane cry and schuik coppis gude speid,°	*energetically*
'Worthie lordis, for Goddis lufe of hevin,	
To us lipper, part° of your almous deid!'°	*give a share; almsgiving*
Than, to thair cry, nobill Troylus tuik heid,	
Having pietie,° neir by the place can pas°	*Feeling pity; passed*
Quhair Cresseid sat, not witting° quhat scho was.	*realising*
70	
Than upon him scho kest° up baith hir ene°	*cast; eyes*
And with ane blenk° it come into his thocht	*one glance*
That he sumtime hir face befoir had sene.	
Bot scho was in sic plye,° he knew hir nocht;	*plight*
Yit than, hir luik into his mynd it brocht	
The sweit visage and amorous blenking°	*glancing*
Of fair Cresseid, sumtyme° his awin darling.	*once*
71	
Na wonder was,° suppois in mynd that he	*It was no wonder that*
Tuik hir figure° sa sone. And lo, now quhy:	*Retrieved her image*
The idole° of ane thing in cace° may be	*image/figure; in (a specific) case*
Sa deip imprentit in the fantasy,°	*imagination*
That it deludis° the wittis° outwardly[31]	*evades; senses*
And sa appeiris in forme° and lyke estait°	*physical shape; condition*
Within the mynd as it was figurait.[32]	
72	
Ane spark of lufe than till his hart culd spring°	*flew*
And kendlit° all his bodie in ane fyre;	*kindled*

30. 'Rank' in Early and Middle Scots may be used, as here, with a pejorative sense.

31. While the senses rely on what they now perceive of the outside world, imagination ignores that outward evidence, working from stored, mental images drawn from the past.

32. 'As it had been inwardly conceived/shaped within the mind.' Troilus wonders whether he is seeing a phantasm.

With hait fevir, ane sweit and trimbling° *a fit of sweating and trembling*
Him tuik, quhill° he was reddie to expyre; *until*
To beir his scheild his breist began to tyre.
Within ane quhyle,° he changit mony hew° *one instance; often changed colour*
And, nevertheles, not ane ane uther knew.° *neither recognized the other*

73

For knichtlie pietie° and memoriall° *pity; remembrance*
Of fair Cresseid, ane gyrdill° can he tak, *girdle/belt*
Ane purs of gold and mony gay jowall,° *many a bright jewel*
And in the skirt of Cresseid doun can swak;° *tossed*
Than raid away—and not ane word he spak,
Pensive in hart, quhill he come to the toun—
And for greit cair, oft syis° almaist fell doun. *often*

74

The lipper folk to Cresseid than can draw° *then drew near*
To se° the equall distributioun *watch/oversee*
Of the almous. Bot quhen the gold thay saw,
Ilk ane to uther prevelie can roun° *secretly whispered*
And said, 'Yone lord hes mair affectioun,
How ever it be, unto yone lazarous° *that leper*
Than to us all; we knaw be° his almous.' *deduce from*

75

'Quhat lord is yone,' quod scho, 'have ye na feill,° *notion/idea*
Hes done to us so greit humanitie?'
'Yes,' quod a lipper man, 'I knaw him weill;
Schir Troylus it is, gentill° and fre.'° *noble; generous*
Quhen Cresseid understude° that it was he, *realized*
Stiffer° than steill° thair stert° ane bitter stound° *Tougher; steel; started up; pain*
Throwout hir hart, and fell doun to the ground.

76

Quhen scho, ouircome° with siching sair and sad, *recovered*
With mony cairfull° cry and cald ochane:°[33] *doleful; restrained cry of grief*
'Now is my breist with stormie stoundis stad,° *pangs beset*
Wrappit in wo, ane wretch full will of wane!'° *hopeless*
Than swounit scho oft or scho culd refrane,° *desist/control herself*
And ever in hir swouning cryit scho thus,
'O fals Cresseid and trew° knicht Troylus! *faithful*

77

'Thy lufe, thy lawtie° and thy gentilnes° *fidelity; nobility*
I countit small in my prosperitie,° *i.e. good fortune*
Sa elevait° I was in wantones *elevated*

33. Literally: 'cold alas'; 'ochane'—a cry of lamentation drawn from Scots and Irish Gaelic. 'Cald' is used in a manner anticipating Douglas's usage in *Conscience*, 'O hungrie ens, cursit with caris calde' (l. 22). 'Quod scho' or its equivalent is assumed.

And clam upon the fickill quheill° sa hie.   *wheel (of Fortune)*
All faith and lufe I promissit to the
Was in the self,° fickill and frivolous: *selfish*
O fals Cresseid and trew knicht Troylus!

78

'For lufe of me thow keipit continence,[34]   *remained faithful*
Honest and chaist in conversatioun;°   *conduct*
Of all wemen protectour and defence
Thou was, and helpit thair opinioun;°   *reputation*
My mynd in fleschelie, foull affectioun°   *passion*
Was inclynit to lustis lecherous:
Fy, fals Cresseid; O trew knicht Troylus!

79

'Lovers, be war and take gude heid about
Quhome that ye lufe, for quhome ye suffer paine.
I lat yow wit, thair is richt few thairout[35]
Quhome ye may traist to have trew lufe agane;°   *trust to return love faithfully*
Preif quhen° ye will, your labour is in vaine.   *Test whenever*
Thairfoir, I reid ye,° tak° thame as ye find,   *advise you; accept*
For thay ar sad° as widdercok° in wind.   *steadfast; weathercock*

80

'Becaus I knaw° the greit unstabilnes,°   *am aware of; extensive instability*
(Brukkil° as glas, into° my self I say)°   *Brittle/Fragile; for...speak*
Traisting in uther als greit unfaithfulnes,
Als unconstant and als untrew of fay[36]—
Thocht *sum*° be trew—I wait richt few ar thay.   *Although* some
Quha findis treuth, lat him his lady ruse;°   *praise*
Nane but my self, as now,° I will accuse.'   *from now on*

81

Quhen this was said, with paper scho sat doun,
And on this maneir maid hir testament:°   *solemn declaration/will*
'Heir I beteiche° my corps° and carioun°   *commit; body; corpse*
With wormis and with taidis° to be rent.°   *toads; torn*
My cop and clapper and myne ornament
And all my gold, the lipper folk sall have,
Quhen I am deid, to burie me in grave.

82

'This royall ring, set with this rubie reid,
Quhilk Troylus in drowrie° to me send,   *as a love token*

34. In Deguileville's *Pilgrimage of the Life of Man*, Bk 1. 4190–4242, Continence is seen as the third branch of Temperance. As a virtue it is set primarily against sexual temptations and so is particularly apposite for Troilus.
35. 'I'll have you know, there are scarcely any in existence (out there).'
36. ll. 3–4: 'Assuming in others the same degree of infidelity, (to be) equally inconstant and as untrue in faithfulness.'

To him agane I leif it quhen I am deid,
To mak my cairfull deid° unto him kend.° *unhappy death; known*
Thus I conclude schortlie° and mak ane end: *briefly*
My spreit° I leif to Diane,[37] quhair scho dwellis, *soul*
To walk with hir in waist woddis° and wellis.° *wild woods; streams*

83

'O Diomeid, thou hes baith broche and belt
Quhilk Troylus gave me in tokenyng° *token*
Of his trew lufe!' And, with that word, scho swelt.° *died*
And sone ane lipper man tuik of the ring,
Syne° buryit hir withouttin tarying.° *Then; delaying*
To Troylus furthwith the ring he bair° *carried*
And of Cresseid the deith he can declair.° *announced*

84

Quhen he had hard° hir greit infirmitie,° *heard of; serious illness*
Hir legacie and lamentatioun,
And how scho endit in sic povertie,
He swelt° for wo and fell doun in ane swoun; *fainted*
For greit sorrow his hart to brist° was boun;° *burst; ready*
Siching full sadlie, said, 'I can no moir;° *I can (do) no more*
Scho was untrew and wo is me thair foir.'

85

Sum said he maid ane tomb of merbell° gray *marble*
And wrait hir name and superscriptioun° *inscription above*
And laid it on hir grave, quhair that scho lay,
In goldin letteris, conteining this ressoun:° *statement*
'Lo, fair ladyis, Cresseid of Troy the toun,
Sumtyme countit the flour of womanheid,
Under this stane, lait lipper,° lyis deid.' *former leper*

86

Now, worthie° wemen, in this ballet schort,° *honourable; brief poem*
Maid for your worschip and instructioun,[38]
Of cheritie,° I monische° and exhort;[39] *Out of/regarding charity; urge*
Ming not° your lufe with fals deceptioun. *Do not mix*
Beir in your mynd° this sore conclusioun° *Remember; grievous end*
Of fair Cresseid, as I have said befoir:
Sen scho is deid, I speik of hir no moir.

37. The penitent Cressida bequeaths her once wanton soul to the goddess of chastity.
38. 'Composed in your honour and for your instruction.'
39. Two senses of this line co-exist. Either the poet has exhorted the ladies in a spirit of charity or his poem has charity as its persuasive end. 'Charity' means God's love for us and so was the highest rung on 'the ladder of love' as described by St Bernard.

§ 6 William Dunbar (c.1460–c.1520): *The Goldyn Targe*

[See also Introductions to § 7 and § 10]

While, unusually for a medieval poet, Dunbar reveals a good deal about himself in his work (see Introduction § 10), the evidence provided by records is—as in the case of Henryson—suggestive rather than precise. His latest biographers are inclined to identify him with the William Dunbar who studied at St Andrews University, taking a bachelor's degree there in 1477 and a master's in 1479. He did receive a royal pension from 1500–1513. This was, at least in part, a payment for his verse. Whether or not Dunbar took priestly orders remains a matter for debate but he is, on one occasion, referred to as a chaplain.

As 'maister poete' or laureate at the court of James IV, Dunbar was necessarily involved in the energetic attempts of that monarch to make it a European political centre, renowned for its cultural and scientific expertise. Dunbar's position guaranteed that he would prove his mastery of his chosen craft, but also implied that he was frequently commissioned to provide entertainment for the courtiers and their influential visitors. Therefore, while welcoming the direct insight he provides into the domestic and historical events of the period, one should guard against making easy assumptions about his objectivity. Also, as the recipient of a court pension, Dunbar was not always free to voice his own views, having to accommodate them to official policy. Dunbar's poetry suggests a sensitive, even touchy individual. His virtuosic mastery of Middle Scots (so highly valued by Hugh MacDiarmid) is a leitmotiv linking all three sections devoted to his work.

The Goldyn Targe *is a dream allegory, which is so intensely dramatic that links between its form and that of pageant and interlude have been highlighted by critics. Formally, Dunbar's story-line merges the waking world into the dream very cleverly. It may help interpretation to read it through ('the natural order') and then re-read it according to the 'artificial ordering'. This involves beginning with the waking world (sts. 1–5 and 28), then taking the outer circle of the dream (sts. 6–15 and 27) and lastly turning to the battle (sts. 16–26) between the Targe (Shield) of Reason and the personified forces intent on piercing its defences. The following questions may then be posed. How, if at all, does the second, 'artificial' reading alter a first impression of the poem? How are the transitions from one world to another achieved imagistically and allegorically? Why call the poem 'The Goldyn Targe', when the shield only enters the field of poetic conflict at the last stage of each reading?*

The Goldyn Targe[1]

1

Ryght as the stern of day° begouth° to schyne, — *day star; began*
Quhen gone to bed war Vesper° and Lucyne,° — *evening star; moon*
I raise° and by a rosere° did me rest; — *arose; rose bush*
Up sprang the goldyn candill matutyne,°[2] — *sun*
With clere depurit° bemes cristallyne, — *purified*
Glading° the mery foulis° in thair nest; — *Gladdening; birds*

1. ED. Copy Text: Chapman and Millar Print. The title means 'The Golden Shield'.
2. 'the golden candill matutyne.' The poem is written in the aureate terms of the High Style. Literally, 'the gold candle of the morning'. The use of gods and goddesses to represent nature is part of the aureate convention.

Or Phebus was in purpur cape revest,[3]
Up raise the lark, the hevyns menstrale° fyne, *minstrel*
In May, in till° a morow° myrthfullest. *upon; morning*

2

Full angellike thir birdis sang thair houris° *church hours/matins*
Within thair courtyns° grene in to thair bouris,° *curtains; bowers*
Apparalit° quhite and rede wyth blomes swete;° *Apparelled; fragrant flowers*
Anamalit° was the felde wyth all colouris, *Enamelled*
The perly droppis schake° in silvir schouris,° *shook; showers*
Quhill all in balme° did branch and levis flete;° *in fragrant moisture…flow*
To part fra° Phebus did Aurora grete.° *from; weep*
Hir cristall teris I saw hyng° on the flouris, *hang*
Quhilk he, for lufe, all drank up wyth his hete.° *heat*

3

For mirth of May wyth skippis and wyth hoppis,
The birdis sang upon the tender croppis° *shoots (highest)*
With curiouse° note, as Venus chapell clerkis;° *skilful; choristers*
The rosis yong, new spreding of thair knopis,° *buds*
War powderit° brycht with hevinly beriall° droppis, *spangled (heraldic); beryl*
Throu bemes° rede birnyng as ruby sperkis;° *sunbeams; flaming like small rubies*
The skyes rang for schoutyng° of the larkis, *rang with the cries*
The purpur hevyn, ourscailit in silvir sloppis,[4]
Ourgilt° the treis branchis, lef° and barkis. *Touched with gold; foliage*

4

Doune throu the ryce° a ryvir ran with stremes, *brushwood*
So lustily agayn° thai lykand lemys° *merrily facing; pleasant beams*
That all the lake as lamp° did leme of° licht, *like a lamp; gleam with*
Quhilk schadowit° all about wyth twynkling glemis, *reflected*
That bewis° bathit war in secund° bemys *boughs; secondary/returned*
Throu the reflex° of Phebus visage brycht. *reflective action*
On every syde the hegies raise on hicht,° *hedges rose on high*
The bank was grene, the bruke° was full of bremys,° *brook; breams*
The stanneris° clere as stern° in frosty nycht. *gravel; stars*

5

The cristall air, the sapher° firmament, *sapphire*
The ruby skyes of the orient
Kest° beriall bemes on emerant° bewis grene; *Cast; emerald*
The rosy garth,° depaynt° and redolent, *garden; brightly painted*
With purpur, azure, gold and goulis gent° *noble gules (heraldic red)*
Arayed was by Dame Flora,° the quene, *goddess of flowers*
So nobily° that joy was for° to sene;° *splendidly; to…behold*
The roch agayn° the rivir resplendent *Against the rock*
As low° enlumynit all the leves schene.° *flame; bright*

3. 'Before Phoebus (the sun-god) was dressed in his deep crimson cloak.'
4. 'The crimson sky, (cloud-)speckled, as with silver scales.'

6

Quhat throu° the mery foulys armony°	*Because of; harmony of birds*
And throu the ryveris soun, rycht ran me by,	
On Florais mantill° I slepit as I lay;	*cloak*
Quhare sone,° in to my dremes fantasy,°	*soon; fantasy (world of)*
I saw approch agayn the orient sky	
A saill als quhite as blossum upon spray,°	*stem*
Wyth merse° of gold brycht as the stern of day,°[5]	*top of mast; day star/sun*
Quhilk tendit° to the land full lustily	*moved towards*
As falcoune swift, desyrouse of hir pray.°	*eager for her prey*

7

And hard on burd° unto the blomyt medis°	*close at hand; meadows*
Amang the grene rispis° and the redis°	*sedge; reeds*
Arrivit sche, quhar fro anone° thare landis°	*at once; disembarks*
Ane hundreth ladyes, lusty in to wedis,°	*arrayed brightly*
Als fresch as flouris that in May up spredis,°	*sprout up*
In kirtillis grene withoutyn kell° or bandis.°	*kirtle; headbands*
Thair brycht hairis hang gleting° on the strandis°	*gleaming; shores*
In tressis° clere, wyppit° wyth goldyn thredis;	*tresses; intertwined*
With pappis quhite° and mydlis° small° as wandis.°	*white breasts; waists; slender; twigs*

8

Discrive I wald, bot quho coud wele endyte[6]	
How all the feldis wyth thai lilies quhite°	*those white lilies*
Depaynt° war brycht, quhilk to the hevyn did glete?°	*Coloured; glisten*
Noucht thou, Omer,° als fair as thou coud wryte,	*Homer*
For all thine ornate stilis° so perfyte;°	*styles; perfect*
Nor yit thou, Tullius,°[7] quhois lippis swete	*Cicero*
Off rethorike did in to termes flete.[8]	
Your aureate[9] tongis, both, bene all to lyte°	*too lightweight*
For to compile° that paradise complete.	*put together (verbally)*

9

Thare saw I Nature and Venus, quene and quene,	
The fresch Aurora and Lady Flora schene,	
Juno Appollo[10] and Proserpyna;°	*queen of underworld*
Dyane, the goddesse chaste of woddis° grene,	*woods*

5. The elements within the landscape are translated into the imaginative logic of the dream. The blossoms become the sail, the sun becomes the top-castle surrounding the mast ('merse') etc.
6. 'I would describe (all this) but who could adequately portray in verse.' Rhetorically, this is the inexpressibility branch of the modesty topos.
7. ll. 4–6: 'Omer... Tullius.' Dunbar invokes Greek and Latin authorities. Homer is not a good example of virtuoso rhetoric; Dunbar only knew of him by reputation. Cicero was known and is a fine example of 'ornate stilis'.
8. ll. 6–7: 'Whose sweet lips made the figures of rhetoric flow.'
9. 'Aureate': the golden high style, sonorous and full of Latinate compounds, archaisms and coinages.
10. The print has no comma between the names. There is, therefore, no need to accuse Dunbar of mixing his divine genders. This is Apollo's Juno or, in terms of the natural translation—the sun's sky.

My Lady Cleo, that help of makaris bene,[11]
Thetes, Pallas and prudent Minerva,
Fair feynit° Fortune and lemand° Lucina. *disguised/fickle; shining*
Thir mychti quenis in crounis mycht be sene,
Wyth bemys blith, bricht as Lucifera.° *the morning star*

10

Thare saw I May, of myrthfull monethis quene,
Betwix Aprile and June hir sistir schene,° *fair sisters*
Within the gardyng walking up and doun,
Quham of the foulis gladdith° all bedene;° *rejoice; entirely*
Scho was full tender in hir yeris grene.
Thare saw I Nature present hir a goune,° *gown*
Rich to behald° and nobil of renoune,° *behold; reputedly splendid*
Off eviry hew° under the hevin that bene,° *hue; which exists*
Depaynt and broud° be gude proporcioun. *embroidered*

11

Full lustily thir° ladyes, all in fere,° *these; together/in a company*
Enterit within this park of most plesere° *pleasure*
Quhare that I lay, ourhelit° wyth levis ronk.°[12] *covered with; dense*
The mery foulis blisfullest of chere° *mood*
Salust° Nature, me thoucht, on thair manere;° *Hailed; after their fashion*
And eviry blome° on branch and eke on bonk° *flower; also on bank*
Opnyt and spred thair balmy levis donk,° *moist*
Full low enclynyng° to thair quene so clere, *inclining/curtsying*
Quham of° thair noble norising° thay thonk.° *for; nurturing; thanked*

12

Syne,° to Dame Flora on the samyn wyse° *Then; same manner*
Thay saluse° and thay thank a thousand syse,° *give greetings; times*
And to Dame Venus, lufis mychti quene,
Thay sang ballettis in lufe,° as was the gyse,° *love lyrics; custom*
With amourouse notis lusty to devise,° *describe*
As thay that had lufe in thair hertis grene;° *green/young*
Thair hony throtis,° opnyt fro the splene,[13] *honey throats/sweet voices*
With werblis° swete did perse° the hevinly skyes *warblings; pierce*
Quhill° loud resownyt° the firmament serene. *Until; resounded*

13

Ane othir court thare saw I, consequent.° *following*
Cupide° the king wyth bow in hand ybent° *god of love; drawn*
And dredefull° arowis grundyn° scharp and square.° *fearsome; ground; squared off*

11. ll. 5–6: 'My lady Cleo, that benevolent aid to poets,' or 'My lady Cleo who is the aid of poets'. Cleo is the goddess of history; Thetis of the sea; Pallas (Greek) and Minerva (Latin) are names for the goddess of wisdom.

12. The poet overhears while concealed. The convention is that of the 'chanson d'aventure'. Cf. *Tretis of the Twa Mariit Wemen and the Wedo* § 7.

13. 'Opened from the spleen'. They are producing their voices properly, from the stomach area. Hence, 'resoundingly' or 'wholeheartedly'.

Thare saw I Mars,° the god armypotent,° *god of war; mighty in arms*
Aufull° and sterne, strong and corpolent.° *Awesome; sturdily built*
Thare saw I crabbit° Saturn,[14] ald and haire°— *ill-natured; grey-haired*
His luke° was lyke for to perturb° the aire!° *aspect; trouble; atmosphere*
Thare was Mercurius,° wise and eloquent *god of eloquence*
Of rethorike, that fand° the flouris° faire. *who discovered; embellishments*

14

Thare was the god of gardingis,° Priapus, *gardens/cultivated land*
Thare was the god of wildernes,° Phanus, *uncultivated land*
And Janus, god of entree,° delytable;° *entrance; delightful*
Thare was the god of fludis,° Neptunus, *waters*
Thare was the god of wyndis, Eolus,
With variand° luke rycht lyke a lord unstable; *changing*
Thare was Bacus,° the gladder° of the table, *god of wine; joy-bringer*
There was Pluto,° the elrich incubus,° *god of hell; elvish demon*
In cloke of grene—his court usit° no sable. *employed*

15

And eviry one of thir,° in grene arayit, *them*
On harp or lute full merily thai playit,
And sang ballettis with michty notis clere;
Ladyes to dance full sobirly assayit,° *gravely proceeded*
Endlang° the lusty ryvir so thai mayit,° *Along; celebrated May*
Thair observance rycht hevynly was to here.° *hear*
Than crap° I throu the levis and drew nere, *crept/crawled*
Quhare that I was rycht sudaynly affrayit°— *startled/(assaulted)*
All throu a luke,° quhilk I have boucht° full dere!° *because of a vision; paid for; dearly*

16

And schortly° for to speke, be lufis quene *briefly*
I was aspyit.° Scho bad° hir archearis kene° *espied; ordered; fierce*
Go me arrest and thay no tyme delayit;
Than ladyes fair lete fall thair mantillis grene,
With bowis big in tressit° hairis schene *braided*
All sudaynly thay had a felde arayit.° *prepared a battle field*
And yit, rycht gretly was I noucht affrayit,° *frightened*
The party° was so plesand for to sene.° *opposing party; behold*
A wonder lusty bikkir° me assayit°— *missile attack; tested/confronted*

17

And first of all, with bow in hand ybent,
Come Dame Beautee,[15] rycht as scho
wald me schent.° *just as if she wanted to drive me off*
Syne, folowit all hir dameselis yfere° *together*
With mony diverse aufull instrument.

14. Malevolent Saturn was the father of Jupiter. He devoured all his other children.
15. Although 'The Goldyn Targe' and the soul-battle between Reason and Beauty do not make their appearance until this stanza, they stand at the formal centre of the poem's circular dream structure. (Nature—Ship/Courts—Targe—Ship/Courts—Nature.)

Unto the pres,° Fair Having°[16] wyth hir went,	*throng; Seemly Behaviour*
Fyne Portrature,° Plesance° and Lusty Chere.°	*Appearance; Delight; Happy Mood*
Than come Resoun with schelde of gold so clere;	
In plate° and maille,° as Mars armypotent,	*plate armour; chain mail*
Defendit me that nobil chevallere.°	*knight*

18

Syne, Tender Youth come wyth hir virgyns ying,	
Grene Innocence and Schamefull Abaising,°	*Modest Bashfulness*
And Quaking Drede with Humble Obedience.	
The goldyn targe harmyt thay no thing,°	*they did not harm at all*
Curage° in thame was noucht begonne to spring.	*The force of Desire*
Full sore thay dred° to done° a violence.	*dreaded; committing*
Swete Womanhede I saw cum in presence;	
Of artilye° a warld° sche did in bring,	*artillery; world/many kinds*
Servit wyth° ladyes full of reverence.	*Displayed by*

19

Sche led wyth hir Nurture° and Lawlynes,°	*Good Breeding; Humility*
Contenence,° Patience, Gude Fame° and Stedfastnes,	*Continence; Good Reputation*
Discrecioun, Gentrise° and Considerance,°	*Gentility; Consideration*
Levefull Company° and Honest Besynes,°	*Lawful Friendship; Diligence*
Benigne Luke, Mylde Chere° and Sobirnes.°	*Mild Mood; Sobriety*
All thir bure ganyeis° to do me grevance;	*carried weapons*
Bot Resoun bure° the targe° wyth sik constance°	*bore; shield; steadfastness*
Thair scharp assayes° mycht do no dures°	*keen assaults; harm*
To me, for all thair aufull ordynance.°	*fearsome battle order*

20

Unto the pres persewit Hie Degree;°	*High Rank entered the fray*
Hir folowit ay° Estate° and Dignitee,°	*always; Rank; High Standing*
Comparisoun,° Honour and Noble Array,	*Distinction*
Will, Wantonness, Renoun and Libertee,	
Richesse, Fredome and eke Nobilitee.°	*Gentility*
Wit ye,° thay did thair baner hye° display!	*You can believe; high/proudly*
A cloud of arowis, as hayle schour,° lousit° thay[17]	*like a hail shower; let loose*
And schot quhill wastit° was thair artilye;°	*until exhausted; weaponry*
Syne went abak,° reboytit° of thair pray.°	*retreated; foiled; prey*

21

Quhen Venus had persavit° this rebute,°	*perceived; setback*
Dissymilance° scho bad° go mak persute°	*Deceptiveness; ordered; pursuit*
At all powere° to perse° the goldyn targe;	*At full force; penetrate*
And scho, that was of doubilnes the rute,°	*root of duplicity*
Askit hir° choise of archeris in refute.°[18]	*Asked for her (own); in order to repel*
Venus the best bad hir go wale at large.°	*freely select*

16. *Le Roman de la Rose* provides most of the characters in the psychomachia.
17. This is not an exaggerated image. Bowmen could fire at an extremely rapid rate.
18. Three tactical changes precede Dissymilance's victory. Beauty organizes the assault; the battle plan is founded on deceit and Dissymilance is given a free choice from among the warriors available.

Scho tuke Presence°—plicht anker° of the barge— *Physical Closeness; main anchor*
And Fair Callyng,° that wele a flayn° coud schute *Friendly Greetings; arrow*
And Cherising,° for to complete hir charge.° *Cherishing; commission*

22

Dame Hamelynes° scho tuke in company, *Familiarity*
That hardy° was and hende° in archery *bold; skilled*
And broucht Dame Beautee to the felde agayn;
With all the choise° of Venus chevalry,° *pride; battle force*
Thay come and bikkerit° unabaisitly;° *attacked; dauntlessly*
The schour of arowis rappit° on as rayn.° *drove; rain*
Perilouse° Presence, that mony syre has slayn, *Dangerous*
The bataill broucht° on bordour hard us by°— *guided; edge of the field near to us*
The salt° was all the sarar,° suth to sayn.° *assault; more bitter; truth to tell*

23

Thik was the schote of grundyn dartis kene,° *javelins ground sharp*
Bot Resoun with the scheld of gold so schene
Warly° defendit, quho so evir assayit. *Prudently*
The aufull stoure° he manly° did sustene° *conflict; manfully; endured*
Quhill Presence kest a pulder° in his ene;° *powder; eyes*
And than, as drunkyn man, he all forvayit!° *lost his way*
Quhen he was blynd, the fule° wyth hym thay playit *fool*
And banyst° hym amang the bewis grene.° *banished; to the greenwood*
That sory sicht me, sudaynly, affrayit.

24

Than was I woundit to the deth wele nere,° *well nigh*
And yoldyn° as a wofull prisonnere *handed over*
To Lady Beautee in a moment space.
Me thoucht scho semyt lustiar of chere° *her face looked more agreeable*
Efter that Resoun tynt° had his eyne clere *lost*
Than of before, and lufliare of face.
Quhy was thou blyndit, Resoun? Quhi, allace,
And gert° ane hell my paradise appere *made*
And mercy seme quhare that I fand° no grace? *found*

25

Dissymulance was besy me to sile,° *deceive*
And Fair Calling did oft apon me smyle,
And Cherising me fed wyth wordis fair.
New Acquyntance° enbracit me a quhile *Acquaintance*
And favouryt me,° quhill men mycht go a myle, *plied me with favours*
Syne tuke hir leve. I saw hir nevir mare.° *never again*
Than saw I Dangere° toward me repair, *Disdain*
I coud eschew° hir presence be no wyle;° *avoid; stratagem/device*
On syde° scho lukit° wyth ane fremyt fare° *Askance; gazed; hostile expression*

26

And at the last Departing coud hir dresse,° *got ready*
And me delyverit° unto Hevynesse° *handed me over to; Depression*

For to remayne, and scho in cure me tuke.° *took charge of me*
Be this° the lord of wyndis wyth wodenes°— *At this; madness*
God Eolus—his bugill blew, I gesse,° *guess*
That with the blast the levis all to-schuke;° *quivered violently*
And sudaynly, in the space of a luke,
All was hyne went;° thare was bot wildernes; *Everything dispersed*
Thare was no more bot° birdis, bank and bruke.° *nothing else but; brook*

27

In twynklyng of ane eye to schip thai went,
And swyth° up saile unto the top° thai stent° *immediately; top-castle; stretched*
And with swift course atour° the flude° thai frak.° *over; water; moved quickly*
Thai fyrit gunnis wyth powder violent
Till that the reke raise° to the firmament. *smoke rose*
The rochis° all resownyt° wyth the rak,° *rocks; resounded; shock*
For rede° it semyt that the raynbow brak.° *Because of the noise; shattered*
With spirit affrayde apon my fete I sprent,° *leapt*
Amang the clewis° so carefull° was the crak.° *cliffs; grievous; explosion*

28

And as I did awake of my sweving,° *dream/vision*
The joyful birdis merily did syng
For myrth of Phebus tendir bemes schene.
Swete war the vapouris,° soft the morowing,° *mists; morning*
Halesum° the vale depaynt° wyth flouris ying, *Wholesome; painted*
The air attemperit,° sobir° and amene.° *temperate; mild; pleasant*
In quhite and rede was all the felde besene,° *arrayed*
Throu Naturis nobil fresch anamalyng° *enamelling*
In mirthfull May, of eviry moneth quene.° *of all months queen*

29

O reverend Chaucere, rose of rethoris° all *rhetoricians*
(As in oure tong° ane flour imperiall)° *vernacular; most excellent*
That raise in Britane evir, quho redis rycht,° *(for) anyone who interprets well*
Thou beris of makaris the tryumph riall;° *bear the victor's crown among poets*
Thy fresch anamalit termes celicall° *polished figures divine (rhet.)*
This mater° coud illumynit have° full brycht. *topic; have shed light upon*
Was thou noucht of oure Inglisch°[19] all the lycht, *English tongue*
Surmounting° eviry tong terrestriall,° *Surpassing; earthly*
Alls fer as Mayes morow dois mydnycht?

30

O morall Gower and Ludgate laureate,° *Lydgate crowned with laurels*
Your sugurit lippis and tongis aureate° *aureate (n. 9)*
Bene to oure eris cause of grete delyte.
Your angel mouthis most mellifluate° *mellifluous*
Oure rude° langage had clere illumynate° *crude; enlightened*

19. The Scots language developed from Northumbrian. It was, therefore, a dialect of English.

And fair ourgilt° oure spech, that imperfyte° — *beautifully gilded over; imperfect*
Stude, or° your goldyn pennis schupe° to write; — *before; prepared/were created*
This ile before was bare and desolate
Of rethorike or lusty fresch endyte.° — *writing*

31

Thou, lytill quair,° be evir obedient, — *book/poem*
Humble, subject° and symple of entent° — *servile; intent*
Before the face of eviry connyng wicht.° — *learned person*
I knaw quhat thou of rethorike hes spent; [20]
Off all hir lusty rosis redolent
Is none in to thy gerland sett on hicht.° — *on high*
Eschame thar of° and draw the out of sicht. — *Be ashamed at that*
Rude is thy wede,°[21] disteynit,° bare and rent;° — *garb; stained; torn*
Wele aucht thou° be aferit° of the licht. — *You ought with reason; frightened*

20. 'I know what you have expended by way of eloquence...' In this variant on the usual modesty topos, Dunbar does not deny all knowledge of rhetoric.
21. Language was conventionally referred to as the clothing of thought. Cf. § 23 Alexander, *Anacrisis*.

§ 7 William Dunbar (c.1460–c.1520): *The Tretis of the Twa Mariit Wemen and the Wedo*

[See also Introductions to § 6 and § 10]

The Tretis *is Dunbar's longest poem. It is based on the* chanson de mal mariée *form as practised by Chaucer in the* **Wife of Bath's** *and* **Miller's Tales**. *Dunbar had read these but he chooses to turn his treatment of the theme into a debate form, led by the redoubtable widow as mistress of ceremonies. After an apparently idealistic opening (1–40), the three women in turn lament the inadequacy of their husbands. While the wives are still trapped within the marriage bond and so can only complain and vituperate (49–149; 157–238) the widow has used her experience with two husbands (270–95; 296–409) to work out a fully-formulated strategy of manipulation and sovereignty (245–69; 410–504).*

The poem satirizes husbands through statement and wives through enactment. It is, therefore, a powerful indictment of medieval marriage. This tended to be an economic arrangement in which women became part of a property deal. As warfare dominated, husbands were often away from home for long periods. Absence provided an opportunity, especially for noble ladies, to look elsewhere. The code of courtly love, whose freedoms the wives covet and whose conventions the widow skilfully manipulates, offered a model of behaviour to fill that gap. Passionate, idealized, secret and adulterous, it transferred sovereignty from man to woman.

The Tretis *follows an overlapping structure. Each contribution to the debate takes up the arguments and imagery which have dominated the previous one, but moves beyond them. To understand the care with which Dunbar 'makes' his verse, it is, therefore, in this case especially instructive to look at the images used by all three characters (e.g. the bonds/chains of marriage; the human as beast) to see if they are employed in the same way or to the same effect. Similarly, the gradually developing arrangement of the three parallel cases highlights any new image lines introduced by a later speaker. Why does the second wife, for example, introduce a series of images and antitheses emphasising the difference between appearance and reality when the first wife had felt no need to do so? Do such additions affect our view of the poem? Most pertinently of all, given the injunction to makars to relate form and meaning carefully, was Dunbar wise to organize his debate on marriage and sovereignty in this way?*

The Tretis of the Twa Mariit Wemen and the Wedo

Apon the midsummer evin,° mirriest° of nichtis,	*evening; merriest*
I muvit° furth allane in meid° as midnicht wes past,	*walked; meadow*
Besyd ane gudlie° grein garth,° full of gay flouris,	*pleasant; garden*
Hegeit of° ane huge hicht° with hawthorne treis,	*Hedged to; height*
Quhairon ane bird on ane bransche so birst out° hir notis	*poured out*
That never ane blythfullar° bird was on the beuche° hard.°	*more joyful; bough; heard*
Quhat throw° the sugurat° sound of hir sang glaid	*What with; sugared/sweet*
And throw the savour sanative° of the sweit flouris,	*restorative*
I drew in derne to the dyk to dirkin efter mirthis.[1]	

1. ED. Copy Text: Maitland Folio 1–103; 'Rouen' Print 104–530. 'I drew secretly towards the wall—to lie low after revelry' or 'in the hope of revelry'.

The dew donkit° the daill, and dynnit the feulis.° — *darkened; birds sang loudly*
I hard, under ane holyn° hevinlie grein hewit,° — *holly tree; coloured*
Ane hie speiche° at my hand with hautand° wourdis. — *loud talking; haughty*
With that, in haist, to the hege° so hard I inthrang° — *hedge; thrust myself*
That I was heildit° with hawthorne and with heynd° leveis. — *enclosed/concealed; pleasant*
Throw pykis° of the plet° thorne I presandlie° luikit, — *spikes; intertwined; quickly*
Gif ony persoun wald approche within that plesand° garding.° — *pleasant; garden*
I saw thre gay ladeis sit in ane grein arbeir,°[2] — *arbour*
All grathit° in to garlandis of fresche gudlie flouris. — *adorned*
So glitterit° as the gold wer° thair tressis° — *glittered; wire; tresses*
Quhill° all the gressis° did gleme of the glaid° hewis; — *Until; plants; lovely*
Kemmit° war thair cleir hair and curiouslie sched° — *Combed; artfully parted*
Attour° thair schulderis doun,° schyre° schyning full bricht — *Around...and over; radiantly*
With curches cassin° thair abone° of kirsp° cleir and thin. — *kerchiefs arranged; above; a fine fabric like gauze*
Thair mantillis° grein war as the gres that grew in May sessoun, — *mantles*
Fetrit° with thair quhyt° fingaris about thair fair sydis. — *Fastened; white*
Off ferlifull° fyne favour° war thair faceis meik,° — *wondrous; aspect; meek*
All full of flurist fairheid° as flouris in June— — *ripe beauty*
Quhyt, seimlie° and soft as the sweit lillies, — *fine/decorous*
Now upspred upon spray° as new spynist° rose, — *stem; newly opened*
Arrayit ryallie° about with mony riche vardour,° — *royally; greenery*
That Nature full nobillie annamalit°[3] with flouris — *enamelled*
Off alkin° hewis under hevin that ony heynd° knew, — *every kind of; genteel person*
Fragrant, all full of fresche odour, fynest of smell.
Ane cumlie tabil coverit wes° befoir tha° cleir ladeis — *fine table was laid out; those*
With ryalle cowpis° apon rawis,° full of ryche wynis. — *ornate goblets; in rows*
And of thir° fair wlonkes° twa weddit war with lordis, — *those; beauties*
Ane was ane wedow, iwis,° wantoun° of laitis.° — *in fact; free; manners*
And, as thai talk at the tabill of mony taill sindry,° — *different*
Thay wauchtit at the wicht wyne and waris out wourdis,[4]
And syn thai spak more spedelie° and sparit no matiris.° — *quickly; no themes were excluded (i.e. no censorship)*

'Bewrie,'° said the wedo, 'ye woddit° wemen ying,° — *Reveal; wedded; young*
Quhat mirth ye fand° in maryage sen ye war menis wyffis.° — *have discovered; men's wives*
Reveill gif ye rewit° that rakles conditioun,° — *rued; calm/reckless state*[5]

2. The setting, with hidden narrator and enclosed garden, suggests the French 'chanson d'aventure' mode and, therefore, a tale of noble love.
3. When Nature has this crystalline aspect in late medieval poetry, divine topics usually follow.
4. 'They took deep gulps at the strong wine and let their words drawl out.'
5. The widow, like an oracle, uses words which may be interpreted in different ways. Here, 'rakles' may either mean 'without rush or strain' or the very opposite, 'reckless'.

Or gif that ever ye luffit leyd upone lyf° mair *any living man; more…*
Nor thame, that° ye your fayth hes festinit° for ever, *…Than those to whom; has bound*
Or gif ye think, had ye chois,[6] that ye wald cheis° better. *choose*
Think ye it nocht ane blist band° that bindis so fast,° *blessed bond/ring; tight*
That none undo it a deill° may bot the deith ane?"° *in the slightest; death alone*

Than spak ane lusty° belyf° with lustie effeiris:° *fair one; at once; bearing*
'It that ye call the blist band that bindis so fast
Is bair° of blis and bailfull° and greit barrat wirkis.° *empty; wretched; creates great misery*
Ye speir,° had I fre chois, gif I wald cheis bettir? *ask*
Chenyeis° ay ar to eschew° and changeis ar sweit. *Chains; be avoided*
Sic cursit chance° till eschew had I my chois anis,° *fortune; once more*
Out of the cheinyeis of ane churle° I chaip° suld for evir. *boor; escape*
God gif° matrimony wer made to mell° for ane yeir! *grant; entwine*
It war bot merrens° to be mair bot gif° our myndis pleisit. *misery; except when*
It is agane the law of luf, of kynd° and of nature, *the species*
Togidder hartis to strene° that stryveis° with uther. *force; battle*
Birdis hes ane better law na bernis° be meikill, *than men*
That ilk yeir with new joy joyis ane maik° *rejoice in a mate*
And fangis° thame ane fresche feyr,° unfulyeit° and constant, *catch; lover; vigorous*
And lattis thair fulyeit° feiris flie quhair thai pleis.[7] *wearied (sexually)*
Cryst gif° sic ane consuetude° war in this kith° haldin. *grant; such a régime; realm*
Than weill war° us wemen that evir we war born. *Then it would be well (for)*
We suld have feiris as fresche to fang° quhen us likit° *prey on/capture; pleased*
And gif all larbaris° thair leveis quhen thai lak curage.° *impotent men; vigour*
My self suld be full semlie in silkis arrayit,
Gymp,° jolie and gent,° richt joyus and gent. *Graceful; elegant*
I suld at fairis° be found new faceis to se, *fairs*
At playis and at preichingis° and pilgrimages greit,° *sermons; large*
To schaw my renone royaly° quhair preis° was of folk, *illustriousness regally; a crowd*
To manifest° my makdome° to multitude of pepill *show off; comeliness*
And blaw my bewtie on breid° quhair bernis° war mony, *display my beauty; men*
That I micht cheis° and be chosin and change quhen me lykit. *choose*
Than suld I waill° ane full weill° our° all the wyd realme *select; one of good quality; over*
That suld my womanheid° weild° the lang winter nicht, *womanliness; use (sexually)*
And quhen I gottin had ane grome° ganest of uther,° *fellow; the fittest of all*
Yaip° and ying, in the yok° ane yeir for to draw,° *Bold; yoke; drive (like an ox)*
Fra° I had preveit his pith° the first plesand moneth, *Once; had tested his virility*

6. In medieval marriage, the woman seldom did have a choice. Most were arranged for economic rather than romantic reasons.
7. Birds were believed to change their mates every year. They were often used poetically as images of freer love arrangements.

Than suld I cast me° to keik° in kirk and in markat, *set myself; to look secretly*
And all the cuntre about, kyngis court and uther,
Quhair I ane galland° micht get aganis° the nixt yeir *gallant; in preparation for*
For to perfurneis furth° the werk° quhen *carry on; business;*
failyeit° the tother: *flagged*
A forky fure, ay furthwart and forsy in draucht,[8]
Nother febill nor fant° nor fulyeit° in labour, *faint; exhausted*
Bot als fresche° of his forme as flouris in May. *youthful*
For all the fruit suld I fang,° thocht he the flour *receive;*
burgeoun.° *cause to burst forth*
I have ane wallidrag,° ane worme, ane auld *worthless man;*
wobat carle,°[9] *hairy caterpillar of a churl*
A waistit wolroun° na worth bot wourdis to clatter,° *wasted wild boar; gibber*
Ane bumbart,° ane dronbee,° ane bag full of flewme,° *lazy chap; drone; phlegm*
Ane scabbit skarth,° ane scorpioun, ane *scabby monster;*
scutarde behind.° *bum shitter*
To se him scart° his awin skyn, grit scunner° I think. *scratch; source of disgust*
Quhen kissis me that carybald,° than kyndillis° all my sorow. *brute; starts up*
As birs° of ane brym bair° his berd° is als stif, *bristle; fierce boar; beard*
Bot soft and soupill° as the silk is his sary lume.° *supple; pathetic tool/penis*
He may weill to the syn assent,° bot sakles° *consent to the sin; guiltless*
is his deidis.
With gor° his twa grym ene° ar gladderit° all about, *slime; grim eyes; besmeared*
And gorgeit° lyk twa gutaris° that war *clogged up; gutters;*
with glar stoppit.°[10] *stuffed full of filth*
Bot quhen that glowrand gaist° grippis° me about, *goggling ghost; seizes*
Than think I hiddowus Mahowne° hes me *hideous Mahomet (= the Devil)*
in armes.
Thair ma na sanyne° me save fra that auld Sathane, *making the sign of the Cross*
For, thocht I croce me° all cleine° fra the *cross myself; all over;*
croun° doun,[11] *top of my head*
He wil my corse° all beclip° and clap° to his breist. *body; embrace; draw quickly*
Quhen schaiffyn° is that ald schaik° with a scharp rasour *shaven; old rascal*
He schowis° on me his schewill° mouth and *thrusts; distorted;*
schendis° my lippis, *forces apart*
And with his hard hurcheone scyn° sa heklis° he my *hedgehog skin; rakes*
chekis
That, as a glemand gleyd,° glowis my chaftis.° *glowing ember; jaws*
I schrenk° for the scharp stound,° bot schout *shrink; sharp pain;*
dar° I nought, *dare*
For schore° of that auld schrew,° schame him betide. *menace; old wretch*
The luf blenkis° of that bogill° fra his blerde° ene *love glances; hobgoblin; bleary*

8. 'A powerful creature, always up front and strong in driving.' Dunbar's language continues the man/ox image while suggesting powerful virility.
9. The first wife's erotic imaginings come face to face with reality as she contemplates her old and impotent husband. The colloquial and vituperative language of the alliterative, staccato low style takes over entirely.
10. His impotence having been dealt with in penitential terms of assent and action, the old husband is now described in the images of decay and decomposition favoured in the medieval death lyric.
11. ED. The Print begins here.

(As° Belzebub had on me blent°) abasit° my spreit. *As if; gazed; depressed*
And quhen the smy° on me smyrkis° with his smake smolet° *knave; smirks; rogue's muzzle*
He fepillis like a farcy aver, that flyrit in a gillot.[12]
Quhen that the sound of his saw° sinkis in my eris,° *speech; ears*
Than ay renewis my noy° or° he be neir cumand.° *annoyance; before; approaches*
Quhen I heir nemmyt° his name than mak I nyne crocis° *named; nine signs of the cross*
To keip° me fra the cummerans° of that carll mangit,° *guard; distress; crazed churl*
That full of eldnyng° is and anger and all evill thewis.° *jealousy; habits*
I dar nought luke to° my luf for that lene gib.° *glance at; scrawny tom-cat*
He is sa full of jelusy and engyne fals,° *false scheming*
Ever ymagynyng° in mynd[13] materis of evill, *imagining*
Compasand° and castand cacis° a thousand, *Encompassing; inventing ways*
How he sall tak me with a trawe,° at trist° of ane othir. *catch me out with a trick; tryst*
I dar nought keik to° the knaip° that the cop° fillis, *glance at; manservant; cup*
For eldnyng of that ald schrew that ever on evill thynkis.
For he is waistit and worne fra Venus werkis° *acts of love*
And may nought beit worth a bene in bed of my mystirs.[14]
He trowis° that young folk I yerne yeild° for he gane is,° *believes; I long to give myself to; is past it*
Bot I may yuke° all this yer,° or his yerd° help. *itch; this entire year; penis*
Ay quhen that caribald° carll wald clym on° my wambe,° *monstrous; mount; womb*
Than am I dangerus° and daine° and dour° of my will. *disdainful; haughty; obstinate*
Yit leit I never that larbar° my leggis ga betwene *impotent fellow*
To fyle° my flesche na fummyll° me without a fee gret,° *defile; nor fumble; large payment*
And thoght his pen° purly° me payis in bed, *penis; poorly*
His purse pays richely in recompense efter.
For, or° he clym on my corse,° that carybald forlane,° *before; body; useless freak*
I have conditioun of a curche, of kersp allther fynest,[15]
A goun° of engranyt claith° right gaily furrit, *gown; dyed scarlet cloth*
A ring with a ryall stane° or other riche jowell, *costly gemstone*
Or rest of° his rousty raid,° thoght he wer rede wod.° *Or (he could) forget; crude assault; steaming mad*
For all the buddis° of Johne Blunt° quhen he abone clymis° *bribes; this fool; gets on top*
Me think the baid° deir aboucht,° sa bawch° ar his werkis,° *delay; dearly purchased; feeble; (sexual) efforts*
And thus I sell him solace,° thoght I it sour° think. *peddle him his pleasure; bitter*

12. 'He makes his lower lip protrude like a diseased horse, leering at a mare.'
13. The imagination was distinguished from the senses by taking its images from within the mind's memory rather than from present sights and sounds.
14. 'And what he does to relieve my sexual needs in bed is not worth a bean.'
15. 'I get, as pre-condition, a kerchief made of the very finest gauze...'

Fra sic a syre° God yow saif,° my sweit sisteris deir! *fellow; preserve*
Quhen that the semely° had said hir sentence° to end, *lovely lady (ironic); speech*
Than all thai leuch apon loft° with latis° full mery, *laughed aloud; gestures*
And raucht° the cop round about, full of riche wynis, *handed*
And ralyeit° lang or thai wald rest with ryatus° speche. *joked; rebellious*

The wedo° to the tothir wlonk° warpit° thir wordis: *widow; beauty; tossed out*
'Now, fair sister, fallis yow° but fenying° to tell. *it's your turn; without pretence*
Sen man ferst with matrimony yow menkit° in kirk, *joined with you*
How haif ye farne,° be your faith, confese us the treuth— *fared*
That band° to blise° or to ban,° quhilk yow best thinkis,° *bond; bless; curse; seems*
Or how ye like lif to leid° into lell spousage?° *to lead your life; lawful matrimony*
And syne° my self ye exem° on the samyn wise,° *then; you may examine me; way*
And I sall say furth the south,° dissymyland° no word.' *truth; dissembling*

The plesand° said, 'I protest,° the treuth gif I schaw, *agreeable soul; I demur unless*
That of your toungis ye be traist.'° The tothir twa grantit.° *trustworthy; consented*
With that sprang up hir spreit° be a span hechar.°[16] *mood; span higher*
'To speik,' quod scho, 'I sall nought spar.° Ther is no spy neir.° *spare; no spy at hand (ironic)*
I sall a ragment° reveil fra rute° of my hert, *catalogue; depths*
A roust° that is sa rankild° quhill risis° my stomok. *rancour; festering; heaves*
Now sall the byle° all out brist,° that beild° has so lang. *bile; burst; suppurated*
For it to beir° on my breist° wes berdin° our° hevy. *carry; breast; burden; too*
I sall the venome devoid° with a vent° large, *poison expel; discharge*
And me assuage° of the swalme° that swellit wes gret. *relieve myself; bulge*
My husband wes a hur maister,° the hugeast° in erd. *client of whores; greatest*
Tharfor I hait him with my hert, sa help me our Lord.
He is a young man, ryght yaip° bot nought in youth flouris, *quick (body and mind)*
For he is fadit full far and feblit of strenth.° *impotent*
He wes as flurising fresche within this few yeris,[17]
Bot he is falyeid° full far and fulyeid° in labour. *has degenerated; wasted*
He has bene lychour° so lang quhill lost is his natur,° *lecher; vigour*
His lume° is waxit larbar° and lyis into swoune.° *tool; grown tired; has passed out*
Wes never sugeorne wer set na on that snaill tyrit,[18]
For efter sevin oulkis° rest it will nought rap anys.° *weeks; drive in once*
He has bene waistit apon wemen or° he me wif chesit,° *before; chose*
And in adultre° in my tyme I haif him tane° oft; *adultery; caught*
And yit he is als brankand° with bonet on syde,° *as proud; at an angle*
And blenkand to° the brichtest° that in the burgh dwellis; *winking at; prettiest (women)*

16. I.e. 'She became noticeably brighter'.
17. 'Only a few years ago, he was as youthfully promising as the new blossom (on plant or flower).'
18. 'Abstinence was never worse wasted than it is on that tired snail [i.e. penis].'

Alse curtly° of his clething° and kemmyng° of his haris,° — *elegant; dress; combing; hair*
As he that is mare valyeand° in Venus chalmer.° — *valiant; bed chamber (i.e. vagina)*
He semys to be sumthing worth, that syphyr in bour,° — *bedroom cipher/zero*
He lukis as he wald luffit be, thoght he be litill of valour.° — *worth*
He dois as dotit° dog that damys° on all bussis,° — *idiotic; urinates; bushes*
And liftis his leg apon loft° thoght he nought list pische.° — *on high; want to piss*
He has a luke° without lust° and lif without curage.° — *looks...being lustful; desire*
He has a forme° without force° and fessoun° but vertu,° — *fair shape; vigour; appearance; potency*
And fair wordis but effect,° all fruster of° dedis. — *result; without any fruition in*
He is for ladyis in luf a right lusty schadow,° — *shadow/companion*
Bot into derne° at the deid he salbe drup fundin.° — *in private; found drooping*
He ralis° and makes repet° with ryatus wordis,° — *rails; uproar; extravagant claims*
Ay rusing him° of his radis° and rageing in chalmer.° — *boasting; forays (sexual); rampaging around the bedroom*
Bot God wait quhat I think, quhen he so thra° spekis — *wildly*
And how it settis him so syde° to sege° of sic materis. — *little it befits him; boast*
Bot gif him self, of sum evin, myght ane say amang thaim;
Bot he nought ane is, bot nane of naturis possessoris.[19]
Scho that has ane auld man nought all is begylit;° — *is not totally deceived*
He is at Venus werkis na war na° he semys. — *no worse than*
I went° I josit° a gem and I haif geit° gottin. — *thought; possessed; black bead*
He had the glemyng of gold and wes bot glase° fundin. — *mere glass*
Thought men be ferse°—wele I fynd fra falye° ther curage°— — *fierce; afterwards declines; prowess*
Thar is bot eldnyng° and anger ther hertis within. — *envy*
Ye speik of berdis on bewch°—of blise may thai sing, — *birds on the bough*
That on Sanct Valentynis day ar vacandis[20] ilk yer.° — *every year*
Hed I that plesand prevelege,° to part° quhen me likit, — *agreeable privilege; separate*
To change and ay to cheise agane, than chastite adew!
Than suld I haif a fresch feir° to fang° in myn armys. — *new mate; clasp*
To hald a freke° quhill he faynt° may foly be calit. — *hold on to a fellow; weaken*
Apone sic materis I mus° at mydnycht full oft — *muse*
And murnys° so in my mynd I murdris° my selfin. — *grieve; torment to death*
Than ly I walkand for wa° and walteris° about, — *awake for woe; toss*
Wariand° oft my wekit kyn° that me away cast,° — *Cursing; wicked kinfolk; cast off*
To sic a craudoune but curage that knyt my cler bewte,
And ther so mony kene knyghtis this kenrik within.[21]
Than think I on a semelyar,° the suth° for to tell, — *more comely one; truth*
Na° is our syre be sic sevin.° With that I syth° oft. — *Than; seven times; Then I sigh*

19. ll. 197–8: 'Unless he might, one evening, achieve even one of them ['materis']. But he is a nothing, without any potency at all.'
20. Literally—'are vacant estates'. That is, on St Valentine's day, they expel their old mate and invite a new one into their home.
21. ll. 215–6: 'Who joined my fair beauty to such a feckless coward with so many bold knights within this kingdom.'

Than he° ful tenderly dois turne to me in his tume° person, *Then he (husband); empty*
And with a yoldin yerd° dois yolk° me in armys, *exhausted twig (penis); grasps*
And sais, "My soverane sweit thing, quhy sleip ye no betir?
Me think ther haldis yow a hete,° as ye sum harme alyt."° *you've got a fever brewing; sickness suffered*
Quod I, "My hony,° hald abak° and handill me nought sair. *Honey/Sweetie; hold off*
A hache° is happinit hastely° at my hert rut."° *ache; suddenly; deep in my heart*
With that I seme for to swoune,° thought I na swerf tak,° *swoon; don't pass out*
And thus beswik° I that swane° with my sweit wordis. *hoodwink; fellow*
I cast on him a crabit e° quhen cler day is cummyn, *crabbed eye*
And lettis° it is luf blenk° quhen he about glemys.° *pretend; fond glance; looks round*
I turne it in tender luke that I in tene warit,° *shot (at him) in anger*
And him behaldis hamely° with hertly° smyling. *intimately; heartfelt*
I wald° a tender peronall° that myght na put thole,° *wish; delicate young girl; no thrusting endure*
That° hatit men with hard geir° for hurting of flesch, *Who; stiff equipment*
Had my gud man to hir gest,° for—I dar God swer— *guest (in body)*
Scho suld not stert° for his straik° a stray breid° of erd!° *flinch; stroke; a straw's breadth; ground*
And syne I wald that ilk band,° that ye so blist° call *same bond; blessed*
Had bund him so to that bryght° quhill° his bak werkit,° *fair one; so long as back heaved (copulation)*
And I wer in a beid broght with berne° that me likit. *taken to bed by a man*
I trow that bird of my blis suld a bourd want.'[22]

Onone° quhen this amyable had endit hir speche, *Forthwith*
Loudly lauchand, the laif allowit hir mekle.° *the rest commended her greatly*
Thir gay wiffis° maid gam° amang the grene leiffis.° *wives; sport; leaves*
Thai drank and did away dule° under derne bewis,° *dispelled misery; concealing boughs*
Thai swapit of° the sweit wyne, thai swanquhit° of hewis. *tossed off; swan-white (formulaic)*
Bot all the pertlyar, in plane, thai put out thar vocis.[23]

Than said the weido: 'I wis° ther is no way othir.° *see; other*
Now tydis° me for to talk. My taill° it is nixt. *betides; tale*
God my spreit now inspir and my speche quykkin,° *invigorate/enliven*
And send me sentence° to say substantious° and noble, *theme; weighty*
Sa that my preching may pers° your perverst° hertis, *pierce; perverse*
And mak yow mekar° to men in maneris and conditiounis.° *meeker; disposition*
I schaw yow,° sisteris in schrift,° I wes schrew ever° *admit to you; sister confessors; always a scold*

22. Literally: 'I believe that maiden of my joy should lack a joke'. Probably 'blis' refers ironically to her husband. If so, the line would mean that, having no earlier lovers with whom to compare him, the young girl would not find his weak efforts laughable.
23. 'But ever more boldly their voices sounded out clearly into the open countryside.'

Bot I wes schene in my schrowd° and schew me° innocent; *brightly robed; presented myself*
And thought I dour° wes and dane,° dispitois° and bald,° *sullen; haughty; contemptuous; forward*
I wes dissymblit suttelly° in a sanctis liknes° *subtly disguised; image of a saint*
I semyt sober and sweit and sempill° without fraud, *innocent*
Bot I couth sexty dissaif,° that suttillar wer haldin.° *deceive sixty; considered*
Unto my lesson ye lyth° and leir at° me wit,° *give ear; learn from; wisdom*[24]
Gif you nought list be forleit with° losingeris untrew:° *have no wish to be abandoned by; false flatterers*
Be constant in your governance° and counterfeit gud maneris, *conduct*
Thought ye be kene,° inconstant and cruell of mynd. *fierce*
Thought ye as tygris be terne,° be tretable° in luf, *fierce as tigers; tractable*
And be as turtoris° in your talk, thought ye haif talis brukill.° *turtle doves; frail tails (sexual)*
Be dragonis baith and dowis° ay in double forme, *doves*
And quhen it nedis yow° onone° note baith ther stranthis.° *you need to; at once; employ both their strengths*
Be amyable with humble face as angellis apperand,° *appearing*
And with a terrebill° tail be stangand° as edderis.° *fearsome; stinging; adders*
Be of your luke like innocentis, thoght ye haif evill myndis.
Be courtly° ay in clething and costly° arrayit— *elegant; expensively*
That hurtis yow nought worth a hen, yowr husband pays for all.
Twa husbandis haif I had; thai held me baith deir.[25]
Thought I dispytit° thaim agane,° thai spyt° it na thing. *despised; in return; suspected*
Ane wes ane hair hogeart that hostit out flewme.[26]
I hatit him like a hund,° thought I it hid preve.° *hound; kept it hidden*
With kissing and with clapping I gert the carill fon.[27]
Weil couth I claw° his cruke bak° and kemm° his kewt noddill,° *scratch; humped back; comb; shaven head*
And with a bukky° in my cheik bo on° him behind, *tongue; boggle at*
And with a bek° gang about and bler° his ald e,° *curtsy; blur; eye*
And with a kyind contynance° kys his crynd° chekis, *kindly expression; withered*
Into my mynd makand mokis° at that mad fader,° *mocking gestures; father*
Trowand° me with trew lufe to treit° him so fair. *Believing; to be dealing with*
This cought° I do without dule° and na dises tak,° *could; grief; get no distress*
Bot ay be mery in my mynd and myrthfull of cher.° *demeanour*
I had a lufsummar leid° my lust for to slokyn,° *more lovable man; slake*
That couth° be secrete and sure and ay saif° my honour, *knew how to; safeguard*
And sew° bot at certane tymes and in sicir° placis. *woo; safe*
Ay quhen the ald did me anger with akword° wordis, *bad-tempered*
Apon the galland° for to goif° it gladit me agane. *gallant; gaze*
I had sic wit that for wo weipit I litill,
Bot leit the sweit ay the sour to gud sesone° bring. *flavour*

24. 'Wit' is used precisely, meaning 'practical knowledge', 'stratagems'.
25. Double sense of 'They both valued me highly' and 'They both embraced me at a cost'.
26. 'One was a grey-haired geriatric, who coughed up phlegm.'
27. 'With kissing and with caressing I make the fellow act the fool.'

Quhen that the chuf° wald me chid° with	*boor; chide;*
girnand chaftis,°	*grimacing jaws*
I wald him chuk,° cheik° and chyn,° and	*fondle; cheek; chin;*
cheris° him so mekill	*cherish*
That his cheif chymys° he had	*manor;*
chevist to° my sone,	*would have provided for*
Supos the churll wes gane chaist or° the child wes	*become chaste before;*
gottin.°	*begotten*
As wis woman ay I wrought° and not as wod fule,°	*contrived; mad fool*
For mar° with wylis° I wan° na wichtnes of handis.°	*more; wiles; won; blows*
Syne maryt I° a merchand, myghti of gudis.°	*Next I married; i.e. wealthy*
He wes a man of myd eld° and of mene° statur;	*middle age; short*
Bot we na fallowis° wer in frendschip° or blud,°	*equals; kinship; blood/breeding*
In fredome na furth bering° na fairnes of persoune—	*nor conduct*
Quhilk ay° the fule did foryet° for febilnes of knawlege.	*kept…forgetting*
Bot I sa oft thoght him on,° quhill angrit°	*made him think of it; grew angry*
his hert,	
And quhilum° I put furth my voce° and	*sometimes; spoke out;*
peddir° him callit.	*pedlar*
I wald ryght tuichandly talk be I wes twyse maryit,[28]	
For endit wes my innocence with my ald° husband.	*old/previous*
I wes apperand to be pert within perfit eild:[29]	
Sa sais the curat° of our kirk, that knew° me full ying.	*curate; knew*
He is our famous° to be fals, that fair worthy prelot.°	*too famous; prelate*
I salbe laith° to lat him le° quhill I may	*reluctant; make him tell lies;*
luke furth.°	*look out for myself*
I gert the buthman° obey—ther wes no bute ellis°—	*merchant; other remedy*
He maid me ryght hie reverens° fra he my	*accorded me fulsome respect;*
rycht° knew,	*status*
For, thocht I say it my self, the severance° wes mekle	*difference*
Betwix his bastard blude and my birth noble.	
That page° wes never of sic price° for	*lower-class fellow; worth;*
to presome anys°	*presume once*
Unto my persone to be peir,° had pete° nought grantit.	*of equal rank; pity*
Bot mercy into womanheid is a mekle vertu,°	*major characteristic*
For never bot in a gentill° hert is generit° ony ruth.°	*noble; born; pity*
I held ay grene° into his mynd that I	*kept ever fresh;*
of grace° tuk him,	*out of grace*
And that° he couth ken° him self I curtasly him lerit.°	*(so) that; know; taught*
He durst not sit anys my summondis° for,	*once disregard my commands;*
or° the secund charge,°	*before; indictment*
He wes ay redy for to ryn,° so rad° he wes for blame.	*run; afraid (of)*
Bot ay my will wes the war°—of° womanly	*grew more vicious; in accord with*
natur;	
The mair he loutit° for my luf, the les of him I rakit!°	*grovelled; esteemed*

28. 'I would talk in a very pointed way by the time I was twice married.'
29. 'I showed signs of forwardness before I was fully of age.'

And eik—this is a ferly° thing—or I him faith gaif,° *strange; made my vows*
I had sic favour to° that freke° and feid° syne for ever.° *kind regard for; fellow; enmity; ever after*
Quhen I the cure° had all clene° and him ourcummyn haill,° *remedy; had worked out perfectly; entirely subdued*
I crew abone° that craudone° as cok that wer victour. *crowed over; coward*
Quhen I him saw subjeit° and sett at° myn bydding, *submissive; disposed for*
Than I him lichtlyit° as a lowne° and lathit° his maneris. *despised; lout; loathed*
Than woxe° I sa unmerciable, to martir him I thought, *grew*
For as a best° I broddit° him to all boyis laubour.° *like a beast; goaded; work*
I wald haif ridden him to Rome with raip° in his heid, *bridle*
Wer not ruffill of° my renounce° and rumour° of pepill. *injury to; reputation; gossip*
And yit hatrent° I hid within my hert all, *hatred*
Bot quhilis it hepit° so huge quhill it behud out.° *piled up; gushed out*
Yit tuk I never the wosp° clene° out of my wyde throte,° *stopper; completely; wide throat*
Quhill° I oucht wantit° of my will or quhat I wald desir. *So long as; lacked*
Bot quhen I severit° had that syre of substance in erd,° *separated; earthly goods*
And gottin° his biggingis° to° my barne° and hie burrow landis,[30] *gained; buildings; for; son*
Than with a stew° stert° out the stoppell° of my hals,° *stench; sprang; stopper; throat*
That he all stunyst° throu the stound° as of a stele wappin.° *was stunned; sharp pain; weapon*
Than wald I, efter lang first,° sa fane° haif bene wrokin° *delay; gladly; avenged*
That I to flyte° wes als fers as a fell° dragoun. *attack verbally; savage*
I had for flattering of that fule fenyeit° so lang— *pretended*
Mi evidentis of heritagis or thai wer all selit[31]—
My breist that wes gret beild,° bowdyn° wes sa huge, *severely inflamed; swollen*
That neir° my baret° out brist or the band makin.° *almost; anger; contract was finalised*
Bot quhen my billis° and my bauchlis° wes all selit,° *documents; charges; sealed*
I wald na langar beir on bridill° bot braid° up my heid. *support the bridle; tossed*
Thair myght na molet° mak me moy° na hald my mouth in. *bit; submissive*
I gert the renyeis° rak° and rif into sondir,° *reins; strain; break asunder*
I maid that wif-carll to werk all womenis werkis,[32]
And laid all manly materis° and mensk° in this eird.° *buried all manly affairs; dignity; earth*
Than said I to my cummaris° in counsall about, *gossips;*
"Se how I cabeld yone cout° with a kene brydill. *tied up that colt*
The cappill° that the crelis kest in° the caf mydding° *horse; creels tipped into; midden*
Sa curtasly° the cart drawis and kennis na plungeing.° *docilely; bucking*

30. Literally—'high burgh lands'. As 'buildings' have already been dealt with, this probably refers to the sites owned in the upper town and ready for development. It may, however, refer to the tenements described in 'To the Merchantis of Edinburgh'.
31. 'Before the legal documents safeguarding my inheritance were sealed up.'
32. 'I turned that wife-man into a house-husband.'

He is nought skeich° na yit sker° na — *given to shying; restive;*
scippis° nought on syd."° — *prances; sideways*
And thus the scorne and the scaith° scapit he nothir.° — *pain; he escaped neither*
He wes no glaidsum gest° for a gay lady, — *welcome guest*
Tharfor I gat him a gam° that ganyt° him bettir. — *sport; suited*
He wes a gret goldit[33] man and of gudis riche;
I leit him be my lumbart° to lous° me all — *financier; free (from);*
misteris,° — *obligations*
And he wes fane for to fang° fra me that fair office, — *acquire*
And thoght my favoris to fynd throw his feill giftis.° — *many presents*
He grathit° me in a gay silk and gudly arrayis,° — *adorned; becoming/fine clothes*
In gownis of engranyt° claith and — *dyed crimson;*
gret° goldin chenyeis,° — *heavy; chains*
In ringis ryally° set with riche ruby stonis, — *nobly*
Quhill hely raise my renoune° amang — *greatly enhanced my reputation;*
the rude° peple — *poor*
Bot I full craftely did keip thai courtly wedis° — *clothes*
Quhill efter dede° of that drupe° that docht° — *death; droopy one; achieved;*
nought in chalmir.° — *bedroom*
Thought he of all my clathis maid° cost and expense, — *undertook*
Ane othir sall the worschip° haif that — *credit;*
weildis° me eftir; — *rules/uses (sexually)*
And thoght I likit him bot litill, yit for luf of othris
I wald me prunya plesandly° in precius° wedis, — *preen pleasurably; costly*
That luffaris myght apon me luke and ying lusty gallandis,
That I held more in daynte° and derer° be ful mekill — *favour; dearer*
Ne° him that dressit me so dink°—full dotit° wes his heyd! — *Than; finely; lovesick*
Quhen he wes heryit° out of hand° to — *plundered; entirely;*
hie up° my honoris,° — *boost; distinctions*
And payntit° me as pako,° proudest of fedderis, — *depicted; peacock*
I him miskennyt,° be Crist, and cukkald° him maid. — *disregarded; cuckold*
I him forleit° as a lad° and lathlyit° him mekle. — *abandoned; like a servant; loathed*
I thoght myself a papingay° and him a plukit herle.° — *parrot; plucked heron*
All thus enforsit° he his fa° and fortifyit in strenth, — *empowered; foe*
And maid a stalwart staff to strik him selfe doune.
Bot of ane bowrd° into bed I sall you breif° yit: — *jape; tell*
Quhen he ane hal° year wes hanyt° and him — *whole; restrained;*
behuffit rage,° — *needed sexual pleasure*
And I wes laith to be loppin with° sic a lob avoir,° — *mounted by; clumsy old horse*
Alse lang as he wes on loft° I lukit on him never, — *on top*
Na leit never enter in my thoght that he
my thing persit.° — *my thing (vagina) pierced*
Bot ay in mynd ane othir man ymagynit that I haid,
Or ellis had I never mery bene at that myrthles raid.° — *joyless invasion*
Quhen I that grome geldit° had of gudis and of natur, — *gelded*
Me thoght him gracelese° one to goif,° sa me God help! — *ill-favoured; gaze at*

33. 'Goldit': An unusual formation. Dunbar may have used it to evoke the sense of 'gilded'—i.e. having a crust of gold now stripped away by the widow. But it also has close and contextually relevant sound associations with 'geldit' (castrated). Cf. l. 392.

Quhen he had warit° all on me his welth and his substance, *laid out/expended*
Me thoght his wit wes all went away with the laif.° *rest*
And so I did him dispise, I spittit quhen I saw
That superspendit,° evill spreit, spulyeit° of all vertu. *bankrupt; despoiled*
For weill ye wait, wiffis, that he that wantis riches
And valyeandnes° in Venus play is ful vile haldin. *vigour*
Full fruster° is his fresch array and fairnes of persoune; *Entirely in vain*
All is bot frutlese° his effeir° and falyeis at the upwith.° *futile; equipment; erection*
I buskit up° my barnis like baronis sonnis, *dressed/bedecked*
And maid bot fulis of the fry° of his first wif. *offspring*
I banyst° fra my boundis° his brethir° ilkane, *banished; lands; brothers*
His frendis as my fais° I held at feid° evir. *foes; maintained hostility to*
Be° this ye beleif may, I luffit nought him self, *From*
For never I likit a leid° that langit° till his blude;° *person; belonged; kin*
And yit thir wismen, thai wait that all wiffis evill
Ar kend with° ther conditionis° and knawin with° the samin. *by; dispositions; recognized by*

Deid is now that dyvour° and dollin° in erd. *bankrupt; buried*
With him, deit° all my dule° and my drery thoghtis. *died; grief*
Now done is my dolly° nyght, my day is upsprungin. *dismal*
Adew, dolour, adew, my daynte° now begynis. *delight*
Now am I a wedow, iwise,° and weill° am at ese. *indeed; completely*
I weip as I were woful bot wel is me for ever.
I busk° as I were bailfull° bot blith is my hert. *dress; grieving*
My mouth it makis murnyng° and my mynd lauchis. *speaks of bereavement*
My clokis thai ar caerfull° in colour of sabill,° *indicate mourning; sable*
Bot courtly° and ryght curyus° my corse° is ther undir.° *elegant; lovely; body; beneath them*
I drup° with a ded° luke in my dule habit,° *languish; lifeless; dress of grief*
As with manis daill I had done for dayis of my lif.[34]
Quhen that I go to the kirk cled in cair weid,° *mourning*
As foxe in a lambis fleise,° fenye° I my cheir.° *fleece; disguise; mood*
Than lay I furth my bright[35] buke on breid° on my kne, *wide open*
With mony lusty letter ellummynit° with gold, *illuminated*
And drawis my clok forthwart our my face quhit,° *white/pale*
That I may spy unaspyit a space me beside.° *a distance around me*
Full oft I blenk by° my buke and blynis of° devotioun, *glance beyond; cease from*
To se quhat berne is best brand° or bredest° in schulderis, *brawniest; broadest*
Or forgeit° is maist forcely° to furnyse° a bancat° *forged; strongly; provide; feast*
In Venus chalmer,° valyeandly, withoutin vane ruse.° *chamber (sexual); vain boasting*
And as the new mone,° all pale, oppressit with change *moon*
Kythis quhilis° her cleir face throw cluddis° of sable, *Sometimes reveals; clouds*

34. 'As if I had finished for ever with sexual intercourse.'
35. The brightness is explained in the next line. This is an illuminated manuscript, related to the spiritual devotion she is intent on enacting. That the widow possesses such a book confirms her claims to wealth. Whether she can read it or is 'playing' this role, as well, remains an open question.

So keik° I throw my clokis and castis kynd lukis — *peep*
To knychtis and to cleirkis° and cortly personis.° — *scholars; courtiers*
Quhen frendis of my husbandis behaldis me on fer,° — *from afar*
I haif a watter spunge for wa° within my wyde clokis. — *(the appearance of) woe*
Than wring I it full wylely° and wetis my chekis; — *cunningly*
With that, watteris myn ene and welteris doune° teris. — *stream down*
Than say thai all that sittis about, "Se ye nought, allace,
Yone lustlese led,° so lelely° scho luffit hir husband. — *joyless creature; faithfully*
Yone is a pete° to enprent° in a princis hert, — *image of pity; imprint*
That sic a perle of plesance suld yone pane dre."° — *endure*
I sane me,° as I war ane sanct,° and semys ane angell; — *cross myself; saint*
At langage of lichory,° I leit as° I war crabit.° — *lechery; act as if; offended*
I sith° without sair hert or seiknes in body, — *sigh*
According to° my sable weid I mon° haif sad maneris, — *In accord with; must*
Or thai will se all the suth;° for certis we wemen, — *truth*
We set us all for the syght, to syle men of treuth.[36]
We dule° for na evill deid, sa° it be derne haldin.° — *grieve; so long as; kept secret*
Wise wemen has wayis° and wonderfull gydingis° — *means; ways of acting*
With gret engyne° to bejaip ther jolyus° husbandis, — *ingenuity; jealous*
And quyetly with sic craft convoyis our materis,° — *conduct our business*
That, under Crist, no creatur kennis of our doingis.
Bot, folk, a cury° may miscuke° that knawlege wantis,° — *cooked dish; spoil; lacks*
And has na colouris° for to cover ther awne° kindly fautis;° — *colours/pretences; own; natural faults (i.e. of species)*
As dois thir damysellis° for derne° dotit° lufe, — *young ladies; secret; foolish*
That dogonis° haldis in dainte° and delis° with thaim so lang, — *rascals; esteem; are involved*
Quhill° al the cuntre knaw ther kyndnes and faith. — *Until*
Faith[37] has a fair name, bot falsheid faris beittir.
Fy on hir that can nought feyne, her fame° for to saif! — *reputation*
Yit am I wise in sic werk and wes all my tyme.° — *all my life*
Thoght I want wit in warldlynes,° I wylis° haif in luf, — *worldly matters; tricks*
As ony happy woman has that is of hie blude.° — *noble blood*
Hutit be the halok lase a hunder yeir of eild![38]
I have ane secrete° servand, rycht sovir° of his toung, — *discreet; secure*
That me supportis of sic nedis, quhen I a syne° mak — *sign*
Thocht he be simpill to the sicht,° he has a tong sickir;° — *simple to look at; safe*
Full mony semelyar sege° wer° service dois mak. — *a more handsome man; worse*
Thoght I haif cair under cloke° the cleir day quhill nyght, — *cloaked care (= feigned)*
Yit haif I solace° under serk° quhill the sone ryse. — *get comfort; (my) chemise*
Yit am I haldin° a haly° wif our all the haill schyre.° — *taken for; pious; shire*
I am sa peteouse° to the pur,° quhen ther is personis mony.° — *compassionate; poor; a large crowd about*
In passing of pilgrymage I pride me full mekle,

36. 'We all prepare a (visual) performance to beguile men away from the truth.'
37. Increasingly the widow's sermon, in its materialistic translation of Christian values, verges on blasphemy. The fair name of Faith derives from its status as one of the three theological virtues.
38. 'May the young girl who lacks guile be mocked until she is a hundred years old!'

Mair for the prese° of peple na° ony perdoun wynying.°[39] *throng; than; pardon gaining*
Bot yit me think the best bourd,° quhen baronis and knychtis *fun*
And othir bachilleris° blith, blumyng in youth, *young knights*
And all my luffaris lele my luging persewis,° *enter my lodging (sexual)*
And fyllis° me wyne wantonly° with weilfair and joy. *pour out; lavishly*
Sum rownis° and sum ralyeis° and sum redis ballatis,° *whisper; quip; poems*
Sum raiffis° furth rudly° with riatus° speche, *declaim; coarsely; wanton*
Sum plenis° and sum prayis, sum praisis mi bewte, *complain*
Sum kissis me, sum clappis° me, sum kyndnes me proferis. *embrace*
Sum kerffis to° me curtasli,° sum me the cop° giffis, *carves for; courteously; cup*
Sum stalwardly steppis ben° with a stout curage, *pass inside*
And a stif standand° thing staiffis° in mi neiff,° *standing/upright; pokes; fist*
And mony blenkis ben our, that but full fer sittis,[40]
That mai for° the thik thrang° nought thrif° as thai wald. *on account of; throng; thrive*
Bot with my fair calling° I comfort thaim all; *warm welcome*
For he that sittis me nixt, I nip° on his finger, *pinch*
I serf° him on the tothir syde on the samin fasson,° *serve; in the same way*
And he that behind me sittis I hard on him lene,
And him befor with my fut fast° on his I stramp,° *firmly; press down*
And to the bernis far but° sweit blenkis I cast. *men on the far outside*
To every man in speciall speke I sum wordis,
So wisly and so womanly quhill warmys ther hertis.
Thar is no liffand leid° so law of degre° *living man; low in rank*
That sall me luf unluffit, I am so loik hertit.° *warm-hearted*
And gif his lust so be lent into° my lyre quhit° *fixed upon; white/fair skin*
That he be lost or with me lak, his lif sall not danger.[41]
I am so mercifull in mynd, and menys° all wichtis, *take pity on*
My sely saull° salbe saif quhen Sabot° all jugis.[42] *innocent soul; the Lord of hosts*
Ladyis, leir° thir lessonis and be no lassis° fundin. *learn; foolish virgins*
This is the legeand° of my lif, thought Latyne° it be nane.' *holy story; Latin*

Quhen endit had hir ornat° speche this eloquent wedow, *elaborate*
Lowd thai lewch° all the laif° and loffit° hir mekle, *laughed; rest; complimented*
And said thai suld exampill tak of her soverane teching° *supreme teaching/lesson in mastery*
And wirk efter° hir wordis, that woman wes so prudent. *act after*
Than culit° thai ther mouthis with confortable drinkis *cooled*
And carpit° full cummerlik,° with cop going round. *chattered; companionably*

39. Pilgrimages were viewed as penitential journeys. Completion of these journeys cancelled out a given number of years in purgatory.

40. 'But and ben' means 'out and in'. Those at the edges of the crowd gaze over towards the centre, hoping to catch the widow's eye.

41. 'That he is lost without me, his life will not be endangered.' The widow is shadowing, carnally, the complete mercy of Christ.

42. The reference is to the Last Judgement. 'Sabot' derives from the Old Testament, 'dominus sabaoth' or 'Lord of hosts'. See Isaiah I. 9; Romans 9. 29. The image is particularly apposite as the widow has just ministered to a 'host' or 'crowd' herself. As they touch her in hope of physical love, one is reminded of those who hoped to be cured spiritually, in the same manner, by Christ.

Thus draif thai our° that deir nyght with danceis full noble, *they passed*
Quhill that the day did up daw° and dew donkit° flouris. *dawned; moistened*
The morow° myld wes and meik° the mavis did sing, *next day; mildly*
And all remuffit° the myst and the meid smellit.° *passed away; meadow was scented*
Silver schouris doune schuke° as the schene° cristall *fell; bright*
And berdis shoutit° in schaw° with ther schill° notis. *birds clamoured; copse; shrill*
The goldin, glitterand gleme so gladit° ther hertis, *gladdened*
Thai maid a glorius gle° amang the grene bewis.° *melody; boughs*
The soft sowch° of the swyr° and soune° of the stremys, *murmuring; wind; music*
The sweit savour° of the sward and singing of foulis *scent*
Myght confort ony creatur of the kyn of Adam,° *Adam's kin (i.e. humanity)*
And kindill agane his curage,° thoght it wer° caldly sloknyt.° *sexual desire; had been; coldly quenched*
Than rais° thir ryall rosis in ther riche wedis° *rose; fine garments*
And rakit° hame to ther rest throw the rise blumys;° *meandered; brushwood blossoms*
And I all prevely past to° a plesand arber,° *secretly went to; arbour*
And with my pen did report ther pastance° most mery. *diversion*

Ye auditoris° most honorable, that eris has gevin *listeners*
Onto this uncouth° aventur, quhilk airly° me happinnit— *strange; recently*
Of thir thre wanton wiffis, that° I haif writtin heir, *about whom*
Quhilk wald ye waill to° your wif, gif ye suld wed one?[43] *choose as*

43. The poet now sets his own 'demande d'amour' for us. So long as the widow asks the wives, we can listen undisturbed. Now we are drawn into the debate, which opens out from art's control into the variety of actual lives.

§ 8 Anonymous (c. 1480): *The Freiris of Berwik*

The Freiris of Berwik *used to be attributed to Dunbar. While this is no longer thought likely, the fact that editors believed it might have been composed by the most accomplished of all early Scots writers offers indirect confirmation of its quality. Certainly, it provides a fine example of the Scottish fabliau form. Its sources are French rather than Chaucerean and there is, therefore, little attempt at extended character description. Action and the farcical spirit dominate as the two friars enter the house of Symon Lawrear in his absence (1–114), witness the love-tryst between his wife and the prior (115–89) then turn the tables on the lovers when Symon returns (190–567).*

The poem's power resides in the precision both of its comic visualisation and of its bawdy wordplay. The images of 'gates' ('He had a prevy posterne of his awin', 129). and lodgings ('herbrye') around which double-entendres are centred, are those used for chivalric or divine purposes in Romance or Legend. The status of the Fabliau as comic counterpoint to these higher modes, is as clear in the Scots tale as in the 'quiting' of Knight by Miller in Chaucer's **Canterbury Tales**.

Structurally, the witty narrative provides a dynamic norm, permitting the lengthier set-pieces (e.g. Robert's conjuration) to slow down the pace without a major loss of momentum. Editorial evidence supports both the popularity and the satirical immediacy of the story. It would seem that the basic tale was well-known and that the religious orders to which the friars and the prior belonged could be adapted by a 'bard', depending on which audience he was addressing and which sect he wished to mock.

The Freiris of Berwik[1]

'As it befell and happinnit° in to deid° — *happened; in fact*
Upoun a rever,° the quhilk is callit Tweid.'° — *river; Tweed*

At Tweidis mowth,° thair standis a nobill toun, — *mouth*
Quhair mony lordis hes bene° of grit renoune,° — *have lived; renown*
And mony worthy ladeis, fair of face;[2]
And mony ane fresche, lusty galland° was — *youthful lusty gallant*
In to this toun—the quhilk is callit Berwik.[3]
Upoun the sey° thair standis nane it lyk, — *On the coast*
For it is wallit weill abowt with stane° — *well fortified by (a) stone wall(s)*
And dowbill stankis castin mony ane; [4]
And syne° the castell is so strang and wicht,° — *then/in addition; substantial*
With strait towris° and turattis he on hicht;° — *upright towers; high turrets above*
The wallis wrocht craftely° withall; — *skilfully*

1. The editors are grateful to Janet Foggie for providing detailed background on the Dominicans. Notes which are indebted to her research are marked: (J.F.)
ED. Copy Text: Bannatyne MS. Maitland MS readings have been introduced where they *significantly* clarify the sense or are demonstrably superior.
2. ED. And mony worthy ladeis, fair of face] M; Quhair mony a lady bene fair of face B.
3. Berwick's geographic position at the mouth of the Tweed made it a key fortress. Surrounded by a wall (l. 9), it frequently changed hands in the border warfare between Scotland and England. As it was in Scottish hands between 1461 and 1482, the poem may be dated towards the end of that period.
4. 'And with a good number of excavated double ditches.'

The portcules most subtelly to fall° — *falling most artfully*
Quhen that thame list to draw thame upoun hicht,[5]
That it micht be of na maner of micht° — *strength*
To win° that hous° be craft° or subteltie. — *conquer; building; (martial) skill*
Quhairfoir, it is maist gud allutirly° — *absolutely the best*
In to my tyme, quhair evir I haif bene°— — *i.e. in my experience*
Moist fair, most gudly,° most plesand to be sene; — *most handsome*
The toun, the wall, the castell and the land,
The he° wallis upoun the upper hand,° — *high walls; level*
The grit croce kirk; and eik the Masone Dew[6]—
The Jacobene freiris;° of the quhyt hew° — *Jacobin friars; white of colour*
The Carmeleitis;° and the Minouris° eik[7]— — *Carmelites; Friars Minor*
The four ordouris wer nocht for to seik° — *did not need to be sought out*
Thay wer all in this toun dwelling.[8]
So appinnit intill° a Maii morning, — *Thus it happened on*
That twa of the Jacobine freiris,
As thay wer wont and usit mony yeiris[9]
To pass° amang thair brethir upaland,° — *journey; in the country districts*
Wer send of° thame best practisit° and cunnand°— — *from among; most skilled; learned*
Freir Allane and Freir Robert the uder.° — *other*
Thir silly°[10] freiris with wyffis° weill cowld gluder;° — *pious (ironic); women/wives; cajole*
Rycht wondir weill plesit thai all wyffis
And tawld° thame tailis and haly sanctis lyffis.°[11] — *told; lives of holy saints*
Quhill° on a tyme thay purposit to pas hame;° — *Until; decided to go home*
Bot verry tyrit° and wett wes Freir Allane, — *tired*
For he wes awld° and micht nocht wele travell, — *old*
And als he had ane littill spyce of gravell. [12]
Freir Robert wes young and verry hett of blude°[13] — *very hot-blooded*

5. 'When they wanted to withdraw on high.' The strategy was to let the portcullis fall, at the last minute, leaving the attacking forces stranded.
6. 'The great church in the shape of a cross and also the hospital.' The first two orders are introduced via the sites of their houses. The Trinitarians inhabited the 'croce kirk'. The hospital ('Maison Dieu') adjoined the Jacobin abbey (J.F.).
7. ED. ll. 24–5. The Jacobene freiris of the quhyt hew /The Carmeleitis and the monkis eik] B; The freiris of Jacobinis quhyt of hew /The carmelitis, augustinianis and als the Minouris eik M. A composite text has been offered. Both scribes rationalize erroneously in finding the four orders (l. 26).The Maitland scribe adds 'augustinianis' because he fails to see that the Trinitarians have already been named. The punctuation of l. 24 separates the clauses because the Jacobins wore black cowls and hoods.
8. Berwick housed all four orders—Dominican (Jacobin) or Black Friars, Carmelites or White Friars, Trinitarians and Franciscans or Brown Friars (Friars Minor). It is an ideal setting for a tale which can be adapted to satirise one group or the other.
9. 'As had been their [the fraternity's] wont and custom over many years.'
10. Throughout the poem, witty use is made of the wide range of meaning then contained by the word 'silly'—innocent, pious, virtuous (good), naive, stupid.
11. ED. and haly] M. B. reads 'of haly', which identifies the tales they tell as saintly legends. While these were in the friars' repertoire, less serious tales would be needed to please the audience as defined.
12. 'And he also had a trace of gravel.' A urinary ailment.
13. The Dominicans sent a young friar out with an older companion (his *socius*). This practice was designed to prevent the sort of licentious behaviour later shown by Friar John (J.F.)

And be the way° he bure° both clothis and hude[14] — *on the journey; carried*
And all thair geir,° for he wes strong and wicht.° — *gear/baggage; sturdy*
Be that° it drew neir towart the nicht, — *When*
As thay wer cumand towart the toune full neir,° — *very close*
Freir Allane said than, 'Gude bruder, deir,
It is to lait.° I dreid° the yet[15] be closit° — *too late; fear; gate is closed*
And we ar tyrit and verry evill disposit° — *ill disposed*
To luge owt of° the toun bot gif that° we — *To lodge outside; unless*
In sume gud hous this nycht mot herbryt° be.' — *sheltered*
Swa wynnit° thair ane woundir gude hostillar° — *lived; innkeeper*
Without° the toun in till a fair manar° — *Outside; fine dwelling place*
And Symon Lawrear wes his name.
Ane fair blyth wyf he had of ony ane° — *compared to any*
Bot scho wes sumthing dynk° and dengerous.° — *difficult to please; haughty*
Thir sillie° freiris come to that mannis hous — *good*
And hailsit° hir richt bayth full curtaslie, — *greeted*
And scho rewardit thame agane° in hy.°[16] — *returned the compliment; hastily*
Freir Robert sperit eftir° the gude man° — *asked about; husband*
And scho agane anserit thame thane,
'He went fra hame, God wait, on Weddinsday,
In the cuntre for to seik corne and hay
And uthir thingis quhairof we haif neid.'
Freir Robert said, 'I pray grit God him speid
And sauf him sound° in till his leil travale,'°[17] — *preserve him; lawful toil*
And hir desyrit the stowp° to fill of aill,° — *pitcher; with ale*
'That we may drink, for I am wondir dry!'
With that the wyfe went furth richt schortly° — *left at once*
And fillit the stowp and brocht in breid and cheis;
Thay eit and drank and satt at thair awin eis.° — *i.e. made themselves comfortable*
Freir Allane said to the gudwyfe in hye,
'Cum hiddir, deme,° and sett yow doun me bye° — *dame; beside me*
And fill the cop° agane anis° to me!' — *cup; one more time*
Freir Robert said, 'Full weill payit° sall ye be.' — *repaid*
The freiris wer blyth and mirry tailis cowld tell,° — *told*
And even with that° thay hard° the prayer bell — *just then; heard*
Off thair awin abbay—and than thay wer agast
Becaus thay knew the yettis[18] wer closit fast,
That thay on na wayis micht gett entre.° — *get in*

14. Dominicans were not allowed to take off their outer, distinguishing garments when outwith the abbey (J.F.). In the Bannatyne version of the tale, this detail is crucial. Once the black hood and cowl are shed, the white habits underneath are revealed. They appear 'white' in this sense when they seek lodging.

15. The listener cannot at this stage know whether the city or the abbey gate is referred to. (See l. 78; n. 18.)

16. 'in hy' may mean 'loudly' or 'hurriedly'. In the *Freiris* it is often used to eke out the metre. Cf. ll. 71; 138; 209; 239; 251 etc.

17. ED. him sound in till his leil travale] M; him haill and sound in to his travell. B.

18. The reference in l. 47 is now clarified. The city gate (then) and the abbey gate (now) are closed. The friars are, of course, not truly 'agast' (l. 77), having already decided to stay elsewhere. Their anxiety is assumed to arouse her pity.

Than the gudewyfe[19] thay prayit for cheritie° — *out of charity*
To grant thame herbrye° that ane nicht.[20] — *lodging*
Bot scho to thame gaif anschir° with grit hicht°— — *replied; very haughtily*
'The gudeman is fra hame,° as I yow tald, — *away from home*
And God it wait gif I durst be so bald° — *bold*
To herbry° freiris in this hous with me. — *As to shelter*
Quhat wald Symon say, ha benedicite,° — *Lord bless me*
Bot° in his absence I abusit his place?° — *If; abused his home/position*
Our deir Lady Mary° keip me fra sic cace° — *i.e. Virgin Mary; (a) situation*
And keip me owt of perrell° and of schame!' — *peril*
Then auld Freir Allane said, 'Na, fair dame,
For Godis saik, heir me quhat I sall say.
In good faith, we will both be deid or day;° — *be dead before morning*
The way is evill and I am tyrit and wett.
Our yettis° ar closit that we may nocht in gett, — *gates*
And to our abbay we can nocht win in;° — *gain entry*
To caus us perreis, but help, ye haif grit syn.[21]
Thairfoir, of verry neid,° we mon byd still° — *utter necessity; remain here*
And us commit alhaill° in to your will.'° — *entirely; (good) will*
The gudewyf lukit unto the freiris tway
And, at the last, to thame this can scho say,° — *she said*
'Ye byd nocht° heir, be Him that us all coft.° — *You are not staying; redeemed*
Bot gif° ye list° to lig° up in yone loft, — *Unless; want; lie*
Quhilk is weill wrocht° in to the hallis° end.[22] — *well built; hall's*
Ye sall fynd stray,° and clathis° I sall yow send; — *straw; bedclothes*
And gif ye list, to pas bayth on in feir,[23]
For on no wayis will I repair haif heir.'° — *have you staying here*
Hir madin° than scho send hir on befoir° — *maid; ahead*
And hir thay followit baith withowttin moir;° — *without more ado*
Thay war full blyth° and did as scho° thame kend° — *pleased; i.e. maid; directed*
And up thay went in to the hallis end
In till a loft, wes maid° for corne and hay. — *(which) was made*
Scho maid thair bed, syne past doun° but° delay, — *then descended; without*
Closit the trop° and thay remanit still — *trap-door*
Into the loft, and had nocht *all* thair will.[24]
Freir Allane lay doun as he best micht.° — *as best he could*
Freir Robert said, 'I hecht to walk° this nicht. — *intend to keep awake*
Quha wait,° perchance, sum sport I may espy!' — *Who knows*
Thus, in the loft, latt I thir freiris ly° — *I leave these friars lying*
And of the gudwyf now I will speik mair.° — *further*
Scho wes richt blyth° that they wer closit° thair — *glad; shut up*

19. 'gudewyfe' (l. 80) and 'gudeman' (l. 83) are colloquial words favoured in fabliaux because they stress the marriage bond, which is usually threatened in such tales.

20. The appeal is made in holy terms. 'Charity' is a theological virtue and the granting of shelter a deed of temporal mercy.

21. 'To cause us to perish through denying aid (without help) places great guilt (sinfulness) upon you.'

22. The wife is of the merchant classes and has a large house. The friars expect to be lodged on ground level in the spare bedroom. Mrs Lawrear, for her own reasons, places them upstairs, cramped, in the loft.

23. I.e. 'And if you both don't mind making a move in that direction.'

24. ED. and had nocht all thair will] M; thay wantit of their will B.

For scho had maid ane tryst° that samyn° nicht — *love-tryst; same*
Freir Johine—hir luvis°—supper for to dicht;° — *lover's; prepare*
And scho wald haif none uder cumpany° — *no one else present*
Becauss Freir Johine, that nicht, with hir sowld ly°— — *was to lie with her*
Quha dwelland° wes in to that samyne toun, — *dwelling*
And ane blak freir he wes of grit renown.[25]
He govirnit alhaill° the abbacy;[26] — *ruled entirely*
Silver and gold he had aboundantly;
He had a prevy posterne° of his awin, — *secret back entrance*
Quhair he micht ische,° quhen that he list,° unknawin[27] — *issue forth; wished*
Now thus, in to the toun, I leif him still—
Bydand his time.° And turne agane, I will — *Awaiting his moment*
To this fair wyfe, how scho the fyre cowld beit° — *stoked*
And thristit° on fatt caponis° to the speit,° — *fixed; capons; spit*
And fat cunnyngis° to the fyre can lay,° — *rabbits; laid on*
And bad° hir madin, in all the haist scho may,[28] — *ordered*
To flawme° and turne and rost° thame tenderly. — *baste; roast*
And to hir chalmer° so scho went in hy. — *bedroom*
Scho pullit hir cunt and gaif hit buffettis tway° — *two slaps*
Upoun the cheikis,° syne till it cowd scho say:° — *labia; then addressed it thus*
'Ye sowld be blyth and glaid at my requeist;° — *at my invitation*
Thir mullis° of youris ar callit° to ane feist.' — *lips; summoned*
Scho cleithis hir° in a kirtill° of fyne reid,° — *dresses herself; gown; red (cloth)*
Ane fair quhyt curch° scho puttis upoun hir heid. — *kerchief*
Hir kirtil belt was silk and silver fyne
With ane proud purs° and keyis gingling° syne; [29] — *costly purse; jingling*
On every finger scho weiris ringis two.
Scho was als prowd as ony papingo.° — *parrot*
The burde° scho cuverit with clath of costly greyne;° — *table; costly green material*
Hir napry aboif° wes woundir weill besene.° — *linen on (table) top; arrayed*
Than but° scho went, to se gif ony come. — *outside*
Scho thocht° full lang to meit° hir lufe, freir Johine. — *had been thinking…of meeting*
Syne schortly° did this freir knok at the yett. — *soon*
His knok scho kend° and did so him in lett. — *recognized*
Scho welcomit him in all hir best maneir.° — *fashion*
He thankit hir and said, 'My awin luve deir,
Haif thair ane ane pair of bossis° gude and fyne— — *small casks/leather bottles*
Thay hald ane gallone full of Gascone° wyne; — *from Gascony*
And als° ane pair of pertrikis° richt new slane° — *also; partridges; newly slain*
And eik ane creill° full of breid of mane.°[30] — *wicker basket; savoury bread*

25. ED. M. here identifies the lover as 'Ane gray freyr', thus directing the satire towards the Franciscan order. B's version works entirely within the Dominican order.
26. Friar John is not called abbot, because the Dominicans used the title 'prior' to describe their leader. This was an elected post, held for a limited term (J.F.).
27. ll. 129–30. Gates (open and shut; front and back) are favoured images in fabliaux as they have sexual connotations.
28. ED. ll. 135–6 M.
29. ED. ll. 145–6 M.
30. 'Breid of mane' probably derives from 'panis dominicus' or 'our Lord's bread'.

This I haif brocht to yow, my awin luve deir;
Thairfoir, I pray yow, be blyth and mak gud cheir.° *make merry*
Sen it is so that Semon is fra hame,
I will be hamely° now with yow, gud dame.' *intimate (pun)*
Scho sayis, 'Ye are full hertly welcome heir
At ony tyme, quhen that ye list appeir.'
With that scho smylit woundir lustely;
He thristit° hir hand agane richt prevely, *squeezed*
Than in hett luve thay talkit uderis till.° *they communed with each other*
Thus, at thair sport, now will I leif thame still
And tell yow off thir silly freiris two
Wer lokit in the loft amang the stro.
Freir Allane in the loft still can ly;
Freir Robert had ane littill jelosy,° *suspicion*
For in his hairt he had ane persaving° *premonition*
And throw the burdis° he maid with his botkin° *floor boards; dagger*
A litill hoill—on sic a wyiss° maid he *manner*
All that thay did thair doun he micht weill se,
And every word he herd that thay did say.
Quhen scho wes prowd, richt woundir fresche and gay,
Scho callit him baith 'hert,' 'lemmane'° and 'luve'. *lover*
Lord God, gif than his curage wes aboif,° *his desire was aloft*
So prelat-lyk° sat he in to the chyre! *i.e. in such a priest-like manner*
Scho rownis° than ane pistill° in his eir— *whispers; i.e. a tender message*
Thus sportand thame° and makand melody. *disporting themselves*
And quhen scho saw the supper wes reddy,
Scho gois belyfe° and cuveris the burde° annon; *swiftly; sets the table*
And syne the pair of bossis hes scho tone° *taken*
And sett thame doun upoun the burde him by.
And evin with that° thay hard the gudman cry, *at that very moment*
And knokand at the yett he cryit fast.° *called out persistently*
Quhen thay him hard, than wer thay both agast
And als Freir Johine wes in a fellone fray,° *dreadful state of fright*
He stert up fast° and wald haif bene away. *got up hastily*
Bot all for nocht, he micht no way win owt.
The gudwyfe spak than with a visage stowt,° *determined*
'Yone is Symone that makis all this fray,° *alarm*
That I micht tholit full weill had bene away![31]
I sall him quyt° and I leif half a yeir, *get even with him*
That cummert° hes us thus, in sic maneir— *disturbed*
Becaus for him° we may nocht byd togidder; *due to him*
I soir repent° and wo is ye come hidder *I sorely regret*
For we wer weill gif that ye wer away.'
'Quhat sall I do, allace?' the freir can say.° *said*
'Hyd yow,' scho said, 'quhill he be brocht to rest,
In to yone troich;° I think it for the best. *trough*
It lyis mekle° and huge in all yone nuke;° *large; corner*

31. 'Whose absence I could have endured quite easily!'

It held a boll of meill° quhen that we buke.'° — *measure of meal; were baking*
Than undir it scho gart him creip in hy
And bad him lurk thair verry quyetly;
Scho closit him° and syne went on hir way. — *concealed him*
And till hir madin smertlie can scho say,[32]
'Away all this and slokin out° the fyre; — *put out*
Go clois the burde and tak away the chyre,[33]
And lok in° all in yon almorie°— — *lock up; cupboard*
Bayth meit and drink—and ga belyf in hy.'° — *set about it very quickly*
Baith connyngis, caponis and wyld fewles fyne,° — *tasty game-birds*
The mane breid, the bossis with the wyne
Scho hid up all; and strowit° the hous so clein — *strewed with sand/rushes*
That no liknes of feist meit° micht be sein. — *semblance of festive fare*
And syne, withouttin ony mair delay,
Scho castis of haill hir fresch array;° — *attractive outfit*
Than went scho to hir bed annone
And tholit him° to knok his fill. Symone, — *allowed/suffered him*
Quhen he for knoking tyrit wes° and cryid, — *was weary of*
Abowt he went unto the udir syd
And on Alesone fast cold he cry;° — *vigorously called*
And, at the last, scho anserit crabitly,° — *irritably*
'Ach, quha be this that knawis sa weill my name?
Go hens,' scho sayis, 'for Symon is fra hame
And I will herbry no geistis heir perfey.° — *in faith*
Thairfoir, I pray yow to wend° on your way, — *proceed*
For at this time ye may nocht lugit be!'
Than Symone said, 'Fair dame, ken° ye nocht me? — *recognize*
I am your Symone and husband of this place.'
'Ar ye my spous, Symone?' scho sayis. 'Allace,
Be misknawlege° I had almaist misgane!° — *misunderstanding; erred*
Quha wend°[34] that ye sa lait wald haif cum hame.' — *would have supposed*
Scho stertis up and gettis licht° in hy — *gets (a) light*
And oppinit than the yet full haistely.
Scho tuk fra him his geir at all devyis,° — *entirely*
Syne welcomit him on maist hairtly wyis.° — *in a most hearty manner*
He bad the madin kindill on the fyre,° — *light up the fire*
Syne, 'Graith me meit and tak the all the hyre.'° — *Speedily prepare me some food*
The gudwyfe said schortly, 'Ye may trow,° — *i.e. Believe me*
Heir is no meit that ganand is° for yow.' — *is suitable*
'How sa, fair deme? Ga, gait me cheis and breid!
Ga fill the stowp!° Hald me no mair in pleid,[35] — *pitcher*
For I am verry tyrit, wett and cauld.'
Than up scho rais and durst nocht mair be bauld,° — *aggressive*
Cuverit the burde,° thairon sett meit in hy— — *Laid the table*

32. ED. ll. 212–22 M.
33. The table would be 'closed' by separating board from trestles, then packing them both against the wall. The armchair had been brought out specially for her lover. See l. 183.
34. ED. wend] M; wenit B.
35. 'Don't continue to hold me ransom to your argument.'

Ane sowsit nolt fute° and scheipheid° haistely— *steeped calf's foot; sheep's head*
And sum cauld meit scho brocht to hym belyve
And fillit the stowp. The gudman than wes blyth.
Than satt he doun and swoir, 'Be all hallow,° *By all the saints*
I fair richt weill and° I had ane gud fallow.° *if; companion*
Dame, eit with me and drink, gif that ye may.'
Said the gudwyf, 'Devill inche cun may I;° *Devil a bit of it, shall I*
It wer mair meit° in to your bed to be *suitable (pun)*
Than now to sit desyrand cumpany.'
Freir Robert said, 'Allace, gud bruder deir,
I wald the gudman wist that we wer heir;
Quha wait, perchance, sum bettir wald he fair,
For sickerly° my hairt will ay be sair *certainly*
Gif yone scheipheid with° Symon birneist be,° *by; is polished off*
Sa mekill gud cheir being in the almerie!'
And with that word, he gaif ane hoist° anone. *cough*
The gudman hard and speirit,° 'Quha is yone?' *asked*
The gudwyf said, 'Yone are freiris tway.'
Symone said, 'Tell me, quhat freiris be thay?'
'Yone is Freir Robert and silly° Freir Allane, *good*
That all this day hes travellit with grit pane.
Be° thay come heir it wes so verry lait, *By the time that*
Houris[36] wes rung and closit wes thair yait
And in yone loft I gaif thame harbrye.'
The gudman said, 'Sa God haif pairt of me,
The freiris twa ar hairtly welcome hidder.
Ga call thame doun that we ma drink togidder.'
The gudwyf said, 'I reid° yow lat thame be. *advise*
Thay had levir° sleip nor° sit in cumpanye.' *rather; than*
The gudman said unto the maid thone,
'Go pray thame baith to cum till me annone.'
And sone the trop° the madin oppinit than *trapdoor*
And bad thame baith cum doun to the gudman.
Freir Robert said, 'Now, be sweit Sanct Jame,[37]
The gudman is verry welcome hame
And for his weilfair dalie do we pray;
We sall annone cum doun to him, ye say.'
Than, with that word, thay start up baith attone° *together*
And doun the trop delyverly° thay come— *speedily*
Halsit° Symone als sone as thay him se, *Greeted*
And he agane thame welcomit hairtfullie° *warmly*
And said, 'Cum heir, myne awin bredir deir
And sett yow doun sone besyd me heir,
For I am now allone, as ye may se;
Thairfoir, sitt doun and beir me cumpanye
And tak yow pairt of sic gud° as we haif.' *fare*

36. ED. Houris] M; Curfur B. 'Curfur' = 'curfew' is possible but 'houris' ('prayers') relates specifically to 'the prayer bell' of l. 76.
37. Ironic. St James was associated with taking moral responsibility for your deeds.

Freir Allane said, 'Schir, I pray God yow saif
For heir is now annuch of Godis gud.'
Than Symon anserit, 'Now be the Rud,°   *holy cross*
Yit wald I gif ane croun of gold for me
For sum gud meit and drink amangis us thre.'
Freir Robert said, 'Quhat drinkis wald ye craif°   *crave*
Or quhat meitis desyre ye for to haif?
For I haif mony sindry practikis seir,°   *many and various skills*
Beyond the sey in Pareis did I leir,[38]
That I wald preve° glaidly for your saik,   *demonstrate*
And for your demys,° that harbry cowd us maik.°   *dame's (sake); provided us with*
I tak on hand° (and ye will counsale keip)   *undertake*
That I sall gar yow se,° or° ever I sleip,   *reveal to you; before*
Of the best meit that is in this cuntre;
Off Gascone wyne, gif ony in it be,
Or, be thair ony within ane hundreth myle,
It salbe heir within a bony quhyle.'°   *short space of time*
The gudman had grit mervell of this taill
And said, 'My hairt neir° will be haill°   *never; whole/at peace*
Bot gif ye preve° that practik or ye pairte,   *demonstrate*
To mak ane sport.'° And than the freir upstart.   *To provide entertainment*
He tuk his buk and to the flure he gais;°   *takes the floor*
And to the eist direct he turnis his face;[39]
Syne to the west he turnit and lukit doun
And tuk his buk and red ane orisoun;°   *recited a prayer*
And ay° his eyne war on the almery   *at all times*
And on the troch, quhair that Freir Johine did ly.
He set him doun and kaist abak his heid;
He girnit,° he glourit,° he gapit as he war weid;°[40]   *snarled; glowered; mad*
And, quhylis, still he satt in studeing°   *meditation*
And uthir quhylis upoun his buk reding;°   *reading aloud*
And with baith his handis he wald clap
And uthir quhylis wald he glour and gaip;
Syne in the sowth he turnit him abowt
Weill thryis° and mair.[41] Than lawly°   *thrice; lowly;*
cowd he lowt,°   *stooped/bowed*
Quhen that he come neir the almery.
Thairat our dame had woundir grit invy°   *rancour*
For in her hairt scho had ane persaving°   *premonition*
That he had knawin all hir govirning.°   *conduct*
Scho saw him gif the almery sic a stait°[42]   *such importance*
Unto hir self scho said, 'Full weill I wait
I am bot schent.° He knawis full weill my thocht.   *It is all up with me*

38. Magic and necromantic practices are usually associated with foreign learning.
39. ED. B. and M. introduce a third rhyming line. This has been omitted.
40. ED. ll. 325–6 heid; weid] M. hude; woid B. Not only is this a poor rhyme, the travelling friars had taken off their hoods. See l. 42.
41. ll. 331–2 Turning in all directions, ending at the east, is in accord with mystical and magical practice. Robert, however, faces south finally, as the food is hidden there.
42. ED. stait] M; straik B.

Quhat sall I do? Allace, that I wes wrocht!° *I was ever born*
Get Simon wit, it wilbe deir doing.'[43]
Be that, the freir had left his studeing
And on his feit he startis up full sture° *very vigorously*
And come agane and seyit all his cure:° *fulfilled his office*
'Now is it done and ye sall haif playntie
Of breid and wyne, the best in this cuntre.
Thairfoir, fair dame, get up deliverlie° *smartly*
And ga belyfe° unto yone almerie *immediately*
And oppin it, and se ye bring us syne
Ane pair of bossis full of Gascone wyne
(Thay hald ane galloun and mair, that wait I weill!)
And bring us als the Mayne breid in a creill,° *creel/basket*
Ane pair of cunyngis, fat and het pypand;° *piping hot*
The caponis als ye sall us bring fra hand;
Twa pair of pertrikis, I wait thair is no ma;
And eik of pluveris,° se that ye bring us twa.' *plovers*
The gudwyf wist it wes no variance.° *argument was pointless*
Scho knew the freir had sene hir govirnance;° *had witnessed her actions*
Scho saw it wes no bute° for to deny. *remedy*
With that scho went unto the almery
And oppinnit it and than scho fand thair
All that the freir had spokin of befoir.
Scho stert abak, as scho wer in a fray,° *state of alarm*
And sanyt hir° and, smyland, cowd scho say,° *crossed herself; said*
'Ha, banedicitie,° quhat may this bene? *Oh, bless me*
Quha evir afoir hes sic a fairly° sene— *wonder*
Sa grit a mervell—as now hes apnit heir?
Quhat sall I say? He is ane haly freir;
He said full suth of° all that he did say.' *He spoke very truthfully in*
Scho brocht all furth and on the burd cowd lay
Baith breid and wyne and uthir thingis moir,
Cunyngis and caponis, as ye haif hard befoir;
Pertrikis and pluveris befoir thame hes scho brocht.
The freir knew weill and saw thair wantit nocht.° *was nothing missing*
Bot all wes furth brocht evin at his devyis.° *according to his design*
And Symone saw it appinnit on this wyis.
He had grit wondir and sweris be the mone,
That Freir Robert weill his dett had done.° *had acquitted himself well*
'He may be callit ane man of grit science,° *knowledge*
So suddandlie that all this purviance°[44] *these provisions*
Hes brocht us heir, throw his grit subteltie
And throw his knawlege in filosophie:
In ane gud tyme it wes quhen he come hidder!
Now, fill the cop that we may drink togidder
And mak gud cheir eftir this langsum° day, *tedious*
For I haif riddin ane woundir wilsome way.° *tortuous route*

43. 'If Simon gets to know, it will be a costly affair.'
44. ED. Sa suddandlie that all this purviance] M; Sa suddanly maid all this purviance B.

Now, God be lovit, heir is suffisance°	*sufficiency*
Unto us all, throw your gud govirnance.'	
And than annone thay drank evin round abowt°	*in turn*
Of Gascone wyne. The freiris playit 'Cop Owt';°	*Drain the Cup*
Thay sportit thame and makis mirry cheir	
With sangis lowd, baith Symone and the freir;	
And on this wyis the lang nicht thay ourdraif°—	*passed*
No thing thay want° that thay desyrd to haif.	*they lack nothing*
Than Symon said to the gudwyf in hy,	
'Cum heir, fair dame, and sett yow doun me by	
And tak pairte of sic gud as we haif heir	
And hairtly I yow pray to thank this freir	
Off his bening° grit besines and cure,°	*gracious; office*
That he hes done to us upoun this flure	
And brocht us meit and drink haboundantlie,	
Quhairfoir of richt, we aucht mirry to be.'	
Bot all thair sport, quhen thay wer maist at eis,	
Unto our deme° it wes bot littill pleis°	*dame; pleasure*
For uthir thing thair wes in to hir thocht.	
Scho wes so red° hir hairt wes ay on flocht°	*so flushed (because); in a flutter*
That, throw the freir,° scho sowld discoverit be.	*i.e. Robert*
To him scho lukit oft tymes effeiritlie°	*fearfully/anxiously*
And ay disparit° in hart was scho,	*despairing*
That he had witt° of all hir purveance to.°	*knowledge; preparation for it*
Thus satt scho still and wist no udir wane.°	*knew no other recourse*
Quhat evir thay say, scho lute him all allane.[45]	
(But scho drank with thame in to cumpany°	*to be convivial*
With fenyeit cheir and hert full wo and hevy.)	
Bot thay wer blyth annuche, God watt, and sang,	
For ay the wyne was rakand° thame amang.	*passing*
Quhill, at the last, thay woix richt blyth ilk one.°	*each one*
Than Symone said unto the freir annone,	
'I mervell mikill° how that this may be,	*greatly*
In till schort tyme that ye sa suddanlye	
Hes brocht to us sa mony denteis deir.'°	*expensive dishes*
'Thairof haif ye no mervell,' quod the freir.	
'I haif ane pege full prevy of my awin,°	*a servant unique to me*
Quhen evir I list, will cum to me unknawin°	*unperceived/unrecognised*
And bring to me sic thing as I will haif;	
Quhat evir I list, it neidis me nocht to craif.°	*I don't long for it in vain*
Thairfoir, be blyth and tak in pacience	
And, trest ye weill, I sall do diligence.°	*I shall do my utmost*
Gif that ye list or thinkis° to haif moir	*desire or intend*
It salbe had and I sall stand thairfoir,°	*I give you my pledge on it*
Incontinent,° that samyn° sall ye se.	*Immediately, that very thing*
Bot, I protest that ye keip it previe;°	*to yourselves*
Latt no man wit that I can do sic thing.'	
Than Symone swoir and said, 'Be hevynnis King,	

45. 'Whatever they might say, she kept her distance from him.'

It sal be kepit prevy as for me.
Bot, bruder deir, your servand wald I se,
Gif it yow pleis—that we may drynk togidder
For I wait nocht gif ye ma ay° cum hidder, — *always*
Quhen that we want° our neidis sic as this.' — *lack*
The freir said, 'Nay, so mot I haif hevynis blis!
Yow to haif the sicht of my servand,
It can nocht be. Ye sall weill undirstand,
That ye *may* se him graithly° in his awin kynd;° — *readily; natural image*
Bot ye, annone, sowld go owt of your mynd!
He is so fowll and ugly for to se,
I dar nocht awnter for to tak on me° — *venture to take it upon me*
To bring him hidder heir, in to our sicht,
And namely now so lait in to the nicht—
Bot gif° it wer on sic a maner wyis — *Unless*
Him to translait,° or ellis dissagyis — *transform*
Fra his awin kynd in to ane uder stait.'[46]
Than Symone said, 'I mak no moir debait.
As pleisis yow, so lyk is it to me;
As evir ye list,° bot fane wald I him se.' — *Do as you please*
Freyr Robert said, 'Sen that your will is so,
Tell on to me withouttin wordis mo,
In till quhat kynd sall I him gar appeir?'
Than Symone said, 'In liknes of a freir
In quhyt cullour—richt as your self it war,[47]
For quhyt cullour will na body deir.'° — *hurt*
Freir Robert said that swa it cowld nocht be
For sic causis° as he may weill foirse:° — *reasons; anticipate*
'That he compeir in to° our habeit quhyt, — *appear in*
Untill our ordour it wer a grit dispyte,
That ony sic unworthy wicht° as he — *being*
In till our habeit men sowld behald or se.
But, sen it pleissis yow that ar heir,
Ye sall him se in liknes of a freir,
In habeit blak it was his kynd to weir[48]
In to sic wyss° that he sal no man deir. — *In such a manner*
Gif ye so do, and rewll yow at all wyiss,° — *govern yourself at all times*
To hald yow cloiss° and still at my devyiss, — *To keep yourself undisclosed*
Quhat evir it be ye owdir° se or heir, — *either*
Ye speik no word nor mak no kynd of steir,° — *disturbance*
But hald yow clois quhill I haif done my cure.'
Than said he, 'Symone, ye mone be on the flure
Neirhand besyd, with staff in to your hand;
Haif ye no dreid! I sall yow ay warrand.'° — *I shall be your guarantor always*
Than Symone said, 'I assent that it be swa.'
And up he start and gat a libberla° — *cudgel*

46. Devils were believed to have the power to change nature and appearance.
47. They are not wearing their black hood and cloak.
48. 'In a black habit suited to his nature.' (ED. M. reads 'In gray habite as is his kynde to weir.')

Into his hand and on the flure he stert,
Sumthing effrayit, thocht stalwart was his hart.
Than to the freir said Symone verry sone,
'Now tell me, maister, quhat ye will haif done.'
'No thing,' he said, 'bot hald yow clois and still.
Quhat evir I do, tak ye gud tent thairtill,° — *pay good heed to it*
And neir the dur ye hyd yow prevely,
And quhen I bid yow stryk,° strek hardely — *strike*
Into the nek! Se that ye hit him richt.'
'That sall I warrand,' quod he, 'with all my micht.'
Thus on the flure I leif him standand still
Bydand his tyme; and turne agane I will
How that the freir did take his buke in hy
And turnit our the levis full besely
Ane full lang space. And quhen he had done swa,° — *so*
Towart the troch, withowttin wordis ma,
He gois belyfe, and on this wyis sayis he:
'Ha, how, Hurlybas!° Now, I conjure the, — *(name for demon)*
That thow uprys and sone to me appeir
In habeit blak, in liknes of a freir!
Owt of this troch, quhair that thow dois ly,
Thow rax the° sone and mak no dyn nor cry; — *stretch yourself*
Thow tumbill our the troch, that we may se,
And unto us thow schaw the oppinlie;
And in this place, se that thow no man greif° — *harm*
Bot draw thy handis boith in to thy sleif° — *sleeve*
And pull thy cowll doun owttour° thy face. — *right over*
(Thow may thank God that thow gettis sic a grace)
Thairfoir, thow turs the to thyne awin ressett!° — *return to your own domain*
Se this be done and mak no moir debait;
In thy depairting se thow mak no deray° — *cause no disturbance*
Unto no wicht, bot frely pas thy way;
And in this place, se that thow cum no moir
Bot° I command the, or ellis the charge befoir;° — *Unless; give you a prior order*
And our° the stair se that thow ga gud speid; — *over*
Gif thow dois nocht—on thy awin perrell beid!'° — *i.e. count on your own peril*
With that the freir, that under the troch lay,
Raxit him sone, bot he wes in a fray!
And up he rais and wist na bettir wayn,° — *recourse*
Bot of the troch he tumlit our° the stane. — *tumbled over*
Syne, fra the samyn, quhairin he thocht him lang,° — *he had been long enough*
Unto the dur he preisit him to gang,° — *hastened to go*
With hevy cheir° and drery countenance — *sad mood*
For nevir befoir him hapnit sic a chance.
And quhen Freir Robert saw him gangand by,
Unto the gudman full lowdly cowd he cry,
'Stryk, stryk herdely, for now is tyme to the!'° — *i.e. the moment is yours*
With that, Symone a felloun flap lait fle.° — *let fly a fierce blow*
With his burdoun,° he hit him on the nek, — *cudgel*
He wes sa ferce, he fell owttour the sek° — *right over the sack*

And brak his heid upoun ane mustard stane.[49]
Be this, Freir Johine attour the stair is gane
In sic wyis, that mist he hes the trap° *small stair at angle to stairway*
And in ane myr° he fell—sic wes his hap— *heap of rubbish*
Wes fourty futis of breid° undir the stair, *in extent*
Yeit, gat he up with cleithing nothing fair;
Full drerelie upoun his feit he stude
And, throw the myre, full smertly than he yude,° *went*
And our the wall, he clam richt haistely,
Quhilk round abowt wes laid with stanis dry.
Off his eschaping in hairt he wes full fane.° *he was heartily glad*
I trow he sall be laith° to cum agane! *reluctant*
With that, Freir Robert stert abak and saw
Quhair the gudman lay sa woundir law
Upoun the flure and bleidand wes his heid.
He stert to him and went° he had bene deid *thought*
And clawcht° him up withowttin wordis moir *snatched*
And to the dur delyverly him bure
And, fra the wind wes blawin twyis in his face,
Than he ourcome within a lytill space.[50]
And than Freir Robert franyt at him fast,° *asked him forcibly*
Quhat ailit him to be so soir agast?
He sayd, 'Yon feynd had maid me in effray.'[51]
'Lat be,' quod he, 'the werst is all away.
Mak mirry, man, and se ye murne na mair!
Ye haif him strikin quyt owttour the stair.
I saw him slip, gif I the suth can tell,
Doun our the stair—in till a myr he fell!
Bot lat him go, he wes a graceles gaist,° *graceless ghost/guest*
And boun yow° to your bed, for it is best.' *take yourself off*
Thus, Symonis heid upoun the stane wes brokin
And our the stair the freir in myre hes loppin° *leapt*
And, tap our taill,° he fyld wes woundir ill,° *top to toe; was very badly befouled*
And Alesone on na wayis gat hir will.
This is the story that hapnit of that freir;
No moir thair is, bot Chryst us help most deir.°[52] *most precious (i.e. Christ)*

49. A stone utensil used to grind mustard-seed.

50. ll. 549–50: 'And the wind had hardly blown twice in his face before, in a short space of time, he regained consciousness.'

51. ED. He sayd yon feynd had maid me in effray] M; He said yone freir hes maid me thuss gait say B.

52. ll. 561–6: cf. stylistically Chaucer *Miller's Tale*, 3850–4; *Reeve's Tale*, 4313–8.

§ 9 Gavin Douglas (1476–1522): *Eneados*

[See also Introduction to § 15]

A younger son of Archibald, 5th Earl of Angus and Elizabeth, daughter of Lord Boyd (leader of the most influential family during the reign of James III), Gavin Douglas belonged to the higher ranks of the Scottish nobility. Born and educated during the reign of James IV, he graduated from the University of St Andrews in 1494. His chosen career was the church and he quickly rose within its ranks, becoming Bishop of Dunkeld in 1515. His family, led by the Earl of Angus, soon lost power and the Regent, Albany, latterly arraigned Douglas on a charge of high treason. The Bishop died as an exile from his homeland, in London—probably of the plague.

P. Vergilius Maro (Vergil), the author of the **Aeneid**, *was a Latin poet born in 70 B.C. who came to Rome to learn oratory and Civil Law during the troubled civil war period dramatized by Shakespeare in* **Julius Caesar.** *Retreating to the area around the Bay of Naples, he published his pastoral poems, the* **Eclogues**, *in 44 B.C., shortly after the murder of Caesar. His second major work, the* **Georgics**, *appeared fourteen years later. The* **Aeneid**, *his last work, is an epic study of Aeneas' journey, away from the ravaged city of Troy, to found a new city and new life for his people in Rome.*

Gavin Douglas's literary fate has been to stand, somewhat undeservedly, in the shadow of the other two great makars, Robert Henryson and William Dunbar. He has no shorter poems to represent him and his earlier, allegorical dream-poem, **The Palice of Honour** *(c. 1501), is highly conventional. Yet his contribution is unique in at least two ways. Douglas is the first major Scottish poet to be heavily influenced by humanist thought—as the lists of authors in the* **Palice** *describe and the* **Eneados** *enacts. He maintains the Christian world-view of his predecessors, but re-interprets it in accordance with these ideas. Secondly, translation is greatly favoured in Scottish Literature, which has an unusually high number of excellent practitioners in this mode. Douglas is the first recorded translator and sets a standard which will seldom, if ever, be matched—even by the finest of his successors (see especially § 17. Stewart and § 22. Urquhart).*

Text: *The hero (Aeneas) is on a journey undertaken for martial reasons—in this case the fall of Troy. He hopes to found a new city but, as the references to divine malevolence remind us, we are in a world ruled by the pagan gods. The many setbacks he encounters are ultimately caused by Juno's malevolence but finally redressed by Jupiter.*

Context: *The* **Aeneid,** *like many classical epics, begins in the middle of events and then looks back. (III.x.121–6) The passage from Book III has been chosen not only because it is self-contained, but also because it underlines that structure—drawing the reader back to the storm, which opened Book I. In addition, it highlights the bardic element within the poem and its relation to the earlier epics of Homer. In recounting his adventures for the benefit of Dido's court, Aeneas is his own storyteller. As such he takes on the voice of Achemenydes, a stranded follower of Homer's hero, Odysseus (III, ix.48–9; x.67–8). From Book IV onwards, the story post-dates Book I. The Chapter divisions are Douglas's own.*

Canto IX, 47–120: 'Of the Greik clepit Achemenydes, rehersyng ene the natur of Ciclopes' (*Aeneid* III, 613–54)[1]

[Aeneid continues the story of his voyages, as told to Dido and her court. Earlier in Book III, he has learned that his new city cannot be sited in the known Greco-Trojan world. He has also discovered that the city cannot be modelled on Troy. With the death of his father Anchises and his entry into unknown waters, he finds himself in a new, frightening world in more senses than one. It is at this stage he reaches Ithaca and meets Achemenydes. An old soldier, deserted by Ulysses on his earlier voyage, Achemenydes lives in constant fear of a race of one eyed-giants (the Ciclopes) who inhabit the island.]

' "Of the realm Itachia° I am, butless,[2]	*Ithaca (island to west of Greece)*
And of the cumpany of fey° Ulixes;[3]	*fated*
And Achemenydes onto name I hait,°	*am called*
Cummyn onto Troy with my fader of lait°	*lately*
(Bot a puyr wageour,° clepyt° Adamastus)	*Only a poor soldier; called*
Wald God yit° the same forton remanyt to us!	*still*
My falloschip onwytting foryet° me heir,	*thoughtless companions left*
Quhen tha,° thir° cruel marchys° left for feir	*those; these; shores*
And in the Ciclopes huge cave tynt° me;	*lost*
A gowsty hald° within, laithly° to se,	*cavernous dwelling; ugly*
Ful of vennom and mony bludy meys.°[4]	*feasts*
Bustuus,° hie Poliphemus set a deys,°	*Massive; dais (which)*
Thar remanys, that may the starnys schaik.[5]	
Ye goddis delyvir this erd from sik wraik°	*destruction*
For he is ugsum° and grysly° forto se,	*ugly; terrible*
Hutyt to speke of and aucht not nemmyt be![6]	
Thir wrachit mennys flesch, that is hys fude—	
And drinkis worsum,° and thar lappyrrit° blude.	*(he) drinks pus; coagulated*
I was my self° quhen, gruflyngis° amyd his cave,	*on my own; prostrate*
Twa bodeys of our sort° he tuke and rayf;°	*company; ripped apart*
Intil hys hyddus hand thame thrymlyt° and wrang,	*squeezed*
And on the stanys owt thar harnys dang,°	*beat out their brains*
Quhil brayn and eyn and blude al poplit owt°[7]—	*popped out*

1. ED. COPY TEXT: Cambridge MS. Our edition follows the practice of Coldwell in his Scottish Text Society edition, though less conservatively. A strong case could be made for using the Elphinstoun MS as Copy. As our extracts are brief, the advantage of keeping the text in close alignment with the fullest critical edition overrode nicety of editorial judgement in a context where five full manuscripts vie for authority.

ED. DOUGLAS'S TEXT: Douglas probably used Ascensius' 1501 text of Virgil with accompanying commentaries. (See Bibliography: Bawcutt, *Douglas*, 1976, pp. 92–127.) Notes marking the variation begin 'ED. Asc.'

2. ED. butless] mss; 'but less' makes no sense. The voice is that of Aeneas, recounting the words of Achemenydes. 'butless': 'aimless' is close to Vergil's 'infelicis [unhappy] Ulixi'.

3. Odysseus (Ulysses) is the hero of Homer's *Odyssey*. His journeying became part of Aeneas's story and his heroism a touchstone against which the later hero's conduct can be compared and contrasted.

4. Blood is a powerful leitmotiv in *Aeneid*, III.

5. ll. 58–9: In Vergil, it is the giant who shakes the stars: 'ipse arduus, altaque pulsat sidera'.

6. ED. Asc. 'effabilis' (capable of being expressed in words) for the more usual 'adfabilis' (courteous). 'Avoided in speech and not to be named aloud.'

7. ED. Asc: 'Expersa' (expelled) for 'aspersa' in phrase 'sanieque expersa natarent limina'—'and the splashed courts swam with gore'.

I saw that cruel fend eik,° that but dowt°	*fiend also; who assuredly*
Thar lymmys ryfe and eyt,° as he war woid;°	*ate; mad*
The youstir° tharfra chirtand,° and blak blude,	*seepage; squirting out*
And the hait flesch undir his teith flykkerand.°	*quivering*
Bot not onwrokyn,° forsuyth, his feste° he fand;	*unavenged; food*
Nor Ulixes list° not lang suffyr this,	*did it please Ulysses*
Ne this kyng of Itachy hym self, nor his°	*his (men)*
Myghtyn foryet, into sa gret a plyght.	
For sammyn° as that horribyll, fendlich° wight	*at the same time; fiendish*
Had eyt his fyll and drunk wyne, he° hym gave	*(which) he*
(Sowpit° in sleip, his nek furth of° the cave	*Sunk; outside*
He straucht,° fordronkyn, lyggyng in his dreym;	*stretched*
Bokkis° furth and yiskis° of yowstyr mony streym,	*Belches; issues*
Raw lumpys of flesch and blude blandyt° with wine)	*mixed*
We the gret goddys besocht° and kavillys° syne	*beseeched; lots*
Kastis,° quhat suld be every mannys part;°	*Cast; role*
Syne, al atanys abowt,° and on hym start,°	*all at once turned; set*
And with a scharpyt and bryntt steyng of tre°	*smouldering wooden stake*
Out dyd we boyr and pyke hys mekill e,°	*poked out his great eye*
That lurkit alane undyr hys thrawyn front large,°	*furrowed forehead broad*
Als braid as is a Gregioun° scheild or targe,°	*Greek; shield*
Or lyke onto the lantern of the moyn.[8]	
And thus, at last, have we revengit soyn,°	*soon*
Blithly the gostis° of our feris° ded.	*spirits; companions*
Bot yhe, onhappy men, fle from this sted,°	*place*
Fle, fle this cost, and smyte the cabill in twane!°	*dash the hawser in two*
For quhou grysly° and how gret,° I you sayn,	*horrible; huge*
Lurkis Polyphemus, yimmand° his beystis rouch,	*tending*
And al thar pappis° mylkis through and throuch.	*teats*
Ane hundreth otheris, als huge of quantite,	
Endlang° this ilk° costis syde of the se,	*Along; same*
Gret Ciclopes inhabitis heir and thar,	
And walkis in thir hie montanys our alquhar.°	*everywhere*
The moyn hes now fyllyt hir hornys thryss	
With new lyght, sen I have on this wys°	*way*
My lyfe in woddis led, but° syght of men,	*out of*
In desert hyrnys° and seyr° wild beistis den,	*retreats; many kinds of*
And far out from my cavern dyd aspy	
The grym Ciclopes, and oft thar grysly cry;	
My wrachit fude was berreis of the brymmyll,°	*brambles*
And stanyt heppis,° quhilk I on buskis° fand,	*hips with stones; bushes*
With rutis of herbis I holkit furth of° land;	*dug out of*
And vyssyand° al about, I se at last	*gazing*
Quhamto I me betaucht° and gan avow,°	*entrusted myself; vowed service*
Quhat flote° at ever it was—for wayt ye quhou	*fleet*
It is enuch that I eschapyt have	
Yone cruel pepill, I set not of the lave;°	*I do not value the rest*

8. Vergil has 'Phoebeae lampadis', 'the lamp of Phoebe'.

For, rather° ye or I fal in syk wraik,° *rather (than); desolation*
Quhat deith ye pless, the lyfe fra me gar taik." '[9]

Book III, Canto X, 1–71; 121–6: 'Of Poliphemus, and mony strange cost' (*Aeneid*, III, 655–91; 716–8)

'Skars° this wes sayd, quhen sone we gat a sycht *Hardly*
Apon ane hyll stalkand, this hydduus wight° *hideous creature*
Amang hys bestis, the hyrd° Poliphemus, *shepherd*
Down to the costis bekend,[10] draw towartis us:
A monstre horrbyll, onmesurabill and myschaip,° *misshapen*
Wanting° hys syght; and gan° to stab and graip° *Lacking; began; grope*
With hys burdon,° that wes a gret fyr tre,° *club; fir tree*
Fermand his steppis,° becaus he mycht not se, *Steadying his footing*
The wollyt scheip him follwyng at the bak,
Quharin his pleasour and delyte gan he tak.
About hys halss° a quhissil° hung had he, *neck; (shepherd's) pipe*
Wes al his° solace for tynsell° of hys e; *(Which) was his only; loss*
And, with his staf fre he the deip flude
Twichit,° and cummyn at the sey-syde stude. *Touched*
Of hys e-dolp° the flowand blude and attir° *eye-socket; pus*
He wysch° away al with the salt wattir *washed*
Grassilland° his teith, and rummysand° full hie.° *Grinding; roaring; loudly*
He wadis furth throu myddis of the see;° *through the open sea*
And yit the watir wet not hys lang syde.
We, far from thens, affrayt, durst not abyde,
Bot fled onon,° and within burd° hes brocht *at once; on board*
That faithful Greik quhilk us of succurss socht,° *sought help from us*
And, prevyly,° we smyte the cabill in twane.° *under cover; cut the cable in two*
Syne, kempand° with aris° in al our mane,° *striving; oars; strength*
Upweltris° watir of the salt sey flude. *Stirs up*
He persavyt the sownd, quhar that he stude,
And, towart the dyn, movis hys pays° onon, *noise strides*
Bot quhen he felt,° at° we sa far war gone, *sensed; that*
Sa that his handis us areke° ne mycht, *reach*
Nor the deip Sey Ionium,° for al hys hycht, *Ionian Sea*
Ne mycht he waid equale us to arest,° *stop*
A fellon bray° and huge schowt up he kest, *savage braying sound*
Quharthrou the sey and al the fludis schuke;
The land alhail of Itail trymlyt and quoyk,
And holl cavernys or furnys of Ethna rownd° *furnesses round Mt Etna*
Rummyst° and lowyt,° fordynnyt° with the sound. *Roared; reverberated; rang*
Bot than, furth of the woddis and hillys hie,
Walkynnyt° with the cry, a huge pepill° we se *Awakened; a gigantic race*

9. 'You may take my life from me, by whatever means of death you please.'
10. ED. The Bath MS has 'beikand', which would suggest that Polyphemus is beckoning. The others have 'bekend', which suggests that Polyphemus was well acquainted with the route. It is tempting, however, to rede 'sekend' or 'seikand', which accurately translate V.'s 'petentem'.

Of Ciclopes cum hurland° to the port, *rushing*
And fillyt all the cost° sydis at schort. *coast*
The elrych bredyr,° with thair lukis thrawyn,° *weird brethren; distorted*
Thocht not avalyt, thar standyng have we knawyn[11]—
Ane horribil sort, with mony camscho beik° *many a deformed nose*
And hedis semand to the hevyn areik,° *reach up*
Siclyke as quhar that, with thar hie toppis,
The byg akis° strekyng in the ayr thar croppys° *oaks; highest branches*
Or than thir cipressis° berand heich thar bewys,° *these cypresses; boughs*
Growand in the woddis or hie up on hewis,° *crags*
In schawys ald,° as men may se from far, *ancient groves*
Hallowyt to Dyane° or yit to Jupiter.[12] *Diana (the huntress)*
The scharp dreid maid us so to cach haist,° *move faster*
Withdrawand fast, as thocht we had bene chaist,
And for to set our sail quhiddir we best mycht,
To follow the wynd, and hald na coursis rycht.° *maintain no set route*
Aganys the counsale of Helenus,[13] our feris
Perswadis to hald furth evyn° the way that steris *head straight ahead*
Mydwart betwix Charibdis and Scylla,[14]
A litil space fra ded by athir of twa,[15]
For, bot we hald that cours, forowtyn fail,
Bakwartis, thai said, on Ciclopes mon we° saill. *we would have to*
Bot lo! onon a fair wynd, or we wist,° *realized*
Rayss of° the north, blawyng evyn as we lyst,° *Rose from; wished*
From the strait° bay of Pelorus the mont° *narrow; Mt Pelorus (in Sicily)*
And sone we swepyt by,° at the fyrst bront,° *swept past; onrush*
The mouth of flude Pantgyas° ful of stanys, *R. Pantagias*
The sownd Megarus,° and Tapsum ile[16] atanys. *Megarian bay*
The namys of thir costis, Achemenydes,
The companyeon of onhappy Ulixes,
Rakynys° to us, as we past ane by ane, *Relates*
For we return the sammyn went agane° *retraced the same route*
Quhar thar° navy had waverit° by thar rays.° *i.e. Ulysses'; strayed; voyage*

[Poetically, Aeneas too 'retraces the route' of his past voyages until he reaches the stage at which the epic had begun in Book I. Lamenting the death of his father, Anchises, he bewails his ill fate so far and, in this way, explains how he and his men reached Dido's land.][17]

11. 'We were aware of them standing there to no avail [i.e. impotently].'
12. The voyages of Aeneas are conducted in opposition to Juno, the wife of Jupiter.
13. Son of Priam, King of Troy.
14. Charibdis was a whirlpool to one side of the straits of Messina. On the other was the nymph Scylla, who had been turned into a sea-monster by Circe, jealous of Glaucus' pursuit of her.
15. 'Narrowly separated from death on either side.'
16. Thapsus is, in fact, a Sicilian peninsula. The description (ll. 63–6) derives from commentary material. See n. 1.
17. This 'in medias res' structuring (starting in the middle of the action, then looking back and only latterly moving forward) was especially favoured in Classical Epic. It is one of the artistic and artificial orderings of material recommended to the medieval artist by Vinsauf in his *Poetria Nuova*.

The prynce Eneas, on this wys, alane
The fatis of goddys and rasys° mony ane — *tribes*
Rehersyng schew, and syndry strange wentis,° — *exotic routes/strange events*
The quene and all the Tyrryanys takand tentis.° — *people of Tyre paying attention*
And at the last he cessyt and said no moir,
Endyng his tayll as ye have hard befor.[18]

18. The stage at which the story-line of the epic, begun in Book I, has now been reached.

§ 10 William Dunbar (c.1460–c.1520): *Lyrics and Ballatis*[1]

[See also introductions to § 6 and § 7]

A number of authorial voices are represented in the later lyrical sections. Dunbar, however, is so varied and superlative a lyricist, that he may represent on his own the spectrum of modes, styles and tones of the earlier Middle Scots period as well. **'The Magryme', 'Ane Dance in the Quenis Chalmer', 'How Sould I governe me?'** *and* **'To the Merchantis of Edinburgh'** *provide poetic insights into the character of the poet, the court of James IV and the outside world of trade under the law. As such, they act as a valuable complement to the biographical material noted in the Introduction to § 6.* **'Ane Ballat of Our Lady', 'Timor Mortis Conturbat Me'** *and* **'Ane Ballat of the Fenyeit Freir of Tungland'** *encapsulate the virtuosity of the 'maister poete' in High, Middle and Low styles; eulogistic, contemplative and satiric voices respectively.*

(i) *'Ane Ballat of Our Lady'*[2]

1	
Hale, sterne superne,° hale in eterne	*celestial star*
In Godis sicht to schyne;	
Lucerne° in derne° for to discerne°	*Lamp; darkness; by which to see*
Be glory and grace devyne;	
Hodiern, modern, sempitern,°	*For this day this age and evermore*
Angelicall regyne;°	*queen*
Our tern inferne° for to dispern,°	*gloom infernal; disperse*
Helpe, rialest rosyne.°	*most royal rose*
Ave Maria, gracia plena.[3]	*Hail Mary full of grace*
Haile, fresche floure femynyne;°	*womanly*
Yerne us guberne,° virgin matern°	*Govern us diligently; maternal*
Of reuth° baith rute and ryne.°[4]	*pity; root and bark*
2	
Haile, yhyng° benyng° fresche flurising,°	*young; gracious; blossoming*
Haile, Alphais habitakle;°	*God's (the Creator's) dwelling place*
Thy dyng° ofspring maid us to syng	*worthy*
Befor His tabernakle;°	*tabernacle*
All thing maling° we doune thring°	*malign; overthrow*
Be sicht of His signakle,°	*sign i.e. the Cross*
Quhilk king us bring unto His ryng°	*kingdom*
Fro dethis dirk umbrakle.°	*From death's dark shade*
Ave Maria, gracia plena.	

1. The use of 'ballat' here and in subsequent sections is to cover the inclusion of rather longer poems, which meet most of the criteria of lyric except the idea that it should be short.
2. ED. (i) Copy Text: MS Asloan. The divine topic warrants the metrical intricacy and Latin rhythms of the high style.
3. The angelic salutation, drawn from Luke 1. 28.
4. St. 1 illustrates in miniature the liturgical, biblical, visual and commentary sources which intertwine to add force to the eulogy. Mary was depicted with a star and a rose as attributes in art. She bore Christ miraculously as a virgin. As mother (root) and penitent at the wooden cross ('ryne') she prays in pity for us.

Haile, moder and maide but makle;° *without spot/pure*
Bricht syng,° gladyng° our languissing *sign/icon; gladdening*
Be micht of thi mirakle.

3

Haile, bricht be sicht in hevyn on hicht;° *clearly visible in highest heaven*
Haile, day sterne orientale;° *rising in the east*
Our licht most richt in clud° of nycht *cloud*
Our dirknes for to scale:° *disperse*
Hale, wicht-in-ficht,° puttar-to-flicht°[5] *soldier-in-combat; putter-to flight*
Of fendis° in battale; *fiends*
Haile, plicht but sicht;° hale, mekle° of mycht; *invisible support; great*
Hale, glorius virgin, hale!
Ave Maria, gracia plena.
Haile, gentill nychttingale;
Way stricht, cler dicht to wilsome wicht[6]
That irke° bene in travale.° *weary; labouring*

4

Haile, quene serene; hale, most amene;° *kindly/pleasing*
Haile, hevinlie hie emprys;° *empress*
Haile, schene° unseyne with carnale eyne;° *bright one; by earthly eyes*
Haile, ros of paradys;° *rose of paradise/without thorns*
Haile, clene bedene° ay till conteyne;° *utterly spotless one; in perpetuity*
Haile, fair fresche floure delyce,° *lily*
Haile, grene° daseyne;° haile for the splene° *green/fresh; daisy; spleen/heart*
Of Jhesu genitrice;° *mother*
Ave Maria, gracia plena.
Thow baire° the prince of prys;° *bore; glory*
Our teyne° to meyne° and ga betweyne° *affliction; intercede for; mediate*
As humile oratrice.° *humble pleader*

5

Haile, more decore than of before° *ever more beautiful*
And swetar be sic sevyne,°[7] *seven times more gracious*
Our glore forlore° for to restore *lost bliss*
Sen thow art qwene of hevyn;
Memore of sore,° stern in aurore,° *Memorial to misery; day-star*
Lovit with angellis stevyne;° *Extolled by angels' voices*
Implore, adore, thow indeflore,° *undeflowered one/i.e. virgin*
To mak our oddis evyne.° *balance the odds against us*
Ave Maria, gracia plena.
With lovingis lowde ellevyn° *eleven loud cries of praise*
Quhill store° and hore° my youth devore° *Until adversity; old age; devour*
Thy name I sall ay nevyne.° *always tell aloud*

5. I.e. combatant and conqueror. As mother of Christ, who defeated Satan and delivered us from hell. Compound words are a feature of the high style.
6. 'Straight pathway, clearly laid out for the wilful individual/errant traveller.'
7. Favourable numbers—3, 7 and 11 (5.10)—are used to translate the divine mysteries surrounding Mary.

6

Empryce of prys,° imperatrice,° — *Esteemed empress; commander*
Bricht polist° precious stane;° — *polished; precious stone*
Victrice° of vyce, hie genitrice° — *Conqueror; noble mother/creator*
Of Jhesu lord soverayne;
Our wys pavys fro° enemys — *shield of prudence against*
Agane the Feyndis trayne;° — *followers of the Fiend/Satan*
Oratrice, mediatrice, salvatrice,° — *Preacher intercessor saviour*
To God gret suffragene;° — *hand-maiden/assistant*
Ave Maria, gracia plena.
Haile, sterne meridiane;° — *star at noon/sun*
Spyce,° flour delice° of paradys[8] — *Spice; lily*
That baire° the gloryus grayne.°[9] — *bore; seed of glory (i.e. Christ)*

7

Imperiall wall, place palestrall° — *palatial dwelling*
Of peirles pulcritud;° — *peerless beauty*
Tryumphale hall, hie trone° regall — *throne*
Of Godis celsitud;° — *majesty*
Hospitall riall,° the lord of all — *royal lodging*
Thy closet° did include;° — *small room (womb); enclose*
Bricht ball cristall,° ros virginall — *crystal globe*
Fulfillit of° angell fude.° — *replete with; food of angels (Christ)*
Ave Maria, gracia plena.
Thy birth° has with His blude — *i.e. the Child you bore*
Fra fall mortall, originall° — *original (in Eden)*
Us raunsound° on the Rude.° — *ransomed; Cross*

(ii) *'Ane Dance in the Quenis Chalmer'*

1

Sir Jhon Sinclair begowthe° to dance — *began*
For he was new° cum owt of France; — *recently*
For ony thing that he do mycht
The ane futt yeid ay onrycht[10]
And to the tother wald nocht gree.° — *keep in harmony with*
Quod ane,° 'Tak up° the Quenis knycht!' — *Said one; Pick up/Give a hand to*
A mirrear° dance mycht na man see. — *merrier*

2

Than cam in Maistir Robert Schau:[11]
He leuket as° he culd lern° tham a,° — *looked as (if); teach; all*
Bot ay° his ane futt did waver;° — *always; wavered/faltered*
He stackeret° lyk ane strummall aver° — *staggered; shambling cart-horse*

8. Imagery from *The Song of Solomon* is traditionally used to express the mysteries of divine love. The spice flowers here and much of the earlier flower imagery derive from this source. The lily, symbol of royalty in France, was one of Mary's attributes in fine art.
9. See John 12. 24–5.
10. ED. (ii) Copy Text: MS Maitland Folio. I.e. In spite of all his efforts, one foot kept going awry.
11. Robert Shaw was the court physician.

That hopschackellt° war aboin° the kne; — *hobbled; above*
To seik fra Sterling° to Stranaver° — *from Stirling; Strathnaver*
A mirrear dance mycht na man see.

3

Than cam in the maister almaser,° — *chief almoner*
Ane hommiltye jommeltye juffler° — *clumsy awkward fellow*
Lyk a stirk° stackerand° in the ry;° — *bullock; staggering; rye*
His hippis° gaff° mony hoddous° cry. — *hindquarters; emitted; hideous*
John Bute the fule° said, 'Waes° me! — *(court) fool; Woe's*
He is bedirtin,° fye, fy!' — *befouled*
A mirrear dance mycht na man see.

4

Than cam in Dunbar the mackar,° — *poet/makar*
On all the flure° thair was nane frackar,° — *(dance) floor; more lively*
And thair he dancet the Dirrye Dantoun;° — *a vigorous dance of the day*
He hoppet° lyke a pillie wanton° — *capered; randy fellow*
For luff of Musgraeffe,[12] men tellis me;
He trippet° quhill he tint° his panton:° — *jigged; lost; slipper*
A mirrear dance mycht na man see.

5

Than cam in Maesteres Musgraeffe;
Scho mycht heff lernit° all the laeffe;° — *instructed; rest*
Quhen I schau° hir sa trimlye° dance, — *saw; so neatly*
Hir guid convoy° and contenance,° — *deportment; bearing*
Than for hir saek I wissitt° to be — *wished*
The grytast° erle or duk in France: — *greatest/most noble*
A mirrear dance mycht na man see.

6

Than cam in Dame Dounteboir[13]—
God waett° gif that scho louket sowr;° — *knows; looked bad-tempered*
Schou maid sic morgeownis° with hir hippis° — *contortions; haunches*
For lachtter nain mycht hald thair lippis;° — *i.e. no one could keep a straight face*
Quhen schou was danceand bisselye° — *dancing busily*
Ane blast of wind son° fra hir slippis:° — *soon; slips/escapes*
A mirrear dance mycht na man see.

7

Quhen thair was cum in fyve or sax
The Quenis Dog[14] begowthe to rax° — *began to stretch*
And of his band° he maid a bred° — *from his leash; spring*
And to the danceing soin° he him med;° — *soon; applied himself*
Quhou mastevlyk° abowt yeid° he! — *mastiff-like; went*

12. A lady at the court.
13. A disparaging name given to court ladies.
14. James Dog was Master of the Queen's Wardrobe.

He stinckett° lyk a tyk,° sum saed: *stank; cur*
A mirrear dance mycht na man see.

(iii) *'The Magryme'*° *headache*

1

My heid did yak° yester nicht,° *ached; last night*
This day to mak° that I na micht, *compose/write poetry*
So sair° the magryme° dois me menyie,° *painfully; migraine; assail*
Perseing° my brow as ony ganyie,° *Piercing; arrow*
That scant I luik may° on the licht. *I may scarcely (bear to) look*

2

And now, Schir, laitlie eftir mes° *mass*
To dyt° thocht I begowthe to dres,° *compose; began to apply myself*
The sentence° lay full evill till° find— *theme; very difficult to*
Unsleipit in my heid behind,[15]
Dullit in dulnes° and distres. *Dulled by sluggishness*

3

Full oft at morow° I upryse *in the morning*
Quhen that my curage° sleipeing lyis:° *creative energy; (still) slumbers*
For mirth, for menstrallie° and play,° *minstrelsy; entertainment*
For din nor danceing nor deray,° *revelry*
It will not walkin° me no wise.° *arouse; in no way*

(iv) *'Ane Ballat of the Fenyeit Freir*° *of Tungland'* *(How he fell in the Myre fleand*° *to Turkiland)*[16] *Feigned Friar* *flying*

1

As yung Awrora° with cristall haile° *goddess of dawn; i.e. dew*
In orient° schew° hir visage paile *east; revealed*
A swenyng° swyth° did me assaile *dream; quickly*
Off sonis of Sathanis seid;[17]
Me thocht° a Turk of Tartary° *It seemed; land of Tartars/hell*
Come throw the boundis° of Barbary° *lands/boundaries; heathendom*
And lay forloppin° in Lumbardy° *a fugitive; in Lombardy*
Full lang° in waithman weid.° *A very long time; outlaw's dress*

2

Fra baptasing° for to eschew° *baptizing; avoid*
Thair a religious man° he slew *man of religion*

15. ED. (iii) Copy Text: MS Reidpeth. The memory was held to occupy the back of the brain, where it provided a treasure house of images. The poet laments that he cannot retrieve any of the ideas embedded 'At the back of (his) sleep-deprived brain'.
16. ED. (iv) Copy Text: MS Bannatyne. The story of John Damian—Italian alchemist and Abbot of Tungland—who tried, unsuccessfully, to fly off the battlements of Stirling Castle, is related by the seventeenth century historian, Bishop Leslie.
17. 'About the offspring of the seed of Satan.' Damian is at once seen as a devil.

And cled him in his abeit° new   *religious garb/habit*
    For he cowth° wryte and reid.   *was able to*
Quhen kend° was his dissimulance°   *revealed; deception*
And all his cursit govirnance°   *accursed conduct*
For feir he fled and come in° France   *came into*
    With littill of Lumbard leid.°[18]   *lore from Lombardy*

3

To be a leiche° he fenyt him° thair,   *doctor; passed himself off as*
Quhilk mony a man micht rew evirmair,°   *rue ever afterwards*
For he left nowther seik° nor sair°   *sick; suffering*
Unslane° or° he him yeid°   *Unslain/Alive; before; left*
Vane organis° he full clenely carvit,°   *The wrong organs; cut out*
Quhen of his straik° so mony starvit,°   *stroke; perished*
Dreid° he had gottin° that he deservit°   *For fear...of getting; deserved*
He fled away gud speid.°   *in haste*

4

In Scotland than° the narrest° way   *then; quickest*
He come his cunnyng° till assay;°   *knowledge; try out*
To sum man° thair it was no play,°   *folk; no laughing matter*
The preving° of his sciens;°   *testing; learning*
In pottingry° he wrocht° grit pyne;   *the apothecary's art; caused*
He murdreist° mony in medecyne;°   *murdered; (name of) medicine*
The jow° was of a grit engyne°   *jew/infidel; ingenuity*
And generit was° of gyans.°[19]   *came from the race; giants*

5

In leichecraft° he was homecyd°—   *medicine; a manslayer*
He wald haif, for a nicht to byd,
A haiknay and the hurtmanis hyd,
So meikle was his myance.[20]
His yrnis° was rude° as ony rawchtir,°   *instruments; rough-hewn; rafter*
Quhair he leit blude° it was no lawchtir;°   *let blood; cause for laughter*
Full mony instrument for slawchtir°   *slaughter*
Was in his gardevyance.°   *(medical) chest*

6

He cowth gif cure for laxatyve
To gar a wicht hors want his lyve;[21]
Quha evir assay wald,° man or wyve,   *would try it out*
Thair hippis yeid hiddy giddy.°   *buttocks went into a spin*

18. He talked in a way which suggested study at Bologna (in Lombardy), one of the earliest Universities to promote medicine as a discipline.
19. See Genesis 6. 1–4.
20. ll. 2–4: 'He was so resourceful that, for one night's attendance, he would procure as payment a horse and the sick person's skin.'
21. ll. 1–2: 'He could prescribe a cure for loose bowels which would make a sturdy steed give up the ghost.'

His practikis° nevir war put to preif° — *methods; tested*
But° suddane deid° or grit mischeif;° — *Without; death; distress*
He had purgatioun° to mak a theif — *purging remedy*
To dee° withowt a widdy.° — *Die; noose*

7

Unto no mess pressit° this prelat° — *To no mass hurried; prelate*
For sound of sacring bel° nor skellat;° — *sacrament bell; hand-bell*
As blaksmyth bruikit° was his pallatt° — *streaked with black; pate*
For battering° at the study.° — *hammering; anvil*
Thocht he come hame a new maid channoun,[22]
He had dispensit with matynnis channoun,
On him come nowther stole nor fannoun
For smowking of the smydy.[23]

8

Me thocht seir fassounis° he assailyeit° — *various methods; tried out*
To mak the quintessence[24] and failyeit
And quhen he saw that nocht availyeit° — *worked*
A fedrem° on he tuke° — *coat of feathers; put on*
And schupe° in Turky for to fle;° — *prepared; fly*
And quhen that he did mont on he° — *mounted on high*
All fowlis ferleit° quhat he sowld be° — *birds wondered; might be*
That evir° did on him luke.° — *continually; gaped at him*

9

Sum held° he had bene Dedalus,° — *maintained; Daedalus*
Sum the Menatair marvelus,° — *mythic Minotaur*
Sum Martis° blak smyth Vulcanus° — *Mars'; Vulcan*
And sum Saturnus kuke;° — *Saturn's cook*
And evir the cuschettis° at him tuggit,° — *wood-pigeons; tugged*
The rukis° him rent,° the ravynnis° him druggit,° — *rooks; tore; ravens; dragged*
The hudit crawis° his hair furth ruggit:° — *hooded crows; yanked out*
The hevin he micht not bruke.° — *enjoy possession of*

10

The myttane° and Sanct Martynis fowle° — *buzzard; type of hawk*
Wend° he had bene the hornit howle;° — *Supposed; long-eared owl*
Thay set aupone him with a yowle° — *screech*
And gaif him dynt° for dynt. — *blow*
The golk,° the gormaw° and the gled° — *cuckoo; cormorant; kite*
Beft him with buffettis° quhill he bled; — *Buffeted him*
The sparhalk° to the spring° him sped — *sparrow hawk; attack;*
Als fers° as fyre of flynt.° — *fiercely; fire from flint*

22. Damian was made Abbot of Tungland in the house of the Premonstratensian canons there in 1504.
23. ll. 6–8: 'He had granted himself dispensation from the prescribed service of matins; stoking the smithy for him had priority over dressing himself in the liturgical vestments of stole and maniple.' (The firing of the smithy is for alchemical purposes.)
24. The mysterious fifth (transcendent) element, production of which was the prime aim of alchemy.

11

The tarsall° gaif him tug for tug,	*tercel*
A stanchell° hang in ilka lug,°	*kestrel; each ear*
The pyot° furth his pennis° did rug,°	*magpie; feathers; pulled out*
The stork straik ay° but stynt;°	*kept striking; without pause*
The bissart,° bissy° but rebuik,°	*buzzard; assiduous; check*
Scho was so cleverus° of hir cluik°	*deft; with her claw*
His bawis° he micht not langar bruik,°	*testicles; enjoy the use of*
Scho held tham at ane hint.°	*grip*

12

Thik was the clud° of kayis° and crawis,°	*cloud; jackdaws; crows*
Of marleyonis,° mittanis and of mawis°	*merlins; gulls*
That bikkrit° at his berd° with blawis	*attacked; beard*
In battell him abowt;°	*around him*
Thay nibbillit° him with noyis° and cry,	*pecked; noise*
The rerd° of thame rais to the sky	*clamour*
And evir he cryit on Fortoun, 'Fy!'	
His lyfe was in to dowt.°	*in jeopardy*

13

The ja° him skrippit° with a skryke°	*jay; mocked; screech*
And skornit° him as it was lyk;°	*jeered at; so it seemed*
The egill° strong at him did stryke	*eagle*
And rawcht° him mony a rowt.°	*landed; blow*
For feir uncunnandly° he cawkit°	*unwittingly; defecated*
Quhill all his pennis° war drownd and drawkit;°	*feathers; drenched*
He maid a hundreth nolt° all hawkit°	*cattle; streaked*
Beneth him with a spowt.°	*discharge*

14

He schewre° his feddreme° that was schene°	*tore at; plumage; fine*
And slippit owt of it full clene	
And in a myre° up to the ene°	*bog; eyes*
Amang the glar° did glyd.°	*slime; slither*
The fowlis all at the fedrem dang°	*lashed out*
As at a monster thame amang	
Quhill all the pennis of it owsprang°	*sprang forth*
In till the air full wyde.°	*far and wide*

15

And he lay at the plunge° evirmair	*was immersed*
Sa lang as any ravin did rair,°	*called out*
The crawis him socht with cryis of cair°	*vexed cries*
In every schaw° besyde;°	*thicket; nearby*
Had he reveild° bene to the ruikis	*revealed*
Thay had him revin° all with thair cluikis	*torn to pieces*
Thre dayis in dub° amang the dukis°	*stagnant pool; ducks*
He did with dirt him hyde.°	*hid himself*

16

The air was dirkit with° the fowlis	*darkened by*
That come with yawmeris° and with yowlis,	*fretful cries*
With skryking,° skrymming° and with scowlis	*shrieking; scudding*
To tak him in the tyde.[25]	
I walknit° with the noyis and schowte,°	*wakened; clamour*
So hiddowis beir° was me abowte;	*hideous din*
Sensyne° I curs that cankerit rowte°	*Since then; malignant crew*
Quhair evir I go° or ryde.	*walk*

(v) *'How sould I Governe me?'*

1

How sould I rewill me° or in quhat wys°	*comport myself; manner*
I wald sum wyse man wald devys,°	*would work out*
Sen I can leif° in no degre°	*live; fashion*
Bot sum my maneris will dispys:[26]	
Lord God, how sould I governe me?°	*conduct myself*

2

Giff° I be lustye,° galland° and blythe,°	*If; charming; gallant; cheerful*
Than will thai say on° me full swythe°	*about; at once*
Yone° man, out of his mynd is he	*That*
Or sum hes done him confort kythe;°	*offered him comfort*[27]
Lord God, how sould I governe me?	

3

Giff I be sorrowfull and sad°	*grave*
Than will thai say that I am mad;	
I do bot drowpe° as° I wald de,°	*droop; as if; die*
So will thai deyme,° bayth man and lad:	*judge*
Lord God, how sall I governe me?	

4

Be I liberall,° gentill° and kynd,	*bountiful; amiable*
Thocht I it tak of nobill strynd,°	*from a noble lineage*
Yit will thai say, baythe he and he,°	*one and all*
Yon man is lyke° out of his mynd:	*appears to be*
Lord God, how sall I governe me?	

5

Giff I be lustie in myne array°	*brightly attired*
Than lufe I paramoris,° say thai,	*take mistresses*
Or in my mynd is proud and he,°	*exalted*
Or ellis° I haif it sum wrang way:°	*else; I am being perverse*
Lord God, how sall I governe me?	

25. 'On that occasion' or 'In due course of time.'
26. ED. (v) Copy Text: MS Maitland Folio. The ordering of this text has also been followed. 'Without some people denigrating my behaviour.'
27. Probably with the sense of a bribe—i.e. that he is in someone's pocket.

6
In court, rewaird° gif purches° I, — *acknowledgement; procure*
Than have thai malice and invy,
And secreitly on me thai lie° — *tell lies about me*
And dois me sklander privaly:° — *slander me in private*
Lord God, how sould I governe me?

7
And gif I be not wele besene° — *properly dressed*
Than twa and twa sayis thame betwene,° — *among themselves*
Evill gydit° is yone man, par de!° — *Ill guided; by God*
Be his clething° it may be sene; — *From his attire*
Lord God, how sould I governe me?

8
Gif I be sene in° court our lang° — *at/around; too long*
Than will thai quhispir° thame amang, — *whisper*
My freindis ar not worthe ane fle° — *flea*
That I sa lang but guerdon gang:° — *have gone without recognition*
Lord God, how sould I governe me?

9
How sould my gyding be devysit?° — *conduct be planned*
Gif I spend litle I am dispysit;
Be I courtas,° nobill and fre,° — *courteous; generous*
A prodigall° man than am I prysit:° — *spendthrift; adjudged*
Lord God, how sould I governe me?

10
Sen all is jugit,° bayth gud and ill, — *judged (unfavourably)*
And no mannis toung I may had still,° — *keep silent*
To do the best my mynd salbe;° — *my intention will be*
Lat everie man say quhat he will,
The gratious God mot governe me![28]

(vi) *'To the Merchantis of Edinburgh'*[29]

1
Quhy will ye merchantis of renoun° — *honourable merchants*
Lat Edinburgh, your nobill toun,
For laik of reformatioun
The commone proffeitt° tyine° and fame?° — *common good; lose; reputation*
  Think ye not schame° — *Are you not ashamed*
That onie uther regioun° — *any other region*
Sall with dishonour hurt° your name?° — *injure; (good) name*

28. 'May I be ruled by gracious God!'
29. ED. (vi) Copy Text: Reidpeth. The old town of Edinburgh in the late fifteenth century stretched from the Castle in the west to Holyrood in the east; from the north loch (now Waverley Gardens) to the south loch and burgh muir (Meadows).

2

May nane pas throw your principall gaittis° — *main streets*
For stink of haddockis and of scaittis,° — *skates*
For cryis of carlingis° and debaittis,° — *old hags; arguments*
For fensum flyttingis of defame;°[30] — *offensive derogatory name-calling*
Think ye not schame,
Befoir strangeris of all estaittis° — *ranks*
That sic dishonour hurt your name?

3

Your stinkand styll° that standis dirk — *stinking alley*[31]
Haldis° the lycht fra your parroche kirk;° — *Keeps; parish church (St Giles)*
Your foirstair° makis your housis mirk° — *outside stairs; dark*
Lyk na cuntray bot° heir at hame; — *As in no country except*
Think ye not schame
Sa litill polesie° to wirk — *improvement*
In hurt and sklander° of your name? — *slander*

4

At your hie croce,° quhar° gold and silk — *high cross; where*
Sould be, thair is bot crudis° and milk; — *curds*
And at your trone° bot cokill° and wilk,° — *weighing beam; cockles; whelks*
Pansches,° pudingis° of° Jok and Jame;[32] — *Tripe; offal puddings; for*
Think ye not schame,
Sen as the world sayis that ilk° — *tells the same story*
In hurt and sclander of your name?

5

Your commone menstrallis° hes no tone° — *public minstrels; can play no tune…*
Bot° 'Now the Day dawis' and 'Into Joun';° — *…Except; (two popular tunes)*
Cunningar° men man° serve Sanct Cloun° — *More talented; must; Saint Clown*
And nevir to uther craftis clame;° — *lay claim to additional skills*
Think ye not schame,
To hald° sic mowaris on the moyne° — *maintain; bayers-at-the-moon*
In hurt and sclander of your name?

6

Tailyouris,° soutteris° and craftis vyll° — *Tailors; cobblers; base crafts*
The fairest of your streittis fyll° — *defile*
And merchandis at the stinkand styll° — *stinking passage*
Ar hamperit in ane hony came;° — *cramped within a honeycomb*
Think ye not schame,
That ye have nether witt° nor wyll° — *common sense; resolution*
To win yourselff ane bettir name?

30. The habit of throwing waste from the upper windows of tenement houses whose front stairs were built outwards (3.3) meant that only the very centre of the narrow streets was safe.
31. The passage leading into the luckenbooths.
32. The contrast is between the craftsmen who bring their stalls into the city and the merchants whose shops are being blocked out by the intrusion of lower tradesmen.

7

Your burgh° of beggeris° is ane nest.[33] — *town; beggars*
To schout, thai swentyouris° will not rest.° — *vagabonds; stop*
All honest folk they do molest,
Sa piteuslie thai cry and rame;° — *shout*
    Think ye not schame,
That° for the poore hes nothing drest° — *You who; devised*
In hurt and sklander of your name?

8

Your proffeit daylie dois incres,° — *increase*
Your godlie workis les and les;
Through streittis nane may mak progres
For cry of cruikit,° blind and lame; — *deformed*
    Think ye not schame
That ye sic substance° dois posses — *wealth*
And will not win ane bettir name?

9

Sen for the court and the sessioun
The great repair of this regioun
Is in your burgh,[34] thairfoir be boun° — *prepared*
To mend° all faultis° that ar to blame,° — *remedy; faults; blameworthy*
    And eschew schame;° — *avoid guilt*
Gif thai pas to ane uther toun,°[35] — *another town*
Ye will decay and your great name.

10

Thairfoir, strangeris° and leigis° treit,° — *visitors; loyal subjects; treat well*
Tak not ouer mekill° for thair meit° — *too much; food*
And gar° your merchandis be discreit;° — *have...show discretion*
That° na extortiounes be, proclame° — *So that; denounce*
    All fraud and schame;
Keip ordour and poore nighbouris° beit,° — *neighbours; assist*
That ye may gett ane bettir name.

11

Singular proffeit° so dois yow blind, — *Personal profit*
The common proffeit° gois behind;° — *common good; lags behind*
I pray that Lord remeid° to fynd — *remedy*
That deit° into Jerusalem — *Who died*
    And gar yow schame;° — *make you penitent*
That sumtyme° ressoun may yow bind° — *some day; control*
For to [win bak to] yow° guid name. — *[regain for] you*

33. Recent outbreaks of the Black Death had intensified this situation.
34. ll. 1–3: 'Because of the king's court and the Court of Session the major focal point of the region lies in your burgh.' James IV had reinforced Edinburgh's position as a legal centre. As burgesses, the merchants had powers and responsibilities for running the town.
35. Presumably Stirling, with its castle-palace and the freer mercantile régime of a baronial burgh.

(vii) *'Timor Mortis Conturbat Me.'*[36]

1

I that° in heill° wes and gladnes° — *who; health; joy*
Am trublit° now with gret seiknes° — *troubled; with serious illness*
And feblit° with infermite:° — *weakened; infirmity*
Timor mortis conturbat me.[37] — *The fear of death troubles me*

2

Our plesance° heir is all vane° glory, — *(time of) joy; empty*
This fals warld is bot transitory,
The flesch is brukle,° the Fend° is sle:° — *frail; Satan; devious*
Timor mortis conturbat me.

3

The stait of man dois change and vary,
Now sound, now seik,° now blith, now sary,° — *sick; wretched*
Now dansand° mery, now like to dee:° — *dancing; likely to die*
Timor mortis conturbat me.

4

No stait in erd° heir standis sickir;° — *earth; stands secure*
As° with the wynd, wavis° the wickir,° — *Just as; sways; willow*
Wavis° this warldis vanite:° — *(Just as) volatile is; empty pride*
Timor mortis conturbat me.

5

One to the ded° gois all estatis,° — *Onwards to death; ranks*
Princis, prelotis° and potestatis,° — *prelates; potentates*
Baith riche and pur° of al degre:° — *poor; every degree*
Timor mortis conturbat me.

6

He° takis the knychtis in to feild° — *i.e. Death; on the battlefield*
Anarmyt° undir helme° and scheild, — *Armed; helmet*
Victour he is at all melle:° — *in every combat*
Timor mortis conturbat me.

7

That strang° unmercifull tyrand° — *strong; tyrant*
Takis one the moderis breist sowkand
The bab full of benignite;[38]
Timor mortis conturbat me.

36. ED. (vii) Copy Text: 'Rouen' Print. This poem is also known as the 'Lament for the Makaris', because it contains a long list of Scots and English poets, dead or dying.
37. The refrain is liturgical, being drawn from the seventh lesson of the Office of the Dead. It is also personal, with each stanza returning finally to the poet's own worries—'troubles ME'.
38. ll. 2–3: 'Seizes the baby, full of graciousness, while it is sucking on its mother's breast.'

8

He takis the campion° in the stour,° — *champion; strife*
The capitane closit° in the tour,° — *enclosed; stronghold*
The lady in bour° full of bewte:° — *enclosed garden; beauty*
Timor mortis conturbat me.

9

He sparis no lord for his piscence,° — *because of his (lord's) power*
Na clerk° for his intelligence; — *scholar*
His awfull strak°[39] may no man fle:° — *terrible stroke; escape from*
Timor mortis conturbat me.

10

Art magicianis° and astrologgis,° — *Magicians; astrologers*
Rethoris,° logicianis and theologgis°— — *Rhetoricians; theologians*
Thame helpis no conclusionis sle:° — *subtle*
Timor mortis conturbat me.

11

In medicyne the most practicianis,° — *greatest practitioners*
Leichis,° surrigianis° and phisicianis, — *Doctors; surgeons*
Thame self fra ded° may not supple:° — *death; may not deliver themselves*
Timor mortis conturbat me.

12

I se that makaris° amang the laif° — *poets; rest*
Playis° heir ther pageant, syne gois to graif;° — *Play out; grave*
Sparit is nought ther faculte:° — *profession/discipline*
Timor mortis conturbat me.

13

He hes done petuously devour° — *piteously devoured*
The noble Chaucer of makaris flour,° — *flower*
The monk of Bery° and Gower, all thre: [40] — *i.e. John Lydgate*
Timor mortis conturbat me.

14

The gud Sir Hew of Eglintoun[41]
And eik° Heryot and Wyntoun[42] — *also*
He has tane° out of this cuntre: — *taken*
Timor mortis conturbat me.

39. 'The stroke' is of death's scythe. Visual images of death influence the poem throughout.
40. As in *The Goldyn Targe*, 29; 30, Dunbar sees himself inheriting an English vernacular tradition beginning with Chaucer (late 14th Century) and continuing through John Lydgate and John Gower (early 15th Century).
41. The roll-call of Scottish poets begins with early poets. Eglinton was brother-in-law of Robert II and therefore a contemporary of Barbour.
42. The identity of Heriot is uncertain. Andrew of Wyntoun wrote a history of Scotland in verse. He was prior of Lochleven until 1422.

15
That scorpion fell° hes done infek° — *cruel; poisoned*
Maister Johne Clerk and James Afflek[43]
Fra balat making and trigide:° — *composing lyrical and tragic verse*
Timor mortis conturbat me.

16
Holland and Barbour he hes berevit:° — *snatched away*
Allace that he nought with us levit° — *did not leave with us*
Schir Mungo Lokert of the Le:[44]
Timor mortis conturbat me.

17
Clerk of Tranent eik° he has tane° — *also; taken*
That maid the anteris° of Gawane; — *composed the adventures*
Schir Gilbert Hay endit° has he:[45] — *terminated*
Timor mortis conturbat me.

18
He has Blind Hary and Sandy Traill
Slane with his schour° of mortall haill° — *shower; lethal hail*
Quhilk Patrik Johnestoun myght nought fle:°[46] — *escape*
Timor mortis conturbat me.

19
He has reft° Merseir[47] his endite° — *torn away (from); writing*
That did in luf so lifly° write, — *vividly*
So schort, so quik,° of sentence hie:° — *lively; noble theme*
Timor mortis conturbat me.

20
He hes tane Roull of Aberdene
And gentill Roull of Corstorphin[48]—
Two bettir fallowis° did no man se; — *companions*
Timor mortis conturbat me.

21
In Dunfermelyne he has done roune° — *whispered...*
With° Maister° Robert Henrisoun; — *...To; Master (of Arts)*

43. John Clerk may be the 'Clerk' to whom some verses in the Bannatyne Manuscript (1568) are attributed. Afflek is unknown.
44. Richard Holland was secretary to the Earl of Moray and wrote *The Buke of the Howlat* in the mid fifteenth century. Mungo Lockhart is not elsewhere identified as a poet but died in 1489.
45. Clerk is unknown. Gilbert Hay (fl. 1450) was a priest and translator.
46. Traill is unknown. Blind Hary is the name usually given to the author of *The Actis and Deidis of Schir William Wallace* (c.1478). Patrick Johnson flourished at the same time and wrote plays or interludes for the court.
47. Probably the Mercer to whom several lyrics in the Bannatyne MS are attributed.
48. Roull of Corstorphine is probably the author of one of the flyting/cursing poems in the Bannatyne MS. Roull of Aberdeen is unknown.

Schir Johne the Ros[49] enbrast° has he: *(embraced)*
Timor mortis conturbat me.

22
And he has now tane last of aw° *(all)*
Gud gentill° Stobo and Quintyne Schaw[50] *(courteous/noble)*
Of quham all wichtis° has pete:° *(everyone; regret)*
Timor mortis conturbat me.

23
Gud Maister Walter Kennedy° *(Walter Kennedy M.A.)*
In poynt of dede° lyis varaly°— *(On the point of death; truly)*
Gret reuth° it wer that so suld be; *(pity)*
Timor mortis conturbat me.

24
Sen° he has all my brether tane, *(Since)*
He will naught lat me lif alane;° *(me alone live)*
On forse,° I man his nyxt pray° be; *(Inevitably; victim)*
Timor mortis conturbat me.

25
Sen for the deid° remeid° is none *(against death; remedy)*
Best is that we for dede dispone—° *(prepare for)*
Eftir° our deid, that lif may we! *((So that) after)*
Timor mortis conturbat me.

49. May be the man referred to as Dunbar's representative at the start of his flyting with Walter Kennedy.
50. 'Stobo' was name given to John Reid of Stobo. He died in July 1505, so the poem may be dated in that year or the next. One of Quentin Shaw's lyrics appears in the Maitland MS.

§ 11 Lyrics and Ballatis of the Reformation and Marian Period

Precise dating is not always possible, but the lyrics in this section represent the troubled rule of two Marys—first, the regency of Mary of Guise (1553–60); secondly the reign (1560–7) of Mary Queen of Scots and the period of her captivity until James VI assumed real power in 1584. The Catholic ambitions of Mary of Guise drove the Protestant lords into an alliance with Elizabethan England and bequeathed to her daughter a particularly difficult inheritance. Mary Stuart failed to meet that challenge and was executed on the orders of Elizabeth in 1587.

The major strains of verse during the period are represented. The courtly lyric is now firmly allied with music. While it remains manneristic, that link guarantees a wider variety of (usually simpler) stanza forms. Little is known about the leading lyricist of the period, **Alexander Scott**, *although he is usually identified with the 'old Scott' referred to in one of Montgomerie's sonnets. A musician and poet, he seems to have had the same senior bardic position in Mary's reign as Montgomerie had with James. This permitted Scott to write public poetry of welcome and warning to the Queen (VIII) as well as the amorous songs (II-V), for which he is best known.*

The Protestant voice is also heard—mainly in broadsheet form or through vernacular renderings of passages from the **Bible** *(IX-XI; XIII). On this side of the divide, the powerful, satirical voice of* **Robert Sempill** *is among the most skilful. Sempill spent some time in France but returned to Scotland in 1572 after the Massacre of St Bartholomew's Eve. His support for the reformers was consistent and he can write seriously on religious and political issues. His ability to handle lighter and more scurrilous topics is exemplified in* **'The Ballat maid upoun Margret Fleming'** *(VII). His use of a female persona in* **'Maddeis Proclamation'** *(X) marks a trend in the male-dominated tradition of early Scottish writing (cf. IX).* **'Haif hairt in hairt'** *(I) appears to have been written by a woman, as does the lesbian lyric,* **'As Phebus in his spheris hicht'** *(VI).*

Less impassioned comments on a time of conflict and cultural deprivation also abound (XII). The compiler of the **Maitland MSS, *Sir Richard Maitland of Lethington*,** *sums up the sense of loss in 'Satire on the Age' (XIV). A Lord of Session and Keeper of the Seal, he lived from 1496–1586, and so would have memories even of Dunbar, to give authority to his comparison with more convivial and optimistic days.*

11a: Ballatis of Love[1]

Anonymous[2]

I

'Haif hairt in hairt'

1

Haif hairt in hairt, ye hairt of hairtis haill,[3]
Trewly, sweit hairt, your hairt, my hairt sal haif.

1. ED. § 11a I-VII. COPY TEXTS: I-V; VII Bannatyne MS; VI Maitland Quarto.
2. As the reply to this poem is given by Alexander Scott (No. II), this poem may well have been written by a woman.
3. Elliptical: literally the sense is—'Receive (my) heart into (your) heart, you (who are the) heart of all hearts'. The first phrase may also mean—'Be emotionally courageous'.

Expell, deir hairt, my havy° hairtis baill,° *sad; sorrow*
Praying yow hairt, my hairt, quhilk hes my hairt in graif,° *grave/tomb*
Sen ye, sweit hairt, my hairt may sla° and saif, *slay*
Lat nocht, deir hairt, my leill° hairt be forloir,° *loyal/faithful; lost*
Excelland hairt of every hairtis gloir.

2
Glaid is my hairt with yow, sweit hairt, to rest
And serve yow, hairt, with hairtis observance.° *devotions*
Sen ye ar, hairt, with bayth our hairtis possest,
My hairt is in your hairtis governance.
Do with my hairt your hairtis sweit plesance,° *pleasure*
For is my hairt thrall° your hairt untill;° *in thrall...to*
I haif no hairt contrair your hairtis will.

3
Sen ye haif, hairt, my faythfull hairt in cure,° *care*
Uphald the hairt quhilk is your hairtis awin.° *own*
Gif my hairt be your hairtis serviture,° *servant*
How may ye thoill° your trew hairt be ourthrawin? *endure*
Quhairfoir, sweit hairt, nocht suffer so be knawin,
Bot ye be, hairt, my hairtis rejosing
As ye ar hairt of hairtis conforting.

II–V: Alexander Scott (c.1515–c.1583)

II

'Reply to Hairtis'[4]

1
Considdir, hairt, my trew intent,
Suppois° I am nocht eloquent *Even if*
To wryt yow anser responsyve:
Your scedull° is so excellent, *manuscript/poem*
It passis° far my wittis fyve,° *transcends; i.e. five senses*

2
For quhy° it is so full of hairtis, *Because*
That myne within my bosum stairtis,
Quhen I behald° it rycht till end, *peruse*
And for ilk° hairt ane hundreth dertis *each*
Outthrow° my hairt to yow I send. *Out the whole of*

3
This woundit hairt, sweit hairt, ressaif° *receive*
Quhilk is, deir hairt, abone the laif,° *more than the rest*

4. Bannatyne has a marginal note, relating the poem to 'Haif hairt in hairt': 'The answeir heirof in the 235 leif.' (Cf. 4. 2–3)

Your faythfull hairt with trew intent.
Ane trewar hairt may no man haif,
Nor yit ane hairt mair permanent.

4

Ane hairt it is without dissait.° — *deceit*
It is the hairt to quhome ye wret° — *wrote*
The misseif° full of hairtis seir.° — *missive; diverse*
It is ane hairt, bayth air° and lait, — *early*
That is your hairtis presoneir.

5

It is ane hairt full of distres,
Ane cairfull° hairt all comfortles, — *full of cares*
Ane penseve° hairt in dule° and dolour,° — *melancholy; grief; distress*
Ane hairt of wo and havines,
Ane mirthles hairt withouttin mesour° — *immoderately*

6

It is ane hairt bayth firme and stabill,
Ane hairt withouttin fenyeit fabill,[5]
Ane constant hairt, bayth trest° and trew, — *trustworthy*
Ane sure hairt set in to sabill,° — *dressed in sable/black*
Ane wofull hairt bot gif° ye rew.° — *unless; are compassionate*

7

It is ane hairt that your hairt servis,
Ane hairt for° lufe of your hairt stervis,° — *(which) without; dies*
Ane hairt that nevir you offendit,
Ane hairt of youris, bayth vane° and nervis, — *vein(s)*
Ane hairt but° solace bot gif ye send it. — *without*

8

It is na gravit° hairt in stone, — *engraved*
In silver, gold nor veir° bone, — *ivory*
Nor yit ane payntit symlitud,° — *representation*
Bot this same verry° hairt allone — *identical/true*
Within my breist of flesch and blude.

9

Thairfoir, sweit hairt, send me the hairt
That is in to your breist inwart,° — *inside/intimate*
And nocht thir writtin hairtis in vane,°[6] — *in vain/futile*
Bot your hairt to my hairt revert° — *change*
And send me hairt for hairt agane.

5. His heart does not tell lies. It is this literal use of the phrase 'fenyeit fabill,' which Henryson redefines in the Prologue to his own fables (§ 14).
6. The other sense of 'vein' has been introduced earlier, allowing an opposition between the 'inky vein of writing' and 'blood from the veins' to be suggested .

III

'It cumis you luvaris to be laill'

1

It cumis° you luvaris to be laill°	*befits; loyal*
Off body, hairt and mind alhaill,°	*entire*
And, thocht ye with your ladyis daill,°	*dally*
'Ressoun',°[7]	*Fair enough*
Bot, and your faith and lawty faill,	
'Tressoun!'°	*Perfidy!*

2

Ye may with honesty persew,°	*pursue/court*
Gif ye be constant, trest° and trew.	*trusty*
Thocht than, unrycht,° thay on you rew,	*wrongly*
'Ressoun'.	
Bot be ye fund dowbill°—'Adew!'	*deceitful*
'Tressoun!'	

3

Your hummill service first resing° thame,	*consign (to)*
For that, to your intent,° sall bring thame.	*purpose*
With leif° of ladeis thocht ye thing° thame,	*permission; copulate with*
'Ressoun',	
Bot eftirwart and° ye maling° thame,	*if; malign*
'Tressoun'.	

4

Do nevir the deid that ma diseis° thame,	*vex/infect (sexually)*
Bot wirk with all your mind to meis° thame.	*soothe*
To tak your plesour quhen it pleis *thame*,	
'Ressoun'.	
Bot with untrewth and ye betrais° thame,	*betray*
'Tressoun!'	

5

Defend thair fame,° quha evir fyle° thame,	*honour; may shame*
And ay with honest havingis° style thame,	*behaviour*
To Venus als° suppois ye wile° thame,	*also; trick*
'Ressoun'.	
Bot be ye fraudfull and begyle thame,	
'Tressoun!'	

7. The words 'ressoun' and 'tressoun' return in each stanza as comments on different aspects of the male lover's fate. This is possible because they are portmanteau terms, covering a variety of possible meanings centred on proper and improper use of the gift of rationality. However, as the ladies accept perfect love as their right but stridently denounce any perceived lapses, there is an intended tonal disparity. The suggested glosses: 'Fair enough.' and 'Perfidy!' mirror this.

6

Ye suld considdir or ye taik thame,
That littill service° will nocht staik° thame.[8] *slight service; suit*
Get ye ane goldin hour to glak° thame, *toy with*
'Ressoun'.
Bot be ye fraudfull and forsaik thame,
'Tressoun!'

7

Be secreit, trew and plane° allwey. *direct*
Defend thair fame baith nycht and day,
In prevy° place suppois ye play— *secret*
'Ressoun'.
Bot be ye ane clattrer,° harmis ay!° *talebearer; alas*
'Tressoun!'

8

Be courtas in thair cumpany,
For that sall caus thame to apply,° *pay attention*
Thocht that thay lat you with thame ly—
'Ressoun'.
Bot be ye fund unfaithfull, fy!
'Tressoun!'

9

Wey° weill thir versis that I wryt you. *Weigh*
Do your devoir° quhen that thay lat you. *duty*
To lufe your ladeis, who can wyt° you? *blame*
'Ressoun'.
Do ye the contrair, heir I quyt° you. *disown*
'Tressoun!'

IV

'Lo, quhat it is to lufe!'

1

Lo, quhat it is to lufe!
Lerne ye that list to prufe,° *experience/test (it)*
Be me,° I say, that no ways may *From me*
The grund° of greif remufe, *cause/source*
Bot still decay both nycht and day.
Lo, quhat it is to lufe!

2

Luif is ane fervent fire.
Kendillit without desire—

8. The more earthy sub-text suggests that a small erection will not satisfy ladies either.

Schort plesour, lang displesour[9]—
Repentence is the hire.° *price to pay*
Ane pure° tresour without mesour,° *poor; without moderation*
Luif is ane fervent fire.

3
To lufe and to be wyis,
To rege° with gud advyis, *regulate your conduct*
Now thus, now than,° so gois the game: *Now this way, now that*
Incertane is the dyis.[10]
Thair is no man, I say, that can
Both lufe and to be wyis.

4
Fle alwayis frome the snair.
Lerne at me° to be ware. *by me*
It is ane pane and dowbill trane° *trap*
Of endles wo and cair.
For to refrane° that denger plane; *avoid*
Fle alwayis frome the snair.

V

'Quha is perfyte'

1
Quha is perfyte° to put in wryt° *skilled (enough); in writing*
The inwart murnyng and mischance,° *misery*
Or to indite° the grit delyte *set down*
Of lustie lufis observance,° *devotions*
Bot he that may certane patiently suffir pane
To win his soverane° in recompance? *sovereign*

2
Albeid° I knaw of luvis law *Although*
The plesour and the panis smart,
Yit I stand aw° for to furthschaw° *(in) awe; represent*
The quiet secreitis of my harte,
For it may Fortoun raith° to do his body skaith,° *anger; harm*
Quhilk wait° that of thame baith I am expert. *Who (Fortune) knows*

3
Scho wait my wo, that is ago;° *who has left*
Scho wait my weilfair and remeid;
Scho wait also I lufe no mo° *no others*
Bot hir, the well of womanheid;

9. ll. 2–3. Elliptical. 'Short pleasure (followed by) lengthy misery (result when) it is kindled without being asked for.'
10. Dice is often used with a singular verb.

Scho wait withouttin faill I am hir luvar laill:
Scho hes my hairt alhaill° till I be deid. *entire*

4
That bird of blis in bewty is
In erd° the only *A per se*° *On earth; paragon*
Quhais mouth to kis is worth, I wis,
The warld full of gold to me.
Is nocht in erd I cure° bot° pleis my lady pure, *care (about); except (to)*
Syne° be hir serviture unto° I de. *Then; servant until*

5
Scho hes my lufe. At hir behufe° *command*
My hairt is subject, bound and thrall,
For scho dois moif my hairt aboif
To se hir proper persoun small.° *slender*
Sen scho is wrocht at will, that natur may fulfill,[11]
Glaidly I gif hir till, body and all.

6
Thair is nocht wie can estimie° *no man (who) can calculate*
My sorrow and my sichingis sair,° *sad sighs*
For so am I done fathfullie
In favouris with my lady fair,
That baith our hairtis ar ane, luknyt° in luvis chene,° *locked; chain*
And everilk greif is gane for evir mair.

Anonymous

VI

'As Phoebus in his spheris hicht'

1
As Phoebus° in his spheris hicht *Sun-god*
Precellis° the kaip crepusculein,° *Outshines; cape of twilight*
And Phoebe° all the starris licht, *Moon-goddess*
Your splendour, so madame I wein,
Dois onlie° pas all feminine *uniquely*
In sapience superlative,
Indewit with vertewis sa devine
As° leirned Pallas[12] redivive.° *As if; were reborn*

2
And as, be hid vertew° unknawin, *property*
The adamant[13] drawis yron thairtill,° *attracts iron*

11. The divine will fulfils its purposes by shadowing the order and love of heaven within Nature's orderliness and beauty. The lady, as *A per se*, is a major example of this.
12. Pallas was not only the goddess of wisdom but represented the moon.
13. 'adamant': a legendary stone to which magic properties were attributed.

Your courtes nature so hes drawin
My hairt youris to continew still;
Sa greit joy dois my spreit fulfill
Contempling your perfectioun,
Ye weild° me holie° at your will — *rule; entirely*
And raviss° my affectioun.[14] — *ravish/take by force*

3

Your perles° vertew dois provoike,° — *peerless; excite*
And loving kyndnes so dois move
My mynd to freindschip reciproc,° — *reciprocal*
That treuth sall try sa far above
The auntient heroicis love[15]
As salbe thocht prodigious,° — *marvellous/portentous*
And plaine experience sall prove
Mair holie and religious.

4

In amitie Perithous
To Theseus wes not so traist,°[16] — *bound in trust*
Nor till Achilles, Patroclus,
Nor Pilades to trew Orest,° — *Orestes*
Nor yit Achates luif so lest° — *intertwined*
To gud Aenee,° nor sic freindschip — *Aeneas*
David to Jonathan profest,
Nor Titus trew to kynd Josip.° — *Josephus*

5

Nor yit Penelope I wiss
So luiffed Ulisses in hir dayis,
Nor Ruth the kynd Moabitiss° — *Moabite woman*
Nohemie°[17] as the scripture sayis — *Naomi*
Nor Portia quhais worthie prayiss
In Romaine historeis we reid
Quha did devoir the fyrie brayiss° — *was consumed by hot coals*
To follow Brutus to the deid.° — *into death*

6

Wald michtie Jove grant me the hap° — *good fortune*
With yow to have your Brutus pairt,
And, metamorphosing our schap,
My sex intill his vaill° convert. — *form*
No Brutus then sould caus us smart

14. 'affectioun': may refer specifically to the affective or non-rational part of the lover's soul.
15. ll. 4–5. Their love 'will test out the truth of the love of ancient heroes so far above'. That is—he will discover whether heroes and heroines really became stars, as the euhemeristic myths taught.
16. The examples of friendship in sts. 4–6 are drawn from the Bible, from classical history and classical mythology. They also, importantly, include homosexual friendships.
17. The love of Ruth for her mother-in-law, Naomi was deduced from Naomi's kiss (Ruth I. 10) and Ruth's vow, 'Where you go I will go, and where you stay, I will stay' (Ruth I. 18).

As we doe now, unhappie wemen,[18]
Then sould we bayth with joyfull hairt
Honour and bliss the band of Hymen.° *bond of marriage (god)*

7

Yea certainlie we sould efface
Pollux and Castoris memorie,[19]
And gif that thay deservit place
Amang the starris for loyaltie,
Then our mair perfyte amitie
Mair worthie recompence sould merit,
In hevin eternall deitie
Amang he goddis° till inherit. *high gods*

8

And as we ar, thocht till our wo
Nature and Fortoun doe conjure° *conspire together*
And Hymen also be our fo,
Yit luif of vertew° dois procuire° *love per se; produce*
Freindschip and amitie sa suire,
Sa constantlie quhilk sall induire
That not bot deid sall us divorce;

9

And thocht adversitie us vex,
Yit be° our freindship salbe sein° *through; demonstrated*
Thair is mair constancie in our sex
Then ever amang men hes bein;
No troubill, torment, greif or tein° *misery*
Nor erthlie thing sall us dissever,°[20] *separate*
Sic constancie sall us mantein
In perfyte amitie for ever.

Robert Sempill (c.1530–95)

VII

'The Ballat maid upoun Margret Fleming, callit "The Flemyng Bark" in Edinburgh toun'[21]

1

I haif a littill Fleming berge,° *Flemish barge*
Off clenkett° work bot scho is wicht;° *riveting; expert*

18. Theirs is a lesbian relationship.
19. Castor and Pollux, the sons of Leda, became the twin constellation, Gemini.
20. The idea of a lesbian marriage, introduced with Hymen, continues in this echoing of the words of the marriage service.
21. This bawdy ballad is a dramatic monologue. It depends, throughout, on sexual double meanings derived from the conceit of the prostitute as boat. (Cf. The hostess sonnets of John Stewart, § 18.15a/b; Allan Ramsay, 'Lucky Spence's Last Advice.') A final marginal addition in a later hand reads, 'To Ioh. Carmichael.'

Quhat pylett° takis my schip in chairge — *Whichever pilot*
Man° hald hir clynlie, trym and ticht,° — *Must; firm and tight*
Se that hir hatchis be handlit richt° — *treated properly*
With steirburd, baburd, luf and lie,°[22] — *i.e. Everywhere*
Scho will sale all the winter nicht
And nevir tak a telyevie.° — *pitch over*

2

With evin keill befoir the wind,
Scho is richt fairdy° with a saill, — *very fast*
Bot at ane lufe scho lyis behind;[23]
Gar heiss° hir quhill hir howbands skaill.° — *Raise; restraining ropes loosen*
Draw weill the takill° to hir taill,° — *tackle; stern*
Scho will nocht miss° to lay your mast,° — *fail; bring your mast down*
To pomp° als oft as ye may haill,° — *Pump/Thrust; heartily*
Yeill nevir hald hir watterfast.° — *watertight*

3

To calfet° hir oft can do non ill — *caulk*
And tailloun° quhair the fludmark flowis, — *tallow/(tail-on)*
But gif scho lekkis,° gett men of skill — *leaks*
To stop hir hoilis laich° in the howiss;° — *low; holds*
For falt° of hemp, tak hary towis,° — *lack; rough ropes*
With stane ballest[24] withouttin uder.° — *anything else*
In moneless° nichtis, it is na mowis° — *moonless; sport*
Except ane stout° man steir hir ruder. — *strong*

4

A fair veschell abone the watter
And is bot laitly reiket to,° — *recently rigged up/young*
Quhairto till deif° you with tome clatter° — *deafen; empty chatter*
Ar nane sic in the floit° as scho. — *fleet*
Plum weill the grund,° quhat evir ye doo, — *Plumb the depths well*
Haill° on the fuk-scheit° and the blind, — *Haul; mainsail/(blanket)*
Scho will tak in at cap° and koo° — *prow; stern*
Without scho ballast be behind.

5

Na pedderis pak,° scho will ressaif[25] — *pedlar's pack*
Althocht hir travell scho sould tyne,° — *lose*
Na coukcald-karle° nor carllingis pet° — *cuckold-boor; hag's pet*
That dois thair corne and caitell cryne,° — *shrivel*
Bot quhair scho finds a fallow fyne
He wilbe fraucht fre° for a souss;° — *treated generously; small coin*

22. 'Starboard, port, windward and leeward.'
23. 'But when sailing close to the wind, she lags behind'/'But when making love, she lies with her bottom upwards.'
24. Broken stone or other heavy material, taken aboard to hold a ship steady.
25. I.e. she is choosy about her clients.

Scho kareis nocht but° men and wyne	*cares for nothing except*
And bulyoun° to the counye-houss.°	*bullion; mint/private parts*
6	
For merchandmen° I may haif mony,	*(As) for merchants*
But nane sic as I wald desyre,	
And I am layth to mell° with ony	*mingle/have intercourse*
To leif my mater in the myre.	
That man that wirkis best for his hyre,	
Syne he salbe my mariner,	
Bot nycht and day mon° he nicht tyre	*must*
That sailis my bony ballinger.°	*pretty little craft*
7	
For ankerhald° nane can be fund,	*anchorage*
I pray you cast the leidlyne° out	*sounding line*
And, gif ye can nocht get the grund,°	*get your bearings*
Steir be the cumpas and keip hir rout;°	*hold steady*
Syne treveiss still° and lay about	*tack gently*
And gar° hir top° tuiche wind and waw;°	*make; crest; wave*
Quhair anker dryvis, thair is na dout	
Thir tripand tyddis° may tyne° us aw.	*surging tides; be the end of*
8	
Now is my pretty pynnege° reddy,	*pinnace*
Abydand° on sum merchand blok;[26]	*Waiting*
Bot (be scho emptie) be our Leddy,°	*Virgin Mary*
She will be kittill° of hir dok.°	*particular/fickle; stern*
Scho will ressaif na landwart Jok,°	*rustic Jimmy*
Thocht he wald fraught° hir for a croun;	*hire*
Thus, 'Fare ye weill!' sayis gude Johne Cok,[27]	
Ane nobill telyeour°[28] in this toun.	*tailor*

11b: Ballatis, Political and Religious[29]

Alexander Scott

VIII

'Ane New Yeir Gift to the Quene Mary, quhen scho come first hame, 1562'

[The extract opens a lengthy welcome to Mary Queen of Scots. Scott does take advantage of his senior bardic position to highlight Scotland's poverty and warn the queen of difficul-

26. 'merchand blok' may mean either that the ship is laid up on a 'nearby block of wood' or that the girl and her procuress only await a suitable 'mercantile arrangement.'
27. 'Cok,' apart from its obvious meaning, had blasphemous undertones, being used as a colloquial reference to 'God.'
28. Tailors and cobblers were traditional comic butts. Their names, therefore, had ribald connotations.
29. ED. § 11b VIII-XIII. COPY TEXTS: VIII: Bannatyne MS; IX, X: Sempill Ballates,* XI–XIII: Ane Compendious Buik of Godlie and Spirituall Sangis 1578. (*The collation of Craigie in *Satirical Poems of the Reformation* has been followed.)

ties facing her. The predominant tone, however, is optimistic and suitably represented by the first two stanzas.]

Welcum, illustrat° ladye and oure Quene! *illustrious*
Welcum oure lyone with the floure delyce![30]
Welcum oure thrissill with the Lorane grene![31]
Welcum, our rubent roiss° upoun the ryce!° *rose; spray*
Welcum, oure jem and joyfull genetryce!
Welcum oure beill° of Albion° to beir! *suffering; England*
Welcum, oure plesand princes, maist of pryce!° *most praiseworthy*
God gif the° grace aganis this gud new yeir. *you*

This guid new yeir, we hoip, with grace of God,
Salbe of peax, tranquillitie and rest;
This yeir sall rycht and ressone rewle the rod,° *hold sway*
Quhilk sa lang seasoun° hes bene soir suppreST; *for so long a time*
This yeir, ferme fayth sall frelie be confest,
And all arronius questionis° put areir;° *false issues; behind*
To laboure that this lyfe amang us lest°— *endure*
God gife the grace aganis this guid new yeir.

Anonymous

IX

'The Lamentatioun of Lady Scotland, compylit be hir self, speiking in maner of ane Epistle, in the moneth of Marche, the yeir of God 1572'

[Ten years later, a very different view of Mary's reign is presented in this extract from a longer allegorical poem addressed to a prominent reformer, John Erskine of Dun (1509–91).]

'I grant° I had ane Douchter was ane Quene,° *admit; i.e. Mary*
Baith gude and fair, gentill and liberall,
Dotit° with vertewis and wit naturall; *Endowed*
Prignant in spreit,° in all thingis honourabill, *Full of spirit*
Lusty, gude; lyke° to all men favourabill; *equally*
Schamefull to° evill; baith honest, meik and law.° *Full of shame at; modest*
Thir vertewis all scho had, quhyls scho stude aw° *stood in awe*
Of God eterne as of hir governour,
And quhen° scho did regaird° hir hie honour. *so long as; pay attention to*
Bot, at the last, throw filthie speiche and counsell,
That scho did heir of sum curst Kittie unsell,[32]

30. At that time, the arms of Scotland showed a lion rampant surrounded by a border of lilies, signifying the alliance with France.
31. The thistle had been the emblem of Scotland since the days of James III at least. The cross of Lorraine was inherited by Mary through her mother, Mary of Lorraine.
32. 'curst Kittie unsell'. Literally, 'some accursed Kitty profligate'. The name 'Kittie' was often used (e.g. § 12, l. 670) to suggest an easily corrupted, worldly woman.

Fra° scho gaif eir to sic vyle bawderie— *Once*
God, schame and honour, scho foryet° all thre.[33] *forgot/renounced*

It wer to lang° the vices to reheirse,° *too lengthy; recite*
Quhairin from thyne° scho did hir self exerce:° *then on; give herself to*
The reidar[34] wald thame think maist insolent,° *arrogant/immoderate*
Bot I thame leif° becaus thay ar recent: *pass over*
For quhilks scho was thocht unworthy to ring,° *reign*
And crown to bruik° or ony royall thing: *enjoy*
Sa, all my children, with hir awin consent,
Desposit hir in opin parliament.[35]
Than wald scho, that thay suld hir awin sone° crowne, *i.e. James VI*
Quhilk thing thay did sa syce up and sink downe.[36]
God save his grace, for quhy the same is he
In me that hes the trew authoritie.

Robert Sempill[37]

X

'Maddeis Proclamatioun'

1

In lofty veirs I did reheirs
My drerie lamentatioun,[38]
And now, allace! maist cairfull cace!
I mak my proclamatioun.
Desyring all, baith greit and small,
That heiris me be narratioun,
Not for to wyte° my rude indyte,° *criticise; rough writing*
Sen maid is intimatioun.° *warning has been given*

2

I do intend nane to offend
That feiris God arycht,
Thocht murtherars and blud scheddars

33. This false trinity of attributes mark her out as a type of the 'Bad Ruler'—the Stuart equivalent of Richard III within the Tudor Myth.

34. The original (lost) text was a broadsheet. Reading, rather than listening, becomes the norm as printing develops.

35. Mary was forced to abdicate on 24 July, 1567. She appealed to Parliament for restoration in 1569. A mini-parliament or convention met in Perth in that year. They rejected her case by 40 votes to 9.

36. 'syce up and sink downe'. This image of a boat being tossed up and then down does not imply negation. Metapahorically, it means that the queen's proposal was considered from all viewpoints; colloquially, 'tossed around.'

37. One of a series of poems attributed to Sempill and lamenting, from the Protestant viewpoint, the murder of the Regent Moray by Hamilton of Bothwellhaugh. St. 5 states the context explicitly.

38. The reference is to another lyric in the Sempill collection, 'Maddeis Lamentatioun'. A female voice and dramatic monologue form are adopted in both. Each uses a different form of eight line interlacing stanza. The shorter rhythms and more down to earth language of the 'Proclamatioun' mark it out as the comic, low-style complement to the 'lofty veirs' of 'The Lamentatioun'.

Wald haif me out of sycht.
Thair malice vane I do disdane,
And curse thair subtell slycht.° *trickery*
My name is knawin, thair bruit is blawin
Abrode,[39] baith day and nycht.

3

For I, a wyfe with sempill lyfe,
Dois wyn my meit° ilk day, *earn my livelihood*
For small availl,° ay selling caill,° *For little return; cabbage*
The best fassoun I may.°[40]
Besyde the throne,° I walt upone° *weighing machine; throw on to*
My mercat° but° delay; *merchandise; without*
Gif men thair walk, I heir thair talk
And beiris it weill away.

4

In felloun° feir at me thay speir,° *extreme; enquire*
Quhat tythands° in this land? *tidings*
Quhy sit I dum and dar not mum?° *speak out*
Oft tymes thay do demand.
To thame agane I answer plane,
Quhair thay beside me stand.
'Na thing is heir bot mortall weir,° *deadly strife*
Wrocht be ane bailfull° hand.' *baleful/destructive*

5

A wickit race of grumis but grace° *graceless rascals*
Of Kedyochis curst clan,[41]
Be tressoun vile, quha dois defyle
Thame self, baith wyfe and man,
As lait is sene° with weiping ene; *As has recently been seen*
Thairfoir I sall thame ban,° *curse/exile*
Caus our Regent° maist innocent *Moray*
That cursit seid° ouer ran. *seed i.e. Hamilton family*

6

Quhat cruelteis thay enemeis
Hes wrocht be tymes past
I lat ouer slyde;° I may not byde°— *pass over; delay*
So fair I am agast°— *So utterly aghast am I*
Thair anterous° actis, thair furious factis,° *reckless; violent deeds*
Auld bukis, quha will ouer cast,° *peruse*
And men on live° can yit discrive° *living; still recount*
Thair doings, first and last.

39. 'thair bruit is blawin abrode.' Two ideas are contained in this phrase. (i) Their (evil) reputations are widely known. (ii) Their (false) rumours are blown around everywhere.
40. 'As best I can'. Lit. '(In) the best manner I can.'
41. The ancient residence of the Hamilton family was at Cadzow Castle.

7

Thairfoir, my Lords, as best accords,° *as is most fitting*
Sen ye are hapnit hidder,
This I will say, twix sport and play,
My wordis weill considder
And ponder thame for your awin schame;
To mark thame be not lidder:° *slothful/apathetic*
Let na mans feid,° throw feirfull dreid, *enmity*
Your hartis mak to swidder.° *hesitate*

8

For I heir say, thay will display
Thair baners on the feild,
Thinkand, but dout, to ruit yow out
Or cause yow seik some beild.° *shelter*
At thame!° rycht fane° or els be slane: *Be at them; keenly*
That ganyell° will thay yeild: *return*
Stand not abak, (oh febill pak!)
Bot swordis leir° to weild. *learn*

9

Defend your richt in Goddis sicht.
Quhome of do ye stand aw?[42]
Richt few, I trow, will yow allow,° *approve of you*
Gif to your selfis misknaw.° *deny yourselves*
Stand to, thairfoir, fyle not the scoir,[43]
But all togidder draw,
Not in cat harrowis lyke cankrit marrowis
For feir of efter flaw.[44]

10

Do ye not se that mad menye° *raving rabble*
How thay ar warin crous?° *growing bold*
To wirk yow tene,° thai mak the Quene— *cause you harm*
Thair strenth and strang blokhous.°[45] *strong fortress*
The murther fy! thay do deny
And countis° yow not ane sous:° *rate (at); small coin (French)*
Thair proude pretence° throw negligence,° *presumption; i.e. if ignored*
Will be maist dangerous.

11

To Lythquo toun,° thay ar all boun,°[46] *Linlithgow town; bound*
Quhair thay the murther wrocht

42. 'Of whom are you so greatly afraid?'
43. 'Do not defile the line.' In a version of tug of war called 'Scotch and English', two teams linked into lines ('scores'). Each tried to pull the other across a line, drawn between them.
44. ll. 7–8: 'Not in opposite directions, like peevish spouses in fear of evil consequences.'
45. Only a staunch protestant could use imagery suggesting that Mary's imprisonment in Linlithgow was, in fact, an advantage for her party!
46. Mary's supporters, then in disarray, attended a conference at Linlithgow Castle in April 1570.

And thinkis to de or fortifie° *build upon*
Thair fellony forethocht;° *pre-planned*
And trewlie I can not not espy
Quhat uther thing thay socht,
Bot—king put doun and clame the croun,
Be bludy murther bocht.

12

I pans° and muse how thay excuse *ponder*
This murther perpetrate,
Or with quhat grace haldis up thair face,
Quhair it is nominate.° *named*
Gif (as I trow) thay it allow
Like wolfis insatiate,
Quho can repent, that thay be schent° *driven off/killed*
With blude commaculate?° *stained*

13

Fall to, thairfoir, I yow imploir
My Lords, with ane assent,
And think it lang, ay quhil ye fang° *ever until you catch*
The feiris° that did invent *people*
This crueltie, be tyrannie
To sla our rycht° Regent, *rightful*
For thay, maist sure, dois still indure° *endure/flourish*
With hartis impenitent.

14

That man in deid is worth sum meid,° *consideration*
His fault that dois confes;
Bot quhat rewarde suld be preparde
For him that dois transgres
And will not graunt°—bot rather vaunt *admit*
In his unhappynes?
Maist sure the gallows, with all his fallows,° *companions*
For thair unthankfulnes!

15

For gif self lufe° was from abufe *self-love*
Dejectit° out of hevin, *Cast down*
Quhen Lucifer[47] wald be ane bar° *barrier*
To God, and think him evin—
Quhat sall we wene° of tratours kene,° *think; cruell*
That ithandly° hes strevin *assiduously*
For to deface the nobill race
Of Stewarts, od and evin?° *i.e. entirely*

47. As the full implications of their evil are explained, the Hamiltons and their supporters are connected with the leader of the fallen angels, Lucifer.

16

Considder weill thair cankrit zeill — *zeal*
Hes thristit mony day
For to possess but° godlynes, — *without*
The crowne withouttin stay;° — *delay*
As now of lait thair curst consait° — *strategy*
With murther thay display,
Quhen thay thocht gude to drink this blude,[48]
Be that ungodly way.

17

Bot Sathan[49] sure dois thame allure
With wordis fals and vane,
Ay promysing thame to be king
Quhairof thay ar full fane.
In Paradice he did intice,
Be subtell craft and trane,° — *plot*
The man first maid, sa God hes said,
In sacrede Scripture plane.

18

He° said that he° suld equall be — *i.e. Satan; i.e. Adam*
To God omnipotent,
The appill sweit gif he wald eit,
Quhairof was maid restraint.
With small defence, he gaif credence,
Bot did he not repent
Quhen efterwart he felt the smart
And God aganis him bent.

19

Sa sall all thay that dois this day
With mischant° mynde maling° — *evil; scheme*
Aganis the treuth, but ony reuth,° — *without any pity*
And crowning of our king.
And this thay mufe° for thair behufe° — *instigate; advantage*
To place thair awin ofspring;
Bot° thay repent, thay will be schent° — *Unless; destroyed*
And hell at thair ending.

20

Authoritie, gif just he be,
Quhy do thay this ill will him?° — *thus hate him*
His graitfull gide, throw pevische pride,
Allace! quhy did thay kill him?

48. Associations with the Antichrist follow those with Lucifer. The murder of Moray becomes an evil, worldly communion.
49. The line of unrepentant, selfish worldly rebellion against divinity ends with Satan and the fall of Adam (Genesis 3). It is an apposite analogy for self-interested opposition to a queen, established by God under divine right.

Thair heid supreme in to this realme
Admit gif thay not will him,
Than ye, my Lords, cut of with cords° *hang*
Thame° will be troublous till him. *Those (who)*

21
Revenge this wrang, lat tratoures hang—
Gods law dois sa requyre:
Lat Caleb eik and Josue seik[50]
The promysit impyre.° *promised land*
Thocht murmurars° and murthgerars *denouncers*
Wald all your deith conspyre,
In wyldernes with cursitnes
At lenth thay will all tyre.° *retire*

22
That campion of Babilon,[51]
That bludy beildar up,
With mytrid° heid, ane homyceid *mitred*
That saikles blude dois sup,
Gar cow° his crowne° or put him doun *Shear; head*
That he may taist the cup,[52]
Quhairwith oft tymes, for saikles° crymes, *guiltless*
Mennis lyves he interup.° *cut short*

23
And se that never ye do dissever
From first contractit band,
Quhen ye our king, of yeiris ying,
Made rewlar of this land.
Lat not invy cause sum ly by,° *stay neutral*
Bot all togidder stand;
Than God the Lord misericord° *merciful*
Will be your sure warrand.

24
From cail mercat,° quhair as I sat, *i.e. vegetable market*
Thir wordis I did indyte° *write down*
The wyfis amang, that thocht greit lang(?)
To se my awin hand wryte,
Gif ony be that will judge me
To speik bot in dispyte,° *only in disdain*
God mend the mis° committit is, *error/evil (which)*
And I na mair sall flyte.° *harangue*

50. Numbers 14.30. God tells Moses and Aaron that only Caleb and Joshua have dared to enter the promised land. The others fear the evil men who currently possess it.
51. Archbishop Beaton of Glasgow, who did know in advance of the plan to murder Moray. Later he would, himself, be murdered.
52. The cup of bitterness, as tasted by Samson, rather than the communion cup of love.

Anonymous

XI

'The Paip, that pagane full of pryde'

1

The Paip, that pagane full of pryde,
He hes us blindit lang,
For quhair the blind the blind dois gyde,
Na wonder thay ga wrang;
Lyke prince and king he led the ring° *government/dance*
Of all iniquitie:
Hay trix, tryme go trix, under the grene wod tré.[53]

2

Bot his abominatioun,
The Lord hes brocht to licht;
His popische pryde, and thrinfalde° crowne, *trinal*
Almaist hes loist thair micht.
His plak pardounis,° ar bot lardounis[54] *farthing pardons*
Of new found vanitie.
Hay trix, tryme go trix, under the grene wod tré.

3

His cardinallis hes caus to murne,
His bischoppis borne aback,° *taken aback*
His abbottis gat ane uncouth° turne, *strange/rough*
Quhen schavelingis° went to sack;° *tonsured clergy; pillage*
With burges wyfis thay led thair lyfis,
And fure° better nor° we, *fared; than*
Hay trix, tryme go trix, under the grene wod tré.

4

His Carmelites and Jacobinis,[55]
His Dominiks had greit do,
His Cordeleiris, and Augustinis,
Sanct Frances ordour to;° *(religious) order also*
Thay sillie° freiris, mony yeiris, *vacuous*
With babling blerit our ee,° *blurred our eyes*
Hay trix, tryme go trix, under the grene wod tré.

5

The sisteris gray,° befoir this day, *i.e. of St Francis' third order*
Did crune° within thair cloister, *sing in low tones*

53. 'Hay trix, tryme go trix, under the grene etc.' The editorial expansion suggested by John MacQueen has been adopted.
54. 'lardounis'. The meaning is uncertain but 'lardon' did mean a gibe and 'lardine' was an inferior substitute for lard. The pardons are, therefore, either 'jokes' or 'shams'.
55. 4:1–4. The various orders of Friars, Jacobins and Dominicans are the same order. Cordeliers are the Franciscan Observantines, so called because of the knitted cord they wore round their waists.

Thay feit° ane freir, thair keyis to beir[56]— *paid*
The feind ressave the foster°— *offspring*
Syne, in the mirk,° sa weill culd wirk, *dark*
And kittill° thame wantounlie, *tickle*
Hay trix, tryme go trix, under the grene wod tré.

6

The blind bischop, he culd nocht preiche,
For playing with the lassis,
The syllie freir behuffit to fleiche,° *had to flatter*
For almous° that he assis,° *alms; seeks*
The curat, his Creid he culd nocht reid,[57]
Schame fall the cumpanie!
Hay trix, tryme go trix, under the grene wod tré.

7

The bischop wald nocht wed ane wyfe,
The abbote not persew ane,
Thinkand it wes ane lustie lyfe,
Ilk day to have ane new ane—
In everie place, ane uncouth° face, *strange/new*
His lust to satisfie.
Hay trix, tryme go trix, under the grene wod tré.

8

The persoun° wald nocht have ane hure,° *parson; whore*
Bot twa, and° thay war bony,° *if; attractive*
The vicar (thocht he wes pure)° *poor*
Behuiffit° to have als mony, *Needed/Wanted*
The pareis° preist, that brutall beist, *parish*
He polit° thame privelie.° *fleeced/stripped; secretly*
Hay trix, tryme go trix, under the grene wod tré.

9

Of Scotlandwell the freiris of Faill,[58]
The lymmerie° lang hes lestit, *villainy*
The Monkis of Melros maid gude kaill,° *broth*
On Frydayis quhen thay fastit,
The syllie° nunnis caist up thair bunnis° *innocent/ simple; bums*
And heisit° thair hippis on hie, *raised*
Hay trix, tryme go trix, under the grene wod tré.

10

Of lait° I saw thir lymmaris° stand, *Recently; rascals*
Lyke mad men at mischeif,° *intent on evil*

56. 'keyis to beir' means that, literally, he can enter their cloisters. It also suggests the handing over of responsibility.
57. Slothfulness and illiteracy are the satiric focuses. Some friars cannot read or recite aloud from memory the most basic statement of faith, the Creed.
58. Scotlandwell (in Kinross) and Faill (in Ayrshire) were houses of the Red Friars.

Thinking to get the upper hand,
Thay luke efter releif;
Bot all in vaine—go tell thame plaine,
That day will never be.
Hay trix, tryme go trix, under the grene wod tré.

11
O Jesu! gif thay thocht greit glie,
To see Goddis word downe smorit,° *smothered*
The Congregatioun[59] maid to flie,
Hypocresie restorit,
With messis° sung and bellis rung *masses*
To thair idolatrie;
Marie, God thank yow, we sall gar brank yow,[60]
Befoir that time, trewlie.

Anonymous

XII

'Musing greitlie in my mynde'

1
Musing greitlie in my mynde
The folie that is in mankynde,
Quhilk is sa brukill° and sa blind— *brittle/frail*
And downe sall cum, downe ay, downe ay.

2
Levand° maist pairt in all vice, *Living*
Nouther sa gracious, nor sa wyse,
As out of wretchitnes to ryse—
Bot downe to cum, downe ay, downe ay.

3
And all this warld to weild thow had,
Thy body perfit and properlie maid,
Yit man, as floure, thow sall faid—
And downe thow sall cum, downe ay,

4
Thocht thow war ever eternall,[61]
As man that never suld have ane fall,
Yit doutles die thow sall—
And downe sall cum, downe ay, downe ay.

59. The Congregation of Christ were an influential Protestant group, founded in 1557.
60. Branking was a public punishment. The culprit was clamped into an iron bridle with side panels and a gag (also of iron).
61. Man's immortality was God's intention through all time. The reference here and in the next line is to the fall of Adam and Eve, as recorded in Genesis 3. See st. 8.

5
Thocht thow war man never sa thrall,
Remember yit, that die thow sall,
Quha hiest clymmis,° gettis greitest fall— *highest climbs*
And downe sall cum, downe ay, downe ay.

6
Thocht thow war never of sa greit degre,
In riches, nor in dignitie,
Remember, man, that thow mon° die— *must*
And downe sall cum, downe ay, downe ay.

7
Thair is na king nor empreour,
Duke nor lord of greit valure,° *worth*
Bot he sall faid as lely° floure— *lily*
And downe sall cum, downe ay, downe ay.

8
Quhair is Adam and Eve his wyfe,
And Hercules[62] with his lang stryfe,
And Matussalem,°[63] with his lang lyfe? *Methuselah*
Thay all ar cum downe ay, downe ay.

Anonymous

XIII

The Lordis Prayer

1
[*Our Father,*][64]
Our Father, God omnipotent,
Quhen Christ Thy sone was heir present,
He bad° us ever pray to Thé. *commanded*
Because we knew not for to pray
He leirnit us quhat we suld say,
Syne hecht° to heir us mercyfullie. *promised*

2
[*that art in hevin*]
Sen Thé to call is Thy command,
Thyne awin wordis than understand,
Quhilk Thow hes promeist for till heir:° *to listen to*
Behald not my unrichteousnes,

62. Hercules was renowned for his size and strength.
63. 'And all the days of Methuselah were nine hundred sixty and nine years…' Genesis 5. 27.
64. A Scots version of the Lord's Prayer (Matthew 6. 9–13) is included in the text. To demonstrate the methods of rhetorical expansion, the relevant extracts have been placed above the apposite stanza.

But luke till Christis richteousnes,
And with Thy faith, my spreit up steir.° *guide my soul upwards*

3
[*hallowit be thy name*]
Lord, Thow will have allanerlie,° *uniquely*
Worschip in spirite and veritie,
And to nane uther give Thy gloir;
Thy Name then let us lufe and dreid° *dread*
And call on it, in all our neid,
And thank and love Thé evermoir

4
[*Thy Kingdome cum*]
Destroy the devill, his realme and reigne,° *rule*
Quhilk° of this warld is prince and king, *Who (Christ)*
And lat Thy gospell be our gyde;
Conforme our lyfe efter Thy word,
That we may reigne for ever, O Lord,
In Thy kinrik with Thé to byde.

5
[*Thy will be done in eirth as it is in hevin*]
God, grant that we may wirk Thy will,
In eird Thy plesure to fulfill,
Siclyke° as in the hevin Impyre, *In like manner*
And quhat that ever we tak on hand,
May be conforme to Thy command
And na thing efter our desyre.

6
[*Give us this day our daylie breid*]
Give us this day our daylie breid,
And all thing that Thow hes maid
For mennis sustentatioun,° *sustenance*
And all thing quhairof we have neid,
Our saull and body for to feid,
But sleuth° or solistatioun.° *Without deceit; inducement*

7
[*Forgive us our trespassis as we forgive them that trespas aganis us*]
Forgive our sinnis and our trespas,
For Christis saik, quhilk gevin° was *given over*
To deid,° for our redemptioun *To death*
As we forgive all creature
Offendand us, baith rich and pure,° *poor*
Hartfully; without exemptioun.° *exception*

8
[*And leid us not into temptatioun*]
Defend us from temptatioun,
The feind° and his vexacioun, *devil*

The warld sa fals, the fragill flesche;
Saif us from schame and from dispair,
From unbeleve° and Lollaris lair,°[65] *unbelief; Lollards' lore*
And devillis doctrine mair or les.

9
[*Bot deliver us from evill*]
Deliver us from evillis all,
Baith spirituall and corporall,
And grant us grace, quhen we sall die,
And fra this present lyfe we wend,
That we may mak ane blyssit end,
Syne reigne with Thé eternallie.

10
[*For thine is the kingdom, the power and the glorie, for ever.* Amen.]
Power nor gloir, impyre nor tryne,° *retinue*
Is nane in hevin, nor eirth, bot Thyne,
And ever mair sall sa remaine;
Thairfoir, Thow may and will releve
All thame, that can in Christ beleve,
From deide, the devill, and hellis paine.

11c: Summation

Sir Richard Maitland (1496–1586)

XIV

'Satire on the Age'[66]

1
Quhair is the blythnes that hes bein
Bayth in burgh and landwart° sein, *country*
Amang lordis and ladyis schein°— *bright*
Daunsing, singing, game and play?
Bot now I wait nocht quhat thai mein,° *intend*
All mirrines is worne away.

2
For now I heir na word of Yule° *Christmas festivities*
In kirk, on cassay° nor in scule, *pavement/the streets*
Lordis lattis thair kitchingis cule° *kitchens grow cold*
And draws thame to° the abbay, *haunt*
And scant hes ane to keip thair mule,° *concubine*
All houshaldaris[67] is worne away.

65. The Lollards were followers of John Wycliffe. The *Compendious Book* is resolutely Calvinist.
66. ED. § 11c COPY TEXT: XIV Maitland Folio MS.
67. 'houshaldaris' is a key word in the poem. It has a variety of senses. All centre on the idea of communal living— the maintenance of a household. It is this caring, lighthearted, gregarious lifestyle which, Maitland protests, has turned into selfishness, solitude and seriousness.

3

I saw no gysaris° all this yeir — *masqueraders*
Bot kirkmen cled° lyk men of weir, — *dressed*
That never cummis in the queir;° — *enter the choir*
Lyk ruffyanis is thair array,
To preiche and teiche that will nocht leir,
The kirk gudis thai waist away.

4

Kirkmen affoir war gude of lyf,
Preichit, teichit and stanchit stryf;° — *staunched strife*
Thai ferit° nother swerd nor knyf, — *carried*
For luif of God, the suyth to say;
All honorit thame, bayth man and wyf,
Devotion was nocht away.

5

Our faderis wyse was and discreit,
Thay had bayth honor, men and meit,
With luif, thai did thair tennents treit
And had aneuche in poiss to lay:° — *to hoard away*
Thay wantit° nother malt nor quheit,° — *lacked; wheat*
And mirriness was nocht away.

6

And we hald nother Yule nor Pace° — *the Easter festival*
But seik our meit from place to place,
And we have nother luk nor grace,
We gar our landis doubill pay;
Our tennentis cryis alace, alace,
That reuth° and petie is away. — *compassion*

7

Now we have mair, it is weill kend,
Nor our foirbearis° had to spend, — *forefathers*
Bot far less at the yeiris end
And never hes ane mirrie day!
God will na rychess to us send,
Sa lang as honour is away.

8

We waist far mar now, lyk vane fulis,
We and our page to turss° our mulis,° — *pack; mules*
Nor thai did than, that held grit Yulis,
Off meit and drink said never nay;
Thay had lang formes° quhair we have stulis[68] — *long benches*
And mirrines was nocht away.

68. The imagistic confirmation of the oppositions discussed in the previous note.

9

Off our wanthrift° sum wytis° playis — *prodigality; blame*
And sum thair wantoun vane arrayis,
Sum the wyt° on thair wyffis layis, — *blame*
That in the court wald gang so gay,
And caris nocht quha the merchant payis
Quhill pairt of land be put away.

10

The kirkmen keips na professioun,° — *i.e. are untrue to their vows*
The temporale men committis oppressioun,
Puttand the pure from thair possessioun;
Na kynd of feir of God have thai—
Thai cummar° bayth the Court and Sessioun — *trouble*
And chassis cheritie away.

11

Quhen ane of thame sustenis wrang,
We cry for justice, heid and hang,
Bot quhen our nychtbor we ourgang° — *outwit*
We laubor justice to delay;
Effectioun° blindis us sa lang, — *Self-interest*
All equitie is put away.

12

To put actis,° we have sum feill°— — *make laws; talent*
God wait gif that we keip thame weill—
We cum to bar° with jake° of steill — *i.e. law court; jacket*
As we wald bost° the juge and fray;° — *threaten; attack*
Off sic justice I have na skeill,
Quhair rewle and ordour is away.

13

Our lawis are lichtleit for abusioun,
Sumtyme is clokit with collusioun,
Quhilk causis of blude the greit effusioun,[69]
(For na man sparis now to slay).
Quhat bringis cuntreis to confusioun
Bot quhair° that justice is away? — *Except where*

14

Quhair is the wyt,° quha can schaw us? — *wisdom*
Quha bot our nobillis that suld knaw us
And, till honorabill deidis, draw us?
Lat never commoun weill° decay — *the common good*
Or ellis sum mischeif will faw us° — *some evil will befall us*
And nobilnes° we put away. — *If noble qualities*

69. ll. 1–3. The general sense is that the laws are disparaged because the abuse of them, which sometimes involves disguise and conspiracy, leads to murder.

15

Put our awin lawis to executioun!
Apone trespassouris mak punitioun!
To cruell folk seik na remissioun!
For peax and justice lat us pray,
In dreid sum strange new institutioun
Cum—and our custome put away.

16

Amend your lyveis ane and all,
And be war° of ane suddane fall, *wary*
And pray to God, that maid us all,
To send us joy that lestis ay;
And let us nocht to syn be thrall,° *in thrall*
Bot put all vyce and wrang away.

§ 12: Sir David Lindsay (c.1486–1555): *Ane Satyre of the Thrie Estaitis, Act I, preceded by the Cupar Banns.*

The life of Sir David Lindsay of the Mount spans the latter days of James IV, culminating with defeat at Flodden and the anarchic Regency under the Duke of Albany. He rose to higher rank under James V, first as herald, then as knight and Lord Lyon King of Arms. James was a shrewd monarch, capable of mingling benevolence with rigour—necessary qualities as the Reformation, with all its tensions, began to make its presence felt during his reign. While Lindsay is the major poet of that reign, he was primarily valued as a courtier and ambassador. In the latter capacity he spent a good deal of time in France, gaining an understanding of that country's culture. This enriched his lyrical, narrative and dramatic verse.

Lindsay is the first major poet to voice Protestant aspirations. His work is also remarkably consistent. Alhough he can adopt lighter tones (as in the **Romance of Squyer Meldrum**) *he is primarily a satirist. There is, too, a consistency of purpose which permits the same character—John the Commonweil—to exit from an early allegorical poem* (**The Dreme**) *in protest against the lack of justice in Scotland, only to leap out from among the audience, as a character within* **Ane Satyre**, *about twenty-five years later, at the very moment when King Humanitie has promised to re-establish that justice within society.*

Text: *An extract from the Banns of the earlier Cupar performance of* **Ane Satyre** *has been provided, along with Act One of the later Edinburgh performance. The action centres on the nature of good kingship. King Humanitie, who at once represents a Scottish king, all kings and (at times) Everyman, falls into sensuality and, misled by vice and bad counsel, abjures the responsibilities of the ruler. By the end of the Act, he has undergone the same recovery as Shakespeare's Hal in* **Henry IV.**

Context: *The action continues with an Interlude on the French moralité-sottie model. It is in the second act alone that the estates as such become the immediate focus of dramatic concern. Act One had accomplished the necessary reformation of the king as 'head' of the body politic. Now the nobles and merchants are shown following his lead. Only the spiritual estate, or clergy, remain recalcitrant. Lindsay's most virulent satire is usually reserved for this group, and in his play, their final entrance into the communal harmony is acccompanied by the 'escape' of the Vice figure associated with them. Flatterie's intention of returning remains in the audience's memory. The scenes within the drama have neatly 'resolved' everything; in the world beyond, the jury is still out.*

Ane Plesant Satyre of the Thrie Estaitis[1]

Proclamatioun (Cupar 1552)[2]

Nuntius:[3]

Richt famous pepill, ye sall understand
How that ane prince rycht wyiss and vigilent

1. ED. COPY TEXT: *Banns*: Bannatyne MS; *Satyre*: Charteris Print (1602) with Bannatyne readings introduced where strong evidence exists. These have been noted only in crucial cases. FORMAT: The text is set out in a manner which emphasizes the stanza divisions of versified drama. Bannatyne Stage Directions have been included. STAGING: Additional editorial Stage Directions are designed to make visualisation easier. These are italicized.
2. The play was presented on Whit Tuesday ('On Witsonetysday' *Banns*, l. 271). Within the relevant period, this only fell on 7 June (*Banns* l. 11) in 1552.
3. The reporter or messenger.

Is schortly for to cum in to this land
And purpossis° to hald ane parliament. *intends*
His Thre Estaitis[4] thairto hes done consent,° *have given consent*
In Cowpar toun in to thair best array
With support of the Lord omnipotent,
And thairto hes affixt ane certane day.

With help of Him that rewlis all abone° *above*
That day sal be within ane litill space.° *short time*
Our purposs is, on the sevint day of June—
Gif weddir° serve and we haif rest and pece— *weather*
We sall be sene in till our playing place,°[5] *acting area*
In gude array, abowt the hour of sevin.
Off thristines° that day I pray yow ceiss,° *thirst; cease*
Bot ordane us gude drink aganis allevin.[6]

Faill nocht to be upone the castell hill[7]
Besyd the place quhair we purpoiss to play.
With gude stark° wyne your flacconis° see ye fill, *strong; flagons*
And hald your self the myrieast that ye may.° *in the merriest state possible*
Be not displeisit quhatevir we sing or say,[8]
Amang sad mater howbeid° we sumtyme relyie;° *although; introduce humour*
We sall begin at sevin houris of the day,
So ye keip tryist°—forsuth, we sall nocht felyie.°[9] *keep the tryst/be there; fail*

Edinburgh (Calton Hill Performance: Edinburgh 1554[10])

Dramatis Personae.[11]
Character Name

Diligence perseverance in good works (1)

4. Parliamentary representation is confined to the clergy (who bear the brunt of the satire), the nobles and the merchants. The voice of the fourth estate is, however, heard in Act 2, when the king is ruling wisely.
5. Lyall (Introduction, p. xxii) notes the existence of officially designated playing places—notably in Edinburgh, Glasgow and Dundee—in the fifteenth and sixteenth centuries.
6. 'Let's get ready good drink for ourselves for eleven o'clock.'
7. The castle hill provided an open-air arena. The spectators sat on the slopes of the hill with the playing area sited beyond the burn. As characters shouted from the top of the hill and one, at least, vaulted across the stream from among the audience, this approximates to theatre in the round.
8. In advertising *Ane Satyre*, the Nuntius is anxious to define it as a popular musical rather than a strict morality drama.
9. A farce (which we have omitted) follows the Banns. While there are bawdy movements within the play proper, these co-exist with serious moral and theological material. The writer, however, knows that fabliau material will attract more people to his playing place than sermonising.
10. DATE: There is some critical disagreement over this date but available evidence suggests that it was most probably performed before the Regent, Mary of Guise, in a newly created playing field on Calton Hill, Edinburgh on 12 August, 1554.
11. DRAMATIS PERSONAE: Within the text character names have not been regularised – but the form noted in the list of Dramatis Personae is used consistently at the head of speeches. The first spoken line of dialogue for each role is noted in brackets.

King Humanitie (Rex Humanitas)	temporal kingship (under God) (78)
Bad Courtiers/Counsellors:	
Wantonnes	wantonness, selfish excess (102)
Placebo	(= I shall please), sycophant (118)
Solace	comfort (unprincipled) (142)
Dame Sensualitie	free love; the senses (271)
Sensualitie's Ladies:	
Hamelines	sexual familiarity (295)
Danger	amorous disdain (299)
Fund Jonet	servant girl/singer (314)
Gude Counsall	good counsel (554)
Vices: identity and later disguise	
Flatterie/Devotioun	flattery (piety) (602/797)
Falset/Sapience	falsehood (wisdom) (635/793)
Dissait/Discretioun	deceit (discreetness) (658/785)
Divine Veritie	theological/ Christian truth (1077)
Spiritualitie	the Spiritual Estate (1105)
Representatives of the clergy:	
Abbot	(1113)
Persone	(1121)
Priores	(1234)
Temporalitie	The Temporal Estates
—Nobleman	(1280)
—Merchant	(1280)
Chastitie	chastity (1200)
Representatives of the common people:	
Sowtar	a cobbler (1292)
Taylour	a tailor (1296)
Jennie	the tailor's daughter (1308)
Taylours Wyfe	tailor's wife (1309)
Sowtars Wyfe	cobbler's wife (1318)
Correctioun's Varlet	Divine Correction's servant (1482)
Divyne Correctioun	Divine Reformation (1580)

Ane Satyre (1554)

Act I

Diligence:

The Father and founder of faith and felicitie,
That your fassioun formed to His similitude[12]
And His Sone, our Saviour, scheild in necessitie,° *in time of need*
That bocht yow from baillis° ransonit° on the Rude°[13] *affliction; redeemed; holy cross*
Repledgeand His presonaris° with His pretious blude.[14] *prisoners/captives*
The Halie Gaist, governour and grounder of grace
Of wisdome and weilfair baith fontaine and flude,° *source and river*
Save yow all that I sie seasit° in this place, *seated*
And scheild yow from sinne;
And with His Spreit yow inspyre
Till I have shawin my desyre.
Silence, soveranis,° I requyre, *masters*
For now I begin![15]

Tak tent° to me, my freinds, and hald yow coy,° *pay heed; keep quiet*
For I am sent to yow as messingeir
From ane nobill and rycht redoubtit roy,° *greatly renowned king*
The quhilk° hes bene absent this monie yeir°— *Who; this many a year*
Humanitie, give° ye his name wald speir°— *if; ask*
Quha bade me° shaw to yow, but variance,° *ordered me; without dispute*
That he intendis amang yow to compeir,° *appear*
With ane triumph and awfull ordinance,[16]

With crown and sword and scepter in his hand,
Temperit with mercie quhen penitence appeiris.
Howbeit that hee lang tyme hes bene sleipand,
Quhairthrow misreull hes rung° thir monie yeiris: *misrule has reigned*
That innocentis hes bene brocht upon thair beiris° *biers*
Be fals reporteris of° this natioun; *those who misrepresent*
Thocht young oppressouris at the elderis leiris,° *learn from their elders*
Be now assurit of reformatioun.

Sie no misdoeris be sa bauld
As to remaine into this hauld:° *place*

12. I.e. 'formed you in His own image.' Genesis 1. 26.
13. ransonit on the Rude] B; ranson rude C.
14. 'Offering to His prisoners a new agreement (sealed) with His own precious blood.' The devil owned fallen man until Christ was crucified and harrowed Hell.
15. The lyrical element is reinforced by the variety of verse forms used in the play. Diligence's opening speech establishes the principle. He introduces three of the most commonly used stanzas, moving from a form of the thirteen line Heliconian stanza (1–13) to the eight line Scottish Ballat Royal (14–29) and then to the six line form of *Rime Couée* (30–45). See James VI, *Reulis*, *Chapter VIII*, § 22.
16. 'At the head of a Triumph and with a dreadful show of sovereign authority.' Scottish Ballat Royal, as James VI confirms, is usually associated decorously with 'heich and grave subjectis'.

For quhy° be Him° that Judas sauld — *Because; i.e. Christ*
Thay will be heich hangit.
Now, faithfull folk for joy may sing;
For quhy it is the just bidding
Of my soveraine lord, the king
That na man be wrangit.° — *wronged*

Thocht he, ane quhyll into his flouris,° — *mature years*
Be governit° be vylde trompouris° — *ruled; vile deceivers*
And sumtyme lufe his paramouris,° — *mistresses*
Hauld ye him excusit;
For quhen he meittis with Correctioun,
With Veritie and Discretioun,
They will be bansiched aff the toun,
Quhilk hes him abusit.°[17] — *misled*

And heir, be oppin proclamatioun,[18]
I wairne in name of his magnificence,
The Thrie Estaitis of this natioun,[19]
That they compeir° with detfull° diligence — *present themselves; dutiful*
And till his grace mak thair obedience.
And first I wairne the Spritualitie,
And sie the burgessis spair not for expence
Bot speid thame heir with Temporalitie.

Als I beseik yow famous auditouris,
Conveinit° in this congregatioun, — *Gathered together*
To be patient the space of certaine houris
Till ye have hard our short narratioun.
And als we mak yow supplicatioun,
That na man tak our wordis intill disdaine:° — *scornfully*
Althocht ye hear, be declamatioun,
The Common-weill[20] richt pitouslie complaine.

Rycht so the verteous ladie Veritie
Will mak ane pitious lamentatioun:
Als for the treuth sho will impresonit be
And banischit lang tyme out of the toun;
And Chastitie will mak narratioun
How sho can get na ludging in this land,
Till that the heavinlie King Correctioun
Meit with the king and commoun, hand for hand.[21]

17. Two forms of *Rime Couée* are regularly used. This six line form—aabccb—vies with the more ambitious eight line—aaabcccb—form.
18. This section repeats many of the 'advertising' features provided by the Cupar Banns.
19. The nobility, clergy and merchants.
20. The laments of John the Common-weill, an estate unrepresented in parliament, will be voiced and addressed in the second act of the play.
21. Anticipation of the final outcome was usual in Morality Drama as a virtuous outcome was guaranteed theologically. With no need to 'guess the ending', the spectators could concentrate on the inventiveness of the unfolding plot.

Prudent peopill, I pray yow all,
Tak na man greif in speciall,° *to himself specially*
For wee sall speik in generall,
For pastyme and for play.
Thairfoir, till all our rymis be rung
And our mistoinit° sangis be sung, *out of tune*
Let everie man keip weill ane toung,° *guard his tongue*
And everie woman tway!° *two*

King Humanitie:
O, Lord of lords and King of kingis all,
Omnipotent of power, Prince but peir,° *without equal*
Ever ringand° in gloir celestiall; *reigning*
Quha be great micht° and haifing na mateir° *power; being immaterial*
Maid heavin and eird, fyre, air and watter cleir,[22]
Send me Thy grace, with peace perpetuall,
That I may rewll my realme to Thy pleaseir,° *as You will*
Syne bring my saull to joy angelicall.

Sen Thow hes gevin mee dominatioun
And rewll of pepill subject to my cure,° *care*
Be I nocht rewlit be counsall and ressoun,
In dignitie I may nocht lang indure.
I grant, my stait my self may nocht assure,
Nor yit conserve my lyfe in sickernes:° *security*
Have pitie, Lord, on mee, Thy creature,
Supportand me in all my busines.

I Thee requeist, quha rent° was on the Rude,° *torn; holy cross*
Me to defend from the deids of defame,[23]
That my pepill report of me bot gude
And be my saifgaird baith from sin and shame.
I knaw my dayis induris bot as ane dreame,
Thairfoir, O Lord, I hairtlie The exhort
To gif me grace to use my diadeame° *crown*
To Thy pleasure and to my great comfort. [24]

[Heir sall the king pass to (the) royall sait and sit with ane grave countenance till Wantones cum. *Enter Wantonnes and Placebo.*]

Wantonnes:
My soveraine lord and prince but peir,°[25] *without peer/equal*
Quhat garris yow mak sic dreirie cheir?° *makes you look so miserable*

22. God rules over the four earthly elements, but transcends them 'quintessentially' in Heaven.
23. Bannatyne reads 'deidis' but 'the' deeds referred to are the evil counterparts of the deeds of temporal mercy as defined by Christ.
24. King Humanitie opens as a good ruler, in a state of grace.
25. The evil counsellor echoes the king's opening words (ll. 79–80), but lowers both their application and the verse form.

Be blyth sa lang as ye ar heir,
And pas tyme with pleasure:
For als lang leifis° the mirrie man — *lives as long*
As the sorie,° for ocht he can; — *miserable one*
His banis full sair, sir, sall I ban[26]
That dois yow displeasure.

Sa lang as Placebo and I
Remaines into your company,
Your grace sall leif richt mirrelye—
Of this haif ye na dout!
Sa lang as ye have us in cure,° — *in charge*
Your grace, sir, sall want° na pleasure: — *lack*
War Solace heir, I yow assure,
He wald rejoyce° this rout!° — *cheer up; company*

Placebo:

Gude brother myne, quhair is Solace,
The mirrour of all mirrines?
I have great mervell, be the mes,° — *mass*
He taries sa lang!
Byde he away, wee ar bot shent:° — *ruined*
I ferlie° how he fra us went. — *I wonder*
I trow he hes impediment
That lettis° him to gang. — *prevents*

Wantonnes:

I left Solace, that same greit loun,° — *rogue*
Drinkand into the burrows toun.° — *in the burgh*
It will cost him halfe of ane croun,
Althocht° he had na mair! — *Even if*
And als,° he said hee wald gang see — *also*
Fair Ladie Sensualitie—
The buriall[27] of all bewtie
And portratour° preclair.° — *appearance; most fair*

Placebo:

Be God, I see him at the last
As° he war chaist,° rynnand richt fast, — *As if; being chased*
He glowris evin as he war agast
Or fleyit of° ane gaist.° — *scared by; ghost*
Na, he is wod drunkin° I trow, — *raving drunk*
Se ye not that he is wod fow?° — *mad drunk*
I ken weill be his creischie mow° — *greasy mouth*
He hes bene at ane feast.

26. 'I'll put a painful curse on his bones (on the man)'
27. ED. B: 'beriall'. The words would sound very similar. Dame Sensualitie is in fact at once the 'beryl' of physical beauty and the tomb of spiritual beauty.

[*Enter Solace.*]

Solace:

Now, quha saw ever sic ane thrang?° *throng*
Me thocht sum said I had gaine wrang.
Had I help, I wald sing ane sang
Wyth ane rycht mirrie noyse!
I have sic pleasour at my hart,
That garris me sing the troubill°[28] pairt:
Wald sum gude fallow fill the quart
It wald my hairt rejoyce.

Howbeit my coat be short and nippit,°[29] *tight-fitting*
Thankis be to God I am weill hippit,° *I have a fine pair of hips*
Thocht all my gold may sone be grippit[30]
Intill ane pennie pursse.° *purse for small change*
Thocht I ane servand lang haif bene,
My purchais° is nocht worth ane preine°— *gain; pin*
I may sing 'Peblis on the Greine'[31]
For ocht that I may tursse.° *carry off*

Quhat is my name? Can ye not gesse?
Sirs, ken ye nocht Sandie Solace?
Thay callit my mother Bonie Besse,
That dwelt betwene the bowis;° *arches/limbs (sexual)*
Of twelf yeir auld sho learnit to swyfe,° *copulate*
Thankit be the great God on lyve!
Sho maid me° fatheris four, or fyve, *gave me (a succession of)*
But dout,° this is na mowis.° *Assuredly; bluff*

Quhen ane wes deid, sho gat ane uther—
Was never man had sic ane mother!
Of fatheris, sho maid me ane futher° *horde*
Of lawit° men and leirit.° *ignorant; learned*
Scho is baith wyse, worthie° and wicht,° *stalwart; strong*
For scho spairis nouther kuik° nor knycht— *cook*
Yea, four and twentie on ane nicht
And ay thair eine scho bleirit[32]—

And gif I lie, sirs, ye may speir!° *make enquiry*
Bot, saw ye noucht the king cum heir?[33]

28. ED. B: 'trebill' (treble) makes more obvious sense. However, Vices in Morality Drama wreak chaos with words and C's 'troubill' may be a pun referring to discordance.

29. Vices are given to wearing scant clothing in the height of fashion (l. 203) to show their interest in appearance (ll. 628–30; 675–6) and as a contrast to the full covering of the armour of faith.

30. 'Although all my money quickly could be held (squeezed)'

31. Two popular pieces describing dramatic performances were extant at this time—'Christis Kirk on the Grene' and 'Peblis to the Play'. The role of the bad counsellor being to mislead in words and deeds, it would be fitting for Solace to mix them up.

32. 'And she always hoodwinked them'.

33. There is an element of parody in Solace's speech. He echoes the key words employed reverently by Diligence, but wittily refers them to this world, to play and slothfulness.

I am ane sportour° and playfeir° — *fellow sportsman; playmate*
  To that royall young king.
He said he wald, within schort space,
Cum pas his tyme into this place.
I pray the Lord to send him grace,
  That he lang tyme may ring.° — *reign*

[*Solace joins the others*]

Placebo:
Solace, quhy taryit ye sa lang?

Solace:
The feind a faster I micht gang:[34]
I micht not thrist out throw the thrang
  Of wyfes fyftein fuder!°[35] — *in number/together*
Then, for to rin° I tuik ane rink°— — *run; set a course*
Bot I felt never sik ane stink!
For our Lordis luif, gif me ane drink,
  Placebo, my deir bruder[36]

[Heir sall Placebo gif Sollace ane drink]

King Humanitie:
My servant, Solace, quhat gart yow tarie?° — *made you delay*

Solace:
I wait° not, sir, be sweit Saint Marie,° — *know; i.e. Virgin Mary*
I have bene in ane feirie farie° — *utter maze*
  Or ellis intill ane trance!
SirI have sene—I yow assure—
The fairest earthlie creature
That ever was formit be nature,
  And maist for to advance.° — *most worthy to be praised*

To luik on hir is gret delyte,
With lippis reid and cheikis quhyte;
I wald renunce all this warld quyte° — *entirely*
  For till stand in hir grace!
Scho is wantoun and scho is wyse,° — *(worldly-)wise*
And cled scho is on the new gyse:° — *latest fashion*
It wald gar all your flesche up ryse
  To luik upon hir face.

War I ane king, it sould be kend,° — *understood*
I sould not spair on hir to spend:
And this same nicht for hir to send
  For my pleasure.

34. 'The devil help me if I could have gone any faster'.
35. ED. fuder] B; fidder C.
36. ED. bruder] B; brother C.

Quhat rak of° your prosperitie—   *What matters*
Gif ye want° Sensualitie?   *lack*
I wald nocht gife ane sillie flie°   *i.e. a jot*
For your treasure.[37]

[*King Humanitie descends from his throne.*]

King Humanitie:

Forsuith my freinds, I think ye ar not wyse
Till counsall me to break commandement,
Directit be the Prince of Paradyce:°   *i.e. Christ*
Considering ye knaw that my intent
Is for till be to God obedient,
Quhilk dois forbid men to be lecherous.
Do I nocht sa, perchance I will repent.[38]
Thairfoir, I think your counsall odious,
The quhilk ye gaif mee till,°   *to me*
Becaus I have bene to this day
Tanquam tabula rasa:[39]
That is als mekill° as to say,   *as much*
'Redie for gude and ill.'[40]

Placebo:

Beleive ye that we will begyll yow,
Or from your vertew we will wyle° yow,   *trick*
Or with evill consell ouerseyll° yow   *deceive*
Both into gude and evill?[41]
To tak your graces part wee grant,°   *agree*
In all your deidis participant;
Sa that ye be nocht ane young sanct
And syne° ane auld devill.   *later on*

Wantonnes:

Beleive ye, sir, that lecherie be sin?
Na, trow nocht that! This my ressoun why:
First at the Romane Court[42] will ye begin,
Quhilk is the lemand° lamp of lechery,   *shining*

37. Lechery was the sin of youth; avarice of age. The temptation accords with the youthful king as represented by King Humanitie at this stage of the play. Cf. ll. 233–4.

38. Lindsay's king, like Milton's Adam, is at once made aware of where his true duties lie. The Reformation's increased emphasis on works made 'responsible' heroes more popular.

39. ll. 223–4: '...until this day, I have been like a writing table scraped of wax.' That is, he will be tested first in innocence (or youth) and then re-tested in experience (or age).

40. By opening with eight lines in the high style of the Ballat Royal, but closing with colloquialisms and a macaronic adaptation of the racy five line (abbba) stanza, the King metrically enacts this moral ambivalence.

41. Personification allegory permits characters to inhabit their roles knowledgably (as here) but, at other times, to be deceived by their defining characteristic. Placebo and Flatterie may warn us conceptually against the false way each represents, but also enact the role of an individual moving blindly down that path—cf. l. 235.

42. ED. Romane Court] B; Romane Kirk C.

Quhair cardinals and bischops generally
To luif ladies, thay think ane pleasant sport
And out of Rome hes baneist° Chastity, — *banished*
Quha with our prelats can get na resort.° — *access*

[*King Humanitie and Wantonnes lie down together.*]

Solace:

Sir, quhill° ye get ane prudent queine, — *until*
I think your majestie serein
Sould have ane lustie concubein,° — *mistress/concubine*
To play yow° withall; — *divert yourself*
For I knaw be your qualitie[43]
Ye want° the gift of chastitie. — *lack*
Fall to,° *in nomine Domini.*° — *Join in; in God's name*
This is my counsall.

I speik sir, under protestatioun,
That nane at me haif indignatioun;
For all the prelatis of this natioun,
For the maist part,
Thay think na schame to have ane huir°— — *whore*
And sum hes thrie under thair cuir.° — *protection*
This to be trew, Ile yow assuir,
Ye sall heir efterwart.

Sir, knew ye all the mater throch,[44]
To play° ye wald begin. — *amuse yourself*
Speir at° the monks of Bamirrinoch[45] — *Enquire of*
Gif lecherie be sin.

Placebo:

Sir, send ye for Sandie Solace,
Or ells your monyeoun° Wantonnes, — *minion*
And pray my Ladie Priores
The suith° till° declair — *truth; to*
Gif it be sin to tak ane Kaity,° — *i.e. a mistress/whore*
Or to leif like ane bummillbaty;° — *feckless person*
The Buik° sayis, '*Omnia probate*'[46] — *i.e. The Bible*
And nocht for to spair.

[Heir sall entir Dame Sensualitie with hir madynnis Hamelines and Danger. *They are unseen by the king and his counsellors.*]

43. 'qualitie' means both nature or character, and natural sexual inclination.
44. 'Sir, if you had an out and out understanding of all the facts.'
45. This reference would have had particular force for the Cupar production, as the Cistercian house of Balmerino stood about five miles from that town.
46. I Thessalonians 5. 21. Characteristically, Paul's advice is misinterpreted by the vicious counsellor. The saint refers to the thorough testing of prophecies, but advises the retention only of the good among them.

Dame Sensualitie:

Luifers awalk, behald the fyrie spheir!
Behauld the naturall dochter of Venus!
Behauld, luifers, this lustie ladie cleir,° *beautiful*
The fresche fonteine of knichtis amorous,
Repleit with joyis dulce° and delicious. *sweet*
Or,° quha wald mak to Venus observance, *Also*
In my mirthfull chalmer° melodious, *chamber*
Thair sall thay find all pastyme and pleasance.

Behauld my heid! Behauld my gay attyre!
Behauld my halse,° lusum° and lilie-quhite! *neck; lovely/lovable*
Behauld my visage, flammand as the fyre
Behauld my papis° of portratour° perfyte! *breasts; beauty*
To luke on mee, luiffers hes greit delyte—
Rycht sa hes all the kinges of Christindome.
To thame I haif done pleasouris infinite,
And speciallie unto the Court of Rome.[47]

Ane kis of me war worth in ane morning
A milyioun of gold to knicht or king;
And yit I am of nature sa towart° *forward/brazen*
I lat no luiffer pas with ane sair hart.
Of my name, wald ye wit the veritie?
Forsuith, thay cal me Sensualitie.
I hauld it best, now or° we farther gang, *before*
To Dame Venus let us go sing ane sang.

Hamelines:

Madame, but tarying,
For to serve Venus deir
We sall fall to and sing.
Sister Danger, cum neir.

Danger:

Sister, I was nevir[48] sweir
To Venus observance
Howbeit I mak dangeir.
Yit, be continuance[49]
Men may have thair pleasance;
Thairfoir, let na man fray,° *be afraid*
We will tak it perchance,
Howbeit that wee say nay.

Hamelines:

Sister, cum on your way
And let us nocht think lang,

47. Dame Sensualitie uses the seven line, *Troilus and Criseyde* stanza to present a formal *descriptio* of herself. This rhetorical figure moves from the head downwards.
48. ED. nevir] B; nocht C.
49. ll. 299–301. 'Sister, I was never slow in my worship of Venus although I show disdain.'

In all the haist wee may,
To sing Venus ane sang.

Danger:
Sister, sing this sang I may not
Without the help of gude Fund-Jonet.
Fund-Jonet, hoaw! Cum, tak a part!
Fund-Jonet:
That sall I do with all my hart
Sister, howbeit that I am hais.° *hoarse*
I am content to beir a bais![50]
Ye twa sould luif me as your lyfe;
Ye knaw I lernit yow baith to swyfe° *copulate*
In my chalmer°—ye wait weill quhair! *bedroom*
Sensyne,° the feind ane man ye spair. *Since then*
Hamelines:
Fund-Jonet, fy, ye ar to blame!
To speik foull wordis, think ye not schame?
Fund-Jonet:
Thair is ane hundreth heir sitand by
That luifis geaping° als weill as I— *copulating*
Micht thay get it in privitie!° *secret*
Bot quha begins the sang, let se.

[*Fund-Jonet looks at the music. King Humanitie gets up.*]

King Humanitie:
Up, Wantonnes, thow sleipis to lang!
Me thocht I hard ane mirrie sang.
I the command in haist to gang
Se quhat yon mirth may meine.
Wantonnes:
I trow, sir, be the Trinitie
Yon same is Sensualitie.
Gif it be scho, sune sall I sie
That soverance[51] sereine.

[Heir sall Wantonnes ga spy thame and cum agane to the king.]

King Humanitie:
Quhat war thay yon, to me declair.
Wantonnes:
Dame Sensuall, baith gude and fair.

Placebo:
Sir, scho is mekill to avance,° *greatly to be praised*
For scho can baith play and dance,

50. 'I am happy to carry the base!' or, equally, 'I am happy to bear the weight of a base!'
51. C's reading combines the double sense of 'empire' and 'queenship'. The latter is continued at l. 418. This reading has been preferred to B's (simpler) 'soverane'.

That perfyt patron of pleasance—
Ane perle of pulchritude.° *beauty*
Soft as the silk is hir quhite lyre,° *complexion*
Hir hair is like the goldin wyre:
My hart burnis in ane flame of fyre,
I sweir yow, be the Rude! *holy cross*

I think scho is sa wonder fair
That in earth scho hes na compair.° *equal*
War ye° weill leirnit at luifis lair° *Were you; lore*
And syne had hir anis° sene, *(but) once*
I wait, be cokis passioun,[52]
Ye wald mak supplicatioun
And spend on hir ane millioun,
Hir lufe for till obteine.

Solace:
Quhat say ye, sir? Are ye content
That scho cum heir incontinent?° *at once*
Quhat vails° your kingdome and your rent *what use are*
And all your great treasure,
Without° ye haif ane mirrie lyfe *Unless*
And cast asyde all sturt° and stryfe? *trouble*
And, sa lang as ye want° ane wyfe, *lack*
Fall to, and tak your pleasure!

King Humanitie:
Gif that be trew, quhilk ye me tell,
I will not langer tarie,
Bot will gang preif that play my sell,° *try out that game myself*
Howbeit the world me warie.° *curse/blame*

Als fast as ye may carie,
Speid with all diligence!
Bring Sensualitie
Fra-hand° to my presence. *At once*

Forsuth, I wait not° how it stands,° *know not; is come about*
Bot, sen I hard of your tythands,° *tidings*
My bodie trimblis, feit and hands,
And quhiles° is hait as fyre. *sometimes*
I trow Cupido with his dart
Hes woundit me out throw° the hart; *throughout*
My spreit will° fra my bodie part° *wants to; separate*
Get I nocht my desyre.

Pas on away with diligence° *assiduity*
And bring hir heir to my presence,

52. 'Cok' is a colloquial means of referring to God. Here, the passion of the second person (Christ) is alluded to irreverently.

Spair nocht for travell nor expence—
I cair not for na cost!
Pas on your way schone,° Wantonnes, *soon*
And tak with yow Sandie Solace,
And bring that ladie to this place
Or els I am bot lost.

[*King Humanitie hands a ruby ring to Wantonnes.*]

Commend me to that sweitest thing
And present hir with this same ring,
And say I ly in languishing
Except scho mak remeid.° *offers a cure*
With siching° sair, I am bot schent,° *sighing; quite undone*
Without° scho cum incontinent *Unless*
My heavie langour to relent,° *relieve*
And saif me now fra deid.° *death*

Wantonnes:
Or ye tuik skaith,° be Gods goun, *Before you came to harm*
I lever° thair war not, up nor doun[53] *(had) rather*
Ane tume° cunt into this toun *vacant*
Nor twentie myle about!
Doubt ye nocht sir, bot wee will get hir!
Wee sall be feirie° for till fetch hir; *keen*
But, faith, wee wald speid all the better
Till gar our pursses rout.° *To have our purses jingle*
Solace:
Sir, let na sorrow in yow sink,
Bot gif us ducats for till drink,
And wee sall never sleip ane wink
Till it be—back or eadge.[54]
Ye ken weill, sir, wee have no cunye.° *ready money*
King Humanitie: [*Handing over purse.*]
Solace, sure that sall be no sunyie;° *hindrance*
Beir ye that bag upon your lunyie.° *loin*
Now, sirs, win° weill your wage— *earn*

I pray yow speid yow sone againe.[55]
Wantonnes:
Ye, of this sang,° sir, wee ar faine. *bargain*
Wee sal nether spair for° wind nor raine *desist for*
Till our days wark be done.

53. 'Up nor doun,' a common formula for 'everywhere' has, here, sexual connotations.
54. 'Until it is achieved—no matter the means.' Lit: '...whether the back or the edge of the sword be employed.' The image (drawn from swordplay) continues the erotic undercurrents of the dialogue.
55. Lindsay follows the pattern of early English Morality Dramas (e.g. *Mankind*) by making his Vices move from lighthearted concentration on sins of the flesh (lechery, sloth, gluttony) to a more peremptory tone and the sins of world (covetousness) and devil (pride, envy, wrath).

Fairweill, for wee are at the flicht!° *i.e. on our way*
Placebo, rewll° our roy at richt.° *govern; correctly*
We sall be heir, man, or° midnicht, *before*
  Thocht wee marche with the mone.

[Heir sall thay depairt, singand mirrelly][56]

[Song

'Was nevir in Scotland haird° nor sene *heard*
Sic dansing nor deray,° *disorderliness*
Nowthir at Falkland° on the grene *Falkland (Fife; site of castle)*
Nor Peblis° at the play *Peebles (near Edinburgh)*
As wes of wowaris,° as I wene,° *suitors; maintain*
At Chryst kirk on ane day.
Thair come out kitteis° weschin° clene *wenches; washed*
In thair new kirtillis° of gray, full gay, *frocks*
  At Chrystis kirk of the grene,
  That day.]

Wantonnes:
Pastyme° with pleasance° and greit prosperitie *Diversion; delight*
Be to yow, Soveraine° Sensualitie. *Sovereign/Ruler*

Dame Sensualitie:
Sirs, ye ar welcum. Quhair go ye, eist or west?

Wantonnes:
In faith, I trow we be at the farrest.

Dame Sensualitie:
Quhat is your name, I pray you, sir, declair.

Wantonnes:
Marie, Wantonnes, the kings secretair.° *secretary*

Dame Sensualitie:
Quhat king is that quhilk hes sa gay a boy?

Wantonnes:
Humanitie, that richt redoutit roy,° *well-renowned monarch*
Quha dois commend him to yow hartfullie° *earnestly/(with all his heart)*
And sends yow heir ane ring with ane rubie.
In takin° that, abuife all creatour, *token*
He hes chosen yow to be his paramour:
He bade me say that he will be bot deid
Without that° ye mak haistelie remeid. *Unless*

Dame Sensualitie:
How can I help him althocht he suld forfair?° *perish*
Ye ken richt weill, I am na medcinair.° *doctor*

Solace:
Yes, lustie ladie, thocht he war never sa seik,
I wait ye beare his health into your breik:° *slit*

56. ED. No song appears in either text. We have inserted the opening stanza of 'Christis Kirk on the Grene', a popular song of the day, as preserved in the Bannatyne MS (cf. § 24) This insertion has not been included in the lineation.

Ane kis of your sweit mow° in ane morning — *mouth*
Till his seiknes micht be greit comforting!
And als, he maks yow supplicatioun,
This nicht to mak with him collatioun.° — *feast with him*

Dame Sensualitie:
I thank his Grace of his benevolence.
Gude sirs, I sall be reddie evin fra hand;° — *right away*
In me thair sall be fund na negligence,
Baith nicht and day, quhen his Grace will demand.
Pas ye befoir and say I am cummand
And thinks° richt lang to haif of him ane sicht; — *intend*
And I to Venus do mak ane faithfull band° — *swear a true oath*
That, in his arms, I think to ly all nicht.

Wantonnes:
That sal be done. Bot yit, or I hame pas,° — *before I go home*
Heir I protest° for Hamelynes, your las. — *put in a claim*

Dame Sensualitie:
Scho salbe at command, sir, quhen ye will.
I traist scho sall find yow flinging your fill.° — *jigging your fill*

Wantonnes: [*Dancing energetically.*]
Now, hay, for joy and mirth, I dance!
Tak thair ane gay gamond of France.[57]
Am I nocht worthie till avance,° — *to be praised*
  That am sa gude a page,
And that sa spedelie can rin
To tyst° my maister unto sin? — *entice*
The feind° a penny he will win° — *devil; gain*
  Of this, his mariage.° — *alliance/union*

I rew° richt sair, be Sanct Michell,[58] — *regret*
Nor I had pearst hir° my awin sell — *I did not penetrate her*
For quhy,° yon king, be Bryds bell,[59] — *Because*
  Kennis na mair of ane cunt
Nor dois the noveis of ane freir.° — *a friar's novice*
It war bot almis° to pull my eir: — *a good deed (ironic)*
That wald not preif yon gallant geir![60]
  (Fy, that I am sa blunt!)

I think this day to win greit thank°— — *gratitude*
Hay, as ane brydlit° cat, I brank.° — *like a bridled cat; cavort*

57. The mixture of modes is nicely illustrated in this section. A formal song is followed by a call to dance. The 'gambade' was a lively French dance, already known in Scotland.
58. St Michael, archangel, chief of the heavenly army and patron of knights, seems an ironic choice for Wantonnes' oath. The Saint is later invoked by Falset (l. 870).
59. St Bride (Bridget) was often depicted with a cow, to represent the belief that she began life as a milk-maid. The associated sense of the bell summoning a 'bride' to church follows from l. 458.
60. ll. 464–5: Extended wordplay. 'It would have been a small act of charity to tug my lug [handle]: that would not put that gallant equipment to the test!'

[*Suddenly stops dancing in pain.*]
Alace, I have wreistit my schank!° *twisted my leg*
[*Begins again.*]
Yit I gang,° be Sanct Michaell! *I'm going again*
[*Coming closer to the audience.*]
Quhilk of my leggis sirs, as ye trow
Was it that I did hurt evin now?
Bot quhairto sould I speir at yow?° *enquire of you*
I think thay baith° ar haill. *both*

[*Stops dancing and approaches King Humanitie.*]

Gude morrow, maister, be the mes! *mass*
King Humanitie:
Welcum, my minyeon Wantonnes.

How hes thow sped° in thy travell?° *succeeded; task*
Wantonnes:
Rycht weill, be him that herryit hell!° *who harried hell (i.e. Christ)*
Your erand° is weill done.[61] *errand/erring*
King Humanitie:
Then, Wantonnes, how weill is mee!
Thow hes deservit baith meit and fie,° *wealth*
Be him that maid the mone.° *moon*
Thair is ane thing that I wald speir:
Quhat sall I do quhen scho cums heir?
For I knaw nocht the craft perqueir° *by heart*
Of luifers gyn;° *stratagem*
Thairfoir, at lenth, ye mon me leir
How to begin.

Wantonnes:
To kis hir and clap° hir, sir, be not affeard *caress*
Scho will not schrink, thocht ye kis her, ane span within the baird;
Gif ye think that she thinks shame, then hyd the bairns eine
With hir taill, and tent hir weill[62]—Ye wait quhat I meine?
Will ye leif° me, sir, first for to go to° *permit; have a go*
And I sall leirne yow all kewis° how to do.° *cues; behave*
King Humanitie:
God forbid, Wantonnes, that I gif the leife:
Thou art over perillous ane page sic practicks° to preife.° *customs; to test*
Wantonnes:
Now, sir, preife as ye pleis, I se hir cumand.° *approaching*
Use your self gravelie; wee sall by yow stand.

61. The blasphemous reference to Christ's victory over Satan (l. 478) brings the vicious counsellors' own errand to completion, by wittily discounting the sins of the Devil as (earlier) those of the Flesh and the World.
62. ll. 490–2 Extended wordplay. 'Though you kiss (embrace) her, she will not shrink to any extent within the beard (bush); if you think that she thinks shame, then hide the infant's eyes [male genitals?] with her bottom, and see well to her.'

[*Dame Sensualitie crosses to them.*]

Dame Sensualitie:

O Queen Venus, unto thy celsitude° *majesty*
I gif gloir, honour, laud and reverence,
Quha grantit me sic perfite pulchritude
That princes of my persone have pleasance;
I mak ane vow, with humill observance° *rite*
Rycht reverentlie thy tempill to visie,° *visit*
With sacrifice unto thy deitie.[63]

Till everie stait° I am so greabill° *estate; agreeable*
That few or nane refuses me at all:
Paipis,° patriarks, or prelats venerabill, *Popes*
Common pepill and princes temporall
Ar subject all to me, Dame Sensuall.
Sa sall it be, ay quhill° the warld indures, *as long as*
And speciallie quhair youthage hes the cures.[64]

Quha knawis the contrair?
I traist few in this companie—
Wald thay declair the veritie,
How thay use Sensualitie—
Bot with me maks repair!° *dwells with/resorts to*

And now my way I man avance
Unto ane prince of great puissance,° *power*
Quhom young men hes in governance,
  Rolland into his rage.° *madness*
I am richt glaid I yow assure
That potent prince to get in cure,° *gain control over*
Quhilk is of lustines the luir° *lure*
  And greitest of curage.° *manly courage/desire*

[Heir sall scho mak reverence and say]

O potent prince of pulchritude preclair,° *fairest handsomeness*
God Cupido preserve your celsitude,
And Dame Venus mot keip your court from cair
As I wald sho suld keip my awin hart blud.

King Humanitie:

Welcum to me, peirles in pulchritude:° *nonpareil in beauty*
Welcum to me, thow sweiter nor the lamber,° *amber*
Quhilk hes maid me of all dolour denude.
Solace, convoy this ladie to my chamber.

[Heir sall scho pass to the chalmer and say:][65]

63. ED. deitie] B; diocese C.
64. I.e. 'And especially where high-spirited youth has charge.'
65. King Humanitie and Dame Sensualitie lie together in his open pavilion until l. 1695—a constant visual reminder of how far the youthful king has fallen since voicing his pious intentions (ll. 78–101).

Dame Sensualitie:

I gang this gait with richt gude will.
Sir Wantonnes, tarie° ye stil, *remain*
And Hamelines, the cap° yeis fill *cup*
  And beir him cumpanie.

Hamelines:

That sall I do withoutin dout,
And he and I sall play *cap out*[66]

Wantonnes:

Now ladie, len me that batye tout;[67]
  Fill in for I am dry!

Your dame,° be this,° trewlie *mistress; by now*
Hes gotten upon the gumis!° *Has got it on the lips*
Quhat rak thocht ye and I
Go junne our justing lumis?° *Join our jousting tools (sexual)*

Hamelines:

Content I am with richt gude will,
Quhen ever ye ar reddie,
All your pleasure to fulfill.

Wantonnes:

Now, weill said, be our Ladie!° *Sensualitie/(Mary)*

Ile bair my maister cumpanie
Till that I may indure°— *As long as I can last*
Gif he be quisland wantounlie,
We sall fling on the flure![68]

[Heir sall thay pass all to the chalmer and Gude Counsale sall *descend from his throne and* say]

Gude Counsall:

Immortall God, maist of magnificence,
Quhais majestie na clark° can comprehend, *scholar*
Must save yow all, that givis sic audience,
And grant yow grace Him never till offend,
Quhilk on the Croce did willinglie ascend
And sched His pretious blude on everie side;
Quhais pitious passioun from danger yow defend
And be your gratious governour and gyde.[69]

Now my gude freinds, considder, I yow beseik,° *beseech*
The caus maist principall of my cumming:

66. This appears to have been a drinking game (cf. *Freiris of Berwik*, l. 1303).

67. This obscure phrase puzzles editors. Suggestions range from drinking cup (Hamer) to lusty drink (Lyall). Possibly it is a suggestive phrase, referring both to the vessel being passed round in the drinking game—'cap out'—and to the physical vessel of Hameliness, which Wantonnes thirstily awaits.

68. ll. 552–3 'Once he (the king) is whistling wantonlie' (i.e. making love), 'then we' (he and Hamelines) 'will dance on the floor' (make love themselves).

69. Gude Counsall, echoing the language and themes of Diligence's opening speech, provides the necessary moral corrective to the teaching of the evil counsellors.

Princis or potestatis° ar nocht worth ane leik,° *rulers; leek*
Be thay not gydit be my gude governing.[70]
Thair was never empriour, conquerour nor king
Without my wisdome that micht thair wil avance—
My name is Gude Counsall, without feinyeing.° *feigning*
Lords, for lack of my lair° ar brocht to mischance.° *lore; misfortune/misery*

Finallie, for conclusioun,
Quha halds me at delusioun° *scorn*
Sall be brocht to confusioun,
  And this I understand;
For I have maid my residence
With hie princes of greit puissance° *power*
In Ingland, Italie and France,
  And monie uther land.

Bot out of Scotland, (wa! alace!)
I haif bene fleimit° lang tyme space, *expelled*
That garris our gyders° all want grace *guides/monarchs*
  And die befoir thair day:[71]
Because thay lychtlyit° gude counsall *treated with contempt*
Fortune turnit on thame hir saill,
Quhilk brocht this realme to meikill baill,° *suffering*
  Quha can the contrair say?

My lords, I came nocht heir to lie:
Wais me° for King Humanitie, *Woe is me*
Ouerset with Sensualitie
  In th'entrie of his ring° *At the start of his reign*
Throw vicious counsell insolent;
Sa thay may get riches or rent
To his weilfair thay tak na tent,° *pay no heed*
  Nor quhat sal be th'ending.

Yit, in this realme I wald mak sum repair,° *resort/residence*
Gif I beleifit my name suld nocht forfair;° *perish*
For, wald this king be gydit yit with ressoun,
And on misdoars mak punitioun,
Howbeit I haif lang tyme bene exyllit
I traist in God my name sall yit be styllit.° *honoured*
Sa, till I se God send mair of His grace,
I purpois til repois me in this place.[72]

70. Both medieval chronicles and early renaissance histories emphasized the power of counsellors to guide or misguide a monarch.
71. *Ane Satyre* belongs to a period of constant warfare and poverty. Scotland's kings from James I to James V had died violently and/or early. As Lindsay allegorically confirms, flatterers and bad counsellors ruled the land.
72. A new set of Vices arrive to provide dramatic variety, to oppose Gude Counsall and to mark the second period of the king's testing.

[Heir entiris Flattery new landit owt of France and stormested at the May.][73]

Flatterie:

Mak roume, sirs (hoaw!) that I may rin.
Lo, se quhair I am new cum in,
Begaryit° all with sindrie hewis.° *Trimmed; various colours*
Let be your din till I begin,
And I sall schaw yow of my newis:

Throuchout all Christindome I have past,
And am cum heir now at the last,
Tostit° on sea, ay sen° Yuill day, *tossed; continually since*
That wee war faine to hew° our mast *glad to hack down*
Nocht half ane myle beyond the May!

Bot now amang yow I wil remaine;
I purpois never to sail againe,
To put my lyfe in chance of watter.
Was never sene sic wind and raine,
Nor of schipmen sic clitter clatter.

Sum bade 'Haill!' and sum bade 'Standby!'
'On steirburd, hoaw! Aluiff,° fy, fy!' *Tack windward*
Quhill all the raipis beguith to rattil.° *ropes began to rattle*
Was never roy sa fleyd° as I *scared*
Quhen all the sails playd brittill-brattill.

To se the waws,° it was ane wonder, *waves*
And wind that raif° the sails in sunder! *tore*
Bot I lay braikand like ane brok° *farting like a badger*
And shot sa fast, ° above and under, *discharged so strongly*
The devill durst not cum neir my dok!° *rump/poop (of ship)*

Now am I scapit fra that effray,
Quhat say ye, sirs? Am I nocht gay?
Se ye not Flatterie, your awin fuill,
That yeid to mak° this new array?° *went to create; new outfit*
Was I not heir with yow at Yuill?[74]

Yes, by my faith, I think on weill!
Quhair ar my fallows?—that wald I feill:°[75] *I'd like to know*
We suld have cum heir for ane cast.° *game of dice*
Hoaw, Falset, hoaw!

Falset:

Wa! Serve the devill!°[76] *i.e. the devil take you*
Quha is that, that cryis for me sa fast?° *shouts so forcibly for me*

73. The Isle of May, in the Firth of Forth, provided a safe haven for boats.
74. In the open theatre of morality drama, the Vices often directed their wit at members of the audience, making them part of the temptation process.
75. ED. fallowis, that wald I feill] B; fallows, that wald nocht fail C.
76. ED. Wa serve the divill] B; Wa sair the devill C.

Flatterie:
Quhy, Falset—brother, knawis thou not me?
Am I nocht thy brother, Flattrie?
Falset:
Now, welcome, be the Trinitie!
This meitting cums for gude.
Now, let me bresse the° in my armis: *embrace you*
'Quhen freinds meits, harts warmis,'
Quod Jok, that frelie fud.°[77] *good fellow*

How happinit yow into this place?
Flatterie:
Now, be my saul, evin on a cace,° *by chance*
I come in sleipand at the port,
Or ever I wist, amang this sort.
Quhair is Dissait, that limmer loun?° *rascally trickster*
Falset:
I left him drinkand in the toun;
He will be heir incontinent.° *directly*
Flatterie:
Now, be the haly Sacrament,
Thay tydingis comforts all my hart.
I wait Dissait will tak my part—
He is richt craftie, as ye ken,
And counsallour to the merchand-men.[78]
Let us ly doun heir baith and spy
Gif wee persave him cummand by.

[*Enter Dissait*]

Dissait:
Stand by the gait, that I may steir!° *navigate my way*
Aisay! Koks bons, how cam I heir?
I can not mis to tak sum feir° *Take fright/get company*
Into sa greit ane thrang.
Marie, heir ane cumlie congregatioun!° *fine assembly*
Quhat are ye, sirs, all of ane natioun?
Maisters, I speik be protestatioun,
In dreid ye tak me wrang.

Ken ye not, sirs, quhat is my name?
Gude faith, I dar not schaw° it for schame: *reveal*
Sen I was clekit of° my dame° *snatched up from; mother*
Yit was I never leill,° *upright/law-abiding*
For Katie Unsell[79] was my mother

77. ll. 642–3. The staccato style and use of simple proverbs (l. 642) clearly sign the Low Style, associated with bawdry, scurrility and viciousness.
78. The Vices associate themselves with individual estates.
79. In this tradition of personification allegory (cf. *Piers Plowman*; Tudor Interludes), individualised characters (Katie Unsell)—sometimes named after local celebrities—mingle with types (Flatterie).

And Common Theif my foster brother.
Of sic freindschip I had ane fither,° *plenty*

Howbeit I can not steill;
Bot yit I will borrow and len.
Als, be my cleathing, ye may ken
That I am cum of nobill men,[80]
And als I will debait° *dispute*
That querrell with my feit and hands—
And I dwell amang the merchands.
My name, gif onie man demands,

Thay call me Dissait.
Bon-jour, brother, with all my hart![81]
Heir am I cum to tak your part° *support you*
Baith into gude and evill.
I met Gude Counsall be the way,
Quha pat° me in a felloun fray,° *put; fearful state*
I gif him to the Devill!

Falset:
How chaipit ye°, I pray yow tell? *did you escape*
Dissait:
I slipit in ane fowll bordell° *brothel*
And hid me in ane bawburds° bed. *whore's*
Bot suddenlie hir schankis° I sched° *legs; parted*
With hoch hurland° amang hir howis;° *hip-thrusting; hollows/stockings*
God wait, gif wee maid monie mowis!° *if we made good sport*
How came *ye* heir, I pray yow tell me?
Falset:
Marie, to seik King Humanitie.
Dissait:
Now, be the gude ladie that me bair,
That samin hors is my awin mair![82]
Now, with our purpois let us mell:° *deal*
Quhat is your counsall? I pray yow tell.
Sen we thrie seiks yon nobill king,
Let us devyse sum subtill thing;
And als, I pray yow as my brother,
That we, ilk ane, be trew to uther.
I make ane vow with all my hart
In gude and evill to tak your part:
I pray to God nor I be hangit,
But I sall die or° ye be wrangit!° *before; harmed*
Falset:
Quhat is thy counsall that wee do?

80. An emphasis on clothing (appearance) was a sign of levity and vice.
81. Dissait's pride in claiming nobility is confirmed by pretentious language.
82. I.e. 'We share a common purpose!' Lit. 'That very same horse is my own mare!'

Dissait:
Marie, sirs, this is my counsall, lo:
Till tak our tyme° quhill wee may get it, *opportunity*
For now thair is na man to let° it. *prevent*
Fra tyme the king begin to steir him,° *bestir himself*
Marie, Gude Counsall, I dreid cum neir him!
And be wee knawin with° Correctioun, *If we are recognised by*
It will be our confusioun.° *downfall*
Thairfoir, my deir brother, devyse
To find sum toy° of the new gyse.° *cap; fashion*
Flatterie:
Marie, I sall finde ane thousand wyles.
Wee man turne our claithis and change our stiles
And disagyse us that na man ken us;
(Hes na man clarkis cleathing to len us?)[83]
And let us keip grave countenance,
As wee war new cum out of France.
Dissait:
Now, be my saull, that is weill devysit!
Ye sall se me sone disagysit.
Falset:
And sa sall I, man, be the Rude.° *holy cross*
Now, sum gude fallow len me ane hude.

[Heir sall Flattry help his twa marrowis.°] *comrades*

Dissait:
Now am I buskit°, and quha can spy, *disguised*
The devill stik me, gif this be I?
If this be I or not, I can not weill say—
Or hes the feind or farie-folk borne me away?
Falset:
And gif my hair war up in ane how,° *cap*
The feind ane man wald ken me, I trow.
What sayis thou of my gay garmoun°? *suit of clothes*
Dissait:
I say thou luikis evin like ane loun!° *just like a rogue*
Now, brother Flatterie, quhat do ye?
Quhat kynde of man schaip ye to be?
Flatterie:
Now, be my faith, my brother deir,
I will gang counterfit the freir.
Dissait:
A freir! Quhairto? Ye can not preiche!
Flatterie:
Quhat rak,° man? I can richt weill fleich.° *What of it; cajole*
Perchance, Ile cum to that honour
To be the kings confessour.

83. The donning of physical disguises marks the growing duplicity of the Vices.

Pure freirs are free at any feast
And marchellit ay° amang the best. *always seated*
Als God hes lent to them sic graces,
That bischops put them in thair places
Out-throw thair dioceis to preiche;
Bot, ferlie° nocht howbeit thay fleich, *marvel*
For, schaw thay° all the veritie, *(if) they reveal*
Thaill want° the bischops charitie. *lack*
And, thocht the corne war never sa skant,° *scarce*
The gudewyfis will not let freirs want° *go without*
For quhy, thay ar thair confessours,
Thair heavinlie, prudent counsalours.
Thairfoir, the wyfis plainlie taks thair parts
And schawis the secreits of thair harts
To freirs (with better will, I trow)
Nor thay do to thair bed-fallow.

Dissait:
And I reft anis° ane freirs coull° *snatched once; cowl*
Betwix Sanct-Johnestoun and Kinnoull:[84]
I sall gang fetch it, gif ye will tarie.

Flatterie:
Now, play me that of companarie![85]
Ye saw him nocht this hundreth yeir,
That better can counterfeit the freir.

Dissait:
Heir is thy gaining, all and sum—
This is ane koull of Tullilum.

Flatterie:
Quha hes ane porteus° for to len me? *portable breviary*
The feind ane saull, I trow, will ken me.

Falset:
Now, gang thy way, quhair ever thow will—
Thow may be fallow to° Freir Gill![86] *(fit) companion for*
But, with Correctioun, gif wee be kend,
I dreid wee mak ane schamefull end.

Flatterie:
For that mater I dreid nathing.
Freiris ar exemptit fra the king,
And freiris will reddie entrie get
Quhen lords ar haldin at the yet.° *gate*

Falset:
Wee man do mair yit, be Sanct James,
For wee mon all thrie change our names.[87]
Hayif° me and I sall baptize thee. *Christen*

84. In Charteris, particular references are often more immediately relevant to the Cupar performance. The Carmelite house at Tullilum, near Perth (Sanct-Johnestoun) is closer to Fife than Edinburgh.
85. 'Now do that (thing) for me out of fellowship!'
86. Possibly a proverbial figure.
87. Disguised names follow disguised bodies in a parody of the sacrament of baptism. The worldly and devilish nature of the Vices becomes overt.

Dissait:
Be God and thair-about may it be.
How will thou call me? I pray the, tell!
Falset:
I wait not how to call mysell!
Dissait:
Bot yit anis name the bairns name.
Falset:
Discretioun! Discretioun, in Gods name.
Dissait:
I neid nocht now to cair for thrift:
Bot quhat salbe my Godbairne gift? *Godchild('s)*
Falset:
I gif yow all the devilis of hell.
Dissait:
Na, brother, hauld that to thy sel!
Now sit doun; let me baptize the—
I wad not quhat thy name sould be.
Falset:
Bot yit anis, name the bairns name!
Dissait:
Sapience,° in ane warlds—schame. *Wisdom*
Flatterie:
Brother Dissait, cum baptize me.[88]
Dissait:
Then, sit doun lawlie on thy kne.
Flatterie:
Now, brother, name the bairns name.
Dissait:
Devotioun, in the devillis name!
Flatterie:
The devill resave the, lurdoun loun!
Thow hes wet all my new schavin croun.° *newly shaved crown*
Dissait:
Devotioun, Sapience and Discretioun:[89]
Wee thre may rewll this regioun.
Wee sall find monie craftie things
For to begyll ane hundreth kingis;
For thow can richt weil crak and clatter° *gossip and chatter*
And I sall feinye and thow sall flatter.
Flatterie:
Bot I wald have, or wee depairtit,
Ane drink to mak us better hartit.

[Now the king sall cum fra his chamber.]

88. ll. 794–99 mock ceremonies and sacraments.
89. An unholy Trinity emerges—Deceit becomes Discretion; Falsehood pretends to be Wisdom and Flattery passes himself off as Devotion.

Dissait:
Weill said, be Him that herryit hell!
I was evin thinkand that my sell.
Now, till wee get the kings presence,
Wee will sit doun and keip silence.
I se ane yonder: quhat evir he be[90]
Ile wod° my lyfe, yon same is he. — *wager*
Feir nocht, brother, bot hauld yow still
Till wee have hard° quhat is his will. — *heard*

King Humanitie:
Now, quhair is Placebo and Solace?
Quhair is my minyeoun, Wantonnes?
Wantonnes, hoaw, cum to me sone.
Wantonnes:
Quhy cryit ye,° sir, till I had done? — *did you call out (for me)*
King Humanitie:
Quhat was ye doand? Tell me that.
Wantonnes:
Mary, leirand° how my father me gat.° — *learning; begot me*
I wait nocht how it stands, but doubt;° — *assuredly*
Me think the warld rinnis round about!
King Humanitie:
And sa think I, man, be my thrift:° — *as I thrive*
I se fyfteine mones in the lift.° — *sky*
Wantonnes:
Lat,° Hamelines my lass, allane![91] — *Let be*
Sho bendit up° ay twa for ane! — *drew (ready to shoot)*
Hamelines:
Gat ye nocht that quhilk ye desyrit?
Sir, I belief that ye ar tyrit!
Danger:
Bot, as for Placebo and Solace,
I held them baith in mirrines,
Howbeid I maid it sumthing tewch,° — *tough/drawn out*
I fand thame chalmer-glew annewch.° — *sufficient love-making*
Solace:
Mary, thow wald gar ane hundreth tyre!
Thow hes ane cunt lyk ane quaw-myre!° — *quagmire*
Danger:
Now fowll fall yow—it is na bourdis,° — *no jesting matter*
Befoir ane king to speik fowll wourdis.
Or evir ye cum that gait agane,
To kiss my cloff,° ye salbe fane!° — *cleft; well-pleased*

Solace:
Now, schaw me, sir, I yow exhort,

90. ED. I se ane yonder: quhat evir he be] B; I see ane yeoman: quhat ever be C.
91. ED. We follow Lyall in introducing Bannatyne ll. 826–7; 832–9. These lines were probably excluded from Charteris because of their indecency.

How ar ye of your luif content?
Think ye not this is ane mirrie sport?

King Humanitie:
Yea, that I do in verament.° *in truth*
Quhat bairnis° ar yon upon the bent?° *people; field*
I did nocht se them all this day.

Wantonnes:
Thay will be heir incontinent.
Stand still and heir quhat thay will say.

[Now the vycis cums and maks salutatioun, saying.]

Dissait:
Laud, honor, gloir, triumph and victory
Be to your maist excellent majestie!

King Humanitie:
Ye ar welcum, gude freinds, be the Rude!
Appeirandlie, ye seime sum men of gude;
Quhat ar your names? Tell me without delay.[92]

Dissait:
Discretioun, sir, is my name perfay.

King Humanitie:
Quhat is your name, sir, with the clipit croun?

Flatterie:
But dout, my name is callit Devotioun.

King Humanitie:
Welcum, Devotioun, be Sanct Jame:
Now sirray, tell! Quhat is your name?

Falset:
Marie,sir, thay call me...Quhat call thay me?
I wat not weill, but gif° I lie.[93] *unless*

King Humanitie:
Can ye nocht tell quhat is your name?

Falset:
I kend it quhen I cam fra hame.

King Humanitie:
Quhat gars ye can nocht° schaw it now? *makes you unable to*

Falset:
Marie, thay call me thin drink, I trow?[94]

King Humanitie:
Thin drink! Quhat kynde of name is that?

Dissait:
Sapiens! [*Aside*] Thou servis° to beir ane plat!° *deserve; receive a blow*
Me think thou schawis the not weill wittit.

Falset:
Sypeins, sir! Sypeins! Marie, now ye hit it!

92. The king's ready acceptance of appearance as truth reminds the audience of his fallen state.
93. ED. B. C omits this line, whose existence can be deduced from the rhyme scheme.
94. Falset's linguistic confusion of wisdom (Sapiens) with sypeins (the sediment of drink) at once confirms his insecurity within his new role and betrays his worldly obsessions.

Flatterie:
Sir, gif ye pleis to let me say:
His name is SAPIENTIA.
Falset:
That same is it be Sanct Michell.
King Humanitie:
Quhy could thou not tell it thy sell?° *yourself*
Falset:
I pray your grace appardoun me
And I sall schaw° the veritie. *reveal*
I am sa full of Sapience
That sumtyme I will tak ane trance.
My spreit was reft° fra my bodie, *seized*
Now heich abone the Trinitie.[95]
King Humanitie:
Sapience suld be ane man of gude.
Falset:
Sir, ye may ken that be my hude.
King Humanitie:
Now have I Sapience and Discretioun,
How can I faill to rewll this regioun?
And Devotioun to be my confessour![96]
Thir thrie came in ane happie hour.
Heir I mak the my secretar
And thow salbe my thesaurar,° *treasurer*
And thow salbe my counsallour
In sprituall things and confessour.

Flatterie:
I sweir to yow, sir, be Sanct An,
Ye met never with ane wyser man
For monie a craft, sir, do I can,
War thay weill knawin.
Sir, I have na feill° of flattrie *knowledge/understanding*
But fosterit° with philosophie— *nurtured*
Ane strange° man in astronomie, *extraordinary*
Quhilk salbe schawin.

Falset:
And I have greit intelligence
In quelling° of the quintessence.[97] *extracting*
Bot to preif my experience,
Sir, len me fourtie crownes
To mak multiplicatioun;

95. Falsehood/Wisdom now claims to have had a revealed vision. These were granted only to the most saintly of individuals. The associated idea of Ascension anticipates St Anne (l. 888).
96. The line of sacramental parody continues with the offering of false confession.
97. Distillation of the 'quintessence', or fifth element after air, fire, water and earth, was a main objective of the practice of alchemy.

And tak my obligatioun,° *pledge*
Gif wee mak fals narratioun,
  Hauld us for verie lownes.° *rogues indeed*

Dissait:
Sir, I ken be your physnomie,
Ye sall conqueis,° or els I lie, *conquer*
Danskin,° Denmark and Almane,° *Danzig; Germany*
Spittelfield and the realme of Spane.
Ye sall have at your governance
Ranfrow and all the realme of France;
Yea, Rugland° and the toun of Rome, *Rutherglen*
Castorphine° and al Christindome![98] *Corstorphine*
Quhairto, sir, be the Trinitie,
Ye ar ane verie *A-per-sie*.° *Paragon*

Flatterie:
Sir, quhen I dwelt in Italie,
I leirit the craft of palmistrie.
Schaw me the lufe,° sir, of your hand *palm*
And I sall gar yow understand
Gif your Grace be infortunat,
Or gif ye be predestinat.° *fortunate*
I se ye will have fyfteine queenes
And fyfteine scoir of concubeines.
The Virgin Mary saife your Grace!
Saw ever man sa quhyte ane face,
Sa greit ane arme, sa fair ane hand?
Thairs nocht sic ane leg in al this land!
War ye in armis,° I think na wonder *engaged in war*
Howbeit ye dang doune° fyfteine hunder. *felled*

Dissait:
Now, be my saull, thats trew thow sayis;
Was never man set sa weill his clais.° *clothes*
Thair is na man in Christintie
Sa meit° to be ane king as ye. *fit*

Flatterie:
Sir, thank the haly Trinitie,
That send us to your cumpanie;
For God, nor I gaip in ane gallows[99]
Gif ever ye fand thrie better fallows.[100]

King Humanitie:
Ye ar richt welcum be the Rude;
Ye seime to be thrie men of gude.

98. Boastful speeches, mingling continents with villages, derive from the Miracle Cycle tradition. They were spoken by evil tyrants (e.g. Herod) or by the Nuntius, preparing the audience for their entry.
99. 'May I gape on the gallows, by God…'
100. In Act 2, Flatterie alone will escape the gallows. He does so to demonstrate the continued power of evil generally. More specifically, as the special Vice of the Clergy, his survival represents their resistance to the king's reforms.

[Heir sall Gude Counsell schaw himself in the feild.]

Bot quha is yon that stands sa still?
Ga spy and speir quhat is his will;
And gif he yearnis my presence,° *seeks audience with me*
Bring him to mee with diligence.

Dissait:
That sall wee do, be Gods breid;
We's bring him eather quick° or deid. *alive*

King Humanitie:
I will sit still heir and repois.
Speid yow agane to me my Jois!

Falset:
Ye, hardlie,°[101] sir, keip yow in clois° *rigorously; inside*
And quyet till wee cum againe.
Brother, I trow be coks toes,
Yon bairdit bogill° cums fra ane traine!° *goblin; trick*

Dissait:
Gif he dois sa, he salbe slaine.
I doubt° him nocht nor yit ane uther: *fear*
Trowit I° that he come for ane traine, *If I believed*
Of my freindis I sould rais ane futher.° *call up a throng*

Flatterie:
I doubt full sair, be God Him sell,
That yon auld churle be Gude Counsell.
Get he anis to the kings presence,
We thrie will get na audience.

Dissait:
That matter I sall tak on hand
And say it is the kings command
That he anone devoyd° this place, *quit*
And cum nocht neir the kings grace,
And that under the paine of tressoun.

Flatterie:
Brother, I hauld your counsell ressoun;
Now, let us heir quhat he will say.
Auld lyart° beard—gude day! gude day! *grizzled*

Gude Counsall:
Gude day againe, sirs, be the Rude!
The Lord mot° mak yow men of gude! *May the Lord*

Dissait:
Pray nocht for us to lord nor ladie,
For we are men of gude alreadie.
Sir, schaw to us quhat is your name.

Gude Counsall:
Gude Counsall, thay call me at hame.

101. ED. C has 'hadlie'.

Falset:

Quhat says thow carle? Ar thow Gude Counsall?
Swyith, pak the sone, unhappie unsell![102]

Gude Counsall:

I pray yow, sirs, gif me licence
To cum anis to the kings presence,
To speik bot twa words to his Grace.

Flatterie:

Swyith, hursone carle,° devoyd this place! — *whoreson villain*

Gude Counsall:

Brother, I ken yow weill aneuch,
Howbeit ye mak it never sa teuch:
Flattrie, Dissait and Fals Report,
That will not suffer to resort
Gude Counsall to the kings presence.

Dissait:

Swyith, hursun carle, gang, pak the hence!
Gif ever thou cum this gait° agane, — *way*
I vow to God, thou sall be slane.

[Heir sall thay hurle away Gude Counsall.]

Gude Counsall

Sen, at this tyme, I can get na presence,
Is na remeid bot tak in patience.
Howbeit Gude Counsall haistelie be nocht hard° — *listened (to)*
With° young princes, yit sould thay nocht be skard;° — *By; scared*
Bot, quhen youthheid hes blawin his wanton blast,[103]
Then sall Gude Counsall rewll him at the last.[104]

[Now the Vycis gangs to ane counsall.]

Flatterie:

Now, quhill Gude Counsall is absent,
Brother, wee mon be diligent
And mak betwix us sikker bands,° — *secure pledges*
Quhen vacands fallis° in onie lands, — *vacant offices occur*
That everie man help weill his fallow.

Dissait:

I had, deir brother, be Alhallow,
Sa ye fische nocht within our bounds.[105]

Flatterie:

That sall I nocht, be Gods wounds,
Bot I sall plainlie tak your partis.

102. 'Be off with you at once, you wretched, wicked person!'
103. I.e. 'But, once youth has given vent to high-spirited behaviour.'
104. As Gude Counsall is defined in terms of practical ethics, he may advocate that a prince sow his wild oats before he assumes power, if that will make him a more capable ruler. Neither Dame Veritie nor Divyne Correctioun, as representatives of Morality and Divinity, could so advise.
105. ll. 997–8. 'I had rather, dear brother, by all that's holy, that you did not poach within my limits.'

Falset:

Sa sall we thyne with all our hartis!
Bot haist us! Quhill the king is young,
Let everie man keip weill ane toung° *guard his tongue*
And in ilk quarter have ane spy,
Us till adverteis° haistelly, *warn*
Quhen ony casualities[106]
Sall happin into our countries;
And let us mak provisioun
Or he cum to discretioun.
Na mair he waits° now nor° ane sant, *knows; than*
Quhat thing it is to haif or want.
Or he cum till his perfyte age° *his maturity*
We sall be sikker of our wage,
And then let everie carle craif uther.° *importune elsewhere*

Dissait:

That mouth speik mair, my awin deir brother!
For God, nor I rax° in ane raip,° *stretch; rope*
Thow may gif counsalll to the Paip.

[Now thay returne to the king.]

King Humanitie:

Quhat gart you bid sa lang fra my presence?
I think it lang since ye depairtit thence.
Quhat man was yon with an greit bostous beird?
Me thocht he maid yow all thrie very feard.

Dissait:

It was ane laidlie, lurdan loun° *repulsive lazy fellow*
Cumde to break buithis° into this toun; *break into shops*
Wee have gart bind him with ane poill° *staff*
And send him to the theifis hoill.° *dungeon/pit*

King Humanitie:

Let him sit thair with ane mischance° *in misery*
And let us go to our pastance.° *pleasure*

Wantonnes:

Better go revell at° the rackat,° *make merry; racquet game*
Or ellis go to the hurlie hackat,° *tobogganing*
Or then—to schaw our curtlie corsses°— *elegant bodies*
Ga se quha best can rin thair horsses.

Solace:

Na. Soveraine, or wee farther gang,
Gar Sensualitie sing ane sang!

[Heir sall the ladies sing ane sang. The king sall ly doun amang the ladies and then Veritie sall enter.][107]

106. 'casualties' were incidental items of revenue, particularly payments from tenants or vassals.
107. ED. The second song-stanza opens Dunbar's poem, 'Of the Solistaris at court'. See n. 56.

[**Song**
Thir ladeis fair, that maks repair
And in the courte ar kend
Thre dayis thair, thai will do mair
Ane mater for to end,
Than thair gudmen will do in ten
For ony craift thai can—
So weill thai ken quhat tyme and quhen
Thair meynis thai sowld mak than.]

Dame Veritie:
Diligite Justitiam qui judicatis terram.[108]

Luif justice, ye quha hes ane judges cure
In earth; and dreid the awfull judgement
Of Him that sall cum judge baith rich and pure,
Rycht terribilly with bludy woundis rent.
That dreidfull day into your harts imprent,
Belevand weill how and quhat maner ye
Use justice heir til uthers. Thair, at lenth,
That day, but doubt, sa sall ye judgit be.[109]

Wo, than, and duill° be to yow princes all, *grief*
Sufferand the pure anes for till be opprest;
In everlasting burnand fyre ye sall
With Lucifer, richt dulfullie° be drest.° *sorely; treated*
Thairfoir, in tyme, for till eschaip that nest,° *infamous resort*
Feir God, do law and justice equally
Till everie man. Se that na puir opprest
Up to the hevin on yow ane vengeance cry.

Be just judges, without favour or fead,° *enmity*
And hauld the ballance evin till everie wicht;° *being*
Let not the fault be left into the head—
Then sall the members reulit be at richt.
For quhy? Subjects do follow day and nicht
Thair governours in vertew and in vyce:
Ye ar the lamps that sould schaw them the licht—
Lo, leid them on this sliddrie° rone of yce.° *slippery; sheet of ice*

Mobile mutatur semper cum principe vulgus;[110]

And gif ye wald your subjectis war weill gevin,° *maintained*
Then verteouslie begin the dance your sell,[111]

108. 'You who are judges of the earth, dedicate yourselves to justice.'
109. The merciful administration of justice is a key topic in Christian literature. Theologically, this is because the movement from Old Testament to New is viewed as a movement from justice to mercy.
110. 'The fickle crowd always changes with the prince.'
111. The First Act of the Satyre enacts the fall and correction of King Humanity as, at once, the ruler of the human soul ('reason') and the ruler of a country. Social reforms are impossible so long as the 'leader of the dance' is a creature of chaos and disharmony.

Going befoir; then they anone, I wein,° *believe*
Sall follow yow, eyther till hevin or hell.
Kings sould of gude exempils be the well;
Bot gif that your strands° be intoxicate,° *channels; toxic*
In steid of wyne thay drink the poyson fell:° *harsh*
Thus pepill follows ay thair principate.[112]

Sic luceat lux vestra coram hominibus ut videant opera vestra bona.[113]

And specially ye princes of the preists,
That of peopill hes spirituall cuir,° *care/charge*
Dayly ye sould revolve into your breistis
How that thir haly words ar still maist sure:
In verteous lyfe, gif that ye do indure,
The pepill wil tak mair tent to your deids
Then to your words, and als baith rich and puir
Will follow yow baith in your warks and words.

[Heir sal Flatterie spy Veritie with ane dum countenance.]

Veritie:
Gif men of me wald have intelligence
Or knaw my name—thay call me VERITIE.
Of Christis law I have experience[114]
And hes ouersaillit many stormy sey.
Now am I seikand King Humanitie,
For of his grace I have gude esperance.
Fra tyme that he acquaintit be with mee,
His honour and heich gloir I sall avance.

[Heir sall Veritie pas to hir sait.]

Dissait:
Gude day, father, quhair have ye bene?
Declair til us of your novels.°[115] *news*
Flatterie:
Thair is now lichtit° on the grene *arrived*
Dame Veritie, be buiks and bels![116]

Bot cum scho to the kings presence,
Thair is na buit° for us to byde: *use/advantage*
Thairfoir, I red° us all go hence. *advise*

112. The image of the well feeding into the rivers of personality or state has associations with the well-springs of Christian grace and mercy. This king is, however, a poisoned well.
113. Matthew 5. 16: 'Let your light so shine before men, that they may see your good works, and glorify your Father which is in heaven.'
114. Dame Veritie represents Truth as taught in the Scriptures. The 'estates' focus of the play does not contradict the medieval hierarchy of Christian values; it is simply the chosen satirical aim within that system.
115. Interest in the latest news (cf. l. 606) was another traditional characteristic of the Vices.
116. Swearing by the books and bells of the Mass was sacrilegious.

Falset:

That will we nocht yit, be Sanct Bride;

But wee sall ather gang or ryde
To Lords of Spritualitie,
And gar them trow yon bag of pryde
Hes spokin manifest heresie.

[Heir thay cum to the Spritualitie.]

Flatterie:

O reverent fatheris of the Sprituall Stait,
Wee counsall yow be wyse and vigilant;
Dame Veritie hes lychtit now of lait,
And in hir hand beirand the New Testament. [117]
Be scho ressavit, but doubt wee ar bot schent!° *undone*
Let hir nocht ludge, thairfoir, into this land;
And this wee reid yow do incontinent—
Now—quhill the king is with his luif sleipand.[118]

Spiritualitie:

Wee thank yow, freinds, of your benevolence;
It sall be done evin as ye have devysit.
Wee think ye serve° ane gudlie recompence *deserve*
Defendand us, that wee be nocht supprysit.° *suppressed*
In this mater wee man be weill advysit,
Now, quhill the king misknawis the Veritie;[119]
Be scho ressavit, then wee will be deprysit.° *despised*
Quhat is your counsell, brother, now let se?

Abbot:

I hauld it best, that wee incontinent
Gar hauld hir fast into captivitie,
Unto the thrid° day of the parlament, *third*
And then accuse hir of hir herisie
Or than° banische hir out of this cuntrie; *Rather than*
For with the king gif Veritie be knawin,
Of our greit gloir wee will degradit be° *ignominiously deprived*
And all our secreits to the commouns schawin.[120]

Persone:

Ye se the king is yit effeminate° *weak*
And gydit be Dame Sensualitie,
Rycht sa with young counsall intoxicate.

117. The text Veritie carries is in English, not Latin.
118. The tension between appearance and reality continues; the clergy use Ballat Royal and the High Style to express evil intentions.
119. Play on 'misknawis'. Verity has not yet gained access to the king; the king is still ignorant of Truth.
120. As reforms beckon, the situation of the Fourth Estate is introduced by a senior cleric, who wishes to keep knowledge and power away from ordinary people.

Swa, at this tyme ye haif your libertie—
To tak your tyme I hauld it best for me,
And go distroy all thir Lutherians,[121]
In speciall, yon Ladie Veritie.

Spiritualitie:

Schir Persone, ye sall be my commissair
To put this mater till executioun;
And ye, Sir Freir, because ye can declair
The haill processe, pas with him in commissioun.° *shared assignment*
Pas all togidder with my braid bennisoun,° *full blessing*
And, gif scho speiks against our libertie,
Then put hir in perpetuall presoun,
That scho cum nocht to King Humanitie.

[Heir sall thay pass to Verity.]

Persone:

Lustie Ladie, we wald faine understand
Quhat earand ye haif in this regioun:
To preich or teich, quha gaif to yow command?
To counsall kingis, how gat ye commissioun?
I dreid, without ye get ane remissioun,[122]
And syne renunce your new opiniones,
The Sprituall Stait sall put yow to perditioun,
And in the fyre will burne yow, flesche and bones.[123]

Veritie:

I will recant nathing that I have schawin.
I have said nathing bot the veritie.
Bot, with° the king fra tyme that I be knawin,° *by; am recognised*
I dreid ye spaiks° of Sprituallitie *shafts*
Sall rew that ever I came in this cuntrie;
For, gif the veritie plainlie war proclamit,
And speciallie to the kings majestie,
For your traditions ye wilbe all defamit.

Flatterie:

Quhat buik is that, harlot, into thy hand?
Out, walloway, this is the New Testament
In Englisch toung, and printit in England!
Herisie, herisie! Fire, fire, incontinent!

Veritie:

Forsuith, my freind, ye have ane wrang judgement,
For in this Buik thair is na heresie,

121. The strongly Calvinist nature of Reformation in Scotland began with Knox in the mid 1550s. Prior to that, Lutheranism was strong. Specifically, they are concerned about the English translation of the New Testament, which Veritie carries.

122. 'I fear that, unless you obtain a release from punishment'. Such releases could be illegally acquired.

123. Only in a world of chaos could Veritie be burned as a witch.

Bot our Christs word, baith dulce° and redolent— *harmonious*
Ane springing well of sinceir veritie.[124]

Dissait:
Cum on your way, for all your yealow locks!
Your wantoun words, but doubt,° ye sall repent. *assuredly*
This nicht, ye sall forfair° ane pair of stocks *endure*
And syne,° the morne, be brocht to thoill° judgment. *then; suffer*

Veritie:
For our Christs saik, I am richt weill content
To suffer all thing that sall pleis His grace;
Howbeit ye put ane thousand to torment,
Ten hundreth thowsand sall rise into thair place.

[Veritie sits doun on hir knies and sayis:]

Get up—Thow sleipis all too lang, O Lord![125]—
And mak sum ressonabill reformatioun° *just redress*
On them that dois tramp doun Thy gracious word,
And hes ane deidlie indignatioun
At them quha maks maist trew narratioun.
Suffer me not, Lord, mair to be molest!
Gude Lord, I mak The supplicatioun,
With Thy unfreinds° let me nocht be suppress.° *enemies; overcome*
Now, Lords, do as ye list:
I have na mair to say.

Flatterie:
Sit doun, and tak yow rest
All nicht till it be day!

[Thay put Veritie in the stocks and returne to Spiritualitie.]

Dissait:
My Lord, wee have with diligence
Bucklit up weill yon bledrand baird.[126]

Spiritualitie:
I think ye serve gude recompence;
Tak thir ten crowns for your rewaird.

Veritie:
The prophesie of the propheit Esay° *Isaiah*
Is practickit, alace, on mee this day,
Quha said the veritie sould be trampit doun
Amid the streit, and put in strang presoun:
His fyve and fiftie chapter, quha list° luik, *wishes*

124. The virtuous characters do not object to the Bible being printed in English rather than Scots.
125. The fact that King Humanitie is still lying with Sensualitie on the playing area adds dramatic irony to this pious exclamation. See also Psalm 44. 23–26.
126. 'Firmly secured that babbling, vagabond minstrel.'

Sall find thir words writtin in his buik.[127]
Richt sa, Sanct Paull wrytis to Timothie
That men sall turne thair earis from veritie.[128]
Bot in my Lord God I have esperance;
He will provide for my deliverance.
Bot ye princes of Spritualitie,
Quha sould defend the sinceir veritie,
I dreid the plagues of Johnes Revelatioun[129]
Sal fal upon your generatioun.
I counsall yow this misse t'amend,° *atone for this sin*
Sa that ye may eschaip that fatall end.

[Heir sall entir Chaistetie and say:]

Chastitie:
How lang sall this inconstant warld indure,
That I sould baneist be sa lang, alace?
Few creatures or nane takis on me cure,° *take heed of me*
Quhilk gars me monie nicht ly harbrieles.° *without shelter*
Thocht I have past all yeir fra place to place,
Amang the Temporal and Spirituall staits
Nor amang princes,I can get na grace,
But boustouslie° am haldin° at the yetis.° *roughly; kept; gates*

Diligence:
Ladie, I pray yow, schaw me your name;
It dois me noy,° your lamentatioun. *pains me*
Chastitie:
My freind, thairof I neid not to think shame !
Dame Chastitie—baneist from town to town.
Diligence:
Then pas to ladies of religioun,
Quha maks thair vow to observe chastitie.
Lo, quhair thair sits ane priores of renown
Amangs the rest of Spritualitie.

Chastitie:
I grant yon ladie hes vowit chastitie,
For hir professioun thairto sould accord:
Scho maid that vow for ane abesie,° *abbey*
Bot nocht for Christ Jesus our Lord.
Fra tyme that they get thair vows, I stand for'd,
Thay banische hir out of thair cumpanie:

127. The reference would seem, in fact, to be to Isaiah 59. 14—'...for truth is fallen in the streets and equity cannot enter'.
128. 2 Timothy 4. 4.
129. In order to persuade the audience to repent, powerful visions of the fate awaiting impenitents at the Day of Judgment were introduced by Miracle and Morality dramatists. Revelation 22.18 promises plagues for those who seek to alter or amend divine truth.

With Chastitie thay can mak na concord
Bot leids thair lyfis in sensualitie.

I sall observe your counsall, gif I may;
Cum on and heir quhat yon ladie will say.

[Chastitie passis to the Ladie Priores and sayis:]

My prudent, lustie Ladie Priores,
Remember how ye did vow chastitie?
Madame, I pray yow of your gentilnes,
That ye wald pleis to haif of me pitie,
And this ane nicht to gif me harberie;[130]
For this I mak yow supplicatioun.
Do ye nocht sa, Madame, I dreid, perdie,° *by God (par Dieu)*
It will be caus of depravatioun.[131]

Priores:
Pas hynd Madame! Be Christ, ye cum nocht heir!
Ye ar contrair to my complexioun;° *constitution*
Gang seik ludging at sum auld monk or freir—
Perchance thay will be your protectioun.
Or to prelats mak your progressioun,
Quhilks ar obleist to yow als weill as I.
Dame Sensuall hes gevin directioun
Yow till exclude out of my cumpany.

Chastitie: [*addressing the audience*]
Gif ye wald wit° mair of the veritie, *know*
I sall schaw yow, be sure experience,
How that the Lords of Sprituality
Hes baneist me, alace, fra thair presence.

[Chastitie passes to the Lords of Spritualitie.]

My Lords, laud,° gloir, triumph and reverence *praise*
Mot be unto your halie, Sprituall Stait!
I yow beseik of your benevolence
To harbry mee, that am sa desolait,

Lords, I have past throw mony uncouth schyre,° *a strange district*
Bot in this land, I can get na ludgeing!
Of my name, gif ye wald haif knawledging,
Forsuith, my Lords, thay call me Chastitie.
I yow beseik of your graces bening,° *benign*
Gif me ludging this nicht for charitie.

130. The test of offering shelter is ontologically contextualised by Christ. In refusing it, the Prioress (l. 1236), Spiritualitie (l. 1256) and Temporalitie (ll. 1280–2) damn themselves by failing to offer the deeds of temporal mercy (Matthew 25. 33–46).
131. 'depravation' is the action of depriving a person of his office or dignity.

Spiritualitie:

Pas on, Madame, we knaw yow nocht;
Or, be Him that the warld hes wrocht,
Your cumming sall be richt deir coft° — *bought*
Gif ye mak langer tarie.

Abbot:

But doubt, wee will baith leif and die
With our luif, Sensualitie.
Wee will haif na mair deall with the
Then with the Queene of Farie.

Persone:

Pas hame amang the nunnis and dwell,
Quhilks are of chastitie the well;
I traist thay will, with buik and bell,
Ressave yow in thair closter.

Chastitie:

Sir, quhen I was the nunnis amang,
Out of thair dortour° thay mee dang°— — *dormitory; drove*
And wald nocht let me bide sa lang
To say my *Pater noster*.

I se na grace thairfoir to get;
I hauld it best, or it be lait,
For till go prove° the Temporall Stait, — *try out/test*
Gif thay will mee resaif.
Gud-day, my Lord Temporalitie,
And yow, merchant of gravitie,
Ful faine wald I have harberie
To ludge amang the laif.° — *rest*

Temporalitie:

Forsuith, wee wald be weil content
To harbrie yow with gude intent,
War nocht we haif impediment.
Forquhy? We twa ar maryit.
Bot wist our wyfis that ye war heir,
Thay wald mak all this town on steir.° — *in a commotion*
Thairfoir, we reid° yow rin areir° — *advise; retreat*
In dreid ye be miscaryit.° — *harmed*

Chastitie:

Ye men of craft, of greit ingyne,° — *skill*
Gif me harbrie, for Christis pyne,
And win° Gods bennesone° and myne, — *gain; blesing*
And help my hungrie hart!

Sowtar:

Welcum, be Him that maid the mone,
Till dwell with us till it be June.

Wee sall mend baith your hois° and schone,° *hose/stockings; shoes*
And plainlie tak your part.[132]

Taylour:
Is this fair Ladie Chastitie?
Now welcum, be the Trinitie!
I think it war ane great pitie
That thou sould ly thairout.
Your great displeasour° I forthink:° *affront; regret*
Sit doun, Madame, and tak ane drink
And let na sorrow in yow sink,
Bot let us play '*Cap out!*'

Sowtar:
Fill in and drink about,
For I am wonder dry!
The devill snyp aff thair snout° *cut off their nose*
That haits this cumpany!

Jennie:
Hoaw, Mynnie! Mynnie! Mynnie!° *Mummy*
Taylours Wyfe:
Quhat wald thow, my deir dochter Jennie?
Jennie, my joy, quhair is thy dadie?
Jennie:
Mary, drinkand with ane lustie ladie;
Ane fair, young mayden, cled in quhyte,
Of quhom my dadie taks delyte.
Scho hes the fairest forme of face,
Furnischit with all kynd of grace;
I traist, gif I can reckon richt,
Scho schaips° to ludge with him all nicht. *plans*
Sowtars Wyfe:
Quhat dois the Sowtar, my gudman?
Jennie:
Mary, fillis the cap and turnes the can.
Or he cum hame, be God, I trow
He will be drunkin lyke ane sow.
Taylours Wyfe:
This is ane greit dispyte,° I think, *outrage*
For to resave sic ane kow-clink.° *whore*
Quhat is your counsell that wee do?[133]
Sowtars Wyfe:
Cummer, this is my counsall, lo:
Ding° ye the tane and I the uther. *Lay on/go for*

132. Only the Fourth Estate, a cobbler and a tailor, follow Christ's commandment in the true spirit of mercy.
133. The wives of cobbler and tailor echo the recalcitrant, worldly reaction of Mrs Noah in the Miracle Cycles.

Taylours Wyfe:

I am content, be Gods mother!
I think, for mee, thay huirsone smaiks,° *worthless fellows*
Thay serve richt weill to get thair paiks.° *get a thrashing*
Quhat maister feind neids all this haist?[134]
For it is half ane yeir almaist
Sen ever that loun laborde my ledder!° *made a sexual move to me*

Sowtars Wyfe:

God, nor my trewker mence ane tedder![135]
For it is mair nor fourtie dayis
Sen ever he cleikit up my clayis,° *hoisted up my clothes*
And last° quhen I gat chalmer-glew,° *the last time; had intercourse*
That foull Sowtar began till spew.
And now thay will sit doun and drink
In cumpany with ane kow-clink!
Gif thay haif done us this dispyte,
Let us go ding° them till thay dryte!° *beat; defecate*

[Heir the wifis sall chase away Chastitie.]

Taylours Wyfe:

Go hence, harlot! How durst thow be sa bauld,
To ludge with our gudemen but our licence?
I mak ane vow to Him that Judas sauld,
This rock° of myne sall be thy recompence. *rod*
Schaw me thy name, dudron,° with diligence.° *slut; readiness*

Chastitie:

Marie, Chastitie is my name, be Sanct Blais.[136]

Taylors Wyfe:

I pray God nor He work on the vengence,[137]
For I luifit never chastitie all my dayes!

Sowtars Wyfe:

Bot my gudeman (the treuth I sall the tell!)
Gars me keip chastitie, sair agains my will;
Becaus that monstour hes maid sic ane mint,
With my bedstaf that dastard beirs ane dint.[138]
And als I vow—cum thow this gait° againe— *way*
Thy buttoks salbe beltit,° be Sanct Blaine![139] *thrashed with a belt*

[Heir sall thay speik to thair gudeman and ding them.]

134. I.e. 'What the devil is all the rush about?'
135. 'By God, may my cheating man grace a gallows rope!'
136. St Blais, a fourth century Armenian Bishop, was renowned as a healer.
137. 'I pray to God that He may wreak vengeance on you.'
138. ll. 1352–3: 'Because that monster has made such a move, that craven fellow will undergo an assault with my bedstaff.' (A bedstaff was the pole used to smooth otherwise inaccessible areas of bed linen in recessed beds.)
139. Scottish saint, traditionally supposed to have been buried at Dunblane.

Taylours Wyfe:
Fals hursoun carle, but dout° thou sall forthink° *assuredly; be sorry*
That evar thow eat or drink with yon kow-clink!
Sowtars Wyfe:
I mak ane vow to Sanct Crispine,[140]
Ise be revengit on that graceles grume,° *fellow*
And to begin the play—tak thair ane platt!° *buffet*
Sowtar:
The feind ressave° the hands that gaif mee that! *devil take*
Sowtars Wyfe:
Quhat now, huirsun, begins thow for til ban?° *to curse*
Tak thair ane uther upon thy peild harne-pan!° *bald skull*
Quhat now, cummer,° will thow nocht tak my part? *friend*
Taylours Wyfe:
That sall I do, cummer, with all my hart!

[Heir sall thay ding thair gudemen with silence.]

Taylour:
Alace, gossop, alace! How stands with yow?
Yon cankart°carling,° alace, hes brokin my brow. *bad-tempered; hag*
Now weils yow,° preists, now weils yow all your lifes, *thrive*
That ar nocht weddit with sic wickit wyfes.
Sowtar:
Bischops ar blist, howbeit that thay be waryit,° *cursed*
For thay may fuck thair fil and be unmaryit.
Gossop, alace, that blak band° we may wary° *wretched contract; curse*
That ordanit sic puir men as us to mary!
Quhat may be done bot tak in patience?
And on all wyfis we'll cry ane loud vengence!

[Heir sall the wyfis stand be the watter syde and say:]

Sowtar's Wyfe:
Sen, of our cairls,° we have the victorie, *husbands*
Quhat is your counsell, cummer, that be done?
Taylors Wyfe:
Send for gude wine and hald our selfis merie;
I hauld this ay best, cummer, be Sanct Clone![141]

Sowtars Wyfe:
Cummer, will ye draw aff my hois and schone?
To fill the quart, I sall rin to the toun.
Taylors Wyfe:
That sal I do, be Him that maid the mone,
With all my hart! Thairfoir, cummer, sit doun;

140. The patron saint of shoemakers.
141. Scholars scour the lists of minor saints and provide a variety of possible names. The literary popularity of Saint Cluanus or Saint Clone lies in having a saint whose name sounds like 'clown' within the inverted worlds of satire, comedy or farce. See Dunbar, 'To the Merchantis of Edinburgh', 5. 13.

Kilt up° your claithis abone your waist — *Tuck up*
And speid yow hame againe in haist,
And I sall provyde for ane paist,° — *pastry*
Our corsses° to comfort. — *bodies*

Sowtars Wyfe:
Then, help me for to kilt my clais.
Quhat gif the padoks° nip my tais?° — *toads; toes*
I dreid to droun heir, be Sanct Blais,
Without I get support.

[Sho lifts up hir claiss above hir waist and enters in the water.][142]

Cummer, I will nocht droun my-sell:
Go east about the nether mill.

Taylours Wyfe:
I am content, be Bryds bell,
To gang with yow quhair ever ye will.

[Heir sall thay depairt and pas to the palyeoun.][143]

Diligence: [*To Chastitie*]
Madame, quhat gars yow gang sa lait?
Tell me how ye have done debait
With the Temporall and Spirituall Stait?
Quha did yow maist kyndnes?

Chastitie:
In faith, I fand bot ill and war.° — *worse*
Thay gart mee stand fra thame askar°— — *apart*
Evin lyk ane begger at the bar[144]—
And fleimit° mair and lesse. — *banished*

Diligence:
I counsall yow, but tarying,
Gang tell Humanitie the King.
Perchance, hee of his grace bening,° — *benign*
Will mak to yow support.

Chastitie:
Of your counsell I am content
To pas to him incontinent,
And my service till him present
In hope of some comfort.

[Heir sall thay pas to the king.]

142. This stage direction comes from the Cupar text and refers to characters crossing the Lady burn.
143. Again the direction comes from the Cupar production. Both texts suggest a mode of performance close to that established for *The Castell of Perseverance*, with seats and pavilion providing set places for characters to remain in sight while the central action continues.
144. 'bar' could mean the bar in a court of justice, or merely any barrier, such as at a city gate.

Diligence:
Hoaw, Solace! Gentil Solace, declair unto the king
How thair is heir ane ladie, fair of face,
That in this cuntrie can get no ludging,
Bot pitifullie flemit from place to place
Without° the king, of his speciall grace, — *Unless*
As ane servand hir in his court resaif.[145]
Brother Solace, tell the king all the cace,° — *situation*
That scho may be resavit amang the laif.

Solace:
Soverane, get up and se ane hevinlie sicht—
Ane fair ladie in quhyt abuilyement;°[146] — *clothing*
Scho may be peir° unto ane king or knicht, — *equal in rank*
Most lyk ane angell, be my judgment.
King Humanitas:
I sall gang se that sicht incontinent.
Madame, behauld gif ye have knawledging
Of yon ladie, or quhat is hir intent.
Thairefter, wee sall turne but tarying.° — *return without delay*

Sensualitie:
Sir, let me se quhat yon mater may meine—
Perchance, that I may knaw hir be hir face.
Bot doubt, this is Dame Chastitie, I weine!° — *surmise*
Sir, I and scho cannot byde in ane place.
But, gif it be the pleasour of Your Grace
That I remaine into your company,
This woman richt haistelie gar chase,
That scho na mair be sene in this cuntry.

King Humanitie:
As evir ye pleais, sweit hart, sa sall it be.
Dispone hir° as ye think expedient— — *Deal with her*
Evin as ye list° to let hir live or die, — *choose*
I will refer that thing to your judgement.
Sensualitie:
I will that scho be flemit incontinent,
And never to cum againe in this cuntrie;
And gif scho dois, but doubt scho sall repent,
As als° perchance a duilfull deid sall die. — *As well as*

Pas on, Sir Sapience and Discretioun,
And banische hir out of the kings presence.
Dissait:
That sall we do, Madame, be Gods passioun!
We sall do your command with diligence,

145. The test of temporal mercy is now faced by the king.
146. Once again clothing has allegorical force. White signs the purity of virginity.

And at your hand serve° gudely recompence. *deserve*
Dame Chastitite, cum on, be not agast!
We sall rycht sone, upon your awin expence,
Into the stocks your bony° fute mak fast. *pretty*

[Heir sall thay harll° Chastitie to the stoks and scho sall say:] *drag*

Chastitie:

I pray yow, sirs, be patient,
For I sall be obedient
Till do quhat ye command,
Sen I se thair is na remeid,° *remedy*
Howbeit it war° to suffer deid *Unless it were*
Or flemit furth of the land.
I wyte° the Empreour Constantine[147] *blame*
That I am put to sic ruine
And baneist from the Kirk;
For, sen he maid the Paip ane king
In Rome, I could get na ludging
Bot heidlangs in the mirk.° *dark*
Bot Ladie Sensualitie
Sensyne hes gydit this cuntrie
And monie of the rest;
And now scho reulis all this land
And hes decryit at hir command
That I suld be supprest.

Bot all comes for the best
Til him that lovis the Lord:
Thocht I be now molest,
I traist to be restorde.

[Heir sall thay put hir in the stocks.]

Sister, alace, this is ane cairful cace,° *unhappy state of affairs*
That we with princes sould be sa abhorde.

Veritie:

Be blyth, sister! I trust within schort space
That we sall be rycht honorablie restorde,
And with the king we sall be at concorde,
For I heir tell Divyne Correctioun
Is new landit,—thankit be Christ, our Lord!
I wait hee will be our protectioun.

[Heir sall enter Corrections Varlet.]

147. As Professor Lyall notes (p. 188), Lindsay often attributes to Constantine 'responsibility for the corruption of the primitive church'—in *The Dreme*, *The Monarche* and 'The Testament of the Papyngo' as well as the *Satyre*.

Varlet:

Sirs, stand abak and hauld yow coy!° *be quiet*
I am the King Correctiouns boy,
Cum heir to dres° his place! *make ready*
Se that ye mak obedience
Untill his nobill excellence
Fra tyme° ye se his face; *From the time that*
For he maks reformatiouns
Out-throw all Christin natiouns
Quhair he finds great debaits.° *dissension*
And, sa far as I understand,
He sall reforme into this land
Evin all the Thrie Estaits.
God, furth of heavin hes him send
To punische all that dois offend
Against His Majestie;
As lyks him best, to tak vengence,
Sumtyme with sword and pestilence,
With derth° and povertie. *famine*
Bot, quhen thee peopill dois repent
And beis to God obedient,
Then will he gif them grace.
Bot thay that will nocht be correctit,
Rycht sudanlie will be dejectit° *cast down*
And fleimit from his face.
Sirs, thocht wee speik in generall,
Lat na man into speciall
Tak our words at the warst.
Quhat ever wee do, quhat ever wee say,
I pray yow tak it all in play
And judg ay to the best.[148]

For silence I protest,
Of lord, laird and leddy![149]
Now, I will rin but rest° *race off without resting*
And tell that all is ready.

Dissait:

Brother, heir ye yon proclamatioun?
I dreid full sair of reformatioun;
Yon message maks me mangit.° *distracted*
Quhat is your counsall, to me tell?
Remaine wee heir, be God Him-sell,
Wee will be all thre hangit!

Flatterie:

Ile gang to Spiritualitie
And preich out-throw° his dyosie,° *throughout; diocese*
Quhair I will be unknawin;

148. The issues being dramatized are opened out to the judgment of the spectators.
149. Of lord, laird and leddy] B; Baith of lord, laird and ladie C.

Or keep me closse into sum closter,
With mony piteous *Pater noster*,
Till all thir blasts be blawin.

Dissait:
Ile be weill treitit, as ye ken,
With my maisters, the merchand-men,
Quhilk can mak small debait.° *little contention*
Ye ken richt few of them that thryfes° *prosper*
Or can begyll the landwart° wyfes *country*
But° me, thair man, Dissait! *Without*
Now, Falset, quhat sall be thy schift?° *device*

Falset:
Na, cuir thow° nocht, man, for my thrift.° *concern yourself; success*
Trows thou that I be daft?
Na, I will leif ane lustie lyfe,
Withoutin ony sturt° and stryfe, *trouble*
Amang the men of craft.

Flatterie:
I na mair will remaine besyd yow
Bot counsell yow rycht weill to gyde yow:
Byd° nocht on Correctioun. *Wait*
Fair-weil! I will na langer tarie;
I pray the alrich° Queene of Farie *elvish/weird*
To be your protectioun.

Dissait:
Falset, I wald wee maid ane band° *alliance*
Now, quhill the king is yit sleipand:
Quhat rak to steill° his box? *What about stealing*

Falset:
Now, weill said, be the Sacrament!
I sall it steill incontinent
Thocht it had twentie lox.

[Heir sall Falset steill the kings box with silence.]

Lo, heir the box! Now, let us ga.
This may suffice for our rewairds.

Dissait:
Yea, that it may, man. Be this day,
It may weill mak us landwart lairds[150]

Now, let us cast away our clais
In dreid sum follow on the chase.

Falset:
Rycht weill devysit, be Sanct Blais,
Wald God, wee war out of this place!

[Heir sall thay cast away thair counterfeit clais.]

150. A reference to the device of boosting the economy by selling minor titles and properties.

Dissait:

Now, sen thair is na man to wrang us,
I pray yow, brother, with my hart,
Let us ga part this pelf° amang us; *loot*
Syne, haistely we sall depart.

Falset:

Trows thou to get als mekill as I?
That sall thow nocht! I staw° the box. *stole*
Thou did nathing bot luikit by,
Ay lurkeand lyke ane wylie fox.

Dissait:

Thy heid sall beir ane cuppill of knox,
Pellour, without I get my part.[151]
Swyth, huirsun smaik,° ryfe up° the lox *rogue; pull out*
Or I sall stick the° throuch the hart! *pierce you*

[Heir sall thay fecht with silence.]

Falset:

Alace for ever, my eye is out!
Walloway, will na man red° the men? *separate*

Dissait:

Upon thy craig,° tak thair ane clout! *neck*
To be courtesse I sall the ken.° *teach you*

Fair-weill, for I am at the flicht;° *on the point of flight*
I will nocht byde on na demands;
And wee twa meit againe this nicht,
Thy feit salbe worth fourtie hands.

[Heir sal Dissait rin away with the box throuch the water.]

Divyne Correctioun:

Beati qui esuriunt et sitiunt Justitiam![152]

Thir ar the words of the redoutit Roy[153]—
The Prince of Peace! above all kings, King!—
Quhilk hes me sent all cuntries to convoye° *lead/guide*
And all misdoars dourlie° to doun thring.° *severely; put down*
I will do nocht without the conveining
Ane parleament of the estaits all.
In thair presence, I sall, but feinyeing,
Iniquitie under my sword doun thrall.° *bring to subjection*

151. '(You) thief, unless I get my share.'
152. 'Blessed are those who hunger and thirst after righteousness.' Matthew 5. 6—the spiritual equivalent of 'herberye'. See Matthew 25. 33–46.
153. In defining himself as the Nuntius of God, Divyne Correctioun echoes the opening of the play (cf. ll. 15–16).

Thair may no prince do acts honorabill
Bot gif his Counsall thairto will assist;
How may he knaw the thing maist profitabil,
To follow vertew and vycis to resist,
Without he be instructit and solist?° *urged*
And quhen the king stands at his counsell sound,
Then welth sall wax° and plentie, as he list, *grow*
And policie° sall in his realme abound. *good government*

Gif ony list my name for till inquyre,
I am callit Divine Correctioun.
I fled° throch mony uncouth land and schyre, *winged my way*
To the greit profit of ilk natioun.
Now am I cum into this regioun
To teill° the ground that hes bene lang unsawin, *till/cultivate*
To punische tyrants for thair transgressioun,
And to caus leill° men live upon thair awin. *virtuous*

Na realme nor land but° my support may stand *without*
For I gar kings live into royaltie.° *conduct themselves regally*
To rich and puir I beir ane equall band,° *compact*
That thay may live into thair awin degrie.
Quhair I am nocht, is no tranquillitie.
Be me, tratours and tyrants ar put doun—
Quha thinks na schame of thair iniquitie,
Till thay be punisched be mee, Correctioun.

Quhat is ane king? Nocht bot ane officiar° *functionary*
To caus his leiges° live in equitie, *subjects*
And under God to be ane punischer
Of trespassours against His Majestie.
Bot, quhen the king dois live in tyrannie,
Breakand justice for feare or affectioun,
Then is his realme in weir° and povertie *strife*
With schamefull slauchter but correctioun.

I am ane judge, richt potent° and seveir, *powerful*
Cum to do justice mony thowsand myle.
I am sa constant baith in peice and weir,
Na bud° nor favour may my sicht oversyle.° *bribe; obscure*
Thair is, thairfoir, richt monie in this ile
Of my repair but doubt that dois repent,[154]
Bot verteous men, I traist, sall on me smyle,
And of my cumming sall be richt weill content.

Gude Counsall:
Welcum, my Lord, welcum ten thousand tyms
Till all faithfull men of this regioun!

154. ll. 1625–6. 'Doubtless there are, therefore, a goodly number within this island who will regret my taking up residence.'

Welcum for till correct all falts and cryms
Amang this cankerd° congregatioun. *affected by evil*
Louse Chastitie, I mak supplicatioun;
Put till fredome fair Ladie Veritie,
Quha (be unfaithfull folk of this natioun)
Lyis bund full fast into captivitie.

Divyne Correctioun:
I mervell, Gude Counsell, how that may be.
Ar ye nocht with the king familiar?
Gude Counsall:
That am I nocht, my Lord, full wa is me,
Bot—lyk ane begger—am halden at the bar.
Thay play bo-keik evin as I war ane skar.°[155] *scarecrow*
Thair came thrie knaves in clething counterfeit
And fra the king thay gart me stand afar,
Quhais names war Flattrie, Falset and Dissait.

Bot quhen thay knaves hard tell of your cumming,
Thay staw away—ilk ane ane sindrie gait[156]—
And cuist° fra them thair counterfit cleithing. *cast*
For thair leving, full weill thay can debait:° *contend*
The merchandmen, thay haif resavit Dissait;
As for Falset, my Lord, full weill I ken
He will be richt weill treitit, air° and lait, *early*
Amang the maist part of the crafts men;

Flattrie hes taine° the habite of ane freir, *taken/adopted*
Thinkand to begyll Spiritualitie.
Divyne Correctioun:
But dout, my freind, and I live half ane yeir,
I sall search out that great iniquitie.
Quhair lyis yon ladyes in captivitie?
How now, sisters? Quha hes yow sa disgysit?
Veritie:
Unfaithfull members of iniquitie
Dispytfullie, my Lord, hes us supprysit.

Divyne Correctioun:
Gang put yon ladyis to thair libertie
Incontinent, and break doun all the stocks!
But doubt thay ar full deir welcum to mee.
Mak diligence! Me think ye do bot mocks;
Speid hand, and spair nocht for to break the locks,
And tenderlie tak them up be the hand.
Had I them heir, thay knaves suld ken my knocks,
That them opprest and banesit aff the land!

155. An image full of powerful penitential associations. In the Miracle Cycles the pathos of the crucifixion was highlighted by showing a blindfolded Christ subjected to cruel games of this sort.
156. 'They stole away—each one taking a different route.'

[Thay tak the ladyis furth of the stocks and Veritie sall say:]

Veritie:
Wee thank you, sir, of your benignitie,
Bot I beseik your Majestie royall,
That ye wald pas to King Humanitie
And fleime° from him yon Ladie Sensuall; *expel/banish*
And enter in his service Gude Counsall,
For ye will find him verie counsalabill.
Divyne Correctioun:
Cum on, sisters, as ye haif said, I sall,
And gar him stand with yow thrie, firme and stabill.

[Correctioun passis towards the king with Veritie, Chastitie and Gude Counsell.]

Wantonnes:
Solace, knawis thou not quhat I se?
Ane knicht or ellis ane king, thinks me,
Wih wantoun wings as he wald fle.
  Brother, quhat may this meine?
I understand nocht, be this day,
Quhidder that he be freind or fay.° *foe*
Stand still and heare quhat he will say;
  Sic ane I haif nocht seine.

Solace:
Yon is ane stranger—I stand forde.° *guarantee it*
He seemes to be ane lustie lord;
Be° his heir-cumming for concorde° *If; (is) for peace*
  And be kinde till our king,
He sall be welcome to this place
And treatit with the kingis grace;
Be it nocht sa, we sall him chace
  And to the divell him ding.

Placebo:
I reid us put upon° the king *I advise we importune*
And walkin him of his sleiping.
Sir, rise and se ane uncouth° thing! *strange*
  Get up! Ye ly too lang!
Dame Sensualitie:
Put on your hude, Johne-Fule; ye raif!
How dar ye be so pert,° Sir Knaif, *forward*
To tuich the king? Sa Christ me saif,
  Fals huirsone, thow sall hang!

Divyne Correctioun:
Get up, Sir King, ye haif sleipit aneuch
Into the armis of Ladie Sensual.

Be suir that mair belangis to the pleuch[157]
As efterward, perchance, rehears° I sall. *enlarge upon*
Remember how the King Sardanapall[158]
Amang fair ladyes tuke his lust sa lang,
Sa that the maist part of his leiges al
Rebeld, and syne him duilfully doun thrang.° *overthrew*

Remember how, into the time of Noy,
For the foull stinck and sin of lechery,[159]
God, be my wande,° did al the warld destroy: *rod*
Sodome and Gomore richt sa, full rigorously,[160]
For that vyld sin war brunt maist cruelly.
Thairfoir, I the command incontinent,
Banische from the that huir Sensualitie,
Or els, but doubt, rudlie thow sall repent.

King Humanitie:
Be quhom have ye sa greit authoritie?
Quha dois presume for til correct ane king?
Knaw ye nocht me, greit King Humanitie,
That in my region royally dois ring?°[161] *reign*
Divyne Correctioun:
I have power, greit princes to doun thring,
That lives contrair the Majestie Divyne,
Against the treuth quhilk plainlie dois maling.° *inveigh against*
Repent they nocht, I put them to ruyne.

I will begin at thee, quhilk is the head[162]
And mak on the° first reformatioun;° *you; (the) first reform*
Thy leiges than will follow the but pleid.° *without argument*
Swyith,° harlot, hence without dilatioun.° *Be off with you; delay*
Sensualitie:
My Lord, I mak yow supplicatioun—
Gif me licence to pas againe to Rome; [163]
Amang the princes of that natioun,
I lat you wit,° my fresche beautie will blume. *I'll have you know*

157. 'Be assured that there is more to that matter than that'. Word play on the sexual connotations of 'ploughing', and reference to ll. 1601–2 and Divyne Correctioun's intention to put the kingdom to the plough.
158. The classical tyrants, Sardanapalus and Tarquin (l. 1769) were often used by Christian writers as examples of lustful power ending in tragedy and damnation. They are fittingly mentioned at a time when the king still allies himself with Sensualitie.
159. St Augustine made the age of Noah the second age after Adam. In it, sinfulness—especially lechery—intensified.
160. Genesis 18. 20–19. 28.
161. The king's spiritual blindness and pride combine.
162. The analogy of the head and the body is used to explain why reformation of the soul and of Scotland must begin with reason and royalty.
163. The Act ends as it began with the fiercest satire directed at the spiritual estate and the (Roman) Catholic church in particular.

Adew, Sir King, I may na langer tary!
I cair nocht that; als gude luife cums as gais.
I recommend yow to the Queene of Farie;
I se ye will be gydit with my fais.
As for this king, I cure him nocht twa strais!
War I amang bischops and cardinals,
I wald get gould, silver and precious clais.° *clothes*
Na earthlie joy but my presence avails.

[Heir sall scho pas to Spiritualitie.]

My Lords of the Sprituall Stait,
Venus preserve yow air and lait
For I can mak na mair debait;
 I am partit with your king
And am baneischt this regioun
Be counsell of Correctioun.
Be ye nocht my protectioun,
 I may seik my ludgeing.

Spiritualitie:
Welcum, our dayis darling,
Welcum with all our hart!
Wee all, but feinyeing,
Sall plainly tak your part.

[Heir sall the bischops, abbots and persons kis the ladies.]

Divyne Correctioun:
Sen ye ar quyte of Sensualitie,
Resave into your service Gude Counsall,
And richt sa this fair Ladie Chastitie,
Till ye mary sum queene of blude royall:
Observe then, chastitie matrimoniall° *marital fidelity*
Richt sa, resave Veritie be the hand;
Use thair counsell, your fame sall never fall.
With thame, tharfoir, mak ane perpetuall band.

[Heir sall the king resave Gude Counsell, Veritie and Chastitie.]

Now, sir, tak tent quhat I will say:
Observe thir same baith nicht and day
And let them never part yow fray;
 Or els, withoutin doubt,
Turne ye° to Sensualitie, *(If) you turn back*
To vicious lyfe and rebaldrie,° *riotous living*
Out of your realme, richt schamefullie,
 Ye sall be ruttit out° *roughly ejected*

As was Tarquine, the Romane king,[164]
Quha was, for his vicious living
And for the schamefull ravisching
Of the fair, chaist Lucres,
He was degraidit° of his croun *ignominiously deprived*
And baneist aff his regioun.
I maid on him correctioun,
As stories dois expres.

King Humanitie:
I am content, your counsall till inclyne,
Ye beand of so gude conditioun.° *constitution*
At your command sall be all that is myne,
And heir I gif yow full commissioun
To punische faults and gif remissioun.
To all vertew I salbe consonable° *in accord*
With yow I sall confirme ane unioun
And, at your counsall, stand ay firme and stabill.

[The king imbraces Correction with a humbil countenance.]

Divyne Correctioun:
I counsall yow, incontinent
To gar proclame ane parliament
Of all the Thrie Estaits,
That thay be heir with diligence
To mak to yow obedience
And syne dres all debaits.° *make ready all arguments*

King Humanitie:
That salbe done but mair demand.
Hoaw, Diligence! Cum heir fra hand
And tak your informatioun.° *instruction*
Gang warne Spiritualitie,
Rycht sa the Temporalitie,
Be oppin proclamatioun,
In gudlie haist for to compeir° *present themselves*
In thair maist honorabill maneir,
To gif us thair counsals.
Quha that beis absent, to them schaw
That thay sall underly° the law, *be subject to*
And punischt be that fails.

Diligence:
Sir, I sall baith in bruch° and land,° *burgh; countryside*
With diligence do your command
Upon my awin expens.
Sir, I have servit yow all this yeir
Bot I gat never ane dinneir
Yit for my recompence.

164. The legendary Roman Tarquinius was notorious for his rape of Lucretia.

King Humanitie:

Pas on and thou salbe regairdit
And for thy service weill rewairdit,
  Forquhy, with my consent,
Thou sall have yeirly for thy hyre
The teind° mussellis of the Fernie myre[165] *tithe*
  Confirmit in parliament.

Diligence:

I will get riches throw that rent
Efter the Day of Dume,° *Doomsday*
Quhen, in the colpots° of Tranent, *coalpits*
Butter will grow on the brume!° *broom (bush)*

All nicht I had sa meikill drouth° *thirst*
I micht nocht sleip ane wink;
Or° I proclame ocht° with my mouth, *Before; anything*
But doubt I man haif drink!

Divyne Correctioun:

Cum heir Placebo and Solace
With your companyeoun Wantonnes.
  I knaw weill your conditioun:
For tysting° King Humanitie *enticing*
To resave Sensualitie
  Ye man suffer punitioun.

Wantonnes:

We grant, my Lord, we have done ill,
Thairfoir, wee put us in your will—
  Bot wee haife bene abusit.
For, in gude faith, Sir, wee beleifit
That lecherie had na man greifit
  Becaus it is sa usit.

Placebo:

Ye se how Sensualitie
With principals of ilk cuntrie
  Bene glaidlie lettin in,
And with our prelatis, mair and les.
Speir at my Ladie Priores
  Gif lechery be sin.

Solace:

Sir, wee sall mend our conditioun,
Sa ye give us remissioun;
  Bot give us leif to sing,
To dance, to play at chesse and tabils,
To reid stories and mirrie fabils,
  For pleasure of our king.

165. The reference is probably to the Ferny Myre near Cupar. Because this is inland, no mussels would be found there, as Diligence's ironic reply confirms.

Divyne Correctioun:
Sa that ye do na uther cryme,
Ye sall be pardonit at this tyme
For quhy, as I suppois,
Princes may sumtyme seik solace
With mirth and lawfull mirrines,
Thair spirits to rejoyis;
And richt sa halking and hunting
Ar honest pastimes for ane king
Into the tyme of peace,
And leirne to rin ane heavie spear,
That he, into the tyme of wear,° *war*
May follow at the cheace.

King Humanitie:
Quhair is Sapience and Discretioun?
And quhy cums nocht Devotioun nar?
Veritie:
Sapience, sir, was ane verie loun
And Devotion was nyne times war.[166]
The suith,° sir, gif I wald report— *truth*
Thay did begyle your Excellence
And wald not suffer to resort
Ane of us thrie to your presence.

Chastitie:
Thay thrie war Flattrie and Dissait
And Falset, that unhappie loun,
Against us thrie quhilk maid debait
And baneischt us from town to town.
Thay gart us twa fall into sowne,° *swoon*
Quhen thay us lockit in the stocks.
That dastart knave, Discretioun,
Full thifteouslie° did steill your box. *thievingly*

King Humanitie:
The devill tak them, sen thay ar gane:
Me thocht them ay thrie verie smaiks!° *veritable rogues*
I mak ane vow to Sanct Mavane,
Quhen I them finde, thays bear thair paiks;° *undergo deserved punishment*
I se thay have playit me the glaiks.° *played the fool with me*
Gude Counsall, now schaw me the best—
Quhen I fix on yow thrie my staiks,
How I sall keip my realme in rest.

Gude Counsall:
'*Initium sapientie est timor Domini.*'[167]

166. ED. And Devotion was nyne times war.] B; And Discretioun was nathing war. C.
167. Psalm 111. 10; Proverbs 9. 10. 'The fear of the Lord is the beginning of wisdom.' Enactment of the horrific implications of evil followed by a catharsis of joy is also the penitential methodology of all of the Miracle Cycles and most Morality dramas.

Sir, gif your Hienes yearnis lang to ring,° *reign*
First dread° your God abuif all uther thing; *fear*
For ye ar bot ane mortall instrument
To that great God and King Omnipotent,
Preordinat be His divine Majestie
To reull His peopill intill unitie.
The principall point, sir, of ane kings office
Is for to do to everilk man justice,
And for to mix his justice with mercie[168]
But rigour, favour or parcialitie.
Forsuith, it is na litill observance
Great regions to have in governance.
Quha ever taks on him that kinglie cuir
To get ane of thir twa he suld be suir—
Great paine and labour—and that continuall!
Or ellis to have defame° perpetuall. *notoriety*
Quha guydis weill, they win immortall fame;° *renown*
Quha the contrair, thay get perpetuall schame,
Efter quhais death, but dout, ane thosand yeir
Thair life at lenth rehearst° sall be perqueir.° *re-iterated; thoroughly*
The Chroniklis to knaw I yow exhort:
Thair sall ye finde baith gude and evill report
For everie prince efter his qualitie;
Thocht he be deid, his deids sall never die.
Sir, gif ye please for to use my counsall,
Your fame and name sall be perpetuall.

[Heir sall the messinger Diligence returne and cry 'A Hoyzes! A Hoyzes! A Hoyzes!'° and say:] *Oyez!/Hear ye!*

Diligence:

At the command of King Humanitie
I wairne and charge all members of parliament,
Baith Sprituall Stait and Temporalite,
That till his Grace thay be obedient
And speid them to the court incontinent,
In gude ordour arrayit royally.
Quha beis absent or inobedient,
The kings displeasure thay sall underly.

And als I mak yow exhortatioun,
Sen ye haif heard the first pairt of our play,
Go tak ane drink and mak collatioun;° *take food*
Ilk man drink till his marrow,° I yow pray. *companion*
Tarie nocht lang, it is lait in the day.
Let sum drink ayle and sum drink claret wine;
Be great doctors of physick, I heare say
That michtie drink comforts the dull ingyne!

168. Dame Veritie's major theme is taken up by Gude Counsall.

And ye ladies that list to pisch,
Lift up your taill, plat in a disch
And, gif your mawkine° cryis 'Quhisch,' *lower gut*
Stop° in ane wusp of stray.° *Bung; wisp of straw*
Let nocht your bladder burst, I pray yow,
For that war evin aneuch to slay yow;
For yit thair is to cum, I say yow,
The best pairt of our play!

[Now sall the peopill mak collatioun. Then beginnis the Interlude, the kings, bischops and principall players being out of their seats.]

§ 13 Thomas Maitland (1522–?72): *The Pretended Conference*

The authorship of this tract is not established beyond doubt, but the evidence strongly suggests Thomas Maitland, brother of the more famous Richard Maitland of Lethington and of John Maitland, Lord Thirlestane. Calderwood, in his **History of the Kirk of Scotland,** *recounts the anger caused when the work was first circulated, and traces it from the hands of the Abbot of Kilwinning to the Earls of Argyll and Mar, and finally to John Knox—who is satirized within it. Knox preached on the subject and Calderwood commented, 'The author, Mr Thomas Matlane, brother to Lethington, was present and heard. When he was going out at the kirk doore, he confessed to his sister, the Lady Trabrowne, that he had forged that letter.' A short flyting by Maitland appears in § 24 and he figures as the interlocutor in George Buchanan's* **De Jure Regni Apud Scotos.**

Vernacular prose in Scotland remained predominantly in the hands of historians and religious controversialists until William Alexander contributed to Sidney's **Arcadia,** *and Urquhart composed his poetic prose fiction,* **The Jewel** *(§ 21).* **The Pretended Conference** *has been selected, in part to signal this trend, in part because its invented, dramatic nature gives it a strong claim to be truly imaginative. It is set in 1569 and therefore relates to a time when the supporters of Mary Queen of Scots were trying to discredit the Regent Moray. Maitland demonstrates literary skill in drawing comic portraits and recreating the speech-styles of those who, supposedly, are conspiring against her and the young James VI. In the extract printed below, the tones of the bluff soldier, Lord Lindsay, and the heaven-addressing, croaking religious leader, Knox, are illustrated. Of the other conspirators represented in the full text, the learned Haliburton's pedantic mode and the deviousness of Moray's secretary, Wood, maintain the wit of the satire. The ardent protestants, John Wishart of Pitarrow and James McGill, complete the cast list.*

The Pretended Conference[1]

'The copey of ane bill of adverteisment° send be ane friend out of court to ane kynisman of the Erle Argillis, the x of December 1569, disclosand the consall of sax personis.'[2]

Eftir maist hartlie comendatioune, as I promeist to adverteise° yow of the proceidingis heir in court, principallie safar as concernit my Lord your cousing,[3] sa will I yow to understand that, at this tyme, thair is no hoipe of guid wayis for him. This I knaw, as not only be dyvers raportts of courteouris, as be sa mekill as I can persave my self be my Lord Regentis[4] awin spekand°—bot also be ane discussion and counsall haldin very secretly, quhairto I trust no man in this realm is previe° bot thame that war callit warily° thairto and I, quha was coverit.°

Aboute four dayis syne,° in this towne, my Lord Regent went unto ane previe chamber,° and with him thir sax personis—my Lord Lindsay, the Laird of Petarro, Mr Jhone Woud, Jhone Knox, Mr James McGill, the Tutor of Petcur—quhilk are the men in the warlde he beleivis maist into. Quhen thay war enterit, he desyrit thame to place thame selvis, for he wald retein thame the space of thrie or four houris. It chancit, I was lyand sleypand in ane bed within the cabinet,° sa weill hyd

adverteisment: *warning*; adverteise: *inform*; awin spekand: *own utterance*; previe: *privy*; warily: *circumspectly*; coverit: *concealed*; syne: *ago*; previe chamber: *secret room*; cabinet: *private apartment*

that no man culd persave me; and, eftir I was walknit with the bruit° quhilk thay maid at thair entrie, I micht esilye heir everie word that thay spak.

Then, first, my Lord Regent sayis to thame, 'I have convenit yow at this tyme—as the men in the warlde in quhome I put greitest confidence and traist in to and quhome, I beleiv, wald fainest have my estait standand°—to gif me your faythfull advice, familiarly,° for my advancement and standing. Ye sie quhow mony lyis out frome° me; and mony that war with me at the beginning of this actione are miscontentit of my proceidingis presently, quhairfor I wald desyr yow to declair to me your opyniones, quhow I may best stand and sett furth the purpois ye wait of.' Quhen eftir he haid this spokin, he comandit my Lord Lyndsay to speik first.

Quha sayis, 'My lord, ye knaw of the ald that I was evir mair rashe nor wyse.[5] I can nocht gif yow ane verray wittie° consall; bot I luif yow weill aneughe. To be schort, quhat suld ye do bot use counsall, quhilk ye did nevir yeit.° Thairfoir, I think the devill causit men cheis yow to be ane Regent. Yet, my Lord, mycht ye be quit of thir Machivellistes[6] and thir bastard lordis, that will circumvein° you with thair policie and wrak° yow with thair force.

'I wald have ane guid hoip of all materis—and, quhen ye fall to° thame, bourd° not with thame for (be Godis breith) and° I persave that, I will pass to the Byris[7] and halk° as I did the last tyme at your being in Streveling.° Gif ye do weill, gar thame dance heidles,° and than ilk guid fallow may get ane loump of thair landis, quhilk will gar them fecht lyke swein; and uther men wilbe warier of the spang° of the taill. And gif thair be ony stout carle, set me till him, and I sall gif him ane callado° with ane stokado.° And gif he be ane het° man, I sall lat him play him ane quhyle and syne sall gif him, behynd the hand, ane coup de jarret,° and lat him ly thair. And quhen the principallis are this wayis dispeschit,° ye may do with the gogie° Lordis quhat yow list. And we haid the auld Crage in oure hands, I wald lyke materis the bettir—bot, ye knaw I will nocht speke aganis Grange.[8] Bot yeit, I think I wilbe evyn with him and gif him ane heill wage° for takin part with the Erle of Rothes aganis me.[9]

Ye will not belief quhen he pat on his bonnet, quhow gret ane lauchter was in the haill hous. And syne my Lord Regent sayis, 'Yea weill Sirs, for all his raitlyng° and raillyng, he kennes weil quhat he wald be.' And than thay sweir all with ane voce, the d(evill) speid thame, bot my Lord haid spokin weill.

Next my Lord Regent causit John Knox to speik,[10] quha luikit up to the hevin, as he haid bene begynand ane prayer before the preching—for, be ane hoill,° I mycht see and behold the continance and persave quhat thay did. And eftir he haid keipit sylence ane guid quhill, he beginnis with ane stur° and kroking voce and sayis, 'I pryss° my God gretfuly that hes hard my prayer, quhilk oftymis I pourit furth befoir the throne of His Majestie in anguiss of my sorrowful hart; and that He hes maid His evangell to be prechit with so notable succes undir so waik instrumentis, quhilk in deid culd nevir haif bene done, except your Grace haid bene constitute rewlar over this kirk, specially indewit with ane singular and ardent affectione to obey the will of God and voce of His ministeris.

walknit with the bruit: *awakened by the noise*; estait standand: *position flourishing*; familiarly: *out of friendship*; lyis out frome: *withhold allegiance from*; wittie: *wise*; yeit: *until now*; circumvein: *fraudulently get the better of*; wrak: *ruin*; fall to: *chance upon*; bourd: *jest*; and: *if*; halk: *hawk*; Streveling: *Stirling*; gar thame dance heidles: *have them beheaded*; spang: *lashing*; callado: *thrust*; stokado: *parry*; het: *hotheaded*; coup de jarret: *punch (i.e. knuckle blow)*; dispeschit: *dispatched*; gogie: *gullible*; ane heill wage: *(his) just deserts*; raitlyng: *chattering*; hoill: *hole*; stur: *harsh*; pryss: *praise*

'In respect quhairof, I, as ane of the servandis of God, imbrace your Grace's guid zeill to the promotione of Godis glorie and—as Johne Knox favoris your Grace better nor ony man apone the face of the erth—accordingly sall explane to your Grace my jugement concerning your awin standing, quhilk is sa conjunit with the establishment of the kirk. Yea, the weilfair of Godis kirke so dependis upon your Grace that, gif ye succumbe, it is not possible for it to induir ony lang tyme. Whairfoir, it semis to me maist necessar—bayth for the honour of God, confort of the puir° bretherin and utilitie of this commoun weill°—that, first your Grace's lyfe, nixt your estait, be preservit in equalitie of tyme, and nocht to prescryf° ane certane dyat° of xvi or xvii yeris lyving mair to the constitutioun of the politik lawis than the sovran operatioun of the eternall God.

'And as I never culd away yet with thir jolie wittis and politik branis,° quhilk my Lord Lindsay callis Machivellistes, sa wald I that thay war furtht of° the way, gif it war possibill. For I traist assuredly, gif first your Grace and syne the rest of the nobilitie of our societie haid passit to wark with als grete magnanimite as I utterit my jugement simply and sinceirly in my sermondis, maid purposly for that causs, that mater had bene forthir avancit nor it is (or salbe this lang tyme°) gif God grant na haistiar succes nor my sorrowfull hart prejugis. Siclyk,° thame of the nobilitie and uthiris, that wald hinder your just pretence,° thocht thay seme nocht sa in the eis of the blin° warlde, I have prechit oppinly, and yeit daly cravis of God that thai may be confondit with that wikkit woman,[11] quhome to thai cleif so obstinatlie; and that thair posteritie may drink of the cowpe preparit for the iniquitie and punisment of thair forfathers. And heir I agre with my Lord Lindsay, that spak immediatlie befoir; bot men suld, to establishe the trew religioun, have ane forther respect and consideratioun. That is, that the governement be establisht in your persone sa lang as ye leif, for quhen this barne, quhome we call king, sall cum to agge, dois ony man think that he will leif of all his royall insolence and suffer him self to be rewllit according to the simplicitie of the evangell?°

'Quhat guid hoip can we have of the child, borne of sic parentis? I will nocht speik of the suspitioun concerning the man that was killit,[12] bot thocht he be his quhois he is callit, quhat can we luik for, bot, as it war, the heretage of the fatheris lychtnes, and iniquitie of the mother. Gif Johne Knox counsall be followit, the estait of the evangell and professouris thairof sall never cum under suche ane hassarde. Bettir it is to content ourselfis with him of quhais modestie we have rycht guid experience, bayth in welth and umbre,° and not to change from that graftit and rowttit° societie, with the intemperance of ane unbrydilt childe.

'Your grace hes persavit quhow my blast of the trumpet set furth aganis the regiment of wemen,[13] is apprevit of° all the godly. I have wretin in lyk manner, and hes it redy for the prenting, ane buik, quhairin I preif by sufficient ressonis, that all kingis, princes and rewlaris, gois nocht be succession, nor that birth hes strynth to promote, nor yeit bastardy to seclude men fra government. This will walkin° utheris to pance° mair deiply upoun the mater. Besyde this we sall set furth ane act in the Generall Assemblie[14] on this mater, and bayth I and all the rest of the bretherin sall repett the same in oure daly sermondis, till it be mair nor sufficientlye persuadit to the pepill. This beand solemnally done and than the buik oppynnit

puir: *poor*; commoun weill: *common wealth*; prescryf: *prescribe*; dyat: *regime*; politik branes: *devious minds*; furtht of: *out of*; this lang tyme: *for a long time to come*; Siclyk: *In the same way*; pretence: *claim*; blin: *blind*; evangell: *gospel;* umbre: *shadow*; rowttit: *(securely) rooted*; apprevit of: *approved by*; walkin: *awaken*; pance: *think*

and laid befoir the nobilitie, quha will say the contrar thairof, except he that will nocht feir the wechtie° hand of the magistratt strikand with the sword, nor yeit to be ejectit from the flok as ane scabit scheip, be exortatioun and wyse customes of the kirk.

This sall also serv in aventure° the king depairt of this lyf, as we ar all mortall, to keip us furth of the handis of the houses of Lennox and Hamiltoun,[15] quhais imperfectionis ar to us contrarious. Then your grace, whan avancit be God, we dout nocht bot ye salbe thankfull to all just deservers. Bot quha yow most offendit, we kurse or slay, as nocht the trew membris thairof and quhairby that the servandis of God may be sufficientlie interteineit° according to their calling.' And so he held his pace.°

Then my Lord Regent said, 'Ye know that I was nevir ambitious and yeit I will not oppoise my self to the will of God reveallit be yow, quhilk are the trew ministeris. Bot Jhone, heir ye, for furtherance of it, tell your oppynioun fra the pulpit.'

wechtie: *weighty*; in aventure: *in the event that*; interteinit: *maintained*; pace: *peace*

NOTES

1. ED. COPY TEXT: MS Cotton Caligula B ix (British Library).
2. ED. 'ane bill of adverteisment'. Perhaps in imitation of a hurriedly composed warning, or of a broadsheet, the text has many contracted forms. These have been expanded.
3. 'cousin' of Archibald, 5th Earl of Argyll, a champion of the Reforming cause. (See heading.)
4. James Stewart, 1st Earl of Moray (1531–70). Earlier he had raised the rebellion against Darnley, the queen's husband. He then fled abroad, returning as Regent in 1567.
5. Wisdom was the second virtue of a leader, after courage. Lindsay, who changed sides twice during the Marian-Reformers controversy, defines himself as a failed hero.
6. Niccolò Machiavelli (1469–1527) was an Italian diplomat, poet and philosopher. His treatise on monarchy, *Il Principe* (*The Prince*), made his name a byword for political deviousness. Ironically, the conspirators reveal themselves as machiavellian in this sense.
7. 'Byris': A nearby estate. The reference satirically calls attention to the fact that Lindsay was not the most committed of reformers, having failed to appear at the recent Battle of Langside.
8. 'the auld Crage...Grange': The old crag refers to Edinburgh Castle, positioned on a rocky outcrop and at that time held on Mary's behalf by Sir William Kirkcaldy of Grange. Grange opposed any move to depose Mary and had changed sides because of this.
9. Andrew, 5th Earl of Rothes, had, like Grange, only recently joined the Marian party.
10. John Knox (?1512–72). By now, Knox had returned to Scotland from the continent and was established there as the leading Calvinist preacher.
11. 'that wikkit woman': Mary.
12. 'the man that was killit': The suspicion that Mary's lover, the Italian secretary Riccio, was James's father, was fostered by the Reformers. Riccio was murdered by the Protestant Lords in 1566.
13. Knox's 'Blast' (1558) was a vitriolic attack on the rule ('regiment') of countries by women. The central focus was English—Mary Tudor and Elizabeth I—although it extended to Mary of Guise's power in Scotland. Later, these prejudices were transferred to Mary Stewart.
14. 'the Generall Assemblie' is the governing body of the Presbyterian Church of Scotland. It originated at the Reformation and is supposed to have been convened for the first time in 1560 in order to represent the three estates of the realm.
15. The bitter rivalry between the houses of Lennox (pro-Mary) and Hamilton (pro-Reformers) was, at this time, headed on the one side by Darnley's father, Matthew Stewart, 4th Earl of Lennox, and on the other by James Hamilton, 2nd Earl of Arran.

§ 14 Robert Henryson (c.1450–c.1505): *Prologue to the Morall Fabillis*

[See also Introductions to § 4 and § 5]

The Fable was regarded as a simple form of allegory by medieval rhetoricians because little effort was asked of the listener. For those who had not understood the implicit message contained in the story, it was provided in the moral section. Henryson, however, is concerned to stress that his stories have not only demanded labour on his part, but will require us to provide a matching intellectual endeavour. The images he uses to explain this—tilling the hard earth and cracking the shell of a nut—also call attention to the double level of reference which caused the Fables to be viewed as a branch of allegory.

The Art of the Makar: *The Beast Fable is a particularly apposite vehicle for rehearsing the basic tenets of the poet-craftsman. The fact that animals do not normally conduct conversations highlights the sensitive question of whether imaginative art should be dismissed as lying. In a brief but thorough defence Henryson moves from text to author to audience. He opens his case (st. 1) by squarely facing the 'lying' charge. Imagined particulars may represent truthful concepts and so draw us to a better life (sts. 2–3). Having defended his text's integrity, Henryson turns to authorial integrity, justifying his role morally as a modest one, pedagogically as reliant on authorities, and linguistically as vernacular translation from Latin (st. 5). Henryson adopts the 'modesty topos'—an acknowledged rhetorical method of humbly but ably demonstrating possession of the poetic skills required to guide others verbally—in a particularly artful manner (st. 6). The 'final cause' of persuasion, however, was the effective moving of the audience. In coming to this, Henryson argues that, as man both shares and does not share qualities with animals, the beast-human analogy is particularly well suited to the imaginative branch of logic (sts. 7–8). The introduction to his first fable (st. 9), therefore, concludes an argument which has successfully transformed a 'lie' into the perfect vehicle of the makar's persuasive craft.*

Moral Fables: 'The Prologue'

1	
Thocht feinyeit fabils° of ald° poetre	*invented tales; from ancient*
Be not al grunded upon truth,[1] yit than,°	*yet nonetheless*
Thair polite° termes of sweit rhetore°	*refined; rhetoric*[2]
Richt plesand° ar unto the eir of man;	*pleasing*
And als° the caus quhy thay first began	*also*
Wes to repreif the°[3] of thi misleving,°	*reprove you; evil living*
O man, be figure of ane uther thing.°	*metaphorically/analogically*
2	
In lyke maner as throw a bustious eird°—	*rough earth*
Swa it be laubourit° with grit diligence—	*toiled at/tilled*

1. ED. Copy Text: Bassandyne Print. 'grunded'—'founded'. As the beast fable has animals talking, that mode is, in a particularly obvious sense, a lie and needs defending in terms of 'higher' allegorical structuring.
2. Rhetoric, with grammar and dialectic, formed the early educational curriculum.
3. The audience, lulled by promises of passive pleasure, are suddenly actively and morally involved through use of the 'you' singular form.

Springis the flouris and the corne abreird,° — *first shoots (of) corn*
Hailsum° and gude to mannis sustenence; — *Wholesome*
Sa springis thair ane morall sweit sentence° — *theme (Lat. sententia)*
Oute of the subtell dyte° of poetry, — *subtle composition methods*
To gude purpois, quha° culd it weill apply.[4] — *whoever*

3

The nuttis schell, thocht it be hard and teuch,° — *tough*
Haldis° the kirnell,° sweit and delectabill; — *Contains; kernel*
Sa lyis thair ane doctrine wyse aneuch° — *enough*
And full of frute, under ane fenyeit fabill;
And clerkis° sayis, it is richt profitabill — *wise men*
Amangis ernist to ming° ane merie sport, — *mingle*
To blyth° the spreit and gar° the tyme be schort. — *gladden; make*

4

For, as we se, ane bow that ay is bent
Worthis unsmart° and dullis° on the string; — *Grows inert; slackens*
Sa dois the mynd that is ay diligent
In ernistfull thochtis and in studying.
With sad materis° sum merines to ming° — *serious topics; mix*
Accordis° weill; this Esope said,[5] I wis,° — *Suits; I am sure*
Dulcius arrident seria picta iocis.[6]

5

Of this poete, my maisteris,° with your leif,° — *masters; permission*
Submitting me to your correctioun,
In mother toung, of Latyng,° I wald preif° — *from Latin; attempt*
To mak ane maner° of translatioun— — *form*
Nocht of my self,° for vane presumptioun, — *of my own volition*
Bot be requeist° and precept of ane lord, — *request (of)*
Of quhome the name neidis not record.[7]

6

In hamelie° language and in termes rude[8] — *homely/vernacular*
Me neidis° wryte for quhy° of eloquence° — *I must; because; (arts of) oratory*
Nor retorike I never understude.[9]

4. If the author has to labour at the skills of Rhetoric, so the audience must labour at interpreting these difficult fables.

5. Henryson credits the Greek author Aesop with authorship of the collection of tales he is retelling, yet thinks Aesop writes in Latin (5.3) and is a Roman ('Fable of Lion and Mouse', 8.2). In fact, he draws his fables from different collections within the broad Aesopic tradition. The earlier analogies of rough ground and hard shell warn readers that these will be more testing allegories than was usual for the Beast Fable form.

6. From the Aesopic source of the 'Prologue' by Gualterus Anglicus. 'More sweetly do serious matters smile at us when they are wittily/joyfully crafted.'

7. By leaving the name undefined, Henryson keeps all possibilities open. His authority may be God, a noble patron or simply an invented authority demanded by the modesty convention.

8. Henryson is referring to his lack of skill in handling rhetorical figures.

9. To deny knowledge of Rhetoric in an ornately crafted stanza like this one was known as a 'Modesty Topos'. It showed that the poet *was* a master of rhetorical skills.

Thairfoir, meiklie° I pray your reverence,°	*humbly; graciousness*
Gif ye find ocht° that throw my negligence	*anything*
Be deminute° or yit superfluous,°	*defective; unnecessary*
Correct it at your willis gratious.°	*as you graciously wish*

7

My author in his fabillis tellis how	
That brutal° beistis spak and understude,	*brutal (= non-human)*
And to gude purpois dispute° and argow,	*in order to dispute profitably*
Ane sillogisme propone° and eik° conclude;	*would propose a syllogism; also*
Putting exempill and similitude°	*Showing by example and analogy*
How mony men in operatioun°	*action*
Ar like to beistis in conditioun.°	*nature/character*

8

Na mervell° is ane man be lyke ane beist,	*marvel*
Quhilk lufis ay° carnall and foull delyte,°	*always loves; pleasure*
That° schame can not him renye nor arreist°	*So that; rein in nor stop*
Bot takis all the lust and appetyte,	
Quhilk throw custum° and the daylie ryte°	*habit; daily ritual*
Syne° in the mynd sa fast is radicate°	*Eventually; is so tightly rooted*
That he in brutal beist is transformate.°	*transformed*

9

This nobill clerk, Esope, as I haif tauld,	
In gay metir° and in facound purpurate[10]	*light metre*
Be figure° wrait° his buke, for he nocht wald	*In metaphorical mode; wrote*
Tak the disdane off° hie nor low estate; [11]	*(To) Be disdained by*
And to begin, first of ane cok he wrate,	
Seikand his meit,° quhilk fand ane jolie stone,°	*food; pretty gem*
Of quhome° the fabill ye sall heir anone.°	*(i.e. cock); hear directly*

10. Purple as the colour of royalty was used to describe the High (aureate) Style. The idea still survives in the term, 'purple prose'.
11. This will be a popular work and so will be written in Scots not Latin. The less intelligent may learn only from the fable, while others may uncover the tougher shell of the morality to extract the more difficult moral discussed in sts. 2; 3.

§ 15 Gavin Douglas (1476–1522): *Eneados*

[See also Introduction to § 9]

The Notes provide detailed comments on Douglas's critical ideas. In more general terms, his views on literature are of especial interest because he is both a Christian and a humanist, intent on accommodating the opinions of Valla (127) with the outlook of Augustine (148) rather than setting one against the other. In the extract, Douglas echoes Henryson's reliance on authority and use of the modesty topos in the **Prologue** *to the* **Morall Fabillis** *(cf.* **Prologue, Eneados I**, *76–86; 19–34, and Henryson § 14 st. 5. 5–6; st. 6). The continuity of another rhetorical idea—that poetry is a branch of imaginative oratory—is revealed when Douglas is seen to echo John Barbour's late fourteenth century claim that its vivid images should make an audience believe they are present at the events described (cf.* **Prologue, Eneados I**, *14—'as quha the mater beheld tofor thar e' and Barbour § 1. 20—'Rycht as thai than in presence war.') At the same time, his concern to advance 'the langage of Scottis natioun' through translation is only one of many recognizably humanist aims within the work.*

In choosing to translate Virgil in the first place, and in calling him 'the poet dyvyne' Douglas continues the tradition of the Christian intellectuals, who from the days of the Early Church onwards, had used incremental thought to accommodate and re-define in this way. He does not, however, return to the extreme allegorical readings of the **Aeneid** *which made the first six books prefigure the six ages of man and Aeneas represent Everyman. In trying to convey the ideas of the Latin poet across the full stylistic range, in as accurate a manner as possible, Douglas focusses more on the story of 'arms and the man' than its covert signing of the 'eternal arms divine'.*

Eneados Book 1: Prologue 1–136[1]

Lawd, honour, praysyngis, thankis infynyte	
To the and thy dulce,° ornat, fresch endyte,°	*melodious; literary composition*
Maist reverend Virgill, of Latyn poetis prynce:	
Gem of engyne° and flude° of eloquens!	*ingenuity; coursing stream*
Thow, peirles perle,° patroun of poetry,	*flawless pearl*
Roys,° regester,° palm, lawrer° and glory,	*Rose; standard-setter; laurel*
Chosyn charbukkill,° cheif flour and cedyr tre,	*carbuncle (gemstone)*
Lantarn, laid stern,° myrrour and A per se!°	*guiding star; supreme one*
Maister of masteris, sweit sours° and spryngand well[2]	*source*
Wyde, quhar (our all)° rung is thyne hevynly bell—	*above all/everywhere*
I meyn thy crafty warkis curyus,°	*elegant/subtle*
Sa quyk,° lusty and maist sentencyus,°	*lively; rich in wisdom*
Plesand, perfyte and feilabill° in all degre,°[3]	*emotive; at all levels*

1. ED. COPY TEXT: Cambridge MS. (See § 9 Douglas, *Eneados* III ix. n. 1 for full discussion of texts.)
2. ll. 5–9: Most of these images are Biblical. The medieval belief that Virgil anticipates 'undir queynt figuris' the truths of Christianity is stated by Douglas later in this Prologue (192–97). Here, he is established more generally as an enlightened guide (the carbuncle was held to glow in the dark) and fruitful source.
3. 'in al degre'. The medieval author linked style to theme in order to persuade. Douglas had read Horace's account of the range of appropriate styles in Horace's *Ars Poetica*. For decorum cf. § 22, James VI, *Reulis*, Chapter III; for audience cf. n. 17 below.

As quha the mater beheld tofor thar e,[4]
In every volume quhilk the lyst do wryte° — *which you wish to write*
Surmontyng fer° all other maner endyte, — *Far surpassing*
Lyk as the roys° in June with hir sweit smell — *rose*
The maryguld or dasy doith excell.
Quhy suld I, than, with dull forhed° and vayn,° — *brain; empty*
With rude engyne° and barrand emptyve brayn, — *inventiveness*
With bad, harsk spech and lewit,° barbour° tong — *unlearned; barbarous*
Presume to write quhar thy sweit bell is rung
Or contyrfate° sa precyus wordys deir?[5] — *counterfeit*
Na, na noth swa, but kneill quhen I thame heir!
For quhat compair betwix mydday and nycht?
Or quhat compair betwix myrknes° and lycht? — *darkness*
Or quhat compar is betwix blak and quhyte?
Fra grettar difference betwix my blunt endyte° — *unsubtle writing*
And thy scharp, sugurate sang[6] Virgiliane,
Sa wyslie wrocht, with nevir a word in vane.[7]
My waverand wyt,° my cunnyng° febill at all, — *understanding; knowledge*
My mynd mysty, thir may nocht mys a fall°— — *i.e. trick*
Stra° for thys ignorant blabryng imperfyte° — *A straw; imperfect babbling*
Besyde thy polyst termys redymyte.° — *ornate*
And netheles with support and correctioun,
For° naturall lufe and frendely affectioun, — *Out of (the)*
Quhilkis I beir to thy warkis and endyte°— — *writing*
(Allthocht, God wait, tharin I knaw full lyte)
And that thy facund sentence° mycht be song° — *eloquent meaning; sung*
In our langage alsweill as Latyn tong—
Alsweill?[8] Na, na, impossibill war, per de!° — *by God*
Yit, with thy leif,° Virgile, to follow the — *by your leave*
I wald into my rurall vulgar gros°[9] — *rustic rough vernacular*
Wryte sum savoryng° of thyne *Eneados*. — *Convey some flavour*
But sair I dreid forto disteyn° the quyte — *stain/discolour (rhet.)*
Throu my corruppit cadens° imperfyte. — *faulty rhythm*
Disteyn the? Nay, forsuyth, that may I nocht!
Weill may I schaw my burall,° bustuus° thocht; — *rustic; rough*
Bot thy wark sall endur, in lawd and glory

4. Cf. § 1, Barbour's *Bruce*, I, 20 'Rycht as thai than in presence war.'

5. ll. 19–24. Douglas probably did believe that Scots was still inferior to Latin as a poetic medium. Nonetheless, the statement follows a fine demonstration of the vernacular's power to praise in the ornate style, via lists, similes and Hebraic parallelisms. Under the rules of Rhetoric, such a protestation of modesty proved rather than disproved a poet's skills within, and awareness of, the conventions of his craft.

6. The medieval view that Rhetoric was a 'sweeter' form of teaching than Philosophy derived principally from the arguments and imagery of Dame Philosophy at the start of Boethius' *De Consolatione Philosophiae*. Cf. 'sugurit tun', l. 59. That long poems might be sung or, at least, have a musical accompaniment, is mentioned here and at ll. 39, 46. The *Aeneid* opens with the word 'Canto…' (I sing).

7. ED. Cambridge: 'invane'. Such compounds are a feature of the Cambridge MS. The practice of the other manuscripts has been followed in such cases and the words separated.

8. 'Alswelll?' and 'Disteyn the?' (l. 47) are examples of the rhetorical device of 'Correctio'. It was advocated as a means of artistically conveying a mind thinking aloud.

9. In calling Scots rustic, Douglas suggests it is best fitted to the low style and simple sayings.

But° spot or falt, condyng° etern memory. *Without; befitting*
Thocht I offend, onwemmyt° is thy fame;° *unblemished; reputation*
Thyne is the thank and myne salbe the schame.
Quha may thy versis follow in all degre
In bewtie, sentence° and in gravite? *thought/sense*
Nane is, nor was, ne yit sal be, trow I,
Had, has or sal have sic craft in poetry.[10]
Of Helicon, so drank thou dry the flude[11]
That of thy copios fouth° or plenitude *abundance*
All mon purches° drynk at thy sugurit tun;° *acquire; sweetened cup*
So, lamp of day thou art, and schynand son.
All otheris, on fors,° mon° thar lycht beg or borrow; *necessarily; must*
Thou art Vesper° and the day stern at morow; *the evening star*
Thow, Phebus, lightnar° of the planetis all— *illuminator*
I not° quhat dewly° I the clepe° sall, *know not; aptly; call*
For thou art all and sum—quhat nedis more?—
Of Latyn poetis that sens was,° or befor. *existed afterwards*
Of the° writis Macrobius sans faill° *you; accurately*
In hys gret volume, clepit *Saturnaill*.[12]
Thy sawys° in sic eloquens doith fleit;° *sayings; flow*
So inventive of rethorik flowris sweit
Thou art, and has so hie, profund sentens° *ornate deep meaning*
Tharto,° perfyte but ony indigens,° *Also; lacking nothing*
That na lowyngis° ma do incres thy fame *praises*
Nor na reproche dymynew° thy gud name. *(may) diminish*
But sen I am compellit the to translait,
(And not only of my curage, God wait,
Durst interprys°[13] syk owtrageus foly) *undertake*
Quhar I offend the, les reprefe serve I.° *the less reproof I deserve*
And that ye° knaw at quhais instans° I tuke *i.e. the audience; entreaty*
Forto translait this maist excellent buke—
I meyn Virgillis volume maist excellent—
Set° this my wark full febill be of rent,° *Suppose; of trifling value*
At the request of a lord of renown
Of ancistry nobill and illustir baroun,
Fader of bukis, protectour to sciens° and lair,° *knowledge; learning*
My speciall° gud lord—Henry, Lord Sanct Clair,[14] *My particular/own*
Quhilk with gret instance° divers tymys seir° *insistence; many*

10. The words and triple syntax, within a Christian, trinitarian context, reinforce the idea of Virgil as Christian prophet. The idea leads on naturally from the claim (l. 50) that his memory is immortal and is again strengthened by Biblical imagery (l. 60) and the preference for 'son' (meaning both 'sun' and 'son') over 'sun'.
11. James VI's Castalian band, when adopting the Heliconian stanza (§ 16 Montgomerie, *Cherrie and Slae*) as their signature tune, confessed their indebtedness to Douglas and earlier Scottish poetry as well as to Du Bartas and the Pléiade.
12. Macrobius (fl. 400) was a Latin scholar. His *Saturnalia* was a compendium of late Latin poetics, much of which was given over to study of Virgil. In the Middle Ages, it was set as part of the grammar curriculum.
13. ED. C 'interpryd'; Bath 'enterpriss'; 'interprys' is a composite reading, which makes good sense and maintains the rhyme scheme.
14. Henry, Lord Sinclair, belonged to a family of book-lovers. The manuscript used as copy text for § 2 (James I, *Kingis Quair*) belonged to him.

Prayt me translait Virgill or Homeir,
Quhais plesour, suythly as I undirstude,
As neir conjunct° to hys lordschip in blude — *conjoined/related*
So that me thocht hys request ane command;
Half disparit,° this wark I tuke on hand — *in despair*
Nocht fully grantand° nor anys sayand 'Yee', — *fully accepting*
Bot only to assay° quhou it mycht be. — *test*
Quha mycht gaynsay a lord so gentill° and kynd — *courteous*
That ever had ony curtasy in thar mynd,
Quhilk besyde hys innatyve pollecy,° — *innate good sense*
Humanyte, curage, fredome and chevalry,
Bukis to recollect,° to reid and se, — *retain in memory*
Has gret delyte as ever had Ptholome?[15]
Quharfor to hys nobilite and estait,° — *rank*
Quhat so it be, this buke I dedicait,
Writtin in the langage of Scottis natioun,[16]
And thus I mak my protestatioun:° — *apologia/justification*

Fyrst I protest, beau schirris,° be your leif, — *good sirs*
Beis weill avisit° my wark or° yhe repreif, — *well counselled; before*
Consider it warly,° reid oftar than anys; — *carefully*
Weill at a blenk° sle° poetry nocht tayn° is,[17] — *glance; subtle; understood*
And yit forsuyth I set my bissy pane
As that I couth° to mak it braid and plane,[18] — *As far as I knew how*
Kepand na sudron° bot our awyn langage, — *southern (dialect)*
And spekis as I lernyt quhen I was page.° — *pageboy*
Nor yit sa cleyn all sudron I refus,
Bot sum word I pronunce as nyghtbouris doys:
Lyke as in Latyn beyn Grew° termys sum,[19] — *Greek*
Some behufyt quhilum° (or than be dum) — *It was sometimes necessary*
Sum bastard Latyn, French or Inglys oyss,° — *use*
Quhar scant was Scottis—I had nane other choys.
Nocht for our tong is in the selvyn° skant° — *same; thin/lacking*
Bot for that I the fowth° of langage want° — *copiousness; lack*
Quhar as the cullour of his properte
To kepe the sentens tharto constrenyt me,[20]

15. Ptolomey was King of Egypt from 285–74 B.C.
16. Douglas's reference to the literary vernacular of Scotland as distinct from Inglis implicitly here and explicitly later (cf. l. 111) is very unusual. He will later, like all the other makars, admit Chaucer to be 'principal poet' within the British tradition (I Prol. 339; 343). The nationalist bias of the translation mode and his antagonism against 'Wilyame Caxtoun of Inglis natioun' (l. 138) probably account for this departure from normal practice.
17. Like Henryson, in the Prologue to the *Morall Fabillis* (§ 14. st. 2. n. 4), Douglas emphasizes the care with which an audience must interpret a text.
18. Douglas translates from Latin into Scots as the 'plain' (i.e. understandable) tongue for Scotland. He is commited to decorum, faced by an 'ornate' text and argues the need for audience as well as author to labour at conveying and extracting complex meanings. Glossing 'braid and plane' as 'broad and simple' would imply contradicting the entire argument.
19. ll. 114–6. The written text, it is assumed, will be heard as well as read. Further, languages overlap as they come from a common root.
20. ll. 121–2: '...wherever the rhetorical figures required by his (Virgil's) decorous argument constrained me in keeping close to his meaning...'

Or than to mak my sayng schort, sum tyme
Mair compendyus° or to lykly° my ryme. *Fuller; approximate*
Tharfor, gude frendis, for a gymp° or a bourd,° *quibble; jest*
I pray you note° me nocht at every word. *check*
The worthy clerk hecht Lawrens of the Vaill,[21]
Amang Latynys a gret patron sans faill,° *without doubt*
Grantis° quhen twelf yheris he had beyn diligent *Admits*
To study Virgill, skant° knew quhat he ment. *scarcely*
Than thou or I, my frend, quhen we best weyn° *think*
To have Virgile red, understand and seyn,
The rycht sentens,° perchance, is fer° to seik. *true meaning; far*
This wark,° twelf yheris first was in makyng eyk° *i.e.* Aeneid ; *as well*
And nocht correct,° quhen the poet gan deces.°[22] *revised; died*
Thus, for smal faltis, my wys frend, hald thy pes.
Adherdand° to my protestatioun°— *Sticking; apologia*
Thocht Wilyame Caxtoun, of Inglis natioun,
In proys° hes prent ane buke of Inglys gros,[23] *prose*
Clepand° it Virgill in Eneados, *Calling*
Quhilk that, he says, of Franch he dyd translait.
It has na thing ado tharwith, God wait,
Ne na mair lyke than the devill and Sanct Austyne.[24]
Have he na thank tharfor, but loys his pyne°— *may his labour lack praise*
So schamefully that story did pervert.
I red his wark with harmys° at my hart— *pains*
That syk a buke (but sentens or engyne)° *(without sense or skill)*
Suld be intitillit eftir the poet dyvyne,
Hys ornate goldyn versis mair than gilt,
I spittit for dispyte° to se swa spilt° *contempt; so wasted*
With° sych a wyght, quhilk trewly be myne entent° *By; in my opinion*
Knew never thre wordis at all quhat Virgill ment—
Sa fer he chowpis, I am contrenyt to flyte.[25]

21. Laurentius Valla (1405–57) was a leading humanist. His *De Lingua Latinae Elegantia* was widely studied in the Middle Ages.

22. Virgil failed to complete the poem to his own satisfaction despite working at it from 30–19 B.C. As such, it justifies from the authorial viewpoint not only Valla's perfectionism but Douglas's earlier, more general, call (l. 107) for everyone to spend long hours studying it.

23. Caxton, in 1490, translated the *Aeneid* at second hand from the *Livre des Eneydes*. The fact that his version was in the easier, less artificial form of prose, is an additional reason for contempt.

24. The prime sense is that Caxton's text is as close to Vergil's as black to white. Augustine is shrewdly chosen, being a saint, whose own spiritual journey through error and suffering was often compared to that of Virgil's hero.

25. The context suggests that 'chops' mean both ' chop up (the sense)' and wander from the point in contrast to Virgil (l. 30) and Douglas (ll. 121–4). Flyting is used in its strict sense of denigrating poetically. The Prologue moves into its own lowest 'degre' to do this—ll. 159–282. It ends positively with Douglas's own practice and praise for God, the first of all Makars.

SECTION C: LATE MIDDLE SCOTS AND ANGLO-SCOTS

§ 16 Alexander Montgomerie (1555?–1598): *The Cherrie and the Slae.*

Montgomerie had made his poetic reputation prior to James VI's vernacular revival of the 1580s and early 1590s. A member of the cadet branch of the powerful Ayrshire Eglinton family, he was a Catholic. His biography's tragic movement from royal favour to exile reflects and is largely determined by changing political attitudes to that religion. At first cherished by the young king, who used many quotations from his verse as models of good practice in the **Reulis and Cautelis** *(§ 22), he was subsequently granted a royal licence to travel throughout Europe. It appears that the poet's mission was part of a foreign policy, designed to give covert support to Philip of Spain. When English forces intercepted a ship off Gravesend in 1586, the account given to Lord Cecil records that there were 'six score Scottish soldiers' aboard, with the poet as their military 'captain'. Montgomerie was still imprisoned in 1589. On his return to Scotland, he found that his pension had passed into other hands. He fought the unsuccessful court case, to which Sonnet 2 in § 18B refers, and later spent time at the Abbey of Würzburg. This period of self-imposed exile was followed by another imposed by the courts. The poet became involved in Catholic attempts to provide aid for the Earl of Tyrone. Called to answer charges, he did not appear and was officially outlawed on 14 July 1597. When he died, James wrote a touching epitaph to the poet, voicing the hope that, 'The bell of fame shall aye his praises knell'. He also gave way to Catholic pressure and permitted the man whom, in earlier, happier days, he had known by the nickname of 'Rob Stene', to be buried in consecrated ground.*

Montgomerie's strengths are lyrical. The bell of critical praise is sounding louder, now that his large and varied collection of songs are being heard in their musical settings. That these melodies embrace a wide range is also important. Some are elaborate chansons, mirroring the influence of the dance on the contrapuntal tradition. Others are much simpler and turn, at least in part, to Scottish folk-song and ballad for their inspiration. Like his fellow Ayrshire poet, Burns, Montgomerie moved to longer forms and the narrative voice only occasionally and always dramatically. **The Cherrie and the Slae** *(like* **The Navigatioun** *or his* **Flyting** *contest with Polwart) is—first and foremost—a courtly entertainment. One should think of it being recited or even sung to the Castalian signature tune of 'The Banks of Helicon'. The mingling of pleasurable persuasion, virtuoso art and an audience 'labour(ing) with grit diligence' remain as firmly the trinity of good making for Montgomerie as they had been for Henryson, when he voiced that triple challenge in the* **Prologue** *to his* **Morall Fabillis** (§ 14).

The Cherrie and the Slae[1]

1

About a bank with balmie bewes,° *boughs*
Where nightingals their nots renews

1. ED. Copy Text: Wreittoun 1636. The earlier Waldegrave texts are incomplete and corrupt. They are, however, not so anglicized. To illustrate this, the first six stanzas from Waldegrave are printed below the equivalent stanza from Wreittoun. N.B. the Waldegrave order is 1, 4, 2, 3, 5, 6.

With gallant goldspinks° gay, *goldfinches*
The mavise, mirle° and Progne° proud, *blackbird; i.e. swallow*
The lintwhite,° lark and laverock° loud, *linnet; skylark*
Saluted mirthful May:
When Philomel° had sweetly sung, *i.e. nightingale*
To Progne she deplored
How Tereus cut out her tongue
And falsely her deflorde;[2]
Which storie, so sorie,
To shew ashamd she seemde,
To heare her, so neare her,
I doubted if I dream'd.

[Waldegrave 1]
[About ane bank, quhair birdis on bewis
Ten thusand tymis thair notis renewis
Ilke houre into the day,
The merle and maveis micht be sene,
The Progne and the Phelomene,
Quilk caussit me to stay.° *stop/delay*
I lay and leynit me to ane bus° *bush*
To heir the birdis beir;° *noise*
Thair mirth was sa melodius
Throw nature of the yeir:
Sum singing, sum springing
With wingis into the sky;
So timlie° and nimlie° *swiftly; nimbly*
The birdis they flew me by.]

2
The cushat crouds,° the corbie° cries, *wood pigeon coos; raven*
The cuckow couks, the pratling pyes° *magpies*
To geck° her they begin. *mock*
The jargoun of the jangling jayes,
The craiking crawes the keckling kayes° *cackling jackdaws*
They deav'd° me with their din. *deafened*
The painted pawne° with Argoes eyes,[3] *peacock*
Can on his mayock cal,° *Called on his mate*
The turtle wailes on withered trees,
And Echo answered[4] all,
Repeiting, with greiting,
How faire Narcissus fell,
By lying, and spying
His shadow in the well.° *fountain*

2. Progne and Philomela were sisters. The former was married to Tereus, who raped Philomela and cut out her tongue. She told the tale in a tapestry; the sisters were turned into birds.
3. Argus the hundred-eyed spy for Juno, was beheaded by Mercury. Juno subsequently transferred his many eyes to the tail of her favourite bird, the peacock.
4. The tree nymph Echo pined and died for love of Narcissus. Nemesis punished Narcissus for his lack of feeling, by making him fall in love with his own image—reflected in a fountain.

[Waldegrave 4]
[The cukkow and the cuschet cryde,
The turtle on the uther syde,
Na plesure had to play;
So schil° in sorrow was her sang, *shrill*
That, throw her voice, the roches rang;
For Eccho answerit ay,
Lamenting sair Narcissus cace,
Quha starvit at the well;
Quha with the shaddow of his face
For lufe did slay himsell:
Quhylis° weiping and creiping *Sometimes*
About the well he baid;° *remained*
Quhylis° lying, quhylis° crying, *Now...now...*
Bot it na answere maid.]

3
I saw the hurcheon° and the hare *hedgehog*
In coverts hirpling° heere and there, *Playing in coverts*
To mak their morning mange;° *chorus*[5]
The con,° the conny° and the cat, *squirrel; rabbit*
Whose dainty dounes° with dew were wat° *furs; wet*
With stiffe mustaches strang;
The hart, the hynd, the dae,° the rae,° *doe; roe deer*
The fulmart° and false foxe; *polecat*
The bearded buck clamb° up the brae° *climbed; hillside*
With birsie° baires and brocks;° *bristly; badgers*
Some feeding, some dreading
The hunters subtile snares,
With skipping and tripping,
They plaid them° all in paires. *gambolled*

[Waldegrave 2]
[I saw the hurcheon and the hair,
Quha fed amangis the flowris fair,
Wer happing° to and fro: *hopping*
I saw the cunning° and the cat, *rabbit*
Quhais downis with the dew was wat,
With mony beistis mo.
The hart, the hynd, the dae, the rae,
The fowmart and the foxe
War skowping° all fra brae to brae *skipping*
Amang the water broxe;° *badgers*
Sum feiding, sum dreiding
In cais of suddain snairis;
With skipping and tripping
They hantit° all in pairis.] *hunted/haunted*

5. Alternatively, this could be a French coinage from *manger* (to eat) and have the sense of taking their morning meal.

4

The aire was sober, soft and sweet
But° mistie vapours, wind and weet *Without*
But quyet, calme and cleare
To foster Floras° fragrant flowres, *Roman flower goddess*
Whereon Apollos° paramours *the sun's*
Had trinckled many a teare;
The which like silver shakers° shynde, *drops of dew*
Imbrodering° beauties bed, *Embroidering*
Wherewith their heavy heads declinde,
In Mayes colours clad:
Some knopping,° some dropping *budding*
Of balmie liquor sweet,
Excelling, in smelling,
Through Phoebus° wholsome heat. *the sun's*

[Waldegrave 3]

[The air was sa attemperate° *temperate*
But ony mist, immaculate° *Unflawed by any mist*
Bot purefeit and cleir;
The flouris fair wer flurischit,
As Nature had them nurischit,
Baith delicate and deir:
And every blome on branche and bewch° *bough*
So prettily wer spred,
And hang their heidis out ouir the hewch° *crag*
In Mayis colour cled;
Sum knopping, sum dropping
Of balmie liquor sweit,
Distelling° and smelling *Distilling*
Throw Phoebus hailsum heit.]

5

Mee thought an heavenly heartsome° thing, *pleasant*
Where dew like diamonds did hing,
Ou'r twinckling all the trees,
To study on the flourishde twists,° *blossoming twigs*
Admiring Natures alcumists,° *alchemists*
Labouring busie bees;
Whereof some sweetest hony sought
To stay their lives to sterve,° *i.e. To stave off starvation*
And some the waxie vessels wrought,
Their purchase to preserve.
So heaping for keeping
It in their hyves they hide;
Precisely and wisely,
For winter they provide.

[Waldegrave 5]

[The dew as diamondis did hing,
Upon the tender twistis and ying,

Ouir-twinkling all the treis:
And ay quhair flowris flourischit faire,
Thair suddainly I saw repaire,
In swarmes, the sownding beis.
Sum sweitly hes the hony socht,
Quhil° they war cloggit soir;° *Until; heavy laden*
Sum willingly the waxe hes wrocht,
To keip it up in stoir:
So heiping, with keiping
Into thair hyvis they hyde it,
Precyselie and wyselie,
For winter they provyde it.]

6

To pen the pleasures of that parke,
How every blossome, branch, and bark
Against the sun did shine,
I passe to poets to compile
In high, heroick, stately stile,
Whose Muse surmatches° mine; *surpasses*
But as I looked mine alone,° *on my own*
I saw a river rinne
Out ou'r a steepie rock of stone,
Syne° lighted in a linne° *Then; waterfall*
With tumbling and rumbling
Amongst the roches° round, *rocks*
Devalling° and falling *Descending*
Into a pit profound.

[Waldegrave 6]

[To pen the pleasures of that park,
How every blossome, branche and bark
Agaynst the sun did schyne,
I leif to poetis to compyle
In staitlie verse and lofty style:
It passis my ingyne.° *ingenuity/invention*
Bot, as I mussit° myne allane, *mused*
I saw an river rin
Out ouir ane craggie rok of stane,
Syne lichtit in ane lin,
With tumbling and rumbling
Amang the rochis round,
Devalling and falling
Into that pit profound.]

7

Through routing° of the river rang *roaring*
The roches,° sounding like a sang, *rocks*
Where descant did abound.
With treble, tenor, counter, meene,° *intermediate part*

An echo blew a basse between
In diapason° sound, *musical harmony*
Set with the C-sol-fa-uth cleife° *i.e. staff notation*
With long and large at list,° *at one's pleasure*
With quaver, crotchet, semi-briefe
And not a minim mist;
Compleetly and sweetly,
She firdound° flat and sharp, *warbled*
Than Muses, which uses
To pin° Apollos harpe. *strike*

8

Who would have tyr'd to heare that tone,° *tune*
Which birds corroborate° ay abone *confirm melodically*
With layes of lovesome° larks; *lovely*
Which climb so high in christal skyes,
While° Cupid wakned with the cryes *Until*
Of natures chappel clarks;° *choristers*
Who, leaving al the heavens above,
Alighted on the eard?° *earth*
Lo, how that little lord of love,
Before me there appeard,
So mild-like, and child-like,
With bow three quarters skant,° *stretched*
Syne moylie° and coylie, *demurely*
Hee looked like a sant.° *saint*

9

A cleanly crispe° hang over his eyes, *neat gauze veil*
His quaver by his naked thyes° *thighs*
Hang in° a silver lace;° *on; cord*
Of gold betweene his shoulders grew
Two pretty wings wherewith he flew,
On his left arme a brace.° *wrist-guard*
This god soone off his geare he shook
Upon the grassie ground:
I ran as lightly for to looke,
Where ferlies° might be found. *wonders*
Amazed, I gazed
To see his geare so gay;
Perceiving mine having,° *behaviour*
He counted mee his prey.

10

His youth and stature made mee stout:° *bold*
Of doublenesse° I had no doubt° *trickery; fear*
But bourded° with my boy. *jested*
Quoth I, 'How call they thee my child?'
'Cupido sir,' quoth he and smilde.
'Please you mee to imploy,

For I can serve you in your sute° *suit*
If you please to impire;° *command*
With wings to flee and shafts to shute
Or flames to set on fire.
Make choise then of those then
Or of a thousand things—
But° crave them and have them!' *Only*
With that I woo'd° his wings. *asked for*

11
'What would thou give, my heart,' quoth he,
'To have these wanton wings to flee,
To sporr° thy sprite a while? *spur on*
Or what if love should send thee heere,
Bow, quaver,° shafts and shooting geare, *quiver*
Somebody to beguile?'
'This geare,' quoth I, 'cannot be bought,
Yet I would have it faine.'
'What if,' quoth he, 'it cost thee nought
But rendring all againe?'
His wings then, he brings then
And band° them on my back, *tied*
'Goe fly now,' quoth he now,
And so my leave I take.

12
I sprang up with Cupido's wings,
Whose shots and shooting geare resignes,° *(he) gives up...*
To° lend me for a day. *(In order) to*
As Icarus with borrowed flight,[6]
I mounted higher than I might°— *should have*
Ou'r° perilous a play!° *Too; ploy*
First foorth I drew the double dart,
Which sometime shot his mother,° *i.e. Venus*
Wherewith I hurt my wanton heart
In hope to hurt another.
It hurt me or burnt mee,
While either end I handle;
Come see now, in mee now,
The butterflee° and candle.[7] *butterfly*

13
As she delites into the low,° *flame*
So was I browden of° my bow *infatuated with*
As ignorant as she;
And as she flyes while she is fir'de,
So with the dart that I desirde

6. Icarus was given waxen wings which melted as he approached the sun. He became a type of ignorant aspiration.
7. Conventional image, depicting desire's power to conquer reason and draw the lover into a lethal trap.

Mine hands hath hurt mee to.
As foolish Phaeton,[8] by sute,° *entreaty*
His father's chaire° obtainde, *chariot*
I longed in loves bow to shoote,
Not marking° what it mean'de.° *realising; involved*
More wilful than skilful,
To flee° I was so fond° *fly; foolishly eager*
Desiring impyring,° *Wanting to hold sway*
And so was seene upond° *upon it*

14

Too late I knew, who hewes° too high *raises himself*
The spaile° shall fall into his eye; *splinter*
Too late I went to schooles,
Too late I heard the swallow preach,[9]
Too late Experience doth teach—
The schoole-master of fooles;
Too late I find the nest I seek,
When all the birds are flowne,
Too late the stable doore I steeke,° *make fast*
When as the steede is stowne;° *stolen*
Too late ay, their state ay,
As foolish folk espy;
Behind so, they finde so,
Remead,° and so doe I. *Cure*

15

If I had ripely° beene advisde, *early on*
I had not rashly enterprisde
To soare with borrowed pens,° *feathers*
Nor yet had sayde° the archer-craft *tried out*
To shoot myselfe with such a shaft
As Reason quite miskens.° *entirely disowns*
Fra° Wilfulnes[10] gave me my wound, *Ever since*
I had no force to flee;
Then came I, groning, to the ground.
'Friend, welcome home,' quoth he.
'Where flew yee? Whom slew yee?
Or who brings home the booting?° *booty*
'I see now,' quoth he now,
'Ye have been at the shooting.'

16

As scorne comes commonly with skaith,° *harm*
So I behovde to bide° them baith; *I had to endure*
So staggering was my state

8. Apollo's son, Phaethon, drove the sun god's chariot so wildly, he scorched the earth.
9. The swallow, as voice of experience, appears in Henryson's *Morall Fabillis*, § 4.
10. Allegorically, the refusal of Will to accept the guidance of Reason often initiates a longer spiritual journey or soul-battle.

That under cure I got such check,[11]
Which I might not remove nor neck° — *cover check (in chess)*
But either staile° or mait.° — *stalemate; checkmate*
Mine agony was so extreame,
I swelt° and swound° for feare. — *became faint; swooned*
But ere I wakned off my dreame,
He spoild° me of my geare. — *despoiled*
With flight then, on hight then,
Sprang Cupid in the skyes,
Forgetting and setting
At nought, my carefull° cryes. — *woeful*

17

So long with sight I followed him,
While both my dazeled eyes grew dimme
Through staring of° the starnes;° — *gazing at; stars*
Which flew so thick before mine eyne,
Some red, some yellow, blew and greene,
Which troubled all mine harnes,° — *brains*
That evry thing appeared two
To my barbuilied° braine; — *muddled*
But long might I lye looking so
Ere Cupid came againe;
Whose thundring, with wondring
I heard up through the aire.
Through clouds so, he thuddes so
And flew I wist not where.

18

Then when I saw that god was gone
And I in langour left alone
And sore tormented too,
Sometime I sigh'd while I was sad,
Sometime I musde, and most gone mad;
I doubted° what to doe. — *was unsure*
Sometime I rav'd halfe in a rage° — *madness*
As one into despare
To be opprest with such a page;° — *young boy (Cupid)*
Lord, if my heart was saire!
Like Dido,[12] Cupido
I widdle° and I wary,° — *bemoan; curse*
Who reft° me and left me — *deserted*
In such a feirie farie.° — *confused state*

19

Then felt I Courage and Desire
Inflame mine heart with uncouth° fire, — *unfamiliar*

11. Chess imagery is used to express his defeated state in 16: 4–6.
12. Queen of Carthage; in Virgil's *Aeneid*, she falls in love with Aeneid, who deserts her. Her prolonged misery followed by suicide provides an apt parallel for the narrator's current state.

To me before unknowne.
But then no blood in me ramaines
Unburnt or boyld within my braines
By loves bellowes blowne.
To drowne it ere I was devorit° — *devoured*
With sighs I went about;
But ay the more I shoope° to smor° it — *strove; quench*
The bolder it brake out—
Ay preasing but ceasing° — *ceaselessly pressing*
While° it might break the bounds; — *Until*
Mine hew° so, foorth shew° so — *complexion; displayed*
The dolour of my wounds.

20

With deadly° visage, pale and wan, — *deathly*
More like an atomie° than man, — *skeleton*
I withered cleane away.
As waxe before the fire, I felt
Mine heart within my bosome melt
And, piece and piece, decay.
My veines by brangling° like to break — *shaking*
My punses lap with pith, — *My pulses galloped fiercely*
So fervency did mee infect
That I was vext therewith.
Mine heart ay, it start ay,
The firie flames to flee;
Ay howping,° through lowping,° — *hoping; jumping*
To leape at libertie.

21

But O, alas, it was abusde!
My carefull° corps kept it inclusde° — *troubled; enclosed*
In prison of my breast,
With sighs so sopped° and ou'rset,° — *waterlogged; weary*
Like to a fish fast in a net,
In deadthraw° undeceast; — *death-throe*
Which though in vaine, it strives by strength
For to pul out her head,
Which profites nothing at the length° — *in the long run*
But hastning to her dead;° — *death*
With thristing° and wristing,° — *thrusting; straining*
The faster° still is sho;° — *more entrapped; she*
There I so, did lye so,
My death advancing to.

22

The more I wrestled with the wind,
The faster stil my selfe I finde;
No mirth my minde could mease.° — *calm*
More noy° than I had never none, — *pain*

I was so alterd and ou'rgone
Through drouth of my disease.
Yet weakly, as I might, I raise;
My sight grew dimme and dark;
I staggered at the windling strayes,° *slightest things*
No token° I was stark.° *In no sense; strong*
Both sightles and mightles
I grew almost at once;
In anguish I languish,
With many grievous groanes.

23

With sober pace yet I approach
Hard to the river and the roch,° *rock*
Whereof I spake before;
The river such a murmure made,
As to the sea it softly slade;° *flowed*
The craige° was stay° and shore.° *crag; steep; sheer*
Then Pleasure did me so provoke
There partly° to repaire *apart*
Betwixt the river and the rocke,
Where Hope grew with Despare.
A tree then, I see then,
Of Cherries on the braes. *hills*
Below too, I saw too
A bush of bitter Slaes.

24

The Cherries hang above mine head,
Like trickling° rubies round and red, *dripping*
So high up in the heugh;° *crag*
Whose shadowes in the rivers shew,
As graithly glansing° as they grew *brightly shining*
On trembling twists° and teugh,° *shoots; tough*
Whiles bow'd through burden of their birth,
Declining downe their tops.
Reflexe of Phoebus° off the firth,° *sun's reflection; river*
Now coloured all their knoppes,° *buds*
With dancing and glancing,
In tirle° as Dornick champe;[13] *rippled effect*
Which streamed and leamed,° *gleamed*
Through lightnes of that lampe.

25

With earnest eye while I espy
That fruite betwixt me and the skye,
Half gate° almost to heaven; *half way*
The craige so cumbersome to climb,

13. Linen cloth originating from Tournai, embroidered with flowers or figures.

The tree so tall of growth and trim
As any arrow even;
I calde to minde how Daphne did
Within the laurel shrinke,
When from Apollo she her hid,[14]
A thousand times I thinke.
That tree there, to mee there,
As shee his laurel thought,
Aspyring but tyring,
To get that fruite I sought.

26

To climb that craige it was no buite,° *advantage*
Let bee to prease° to pul the fruite *press forward*
In top of all the tree;
I know no way whereby to come,
By any craft to get it clum,° *climbed*
Apperandly to mee.
The craige was ugly, stay and dreigh,° *wearisome*
The tree long, sound° and small;° *smooth; slender*
I was affraide to climb so high,
For feare to fetch a fall.
Affrayed, I stayed
And looked up aloft,
Whiles minting,° whiles stinting,° *venturing on; holding back*
My purpose changed oft.

27

Then Dread with Danger° and Despare *Disdain*[15]
Forbade me minting° any mare,° *trying; more*
To raxe° above my reach. *stretch*
'What? Tush!' quoth Courage, 'Man go to,
He is but daft that hath to doe
And spares for everie speach,
For I have oft heard sooth men° say *truthful men/seers*
(And we may see't ourselves)
That Fortune helps the hardie ay
And pultrons° ay repels. *cowards*
Then care not and feare not
Dread, Danger nor Despare;
To fazards,° hard hazards *weaklings*
Is death, or° they come there. *before*

28

'Who speeds° but such as high aspyres? *succeeds*
Who triumphs not but such as tyres

14. Daphne is turned into a laurel to defeat Apollo's pursuit in Ovid's *Metamorphoses*.
15. Many of the personifications at this stage are drawn from the French love allegory, *Le Roman de la Rose*. Danger particularly refers to amorous disdain.

To win a noble name?
Of shrinking what but shame succeeds?° *follows*
Then doe as° thou would have thy deeds *as if*
In register of Fame.
I put the case° thou not prevailde, *i.e. Let us suppose*
So thou with honour dies—
"Thy life but not thy courage failde,"
Sall poets pen of thee.
Thy name then, from Fame then,
Can never be cut aff;
Thy grave ay, shal have ay,
That honest epitaph.

29

'What canst thou losse when honour lives?
Renowne thy vertue ay revives,
If valiantly thou end.'
Quoth Danger, 'Huly° friend, take head; *Slowly*
Untimous° spurring spilles° the stead;° *Untimely; upsets; steed*
Tak tent° what yee pretend.° *care; claim*
Though Courage counsel thee to climb,
Bewar thou kep no skaith;° *harm*
Have thou no helpe but Hope and him,
They may beguile thee baith.
Thysell now can tell now
The counsel of these clarkes;° *academics*
Wherethrow yet, I trow yet,
Thy breast doth beare the marks.

30

'Burnt bairne° with fire the danger dreads, *(Like a)...child*
So I believe thy bosome bleeds,
Since last that fire thou felt:
Besides that seindle time° thou sees, *seldom*
That ever Courage keeps the keyes
Of knowledge at his belt.
Though he bid,° "Fordward with the gunnes!," *may order*
Smal° powder he provides; *Scant*
Be not a novice of that nunnes,
Who saw not both the sides;
Fooles haste ay, almaist ay
Ou'rsyles° the sight of some, *Beguiles/Obscures*
Who luikes not or huikes° not, *takes into account*
What afterward may come.

31

'Yet Wisedome wisheth thee to wey° *weigh up*
This figure° in Philosophy, *proposition*
A lesson worth to leare,° *worth learning*
Which is, "In time for to take tent° *take care*

And not, when time is past, repent
And buy repentance deare."
Is there no honour after life
Except thou slay thy sel?° *yourself*
Wherefore hath Atropus that knife?[16]
I trow thou canst not tell.
Who, but it, would cut it
Which Clotho scarce hath spun;
Destroying the joying
Before it be begun.

32

'All ou'rs° are repute to be vice,[17] *excesses*
Ou'r high, ou'r low, ou'r rash, ou'r nice,
Ou'r hote or yet ou'r cold;
Thou seemes unconstant by thy signes,
Thy thought is on a thousand things,
Let Fame her pitty on thee powre° *pour*
When all thy bones are broken;
Yon Slae, suppose° thou think it sowre, *even if*
Would satisfy to sloken° *slake*
Thy drouth now, of youth now,
Which dries thee with desire;
Assuage then, thy rage then,
Foule water quencheth fire.

33

'What foole art thou to die a thrist,
And now may quench it if thou list° *wish*
So easily but paine?
More honour is to vanquish ane
Than fight with tensome° and be tane° *ten or so; taken*
And either hurt or slay[ne];
The practick° is to bring to passe° *practical aim; achieve*
And not to enterprise;° *(merely) to attempt*
And as good drinking out of glasse
As gold in any wise;
I lever° have ever *I'd rather*
A fowle in hand or tway,
Then° seeing ten flying *Than*
About me all the day.

34

'Looke where thou lights° before thou loupe° *may land; leap*
And slip no certainty for Hope,[18]

16. There were three Fates, ruling death (Atropos), birth (Clotho, l. 12) and life (Lachesis).

17. The classical doctrine of the golden mean influenced James VI's political philosophy greatly.

18. Danger counsels the poet to check even those things which seem certainties, when viewed in a spirit of optimism and wish fulfilment (Hope).

Who guides thee but be gesse.'° *by guessing*
Quoth Courage, 'Cowards take no cure
To sit with shame, so they be sure;
I like them all the lesse.
What pleasure purchast is but° paine *without*
Or honour won with ease?
He wil not lye where he is slaine,
Who doubts before he dies.
For feare then, I heare then,
But onely one remead
Which lattis,° and that is *brings release*
For to cut off the head.

35

'What is the way to heale thine hurt?
What way is there to stay° thy sturt?° *hold off; trouble*
What meanes to make thee merrie?
What is the comfort that thou craves?
Suppose these sophists thee deceaves,
Thou knowes it is the Cherrie.
Since for it onely thou but thirsts,
The Slae can be no buite.° *remedy*
In it also thine health consists
And in none other fruite.
Why quakes thou and shakes thou
Or studies° at our strife? *think inconclusively*
Advise thee, it lyes thee[19]
On no lesse than thy life.

36

'If any patient would be pansde,° *cured*
Why should he loupe° when he is lansde° *start (in pain); lanced*
Or shrink when he is shorne?° *cut*
For I have heard chirurgians° say, *surgeons*
Oft-times deferring of a day
Might not be mend° the morne. *amended*
Take° time in time ere time be tint° *Seize; lost*
For time will not remaine.
What forceth fire out of the flint
But as hard match againe?
Delay not, nor fray° not, *fear*
And thou shall see it sa;
Such gets° ay, as sets ay *Such a one achieves*
Stout stomackes to the brae.° *hill*

37

'Though all beginning be most hard,
The end is pleasant afterward;

19. ll. 13–14: 'Reconsider, it is a matter for you of no less concern than your life.'

Then shrinke not for no showre;
When once that thou thy greening° get, *what you long for*
Thy paine and travel° is forget, *labour*
The sweet excels the sowre.
Goe to then quickly, feare no thir° *these*
For Hope good hap hath height.'° *promised*
Quoth Danger, 'Be not sudden, sir;
The matter is of weight.
First spy both, then try both,
Advisement° doth none ill: *Taking counsel/Reflection*
Thou may then, I say then,
Be wilful when thou will.

38

'But yet to minde the proverbe call,
"Who uses perils perish shal";
Short while their life them lasts.'
'And I have heard,' quoth Hope, 'that he
Should never shape° to saile the sea *set out to*
That for all perils casts.° *casts around for dangers*
How many through Despare are dead,
That never perils priev'd!° *experienced*
How many also, if thou read,
Of lives have we releiv'd,° *rescued*
Who being even dying,
But danger but desparde?[20]
A hunder, I wonder° *would be surprised*
But thou hast° heard declarde. *If you have not*

39

'If we two hold not up thine heart,
Which is the chiefe and noblest part,
Thy works would not goe well;
Considering thae[21] companions can
Dissuade a silly,° simple man *innocent*
To hazard for his heale.° *well-being*
Suppose they have deceived some
Ere we and they might meete,
They get no credance where we come
In any man of spreit.° *spirit*
By reason, their treason
By us is plainely spyde;
Revealing their dealing,
Which dow not be denyde.

20. ll. 11–12: The general sense of these epigrammatical lines is that Hope has rescued those who, when no danger existed ('But danger') still despaired ('but desparde') and so brought themselves to the point of death ('being even dying').
21. ED. thae] Wald II; the Wr.

40

'With sleekie sophismes° seeming sweete, *slick sophistries*
As° all their doing were discreet, *As if*
They wish thee to be wise,° *i.e. falsely wise*
Postponing time from houre to houre.
But faith, in underneath the flowre
The lurking serpent lyes[22]—
Suppose thou seest her not a stime,° *particle*
While that° she sting thy foote! *Until*
Perceives thou not what precious time
Thy sleuth° doth overshoote? *sloth*
Alas man, thy case man,
In lingring I lament:
Goe to now and doe° now, *act (in such a way)*
That Courage be content.

41

'What if Melancholy come in
And get a grip ere thou begin?
Then is thy labour lost;
For he will hold thee hard and fast,
Til time and place and fruite be past
And thou give up the ghost.
Then shal be graven upon that place
Which on thy tombe is laid:
"Sometime there liv'd such one." Alas,
But how shal it bee said?
"Heere lyes now, but prise° now, *without renown*
Into dishonours bed,
A cowart,° as thou art, *coward*
Who from his fortune fled."

42

'Imagine, man, if thou were laid
In grave, and syne might heare this said,
Would thou not sweat for shame?
Yes, faith, I doubt not but thou would;
Therefore if thou have eyes, behold
How they would smore° thy fame.° *extinguish; (good) reputation*
Goe to and make no more excuse;
Now[23] life and honour losse
And either them or us refuse;
There is no other chose.° *choice*
Considder, togidder° *together*
That we doe never dwell;
At length ay, but strength ay,
The pultrons° we expell.' *cowards*

22. Imagery from Genesis suggests Satan waiting to tempt Eve and initiate the Fall. 'But faith' has, in this context, the double sense of 'In faith!' and 'Lacking faith'.
23. ED. Now] Wald II; Ere Wr.

43

Quoth Danger, 'Since I understand
That counsell can be no command,
I have no more to say;
Except if that you thinke it good
Take counsel yet ere ye conclude
Of wiser men then they.
They are but rackles,° young and rash, — *imprudent*
Suppose they thinke us fleit;° — *scared*
If of our fellowship ye fash° — *are troubled (about)*
Goe with them hardly be it.° — *boldly by all means*
God speed you, they lead you,
Who have not meekle wit.° — *much common sense*
Expel us, yeeil°[24] tell us, — *you'll*
Heerafter comes not yit.'° — *The future hasn't yet arrived*

44

While Danger and Despare retir'de,
Experience came in and spear'de° — *asked*
What all the matter meande;
With him came Reason, Wit and Skill.° — *Practical knowledge*
Then, they began to aske at Will,
'Where make you to, my friend?'
'To pluck yon lustie° Cherrie, loe,' — *delightful*
Quoth he, 'and quyte° the Slae.' — *renounce*
Quoth they, 'Is there no more adoe
Ere yee win up the brae,
But doe it and to it,
Perforce, your fruite to pluck?
Well, brother, some other
Were better to conduct.° — *give a lead*

45

'We grant yee may be good enough
But yet the hazard of yon heugh° — *crag*
Requyres a graver guide.
As wise as yee are° may goe wrang; — *(i.e. not very wise)*
Therefore, take counsell ere ye gang
Of some that stands beside.
But who were yon three yee forbade° — *rejected from*
Your company right now?'
Quoth Wil, 'Three preachers to persuade
The poysonde Slae to pull.
They tratled° and pratled° — *tattled; prattled on*
A long half hour and mare;
Foul fal them! They call them° — *themselves*
Dread, Danger[25] and Despare.

24. The form indicates that two syllables should be voiced.
25. While the amorous context gives Danger the particular sense of 'Luf-Daungere' or Disdain, the surface meaning of a heightened sense of danger is also present.

46

'They are more fashious° than of feck° *annoying; value*
Yon fazards° durst not for their neck *weaklings*
Climbe up the craige with us.
Fra we determined° to die *Since we decided*
Or then° to climbe the Cherrie tree, *Or else*
They bode° about the bush° *stayed; (sloe)bush*
They are conditinde like the cat,
They would not weet their feet;
But yet if any fish we gate° *get*
They would be apt° to eate. *ready*
Though they now, I say now,
To hazard have no heart;
Yet luck we,° or pluck wee, *should we succeed*
The fruite, they would [have] part.°[26] *have a share*

47

'But when we get our voyage wun,
They shal not then a° Cherrie cun,° *one single; taste*
Who would not enterprise.'° *venture forth*
'Well,'° quoth Experience, 'ye boast; *Impressively*
But he that reckon'd but his hoast° *without due consideration*
Oftimes he counteth twise.
Ye sell the baires skin on his back[27]
But bide while° ye it get; *wait until*
When ye have done, its time to crack°— *tell tales about it*
Ye fish before the net.
What haste, sir! Ye taste, sir,
The Cherrie ere yee pow° it! *pull it off*
Beware, sir, ye are, sir,
More talkative nor trowit.'° *than believed*

48

'Call Danger back againe,' quoth Skil,
'To see what he can say to Wil;
We see him shoad° so straite,° *cast off; quickly*
We may not trow what each one tels.'
Quoth Courage, 'We concluded els;° *otherwise*
He serves not for our mate,
For I can tel you al perquiere° *exactly*
His counsel ere he come.'
Quoth Hope, 'Whereto should he come here?
He cannot hold him dum.° *keep himself dumb*
He speaks ay, and seeks ay,
Delayes° oft times and drifts,° *Defers (sense); meanders*

26. ED. have part] Wald II; not part Wr.
27. To sell the bear's skin while he is still alive has the same proverbial force as counting one's chickens before they are hatched. Montgomerie makes frequent and fitting use of simple proverbs at this early stage in the intellectual journey.

To grieve us and dieve° us — *deafen*
With sophistrie and shifts.'° — *evasions*

49

Quoth Reason, 'Why was he debarde?
The tale is ill° cannot be heard, — *bad (which)*
Yet let us heare him anes.°' — *once*
Then Danger to declare began,
How Hope and Courage tooke the man
To leade him all their lanes;° — *on their own*
How they would have him up the hill
But° either stoppe or stay,° — *Without; delay*
And who was welcomer than Will,
He would be foremost ay.
He could doe and should doe,
Whoever would or nought.
'Such speeding, proceeding,
Unlikely was, I thought.[28]

50

'Therefore I wisht him to beware
And rashly not to run ou'r far,
Without such guides as yee.'
Quoth Courage, 'Friend, I heare you faile;° — *speak falsely*
Tak better tent unto your tale—
Ye said it could not bee.
Besides that, ye would not consent,
That ever we should clim.'
Quoth Wil, 'For my part I repent,
We saw them more than him;
For they are the stayare° — *sustainer*
Of us as well as hee;
I thinke now, they shrinke now:
Goe forward, let them bee.

51

'Goe, goe, we nothing do but guckes;° — *talk foolishly*
They say the voyage never luckes° — *is fortunate*
Where each one hath a vote.'
Quoth Wisedome gravely, 'Sir, I grant
We were no worse your vote to want,° — *lack*
Some sentence° now I note; — *sense*
Suppose you speake it but be gesse,
Some fruite therein I finde.
Ye would be foremost I confesse
But comes oft-times behind.
It may be, that they bee
Deceiv'd that never doubted;

28. Danger now speaks directly.

Indeed sir, that head,° sir, *point*
Hath meekle° wit about it.' *much*

52

Then wilful Will began to rage
And swore he saw nothing in age
But anger, yre and grudge.
'And for myselfe,' quoth he, 'I sweare
To quyte° all my companions heere, *abandon*
If they admit you judge.
Experience is growne so old,
That he begins to rave;
The rest, but Courage, are so cold
No hazarding° they have, *desire to take risks*
For Danger, farre stranger° *stronger*
Hath made them than they were;
Goe fra them, we pray them,
Who neither dow nor dare.

53

'Why may not wee three leade this one?
I led an hundreth mine alone
But counsel of them all.'
'I grant,' quoth Wisedome, 'ye have led;
But I would speere° how many sped° *ask; succeeded*
Or furthered but° a fall? *progressed without*
But either few or none, I trow,
Experience can tell.
He sayes that man may wite but you,° *blame you alone*
The first time that hee fell;
He kens then, whose pens° then, *feathers*
Thou borrowed him to flee.
His wounds yet, which stounds° yet, *ache*
He got them then through thee.'

54

'That,' quoth Experience, 'is true.
Will flattered him when first he flew,
Wil set him in a low,° *aflame*
Will was his counsell and convoy,° *companion*
Will borrowed from the blinded boy° *i.e. Cupid*
Both quaver,° wings and bow, *quiver (of arrows)*
Wherewith, before he say'd° to shoote, *tried*
He neither yeeld° to youth *yielded*
Nor yet had need of any fruite,
To quench his deadly drouth;
Which pines him, and dwines him,° *wastes him (away)*
To death, I wot not how.
If Will then, did ill then,
Himselfe remembers now.

55

'For I, Experience, was there,
Like as I use to bee all where,° *everywhere*
What time hee wited° Will *blamed*
To be the ground° of all his griefe, *source*
As I myself can bee a priefe° *witness*
And witnes thereuntill.
There are no bounds° but I have beene, *boundaries*
Nor hidlings° from mee hid, *secret places*
Nor secret things but I have seene,
That hee or any did.
Therefore now, no more now,
Let him thinke to° conceal it; *suppose he may*
For why now, even I now,
Am debtbound to reveal it. '

56

'My custome is for to declare
The truth, and neither eke° nor paire° *enlarge; pare down*
For any man a joate:° *jot*
If wilful Will delytes in lyes,
Example in thy selfe thou sees,
How he can turne his coate,
And with his language would allure
Thee yet to breake thy bones.
Thou knowes thyself if he be sure—
Thou usde his counsell ones°— *once*
Who would yet, behold yet,
To wreak° thee were not wee,° *destroy; we (here)*
Thinke on you, on yon now,'
Quoth Wisedome, then, to mee.

57

'Wel,' quoth Experience, 'if hee
Submits himselfe to you and mee,
I wait°[29] what I should say. *know*
Our good advise he shall not want,
Providing alwayes that hee grant
To put yon Will away,
And banish both him and Despare,
That all good purpose spils;° *destroys*
So° he will mell° with them no mare,° *So long as; mix; more*
Let them two flyte° their fils. *exchange insults*
Such cossing,° but lossing,° *exchanging; loss*
All honest men may use.'
'That change now, were strange now,'
Quoth Reason, 'to refuse.'

29. ED. wait] Wald II; wote Wr.

58

Quoth Will, 'Fy on him when he flew,
That powde° not Cherries then anew — *pulled/plucked*
For to have staide° his hurt.' — *staunched*
Quoth Reason, 'Though he beare the blame,
He never saw nor needed them,
While° he himselfe had hurt. — *Until*
First,° when he mistred not,° he might; — *Originally; did not need to*
He needs and may not, now.
Thy folly, when he had his flight,
Empashed° him to pow; — *Prevented*
Both hee now, and we now,
Perceives thy purpose plaine,
To turne him and burne him,
And blow on him againe.'

59

Quoth Skil, 'What would wee longer strive?
Far better late than never thrive.
Come let us helpe him yit.
Tint° time we may not get againe, — *Lost*
We waste but present time in vaine.'
'Beware with that,' quoth Wit.
'Speake on, Experience, let see;
We think you hold you dumb.'
'Of bygones I have heard,' quoth he,
'I know not things to come.'
Quoth Reason, 'The season,
With slouthing° slydes away. — *slothfulness*
First take him and make him
A man, if that you may.'

60

Quoth Will, 'If he be not a man,
I pray you, sirs, what is he than?
He lookes like one at least.
Quoth Reason, 'If he follow thee—
And minde° not to remaine with mee— — *intend*
Nought but a bruital° beist. — *i.e. without reason*
A man in shape° does nought consist — *i.e. in shape alone*
For all your taunting tales;
Therefore, Sir Will, I would yee wist,
Your Metaphysick failes.
Goe leare yet, a yeare yet,
Your Logick at the schooles,
Some day then, yee may then,
Passe master with° the mules!'[30] — *graduate among*

30. Reason satirically suggests a philosophical education for Will, including Logic and Metaphysics.

61

Quoth Will, 'I marvel what you meane;
Should I not trow° mine own two eyne — *trust*
For all your logick schooles?
If I did not, I were not wise.'
Quoth Reason, 'I have told you thrise,
None ferlies° more than fooles; — *wonders*
There be more senses than the sight,
Which ye ou'rhaile° for haste. — *overlook/disregard*
To wit—if ye remember right:
Smel, hearing, touch and taste.
All quick° things have sic things, — *living*
I meane both man and beast,
By kinde° ay, we finde ay, — *(their) nature*
Few lackes them at the least.'

62

'So, by that consequence° of thine, — *deduction (in st. 61: 1–4)*
Or syllogisme, said like a swine,
A kow may learne the laire.° — *teach you scholarship*
Thou uses onely but the eyes,
She touches, tastes, smels, heares and sees,
Which matches thee and maire.° — *more*
But since no triumph yee intend,
As presently appeares,
Sir, for your clergie° to be kend — *learning*
Take yee two asses eares!
No miter, perfyter,° — *more perfect mitre*
Got Midas for his meed;°[31] — *reward*
That hood, sir, is good, sir,
To hap° your braine-sick head. — *cover*

63

'Ye have no "feele"° for to defyne, — *feeling (ironic)*
Though yee have cunning to decline° — *ability to deduce*
A man to bee a moole;° — *mule*
With little work, yet, yee may vowde° — *solemnly undertake*
To grow a gallant horse and good,
To ride thereon at Yoole.
But to our ground° where wee began: — *premise*
For all your gustlesse° jests, — *tasteless*
I must be master° of the man — *teacher*
But thou to bruital beasts;
So wee two must bee two,
To cause both kinds be knowne;
Keep mine then, from thine then,
And each one use their owne.'

31. Reason is dealing with use and misuse of the senses; ll. 11–12: Midas, in Ovid's *Metamorphoses* XI, was given the ears of an ass for preferring Pan's music to Apollo's.

64

Then Wil, as angry as an ape,
Ran ramping,° swearing rude° and rape,° *wildly; roughly; rapidly*
Saw he none other shift.° *strategy*
He would not want° an inch his wil° *deny; wilfulness*
Even whether't did him good or ill,
For thirty of his thrift;° *position*
He would be foremost in the field
And master if he might;
Yea, hee should rather die than yeeld,
Though Reason had the right.° *right on his side*
'Shal he now, make mee now
His subject or his slave?
No, rather my father
Shal quick° goe to the grave. *quickly/alive*

65

'I height° him while mine heart is haile, *promised*
To perish first ere he prevaile,
Come after what so may.'
Quoth Reason, 'Doubt yee not indeed,
Yee hitte the naile upon the head;
It shall bee as yee say.
Suppose yee spur for to aspire,
Your bridle wants a bit;
That marke° may leave you in the myre° *aim; i.e. bogged down*
As sicker° as yee sit. *certainly*
Your sentence, repentance,
Shall leave you, I believe,
And anger you langer,° *(for) longer*
When yee that practick prieve.° *put that into practice*

66

'As yee have dyted° your decreet,° *composed; pronouncement*
Your prophecy to bee compleat,
Perhaps and to your paines;
It hath beene said and may be so,° *be the case*
"A wilful man wants never woe,
Though he get little gaines."° *few rewards*
But since ye think't an easie thing
To mount above the moone,
Of your owne fiddle take a spring° *lively tune*
And dance when yee have done.
If than, sir, the man, sir,
Like of your mirth hee may;
And speare first, and heare first,
What he himselfe will say.'

67

Then altogether they began
And said, 'Come on, thou martyrde man,

What is thy will, advise.'
Abasde° a bony while° I stood — *Dejected; fair time*
And musde ere I mine answere made.
I turnd me once or twise,
Beholding everyone about,
Whose motions mov'd me maist.
Some seem'd assured, some dread for doubt,
Will ran red-wood for haist,° — *mad with rage*
With wringing and flinging
For madnes like to mang;° — *go frantic*
Despare too, for care too,
Would needs himselfe goe hang.

68

Which, when Experience perceiv'd,
Quoth he, 'Remember, if I rav'de
As Will allegde of late,
When, as he swore, nothing he saw
In age but anger, slack° and slaw° — *untrustworthy; spineless*
And cankred in conceite,° — *corrupt in mind*
Ye could not lucke° as alledgde, — *succeed*
Who all opinions spearde,
Hee was so frack° and firie edg'd, — *bold*
He thought us foure but feard.° — *(were) simply afraid*
"Who panses what chanses,"° — *ponders over fortune*
Quoth hee, "no worship° wins; — *honour*
To some best, shal come best,
Who hap wel, rack well rins."[32]

69

'Yet,' quoth Experience, ' behold,
For all the tales that ye have told,
How hee himselfe behaves;
Because Despare could come no speed,
Loe, heere he hings all but the head,
And, in a widdy,° waves.° — *gallows' rope; sways*
If you be sure, once thou may see,
To men that with them mels;° — *involve themselves*
If° they had hurt or helped thee — *Whether*
Consider°—by themsels.° — *Judge; their intrinsic natures*
Then chuse thee, to use thee
By us or such as yon;
Syne soone now, have done now,
Make° either off or on.' — *Do/Decide*

70

'Perceiv'st thou not, wherefra proceeds
The frantick fantasie that feeds

32. I.e. 'He who ventures wins'.

Thy furious flamming fire,
Which doth thy bailfull° brest combur,° *wretched; burn*
That none indeed,' quoth they,[33] 'can cure
Nor helpe thine hearts desire?
The piercing passions of the spreit,
Which wastes thy vitall breath,
Doth hold thine heavy heart with heate;
Desire drawes on thy death.
Thy punces pronunces° *pulses speak out against*
All kinde of quyet rest;
That fever hath ever
Thy person so opprest.

71

'Couldst thou come once acquaint with Skil,
Hee knowes what humours[34] doth thee ill
And how thy cares contraks;° *are incurred*
Hee knowes the ground of all thy griefe
And recipies of° thy reliefe; *prescriptions for*
All medicines hee maks.'
Quoth Skill, 'Come on, content am I
To put° mine helping hand, *provide*
Providing alwayes hee apply
To counsel and command.
While° wee, then,' quoth he then, *So long as*
'Are minded to° remaine, *intend to*
Give place now,° in cace now, *Give way*
Thou get us not againe.

72

'Assure thy selfe° if that we shed,° *Be sure; part*
Thou shalt not get thy purpose sped;° *aim achieved*
Take heede, wee have thee told.
Have done and drive not off the day;
The man that will not when he may,
He shal not when hee would.
What wilt thou doe, I would we wist:° *wish we knew*
Accept or give us ou'r?'
Quoth I,[35] 'I think me more than blest
To finde such famous foure
Beside mee, to guide mee,
Now when I have to doe;° *act*
Considering what swidering° *hesitating*
Ye found me first into.

33. The four counsellors speak/sing together at this point.
34. The four humours—sanguine, melancholic, choleric, phlegmatic—were held to influence behaviour, depending on which was dominant.
35. The poet here dissociates the total self ('I') from its personified constituents ('Hope', 'Despair' etc.).

73

'When Courage crav'd a stomack° stout — *(as seat of courage)*
And Danger drave mee into doubt
With his companion Dread;
Whiles° Wil would up above the aire, — *Now...*
Whiles° I am drownde in deep Despare, — *Now...*
Whiles Hope held up mine head.
Such pithie reasons and replies
On every side they shew,
That I, who was not very wise,
Thought all their tales were true.
So mony and bony,
Old problems they proponit,° — *proposed*
But quickly° and likely,° — *vitally; with feeling*
I marvell meekle° on it. — *greatly*

74

'Yet Hope and Courage wan the field,
Though Dread and Danger never yeeld,
But fled to finde refuge.
Yet when ye foure came, they were faine° — *glad*
Because ye gart them° come againe; — *caused them (to)*
They griende° to get you judge. — *agreed*
Where they were fugitive before,
Yee made them frank and free
To speak and stand in aw no more.'
Quoth Reason, 'So should bee.
Oft-times now, but crymes° now, — *without accusations*
But even, perforce, it fals° — *(still) falls out that*
The strong ay, with wrong ay,
Puts weaker to the wals,

75

'Which is a fault, ye must confesse;
Strength was not ordained to oppresse
With rigour by the right,
But, by the contrare, to sustaine
The loaden, which ou'rburthend beene,[36]
As meckle° as they might.' — *much*
'So Hope and Courage did,' quoth I,
'Experimented like,° — *Similarly taught by experience*
Show skilde and pithy reasons why
That Danger lap the dyke.'° — *ditch/turf wall*
Quoth Dreid, 'Sir, take heed, sir;
Long spoken part must spill;° — *(Too) long a plea must fail*
Insist not, we wist not
Ye went against our will.

36. See Matthew 11. 28–30.

76

'With Courage ye were so content,
Ye never sought our smal consent;
Of us ye stood not aw.° *in awe*
Then Logick lessons ye allowit
And was determined to trow it;° *believe it to be true*
Alleageance past for law.[37]
For all the proverbs wee perusde,
Yee thought them skantly skild° *poorly framed*
Our reasons had been as well rusde,° *concocted*
Had ye beene as well wil'de° *favourably inclined*
To our side, as your side;
So truely I may tearme it;
I see now, in thee now,
Affection doth affirm't.'° *determine it (choice)*

77

Experience then smirking smilde.
'We are no bairnes° to be beguild,' *children*
Quoth he and shooke his head;
'For authors who alledges° us, *cite*
They stil would win about the bus° *bush*
To foster deadly feede;° *feuding*
For wee are equal for you all,
No persons wee respect.
We have been so, are yet and shall
Be found so in effect.
If we were, as ye were,
We had comde unrequyrde;
But wee now, ye see now,
Doe nothing undesirde.

78

'There is a sentence said by some,
"Let none uncald to counsell come,
That welcome weines° to bee." *hopes*
Yea, I have heard another yit,
"Who came uncald, unserv'd shuld sit."
Perhaps, sir, so may yee.'
'Goode man, grande mercie° for your gecke,'° *thank you; taunt*
Quoth Hope and lowly lowts;° *bows*
'If yee were sent for, we suspect,
Because the doctours doubts,
Your yeares now, appeares now
With wisedome to be vext,
Rejoycing, in gloysing,° *glossing*
Till you have tint° your text. *obscured*

37. 'Allegation assumed the place of legal right.'

79

'Where yee were sent for, let us see
Who would be welcomer than wee.
Prove that and we are payde.'
'Wel,' quoth Experience, 'beware;
You know not in what case you are;
Your tongue hath you betrayde.
The man may ablens°[38] tine a stot° — *perhaps; lose an ox*
Who cannot count his kinch.° — *cannot count up his cattle*
In your owne bow you are ou'rshot
By more then halfe an inch.
Who wat, sir, if that, sir,
Is sowre which seemeth sweet;
I feare now, ye heare now,
A dangerous decreete.° — *decree*

80

'Sire, by that sentence yee have said,
I pledge ere all the play° be plaid — *game*
That some shall lose a laike.° — *stake*
Since yee but put me for to prove,
Such heads° as help for my behove,° — *points; need (behoof)*
Your warrand° is but waike;° — *warrant; weak*
Speare at the man youre selfe and see,
Suppose you strive for state,
If hee regrated not how hee
Had learned my lesson late;
And granted, hee wanted° — *lacked*
Both Reason, Wit and Skill,
Compleaning° and meaning° — *Bemoaning; lamenting*
Our absence did him ill.

81

'Confront him further face for face,
If yet hee rewes° his rackles° race, — *regrets; reckless*
Perhaps and ye shall heare.
For ay since Adam and since Eve,
Who first thy leasings° did believe — *lies*
I sold thy doctrine deare.
What hath beene done even to this day
I keepe in minde almaist;
Ye promise further than ye pay,
Sir Hope, for all your haste.
Promitting,° unwitting, — *Promising*
Your heghts° yee never hooked;° — *promises; recorded*
I show you, I know you,
Your bygones° I have booked.° — *history; recorded*

38. ED. ablens] WII; able Wr.

82

'I would, incace a count° were crav'd, *account*
Shew thousand thousands thou deceivde,
Where thou was true to one;
And by the contrare I may vant,° *boast*
Which thou must (though it grieve thee) grant,
I trumped° never a man, *deceived*
But truely told the naked trueth
To man that meld° with mee: *mixed*
For neither rigour nor for rueth,
But onely loath to lie.
To some yet, to come yet,
Thy succour shall be slight;
Which I then, must try then
And register it right.'

83

'Ha, ha!' quoth Hope and loudly leugh;° *laughed*
'Ye'r but a prentise° at the pleugh,° *apprentice; plough*
Experience yee prieve.
Suppose all bygones as yee spacke,° *stated*
Ye are no prophet worth a plack,° *farthing*
Nor I bound to believe.
Yee should not say, sir, till yee see,
But when ye see it, say.'
'Yet,' quoth Experience, 'at thee
Make many mints° I may: *attempts*
By sings° now, and things now, *signs*
Which ay before mee beares,
Expressing, by gessing,
The perill that appeares.'

84

Then Hope replyde, and that with pith,° *forcefully*
And wisely weigh'd his words therewith,
Sententiously and short;
Quoth hee, 'I am the anchor grip,
That saves the sailers and their ship
From perill to their port.'
Quoth hee,° 'Oft times that anchor drives, *i.e. Experience*
As wee have found before,
And loses many thousand lives
By shipwrack on the shore.
Your grips oft but slips oft,
When men have most to doe,
Syne leaves° them, and reaves° them *deserts; steals from*
Of my companion too.'

85

'Thou leaves them not thy selfe alone,
But to their griefe when thou art gone

Gars° Courage quite° them als.'° *Make; abandon; also*
Quoth Hope, 'I would ye understood.
I grip fast if the ground be good,
And fleets° where it is false. *shift my ground*
There should no fault with mee be found,
Nor I accusde at all.
Wyte° such as should have sound° the ground, *Blame; sounded (lit.)*
Before the anchor fall.
Their leed° ay, at neede ay, *lead (ship's)*
Might warne them if they would;
If they there, would stay there,
Or have good anchor-hold.

86

'If yee read right, it was not I,
But onely Ignorance whereby
Their carvels° all were cloven.° *light vessels; split*
I am not for a trumper tane.'° *held to be a deceiver*
'All,' quoth Experience, 'is ane;
I have my processe° proven, *case*
To wit, that we were cald each one,
To come before wee came;
That now objection ye have none,
Your selfe may say the same.
Ye ar now, too farre now
Come forward for to flee;
Perceive then, ye have then
The worst end of the tree.'

87

When Hope was gald into the quick,° *hurt to the quick*
Quoth Courage, kicking at the prick,° *i.e. reacting violently*
'Wee let you well to wit:° *We give you due warning*
Make hee you welcomer than wee,
Then bygones bygones, farewell he,
Except hee seeke us yit.
Hee understands his own estate,° *position*
Let him his chiftanes chuse;[39]
But yet his battel will bee blate,° *hard*
If hee our force refuse.
Refuse us, or chuse us,
Our counsel is hee clim;° *that he should climb*
But stay° hee, or stray hee, *delay*
We have none help for him.

88

'Except the Cherrie be his chose,° *choice*
Bee ye his friend, wee are his foes;

39. Leading combatants. Courage is thinking in terms of a battle decided by single combat between representative warriors for either side.

His doings° we despite.° *behaviour; despise*
If we perceive him satled sa° *thus inclined*
To satisfie him with the Slae,
His company we quite!'° *leave/quit*
Then Dread and Danger grew so glad,
And wont° that they had wun; *thought*
They thought all seald,° that they had said *agreed under seal*
Sen° they had first begun. *Since*
They thought then, they mought then
Without a partie plead[40]
But yet there, with Wit there,
They were dung° downe indeed. *knocked*

89

'Sirs Dread and Danger,' then quoth Wit,
'Ye did yourselves to mee submit;
Experience can prove.'
'That,' quoth Experience, 'I past.° *confirmed*
Their owne confession made them fast,° *entrapped them*
They may no more remove;° *shift ground (of case)*
For, if I right remember mee,
This maxime then they made,
To wit: "The man with Wit should wey
What philosophs had said." '
Which sentence, Repentance
Forbade him deare to buy.
They knew then, how true then,
And preasde not° to reply. *did not rush*

90

Though hee dang° Dread and Danger down, *knocked*
Yet Courage could not overcome,
Hope heght° him such an hyre;° *promised; reward*
Hee thought himselfe, so soone he saw
His enemies were laid so law,
It was no tyme to tyre.
Hee hit the yron while it was hait,
Incace it might grow cold;
For he esteemde his foes defaite,° *defeated*
When once he found them folde.° *having given way*
'Though we now,' quoth hee now,
'Have beene so free and franke,
Unsought yet, ye mought yet,
For kindnesse cund° us thanke. *experienced*

91

'Suppose it so as thou hast said,
That unrequyrde wee offered aide,

40. I.e. 'Plead their case without an opposing case being put forward.'

At least it came of° love. *derived from*
Experience, yee start too soone:
Yee dow nothing while° all be done, *until*
And then perhaps yee prove
More plaine than pleasant, too, perchance;
Some tell that have you tryit,° *tested*
As fast as you your selfe advance,
Ye dow not wel deny it.
Abide then, your tide then,
And waite upon the wind;
Ye know sir, ye ow° sir, *must*
To hold you ay behinde.

92

'When yee have done some doughty deeds,
Syne ye should see how all succeeds,
To write them as they were.'
'Friend, huly,° haste not halfe so fast, *slowly*
Lest,' quoth Experience, 'at last,
Ye buy my doctrine deare.
Hope puts that haste into your head,
Which boyles your barmie° braine. *frothy*
Howbeit fooles haste, comes hulie speede,° *success comes slowly*
Faire heights make fooles be faine;° *glad*
Such smyling, beguiling,
Bids feare not for no freets;° *omens*
Yet I now, deny now,
That al is gold that gleets.° *glitters*

93

'Suppose not silver all that shines,
Ofttimes a tentlesse° merchant tines° *careless; experiences a loss*
For buying geare° be gesse;° *goods; by guess(ing)*
For all the vantage and the winning,
Good buyers gets at the beginning.'
Quoth Courage, 'Not the lesse,
Whiles as good merchant tines as wins,
If old mens tales be true;
Suppose the pack come to pins,[41]
Who can his chance es[c]hew?° *avoid his fate*
Then, good sir, conclude, sir,
Good buyers have done baith;
Advance then, take chance then,
As sundry good ships hath.

94

'Who wist what would bee cheape or deare
Should neede to traffique but a year,

41. ED. Most editors insert 'the' before pins, but a pause after 'suppose' keeps the rhythm without emendation. The proverb means, 'Suppose he dissipates his wealth.'

If things to come were kend;
Suppose all bygone things be plaine,
Your prophecy is but prophane,° *profane/blasphemous*
Ye're best behold the end.
Yee would accuse mee of a crime
Almost before wee met;
Torment you not before the time,
Since dolour payes no debt.
What by past, that I past,
Ye wot if it was well;
To come yet, by doome° yet, *judgment*
Confesse ye have no feele.'° *instinctive idea*

95

'Yet,' quoth Experience, 'what than?
Who may be meetest° for the man, *most appropriate*
Let us his answere have.'
When they submitted them to mee,
To Reason I was faine to flee,
His counsell for to crave.
Quoth he, 'Since you yourselves submit
To doe as I decreet,° *ordain*
I shall advise with Skil and Wit,
What they thinke may be meete.'° *suitable*
They cryde then, 'We byde° then *remain*
At Reason for refuge;
Allow him, and trow him,
As governour and judge.'

96

So said they all with one consent,
'What° he concluds we are content, *Whatever*
His bidding to obey;
Hee hath authority to use,
Than take his chose whom he would chuse
And longer not delay.'
Then Reason rose and was rejoysde;
Quoth he, 'Mine hearts, come hither!
I hope this play° may bee composde° *quarrel; resolved*
That we may goe together.
To all now, I shall now
His proper place assigne;
That they heere, shal say heere,
They thinke none other thing.

97

'Come on,' quoth he, 'companion Skill,
Ye understand both good and ill;
In physick° yee are fine. *medicine*
Be medciner° unto this man *doctor*

And shaw such cunning° as yee can, *knowledge*
To put him out of paine.
First, gard° the ground° of all his griefe, *pay attention to; root*
What sicknes ye suspect;
Syne looke what hee lackes for reliefe,
Ere further he infect.
Comfort him, exhort him,
Give him your good advice;
And panse° not, nor skanse° not, *ponder; consider*
The perill nor the price.

98

'Though it be cumbersome what recke?° *matter*
Finde out the cause by the effect
And working of his veines.
Yet, while we grip it to the ground,
See first what fashion may bee found
To pacifie his paines.
Doe what ye dow to have him haile
And for that purpose prease;° *strive*
Cut off the cause, the effect must faile,
So all his sorrowes cease.
His fever shall never
From thencefoorth have no force;
Then urge him, to purge him,
He will not waxe° the worse.' *grow*

99

Quoth Skil, 'His senses are so sicke,
I know no liquor worth a leeke
To quench his deadly drouth;
Except the Cherrie help his heat,
Whose sappy sloking° sharp and sweet, *juicy quenching*
Might melt into his mouth,
And his melancholy remove,[42]
To mitigate his minde.
None wholesomer for your behove,
Nor more cooling of kinde;
No nectar directar
Could all the gods him give;
Nor send him to mend him,
None like it, I believe,

100

'For drouth decayes° as it digests.'° *Since thirst declines; is slaked*
'Why then,' quoth Reason, 'nothing rests° *remains (to be decided)*
But how it° may bee had.'° *i.e. cherry; gained*
'Most true,' quoth Skil. 'That is the scope,

42. A return to the theory of the humours. See n. 33.

Yet we must have some helpe of Hope.'
Quoth Danger, 'I am rad,° *advised*
His hastines breeds us mishap,
When he is highly horst;° *on his high horse*
I would wee looked ere wee lap.'
Quoth Wit, 'That were not worst.
I meane now, conveene now
The counsell one and all;
Begin then, cal on then.'
Quoth Reason, 'So I shall.'

101

Then Reason rose with gesture grave,
Belyve° conveening all the lave° *At once; rest*
To see what they would say;
With silver scepter in his hand,
As chiftane chosen to command
And they bent to obey.
He pansed° long before he spake *reflected*
And in a study stood;
Syne hee began and silence brake:
'Come on,' quoth he, 'conclude!
What way now, we may now,
Yon Cherrie come to catch;
Speak out sirs, about sirs,
Have done, let us dispatch.'

102

Quoth Courage, 'Scourge him first that skars;° *takes fright*
Much musing memory but marres.'
'I tell you mine intent,'
Quoth Wit. 'Who will not partly panse° *give some thought*
In perils, perishes perchance,
Ou'r rackles° may repent.' *(He who is) too reckless*
'Then,' quoth Experience, and spake:
'Sir, I have seene them baith,
In braidiness°[43] and lye aback° *recklessness; laggardliness*
Escape and come to skaith.°[44] *injury*
But what now, of that now?
Sturt° followes all extreames. *Vexation/strife*
Retaine then, the meane then,
The surest way it seemes.[45]

103

'Where some hes further'd, some hes faild,
Where part hes perisht, part prevaild,

43. ED. braidiness] Eds; braidieness Ramsay 1724; bairnliness Wr.
44. ll. 8–10: Experience balances earlier arguments of Courage and Wit. The general sense is, 'Sir, I have seen both reckless and over-cautious behaviour, avoiding and hurtling towards injury.'
45. Reconfirmation of the doctrine of the mean.

Alike all cannot lucke.° *be equally fortunate*
Then either venture with the one
Or, with the other, let alone
The Cherrie for to plucke.'
Quoth Hope, 'For feare folke must not fash.' *worry*
Quoth Danger, 'Let not light.'° *Do not lightly refrain*
Quoth Wit, 'Bee neither rude nor rash.'
Quoth Reason, 'Yee have right.'
The rest then, thought best then,
When Reason said it so,
That roundly and soundly,
They should together goe,

104
To get the Cherrie in all haste,
As for my safety serving maist—
Though Dread and Danger feard
The peril of that irksome way—
Lest that thereby I should decay
Who then so weake appearde.
Yet, Hope and Courage hard beside,
Who with them wont contend,° *usually fought with*
Did take in hand us for to guide
Unto our journeyes end;
Impleadging° and waidging° *Guaranteeing; staking*
Both two their lives for mine,
Providing the guiding
To them were granted syne.° *directly afterwards*

105
Then Dread and Danger did appeale,
Alledging it could not be well,
Nor yet would they agree.
But said they should sound their retreate,
Because they thought them no wise meete° *fitting*
Conductores° unto mee, *Guides*
Nor to no man in mine estate° *condition*
With sicknes sore opprest;
For they tooke ay the nearest gate,° *way*
Omitting oft the best.
'Their nearest, perquearest,° *most exactly*
Is alwayes to them baith,
Where they sir, may say sir,
What recks them of° your skaith?° *do they care about; injury*

106
'But as for us two, now we sweare
By him before whom we appeare:
Our ful intent is now
To have you whole° and alway was, *entire/cured*

That purpose for to bring to passe—
So is not theirs I trow.'
Then Hope and Courage did attest
The gods of both these parts,° *upper and under world*
If they wrought not all for the best
Of mee with upright hearts.
Our chiftane than liftane° *then raising*
His scepter did enjoyne,
'No more there, uproare there!'
And so their strife was done.

107
Rebuiking Dread and Danger sore—
Suppose they meant well evermore
To me as they had sworne—
Because their neighbours they abusde,
In so farre as they had accusde
Them, as ye heard beforne.
'Did ye not else,' quoth he, 'consent
The Cherry for to pow?'
Quoth Danger, 'We are well content;
But yet the maner how?
We shal now, even all now,
Get this man with us there.
It restis and best is
Your counsel shall declare.'

108
'Wel said,' quoth Hope and Courage. 'Now,
We thereto will accord with you
And shall abide by them;
Like as before we did submit,
So wee repeate the samine° yit, *same*
We minde° not to reclaime.° *intend; protest*
Whom they shal chuse to guide the way,
Wee shal him follow straight,
And further° this man what we may° *aid; however we can*
Because wee have so height.° *promised*
Promitting, but flitting,° *without changing position*
To doe the thing we can
To please both and ease both,
This silly,° sickly man.' *feeble*

109
When Reason heard this, 'Then,' quoth hee,
'I see your chiefest stay° to bee, *main hindrance*
That wee have nam'd no guide;
The worthy counsel hath, therefore,
Thought good that Wit should goe before
For perils to provide.'

Quoth Wit, 'There is but one of three,
Which I shall to you show,
Whereof the first two cannot bee
For any thing I know.
The way heere, to stay° heere *too steep*
Is, that wee cannot clim
Even ou'r now, we foure now;
That will bee hard for him.

110

'The next, if we goe downe about,
While that this bend° of craiges run out *incline*
The streame is there so starke,
And also passeth wading deepe
And broader farre than we dow leape,
It should be idle wark.° *useless endeavour*
It growes ay broader nere the sea,
Sen over the lin° it came; *waterfall*
The running dead[46] doth signifie
The deepnes of the same.
I leave now, to deave° now, *annoy (with talk)*
How that it swiftly slides,
As sleeping and creeping,
But nature so provides.

111

Our way then lyes about the lin,
Whereby a warrand° we shal win, *warrant/secure place*
It is straight and plaine;
The water also is so shald,° *shallow*
We shal it passe° even as we wald *cross*
With pleasure and but paine.
For as we see the mischief grow,
Oft of a feckles° thing. *futile*
So, likewise doth this river flow
Fourth of a pretty spring,
Whose throat, sir, I wot sir,
You may stop with your neive;° *fist*
As you, sir, I trow, Sir
Experience can prieve.'° *vouch for*

112

'That,' quoth Experience, 'I can.
All that yee said sen yee began,
I know to be of truth.'

46. 'The course of death.' The image evokes Dante's depiction of dead souls being ferried across the rivers of the Underworld. The theological sense of the poem teaches that divine grace is offered after death. This does not negate the romantic and moral lessons of the poem; it adds another, transcendant, perspective within an accretive allegory.

Quoth Skill, 'The samine I approve.'
Quoth Reason, 'Then let us remove
And sleepe no more in sleuth.° *slothfulness*
Wit and Experience,' quoth he,
'Shall come before apace;
The man shall come with Skill and mee
Into the second place.
Attour° now, you foure now, *Across*
Shall come into a band;
Proceeding and leading
Each other by the hand.'

113

As Reason ordeinde all obeyde;
None was ou'r rash, nor none affraide—
Our counsel was so wise.
As of our journey Wit did note,
We found it true in every jote;° *detail*
God bles'd our interprise;° *enterprise*
For, even as wee came to the tree,
Which (as yee heard me tell)
Could not be clum—there, suddenly,
The fruite for ripenes fell.
Which hasting and tasting,
I found my selfe relievde
Of cares all and sares° all, *griefs/pains*
Which mind and body grievde.

114

Praise be to God, my Lord, therefore,
Who did mine health to mee restore,
Being so long time pinde.° *punished*
Yea, blessed bee His holy name,
Who did from death to life recleame
Mee, who was so unkinde.° *unnatural*[47]
All nations also magnifie
This everliving Lord.
Let me with you and you with mee,
To laude° Him ay accord. *praise*
Whose love ay, wee prove ay
To us above all things;
And kisse Him and blesse Him,
Whose glore eternall rings.° *reigns*

47. This is the conventional idea of man being out of tune with the law of nature (kynde) and so unable to read God's benevolent intentions correctly.

§ 17: John Stewart of Baldynneis (?1550–?1605): *Roland Furious*

John Stewart specifically set out to be James VI's obedient poetic apprentice at the start of the Castalian movement. In part, he may have hoped that such obedience would result in political preferment. He was, after all, the son of James V's mistress, Elizabeth Betoun and, therefore, in a rather vulnerable position at court. If this were an aim, it was not achieved. Although he belonged to a noble family, was well educated and travelled widely, Stewart never gained the status of Fowler (Introduction § 18) or Alexander (Introduction § 23). He was even imprisoned during a bitter dispute between his mother and her second husband, Lord Gray. It would appear that he died in a pub-brawl.

Stewart was, however, one of the most talented of the Castalians, ranging through a wide variety of lyrical forms and composing, in **Ane Schersing out of Trew Felicitie**, *a Scottish version of the spiritual journey form.* **Roland Furious** *remains his most ambitious work. Based on Ariosto's* **Orlando Furioso**, *but relying on intermediary French sources, it seeks to simplify and moralize the original Italian epic. The first of the chosen extracts (from* **Canto 5***) discusses this methodology. The second (***Canto 11***), constitutes the poem's dramatic climax —the madness of Roland/Orlando.*

Context: *Broadly, the twelve Cantos are concerned with the power of love to overwhelm reason. The amorous adventures of Roland and the heroine (Angelique/Angelica) are for the most part kept separate in Stewart's version. Only Canto 7 draws them together evenhandedly. Angelique's attempts to preserve her chastity against the advances of various knights, an old hermit and even a monster, are the major topic of Cantos 2, 3 and 5. This line culminates with the proud noblewoman falling for an ordinary soldier, Medoro. Their meeting is idyllically described against a pastoral setting in Cantos 9 and 10. Stewart's reordering of Ariosto's material allows the hero's mad discovery of that trysting place, in Canto 11, to be at once the nadir of his tragic fall as traced in Cantos 1,4,6 and 8 and a contrast in chaos and barbarism to his lady's new-found harmony and charity. In the last, and the most original, of the twelve Cantos, Stewart shows Roland's 'maladie' being divinely cured.*

Roland Furious[1]

The Fifth Cant.[2]

[*Stewart opens this Canto with a brief comment on his techniques of 'abbregement'.*]

As painfull pilgrim, pressing to fulfill° — *striving to complete*
His irksum° journay, passing° to and fro — *tiresome; wandering*
In dririe nycht—so I, agains my will,
Dois stot° and stummer° in my mateir low.[3] — *stagger; stumble*

1. ED. COPY TEXT: *Nat Lib of Scotland MS Adv. 19.2.6. Roland* is an abridgement (with the help of French intermediary texts) of Ariosto's *Orlando Furioso*. 'Furious' may mean 'violent' or 'mad'. For Ariosto's hero, as the second extract confirms, the combination of both senses is apposite. The paragraphing of the texts is editorial but coincides with the ballat royal stanzaic structure. See. n. 7.
2. Stewart presented the manuscript, which contains *Roland* and a group of lyrics, as a personal present to James VI. In it, he vowed 'to becum your hienes scholler' out of admiration for the king's precepts, as expressed in the *Reulis and Cautelis* and *The Essayes of a Prentise* generally. The word 'Cant'—a hybrid between Italian 'Canto' and French 'Chant'—may be an (unhappy) attempt to follow the king's critical practice of adopting Franco-Scottish coinages into his Literary Theory.
3. The sense, as in the Dedication, is that the topic is too 'mightie' for his own limited skills so he sinks deep ('low') into it.

I haif no way° quhairbe derect to go, — *means*
But (as the wycht,° quho wanders wilsum° blind) — *person; wilfully*
This work of myn behuifs me schers° it so, — *forces me to search through*
Quhyls heir, quhyls thair, quhyls fordwart and behind.
The historie all interlest° I find[4] — *interlaced*
With syndrie sayings of so great delyt,
That singlie, most I from the rest out spind,[5]
As the unskilful prentes imperfyt,°[6] — *imperfect apprentice*
Quho fyns° the gould frie from the laton quyt.° — *refines; white lead (alchemy)*
No wonder thocht° my wittis waver will, — *if*
In flowing field of sic profound indyt° — *(a) deep work*
My minschit° meitir may bot mank° and spill.°[7] — *chopped up; fall short; waste*
Yit, as the painter stairing stedfast still,
With trimbling hand, his dracht° perfyt to draw, — *design*
So indevoir° I with my sklender skill — *endeavour*
For to do better than my breath may blaw.[8]
Accept guid will, for I guid will sall schaw
To fram so furth as I haif done intend.[9]

The Eleventh Cant.

[*The hero Roland (Orlando) is searching for his enemy Mandricard (Mandricardo). By chance he enters the grove where his lady Angelique (Angelica) has recently been wooed and won by the young Moor, Medor (Medoro). Discovering the evidence of their affair, the hero literally becomes 'furious' or 'violent in madness'. Cf. Ariosto,* Orlando Furioso, *Canto 23.100–Canto 24.13; Canto 29.57–64.*]

Major characters:

Roland (Orlando): Nephew to Charlemagne and leading warrior in his cause. Married to Aude (Alda), he falls in love with Angelique (Angelica).

Angelique (Angelica): Daughter of Galafron, Emperor of Cathay, she is sent to Charlemagne's court to destroy it by captivating the leading warriors within it.

4. This is not necessarily a criticism of Ariosto's practice. Interlaced structures were popular in both Middle Ages and Renaissance.
5. 'That I had to tease single strands out from the rest.' Stewart will adopt different principles from Ariosto. He will simplify the story by teasing out the tales of Orlando and Angelica from the others. In doing this he relied on Desportes' earlier, simplified tales, *Roland* and *Angelique*.
6. A reference to the title (*Essayes of a Prentise*) in which James's *Reulis* were contained. Stewart took pride in being the apprentice's apprentice. His epic is preceded by an Address, an Introduction, a Dedication, an Invocation and two lyrics, all of which establish his unworthiness as a writer in contrast to the brilliance of James.
7. ll. 15–16. James uses 'flowing' to mean 'rhythm' generally and smooth musical rhythms specifically. Chopped up metre is, therefore, the antithesis of the 'flowing' ideal set out by the king. To translate the 'ottava rima' of the Italian Epic, Stewart chooses the eight line Scottish Ballat Royal Stanza as defined and exemplified in James's *Reulis* (§ 23). The king suggests its use for 'any heich and grave subjectis, specially drawin out of learnit authouris'. Stewart interlinks the stanzas, producing the rhyme scheme: *a—ababbcbc—cdcddede—e*.
8. The distinction is between spontaneous/aural and considered/written tale-telling.
9. 'To represent it in the same way as I conceived it.' Both the relationship between form and content, and the benevolent intention of the author (ll. 19–20) were crucial in Christian poetics.

Medor (Medoro): Young African soldier, with whom Angelica falls in love and whom she later marries.

(The Italian forms for character names are employed in the Notes and Glosses.)

Perplexit pen againe to paine° apply;	*i.e. tragic matters*
Denunce° the teirs that from thy dyt distels!°	*Convey; writing are distilled*
Now, for your ayde, Ramnusia[10] I cry,°	*call upon*
To reule arycht—the rancor intermels.[11]	
This trublous teine° my tyrit toung compels	*painful misery*
To dry for drouth,° that I may not declair°	*dry up for thirst; speak out*
Within this goulf,° quhair source of sorrow swels,	*ravine*
My sensis so suffuscat° ar with cair.	*suffocated*
Wold God, Bocace° mycht in my place repair,[12]	*Boccaccio*
This tragedie perfytelie to compyle,	
Or reverent Ovid wold the sammyng spair°	*spare (time to do) the same*
In metamorphois of° his steitlie° style;	*By varying; dignified*
For, lyk as myrth dois mak the visage smyle,	
Or plesand lycht rejosis moir the ie	
Than deip perbrouilyeit° dungeons dark and vyle,	*boiled up (i.e. bubbling)*
So wanton° verse moir aptlie dois aggrie	*loose (metrically)*
To pouse° the pithles° spreit with sum supplie,	*encourage; weak*
Quhilk I posses—laiking the curius vaine°—	*elegant vein (poetic)*
Than° mirthles mateirs that amazis° me	*(More) than; astound*
And doubill duls my dolorus, dullit braine.[13]	
Yit, sen the burding° dois on me remaine	*burden*
To sport° my prence,[14] quhois courtasie bening	*celebrate*
May mak me aide, as meed° the gowldin graine,[15]	*did*
Quhilk did Eneas to his journay bring,	
I indevoir the remanent° to sing	*remainder*
Of Rolands fall in furie° at the last.	*violent madness*
Help at this neid, O greizlie ghests maling,°	*ghastly malign spirits*
With spedie pen to mak this propose past,°	*bring this purpose to an end*
Compact in breiff this bailfull bittir blast°	*time/blow*
Quhilk dois my style renverse° in disaray	*overturn*
And all my sensis na les maks agast	
Than Nabuchadnosors great decay.[16]	

10. I.e. Nemesis, the avenger, who was believed to come from Rhamnus in northern Attica.
11. ll. 3–4 One sense of these lines could be, 'Now I call upon your help Ramnusia, (for) rancour intervenes in my attempts to gain proper control of my verse.'
12. ll. 9–12. Boccaccio's *De Casibus Virorum Illustrium* and *De Claris Mulieribus* deal with the tragic fall of heroes and heroines as do Ovid's *Metamorphoses*. Canto 11 charts the extreme fall of Orlando from heroism into madness and, as such, is a fine example of the mode.
13. ll. 13–20. He finds comic topics easier to write than tragic or pitiful ones.
14. James VI. Stewart is not above interrupting his tale to praise his patron.
15. ll. 23–4. The golden bough of knowledge allowed Aeneas to enter the underworld (*Aeneid* Book VI).
16. ll. 32–152. Stewart may abridge the story told by Ariosto but he also introduces a good deal of literary, moral and theological commentary. This long list of tragic types is not present in *Orlando Furioso*. Such authoritative universalising is, however, essential to Stewart's more overtly allegorical reworking. Nebuchadnezzar's fall into bestiality is recorded in Daniel 4. 33.

The monarck Ninus,[17] that in preson lay
Of croune bereft and captive to the deed;° *until death*
The puissant Cyrus, King of Perse, I say,
Quho vincust° Cresus, syn° did lose his heed; *conquered; then*
Great Alexander, poysand but remeed;° *without cure*
Nor mychtie Cesar, quho was schortlie° slaine, *quickly*
Skairse represents so lairge° of Fortouns feed,° *broadly; enmity*
As our Comte Roland, quho did lose his braine.
O, frivole Fortoune, fikile, false and vaine!
Quhy dois thou vex this world with sic annoy?
Thou hich exalts, law to deject° againe *cast down*
Thy quheile,° ay tumbling° with decetfull toy;° *wheel; causing to fall; trifle*
All that suppons° maist suirlie° till injoy, *who suppose; confidently*
Thy hautie, wavering hairis with the wind,
With subtile smyle oft tyms thou dois distroy
And for reward presents thy pow° behind.[18] *bald head*
No force avails, thy fikilnes to bind;
Dame Indiscreit,° I sute of° the no grace, *Lady Haphazard; seek from*
Thou art my fo, for I culd nevir find
No kynd of favor in thy fenyeit° face. *deceitful*
His majestie hes power in this cace
With sweit regarde, thy sournes till assuadge,
Quhois royale feit maist humylie° I imbrace *humbly*
To saif me from thy rancor and thy radge.
Thy course inconstant in till everie adge
Pruife dois record, thocht I not specefie:
Great Bajacet[19] that Turk thou did incadge° *encage/imprison*
Quhom Tamberlan maist duilfullie meed drie° *endure*
Ane extreme slavrie till that he did die;
The one thou did from bass° estait avance *low*
And dang° the uther doune from hich degrie, *struck*
So is the coustume of thy fatall° chance. *fateful/fatal*
For to record that potent King of France,[20]
Quho in the sporting of his manlie spreit
Unto the deed wes percit with ane lance,
Is pruife that thou in variance dois fleit.° *change ground*
King Alexander is exemple meit,° *fitting*
Quho reuld above the antique° Scottis keine;° *ancient; bold*
The hardie force quhairwith he was repleit,
Nor yit the prudence quhilk did in him scheine,
Could not eschew° the rigor of thy teine° *avoid; rage*

17. ll. 33–8. Male types of tragic fall. *Ninus*, the mythical founder of Nineveh, was murdered by his wife Semiramis; *Cyrus*, King of Persia, was beheaded after defeat by Tomyris, queen of the Massagetae; *Julius Caesar* was slain by conspirators. *Alexander* died of fever but among rumours that he had been poisoned by Antipater or Olympias.
18. ll. 46–8. Fortune is now imagined as the goddess, Occasio. She had long hair in front to prevent identification and no hair behind, so that she could not be caught.
19. ll. 59–61 Bajazet I, was defeated by Tamburlaine (l. 60) in 1402. This transfer of power in the Ottoman Empire shows the contrasted effects of good and bad fortune.
20. ll. 65–76 Henri II of France, who died during a tournament in 1559, and Alexander III of Scotland (see n. 21), show Fortune's ability to strike when least expected.

But creuallie, be the,° he was forlorn — *because of you*
In p[r]icking° of his horse, as mycht be seine — *spurring*
Above the rock thair situat at Kingorn.[21]
For, as the rose annexit to the thorn,
So is thy plesour with sum paine prepaird;
Or, as the wyde increscis with° the corn, — *weed multiplies along with*
So thou perturbs the cheifest but regaird.° — *the noblest one regardless*
Quho walks at will within thy wavering yaird° — *erratic realm*
And dois delyt° to smell thy suggurit° gall, — *delights; sugared/sweet*
With suddan storm his stait sall not be spaird,
Bot as Pompey or hardie Hanniball[22]
So sall occur in fin° thair fatale fall. — *at the end*
The strong redouttit, dochtie° Darius, — *redoubtable*
Quho lang° did dant° his mychtie nychtbours all — *for a long time; subdued*
Be venim of thy visage varius,
Quhan force of fois he fand contrarius,° — *in opposition*
New battell thryse he bauldlie did conveine,
Bot ruittit out he was as° Arius. — *as was*
First, did he lose his kingdome and his queine,
His mother, guids and childrine all was seine
In the possession of his enemie;
Syn lost his lyf and mycht na wayis obteine
At his last breath so meikile laser frie° — *spare time*
As native freind or serviteur to sie,
Bot in his chariot, wondit to the deed,° — *mortally wounded*
He thocht it° did his painfull spreit supplie, — *believed it (Fortune)*
Quhan till his fo his last regrait° he meed. — *lamentation*
Queine Semerame,[23] thou lang did welthie leed,
Quha in hir courage disaguisde hir kynd° — *(female) nature*
Bot all thy favor turnit in to feed,° — *feud/emnity*
At her last battell with the King of Ynd.° — *i.e. Stabrobates*
Dame Panthasile, quhais high magnanime mynd
Did thrall° the boldnes of the Grecians stout,° — *captivate; hardy*
Thocht for ane space thou° prosperus inclynd — *(Fortune)*
With blast of fame to sound hir praisis out,
In tragedie alwayis thou brocht about° — *around/full circle*
Hir proud attempt and mychtie mundan° gloir; — *worldly*
Scho and hir ladies, all that seimlie rout° — *band*
Did vincust° die, quhilk dewlie° I deploir. — *vanquished; fittingly*
Zenobia, quham beuteis did decoir,° — *did adorn*
Hir profund prudence nor hir hardie hand
Mycht not resist thy malice onie moir

21. Alexander III was thrown to his death by his horse at Kinghorn in 1286.
22. ll. 84–100: Pompey, Hannibal and—as major example—Darius (ll. 86–100) are, respectively, Roman, Carthaginian and Persian illustrations of Fortune suddenly deserting long-favoured leaders. Arius (l. 91), driven into exile by the Nicene Council, provides the Christian complement to the pagan examples.
23. ll. 101–24. The first female example of unexpected misfortune, Semiramis, was the wife of Ninus (l. 33). This brings the reader full circle. The Amazon queen, Panthasile, died in war against the Greeks; Zenobia, Queen of Palmyra (major example; ll. 113–24), was defeated and humilated by the Romans under the Emperor Aurelian (l. 116).

Fra ans° scho did Aurelius gainstand,°	*From the time when; oppose*
Quha brocht hir captiv from hir native land	
And, till triumphe[24] above this cairfull° queine	*miserable*
Hir persone fixit at ane chariot band[25]	
And drew hir so throch Rome apertlie° seine.	*overtly/openly*
O crewall Fortoune, noysum° was thy teine;°	*harmful; rage*
Thocht scho presumd° all Asia to gyd,	*was presumptive enough*
Thy recompance maist freuch° and frivole° beine.	*brittle; fickle/of little worth*
So all are served that dois in the confyd.	
Thy slipprie solas° dois als schortlie slyd	*comfort*
As yse dissolves with flam of fervent fyre;	
Thy douce° delyt with dolor is devyd°—	*sweet; divided/mixed*
Quhan we belive to find our harts desyre	
With fikile fassone so thou dois impyre,°	*rule*
Quhill everie stait° may sie the facill flot:°[26]	*rank; easily drift around*
Thou gifs no gaine° to him quho merits hyre°	*profit; payment*
Bot at thy lust dois attribute the lot; [27]	
Thou maks the giltie sum tyme seime but spot°	*without stain*
And guid desert° in to the dust dings downe:°	*merit; (you) cast down*
Wit° walkith oft in till ane raggit cot°	*Common sense; coat (prov.)*
And Folie set up in ane velvet goune:	
Ane laird be the becums ane meschant lowne,°	*worthless servant*
Ane loune againe be the is meed ane laird,	
So in all thing thou art ay blindlie bowne°—	*blindly ready for action*
To rycht nor resone haifing no regaird.	
Thou rakles° rins as rasche and restles baird,°	*uncaringly; vagabond*
Both up and doune, befoir° and now abak;°	*in front; behind*
I knaw no puissant, erdlie pomp prepaird,	
Thy frivole frailnes firmlie to coak.°	*coerce*
Gif either wisdome, force or wordie fak°	*worthy deed*
Mycht haif rebellit, quhaire thy baile is boune,[28]	
Than° Roland haid, be the, susteind na lak°	*Then; suffered no set back*
Bot evir hichlie borne the palmie croune,°	*crown of palms/victor's wreath*
Quhom thy deceit degressis na les doune,°	*no less draws down*
Nor° Hector, traillit at° Achylles steid,°[29]	*Nor (would); dragged by; steed*
Was changeit° from that Hector of renoune,	*i.e. Have been changed*
Quho umquhyle reft° Achylles of his weid.°	*earlier deprived; armour*
Impolist° pen to propose° new proceid,	*Unpolished/Crude; purpose*
Returne to text and dyt of Roland rycht.[30]	

24. Two senses of 'triumphe' intermingle. Zenobia is paraded in a martial procession (or 'Triumph') in order to be publicly humilated ('triumphed over').
25. Zenobia was firmly positioned ('persone fixit') and then dragged behind the chariot.
26. Her drifting implies a lack of principles.
27. 'But deal out each individual fate according to your own desire.'
28. '(If Wisdom...) could have offered resistence at the point when your misery was ready to take off.'
29. Achilles dragged the body of Hector round the wall of Troy. This example parallels the case of Zenobia.
30. Although Stewart has deserted his sources ('text') and left the tale proper of Roland ('dyt of Roland rycht') his 'exemplary' introduction has carefully followed all the rhetorical rules set down for universalizing a topic in this way. This is, therefore, only a 'modesty topos' and not genuine humility.

He most induir° and I most schaw indeid	*must endure*
This alteration quhilk did on him lycht.°	*befell him*
Now eftir that this strong redouttit° knycht	*dreaded/respected/distinguished*
Be ampill pruife all uthers did precell,°	*surpass*
Quhill all the world abaisit of° his mycht,	*did reverence to*
At last in schersing° Mandricard[31] so fell°	*seeking out; cruel*
He sees ane christall revere° douce distell°	*river; fall in drops*
About the bordour of ane mydow fair,	
Quhair flouris fresche maist savoruslie did smell	
And monie seimelie, frondise° trie preclair°	*leafy; magnificent*
Obumbrat° all this situation° rair.	*Shadily surrounded; place*
Doune he desends amyds the blossoms greine	
For to refresche him in the temperat air,	
Sen dayis two he haid in travell beine	
In sutting° of the foirsaid Sarraseine.°	*pursuit; Saracen*
Bot heir depryvit was he of repois	
And all his confort turnit in to teine,°	*misery/suffering*
Quhan that his wofull eine haid done disclois°	*had been opened to*
The vive° handwreting of his onlie chois,°	*clear; choice (Angelica)*
Ingravit thair on monie growand graine;°[32]	*growing plants*
For this was even the veirray place formois,°	*lovely*
Quhair scho and Medor[33] wont was to remaine.	
In thousand wayis that part° did all explaine	*area*
Thair schypert° nams,[34] as I haif schawne befoir,	*intertwined*
Bot everie lettir bruist his bailful braine	
And percit throch his wondit hart als soir	
As duilfull deedlie dart him to devoir.°	*devour*
With monie wayis maist cairfullie he socht	
Till schift the sorrow that so did him schoir°	*threaten*
And not to credit sic ane noysum° thocht,	*grievous*
Efforcing him with feirfull spreit afflocht°	*distressed*
For to belive° that scho of hir guid grace	*To believe*
In his remembrance° haid thois wordis wrocht,°	*his own memory; carved*
Him so surnaming Medor in this place;	
Or that sum uther Angelique percace,°	*perchance*
So, in this sort,° haid done thair luif furthschaw.°	*manner; broadcast*
Not[35] full assuirit° was he yit alace,	*fully reassured*
For the characters° suirlie did he knaw	*i.e. her writing*
Quhilk his awne ladie usit ay to draw;	
Bot could nawayis him self belive at all.	
So with opinions he the treuth did thraw,°	*contest*
As doutfull trust did in his fancie° fall	*fancy/imagination*

31. Mandricardo became Orlando's enemy when that knight killed his father, Agrican. At this point, they have been separated and Orlando seeks out his foe—*Orlando Furioso*, Canto 23. 99ff. 'e dove meglio col pagan pensosse/di potersi incontrare, il destrier mosse.'
32. The lovers had carved poems and expressions of love on the trees in their woodland retreat.
33. Medoro is a young Moor of humble origin, who followed Prince Dardinello into the French wars.
34. The entire names, rather than the first letters only, are interlaced. Cf. l. 328.
35. ED. Not] ed; Bot MS.

Him self to suadge,° with sum assurance small. — *assuage*
Bot as hote collis with sum wattir cold
First seims to slaik,° yit eftirwart they sall — *quench/slake*
Upblais in fyre more ferventlie and bold,
Even so the moir that he extinguise wold
His glowing greif, the sam the moir did ryis.
As feltert° foule, quhilk glew° or girn° dois hold, — *entangled; birdlime; snare*
The moir scho flychters° scho the faster lyis, — *flutters*
The moir also that he did deip devyis
This mortall pansive° terror till eschew,° — *melancholy; escape*
The moir profound his paine did him suppryis,° — *attack*
Quhilk force nor wisdom mycht nawayis reskew.
In this estate,° approtching neir he drew — *state of mind*
Till the caverne above ane fontane cleir,
Quhair wodbind° and vyn brainchis linkit° threw — *woodbine; interlaced*
Ane plesand tortur at the entress° heir, — *entrance*
Decoring° all this proper part° so deir — *Adorning; particular spot*
To both the foirsaid luifers everie day;
For quhan fair Phebus° with his heit seveir — *i.e. the sun*
Did brymlie byrne,° heirin imbrast they lay; — *fiercely burn*
Quhairfoir thair nams both in and out I say
Heir drawne was ofter than in onie place
With cake,° with coll° and pensile sharp alway, — *chalk; charcoal*
Both heir and thair was schawne thair happie cace.
The cairful comte,° with sad dejectit face — *woeful count*
Ful monie luiflie dictums° heir did vew — *amorous sayings*
Be Medor wrocht, quhilks at the sammyng space
Als recent, fair and vivelie formit° schew — *clearly formed*
As instantlie° they haid beine forgit new. — *As if just then*
And for the fervent wonderful delyt
That heir did to this Adonis° insew, — *i.e. beautiful youth (Medoro)*
In verse he drew this subsequent indyt,° — *following poem*
Quhilk wretin was maist plainlie and perfyt
In his awne langage,° as I do suppois, — *i.e. Arabic*
Quhairof the sentence° I sall heir recyt, — *general content*
Thocht I exactlie may it not disclois.

'O herbis greine and prettie plants formois,° — *attractive*
O limpid wattir, springing suave° and cleir, — *pleasant*
O cave obscuir, aggriabill to thois
Quho wold tham cuile° in thy fresche umber° deir, — *cool themselves; shade*
Quhair Angelique maist beutifull but peir° — *peerless*
In vaine desyrd be uthers monie mo,
Oft nakit lay betwixt my armes heir.
I, Medor puir,° quhom ye haif eisit so — *poor*
May not requyt you moir; bot quhair I go
Your praise sall evir stedfastlie induir.
Lords, ladies, knychts and lustie luifers tho
And everie gentle hart, I will procuir
To wiss° you weill and frie of dainger suir. — *wish*

Both sone and mone and nymphs you saif from tort,°[36] — *wrong*
And nevir pastor°[37] *with his troup injuir* — *shepherd*
Your verduir ritche, O seimlie fair resort.
Bot ay about you, birdis blythlie sing,
And unmolestit be° *your silver spring.'* — *may be*

In toung Arabic wretin was this thing,
Quhilk langage Roland rycht expertlie knew,
And oft he red it contrarie,° to wring — *against the sense*
The veirray sentence° from the mening trew. — *desired message*
Bot ay the moir that he did so persew,
Moir plaine and ampill° did the text appeir, — *complete/fulsome*
Quhilk to the death his thirlit° hart neir threw.° — *enslaved; overthrew*
Assault of sorrow socht him so seveir
That staring, still, he stuid astonist heir
For wo almaist void of his wittis° all, — *out of his wits*
With havie fixit eis° and cairfull cheir — *sad staring eyes*
Upon the stone as sensles stonie wall;
His chin declyning on his brest did fall
And cloud of cair held doune° his cumlie front,° — *drew down; handsome brow*
Quhair left was no audacitie to brall° — *soar*
For boyling bail his boudin° braine haid blont.° — *grief-affected; blunted*
Great, egar° greif so grivous did surmount, — *sharp*
That he onnawayis° mycht relasche° his wo — *in no way; relax/relieve*
With wofull words, as umquhyle° he was wont; — *once*
Nor yit no teiris from his eine could go,
His liquid humor suffocat° was so,[38] — *stifled*
As quhan in veschell wyd° with narrow throt° — *broad vessel; throat/stem*
The wattir choks and may not flow thairfro
For great aboundance that dois in it flot.° — *flow*
No wonder now althocht his brest be blot° — *stained*
With dainger deip of deedlie duill in deid,
Bot yit his hoip could not dissolve the knot
Quhilk in his ladies° loyaltie did breid.° — *lady's; originate*
So with sum trust betosd° and meikill dreid° — *tossed about; much fear*
He scherst° his thochts to think this thocht untrew — *searched among*
(Quhairon his fancie for ane space did feid)
And ferventlie, dois wiss it till insew° — *follow (logically)*
That sum evilwiller all thois dictums° drew, — *statements*
For to diffame° his constant ladie frie,° — *defame; noble*
And, be sic bittir blame, his baile to brew,° — *to stoke up his misery*
That, suddanlie, quhan he the sam° suld sie, — *same*
For percing paine mycht at that instant die:
'O Lord,' sayis he, 'quhat vehement dispyt° — *animosity*
Hes he declaird, quhom evir so it be?

36. 'tort'—the many French coinages in Stewart's work (cf. 'renverse' l. 30; 'Obumbrat' l. 165) follow James's guidelines in the *Reulis*.
37. The pastoral motif in this section derives directly from Ariosto.
38. Psychologically, Orlando's well-balanced humours have become upset. The dry, hot humours now dominate, bringing melancholy and anger in their wake.

Weill imitat hes he hir hand° perfyt	*hand(writing)*
In drawing of this nochtie° noysum° dyt.'	*nasty; harmful*
So with this feibile esperance° at last	*weak hope*
Sum thing assuagit was his former fyt,°	*fit*
And thus againe on Bridedor[39] he past.°	*rode off*
The day declynd and nycht approtchit fast;	
Fair Tytans steids° haid rune thair utter° race,	*Titan's steeds; last (i.e. sunset)*
Quhois giltit hairs disparpling,° bak did cast°	*scattering; cast(themselves)*
Throche asurit° sky, quhilk elss° obscuird his face,	*azure-coloured; otherwise*
Till his palle sister Phebe[40] giffing place,	
Quhan that the pynit° paladeine[41] did tend°	*tormented; direct*
His course, na les incertaine° at this space°	*uncertainly; time*
Than schip but rudder quhilk dois wilsum wend.°	*turn of its own accord*
Bot yit, or° he his voyage far did spend,°	*before; went far (on)*
From tops of houssis till him did appeir	
The smok of fyrie vapeur up ascend;	
Bald,° barking doggis also did he heir	*Bold*
And monie flokis° making meikill beir,°	*flocks; noise*
Sum routting° loud and sum did semplie blait.	*baaing*
Unto the village quhan the compt° cam neir,	*count (Orlando)*
He lychtit doune° because it was so lait,	*alighted*
Quhair radelie° ane boy, discreit° and fait,°	*eagerly; responsible; smart*
Did tak the gydment of his horse in cuir.[42]	
Sum did disarme his person of estait,°	*noble/worthy*
Sum loust the giltit spurris quhilk he buir°	*wore*
And sum, attending, stuid upon the fluir°	*waited in the hall*
For till obey as plesit him command.	
Now this was even the verray ludging° suir,	*actual lodging house*
Quhair wondit° Medor all his weilfair fand.[43]	*wounded*
The stressit knycht all stupefact did stand	
And wold to bed but° onie kynd of fuid;	*without*
Sic gripping greif about his bosom band°	*lay tightly*
That appetyt from meit was far excluid.°	*removed*
For, fillit full of havie rancor ruid,°	*forceful festering hatred*
He did behold with goustlie° visage palle	*ghastly*
The wofull wreat,° quhilk frizit up° his bluid;	*writing; turned to ice*
Depaint° on posts and windocks° of the hall,	*Depicted; windows*
On durs, on tabils and on everie wall,	
Both 'Angelique' and 'Medor' schyphert beine°	*were intertwined*
With luifflie knottis° interlasit small,	*love-knots*
In thousand sorts apertlie° to be seine.	*overtly*

39. Literally, 'Golden Bridle', Orlando's horse.
40. One of numerous instances where Stewart follows the French prose of Jean Martin's *Roland Furieux* (1.543). Stewart translates Martin's 'Donnant lieu à sa soeur Phèbe.' Ariosto has no reference to the goddess, 'Dando già il sole alla sorella loco.'
41. 'paladeine': paladin—one of the twelve peers/famous warriors of Charlemagne's court.
42. 'Took the management of his (Orlando's) horse into his care.'
43. Angelica first meets Medoro, lying injured between two dead soldiers, in *Orlando Furioso*, Canto 12. 165. His conqueror proves to be a Scottish knight.

The trublit comte could not abstract° his eine	*withdraw*
From sycht of that quhilk wrocht him greattest paine,	
And, tending° oft to crave quhat it sould meine,	*inclining*
Feir for to find his feirfull thocht meed plaine	
Caust him againe his lippis close restraine.	
So° from him self he wold the truith oscuir,°	*Thus; obscure*
With trimbling dreid in his perturbit braine	
Sum suadgement schersing, be consait unsuir.[44]	
Bot crewall fortone at sic feid him buir,°	*bore such enmity toward him*
That scho no paine wold from his persone spair	
But tuik delyt this chiftan° til injuir.	*leader/general*
His musing mynd, mischiving° mair and mair,	*instigating his own ruin*
No thing avalit his obfuscat cair,[45]	
With cloud of dout, quhairin he held his pace,°	*retained his peace of mind*
For ane at lenth° did all the trewth declair[46]—	*finally someone*
But inquisition—of this cairfull cace;	
Quhilk was the pastor quho, in to that place,	
Be° broikin sychis did persave° his wo,	*From (Orlando's); perceive*
And, till appaise° his pansive° spreit ane space,°	*appease; melancholy; a while*
Began the histoir of the luifers two:[47]	
First quhow that Medor, deedlie wondit so,	
He thair did bring at Angeliques desyre,	
Quha° cuird his hurt;° than quhow that scho did go,	*i.e. Angelica; injury*
For him consuming all in luifis fyre	
Swa that, of honor thochtles° or impyre,°	*oblivious; rank/sovereignty*
Scho to this sempill souldart° did inclyn,	*soldier*
And band up mariage for to quenche desyre.[48]	
Thus he the histoir,° rycht° in everie lyn	*story; accurate*
Did so discus° quhill that hir braslat fyn°[49]	*relate; precious bracelet*
He representit at that instant steed.°	*aforementioned place*
This was the ax at last descendan syn°[50]	*descending then*
With deedlie dint° quhilk did ding of° his heed.	*blow; struck off*
Lang speichles lay he strukin almaist deed,	
Quhill source° of sorrow mycht no moir susteine,	*well-spring*
Bot furiuslie outbirstit° but remeed	*fiercely burst forth*
Sobs from his mouth and teiris from his eine.	
Bot most of all quhan solitar he beine	
Ane floud aboundant, bouting° out besprent°	*springing; besprinkled*

44. 'Seeking some relief through insecure imagining(s).'

45. Literally: 'In no way aided his obfuscated care.' I.e. 'In no way lightened his dark misery.'

46. ll. 345–50. Ironically the shepherd tells the story of Medoro, intending to relieve Orlando's suffering. 'But inquisition' (l. 346) means, literally, 'without formal investigation'—i.e. the shepherd volunteers unsolicited information.

47. In Ariosto, Medoro's wounds are tended by Angelica. Sought by heroes, she loves and marries an ordinary soldier. Earlier these two have come to the grove and written their names on the trees (*Orlando Furioso*, Canto 19. 17–42).

48. The imagery of 'binding up' and 'quenching' skilfully links the illness motif to the Pauline view of marriage.

49. Cf. Ariosto, *Orlando Furioso*, Canto 19. 40.5–8.

50. Ariosto uses the same physical image of the 'lost head' to introduce Orlando's madness. 'Questa conclusion fu la secure/che 'l capo a un colpo gli levò dal collo.' Canto 23. 121.1–2.

His boudin° brest, all swellit up in teine — *affected by grief/distended*
And, both his cheaks bebathing but relent,° — *relentlessly*
Deip in him now was cauld dispair imprent;° — *imprinted*
Yit from his birnand bosome fast did flow
Hote flammyng sychs,° quhilk nevir could be spent,° — *sighs; exhausted*
So fell and fervent was the fyrie low,° — *flame*
Quhilk in his hart ay moir and moir did grow.
But onie slaking thocht it fumit out,° — *burst out angrily*
His breath bot onlie did as belleis° blow — *bellows*
To kendle all his bodie round about;
And als his eine did serve bot for ane spout° — *waterspout*
The vitale humeur° from his lyf to draw, — *humour (bodily)*
For sorrow suir—not cled with° former dout— — *dressed in*
Did all his arters vive° aschunder thraw. — *arteries sharply*
Quho may the strese° intolerabile schaw, — *stress*
Quhilk did this valyant warior so torne?° — *transform*
Leile,° lychtleit° luifers onlie may it knaw, — *Faithful; disdained*
Quho haples° fruite of jelousie hes schorne.° — *luckless; pierced*
In bed he restles tumblit thus folorne,
Quhilk did moir dour than dourest stone appeir;[51]
Ilk softest fedder was, as poyntit thorne
To prick his persone, or the scharpest breir;° — *briar*
The walkryf° thochtis of his cair seveir — *wakeful*
Permits him nocht to sleip ane moment space.
Turne as he wold both hither, thair and heir,
Raidge of his rancor did him ay imbrace
And in this torment he bethocht,° alace, — *realized*
That his unkyndlie, darrest ladie quhyt
Haid interteind hir Medor in this place;
Heirfoir the sammyng° (plinist° with dispyt°) — *same place; filled; scorn*
He did abhorre and from it bendit quyt.° — *leapt off it with alacrity*
As quhan ane pastor, schersing eisment,° lyis[52] — *comfort*
Amongs the tender flouris of delyt,
Syn at his feit ane yssing° serpent spyis° — *hissing; espies*
Maist quyklie and astonist up will ryis,
So Roland full of dolor and desdaine
With diligence for all his harneis° cryis — *armour*
And in that ludgeing wold no moir remaine,
Bot montit on his Bridedor againe,
And wold not tarie quhill Aurora brycht
Haid spred hir silver schaddow on the plaine,
Bot throch the feilds ryds all this vilsum° nycht. — *evil/accursed*
He plains,° he pains and—as ane furious wycht°— — *laments; madman*
Blasphems the heavens, the stars and gods devyn,
With trickling teirs beblubring° all his sycht° — *obscuring; vision*
And syching ay insatiantlie° for pyn.° — *unrelievedly; pain*
Yea, thocht the morrow cleir arryvit° syn — *next day brightly dawned*

51. In Epic and Romance, the most hardened of warriors traditionally become the most affected by love.
52. ll. 400–6. Homeric similes play a large part in Stewart's poem. Cf. 559–69.

But intervall° his sorrow did induir. — *Ceaselessly*
From brochs° and citeis far he did declyn,° — *towns; turned away*
Eschewing° sycht of everie creatuir, — *Avoiding*
To dern° deserts and partis° maist obscuir — *remote; areas*
With wofull vult° he wandrit all the day, — *countenance*
But onie knawleidge, quhair his horse him buir;° — *carried him*
And with maist grivous great,° regraitting° ay — *lament; expressing regret*
Did fill the heaven, the air and feilds alway.° — *endlessly*
He fround for furie, feilling in his heed
The storms of raidge, pelmell, about fast play.
In winter, bald° Neptunus[53] nevir meed — *bold*
Mair motion fell° in fomie fluidis reed,° — *dire; red*
As tumults strong, tormoyling° to and fro, — *driving restlessly*
Of braying[54] baile quhilk in his brest abeed° — *remained*
With trublit tempest him tormenting so.
Than, in the nycht, quhan all to rest did go
He doune discendit in ane bocage° greine, — *grove*
With cairfull skrychis° evir waltring° tho, — *shrieks; tottering*
And sic scharp schours of sorrow did susteine
That sleip mycht nevir close his weping eine,
Quhairfra ten thousand teiris did distell—
As quhan, from bourn° that lang hes dammit beine,° — *stream; been dammed up*
Streams breaks° aboundant quhilk thairin did swell. — *break forth*
Him self astonit could not think, nor tell
Quhow possibill so monie teiris mycht
Poure from his eis, quhilks lyk ane springing well
Did nevir stay° thair rynning,° day nor nycht. — *cease; flowing*
Than, syching soir, he said, 'This liquor brycht
Is no moir° teirs! Teirs may not end my wo[55] — *no longer*
Quhilk bot begins; and spent° ar, from my sycht, — *exiled*
My teirs all. This source, quhilk springis so,° — *bubbles up so much*
I knaw it is vive vapor° fleing° fro — *living steam; escaping*
The fervent flams, quhilk birns° my hart to deed° — *burn; death*
Up throch my soddin° brest, syn out dois go — *soaked/sodden*
At my two eis, and sall draw but remeed
My lyf and dolor, both at ons° to feed; — *at once*
Bot sen so is, sched out° thy course with speid — *cover the stages of*
And my unhappie dayis to end soon leed.° — *lead/draw*
And ye, o sychs, quhairwith° my cair° dois feid, — *on which; misery*
Ye ar no sychs! Sychs may not ay proceid
But onie cease as thois that I exspyre.° — *breathe out*
The moir I sych, moir panting breath dois breid.° — *is generated*

53. Neptune, king of the sea.
54. While braying has the overt sense of 'making harsh sounds like a donkey', it also (appositely) means 'grinding into small pieces'.
55. ll. 444–57. Ariosto also invokes and rejects tears and sighs (Canto 23. 126–7). An earlier example of the device is found in Sannazaro's sonnet, 'O vita, vita non ma vivo affanno'. Cf. also the grief of Hieronimo as expressed in Act 3 of Kyd's *Spanish Tragedy*, 'O eyes! no eyes but fountains fraught with tears…' (This play belongs to the decade 1582–1592, and is, therefore, contemporaneous with Stewart's poem.)

The lord of luife,° quho birns me all in fyre, *i.e. Cupid*
Maks with his wings this wind, and will not tyre
To cause my kendlit° flammes evir flow, *kindled/liquid*
Quhill I destroyit be both bon and lyre.° *bone and flesh (formulaic)*
Bot O great mervell, that my hart now dow
So long induir in luifis fervent low° *flame*
And unconsumit utterlie to nocht!
Bot quhom am I in quhom sic raidge dois grow?
Am I that Roland quho hes wonders wrocht?° *achieved marvels*
No! Roland treulie in his grafe is brocht;
His dame ingrait° hes wranguslie him slaine. *ungrateful lady (Angelica)*
I am bot onlie his puir spreit afflocht,° *afflicted*
In wildernese heir forcit to complaine
My desperat, maist great, infernale paine;
To beir record, be my profoundest wo,
Quhat everie ane may hoip for till attaine,
Quho thrallit° in the links° of luife dois go.' *held captive; (of chain)*
This nycht til end, Roland lamentit so;
And quhan the vermell matutina sched° *crimson dawn parted*
In celest hews hir adgeit husband fro[56]
Him leving sleipand in his donckie° bed; *dampish*
And quhan the worldis lycht began to spred
Brycht rubie sparkis° throch the purpur° sky, *splashes; dark red*
Be destenie, the comte° haid so beine led, *(Orlando)*
That, in the part° he him persavit ly,° *area; found himself lying*
Besyd the rock, quhilk he befoir° did spy *earlier*
With Angelique and Medor gravit all;[57]
For force of furie than his flesche did fry![58]
Be dint° and stogs° of dochtie° Durandal,[59] *heavy blows; thrusts; valiant*
The craig and wreat° he claive° in skelpis° small: *writing; cleft; fragments*
So dois he go hich radgeing° in dispyt°— *loudly raging; contempt*
And, suddanlie, to ground renversit all,
Quhair onie trait° was of the luiflie dyt.° *line; amorous composition*
The savage pastor° and his troup may quyt *shepherd*
Cauld, cumlie° umbrage° of this cave for ay, *pleasing; shade*
And that fair fontan, springand silver quhyt[60]
With restles rumor° throch the sprutand° spray. *tumult; spurting*
Thocht recent° liquor clarifeit° alway, *fresh; made clear*
(It spoutit out as colorit christall cleine)
Yit could the same in nothing° quenche, I say, *to no extent*
The coler fell,° quhilk in him birnand beine.° *fierce rage; is burning*
Great stoks° and stons and monie brainchis greine *trunks*

56. According to Greek mythology, Aurora, goddess of the dawn, arose each morning, leaving her aged husband Tithonus in order to lead her brother, the sun-god Helios, into the heavens.
57. See ll. 209–25. On the previous day, Orlando had, by chance, come to the same place.
58. Orlando's flesh burns with hot rage due to an imbalance of the humours. The hot and dry components of choler have become so dominant that even the contrasting, yet complementing, properties of cool and moist are ineffectual. See l. 498.
59. The name given to Orlando's sword.
60. See § 18 B. 13, ll. 1–2.

Thairin he swackit,° and did nevir spair *struck*
Quhill all that wattir, cleir as saphir scheine,° *bright sapphire*
Was drumlie trublit° in ilk conduict° clair; *darkly ruffled; conduit*
Than irkit,° full of swet° and havie cair, *exhausted; anxiety*
But poust° he breathles on the mydow° fell— *strength; meadow*
In sorrow sowpit,° syching sad and sair— *bowed down*
Concluding° heir continewallie to dwell. *Deciding*
No heit, no cauld, no raine nor windis snell° *bitter*
Mycht mak him ons° to leif againe this place, *once*
Quhairin he lay (as dois the histoir tell)
But speitche° and evir, with affixit face,° *Speechless; stony gaze*
The firmament beholding all the space;° *time*
And so but meet or drink did still induir,
Quhill that the dririe nycht haid rune hir race
Thryse cled in till hir clouddie robbe obscuir,° *dark robe*
And quhill Apollo thryse haid montit suir° *risen assuredly*
In gouldin cart to luminat the day.
And grevous rigor, quhilk his bodie buir,
In feibling him it moir agmentit° ay, *increased*
Quhill at the last all vincust quhair he lay,
Be paine heirof out of his sens he start
And all his judgement from him fled away.
Than, the fourt day, working° his proper smart° *creating; own pain*
His hands outragius° did his visage skart° *unrestrained; tear*
Maist horribile, and with ane hiddeus brall° *noise*
For raidge he roird and restles did dispart° *break up*
His scheild, his gantlat° and his corslat° tall. *gauntlet; body armour*
Heir fell the brassats,° thair lyis Durandal, *arm-pieces*
Strong nails he breaks, his cuissots° aff did slyd, *thigh-pieces*
His helm, his gorget° and his harneis° all *throat-piece; armour*
In thousand peicis he disparplit° wyd. *scattered*
Ay moir and moir his furie did hym gyd
From hour till hour, quhill it increscit so
That in no part he permanent wold byd,
Bot ravand wodlie° swift and rasche did go. *raving madly*
His clothing all and sark° he reft° him fro *garment next skin; tore*
And nakit schew his wombe,° his brest and bak. *abdomen*
With flyring° face his mouth did morgeon tho° *mocking; grimace then*
And syndrie sounds maist terribile did mak,
Ay claverand° loud and not to propose° spak. *raving; not to the point*
Syn, quhan his raidge wold reull him moir seveir,
He at ane pull wold suddanlie uptak° *pick up*
The greatest oike or fir that he cam neir,
As bled of buss° or berrie aff the breir; *As if a leaf from a bush*
Great rocks, caverns and montans all about
He meed resound, and with ane luik austeir
Abaist° the pastors, chaceand° everie rout,° *Cowed; following; uproar*
That for to spy his folie ischit out;° *issued forth*
And quhair he cam, but mercie or remeed,
Uprais° amongs tham ane maist feirfull schout; *There arose*

Sum with his fist lay fellit in that steed,° — *place*
Sum dammest doune,° sum bruisit to the deed, — *knocked down senseless*
Sum gat thair brest quyt broikin or thair bak;
Fra sum he puld the arme, the leg or heed,° — *head*
Syn, in his hand the bluidie boulk° wold tak — *bloody implement*
And at ane uther egarlie it swak.° — *(would) brandish*
Tham ranging° thus, with ronklit front upbend° — *scattering them; louring brow*
He meed great heaps of this unhappie pak,
And nane of all agains him durst pretend.
For, as the weyld and furius ours° dois stend°[61]— — *bear; leap forward*
But onie feir or sussie°—for to sie° — *anxiety; watch*
The Russians hunters tym and travell spend,° — *expend(ing) labour*
For to persew hir throche the montans hie,
Thocht than approtche hir ane great cumpanie
Of little hounds, quhowsoon scho° blinks about, — *the moment she (i.e. bear)*
That feibile sort all skattrit bak dois flie;
Even so, quhan raging Roland ruschit out,
The peuple all fast fled in deedlie dout° — *mortal fear*
With all the speid and diligence thay mycht,
And so dissoverit° was this rakless rout:° — *broken up; reckless band*
Sum closit tham° in ludgeings strong and wycht,° — *locked themselves; secure*
Sum montit up on tours or templs hicht,° — *on top of tower or temple*
And sum, low spying, under covert° lay — *in a hiding place*
Of this maist sensles fole° till haif ane sycht, — *madman*
Quho on the feilds dismembrit everie day
Bauld buls° and beufils° in his sport and play. — *bulls; oxen*
He raifs,° he rugs,° he bruisis, breaks and ryfs°[62] — *raves; tears; splits*
With hands, with feit, with nails and teith alway;
He byts, he stricks,° he tumbls, he turns, he stryfs,° — *strikes; strives*
He glaiks,° he gaips, he girns,° he glours, he dryfs — *gawps at; moans*
Throw moss and montane, forrest, firth and plaine,
The birds, the beists, the boyes, the men and wyfs,
With bruit° moir hiddeus from his troublit braine — *noise/clamour*
Than force of fluidis hurlland° in great raine. — *hurtling down*
Foull glar° and dust his face all filthie meed, — *Filthy mud*
Quhairin no former beutie did remaine
And both his eis for wraith was boudin reed,° — *swollen red*
Quhilks up and doune ay turnit° in his heed — *kept circling*
With fearce regard upcasting all the quhyt.° — *white (of the eye)*
Both nycht and day he in the feilds abeed° — *remained*
And, for to fill his houngrie appetyt,
Fuid quhair he mycht, he reft° with great dispyt. — *seized*
Swyft harts and hynds he also wold devoir,
And to the death in rageing furie smyt
The sangler° strong, the tygar or the boir — *adult boar*

61. ll. 559–69. A homeric simile, couched in complex, Latinate syntax. Orlando's animalistic bravery (ll. 566–9) is compared to that of a Russian bear during the hunt (ll. 559–65).

62. ll. 575–81. Stewart becomes more virtuosic as Orlando's madness reaches its zenith. This technique of successive listings was known as *Underwriting*, because it can also make sense vertically: 'He raifs...with hands...he byts,...he glaiks...throw moss...the birds'.

And tham in gobbats° gredelie all toir, — *large pieces*
Thair° bluid upsucking, quhairwith blubbrit° beine — *Their; besmeared*
His visage quhilk appeird so bauld° befoir. — *nobly courageous*
Far mycht he now defigurat° be seine — *disfigured*
From that renownit, wordie,° chiftane keine, — *worthy*
Umquhyle° the beild° and piller firm of France. — *Once; protector*
In this estate perbrouilyit,° all uncleine, — *besmeared/disordered*
Upon the bounds of Spaine he cam be chance,[63]
Quhair Angelique and Medor did advance
Thair journay rycht alongs the rivage° fair. — *bank*
Bot quhan the fole beheld hir beutie glance,° — *shine*
Hir to persew he did with speid prepair.
Not that he knew hir persone maist preclair;° — *illustrious*
Bot, as ane chyld sum bonie bird wold crave
To sport thairwith and kill it syn but mair,° — *without further intent*
For sic effect° fast eftir hir he drave — *such reason*
And Medor all astonist did he lave,° — *leave*
Quhois horse lay fellit with his fist so snell.[64]
Bot be the ring, quhilk did sic vertew have,[65]
The ladie fred was from his furie fell.
This was the fole of quhom I erst did tell,[66]
That rageit on the luifers passand by;
With the quhilk two no moir I will me mell.° — *concern myself*
Sum spreits poetique moir perfyt than I
To paint expertlie, may thair pen apply[67]
Quhow thay did both from thence directlie dres,° — *proceed (to)*
Quhair hir great kingdome welthelie did ly,
That Medor mycht the croune thairof posses.
I lave° also for to declair expres — *pass over*
His faictes all° that did sic furie drie,° — *All his deeds; endure*
For imperfyt and tedius I confes
The mateir els° all manckit[68] is be me; — *remaining material*
Waeik,° crezit° barge upon the swelling sie — *Weak; damaged*
To everie wind will not hir saell upbend,° — *turn up/accommodate*
So may I not expone in ilk degrie
The histoir, weill as it at lenth is pend.[69]

63. ll. 602–14: Ariosto switches, at this point, to the story of Orlando's dealings with the Scottish knight Zerbino (Canto 24. 14 'di Zerbin mi convien prima dire'). Stewart picks up the story of Angelica again in an extreme condensation of the material covered from Canto 29: 57 ('...alla terra di Spagna') to Canto 29: 64 ('e l'annel...la fa sparir come ad un suffio il lume').

64. 'snell' may have either of two senses—'so quickly' (the horse fell) or 'so severely' (the blow descended).

65. Angelica's ring could make her invisible.

66. Stewart, Canto 10. 241, 'Ane furius fole did interchainge thair cheir.'

67. Stewart first praises Ariosto explicitly for being able to sustain a broader, more complex tale.

68. If 'manckit' is translated as 'omitted' and the reference assumed to be to the original work, then Stewart blames Ariosto for being boringly parenthetical. This is at odds with all his other expressions of humility before a superior talent and so it probably refers (as either 'omitted' or 'ruined') to an earlier draft, later abandoned, by Stewart himself.

69. ll. 629–30: 'In the same way, I cannot expound the (original) story to the same high standard, so well composed it is from opening to conclusion.'

§ 18: The Sonnet

To introduce the first of the lyrical sections of the later Renaissance with the voice of Mary, Queen of Scots, is appropriate. During her personal reign from 1560–67 the culture of France, poetic and musical, entered the Scottish court. James VI would build on this—expand the Chapel Royal and invite 'violaris and makars' to join his planned Renaissance—but the French love poems attributed to Mary and found among the 'casket letters' are not only the source of the varied and distinctive Scottish sonnet form, they are a poignant example of the way in which verse forms at this time could be used for political purposes. The sonnets of Mary would be used to justify her deposition, by demonstrating her infatuation with her third husband, Bothwell, and their implication in the murder of Darnley. The strength of the female voice—actual or assumed by male writers—within the Scottish lyric of that period has been exemplified earlier in § 11.

The sonnet selection has been designed to trace the variety of the form. In so doing, a body and a name is given to the specifically highlighted 'Scottish' distinctivenesses defined by James in his **Reulis and Cautelis** *and discussed in the Critical Introduction (p.xxviii). These dominate the form until the mid-1590s, when the theme of love (discouraged by the king—even in his own* **Amatoria** *to Anne of Denmark) regains dominance within a series of Scottish love sequences. Extracts from all of these are provided and contextualised in the Notes. After the nationalist dramas of the Union had passed, the Drayton-Donne division in English poetics finds its Scottish mirror in the greater simplicity and 'strong lines' of Ayton (also § 19). The 'strong lines' of Alexander Craig or William Mure of Rowallan may, on the other hand, owe as much to the earlier Scottish traditions of classical erudition and polemical Calvinism respectively, as to any aesthetically based court allegiances.*

Biographical Background:

See Sectional Introductions for Montgomerie, § 16; James VI, § 22; Stewart, § 17; Alexander, § 23; Ayton, § 19; Drummond, § 19.

Of the other sonneteers, the most important in the pre-1603 period was **William Fowler,** *who sustained the Italian line within the Castalian lyric, even when France and the Pléiade were favoured by the group's royal patron. Born in 1560, he graduated from St Andrews University in 1578. He continued his studies at Navarre and Padua, became an undercover Protestant spy, but made his name at court in the service of Henry, Prince of Wales and, latterly, Anne of Denmark. He went south with the king, but illness soon forced him to return to his homeland. On his death in 1612, his job passed to John Donne; his mantle as poetic polymath having already been assumed by his nephew, William Drummond.*

After 1603, the most ambitious lyrical sequence of all was composed by **Alexander Craig,** *whose* **Amorose Songes, Sonets and Elegies** *appeared in 1606. Its 108 poems are addressed to seven ladies, some of whom are easily identified with noblewomen at court (e.g. 'Penelope' = Lady Penelope Rich); others suggest types of loving from ideal ('Idea') to lusty ('Lais'). Born in Banff in 1567, Craig graduated MA from the University of St Andrews in 1586. A qualified notary, he followed James to London, as Fowler had done, but seems never to have settled down there. The* **Amorose Songes** *are dedicated to the Earl of Dunbar. When Dunbar returned north, Craig was part of his retinue. He remained in his estates at Rose Craig until his death in 1627.*

For Hugh Barclay, David Murray and William Mure see Notes.

18A: *Earlier Sonnets*

Mary Queen of Scots (1542–1587)[1]

[*These French love sonnets are the eighth and ninth in the sequence of eleven plus sixain, attributed to Mary. They are known as the Casket sonnets because they were discovered in 'one small gilt cofer nat fully ane foote lang' and used at her trial as supposed evidence of her 'mad love, infamous adulterie and vile passione' for Bothwell. The evidence was carefully presented in order to suggest that Bothwell and the queen were both involved in the recent murder of her second husband, Darnley.*]

1

Mon amour croist, et plus en plus croistra
Tant que je vivray, et tienray à grandheur
Tant seulement d'avoir part en ce coeur,
Vers qui, en fin, mon amour paroistra
Sy tres à clair, que jamais n'en doutra.
Pour luy je veux faire teste au malheure,
Pour luy je veux rechercher la grandeure
Et feray tant qu'en vray cognoistra
Que jy n'ay bien, heur, ne contentement,
Qu'a l'obeyr et servir loyaument.
Pour luy j'attendz toute bonne fortune;
Pour luy je veux garder santé et vie;
Pour luy tout vertu de suyvre j'ay envie
Et, sans changer, me trouvera tout une.

[My love increseth, and more and more wil increase
So long as I shall lief; and I shall holde for° ane greit felicitie,° *view as; happiness*
To have, onely, pairt° in that hart, *uniquely a place*
To the quhilk, at length, my love sall appeare° *reveal itself*
So clearely, that he[2] sall never doubt.
For him I will strive aganis wan weard,° *dark fate/despair*
For him I will recerfe° greitnes, *seek out*
And sall do so mikle° that he shall know *much*
That I haif no wealth, hap,° nor contentation, *good fortune*
But to obay and serve him truely.
For him I attend° all gude fortune; *look out for/await*
For him I will conserve health and life;
For him I desire to ensew courage,°[3] *cultivate courage*
And he shall ever find me unchangeable.]

1. ED. COPY TEXT: 'Ane Detectioun of the duinges of Marie Quene of Scottes, touchand the murder of hir husband, and hir conspiracie, adulterie and pretensed mariage with the Erle of Bothwell...Translated out of the Latine quhilke was written by G.B.' This 1571 text is slightly corrupt but has been preferred to Cambridge University MS (Oo. 7.47) in order to preserve the 'case' as presented. A modernized version of the Cambridge text exists in *Bittersweet Within my Heart*, edited by Robin Bell (Pavilion, 1992).
2. James Hepburn, 4th Earl of Bothwell (c.1535–78), who became Mary's third husband, by Protestant rite, in May, 1567.
3. In a manner which anticipates Shakespeare's Lady Macbeth, she vows to adopt (follow) the manly courage for which Bothwell was himself renowned.

2

Pour luy aussi je jette mainte larme:
Premier, quand il se fist de ce corps possesseur,
Duquel, alors, il n'avoit pas le coeur;
Puis, me donna un autre dur alarme,
Quand il versa de son sang mainte dragme,[4]
Dont de grief il me vint lesser doleur,
Qui m'en pensa oster la vie et frayeur
De perdre, las, le seul rampar qui m'arme.
Pour luy, depuis, jay mesprisé l'honneur
Ce qui nous peut seul pourvoir de bonheur;
Pour luy, j'ay hazardé grandeur et conscience;
Pour luy, tous mes parentz j'ay quité, et amis,
Et tous autres respectz sont apart mis:
Brief, de vous seul je cerche l'alliance.

[For him also I powred out many tearis:
First, quhen he made himselfe possessor of thys body,
Of the quhilk, then, he had nat the hart;[5]
Efter,° he did geve° me one uther hard charge,° *Later; did impose on; duty*
Quhen he bled of his blude great quantitie,[6]
Through the great sorrow of the quhilk came to me that dolour,
That almost caryit away my life and the feire° *fear...*
To lese° the onely strength that armit me. *...Of losing*
For him, since, I haif despisit honour,[7]
The thing onely that bringeth felicitie;
For him, I have hazardit greitnes and conscience;
For him, I have forsaken all kin and frendes,
And set aside all uther respectes:° *considerations/favours*
Schortly,° I seke the aliance of yow onely.°] *In brief; alone*

18B: *Jacobean Sonnets*

Alexander Montgomerie (1555?–98)[8]

1

Iniquitie on eirth is so increst,° *increased*
All flesh bot few° with falset is defyld, *with few exceptions*
Given ou'r of° God, with gredynes beguyld, *Having abandoned*
So that the puir,° but pitie, ar opprest. *poor*
God in His justice dou na mair digest° *make allowances for*

4. 'mainte dragme': 'dragme' is an alternative form of 'drachme', or 0.125 of an ounce according to the apothecaries' measure. As the 'r' in 'alarme' would not be sounded the rhyme is an exact one. The literal sense is 'many a small liquid measure'.
5. ll. 2–3: Bothwell was rumoured to have raped the queen.
6. The reference is to an occasion when the queen rode twenty miles to tend the wounded Bothwell after he had killed an outlaw.
7. The admission in the sestet that love of Bothwell supersedes morality, kinship and country, was the most damaging of all the 'revelations' in the casket sonnets.
8. ED. COPY TEXTS (Montgomerie): Nos 1–5 Drummond MS; No. 6 Laing III, 447.

Sik sinfull swyn with symonie[9] defyld
But must revenge—thair vyces ar so vyld;
And pour doun plagues of famin, sword and pest.° *plague*
Aryse O Lord, delyver from the lave° *rest*
Thy faithfull flock befor that it infect!° *becomes infected*
Thou sees how Satan sharps° for to dissave,° *cleverly cheats; deceive*
If it were able,° even Thyn awin elect. *possible*
Sen conscience, love and cheritie all laiks,
Lord, short the season for the chosens saiks.[10]

2

A Baxters bird, a bluiter° beggar-borne,[11] *babbler*
Ane ill heud huirsone° lyk a barkit° hyde, *ill-formed bastard; tanned*
A saulles swinger,° sevintie tymes mensworne,° *soulless scoundrel; perjured*
A peltrie pultron° poyson'd up with pryde, *paltry coward*
A treuthles tongue that turnes with eviry tyde,
A double deillar with dissait indeud,
A luiker bak whare he wes bund to byde,
A retrospicien[12] whom the Lord outspeud,° *spat up*
A brybour baird° that mekle baill hes breud,° *known bribe-taker; brewed up*
Ane hypocrit, ane ydill atheist als,
A skurvie skybell° for to be esheu'd,° *contemptible rascal; avoided*
A faithles°—fekles, fingerles[13] and fals, *An unreliable one*
A Turk that tint° Tranent for the Tolbuith. *left/sacrificed*
Quha reids this riddill, he is Sharpe forsuith.[14]

3

So swete a kis yistrene fra thee I reft° *stole*
In bouing doun thy body on the bed,
That evin my lyfe within thy lippis I left.[15]
Sensyne from thee my spreits wald never shed;° *sever*
To folow thee it from my body fled
And left my corps als cold as ony kie.° *key*
Bot when the danger of my death I dred,° *feared*
To seik my spreit I sent my harte to thee;

9. The buying of positions within the church. See Acts 8. 18–20.
10. From a general lament in the octet, Montgomerie moves in the sestet to a particular plea, following James's advice that the sonnet's form lent itself to argumentation. As a Catholic, he had personal experience of persecution, exclusion from office and imprisonment.
11. During Montgomerie's unsuccesful attempt to regain his pension through litigation, he produced a set of sonnets, moving from early confidence in king and lawyers to later fury. This poem attacks his own lawyer (see l. 14). It opens by making him a bird belonging to Mr Baxter, one of the opposing legal team.
12. 'Luiker bak' and 'retrospicien' are vernacular and Latin forms with the same meaning—'one who looks back', or, in this case, 'looks over his shoulder' in self-protection. This was a popular rhetorical device of the time.
13. As cloth was often measured in fingerlengths, a 'fingerless' merchant was, colloquially, one who gave false measure.
14. ll. 13–14: A riddle on his lawyer's name. 'Whoever solves the riddle is sharp' but the solution is also 'Sharpe', the poet's advocate. He moved from his East Lothian home, near Tranent, to 'greater things' in Edinburgh. The tolbooth stands for that city but is also the prison he ought to inhabit.
15. One of Montgomerie's free Ronsardian translations. The source is 'Hier soir Marie, en prenant maugré toy'.

Bot it wes so inamored with thyn ee,
With thee it myndit° lykwyse to remane; *decided*
So thou hes keepit captive all the thrie,
More glaid to byde° then to returne agane. *remain*
Except thy breath thare places had suppleit,
Even in thyn armes thair, doutles, had I deit.

4

Swete nichtingale, in holene° grene that ha[nts.][16] *holly*
To sport thy self and speciall in the spri[ng];
Thy chivring chirlis,° whilks chainginglie thou [chants],° *tremulous trills; sing*
Maks all the roches round about the ring,
Whilk slaiks my sorow so to heir the sing
And lights my loving langour at the leist.
Yit thoght thou sees not, sillie,° saikles° thing, *simple; guiltless*
The peircing pykis° brods° at thy bony breist.[17] *thorns; pierce/prick*
Evin so am I by plesur lykwyis preist,° *urged*
In gritest danger whair I most delyte.
Bot since thy song, for shoring° hes not ceist, *in face of threats*
Suld feble I, for feir, my conqueis quyt?° *give up my (hope of) conquest*
Na, na, I love the—freshest Phoenix fair[18]—
In beuty, birth, in bounty but compair!° *incomparable*

5

The lesbian lad,° that weirs the wodbind wr[eath] *Bacchus*
With Ceres and Cylenus,[19] gled your ging.° *gladden your path*
Be blyth Kilburnie° with the bairns of Be[ath]° *Kilbirnie; Beith*
And let Lochwinnoch lordie lead your rin[g]![20]
Be mirrie men, feir God and serve the Ki[ng]
And cair not by Dame Fortuns fead° a fl[ea]! *enmity*
Syne, welcome hame swete Semple, sie ye sin[g]
Gut ou'r and let the wind shute in the s[ea]![21]
I Richie, Jane and George are lyk to d[ee],
Four crabit crippilis crackand° in our crouch.° *gossiping; (lit)crouching place*
Sens I am trensh-man° for the other thrie, *lord of the feast/spokesman*
Let drunken Pancrage[22] drink to me in D[utch].
Scol frie, al out, albeit that I suld brist
Ih wachts hale beir, fan hairts and mych[sum] drist.[23]

16. ED. The MS pages for this sonnet (also nos. 5 and 7) are torn. The letters in square brackets are editorial.
17. The reference is to the nightingale as Philomela, raped by her brother-in-law.
18. The phoenix was a type of resurrective promise because the young bird was thought to arise from the ashes of the old.
19. Ceres was the corn goddess. Cylenus was the tutor of Bacchus, in Roman mythology, the god of wine.
20. Towns in Ayrshire and Renfrewshire site the poem in Montgomerie's homeland. Landowners are still identified by the names of their estates in rural Scotland.
21. ll. 7–8: Lord Robert Semple, a noted Catholic and friend of the poet, is told to 'be sure to sing (be sick), bent over' and with the wind behind him.
22. While this may be the name of another friend, 'Pan-crache' in Scots had the sense of 'toilet pot-filler'.
23. Imitates the slurred speech of a drunken man. The general sense is—'I hope for good beer, loving hearts and a huge thirst.'

6

I dreamit ane dreame; o that my dreame wer trew![24]
Me thocht my maistres to my chalmer° came — *bedroom*
And with hir harmles handis the cowrteingis° drew — *curtains*
And sweitlie callit on me be my name.
'Art ye on sleip?' quod sche. 'O, fy for schame!
Have ye nocht tauld° that luifaris takis no rest?' — *said (in your verse)*
Me thocht I answerit, 'Trew it is, my dame;
I sleip nocht, so your luif dois me molest.'
With that me thocht hir nicht-gowne of she cuist,° — *cast*
Liftit the claiss° and lichtit° in my armis; — *bed clothes; settled/alighted*
Hir rosie lippis me thocht on me sche thrist
And said, 'May this nocht stanche you of your harmes!'° — *wounds*
'Mercy Madame,' me thocht I menit to say;
Bot quhen I walkennit—alace, sche was away!

Hugh Barclay (1560?–1597)[25]

7

My best belovit brother of the craft,[26]
God, if ye knew the stait that I am in!
Thocht ye be deif, I know ye ar not daft
Bot kynd aneugh to any of your kin.
If ye bot saw me in this winter win° — *wind*
With old bogogers° hotching° on a sped,° — *leggings; digging; spade*
Draiglit in° dirt, whylis wat evin to the [skin] — *Bedraggled with*
I trow thair suld be tears or° we twa shed.° — *before; parted*
Bot maist of all, that hes my bailis° bred° — *misery; given rise to*
To heir how ye on that syde of the m[ure]° — *moor*
Birlis° at the wyne, and blythlie gois to [bed], — *Carouse*
Foryetting me, pure pleuman, I am sure.
So, sillie I, opprest with barmie jugg[is],° — *yeasty dregs*
Invyis° your state that's pouing Bacchus [luggis].° — *Envy; ears/handles*

James VI (1566–1625)[27]

8

That blessed houre, when first was broght to light
Our earthlie Juno° and our gratious Queene![28] — *wife of the chief god, Jove.*

24. Cf. Wyatt, 'They fle from me that sometyme did me seke.'
25. ED. COPY TEXT (Hugh Barclay): Drummond MS.
26. The sonnet is addressed to Montgomerie. Both poets suffered for their Catholic faith, so 'craft' while overtly referring to the poetic craft, may have a covert religious connotation. In the late 1590s, the two men were involved in a conspiracy aimed at aiding the rebellion of Lord Tyrone in Ireland. Barclay was killed in one of the conflicts.
27. ED. COPY TEXTS (James VI): Nos. 8–11, British Library Add. MS 24195; No. 12, Nat. Library of Scotland Adv. 19.2.6. See Introduction § 22.
28. One of a series of sonnets entitled *Amatoria* and addressed to his fiancée, Anne of Denmark.

Three goddesses, how soone they hade her seene,
Contended who protect her shoulde by right;
Bot being as goddesses of equall might
And as of female sexe like stiffe in will,°[29] *obstinate*
It was agreed by sacred Phoebus skill
To joyne there powers to blesse that blessed wight.° *being/person*
Then happie monarch, sprung of Ferguse race,[30]
That talkes with wise Minerve when pleaseth the,
And when thou list° sum princelie sporte to see, *wish*
Thy chaste Diana rides with the in chase,° *the hunt*
Then, when to bed thou gladlie does repaire,
Clasps in thine armes thy Cytherea° faire.[31] *i.e. Venus*

9

Although that crooked, crawling Vulcan[32] lie
An-under ashes colde, as oft we see,
As senseles,° deade—whill,° by his heate, he drie *As if insensible; until*
The greene and fizzing faggots made of tree,
Then will that litle sponke° and flaming eye *spark*
Bleaze bravelie forth and, sparkling all abreed° *abroad*
With wandling° up a wondrous sight to see, *flickering*
Kithe° clearlie then and on the faggots feede. *Reveal (himself)*
So am I forced for to confesse indeede:
My sponke of love, smor'd° under coales of shame, *smothered*
By beauties force, the fosterer of that seede,
Now budds and bursts in an appearing° flame; *visible*
Bot since your beautie hath this wonder wroght,
I houpe Madame it shall not be for noght.

10

Haill mirthfull May, the moneth full of joye![33]
Haill mother milde of hartsume° herbes and flowres! *pleasant*
Haill fostrer faire of everie sporte and toye
And of Auroras[34] dewis and summer showres!
Haill friend to Phoebus and his glancing° houres! *shining*
Haill sister scheine° to Nature breeding all, *bright*
Who—by the raine that cloudie skies out pouris,
And Titans heate—reformes the faided fall
In woefull winter, by the frostie gall

29. These are not the most romantic of sonnets! The king had still to meet his queen, but even in those circumstances his application of the doctrine of the 'middle way' to love-poetry seems ill-advised.
30. Fergus was the legendary first king of Scotland.
31. The king's vast classical knowledge informs most of his vernacular verse. The goddesses listed grant to Anne: wisdom, chastity and beauty.
32. Roman god of fire and metal-working, Vulcan was hurled from heaven by Jupiter/Jove. On crashing to earth he broke a leg and so become lame.
33. One of James's more successful French adaptations. The source is Desportes, *Diane* I,5.
34. ll. 4–10: Aurora is the goddess of dawn; Phoebus and Titan are sun gods; malevolent Saturn was the god of time.

Of sadd Saturnus tirrar° of the trees! *stripper*
And now, by Natures might and thine, they shall
Be florish'd faire with colours that agrees;° *harmonize*
Then lett us all be gladd to honour the,° *you*
As in olde tymes was ever wonte to be.

11

All kinde of wronge, allace, it now aboundes,
And honestie is fleemed° out of this land. *banished*
Now trumprie° ouer trueth his triumphe soundes, *deceit*
Who now can knowe the hart by tongue or hand?
Cummes ever justice at the barre° to stande? *bar (legal)*
Where can she be in these our later dayes?
Alike in water for to wagg a wande[35]
As speare for° her if, truelie, sundrie sayes,° *(to) enquire for; speak*
For manie now abroade doe daylie blaize° *spread abroad*
That justice hath her hart infected sore.
How can she then be cleane in anie wayes
Bot must become corrupted more and more?
Sume lockman now hath locked up apart
Poore justice, martyr'd with a meschant° hart. *miserable*

12

A Sonett: On Sir William Alexanders harshe vearses after the Inglishe fasone.[36]

Hould, hould your hand! Hould, Mercy, mercy° spare *please*
Those sacred nine° that nurst you many a yeare! *i.e. Muses*
Full oft alas with comfort and with care
Wee bath'd you in Castalias fountaine[37] cleare;
Than on our winges aloft wee did you beare
And set you on our stately forked hill,
Where you our heavnly harmonyes did heare
The rockes resoundinge with there° echoes still. *their*
Although your neighbours° have conspir'd to spill° *i.e. English; waste*
That art which did the Laurel crowne obtaine,
And borowing from the raven there ragged quill° *tuneless pen*
Bewray° there harsh hard trotting tumbling vayne, *Reveal*
Such hamringe hard the mettalls hard require—,
Our songs ar fil'd with smoothly flowing fire.[38]

35. Elliptical. The extended sense is: 'It would be as useful to try to hold back water by waving a stick in it' as to seek justice in Scotland just now.

36. William Alexander, Earl of Stirling, was one of the Castalian band (see l. 4). He wrote a more anglicised form of Scots than most of the others. See § 23 Introduction.

37. James's poetic band was named after this fountain on Mount Parnassus, sacred to Apollo and the Muses.

38. All three alliterating words have double meanings. Literally, the 'flowing' metal is shaped and 'filed' in 'fire'. As James used 'flowing' critically to mean 'rhythmical', the songs are also 'filled' with 'rhythmic' expressions of 'passion'.

John Stewart of Baldynneis (1550–1605)[39]

13
'Of Ane Fontane.'

Fresche fontane fair[40] and springand cald and cleine
As brychtest christall cleir[41] with silver ground,° *silver base*
Close cled about° be holsum herbis greine, *Closely covered round*
Quhois twynkling streames yeilds ane luiflie sound;
With bonie birkis° all ubumbrat round° *birches; shaded all round*
From violence of Phebus visage fair,
Quhois smelling° leifs suave Zephir° maks rebound° *fragrant; west wind; flutter*
In doucest souching° of his temperat air; *moaning*
And Titan° new hich flammyng in his chair° *morning sun; chariot*
Maks gaggit° erth for ardent heit to brist.° *cracked; burst*
Than, passinger, quho irkit dois repair,° *exhausted retires to rest*
Brynt be the son and dryit up with thrist,
Heir—in this place—thou may refreschment find
Both be the well, the schaddow and the wind.

14
'Of Ambitious Men.'

As dryest dust—winddrift° in drouthie° day— *wind-driven; rainless/dry*
Quhyls lychts° on lords and ladies of renoune, *Sometimes lands*
Quhyls on thair face and quhyls on thair array
And quhyls upon ane kingis statlie croune;
Yit as it cums, sum ay are bussie boune° *busily engaged*
To cleinge it thence,° so that it find no rest *brush it off*
Quhill to the erth it be againe snipt° doune; *snatched*
So mortall men, quho dois thair mynd molest
To be in gloir coequall with the best,
Thocht for ane space thay volt° with waltring° wind, *whirl up; tossing*
Doune to the ground thay sall againe be drest,° *brought*
For few aloft may fortouns firmtie° find. *security*
Bot ay the swyfter and moir hich thay brall,° *soar*
Moir low and suddane cums thair feirfull fall.[42]

15a
'Of Ane Salutation of Ane Host to his Hostes.'[43]

Guid day madam, with humyll thanks also,
That me unto your ludgeing lairge° did gyd. *roomy hostelry*

39. ED. COPY TEXT (Stewart): Nat. Library of Scotland Adv. 19.2.6.
40. Stewart has been called 'the Scottish Desportes'. This sonnet is based on the French poet's 'Cette fontaine est froide'.
41. Stewart followed James VI's literary rules with self-interested humility. As the king had warned against making the Scottish sonnet too derivative and too amorous, he replaces Desportes' 'semble parler d'amour' with an expanded description of the fountain.
42. Stewart has a series of moral sonnets of which this is one of the most powerful.
43. Greeting and reply are united by the same bawdy analogy. The 'hostess-prostitute' invites the 'traveller-customer' to her 'lodging-vagina'.

Yea skairs° I knew, quhan I thairin did go,	*hardly*
Quhair I sould wend°—the wallis war so wyd!	*go*
Thocht than I slippit, quhan ye bad me byd,°	*stay (up)*
Excuise my part,° the falt was not in me;	*part/member*
Your pathed pathment meid my paessis slyd,[44]	
That I was forst to bow upon my kne.	
Bot yit I thank you for your ludgeing frie;°	*generous*
I grant° in deid ye hold ane oppine port,°	*accept; harbour*
Bot inexpert I am to swyme the sie,	
Quhilk flows on bordor of your brod resort,	
Quhairin I wat° is furnissing° but dout	*know; equipment*
To serve the Turck° and all his camp about!°	*Grand Turk; retinue*

15b

'The Ansuir of the Foirsaid Hostes.'

Your fervent, folische furreour° far feils,	*quartermaster*
Quho, for your herbrie,° meid so meikill beir,°	*lodging; much noise*
Be feckles tratils of his trifling teils—	
I thocht your tryn sould haif cum greater heir.[45]	
None sutche as yow sould to my palice speir	
Quho may be eisit° soon in smallest hall,	*at ease/eased*
Your sthomack servith bot for sempill cheir,°	*fare*
I yow againe sall not to banket° call,	*(love's) feast*
Quhan on your kneis for foibilnes° ye fall!	*feebleness/impotence*
Ye say, my pathed pathment meid yow slyd—	
Bot laik of boldnes on the same to brall°	*rise up*
Meid yow to slip. Ye haid no strenth to byd.	
Heirfoir,° your pithles person to repois,	*From now on*
Tak my bak chalmer° for your guckit° nois.	*back room; silly/foolish*

16

'In Going to his Luif.'

O silver hornit Diane, nychtis queine,	
—Quha for to kis Endimeon, did discend[46]—	
Gif flamme of luif thou haid don than susteine°	*experienced then*
(As I do now, that instant dois pretend°	*who currently seeks*
T'embrasse my luif, not willing to be kend,°)	*recognized*
With mistie vaill thou wold obscuir thy face	

44. 'Your well trodden pavement made me (my paces) slide' but also erotically 'Your wellworn pathway made me slip in my progress.'

45. The hostess whore's opening quatrain subtly plays on the ideas of quartermaster and penis as scouts. 'Your zealous, foolish quartermaster (hot foolish forayer) who made such a fuss about your (its) accommodation is wide of the mark (loses vigour badly) in the feckless prattlings of his useless accounts (ineffectual efforts of his feeble lower parts.) I thought your retinue (appendage) when it came here would have been bigger.'

46. Diana (the moon) loved the shepherd Endymion and put him to sleep, so that she might come down and kiss him each night. Ovid, *Amores* I, xiii. The pastoral line in Scottish Renaissance verse is fully represented in § 19.

For reuth° of me that dois sic travell spend!° — *pity; labour undergo*
And finding now this vissit grant of° grace, — *favoured by*
Bot lettit° be thy borrowit lycht alace, — *Only prevented*
I staying stand in feir for to be seine.
Sen yndling eine invirons° all this place, — *jealous eyes surround*
Quhois cursit mouths ay to defame dois meine.
Bot nether thay nor yit thy schyning cleir
May cause appeir° my secreit luif synceir.[47] — *make (me) reveal*

17
'Ane Literall° Sonnet.' — *Alliterative*

Dull dolor dalie dois delyt destroy,[48]
Will wantith° wit, waist worn with wickit wo, — *lacks*
Cair cankert° causith confortles convoy,° — *ill-natured; companionship*
Seveir sad sorrow scharplie schoris° so, — *threatens*
My myrthles mynd may mervell° monie mo; — *imagine*
'Promp!'° peirles, proper, plesand, perll preclair,° — *Help; lustrous pearl*
Fair fremmit freind, firm fellest° frownyng fo, — *most cruel*
Ryche rubie—rycht renownit,° royall, rair— — *justly renowned*
Send succor soone, so suadge sall° sourest sair,° — *may be assuaged; pain*
Grant grivous gronyng gratious guerdon° guid, — *reward*
For° favor flowing from fresche faces fair — *Because*
Restoris rychtlie, restles rancor ruid,
Bot beutie, breding° bittir boudin° baill — *which breeds; grievous*
Dois (dalie) deedlie, dwynyng° dartis daill.° — *debilitating; distribute*

William Fowler (1560–1612)[49]

18
The day is done, the sunn dothe ells declyne,[50]
Night now approches and the moone appeares,
The twinkling starrs in firmament dois schyne,
Decoring° with the poolles° there circled spheres; — *Adorning; pole stars*
The birds to nests, wyld beasts to denns reteirs,
The moving leafs unmoved now repose,
Dew dropps dois fall, the portraicts of my teares;
The waves within the seas theme calmlye close.
To all things, Nature ordour dois impose—
But not to love, that proudlye doith me thrall,° — *enslaves me*
Quho all the dayes and nights, but chainge or choyse
Steirs up the coales of fyre unto my fall

47. Secrecy was one of the conventions of courtly love. Stewart will not identify his lady however steadfastly the fates oppose him.
48. One of Stewart's many virtuoso lyrics. James VI, in the *Reulis*, Chapter 3, urged Scottish poets to emphasise the strong sounds of Scots by making their verse as 'Literall [i.e. alliterative], sa far as may be.'
49. ED. COPY TEXTS (Fowler): Nos. 18–20, Drummond MS No. 21, Hawthornden MS XI.
50. This is the twenty-second sonnet in Fowler's love sequence, *The Tarantula of Love*. The source of the sonnet is Petrarch's 'Or che'l ciel e la terra e 'l vento tace', which itself stems from Statius' 'Crimine quo merui'.

And sawes his breirs and thornes within my hart,
The fruits quhairoff ar duile,° greiff, grones and smart. *misery*

19

O nights, no nights bot ay a daylye payne![51]
O dayes, no dayes bot cluddie nights obscure!
O lyfe most lothd, transchangde[52] in deathe againe!
O doole, no doole but certain deathe and suire!
O hart, no hart bot rok and marble dure
Quhair waves of woe with tempests stryketh soare!
O eyes, which ay against my harte conteure!° *strive*
O teares, no teares bot of salt streames the store!
O heavens, no heavens bot cahos of disglore!° *dishonour*
O godds, the guyders of my best hard happ!
O dame, quho dothe depress all reuthe and smore!° *smother*
O nights, day, lyfe, o doole of deathe the trapp,
O harte, o eyes, o teares, o godds and dame,
Quhen sal her frosts be warmed be my flame?

20

As that poure, foolisch fliee, quhase custome is
By flams to fyre° her wings and lyfe to lose, *set fire to*
Dothe fondlye° flie to her conceated° bliss *foolishly; imagined*
And purches deathe in place of her repose[53]—
So, in beholding thee: my fragrant rose,
The sweit aspect hethe quikned up° desyre, *wakened up*
Which of my ruyne doth the cause disclose[54]
And forceth me for to refanne my fyre;
So that, in this, for quhilk we both aspyre,
We equall doole° and disadvantage prove;° *grief; experience*
With lyke effects of our imagind hyre° *agreement/bargain*
We lose our lyfe and onlye bot by love.
Disequall yet in this ar thow and I—
Thou, quicklye,° dees; I deing never die. *speedily/while living*

21[55]

Upon the utmost° corners of the warld *extreme*
And on the borders of this massive round,
Quhaire fates and fortoune hither hes me harld,° *hurled*
I doe deplore° my greiffs upon this ground, *lament (aloud)*
And (seing roring seis from roks rebound

51. *Tarantula* 42. Cf. Sannazaro, 'O vita, vita non ma viva affanno.'
52. ED. transchangde] ed.; transchandge MS.
53. *Tarantula* 60. The image of the fly seeking its own destruction in light or fire is a commonplace of Petrarchan love poetry. Cf. Petrarch, 'Son animali al mondo de sì altera' and 'Come talora al caldo tempo sole'.
54. The poet's lady—Bellisa—has a name combining her major attributes of beauty (Fr. *belle*, lovely) and aggression (Lat. *bellum*, war). At this stage in the sequence (*Tarantula* 60) the latter is dominant again.
55. The seventh sonnet in Fowler's brief Hawthornden MS sequence. The setting is noted in the margin—'orknay'.

By ebbs and streames of contrair routing° tyds — *rushing in opposed direcions*
And Phebus chariot in there waves ly dround,
Quha equallye now night and day devyds)
I cal to mynde the storms my thoughts abyds,° — *(which) control my thoughts*
Which ever wax and never dois decress;
For nights of dole,° dayes joys ay ever hyds, — *suffering*
And in there vayle° doith al my weill suppress. — *valley*
So this I sie: quhaire ever I remove,
I chainge bot sees, but can not chainge my love.

Sir William Alexander (1567–1640)[56]

22

Huge hosts of thoughts imbattled in my brest,
Are ever busied with intestine warres,°[57] — *internal/civil wars*
And, like to Cadmus earth-borne troupes, at jarres,° — *at loggerheads*
Have spoil'd my soule of peace, themselves of rest.
Thus forc'd to reape such seed as I have sowne,[58]
I (having interest in this doubtfull strife)
Hope much, feare more, doubt most! Unhappie life!
What ever side prevaile, I'm still orethrowne!
O neither life nor death! ô both, but° bad; — *equally*
Imparadiz'd whiles,° in mine owne conceit,° — *sometimes; fancy*
My fancies straight againe imbroyle my state,
And in a moment make me glad and sad.
Thus, neither yeelding quite to this nor that,
I live, I die, I do I wot° not what. — *know*

23

Oft have I heard, which now I must deny,
That nought can last if that it be extreame:[59]
Times dayly change and we likewise in them,
Things out of sight do straight forgotten die;
There is nothing more vehement then love,
And yet I burne, and burne still with one flame.
Times oft have chang'd, yet I remaine the same,
Nought from my mind her image can remove;
The greatnesse of my love aspires to ruth,° — *pity*
Time vowes to crowne my constancie in th'end,
And absence doth my fancies but extend;
Thus I perceive the poet spake the truth,
That who to see strange countries were inclin'd,
Might change the aire, but never change the mind.

56. ED. COPY TEXT: *Aurora*, 1604.
57. The sixth sonnet in Alexander's philosophical love sequence, *Aurora*. Cf. Petrarch, 'Amor mi sprona in un tempo et affrena.'
58. ll. 2–5: Cadmus created his troops by sowing the teeth of a dragon in the earth. On arising from the soil, they began to kill one other. Ovid, *Metamorphoses*, III.
59. Alexander continues his friendly battling with James, who upheld the doctrine of the golden mean.

24

Awake my muse and leave° to dreame of loves, *cease*
Shake off soft fancies chaines—I must be free!
Ile perch no more upon the mirtle tree,[60]
Nor glide through th'aire with beauties sacred doves;
But, with Joves stately bird,° Ile leave my nest *i.e. eagle*
And trie my sight against Apolloes raies.
Then, if that ought my ventrous course° dismaies, *adventurous journey*
Upon the olives[61] boughes Ile light and rest:
Ile tune my accents to a trumpet now,
And seeke the laurell in another field.[62]
Thus I that once, as beautie meanes did yeeld,
Did divers garments[63] on my thoughts bestow,
Like Icarus[64] I feare, unwisely bold,
Am purpos'd others passions now t'unfold.

Sir David Murray of Gorthy (1567–1629)[65]

25

My Caelia sat once by a christal brooke,
Gazing how smoothly the cleere streams did slide,
Who° had no sooner her sweet sight espi'd, *i.e. the streams*
When with amazement they did on her looke.
The waters slyding by her seem'd to mourne,
Desirous stil for to behold her beauty,
Neglecting to the ocean their duty,
In thousand strange meanders made returne;
But oh! againe, with what an heavenly tune,
Those pleasant streames that issued from the spring,
To see that goddesse did appeare to sing;
Whom having view'd, did as the first had done.[66]
If those pure streams delighted so to eye her,
Judge how my soule doth surfet when I see her.

26

Gazing from out the windowes of mine eyes,
To view the object of my hearts desire,

60. The tree and symbol of Venus.
61. The tree and symbol of Minerva.
62. This is the last sonnet in *Aurora*. It leads to a song celebrating marriage. Cf. Spenser's avowed intention in *Amoretti* 80 of returning to composition of *The Faerie Queene*. Alexander is probably referring to drama and his first Senecan Tragedy, *Darius*.
63. In *Anacrisis*, Alexander refers to words and styles as the garments of thought. He is here abjuring writing in favour of warfare and voyages of discovery.
64. Icarus, see Montgomerie, *Cherrie and Slae* st. 12, n. 6.
65. ED. COPY TEXT: *The Tragicall Death of Sophonisba*, 1611. Murray probably attended Glasgow University. He was involved with James's court in his early life, moving into the service of the Prince of Wales in 1599. After Henry's death in 1612, he turned to business ventures.
66. The syntax is complex. Her beauty causes the stream to return, over and over again, to its source, rather than reach the ocean.

My famish'd lookes in wandring troupes forth flies,
Hoping by some good fortune to espie her;
But, having flowne with staring wings long space,
And missing still the aime that caus'd them soare,
Scorning to feed on any other face,
Turnes to their cabins backe and flies no more,
And (there enclos'd) disdaines to view the light,
Shadowing my face with sable cloudes of griefe:
And thus I breath in cares continuall night,
Till that her sight afford me some reliefe.
Sweet, then, make hast these cloudy cares to cleare
And glad those eyes that holds thy sight so deare.

27

Stay passenger and with relenting looke,
Behold heere Bellizarius, I pray,[67]
Whom never-constant fortune, changing aye,
Even at the top of greatnesse quite forsooke,
And, which is wondrous, in a moment tooke
Mee from the hight of an imperiall sway,
And plac'd me heere—blind, begging by this way—
Whose greatnesse sometime scarce the world could brook.
And while thou daignes° the pittifull aspect,° *disown; sight*
Ah sorrow not so much my fortunes past,
As I beseech thee to bewaile this last:
That, from such honour abjectlie deject,° *cast aside*
I yet am forc'd, a spectacle, to live,
Glad to receive the meanest almes thou't give.

Alexander Craig of Rosecraig (1568?–1627)

28

'To Pandora'[68]

O watchfull bird° proclaymer of the day, *i.e. the cockerel*
Withhold, I pray, thy piercing notes from me;
Yet crow and put the pilgrime to his way
And let the worke-man rise to earn his fee.
Yea, let the lion fierce be feard of thee,
To leave his prey and lodge him in his cave,
And let the deepe divine° from dreaming flie, *profound theologian*
To looke° his leaves within his close conclave:° *consult; private cell*

67. Bellizarius, Lieutenant to the Emperor Justinian, was cruelly cast aside after he had outserved his usefulness. Murray, who was close to Henry, Prince of Wales, and unwelcome at court after his death, may see an autobiographical parallel.

68. ED. COPY TEXT: *The Amorose Songes, Sonets and Elegies*, 1606. Craig addresses seven differently named mistresses in an intertwined series of sonnets and lyrics. Some are lightly disguised portraits of contemporaries at court; others represent 'kinds' of love from prostitution through pastoral to platonism.

Each man, save I, may some remembrance have,
That gone is night and Phosper° draweth nie. *morning star*
Beat not thy breast for mee, poor sleepeles slave
To whome the fates alternall° rest denie: *alternate/recurring*
But, if thou wouldst bring truce unto my teares,
Crow still for mercie in my mistris[69] eares.

29
'To Stella.'[70]

The Persian king, in danger to be dround,
Ask'd if no helpe in humane° hands did stand. *human/merciful*
The skipper then cast in the salt profound
Some Persians brave and brought the king to land.
Then Xerxes[71] crowns the skipper with his hand:
'Who saves the king deserv's,' quoth he, 'a crowne!'
But he° at once to kill him gave command, *i.e. Xerxes*
'Die, die,' said he, 'who did my Persians drowne!'
My ladie faire a Xerxes proud doth prove.
My worthless verse she doth reward with gold,
But O, allace, she lets me die for love
And now I rew that I have bin so bold.
As Xerxes crownd and kild his man, right so
Shee seemes a friend and proves a mortall foe.

30
'To Lais'[72]

How oft hast thou, with sweit smelling breath,
Told how thou lovd'st me—lovd'st me best of al;
And (to repay my love, my zeale, my fayth)
Said to thy captive thou wast but a thrall?
And when I would for comfort on thee call,
'Be true to mee, deare to my soule,' said I;
Then, sweetly quhespering,° would thou say, 'I shall,' *whispering*
And, echo-like, 'Deare to my soule,' replie.
But breach of fayth now seemes no fault to thee—
Old promises, new perjuries do prove.
Apes turfe° the whelps they love from tree to tree *toss*
And crush them to the death with too much love.
My too much love I see hath chang'd thee so,
That from a friend thou art become a foe.

69. A riddle-sonnet reveals that the heroine of the poems addressed to 'Pandora' is Agnes Hay, later wife of James sixth Earl of Glencairn.

70. The sonnets in this group are addressed to Penelope Rich, daughter of the first Earl of Essex and Sidney's 'Stella'.

71. Craig was renowned for his classical knowledge. The story of Xerxes comes from Herodotus, *History*, VIII, 118.

72. The name of two notorious Corinthian courtesans.

31
'To Idea'[73]

My wandring verse hath made thee known allwhare° *everywhere*
Thou known by them and they are known by mee:
Thou, they and I a true relation beare,
As but° the one an other can not bee; *without*
For if it chance by thy disdane I die,
My songs shal cease and thou be known no more.
Thus by experience thou mayst plainly see,
I them, thou mee, and they do thee decore.°[74] *invest with honour*
Thou art that dame whom I shall ay adore
In spight of fortune and the frowning fates,
Whose shining beautie makes my songs to sore
In hyperbolik, loftie, heigh conceits:
Thou, they and I throughout the world be known;
They mine, thou theirs and last I am thine own.

Sir Robert Ayton (1569–1638)[75]

32
[Upone King James]

The old records of annalized° fame *chronicled*
Confirmes this wonder with the worlds assent,
That once that ile, which Delos height by name,
In Neptun's bosome like a pillgryme went.[76]
After, when greate Appollo was content
To grace it with the bliss of his birth day,
Then those inconstant motions did relent
And it began to rest, to stand and stay.
Delos, while I admire the, I must say,
In this our Albion° may with the compare: *Scotland*
Before our Phebus° birth we were a prey *i.e. James VI*
To civill motions, tossed here and there,
Bot since his birthstarre[77] did oreshine our state,
Wee stand secure, redeem'd from all debate.

33
Pamphilia hath a number of gud pairtes° *accomplishments*
Which comendatione to hir worth impairtes,

73. If Lais represents one extreme, Idea represents the other. As the Platonic 'idea' or 'form' of love, she leads the poet higher towards contemplation and holiness. Craig's humanist leanings encourage him to attribute her literary immortalisation to himself.
74. This witty presentation of love's 'logic' characterizes the Idea sonnets, which often discuss the passion's moral and metaphysical implications.
75. ED. COPY TEXT (Ayton): Nos. 32; 34–6, British Library Add. MS 10308; No. 33, Laing MS III, 436.
76. ll. 3–4. Delos, a small Aegean island, was the legendary birthplace of Apollo. It was held to appear and disappear like the island in J.M. Barrie's *Mary Rose*.
77. ED. birthstarre] ed.; birthscore MS.

But amongst all, in one sho doth excell,
That sho can paint inimitablie well;
And yet so modest, that if praisd for this
Sho'le sweare sho doth not know what paintinge is,
But straight will blush with such a pretie grace
That one wold think vermelion dyed hir face.
One of hir pictures I have oftymes seene
And wold have sworne that it hir self had bein,
Yet when I bade hir it one me bestowe,
I'le sweare I heard the picturs self say no.
What, think you this a prodegie? It's non:° *none*
The painter and the picture were both one.

34

To view thy beauty well, if thou be wise,
Come not to gaze upon this glass of thyne
But come and looke upon these eyes of myne,
Where thou shalt see thy true resemblance twyce;
Or if thou thinkes that thou profaines thy eyes
When on my wretched eyes they daigne to shyne,
Looke on my heart, wherein, as in a shryne,
The lively picture of thy beauty lyes:
Or if thy harmless modesty thinkes shame
To gaze upon the horrours of my heart,
Come, read those lynes, and reading, see in them
The trophies of thy beautie and my smart;
Or if to none of those thou'l daigne to come,
Weepe eyes, breake heart, and you my verse be dumbe.

35

Faire famous flood, which sometyme did devyde
But now conjoynes two diadems in one,[78]
Suspend thy pace and some more softly slyde;
Since wee have made the° trinchman° of our mone,° *you; spokesman; complaint*
And since non's left but thy report alone
To show the world our captaines last farewell,[79]
That courtesye I knowe when wee are gon
Perhapps your lord the sea will it reveale,
And you againe the same will not conceale,
But straight proclaim't through all his bremish° bounds, *raging*
Till his high tydes these flowing tydeings tell;
And soon will send them with his murmering sounds
To that religious place, whose stately walls
Does keepe the heart which all our hearts inthralls.

78. ll. 1–2. The reference is to the River Tweed, which no longer separates Scotland from England, but joins them in political union under James VI and I.
79. James crossing the Tweed on his way to London; an event worthy of universal recognition.

36[80]

Forsaken of all comforts but these two,
My faggott° and my pipe, I sitt and muse *burning wood/fire*
On all my crosses and almost accuse
The heavens, for dealing with me as they doe.
Then Hope steps in and, with a smyling[81] brow,
Such chearfull expectations doth infuse
As makes me think ere long I cannot chuse
But be some Grandie,° whatsoever I'm now. *Grandee*
But haveing spent my pype, I then perceive
That hopes and dreames are couzens, both deceive.
Then make I this conclusion in my minde:
Its all one thing, both tends unto one scope,
To live upon tobacco and on hope—
The ones but smoake, the other is but winde.

William Drummond of Hawthornden (1585–1649)[82]

37

I know that all beneath the moone decayes,
And what by mortalles in this world is brought,
In Times great periods shall returne to nought;
That fairest states have fatall nights and dayes.
I know how all the Muses heavenly layes,°[83] *songs*
With toyle of spright° which are so dearely bought, *spirit*
As idle sounds of few, or none, are sought
And that nought lighter is than airie praise.
I know fraile Beautie like the purple flowre,
To which one morne oft birth and death affords,[84]
That Love a jarring is of mindes accords,
Where Sense and Will invassall° Reasons power: *usurp*
Know what I list, this all can not mee move,
But that (ô mee!) I both must write and love.

38

Slide soft, faire Forth, and make a christall plaine,
Cut your white lockes, and on your foamie face
Let not a wrinckle bee, when you embrace
The boat that earths perfections doth containe.
Windes, wonder!—and, through wondring, holde your peace.
Or, if that yee your hearts cannot restraine
From sending sighes, mov'd by a lovers case—
Sigh!—and, in her faire haire, your selves enchaine.
Or take these sighes which absence makes arise

80. A translation of Saint Amant's 'Assis sur un fagot, une pipe à la main'.
81. ED. smyling] Add. 28622; simple MS.
82. ED. COPY TEXT (Drummond): Nos. 37–9, *Poems*, 1616; 40, 42, *Flowres of Sion*, 1630; 41, *Works*, 1711.
83. The opening quatrain is based on Passerat's 'Je sçay bien qu'icy bas rien ferme ne demeure.'
84. ll. 9–10 refer to the day lily (hemerocallis), each of whose trumpet shaped flowers live for just one day.

From mine oppressed brest and wave the sailes,
Or some sweet breath new brought from Paradise.
Flouds seeme to smile, love o're the winds prevailes,
And yet hudge waves arise—the cause is this:
The ocean strives with Forth the boate to kiss.

39

As in a duskie and tempestuous night,
A starre is wont to spreade her lockes of gold,
And while her pleasant rayes abroad are roll'd,
Some spitefull cloude doth robbe us of her sight:
(Faire soule) in this black age so shin'd thou bright,
And made all eyes with wonder thee beholde,
Till uglie Death, depriving us of light,
In his grimme, mistie armes thee did enfolde.[85]
Who more shall vaunt true beautie heere to see?
What hope doth more in any heart remaine,
That such perfections shall his reason raine,
If beautie with thee borne, too died with thee?
World, plaine° no more of love, nor count his harmes, *complain*
With his pale trophees Death hath hung his armes.

40

'Runne (sheepheards) run, where Bethleme blest appeares!
Wee bring the best of newes, bee not dismay'd![86]
A saviour there is borne, more olde in yeares,
Amidst heavens rolling hights this earth who stay'd;
In a poor cotage inn'd, a virginie maide,
A weakling did him beare, who all upbeares,
There is hee poorelie swadl'd, in manger lai'd,
To whom too narrow swadlings are our spheares.
Runne (sheepheards) runne, and solemnize his birth!
This is that night, no, day growne great with blisse,
In which the power of Sathan broken is,
In heaven bee glorie, peace unto the earth.'
Thus singing, through the aire the angels swame,[87]
And cope of starres re-echoid the same.

41

'Saint Peter, after the denying his master'

Like to the solitarie pelican,[88]
The shadie groves I hant and deserts wyld;

85. The octet derives from Tasso's 'Come in turbato ciel lucida stella'; the sestet from Tasso's 'Quasi celeste Diva, alzata à volo'.
86. Drummond's lyrical sequences move from earthly to divine love. This dramatic evocation of Christ's nativity may be studied in relation to his pastoral writing as exemplified in § 19.
87. The dramatic power in part derives from the poet echoing the words spoken by the angels in Luke 2. 10–14.
88. The motif of the pelican feeding its young with its blood was a type of Christ's sacrifice on the cross and of charity. The simile fittingly introduces Drummond's dramatisation of Peter's guilt. See Luke 22. 34, 56–62.

Amongst woods burgesses,° from sight of man, *citizens/inhabitants*
From earths delights, from myne owne selfe exild.
But that remorse, which with my falle beganne,
Relenteth not, nor is by change beguild,
But rules my soule and, like a famishd chyld
Renewes its cryes, though nurse doe what shee can.
Looke how the shricking bird that courts the night
In ruind walles doth lurke, and gloomie place:
Of sunne, of moone, of starres, I shune the light,
Not knowing where to stray, what to embrace;
How to heavens lights should I lift these of myne,
Since I denyed Him who made them shine?

42

Why (worldlings) do ye trust fraile honours dreams
And leane to guilted° glories, which decay? *gilded*
Why doe yee toyle to registrate your names
On ycie pillars, which soone melt away?
True honour is not heere;[89] that place it clames
Where black-brow'd night doth not exile the day,
Nor no farre-shining lamp dives in the sea,
But an eternall sunne spreades lasting beames.
There it attendeth you, where spotlesse bands
Of spirits stand gazing on their soveraigne blisse,
Where yeeres not hold it in their canckring hands,
But who once noble, ever noble is.
Looke home, lest hee your weakned wit make thrall,
Who[90] Edens foolish gardner earst made fall.

Sir William Mure of Rowallan (1594–1657)[91]

43

O three times happie, if the day of grace
In my darke soule did (though but dimly) dawne,
If to my strugling thoughts proclamd were peace,
If from mine eyes the vaile of darknesse drawne,
If once the seed of true repentance sawne
Made gushing streames leave furrowes on my face,
Sinnes menstruous rags in pure transparent laune°[92]
Were chang't, O then how happie were my cace!

89. In *Flowres of Sion*, Drummond probes metaphysical problems from a Christian perspective. True love of his lady has led him to seek the higher love of God.
90. Satan, who brought about the fall of Adam.
91. ED. Copy Text: No. 43, *The True Crucifixe for True Catholickes*, 1629; No. 44, *The Joy of Tears*, 1635. Mure was Montgomerie's nephew. Of his own verse, he wrote 'from Montgomery sche hir birth doth clayme.' He was, unlike Montgomerie, a staunch Protestant. After attending Glasgow University, he represented Ayrshire in the Scottish parliament.
92. 'Sinnes menstruous rags,' Isaiah 30. 22. 'transparent laune,' Revelation 15. 6. Mure, a dedicated covenanter, sounds out the direct, bible-echoing strains of protestant verse.

So darknesse paths no more my feete should trace,
So ever on a quyet conscience feast,
Repentance planted so should vice displace,
So clenst from sinne, sinne's filth I should detest!
Grace, light, repentance, inward peace I crave,
Grant these, good Lord, for mee Thy selfe who gave.

44

Jerusalem is of her freedome spoil'd,
Orders of mens devising there bee plac'd:
True Christ is bound, thief Barrabas assoil'd,°[93] *absolved*
Esau much praised, Jacob much disgracd.
The heritage of God is all defacd,
Formalities to substance are preferd:
Lawes are imposd grievous to bee embracd,
Earths fatnesse upon Judas is conferd.
Eye weep, heart groan, black birds my mirth have mard,
Moon hath no light, the sun his beames withdraweth:
The mouth of godly Zephanie is bard[94]
Because the truth in honestie hee showeth.
Fountains of life, which make Gods citie glad,
Are fild with earth, clear springs can not bee had.[95]

93. In the octet, chaos is suggested through Biblical examples of evil flourishing at the expense of virtue.
94. The Old Testament prophet, Zephanaiah, predicted the coming of the day of wrath on Judah.
95. This extended conceit is directed at Charles I, whom Mure sees as the protagonist of chaos and vice.

§ 19: Pastoral Verse

The two poets who dominate this section are also the leading Scottish poets of the later Renaissance. The early lives of **Sir Robert Ayton** *(1569–1638) and* **William Drummond of Hawthornden** *(1585–1649) run parallel. Each was born into a noble family and attended University—Ayton gaining his M.A. from St Andrews; Drummond from Edinburgh. Poetically, too, they begin as followers of the aureate, late Petrarchist tradition. Later, both their lives and poetry moved apart. While Drummond stayed in his Scottish estates, Ayton went south with James. The latter's political career at the London court included appointments as Groom of the Privy Chamber in 1608 and as Secretary to Queen Anne. At the same time, Ayton mixed with the English literati, coming under the influence of Donne especially. While Drummond, throughout his life, remained true to the school of Drayton, Ayton discarded the aureation of his earlier work and began to cultivate a tighter form of witty, epigrammatic composition. Each died peacefully in the role he had chosen for himself; Ayton as British courtier; Drummond as Scottish laird.*

*Their work—in Latin as well as the vernacular—ranges widely. Drummond also wrote in prose; his reflection on death (***A Cypresse Grove***) being particularly memorable. An idea of their contribution to the Scottish Sonnet and of their part in shaping the literature of the early eighteenth century may be gained by looking at § 18 and § 24. As writers of Pastoral verse, they develop a mode, whose earlier popularity in Scotland is witnessed by the practice of Henryson (§ 19A) and others. It is in the Renaissance, however, that it achieved its greatest popularity. Its origins in the classical writings of Theocritus and Virgil appealed to the early humanists. These sources had employed the shepherd motif to combine and counterpoint serious, witty and erotic views of love as variously practised by vulgar, innocent and sophisticated groups in society. Ayton rejoices in such transferences. He delights in using a single conceit to suggest serious and bawdy readings of the same tale as in* **'The Shiphird Thirsis'***. His verse is also intensely dramatic—in part because he is ever conscious of the plots and characters of European Pastoral Drama; in part because he is skilled in imitating the modulations of the speaking voice. Although Drummond's touch is not so light his pastorals share this theatrical quality. In* **Forth Feasting,** *even the River Tweed is given a persuasive voice. Neither poet, however, attempts to deny the stylization and artifice of the mode in which he is writing. Even in* **Moeliades,** *Drummond's early elegy on Prince Henry, he subdues any personal grief to classical rules and conventions.*

19A: *Earlier Pastoral*

Robert Henryson (c.1420–c.1490): 'Robene and Makyne'[1]

1

Robene sat on gud grene hill
Kepand a flok of fe;° — *sheep*
Mirry Makyne said him till,
'Robene, thow rew on me!° — *have pity on me*
I haif the lovit lowd and still°[2] — *i.e. constantly (formulaic)*

1. ED. COPY TEXT: Bannatyne MS (B). Of all Henryson's verse, this poem was the most frequently reprinted in the eighteenth century. Composed in the French *pastourelle* form, it anticipates many of the characteristics of later pastoral verse and drama.
2. One of several Romance formulae, incongruously applied—see also 2.3; 2.4; 5.7–8; 9.5; 12.2; 12.8.

Thir yeiris two or thre;
My dule in dern°[3] bot gif thow dill,° — *in secrecy; diminish*
Dowtles but dreid° I de. — *Doubtless without dubiety*

2

Robene answerit, 'Be the Rude,° — *holy cross*
Na thing of lufe I knaw,
Bot keipis my scheip undir yone wid;° — *in those woods*
Lo, quhair thay raik° on raw. — *roam*
Quhat hes marrit the in thy mude,° — *put you out of humour*
Makyne, to me thow schaw;
Or quhat is lufe, or to be lude?° — *loved*
Fane wald I leir° that law.' — *learn*

3

'At luvis lair gife thow will leir,
Tak thair ane A B C:
Be heynd,° courtas and fair of feir,° — *gracious; in conduct*
Wyse, hardy and fre,° — *generous*
So that no denger° do the deir,° — *disdain; harm*
Quhat dule in dern° thow dre;° — *secret; suffer*
Preis the° with pane at all poweir,° — *Press on; with all vigour*
Be patient and previe.'

4

Robene answerit hir agane,
'I wait° nocht quhat is luve, — *know*
Bot I haif mervell in certane
Quhat makis this wanrufe.° — *causes this despair*
The weddir is fair and I am fane,° — *well-pleased/satisfied*
My scheip gois haill° aboif; — *safely*
And° we wald play us[4] in this plane, — *If*
Thay wald us bayth reproif.'° — *reprove*

5

'Robene, tak tent unto° my taill — *heed of*
And wirk all° as I reid,° — *do exactly; counsel*
And thow sall haif my hairt all haill,
Eik and[5] my madinheid.° — *virginity*
Sen God sendis bute for baill,° — *(a) remedy for sorrow*
And for murning remeid,
I dern with the bot gif I daill,
Dowtles I am bot deid.'[6]

3. 'In dern' usually has sexual connotations. The popularity of later pastoral verse rested largely on this subversive line of eroticism. Cf. 3.5–6; 10.7–8.
4. Sexual pun. 'play us' can mean 'divert ourselves sexually'.
5. Usually, 'And eik'. Henryson is lightly parodying the excesses of the high romantic style.
6. ll 7–8: 'Unless I deal with you in secret, I am surely as good as dead.' The erotic sub-text reads: 'Unless we make love I shall certainly lack (be without) any sexual experience.' 'Death' was a common metaphor for the sexual act. Cf. Ayton, 'The Shiphird Thirsis'.

6

'Makyne, to morne this ilk a tyde,° *same time*
And ye will meit me heir,
Peraventure my scheip ma gang besyd° *may keep nearby*
Quhill we haif liggit full neir.° *lain very closely together*
Bot mawgre° haif I and I byd,° *blame; if I remain*
Fra° thay begin to steir;° *Once; move (away)*
Quhat lyis on hairt I will nocht hyd,
Makyn, than mak gud cheir!'° *cheer up*

7

'Robene, thow reivis me roif° and rest; *steal peace from me*
I luve bot the allone.'
'Makyne, adew, the sone gois west,
The day is neir hand gone.'° *almost over*
'Robene, in dule I am so drest° *set*
That lufe wilbe my bone.'° *bane/destroyer*
'Ga lufe,° Makyne, quhair evir thow list; *Go and love*
For lemman I bid none!'° *For no lover do I argue terms*

8

'Robene, I stand in sic a styll;° *such a state*
I sicht,° and that full sair.' *sighed*
'Makyne, I haif bene heir this quhyle;
At hame, God gif I wair.'° *God grant I were*
'My huny Robene, talk ane quhyll,
Gif thow will do na mair.'
'Makyne, sum uthir man begyle,
For hamewart I will fair.'° *go*

9

Robene on his wayis went,
Als licht° as leif of tre; *light(hearted)*
Mawkin murnit in hir intent,° *i.e. grieved for her future*
And trowd° him nevir to se. *believed (she would)*
Robene brayd attour the bent;° *hurried off over open ground*
Than Mawkyne cryit on hie,° *aloud*
'Now ma thow sing, for I am schent;° *undone*
Quhat alis lufe at me?'° *What does love have against me?*

10

Mawkyne went hame, withowttin faill,
Fully wery, eftir cowth weip.
Than Robene in a ful fair daill[7]
Assemblit all his scheip;
Be that,° sum pairte of Mawkynis aill° *Thereupon; ailment*
Outthrow *his* hairt cowd creip.

7. ll. 3–4: Literally, 'Robin gathered his sheep in a very pleasant valley.' But he has just talked himself out of 'ful fair daill', in its other sense of 'enjoyable sexual intercourse'.

He fallowit hir fast thair till assaill,° *confront/assail (sexual)*
And till hir tuke gude keip:° *paid close attention to her*

11
'Abyd, abyd, thow fair Makyne,
A word for ony thing!
For all my luve it salbe thyne,
Withowttin depairting:°[8] *Undivided*
All haill thy harte for till haif myne
Is all my cuvating;° *craving*
My scheip to morne quhill houris nyne° *until nine o'clock*
Will neid of no keping.'

12
'Robene, thow hes hard soung and say° *recited*
In gestis° and storeis auld, *tales (usually chivalric)*
"The man that will nocht quhen he may
He sall nocht quhen he wald."[9]
I pray to Jesu every day,
Mot eik° thair cairis cauld *increase*
That first preisis with the to play,
Be firth,° forrest or fawld.'° *wood; field (formulaic)*

13
'Makyne, the nicht is soft and dry,
The wedder is warme and fair,
And the grene woid rycht neir us by
To walk attour all quhair;° *everywhere*
Thair ma na janglour° us espy, *mischief-maker/gossip*
That is to lufe contrair:° *opposed*
Thairin, Makyne, baith ye and I,
Unsene we ma repair.'

14
'Robene, that warld is all away
And quyt brocht till ane end,
And nevir agane thairto perfay
Sall it be as thow wend,° *hope*
For of my pane thow maid it play,° *turned it into sport*
And all in vane I spend;
As thow hes done, sa sall I say,
"Murne on! I think to mend." '° *intend to recover/improve*

15
Mawkyne, the howp of all my heill,° *being/welfare*
My hairt on the is sett,

8. The tables being turned, Henryson highlights the pattern of repetition and variation. The technique is sometimes, as here, underlined by verbal echoing—cf. Robene's protestation 11.3–5 with Makyne's 5.3.
9. ED. he sall] original B. text; sall haif MS. (Proverbial.)

And evirmair to the be leill° *loyal*
Quhill° I may leif but lett;° *Until; without hindrance*
Nevir to faill as uthiris feill,° *as (do) many others*
Quhat grace that evir I gett.'
'Robene, with the I will nocht deill!° *deal*
Adew, for thus we mett.'

16
Malkyne went hame blyth annewche,
Attour the holttis hair;° *hoary woods (formulaic)*
Robene murnit and Malkyne lewche;
Scho sang; he sichit sair—
And so left him° bayth wo and wrewche,°[10] *gave back to him; incivility*
In dolour and in cair,
Kepand his hird under a huche,° *crag*
Amangis the holtis hair.'

19B: *Renaissance Pastoral*[11]

Sir Robert Ayton (1569–1638)

Sonnet: The Second Scene of Baptista Guarini his Pastor Fido, *Paraphrased.*[12]

Faire cruell Silvia,[13] since thou scornes my teares
And over lookes my cares with careless eye,
Since my request in love offends thy eares,
Hence forth I vow to hold my peace and dye.
But while I hold my peace, those things shall cry:
The brookes shall murmur and the winds complaine,
The hills, the dales, the deserts where I lye
With echhoes of my sighes shall preach my paine.
Yea,°[14] put the case, they silent would remaine— *Very well/Suppose we*
Imagine brookes and windes should hold ther peace,
Say that hills, vallies and deserts would disdaine
T'acquaint thy deafe disdaines with my disgrace,

10. 'Wrewche' also refers to sheep in unshorn state.
11. ED. Capitalisation. In this section, the older capitalization has been retained where especial emphasis is intended.
12. ED. COPY TEXT: Brit. Lib. Ad. MS 10308. The source is the section in Guarini's *Pastor Fido*, beginning 'Cruda amarilli, che col' nome ancora...' and ending 'e ti dirà la morte il mio martire'. 'Paraphrased' indicates that Ayton is not attempting a word for word translation. It does not mean an expansion on the original; in fact Ayton's version is shorter than Guarini's.
13. Ayton substitutes 'Silvia' (Tasso's shepherdess-heroine in his pastoral drama *Aminta*) for Guarini's Amarillis.
14. ED. Yea] Ad; Yet Hawthornden and Laing. The Ad reading highlights the fact that the sestet presents an 'argument'. This is in strict accordance with James VI's critical intentions. The Scottish sonnet should deal with 'argumentis' where 'change of purposis' were contemplated (*Reulis*, Chapter 8).

Yet when they dumbe, thou deafe to me shall prove,
My death shall speake and let the know my love.

Amintas[15]

Amintas, on a summer day,
To shunn Appollos° beames *the sun's*
Was dryving of his flocks away
To tast some cooling streames;
And through a forrest as he went
Neare to a river side,
A voice, which from a grove was sent,
Invited him to bide.° *stay*
The voice well seem'd for to bewray° *reveal*
Some male° contented minde, *ill*
For oft tymes did he heare it say
'Ten thousand tymes unkinde!'
The remnant of that ragged mone
Did all escape his eare,
For every word brought forth a grone
And every grone a teare.
But nearer, when he did repaire,
Both voice and face he knew.
And see[16] that Phillis was come there,
Her plaints° for to renew! *complaints*
Soe, leaving her to her complaint
And murrmering ragged mones,
He heard her deadly[17] discontent,
Thus all burst forth at once:

'Amintas, is my love to the
Of such a small account,
That thou disdaines to looke on mee
Or love mee as thou wont?° *used to*
Were those the oathes that thou did make,
The vowes thou did conceive,° *formulated*
When I, for thy contentments sake,
My hearts delight did leave?
How oft did thou protest to mee
The heavens should turne to nought,
The sunn should first obscured be
Or thou should change thy thought?
Then, heavens dissolve without delay,
Sunn show thy face noe more,

15. ED. COPY TEXT: Brit. Lib. Ad. MS 10308. Title: Ad.27879. The name Amintas comes from the shepherd Amyntas in Vergil, *Eclogues*, 2, 3, 5, 10.
16. The call for the audience to 'See', and the direct speech which follows, suggests that this piece may have been performed with speaking or singing voices.
17. ED. deadly] Ad.27879; fully Ad.10308.

Amintas love is lost for aye,
And woe is mee therefore.
Well might I, if I had been wise,
Foreseene what now I finde,
But too much love did seale myn eyes
And made my judgement blinde.
All thy behaviours were, God knowes,
Too smooth and too discreete,° *rational*
Like sugar, which impoyson'd growes
Unspy'd, because it's sweete.
Thy oathes and vowes did promise more
Nor° well they could performe, *Than*
Most like a calme, which comes before
An unexpected storme.
God knowes, it would not greive mee much
For to be kill'd for thee,
But, ah, how neare it doth me tuch° *touch*
That thou should murther mee.
God knowes, I care not—for noe paine
Can come for loss of breath!
It's thy unkindnes, cruell swaine,
That greives mee to the death.
Amyntas, tell me if thow may,
If any fault of myn
Hath giv'n the° cause, thus to betray *you*
My hearts delyt and thyn?
No, no, alas! It could not be!
My love to the was such,
Unles if that thow loathed me
For loving the too much.
But, ah alas, what doe I gaine
By those my fond° complaints? *foolish*
My dolour doubles his disdaine,
My greife his pride augments
Although it yeeld noe greater good,
It oft doth ease my minde
For to reproach the ingrattitude
Of him who is unkinde.'

With that, her hand—cold, wan and pale—
Upon her breast she layed
And, finding that her breath did faile,
She sight° and then she sayed, *sighed*
'Amintas!' And with that, poore maid,
She sight again, soe sore,
That after that she never said,
Nor sight, nor breath'd noe more.[18]

18. Ayton's love of formal balance is evident. Phyllis's plea (ll. 25–76) is introduced (ll. 1–24) and concluded (ll. 76–84) by the Narrator, each of whose contributions is briefly interrupted by a cry of grief from the shepherdess (l. 12; l. 81).

'The Shiphird Thirsis'

The shiphird Thirsis longed to die,
Gazeinge upon the gratious eye
Of hir[19] whome he adored and loved,
When sho, whom no les passion moved,
This said: 'O die not yet I pray!
I'le die with the if thou wilt stay.'[20]
Then Thirsis for a while delayes
Tho haist he had to end his dayes,
But while he thus protractes his breathe
Not deyinge unto him was deathe.[21]
At last, while languishinge he lyes
And suckes sweete nectar from hir eyes,
The lovelie shipherdes,° who fand° *shepherdess; found*
The harvest of hir love at hand,
With trimblinge eyes straight falls a cryinge,
'Die, die sweete hart, for I am dieinge!'
And as the swaine did straight reply,
'Behold sweete hart, with the I die!'
Thus spent these happie two there breath
In such a sweet and deathles death,
That they returned to lyf againe,
Againe to try deathes pleasant paine.

'An Epigram'[22]

Philo lov'd Sophia and she againe
Did pay him home° with coy disdaine. *requite*
Yet, when he dye'd, he left her all he had.
What do you thinke? The man was mad.

William Drummond of Hawthornden (1585–1649)

Madrigals

Madrigal XV: 'Of Phillis'[23]

In peticote of greene,
Her haire about her eine,
Phillis, beneath an oake

19. ED. COPY TEXT: Laing MS III, 436. This has been preferred to Ad. 10308 in this instance to show the linguistic differences in a text of Scottish rather than English provenance. Ad 10308, for example, has 'sheppherd' for 'shiphird' (l. 1), 'her' for 'hir' (l. 3), and 'found' for 'fand' (l. 13). Thirsis was the shepherd-friend of Aminta in Tasso's pastoral drama, *Aminta*.
20. The undertones of bawdry in pastoral verse become dominant in this poem. 'Die,' as sexual pun, is the conceit which unifies the work. Here, the lady asks Thirsis to maintain his erection until they reach a mutual climax.
21. ED. ll. 9–10 are omitted from Ad. 10308.
22. ED. COPY TEXT: Brit Lib Ad MS 10308.
23. ED. COPY TEXT: *Poems, 1616*, ed. Andro Hart, 'Madrigalls and Epigrammes'. The source is Marino's 'Mentre Lidia premia'.

Sate milking her faire flocke:
Among that strained moysture (rare delight!)
Her hand seem'd milke in milke, it was so white.

Madrigal XXI: 'Unpleasant Musicke'[24]

In fields, Ribaldo stray'd
Mayes tapestrie to see,
And hearing on a tree
A cuckooe sing, hee sigh'd and softly said:
'Loe, how (alas) even birds sit mocking mee!'

Poems, Part 1, Madrigal IV

When, as she smiles, I finde
More light before mine eyes,
Nor when the Sunne from Inde[25]
Brings to our World a flowrie Paradise:[26]
But when shee gently weepes
And powres foorth pearlie showres
On cheekes faire blushing flowres,
A sweet melancholie my senses keepes.[27]
Both feede so my disease,
So much both doe me please,
That oft I doubt which more my heart doth burne—
Like Love to see her smile or Pitie mourne.

Pastoral Elegy

Poems, Part 2: 'Songe 1'

Sad Damon,[28] beeing come
To that for-ever-lamentable tombe
(Which those eternall Powers, that all controule,
Unto his living soule
A melancholie prison had prescriv'd) *ordained*
Of hue, of heate, of motion quite depriv'd,
In armes wake,° trembling, cold, *weak*
A marble hee, the marble did infold;[29]

24. ED. COPY TEXT: *Poems*, *1616*, ed. Andro Hart, 'Madrigalls and Epigrammes'.
25. ED. COPY TEXT: *Poems*, *1616*, ed. Andro Hart, *Poems*, Part 1, Madrigal IV. India. Used usually to indicate southern lands as opposed to east and west. See *Exequies of Anthony Alexander*, l. 104.
26. The earthly paradise in pastoral verse represented the lost age of innocence.
27. The pastoral ideal of leisure was associated with the melancholic mood.
28. ED. COPY TEXT: *Poems*, *1616*, ed. Andro Hart, *Poems*, Part 2, Songe 1. Damon was a goatherd in Vergil's third eclogue. The death of the heroine of *Poems*, Part 1 is announced at the start of Part 2. This song is an early expression of the poet's grief.
29. Elliptical. The expanded meaning is—'Himself cold as marble, he embraced the marble tomb'.

And, having made it warme with many a showre
Which dimmed eyes did powre,
When griefe had given him leave and sighes them stay'd,
Thus, with a sad 'Alas!' at last he said:

'Who would have thought, to mee
The place where thou didst lie could grievous bee?
And that (deare body) long thee having sought
(O mee!) who would have thought
Thee once to finde, it should my soule confound
And give my heart than death a deeper wound?[30]
Thou didst disdaine my teares,
But grieve not that this ruethfull° stone them beares; *pitiful/piteous*
Mine eyes serve only now for thee to weepe,
And let their course them keepe,
Although thou never wouldst them comfort show,
Doe not repine, they have part of thy woe.

Ah wretch! too late I finde,
How Vertues glorious titles prove but winde;
For, if shee any could release from Death,
Thou yet enjoy'd° hadst breath; *would still have enjoyed*
For, if shee ere appear'd to mortall eine,° *eyes*
It was in thy faire shape that shee was seene.
But ô! if I was made
For thee—with thee why too am I not dead?
Why doe outragious° Fates[31] which dimm'd thy sight, *intemperate*
Let mee see hatefull light?
They, without mee, made death thee to surprise,
Tyrants (perhaps) that they might kill mee twise.

O griefe! and could one day
Have force, such excellence to take away?
Could a swift-flying moment (ah!) deface
Those matchlesse gifts; that grace,
Which Art and Nature had in thee combinde,
To make thy body paragone° thy minde? *match*
Have all past like a cloud,
And doth eternall silence now them shroud?
Is that, so much admir'd, now nought but dust,[32]
Of which a stone hath trust?[33]
O change, ô cruell change! thou, to our sight,
Shewes Destines rigour equall doth their might.

30. ll. 15–19: Drummond's loose, repetitive style may be an attempt to imitate uncontrolled grieving but it makes for complexity. In essence he notes that the pain caused by her attainable dead body is worse than that caused by her unattainable live one.
31. The three Fates, Clotho, Lachesis and Atropos, were held to control the birth, life and death of man.
32. ED. Is that, so much admir'd, now nought but dust] *Poems* 1656; Is what so much admir'd was nought but Dust. *Works* 1711. 1616.
33. 'Which is entrusted to a stone.'

When thou from earth didst passe
(Sweet nymph) perfectiouns mirrour broken was,
And this of late so glorious World of ours,
Like meadow without flowrs
Or ring of a riche gemme made blind appear'd,° *i.e. seemed dark*
Or night, by starre nor Cynthia neither clear'd.[34]
Love, when hee saw thee die,
Entomb'd him in the lidde of either eye
And left his torch within thy sacred urne,
There for° a lampe to burne. *in place of*
Worth, honour, pleasure with thy life expir'd;
Death since (growne sweet) beginnes to bee desir'd.

Whilst thou to us wast given,
The earth her Venus had as well as heaven:
Nay, and her sunne, whiche burnt as many hearts
As hee doth easterne parts;
Bright sunne, which—forc'd to leave these hemispheares—
Benighted° set into a sea of teares. *Dismayed/At night*
Ah death! who shall thee flie,° *flee from*
Sith° the most worthie bee o'rethrowne by thee? *Since*
Thou spar'st the ravens, and nightingalles dost kill[35]
And triumphes at thy will;
But give thou canst not such an other blow,
Because, like her, earth can none other show.

O bitter-sweets of Love![36]
How better is 't at all you not to prove,° *experience*
Than when wee doe your pleasure most possesse,
To find them then made lesse!
O! that the cause which doth consume our joy,
Remembraunce of it too, would too destroy!
What doth this life bestow
But flowrs, on thornes which grow,
Which (though they sometime, blandishing,° delighte) *flattering*
Yet afterwards us smite?
And, if the rising sunne them faire doth see,
That planet, setting, too beholdes them die.

This world is made a hell,
Depriv'd of all that in it did excell.
O Pan! Pan![37] Winter is fallen in our May,

34. 'Neither star nor moon brightened up the night.'
35. The raven's coarse song and selfish nature are conventionally set against the nightingale's sweet voice and its power to evoke loving harmony in others.
36. 'bitter-sweets.' Pastoral writing was influenced by the Petrarchan tradition of love poetry, which emphasised the passion's contrarieties.
37. ll. 85–96. Chaos is invoked by imagining Pan, the god of nature, of song and of shepherds, taking off his garland and pursuing power politics as the evil 'black' equivalent of the, usually benign, Jupiter (Jove).

Turn'd is in night our day;
Forsake thy pipe; a scepter take to thee;
Thy lockes disgarland, thou black Jove shalt bee.
The flockes doe leave the meads
And (loathing three-leaf'd grasse) hold up their heads;
The streames not glide now with a gentle rore,
Nor birds sing as before,
Hilles stand with clouds like mourners, vail'd in blacke
And owles on caban° roofes fore-tell our wracke.° *cabin/hut; destruction*

That Zephyre,° everie yeere *god of west wind*
So soone was heard to sigh in forrests heere,
It was for her! That, wrapt in gownes of greene,
Meads were so earelie seene;
That, in the saddest month, oft sang the mearles°— *blackbirds*
It was for her! For her, trees dropt foorth pearles!
That prowde and statelie courts
Did envie those our shades and calm resorts,
It was for her—and she is gone—ô woe!
Woods cut, againe doe grow;
Budde doth the rose and dazie,° Winter done; *daisy*
But wee, once dead, no more doe see the sunne.

Whose name shall now make ring
The ecchoes? Of whom shall the nymphettes sing?
Whose heavenlie voyce, whose soule-invading straines
Shall fill with joy the plaines?
What haire, what eyes can make the morne in east
Weepe, that a fairer riseth in the west?
Faire sunne, poste° still away— *hurry*
No musicke heere is found thy course to stay.
Sweet Hybla swarmes,[38] with wormewood fill your bowrs—
Gone is the Flowre of Flowrs!
Blush no more rose, nor lillie pale remaine,[39]
Dead is that beautie, which yours late did staine.° *mar (in comparison)*

Aye mee! To waile my plight,
Why have not I as many eyes as night,
Or as that shepheard which Joves love did keepe,[40]
That I still, still may weepe?
But though I had, my teares unto my crosse
Were not yet equall, nor griefe to my losse;
Yet of you brinie showrs,
Which I heere powre,° may spring as many flowrs, *pour*

38. Hybla was a common name for towns in Sicily. Drummond is, more generally, associating bees with a warm, southern climate.

39. ll. 119–20: i.e. because you are no longer overshadowed by the lady's beauty.

40. Io, priestess of Hera at Argos, was loved by Zeus/Jove. Hera turned her into a white heifer and set Argus of the hundred eyes to watch over her.

As came of those which fell from Helen's° eyes; *Helen of Troy*
And, when yee doe arise,
May everie leafe in sable letters beare° *carry*
The dolefull cause for which yee spring up heere.

The Pastoral in Public Verse and Entertainment

Teares on the Death of Moeliades[41]

O heavens! then is it true that Thou art gone,
And left this woefull Ile° her losse to mone, *i.e. Britain*
Moeliades[42]—bright day-starre of the west,
A comet, blazing terrour to the east?
And neither that thy spright° so heavenly wise *soul*
Nor bodie (though of earth) more pure than skies,
Nor royall stemme, nor thy sweet, tender age,
Of adamantine° Fates could quench the rage? *unalterable*
O fading hopes! O short-while-lasting[43] joy
Of earth-borne man, which one hour can destroy!
Then even of Vertues spoyles, Death trophees reares,[44]
As if hee gloried most in many teares.
Forc'd by grimme Destines, heavens neglect our cryes,
Starres seeme set only to act tragoedies:
And let them doe their worst, since thou art gone,
Raise whom they list° to thrones; enthron'd dethrone; *wish*
Staine princely bowres with blood and even to Gange,° *River Ganges*
In° Cypresse sad, glad Hymens torches change. *Into*
Ah! thou hast left to live,° and in the time, *ceased living*
When scarce thou blossom'd in thy pleasant prime;[45]
So falles, by northerne blast, a virgine rose,
At halfe that doth her bashfull bosome close:
So a sweet flourish,° languishing, decayes *blossom*
That late did blush when kist by Phoebus rayes:° *kissed by sunbeams*
So Phoebus, mounting the meridians hight,
Choack'd by pale Phoebe,° faints unto our sight. *moon*
Astonish'd Nature, sullen, stands° to see *waits/stands by*
The life of all this All, so chang'd to bee.
In gloomie gownes, the starres about deplore,
The sea with murmuring mountaines beates the shore;

41. ED. COPY TEXT: *Mausoleum* 1613. This elegy on the death of Henry, Prince of Wales (6 November 1612) is the first of Drummond's published works.
42. In the margin there is an explanation of the name. In challenges, Henry identified himself as 'Moeliades, Prince of the Isles'. Anagrammatically, this becomes '*miles a deo*', or 'a soldier through God'.
43. Compound words were often used to give a sense of archaism to pastoral writing. They are also linked with the High style. The death of the Prince of Wales warranted extreme use of the device.
44. The idea of the martial triumphal procession underlines the poem—fittingly, in view of Henry's reputation as a soldier.
45. *Moeliades* pre-dates Milton's *Lycidas*, with which it has much in common, modally, thematically and structurally. See also ns. 48; 70.

Blacke darknesse reeles o're all, in thousand showres
The weeping aire on earth her sorrow powres,
That (in a palsey)° quakes to finde so soone *paralysed*
Her lover set,° and night burst foorth ere noone.[46] *sunk down*

If heaven (alas!) ordain'd thee young to die,
Why was it not where thou thy might did'st trie?
And to the hopefull world at least set forth
Some little sparke of thine expected worth?
Moeliades, ô that by Isters° streames *River Danube*
Amongst shrill-sounding trumpets, flaming gleames
Of warme encrimson'd swords and cannons roare,
Balls thicke as raine pour'd by the Caspian shore,
Amongst crush'd lances, rising helmes and shields,
Dismembred bodies ravishing the fields;
In Turkish blood made red like Marses starre,
Thou ended hadst thy life and Christian warre!
Or, as brave Burbon,[47] thou hadst made old Rome
Queene of the world, thy triumphs place and tombe!
So heavens faire face to the unborne which reades,
A booke had beene of thine illustrious deedes: [48]
So to their nephewes°[49] aged syres had told *grandchildren*
The high exploits perform'd by thee of old—
Townes raz'd and rais'd, victorious, vanquish'd bands,
Fierce tyrants flying, foyl'd, kill'd by thy hands.
And in dear Arras,[50] virgines faire had wrought
The bayes,° and trophees to thy countrey brought: *laurel wreaths*
While some new Homer, imping pennes° to Fame, *grafting quills/wings*
Deafe Nilus° dwellers had made heare° thy name. *River Nile; to hear*
That thou didst not attaine those honours spheares
It was not want of worth, ô no but yeares.
A youth more brave, pale Troy with trembling walles
Did never see, nor shee° whose name apalles *Rome*
Both Titans golden bowres° for bloody fights, *i.e. East and West*
Mustring on Marses field such Marse-like knights.
The heavens had brought thee to the highest hight
Of wit and courage, shewing all their might
When they thee fram'd. Ay mee, that what is brave
On earth, they as their owne so soone should crave!

46. The first of six verse paragraphs ends its images of disorder with an evocation of the darkness-in-day, which marked the crucifixion of Christ. This provides a clear link with l. 35.
47. The transition to the Constable de Bourbon after contemplating a crusade as the proper end to so promising a life (ll. 40–6) seems strange. Although he is a fine example of courage, he was also a mercenary and traitor.
48. The idea of the Book of Nature confirms the strong Christian undertones of the poem. As in *Lycidas*, these become dominant in the final movement of the poem.
49. While the sense 'nephews' is current, in the sixteenth century the word retained the older meaning of grandchildren of either sex (Lat. *nepos*).
50. Arras was the centre of tapestry making. By transference, the sense becomes—'in expensive tapestries'.

Moeliades, sweet, courtly Nymphes deplore,° *water spirits lament*
From Thuly to Hydaspes pearlie shore.[51]

When Forth,° thy nurse;[52] Forth, where thou first didst passe *River Forth*
Thy tender dayes (who smyl'd oft on her glasse
To see thee gaze) meandring with her streames,
Heard thou hadst left this Round°—from Phoebus beames *i.e. earth*
Shee sought to flie. But, forc'd to returne,
By neighbour brookes, shee gave herself to mourne.
And, as shee rush'd her Cyclades° among, *Aegean Islands*
Shee seem'd to plaine,° that heaven had done her wrong. *voice a complaint*
With a hoarse plaint, Cleyd° downe her steepie rockes *River Clyde*
And Tweed through her greene mountaines
cled with flockes,° *covered with sheep*
Did wound the ocean (murmuring° thy Death) *rumouring*
The ocean that roar'd about the earth
And it to Mauritanian Atlas[53] told,
Who shrunke through griefe, and downe his white haires roll'd
Hudge streames of teares, that changed were in flood,
With which hee drown'd the neighbour plaines and woods.
The lesser brookes, as they did bubbling goe,
Did keepe a consort° unto publicke woe: *accompaniment*
The shepheards left their flockes with downe-cast eyes,
Disdaining to looke up to angrie skies:
Some broke their pipes, and some in sweet-sad layes,
Made senselesse things amazed at thy praise.
His reed, *Alexis* hung upon a tree,
And with his teares made Doven° great to bee.[54] *River Devon*
Moeliades, sweet, courtly Nymphes deplore,
From Thuly to Hydaspes pearlie shore.

Chaste maides, which haunt faire *Aganippe* well,[55]
And you in *Tempes*° sacred shade who dwell, *valley in Thessaly*
Let fall your harpes, cease tunes of joy to sing,
Discheveled make all *Parnassus* ring
With anatheames° sad, thy musicke *Phoebus* turne *anthems*
In dolefull plaints, whilst Joy it selfe doth mourne.
Dead is thy darling, who decor'd thy bayes,° *laurel wreath*
Who oft was wont to cherish thy sweet layes
And to a trumpet raise thine amorous stile,

51. Drummond sets out his verse paragraphs as if they were musical movements. Movements two to five—ll. 69–70; 95–96; 119–20; 141–2—share this couplet refrain. 'Thuly', the island of Thule, here provides the extreme northern equivalent to Nile (South) and the extremes of the rising and setting sun (East and West). Hydaspes is a tributary of the River Indus, on the banks of which Alexander the Great defeated Porus in 326 BC.
52. A reference to Henry's early upbringing in the Scottish Court.
53. 'Mauritanian' continues the geographic spread of the sad news. In classical myth, 'Atlas' held the world on his shoulders. The load is now too heavy for him.
54. ll. 93–4: 'Alexis' is William Alexander, who also wrote an elegy on Henry's death. The River Devon, a tributary of the Forth, runs close to his ancestral home at Menstrie.
55. A well dedicated to the Muses.

That floting *Delos*[56] envie might this Ile.
You *Acidalian* archers[57] breake your bowes,
Your brandons° quench; with teares blot Beauties snowes *torches*
And bid your weeping mother yet againe
A second *Adons* death—nay, *Marses*, plaine![58]
His eyes once were your darts—nay, even his name
Where ever heard, did every heart inflame!
Tagus did court his love with golden streames,
Rhein with his townes, faire *Seine* with all shee claimes.[59]
But, ah, (poore lovers!) Death did them betrey,
And (not suspected) made their hopes his prey!
Tagus bewailes his losse with golden streames,
Rhein with his townes, faire *Seine* with all she claimes.
Moeliades sweet courtly Nymphes deplore,
From Thuly to Hydaspes pearlie shore.

Delicious meads, whose checkred plaine foorth brings[60]
White, golden, azure flowres, which once were kings,[61]
In mourning blacke their shining colours dye,
Bow downe their heads, whilst sighing Zephyres° flye. *west winds*
Queene of the fields, whose blush makes blushe the morne,
Sweet rose, a princes death in purple mourne.[62]
O hyacinthes, for ay your AI keepe still[63]—
Nay, with moe markes of woe your leaves now fill:
And you, O flowre of Helens teares° first borne, *i.e. the elecampane*
Into those liquide pearles againe you turne.
Your greene lockes, forrests, cut in weeping myrrhes,
The deadly cypresse and inke-dropping firres,
Your palmes and mirtles[64] change; from shadows darke
Wing'd Syrens[65] waile and you, sad Ecchoes, marke
The lamentable accents of their mone,
And plaine° that brave *Moeliades* is gone. *complain/lament*
Stay, skie, thy turning course, and now become
A stately arche, unto the earth, his tombe,

56. The central island of the Cyclades (l. 77) and supposed birthplace of Apollo.
57. 'Acidaly' is a fountain consecrated to Venus. Therefore the 'Acidalian archers' are cupids.
58. Adonis was a beautiful youth, loved by Venus. Drummond calls attention to the fact that Henry as shepherd is a poetic convention—the reality of his earthly fame is martial ('nay *Marses* plaine!'). Mars was also a lover of Venus.
59. The rivers cover Germany, France, Spain and Portugal.
60. ll. 121–42: Kastner notes the similarity between this passage and the shepherd's lament on the death of Basilius in Sidney's *Arcadia*.
61. The anemone, narcissus and hyacinth were, mythologically, supposed to be the resurrected forms of three youthful princes.
62. ll. 125–6: Venus, hurrying to help the stricken Adonis, pierced her foot on a thorn. The ensuing blood dyed the—originally—white roses red.
63. Hyacinth was accidentally killed by Apollo. The letters 'AI', representing a sighing sound, were held to be signed by his blood on the flower. Cf. Sidney, *Arcadia*: 'Lily, in mourning black thy whiteness die; O Hyacinth let AI be on thee still.'
64. 'palmes'—palms—symbol of victory and triumph; 'mirtles'—the myrtle was an emblem of love, held sacred to Venus.
65. Mythical creatures, half-bird, half-women, reputed to lure seamen to death by their song.

Over which ay the watrie Iris° keepe°[66] *rainbow; may stand guard*
And sad Electras sisters[67] which still weepe.
Moeliades, sweet, courtly Nymphes deplore,
From Thuly to Hydaspes pearlie shore.

Deare ghost, forgive these our untimely teares,
By which our loving minde, though weake, appeares.
Our losse, not thine! When wee complaine, wee weepe.
For thee, the glistring walles of heaven doe keepe,
Beyond the planets wheeles, above that source
Of spheares, that turnes the lower in its course,
Where sunne doth never set nor ugly night
Ever appeares in mourning garments dight.° *clad*
Where Boreas° stormie trumpet doth not sound, *north wind*
Nor cloudes in lightnings bursting, minds astound.
From cares cold climates farre, and hote desire,
Where time is banish'd, ages n'er expire:
Amongst pure sprights environed° with beames, *surrounded/haloed*
Thou think'st all things below to bee but dreames,
And joy'st to looke downe to the azur'd barres
Of heaven, indented all with streaming starres;
And in their turning temples to behold,
In silver robe the moone, the sunne in gold,
Like young eye-speaking lovers in a dance,
With majestie (by turnes) retire, advance;
Thou wondrest,° earth to see, hang like a ball, *are amazed*
Clos'd in the gastly° cloyster of this All: *spiritual*
And that poore men should prove so madly fond,° *foolish*
To tosse themselves for a small foot of ground.
Nay, that they even dare brave the powers above,
From this base stage of change, that cannot move.
All worldly pompe and pride thou seest arise
Like smoake, that scattreth in the emptie skies.
Other hilles and forrests, other sumptuous towres:
Amaz'd thou find'st, excelling our poore bowres,
Courts voyde of flattrie, of malice mindes,
Pleasure which lasts, not such as reason blindes;
Farre sweeter songes thou hear'st and carrolings,
Whilst heavens doe dance and quire of angells sings,
Than moldie° mindes could faine; even our annoy *worldly*
(If it approach that place) is chang'd in Joy.[68]

Rest, blessed spright, rest saciate with the sight
Of Him, whose beames both dazell and delight—

66. The redemptive promise of the rainbow anticipates the divine triumph in immortal joy celebrated in the last two movements.
67. Electra was one of the seven Pleaides, daughters of Atlas and the ocean-nymph Pleione. They killed themselves and were turned into stars. This anticipates the movement upwards beyond time into the harmony of the spheres. See especially ll. 147–64.
68. The earthly paradise becomes the divine.

Life of all lives! Cause of each other cause!
The spheare and center, where the minde doth pause:
Narcissus of Himselfe, Himselfe the Well,
Lover and Beautie, that doth all excell.
Rest, happie ghost, and wonder in that glasse,[69]
Where seene is all that *shall be*, *is* or *was*,
While *shall be*, *is* or *was* doe passe away
And nought remaine but an Eternall Day.[70]
For ever rest! Thy praise, Fame may enroule
In golden annalles,° whilst about the Pole *chronicles*
The slow Boôtes° turnes, or sunne doth rise *stars in Great Bear*
With skarlet scarfe to cheare the mourning skies:
The virgines to the tombe may garlands beare
Of flowres, and on each flowre let fall a teare.
Moeliades, sweet courtly Nymphes deplore,
From Thuly to Hydaspes pearlie shore.

Forth Feasting: A Panegyricke to the Kings Most Excellent Majestie[71]

What blustring noise now interrupts my sleepe?
What echoing shouts thus cleave my chrystal deep
And call mee hence from out my watrie court?
What melodie, what sounds of joy and sport
Bee these heere hurl'd from ev'rie neighbour spring?
With what lowd rumours doe the mountaines ring,
Which in unsuall pompe on tip-toes stand
And (full of wonder) over-looke the land?
Whence come these glittring throngs, these meteors bright,
This golden people set unto my sight?
Whence doth this praise, applause and love arise?
What load-starre° east-ward draweth thus all eyes? *guiding star*
Am I awake, or have some dreames conspir'd
To mocke my sense with shadowes much desir'd?
Stare° I that living face? See I those lookes, *Gaze upon*
Which, with delight, wont° to amaze my brookes? *used*
Doe I behold that worth, that man divine,
This ages glorie, by these bankes of mine?
Then, is it true what long I wish'd in vaine[72]—
That my much-loving prince is come againe?

69. Narcissus (cf. l. 122) fell in love with his own image as reflected in a pool.
70. Drummond anticipates Milton in *Lycidas* by transcending the problem of youthful death beyond time from a divine perspective faithfully interpreted. God sees and determines instantaneously, what we perceive and live through sequentially. (See Boethius, *De Consolatione Philosophiae*.)
71. ED. COPY TEXT: *The Muses Welcome*, Adamson, 1618. The voice of the River Forth welcomes King James VI on his return to Scotland in May 1617. The title was probably suggested by Marino's *Tebro Festante*, which celebrated the election of Pope Leo XI. Ronsard's eulogy on Henri III influences the work.
72. It had taken James fourteen years to fulfil his promise, given in 1603, to return to Scotland at the earliest opportunity.

So, unto them whose zenith is the Pole,° *pole star*
When sixe black months are are past, the sunne doeth rolle;
So, after tempest, to sea-tossed wights
Faire Helens brothers° show their chearing lights; *Castor and Pollux*
So, comes Arabias mervaile[73] from her woods
And farre, farre off is seene by Memphis floods,° *Mesopotamian river*
The feather'd sylvans,° clowd-like, by her flie *goddesses of the woods*
And, with applauding clangors, beate the skie.
Nyle wonders, Seraps° priests (entranced) rave, *Egyptian god*
And in Mygdonian[74] stone her shape ingrave;
In lasting cedars marke the joyfull time
In which Apollos bird° came to their clime.° *i.e. phoenix; region*
....

....
Ah, why should Isis[75] only see thee shine?
Is not thy Forth, as well as Isis, thine?
Though Isis vaunt shee hath more wealth in store,
Let it suffice thy Forth doth love Thee more.
Though shee, for beautie, may compare with Seine,
For swannes and sea-nymphes with imperiall Rhene,° *River Rhine*
Yet, in the title may bee claim'd in thee,
Nor shee, nor all the world can match with mee.
Now when (by honour drawne) thou shalt away
To her—alreadie jealous of thy stay°— *delaying*
When in her amourous armes shee doth thee fold
And dries thy dewie haires with hers of gold,
Much questioning of thy fare,° much of thy sport, *prosperity*
Much of thine absence long (how e're so short)[76]
And chides, perhaps, thy comming to the north—
Loathe not° to thinke on thy much-loving Forth. *Do not disdain*
O love those bounds,° whereof thy royall stemme° *boundaries; ancestors*
(More then° an hundreth)[77] wore a diademe. *than*
So, ever gold and bayes° thy browes adorne, *laurel leaves*
So, never Time may see thy race out-worne,° *i.e. line usurped*
So, of thine owne,° still mayst thou bee desir'd, *by your own (people)*
Of strangers fear'd, redoubted and admir'd—
So Memorie the° praise, so precious houres[78] *you*
May character° thy name in starrie flowres; *set out*
So may thy high exployts at last make even,° *be justly balanced*
With earth,° thy empyre,° glorie with the heaven. *On earth; power*

73. The snow white swan is suitably invoked, being seldom seen and one of a species which was held to sing prophetically before its death.
74. King Mygdon, who ruled over part of Phrygia, is mentioned in the *Iliad*. He came to the aid of Troy when it was attacked by the Greeks.
75. The poem is not a piece of unrelieved praise. The Forth expresses Scotland's disappointment at James's tardy return (l. 19) by asking why Oxford (River Isis)/England attracts him more than his native river and land.
76. ll. 393–6: Isis is depicted as a temptress analogous to Lindsay's Dame Sensualitie, 'how e're so short'.
77. In the mythic histories, tracing the Scottish kingship back to Adam.
78. 'In such a way that Memory and sweet songs of devotion may praise you.'

The Entertainement of the High and Mighty Monarch, Prince Charles, King of Great Brittaine, France and Ireland

[On the 15th June, 1633 Charles I was welcomed into Edinburgh in a triumphal procession. The king, on a Barbary horse, passed from the West Port to the gates of Holyrood, stopping in turn at five points, where arches had been erected. There he watched a series of enacted tableaux composed by Drummond and designed by the portrait painter Jamesone. The extract comes from the fourth of these. It was performed at the Nether Bow.]

(At a corner of the Theater, from out a verdant grove came Endymion; hee was apparelled like a Shepheard in a long coat of crimson velvet comming over his knee; hee had a wreath of flowers upon his head, his haire was curled and long; in his hand he bare a Sheep-hooke, on his legs were buskins of gilt leather. These before the King had this actioune.)[79]

Endymion:

Rows'd from the Latmian cave where, many years,
That Empresse of the lowest of the Sphaeres,°[80] — *i.e. Cynthia/moon*
Who cheeres the night and kept me hid, apart
From mortall wights,° to ease her love-sicke heart, — *folk*
As young as when she did me first inclose,° — *imprison*
As fresh in beauty as the Maying rose,
Endymion; that whilome kept° my flockes — *who once guarded*
Upon Ionas° flowry hills and rockes — *Ionia (Greek islands)*
And, warbling sweet layes[81] to my Cynthea's beames,
Out-sang the swannets° of Meanders[82] streames; — *cygnets*
To whome (for guerdon)° she, heavens secret barres° — *reward; barriers*
Made open,° taught the paths and powers of starres.[83] — *Disclosed*
By this deare ladies° strict commandement, — *lady's*
To celebrate this day I here am sent—
But whether is this heaven, which starres doe crowne,
Or are heavens flaming splendors here come downe
To beautify this neather° world with me[84]— — *lower*
Such state and glory did e're shepheard see!
My wits my sense mistrust and stay amaz'd;
No eye on fairer objects ever gaz'd.
Sure, this is heaven, for every wandring starre
(Forsaking those great orbes where whirl'd they are,
All dismall, sad aspects abandoning)
Are here assembled, to greet some darling!
Nor is it strange if they heavens hight° neglect, — *height*

79. ED. COPY TEXT: *Entertainement*, Wreittoun 1633.
80. ll. 1–2 combine the two myths centred on Endymion—that he was loved by the Moon (Cynthia) and granted immortality, keeping his sheep eternally on Mount Latmos.
81. Short verse-tales set to music. The specific mode originated in Britanny.
82. Meander: a winding river in ancient Phrygia.
83. The reference is to the myth that the soul of Apollo passed into swans, giving them the power to sing beautifully and to prophesy when dying (swan-song).
84. Another pastoral invocation of the terrestrial paradise/golden age, this time referring dramatically to Charles and the festivities surrounding him.

Unwonted worth produceth like effect;
Then this it is—thy presence (royall youth)
Hath brought them here within an Azymuth,[85]
To tell° (by me, their herauld) comming things° — *record; events to come*
And what each Fate to her sterne distaffe sings; [86]
Heavens volume to unclaspe, vast pages spread,
Mysterious golden cyphers° cleere to reade: — *signs/figures*
Heare then the augur° of the future dayes. — *augury*
And all the starry Senate of the Skyes;° — *Stellar Parliament*
For what is firme° decreed in heaven above, — *unchangingly*
In vaine, on earth, strive mortalls to improve.

[*In turn, Saturn, Jove, Mars, the Sun, Venus, Mercury and the Moon map out an optimistic horoscope for Charles and the realms under his control.*]

Endymion:
That, heretofore, to thy heroicke mind,
Haps hopes not answer'd as they were design'd—
O doe not thinke it strange; times were not come[87]
And these faire starres had not pronounc'd their doome.° — *judgment*
The destinies did on that day attend
(When to this Northren Region° thou should lend — *Scotland*
Thy cheering presence, and charg'd° with renowne, — *(divinely) entrusted*
Set on thy browes the *Caledonian* crowne)
Thy vertues now thy just desire shall grace;
Sterne Chance shall change and to Desert° give place. — *Merit*
Let this be knowne! To all the Fates admit,
To their grave counsell and to every witt° — *person*
That spies Heavens inside! This, let Sibilles° know — *Prophetesses*
And those mad Corybants which dance and glow
On Dindimus high tops with frantick fire![88]
Let this bee knowne to all Apollo's quire!° — *choir*
And, people, let it not be hid from you,
What mountaines noyse and floods proclaime as true:
Where ever fame abroad his prayse shall ring,
All shall observe, and serve this blessed king.

85. Azymuth: an arc of the heavens measured from zenith to horizon. The reference is to the arch erected at the Nether Bow under which this part of the pageant takes place.
86. The Fates were imagined to sit at their spinning wheels, deciding the destined thread of individual lives.
87. ll. 1–3: Elliptical. The expanded general sense is: 'O, do not think it strange that, before now, it has not appeared to your heroic mind that your hopes of fortune have turned out as they were conceived; the time was not right…' (cf. l. 10). The horoscopal pageant, which preceded, represents the moment of revelation and Scotland becomes the ordained place for kingly enlightenment.
88. ll. 14–15: The Corybantes, priests of Cybele, worshipped her in wild, orgiastic dances. Dindymus, in Asia Minor, was renowned for the cult of Cybele.

§ 20: Anonymous (c.1584?): *Philotus*

In the mid-sixteenth century Scotland's dramatic reputation was high. It was based firmly on George Buchanan's Latin translations of Euripedes' **Medea** *and* **Alcestis** *as well as his original plays,* **Baptistes** *and* **Jephthes** *(§ 24). The anonymous farce,* **Philotus**, *although a much more modest endeavour, is also classical in derivation. Its structure and many of its characters are based on the Latin dramas of Plautus and Terence, whose work was currently enjoying a vernacular revival throughout Europe. In Britain, the 'commedia erudita' was closely connected with school performances in its early days but, by the time of* **Philotus,** *the mode had been transferred to the public and professional stage.*

As the end of farce is laughter and the principal means of evoking it are trickery and disguise, the plot of **Philotus** *is prodigiously complicated. Although its author shows considerable theatrical skill in controlling the development from incident to incident, he does rely on the visual effects proper to drama. In this instance, the best preparation for readers of the play may also be the simplest—a précis of the action.*

Philotus, an old rich man, woos young Emilie using a bawd ('macrell'). The girl's father, Alberto, agrees to the arrangement. Meanwhile Emilie elopes with Flavius and Philerno, her brother, returns from abroad. Her father and Philotus are told that Emilie is now dressed as a man and so, on meeting Philerno, think he is his sister. He humours them (farce delights in improbabilities as long as they produce hilarious situations) and so is put under the guardianship of Philotus' daughter, Brisilla. He falls in love with her and enacts a miraculous 'transformation' to masculinity, attributing it to the gods' pity for him. For Philotus he maintains his female role and undergoes a form of marriage with the old man. Then he threatens his 'husband' physically and sends him to bed with a whore. Flavius, after naively witnessing the marriage, believes Emilie is a sorceress, proclaims a comic exorcism and expels her from his house. In the end, all is explained and the two young couples marry, leaving Philotus to bewail his fate and warn other ancient lovers against following his example.

Philotus[1]

The names of the *Interloquiturs*:[2]

Philotus, a rich old man besotted with Emilie	1
Plesant, the jester, who, remaining onstage, comments on the action	25
Emilie, daughter of Alberto	41
The Macrell, a procuress hired by Philotus	57

1. ED. COPY TEXT: Charteris, 1603. A few readings from the later, anglicized Hart edition (1612) have been introduced. STAGE DIRECTIONS: Additional editorial stage directions, designed to make the action more easily understandable, have been provided. These are in italics. AUTHOR: Although names have been suggested including Alexander Montgomerie, the identity of the author remains a mystery. DATING: No definite date has been provided but the early years of James VI's personal rule seem likely, as one of the major sources, Barnabe Riche's *Farewell to Military Profession*, appeared in 1581. Jamie Reid Baxter (JRB) has, however, adduced a good deal of circumstantial evidence suggesting an earlier date at the end of Mary's reign. Other SOURCES and INFLUENCES include the classical comedies of Plautus and Terence and the Italian 'commedia erudita' (especially *Gl'Ingannati*, 1532). The Italian *novelle* tradition is also relevant.
2. CAST LIST: '*Interloquiturs*' means 'disputants'; 'those who discuss' [see n.3]. The character names and descriptions already confirm the strong links between *Philotus* and the classical comedy of Terence and Plautus.

Alberto, friend of Philotus	345
Flavius, lover of Emilie	433
Stephano, servant of Alberto	641
Philerno, long-lost son of Alberto	697
Brisilla, daughter of Philotus	809
The Minister	929
The Huir (Whore)	1111

(The numbers refer to the lines of text, at which point the characters speak for the first time.)

Ane verie excellent and delectabill Treatise[3] intitulit, Philotus.

[*Enter Philotus and Emilie*. Philotus directis his speich to Emilie.]

1

Philotus:

O lustie° luifsome° lamp of licht, — *delightful; loveable*
Your bonynes,° your bewtie bricht, — *beauty*
Your staitly stature trym and ticht° — *well-formed*
With gesture grave and gude;
Your countenance, your cullour cleir,
Your lauching lips, your smyling cheir°— — *expression*
Your properties° dois all appeir — *attributes*
My senses to illude.° — *delude*

2

Quhen I your bewtie do behald,
I man° unto your fairnes fald:° — *must; yield*
I dow not flie° howbeit° I wald, — *flee; although*
Bot bound I man be° youris: — *I am bound to be*
For you, sweit hart, I wald forsaik° — *reject*
The empryce° for to be° my maik,° — *empress…as; consort*
Thairfoir deir dow,° sum pitie tak, — *dove*
And saif° mee fra the schowres.° — *preserve; pangs (of love)*

3

Deme na ill of° my age, my dow— — *Don't look judgmentally at*
Ise° play the yonkeris part° to yow; — *I'll; role of youth*
First try the treuth, then may ye trow,° — *truly ascertain*
Gif I mynd to desave:° — *intend to deceive*
For gold nor geir° ye sall not want,° — *goods; lack*
Sweet hart, with me thairs be na scant° — *pennypinching*
Thairfoir some grace unto me grant,
For courtesie I crave.

3. The same modal description—'treatise'—is given to this play in the edition of 1603 as to Dunbar's lyrical debate between the widow and the two married women (§ 7). The author, however, calls *Philotus* a farce (l. 1341) and it is set in stanzas like a poem.

[*Plesant addresses the audience.*]

4

Plesant:

Ha ha, quha brocht thir kittocks° hither? — *these wantons*
The mekill feind resave the fithir:° — *The devil take the lot of them*
I trow ye was not al together,
This twel-month at ane preiching![4]
Allace, I lauch for lytill lucke,°[5] — *at ill-fortune*
I lauch to sie ane auld carle° gucke:° — *fellow; act the fool*
Wow, wow, sa faine° as he wald fucke, — *keenly*
Fra he fall till his fleitching!° — *Once he begins cajoling*

5

Now, wallie! as the carle he caiges,[6]
Gudeman, quha hes maid your mustages?° — *been grooming your moustaches*
Lo as the boy of fourescoir° rages, — *stripling of eighty*
As he micht not be biddin;° — *advised*
Came ye to wow° our lasse, now lachter°— — *woo; what a joke*
Ye ar sa rasch thair will be slachter!° — *bloodshed*
Ye will not spair nor speir quhais aucht hir,[7]
Ye ar sa raschlie riddin.° — *hotly driven*

6

Emilie:

I wait not weill sir quhat ye meine,
Bot suirlie,° I have seindill° seine — *surely; seldom*
Ane wower° of your yeirs, sa keine° — *wooer; as keen*
As ye appeir to be.
I think ane man, sir, of your yeiris,
Sould not be blyndid with the bleiris,° — *bleared vision*
Ga seik ane partie of° your peiris,° — *match among; contemporaries*
For ye get nane of mee.

[*Exit Emilie*. The auld man speikis to the Macrell to allure the Madyn.]

7

Gude dame, I have yow to imploy° — *I am hiring you*
Sa ye my purpose can convoy;° — *convey*
And that° yon lasse I micht injoy — *And if*
Ye sould not want° rewaird; — *lack*
Give hir this tablet° and this ring, — *precious ornament/locket*

4. ll. 27–28: 'I do believe that not one of you has attended a church service (preaching/sermon) during the past twelve months.'

5. The constant presence on stage of the jester figure links the courtly and stage worlds. As 'wise' commentator on the folly of others his role is reminiscent of the French 'sottie' tradition, represented by Folie in Lindsay's *Satyre* (§ 12).

6. 'Now, gracious me, how randy the old fellow is becoming!'

7. A difficult line. 'You will not be backward in asking for her hand in marriage from the one who owns her.'

This pursse of gold, and spair nathing;
Sa ye about all weill may bring[8]
Of gold tak na regaird.° *Don't worry about costs*

8

Macrell:[9]

Na sir, let me and that allane,° *leave me and that (one) alone*
Suppose scho war maid of a stane,
Ise gar hir grant or all be gane,
To be at your command:[10]
Thocht scho be strange,° I think na wonder, *distant*
Blait° things is sone brocht in ane blunder,° *Bashful; made to blunder*
Scho is not the first, sir, of ane hunder,
That I have had in hand.

9

I am ane fische I am ane eile,° *eel*
Can steir° my toung and tayle richt weill— *direct*
I give me to the mekill Deill,° *great Devil/Satan*
Gif onie can do mair!° *If any can better me*
I can with fair anis° fleitch° and flatter, *ones (women); cajole*
And win° ane crown bot with ane clatter,° *gain; with slick talk alone*
That gars me° drink gude wyne for° watter, *lets me; instead of*
Suppois my back ga bair.° *bare*

[The Macrell intends to allure the Madyn, *who is reading aloud from her book.*]

10

God blis yow maistres with your buik,° *book*
Leise° me thay lips that I on luik;°[11] *How sweet (are); gaze at*
I hope in God to sie yow bruik° *enjoy the use of*
Ane nobill house at hame.
I ken ane man into this toun,
Of hyest honour and renoun,
That wald be glaid to give his gowne,
For to have yow his dame.

11

Emilie:

Now be my saull, I can not sie
That thair sik vertew is in me,
Gudwyfe, I pray yow quhat is he,
That man, quhome of ye meine?° *to whom you refer*

8. 'As long as you bring everything to a favourable conclusion.'
9. In the Renaissance, 'la maquerelle' proved popular in both the European *commedia erudita* tradition and in the Scots dramatic lyrics of Sempill and Stewart of Baldynneis.
10. ll. 59–60: 'I'll have her agree, before it's all over, to be at your bidding.'
11. Solitary reading aloud remained the norm even after the printing presses had begun to make books available.

Macrell:

Philotus is the man, a faith,° *indeed*
Ane ground-riche° man and full of graith:° *solidly rich; wealth/goods*
He wantis° na jewels, claith nor waith,° *lacks; goods*
Bot is baith big° and beine.° *generous; well-to-do*

12

Weill war the woman all hir lyfe,
Had hap° to be his weddit wyfe, *(Who) was lucky enough*
Scho micht have gold and geir° als ryfe,° *goods; abundantly*
As copper in hir kist:° *chest*
Yea, not a ladie in all this lane,° *street*
I wait° micht have mair wealth in hand, *know*
Nor micht have mair at hir command,
To do with quhat scho list.° *wishes*

13

Fair floure, now sen ye may him fang,° *catch*
It war not gude to let him gang,
Unto your self ye'ile do greit wrang
Sweit hart, now and° ye slip° him. *if; let slip (through net)*
Now thair is twentie into this toun,
Of greitest riches and renoun,
That wald be glaid for to sit doun,
Upon thair kneis to grip him!° *seize/grasp him*

14

Thocht he be auld, my joy, quhat reck?° *what of it*
Quhen he is gane give him ane geck,° *derisory gesture*
And tak° another be the neck, *clasp*
Quhen ye the graith° have gottin. *money*
Schaw me your mynd and quhat ye meine,° *intend*
I sall convoy° all this sa cleine,° *bring about; entirely*
That me yee sall esteme ane freine,° *consider a friend*
Quhen I am deid and rottin.

15

Emilie:

I grant, gude-wyfe, he is richt gude,
Ane man of wealth and nobill blude,
Bot hes mair mister° of ane hude° *need; hood*
(And mittanes till his handis)
Nor° of ane bairnelie° lasse lyke mee— *Than; young*
Mair meit his oy nor wyfe to be:[12]
His age and myne cannot agrie
Quhill that the warld standis.

12. (Who am) 'More suited to be his grandchild (or niece) than his wife'.

16

Macrell:

Let that allane! He is not sa auld,
Not yit of curage° half sa cald, — *vigour*
Bot gif ye war his wyfe ye wald
Be weill aneuch content;
With him mair treitment° on ane day, — *entreaty/beseeching*
And get mair making off° ye may, — *sexual satisfaction*
Nor° with ane wamfler,° suith to say, — *Than; young wooer*
Quhen twentie yeiris ar spent.

17

Ye neyther mell° with lad nor loun,° — *mix; lowborn fellow*
Bot with the best in all this toun—
His wyfe may ay sit formest doun° — *take the foremost place*
At eyther burde° or bink;° — *table; bench*
Gang formest in° at dure or yet,° — *Enter first/ahead; gate*
And ay the first gude-day wald get,[13]
With all men honourit and weill tret,° — *well-looked after*
As onie hart wald think.

18

Se quhat a womans mynde may meise° — *appease*
And heir quhat honour, wealth and eise
Ye may get with him, and° ye pleise — *if*
To do as I devyse:
Your fyre° sall first be birnand cleir,° — *fire; burning brightly*
Your madynis than sall have your geir° — *clothes*
Put in gude ordour and effeir,° — *array*
Ilk° morning or° yow ryse. — *Each; before*

19

And say, 'Lo maistres, heir your muillis,° — *slippers*
Put on your wylicote° for it cuillis,° — *under-petticoat; gets chilly*
Lo, heir ane of your velvote stuillis,° — *velvet stools*
Quhairon ye sall sit doun.'
Than twasum cummis° to cambe your hair, — *two together come*
Put on your heidgeir,° soft and fair— — *head-dress*
Tak thair your glasse° sie all be clair°— — *glass/mirror; fine*
And sa gais on your goun.° — *gown*

20

Than tak to stanche° the morning drouth,° — *quench; drought*
Ane cup of mauesie° for your mouth; — *Malmsey wine*
For fume cast sucker in at fouth,[14]
Togidder with a toist.° — *sop of toast*
Thrie garden gowps° tak of the air, — *gulps*

13. 'And would be accorded always the first greeting.'
14. 'To make it fume, throw in copious amounts of sugar.'

And bid your page in haist prepair,
For your disione° sum daintie fair, — *breakfast*
And cair not for na coist:° — *do not trouble about the cost*

21

Ane pair of plevaris pypping hait,° — *plovers piping hot*
Ane pertrick° and ane quailyie° get, — *partridge; quail*
Ane cup of sack,° sweit and weill set, — *sack (wine)*
May for ane breckfast gaine.° — *be fitting*
Your cater° he may cair for syne,° — *caterer; attend to then*
Sum delicate agane ye dyne,° — *Some delicacy for your dinner*
Your cuke to seasoun all sa fyne,
Than dois imploy his paine.° — *takes pains*

22

To sie° your servantes may ye gang, — *oversee*
And luke your madynis all amang—
And gif thair onie wark be wrang,
Than bitterlie them blame.
Than may ye have baith quaiffis° and kellis,° — *coifs; head-dresses*
Hich candie ruffes and barlet bellis,[15]
All for your weiring and not ellis,° — *All for your unique wear*
Maid in your hous at hame.

23

And now quhen all thir warks is done,
For your refresching efternone,° — *afternoon refreshment*
Gar bring unto your chalmer sone,
Sum daintie dische of meate:
Ane cup or twa with muscadall,° — *sweet wine*
Sum uther licht thing thairwithall—
For rasins or for capers call,
Gif that ye please to eate.

24

Till suppertyme then, may ye chois,
Unto your garden to repois,
Or merelie to tak ane glois,° — *to have a gossip*
Or tak ane buke and reid on;
Syne to your supper ar ye brocht,
Till fair° full far that hes bene socht,° — *To fare; sought out*
And daintie disches deirlie bocht,
That ladies loves to feid on.

25

The organes than into your hall,
With schalme° and tymbrell° sound thay sall, — *shawm; timbrel*

15. High ruffs made of 'Cyprus lawn' were the height of fashion in the Scotland of the later sixteenth century. 'Candie' (= Crete) suggests the mediterranean origin of the new mode (JRB). Barlet bellis—obscure.

The vyole° and the lute with all,[16] — *viol*
To gar your meate disgest.° — *To make you digest your food.*
The supper done, than up ye ryse
To gang° ane quhyle—as is the gyse;° — *walk/promenade; custom*
Be° ye have rowmit° ane alley thryse, — *By the time; roamed*
It is ane myle almaist.

26

Than may ye to your chalmer° gang, — *bedroom*
Begyle° the nicht, gif it be lang, — *Beguile*
With talk and merie mowes° amang, — *jests*
To elevate the splene:
For your collation,° tak and taist — *refreshment before bed-time*
Sum lytill licht thing till disgest,
At nicht use rense° wyne ay almaist, — *Rhenish*
For it is cauld and clene.

27

And for your back,° I dar be bould° — *clothing; bold*
That ye sall weir, even as ye would,
With doubill garnischings of gould,
And craip.° Above° your hair — *crepe; Over*
Your velvote hat, your hude of stait,
Your myssell° quhen ye gang to gait,° — *veil; are ready to go out*
Fra sone and wind, baith air° and lait, — *early*
To keip that face sa fair.

28

Of pareis wark wrocht by the laif,
Your fyne half-cheinyeis ye sall have,
For to decoir ane carkat.[17] Craif° — *Craves*
That cumlie collour bane° — *collar-bone*
Your greit gould cheinyie for your neck?
Be bowsum° to the carle,° and beck,° — *(Then) be submissive; boor; curtsey*
For he hes gould aneuch, quhat reck?° — *so what*
It will not stand on nane.° — *It won't hurt anyone.*

29

And for your gownes, ay the new guyse° — *fashion*
Ye with your tailyeours may devyse—
To have them louse,° with plets and plyis° — *loose-fitting; pleats and folds*
Or clasped clois behind.
The stuffe,° my hart, ye neid not haine:° — *material; stint*
Pan velvot,[18] raysde,° figurit or plaine — *raised*
Silk, satyne, damayse° or grograine,° — *damask; grogram*
The fynest ye can find.

16. The shawm is a wind instrument, the timbrel percussion and the viol and lute are strings.
17. ll. 217–9: 'Of Paris-work [gold and silver smith's work], made of gold or silver leaf, you shall have your fine half chains, to embellish a jewelled head ornament.'
18. 'Pan velvot,' Fr. 'panne de velours', a material like velvet with a longer nap.

30

Your claithes on cullouris cuttit out,° *slashed to show colours underneath*
And all pasmentit° round about, *i.e. decoratively trimmed*
My blessing on that semelie snout,° *pretty mug (face—colloq.)*
  Sa weill I trow sall set them.° *set them off*
Your schankis°of silk, your velvot schone,° *legs; shoes*
Your borderit wylicote° abone,° *embroidered waistcoat; on top*
As ye devyse° all sall be done, *envisage*
  Uncraifit° quhen ye get them. *No longer desired*

31

Your tablet° be your hals° that hings,° *locket; neck; hangs*
Gould bracelets and all uther things,
And all your fingers full of rings,
  With pearle and precious stanes:
Ye sall have ay quhill ye cry ho,° *You shall always have for the asking*
Rickillis° of gould and jewellis, jo.° *Heaps; darling*
Quhat reck to tak the bogill-bo,° *It is pointless to take the huff*
  My bonie burd,° for anis! *pretty maid*

32

Sweit hart, quhat farther wald ye have?
Quhat greiter plesour wald ye crave?
Now be my saull, yow will desave
  Your self, and ye forsaik him:° *if you let him go*
Thairfoir, sweit honie, I yow pray,
Tak tent in tyme° and nocht delay, *Take timely heed*
Sweit sucker,° neck me not with nay,° *sugar; do not say no to me*
  Bot be content to tak him.

33

Plesant:

The devill cum lick that beird° auld rowan.° *bearded; old hag*
Now sie the trottibus and trowane,[19]
Sa busilie as sho is wowane,° *wooing/enticing*
  Sie as the carling craks.° *Look how the old wife chats*
Begyle the barne°—sho is bot young! *Deceive the child*
Foull fall thay lips. God! nor that toung[20]
War doubill gilt with nurisch doung,
  And ill cheir on thay cheikis!

34

Emilie:

Gude-wyfe, all is bot gude I heir,
For weill I lufe to mak gude cheir;
For honouris, gould and uther geir

19. 'trottibus' and 'trowane' are obscure abusive terms, referring to someone who is roaming and vagrant.
20. ll. 262–4: 'Ill-fortune to those lips. God! would that tongue were doubly plastered with ripe compost, and bad cess to those cheeks!'

Thay can not be refusit.
I grant indeid, my daylie fair
Will be sufficient and mair—
Bot be it gude, ye do not spair,
As royallie to ruse it![21]

35

I grant all day to be weill tret,
Honours anew and hicht upset,[22]
Bot quhat intreatment sall I get,
I pray yow, in my bed?
Bot with ane lairbair° for to ly, *impotent person*
Ane auld deid stock,° baith cauld and dry,[23] *stick*
And all my dayes heir I deny,° *refuse*
That he my schankes sched.° *gets to part my thighs*

36

His eine half sunkin in his heid,
His lyre° far caulder than the leid,° *body; lead*
His frostie flesch, as° he war deid, *as if*
Will for na happing° heit.° *event; become warm*
Unhealthsum hosting° ever mair, *coughing*
His filthsum flewme° is nathing fair, *filthy phlegm*
Ay rumisching° with rift° and rair,° *producing noise; rift; rumble*
Now, wow gif that be sweit!° *how sweet that would be*

37

His skynne hard clappit° to the bane; *tautly stretched*
With gut and gravell baith ouirgane[24]—
Now quhen thir troubles hes him tane,° *killed him*
His wyfe gets all the wyte!° *blame*
For° Venus games I let them ga,° *As for; pass*
I gesse hee be not gude of thay°— *at them*
I could weill of his maners ma,
Gif I list till indyte.[25]

38

Macrell:
For Venus game cure not a cuit,° *don't worry a jot*
Waill me° ane wamfler° that can do it; *Pick out for me; young buck*
Sen thair may be na uther buit,° *remedy*
Plat° on his head ane horne:° *Place...horn (i.e. cuckold him)*
Handill me that° with wit and skill, *Let me take care of that*

21. ll. 271–2: 'But however good it is, you do not deprive yourself of richly praising it!' 'Rusit' can also mean 'artful' or 'cunning', giving a potential play on words.
22. ll. 273–4: 'I accept that I shall be well treated every day, and well set up (with) honours ever new.'
23. ll. 278–92. Emilie confirms the conflict between age and youth by using images of decay, drawn from medieval death lyrics, to describe her aged suitor.
24. 'Overcome with troubles of both the gut and gravel.'
25. ll. 295–6: 'I could elaborate further upon his characteristics, if I wanted to recite them.'

Ye may have easments at your will,
At nicht gar° young men cum yow till,° *have; to you*
Put them away at morne.

39

Emilie:
Gude-wyfe, all is bot vaine ye seik,
To mee of sik maters to speik,
Your purpois is not worth ane leik,° *leek*
I will heir yow na mair.
Mark, dame—and this is all and sum—
If ever ye this earand cum,° *come on this errand (again)*
Or of your head I heir ane mum,° *the least sound*
Yea sall repent it sair.

[*Exit Emilie.*]

40

Macrell:
Yon daintie dame scho is sa nyce° *fastidious*
Sche'ill nocht be win be na devyce,
For nouther prayer nor for pryce,° *bribe*
For gould nor uther gaine.
Scho is sa ackwart° and sa thra,° *perverse; stubborn*
That with refuse I come hir fra,
Scho, be Sanct Marie, sayde mee sa,° *spoke to me in such a way*
I dar not ga agane.

[*Exit Macrell.* Philotus enteris in conference with the Madynis father.]

41

Philotus:
Gude gosse,° sen ye have ever bene *gossip/pal*
My trew and auld familiar freind,
To mak mair quentance° us betwene, *intimacy*
I glaidly could agrie:
Ye have ane douchter quhome untill,
I beare ane passing grit gude will,
Quhais phisnomie prefigures° skill *features indicate*
With wit and honestie.

42

Gif mee that lasse to be my wyfe,
For tocher-gude° sall be na stryfe *dowry*
(Beleive mee scho sall have ane lyfe!)
And for your geir I cair not.
Faith, ye your self sall modifie° *assess*
Hir lyfe-rent, land and conjunctfie[26]—

26. '(assess) The amounts she enjoys from her rights for life on all her possessions, her land and her joint holdings.'

And, gossop, quhair thay same° sall be, *those same*
  Appoynt° the place and spair not.[27] *Designate*

43

Betwixt us twa the heyris-maill° *male heirs*
Sall bruik° my heritage,° all haill, *enjoy use of; heritable estate*
Quhilks, gif that thay happen to faill,
  To her heyris quhat saever.° *whosoever*
My moveables I will devyde:
Ane part my douchter to provyde,
Ane pairt to leave sum freind° asyde *(i.e. Alberto)*
  Quhen deith sall us dissever.

44

Alberto:
Gude sir and gossop, I am glaid
That all be done as ye have said,
Tak baith my blissing and the mayd
  Hame to your hous togidder.
And gif that scho play not hir pairt,
In onie lawfull honest airt, *art/manner*
And honour yow with all hir hairt,
  I wald sho gaid not thither!

[*Exit Philotus*. Alberto speiks to his Dochter:]

45

For the° ane man I have foreseine° *you; made provision of*
(Ane man of micht and welth I meine)
That staitlier may the susteine,
  Nor ony of all thy kin;
Ane man of honour and renoun,
Ane of the potentes° of the toun, *influential people*
Quhair nane may beinlier° sit doun, *more comfortably/affluently*
  This citie all within.

46

Emilie:
God and gude nature dois allow,
That I obedient be to yow,
And father, hithertils I trow,
  Ye have nane uther seine;
And als° estemis yow for to be *also*
Ane loving father unto mee,
Thairfoir, deir father, let mee see,
  The man of quhome ye meine.

27. ll. 335–6. Alberto is not to 'spare' in minimising his daughter's dowry rights so that he may gain as much from the deal as possible.

47

Alberto:

Philotus is the man indeid,
Qhair thow ane nobill lyfe may leid,
With quhome I did sa far proceid,
Wee want bot° thy gude will; *only*
Now give thy frie consent thairfoir,
Deck up,° and do thy self decoir°— *Dress up; adorn yourself*
Gang quickly to, and say no moir,
Thow man° agrie thairtill! *must*

48

Emilie:

Gif ye fra furie wald refraine,
And patientlie heir me agane,
I sould yow schaw in termis plane,
With reason ane excuse:
Sen mariage bene but thraldome free,° *is only a form of free servitude*
God and gude nature dois agree,
That I quhair as it lykes not mee,
May lawfullie refuse.

49

I am fourtene, and hee fourescoir,° *eighty*
I haill and sound, hee seik and soir,
How can I give consent thairfoir,
Or yit till him agree?
Judge gif Philotus be discreit° *in possession of all his faculties*
To seik ane match sa far unmeit,° *so greatly unsuitable*
Thocht I refuse him, father sweit,
I pray yow pardon mee.

50

Alberto:

How durst thow, trumper,° be sa bald *deceiver*
To tant° or tell that he was ald, *argue/dispute*
Or durst refuse ocht that I wald
Have biddin the obey?
Bot sen ye stand sa lytill aw,° *in so little awe*
Ise gar yow, maistres, for to knaw° *I'll have you know, mistress,*
The impyre° parents hes, be law, *power*
Abuif° thair children ay! *Over*

51

And heir to God I mak ane vow,
Bot gif thow at my bidding bow,
I sall the dresse°—and harkin how, *punish*
And syne advyse the better!° *And then think better of it*
I sall thee cast intill ane pit,
Quhair thow for yeir and day sall sit

With breid and water, surely knit° — *firmly tied*
Hard bound intill ane fetter.

52

Thow sat sa soft upon thy stuill,
That making off° maid the ane fuill, — *upbringing*
Bot I sall mak thy curage cuill,
For all thy stomack stout!° — *i.e. brave words*
That efterwards, quhill that° thow leif, — *for as long as*
Thou's be agast° mee for to greif. — *terrified*
Perchance thow greines that play to preif,° — *long to test that game*
Advyse thee and speik out!

53

Emilie:
Sweit father, mitigate your rage,
Your wraith and anger sir, asswage,
Have pitie on my youthlie age—
Your awin flesch and your blude.
Gif in your yre° I be ouerthrawin, — *ire*
Quhome have ye wraikit° bot your awin? — *destroyed*
Sic creweltie hes not bene knawin,
Amang the Turkes° sa rude.° — *Turks/infidels; violent*

54

The savage beists into thair kynde,° — *by nature*
Thair young to pitie ar inclynde,
Let mercie thairfoir muif° your mynde — *move compassionately*
To° her that humblie cryis: — *Towards*
Tak up° and lenifie° your yre, — *Take hold of; mitigate*
Suspend the furie of your fyre,
And grant me layser,° I desyre, — *leisure*
Ane lytill to advyse.° — *think things over*

[*Exit Emilie and Alberto.* Heir followis: the oratioun of the yonker Flavius to the madyn, hir answer and consent, the convoying of her from her father. Her father and the auld wower followis and finds Philerno the madyns brother, laitlie arryved, quhome thay tak to be the madyn, and of his deceit.][28]

55

Flavius:
The raging low,° the feirce and flaming fyre — *flame*
That dois my breist and body al combure,° — *burn up*
Incendit with the dart of grit desyre
Fra force of these twa sparking eyis ful sure,
Hes me constraynit to cum and seik my cure
Of her, fra quhom proceidit hes my wound—

28. This footnote marks the end of the introduction ('protasis'). The changed stanza form begins the complication ('epitasis') with its inevitable misunderstandings and disguises.

Quhom neyther salve nor syrop can assure[29]
Bot only sho can mak me saif and sound!

56

Lyke as the captive with° ane tyrant taine, *by*
(Perforce with promise toistit° to and fro) *tossed*
Quhen that he seis° all uther graces gaine,° *sees; mercies by-passing him*
Man succour° seik of him that wrocht° his wo, *help; caused*
So mon I fald° to my maist freindly fo, *yield*
To seik for salve of her that gave the sair:° *wound*
To pray for peace, thocht rigour° bid me go *violent energy*
To cry° for mercie, quhen as I may na mair.° *appeal; can no longer*

[*Enter Emilie. Flavius addresses her.*]

57

Sa, sen ye have me captivate as thrall,° *captured as a slave*
Sen ye prevaill, let pitie now have place:
Have mercie, sen ye maistres ar of all,
Grudge not to grant your supplicant sum grace.
To slay ane taine man,° war bot lack,° allace, *captive; blameless*
Fra that° he cum voluntarlie in will; *Unless*
Sen I am, mistres, in the self same cace—
Ane thrall consenting—pitie war to spill!° *kill*

58

Quhat ferly thocht puir I, with luif opprest,
Confes the force of the blynd archer boy:[30]
How was Appollo for his Daphne drest° *punished*
And Mars amasit° his Venus to enjoy; *confounded*
Did not the thundering Jupiter convoy
For Danae him self into ane showre?[31]
The gods above, sen luif hath maid them coy° *silenced them*
Unto his° law, then quhy sould I not lowre?° *i.e. Cupid's; yield*

59

As taine with° ane nor Daphne mair decoir° *captivated by; decorative*
Quhais vult° to Venus may compairit be, *countenance*
And bene in bewtie Danae befoir
Suppose the god on hir° did cast his eye; *i.e. Emilie*

29. 'Which neither external (salve/ointment), nor internal (syrup/soothing liquid) medication can heal.'
30. ll. 457–8: 'It is no marvel if poor I, with love oppressed, admit to the power of the blind archer boy...' (i.e. Cupid).
31. ll. 459–62. Apollo, the sun god, was struck by one of Cupid's arrows, making him fall passionately in love with the nymph Daphne. She tried to escape his advances and was turned into a laurel tree. Mars and Venus were trapped by an invisible net, forged by Venus' jealous husband, Vulcan. Danae, imprisoned by her father in a bronze tower, was seduced by Jupiter, who transformed himself into a shower of gold.

Quhais graces to hir bewtie dois agrie,
And in quhais fairnes is no foly found.
Quhat mervell mistres, than,° suppose ye se, *then*
With willing band° me to your bewtie bound, *bond*

60

Quhais bricht, conteyning° bewtie with the beamis *all-encompassing*
Na les al uther pulchritude dois pas:° *surpass*
Nor to compair ane clud with glansing° gleames, *shining*
Bricht Venus cullour with ane landwart las,° *country girl*
The quhytest layke° bot with the blackest asse,° *whitest bleached linen; ash*
The rubent rois° bot with the wallowit weid.° *ruby rose; withered weed*
As purest gold is preciouser nor° glasse, *than*
Your bewtie sa all uther dois exceid:

61

Your hair lyk gold and lyke the pole° your eye,[32] *pole star*
Your snawisch° cheiks lyke quhytest allabast,° *snowy; alabaster*
Your lovesum lips, sad, soft and sweit wee sie,° *we see*
As roses red quhen that ane showre is past;
Your toung micht mak Demosthenes[33] agast,
Your teith the peirls micht of thair place depryve;
With buillis° of Indian ebur,° at the last, *globes; ivory*
Your papis° for the prioritie dois stryve. *breasts*

62

And lyke as quhen the stamping seale is set
In wax weill wrocht—quhill it is soft, I say,
The prent thairof remayning may ye get,
Suppois the seale it self be tane away—
Your semlie shaip° sa sall abyde for ay, *lovely form*
Quhilk throw the sicht my sensis hes ressaifit,° *received*
Thocht absent ye, yit I sall nicht and day,
Your presence have as in my hart ingraifit.° *engraved*

63

Thocht fansie be bot of ane figure° fainit,° *image; counterfeit*
Na figure feids° quhair thair is na effect:° *is nourished; substance*
Evin sa, sweit saull, I perisch bot as painit,° *tormented*
With fansie fed that will na fasting breck.° *brook*
Suppois I have the accident, quhat reck?[34]
Grant me the solide substance to atteine,
Gif not, quhen ye to deith sall me direct,
Quhom bot your awin have ye confoundit° clein? *brought to confusion*

32. A rhetorical 'descriptio' of the lady moving from head downwards. Decorously suited to the higher style and dignified stanza form.
33. Greek politician and outstanding orator of the 4th century A.D.
34. '(Even) Supposing I possess the non-substantial, of what value is it?'

64

Last, sen ye may my meladie° remeid, *sickness*
Releive your Sysiphus[35] of his restles stane:
Your Titius'[36] breist that dois full ryfely bleid,° *copiously bleed*
Grant grace thairto, befoir the grip° be gane; *clawing/pang*
Cum stanche the thrist of Tantalus[37] anone,° *at once*
And cure ye wounds gevin with Achilles[38] knyfe.
Accept for yours, fair maistres, such a one,
That for your saik dar sacrifice his lyfe!

65

Emilie:

Your orisoun,° sir, sounds with sic skil *declamation*
In Cupid's court as ye had bene upbrocht,
Or fosterit in Parnassus'[39] forkit hill,
Quhair poetis hes thair flame and furie socht
(Nocht taisting of sweit Helicon[40] for nocht,
As be your plesant preface dois appeir)
Tending thairby, quhill as we have na thocht,° *while we are unaware*
To mak us to your purpois to adheir.

66

With loving language tending till allure,° *to entice*
With sweit discourse the simpill till ouirsyle,° *to delude*
Ye cast your craft, your cunning and your cure[41]
Bot° puir orphanes and madynis to begyle: *Only*
Your waillit out° words, inventit for a wyle,° *carefully chosen; trick*
To trap all those that trowis° in yow na traine:° *believe; treachery*
The frute of flattrie is bot to defyle
And spred that° wee can never get agane. *disperse what*

67

Ye gar us trow that all our heids be cowit,° *trimmed*
In praysing of our bewtie by the skyis;° *to the skies*
Quhen with your words we are na mair bot movit
This way, to sie gif us ye may suppryse.
Your doubill hart dois everie day devyse,
Ane thowsand shifts° was never in your thocht: *sleights*

35. Sisyphus, King of Corinth, punished in the after-life for his cunning, had to roll a heavy boulder up a hill—the boulder always rolling down again, just as he reached the summit.
36. Tityus was punished in the after-life for having tried to rape the mother of Apollo and Diana, by being pegged to the ground while two vultures tore eternally at his liver.
37. In Hades, Tantalus was made to stand in a pool of water, which receded when he tried to drink, and under bunches of fruit which moved when he tried to eat.
38. Legendary Greek hero, who is one of the main characters of Homer's *Iliad*.
39. A mountain range in Greece, sacred to Apollo and the Muses—hence connected with music and poetry.
40. Fountain of the Muses.
41. 'You put forward/cast your skill/craftiness, knowledge/trickery and concern/false cure.' The context suggests that the second senses are in each case intended.

Ye labour thus with all that in yow lyis
For till undo, and bring us all to nocht—

68

And this conceate is common to yow all!
For your awin lust, ye set not by° our schame: *disregard*
Your sweitest words ar seasonit all with gall,
Your fairest phrase disfigures bot defame.° *disgrace*
I think, thairfoir, thay gritlie ar to blame
That trowis° in yow mair nor the thing thay se. *believe*
Boit I, quhill that Emilia is my name
To trow I sall like to Sanct Thomas[42] be!

69

Flavius:
For feir, sweit maistres, quhat remeid?
Quha may perswade quhair thair is dreid?
Yit deme ye wrangouslie° in deid, *you judge unjustly*
Now be my saull, I sweir!
Your honour, not your schame, I seik:
I count° not by my lust ane leik;° *value; leek*
It was na sik thing, maistres meik,
That maid me to cum heir!

70

This is my sute,° ye sall me trust, *suit*
(Judge ye your self gif it be just)
In honest luif and honest lust,
With yow to leid my life:
This is the treuth of my intent,
In° lawfull lufe bot onlie bent,° *On...set*
Advyse yow gif ye can consent,
To be my weddit wyfe.

71

Emilie:
Sir, surelie gif I understude
Your meining for to be as gude,
I think in ane° wee sould conclude, *unanimously*
Befoir that it wer lang.
I am content to be your wife,
To lufe and serve yow al my lyfe,
Bot rather slay me with a knyfe,
Nor offer me ane wrang.

72

Bot sir, ane thing I have to say,
My father hes this uther day,

42. Like St Thomas the doubter, she will believe nothing without proof.

In mariage promisit me away
Upon ane deid auld° man, *extremely old*
With quhome—thocht I be not content—
Till nane uther he will consent;
Mak to thairfoir for till invent
Ane convoy, gif yow can.[43]

73

Lykewayis yow mon° first to me sweir *must*
That ye to me sall do na deir,° *harm*
Nor sall not cum my bodie neir,
For villanie nor ill,
Ay quhill the nuptiall day sall stand;
And farther sir, gif mee your hand,
With me for to compleit the band,
And promeis to fulfill.

74

Flavius:
Have thair my hand with al my hart,
And faithfull promeis for my part,
Na tyme to change, quhill° deithis dart *until*
Put till my lyfe ane end;
Bot be ane husband traist and trew,
For na suspect that anis° sall rew,° *even once; repent*
Bot readie ay to do my dew,° *do what I ought to*
And never till offend.

75

Emilie:
All day quhairto the treuth to tell,
I dar nocht with that matter mel,° *concern myself unduly*
Bot yit I sall devyse my sell,
Ane schift to serve our turne:
For keiping strait,° baith lait and air,° *being closely guarded; early*
Unsend-furth° may I never fair,° *Unsummoned; go out*
Make I ane mint° and do na mair, *attempt*
I may for ever murne.

[*She paces around pensively.*]

76

Quhen I have unbethocht me° thryse, *considered*
I can na better way devyse,
Bot that I man° me disagyse *must*
In habite° of ane man. *clothing*
Thus I but danger, or but dout,° *with no dubiety*
This busines may bring about;

43. ll. 575–6: 'Therefore, set yourself to devise a way out of this, if you can.'

In mans array unkend pas out,° *leave unrecognised*
For ocht my keipars can.° *Despite the efforts of my warders*

77

Thairfoir, ye sall gang and provyde
Ane pages claithis in the meine tyde,° *meantime*
For all occasions me besyde,° *(to have) at hand...*
Against° I have ado: *...in preparation for (what)*
Let thame, evin as thay list, me call,[44]
Or quhat sumever me befall,
I hope within thrie dayis I sall
Cum quyetly yow to.

78

Flavius:

Be my awin meins I sall atteine,
And send to yow thay claithis unsene,
Convoy° lat sie all things sa cleine,° *Carry out; faultlessly*
That never nane suspeck.
I will wait on my self, and meit yow,
To se your new claiths as thay set yow,° *how they suit you*
The carle° that hecht° sa weill to treit yow, *old fellow; promised*
I think sall get ane geck.° *i.e. be made to look a fool*

[*They separate. Time is presumed to have passed. Flavius is seen to wait for Emilie.*]

79

Emilie:

I have won narrowlie away,[45]
Yon carle° half put me in effray, *i.e. Stephano*
He lay in wait and waiting ay,
In changing aff my claithis.
Sir, let us ga out of his sicht,
Sen I am frie, 'My freind, gude-nicht!'
He lukis as all things war not richt,[46]
Lo yonder quhair he gais!

80

Flavius:

My onlie luif and ladie quhyte,° *white (i.e. fair)*
My darling deir and my delyte,
How sall I ever the requyte° *repay you*
This grit gude, will let see,
That, but respect that men callis schame,
Nor hazart of thy awin gude name,

44. The meaning is ambivalent. 'Let them call for me, as much as they want' or 'Let them call me whatever they want.'
45. 'I have just managed to get away.'
46. I.e. 'He looks as if he knew something were up.'

For brute, for blasphemie nor blame,
 Hes venterit all for mee.[47]

[*Exeunt Flavius and Emilie. Enter* Stephano, Albertus Servant *with Alberto and Philotus*.]

81

Stephano:[48]
Maister, full far I have yow socht,
And full ill newes I have yow brocht—
The thing, allace, I never thocht,° — *believed possible*
 Hes happinnit yow this day!
Your douchter, sir, (ye had bot ane)
Ane mannis claithis hes on hir tane° — *assumed*
And quyetlie hes hir earand gane,° — *gone about her business*
 I can not tell quhat way!

82

I wonderit first, and was agast,
Bot quhen I saw that sho was past,° — *had gone*
I followit efter wonder fast,
 Yit was I not the better!
Scho schiftit hes hir self° asyde, — *has dodged /changed clothes*
And in sum hous sho did hir hyde,
Na sir, quhat ever sall betyde,
 It will be hard to get her.

83

Alberto:
Fals pewtene,° hes scho playit that sport? — *whore*
Hes scho me handlit in this sort?° — *manner*
To God I vow, cum I athort° — *(if) I come across her*
 And lay on hir my handis,
I sall hir ane exampill mak
To trumpers all durst° undertak, — *all deceivers (who) dare to*
For to commit sa foull ane fack,° — *deed*
 Quhill that this citie standis!

84

Vylde° vagabound, fals harlot, hure!° — *Vile; whore*
Had sho na schame, tuke sho na cure° — *no consideration*
Of parentis, that hir gat° and bure,° — *conceived; bore*
 Nor blude of quhilk sho sprang?
All honest bewtie to dispyse,

47. ll. 637–40: elliptical. '(repay you) Who have ventured all for me without taking into account either what people might call shameful, or the risk to your own good reputation through rumour, slander or censure.'

48. Although Stephano has the same position as the slave in classical comedy, he remains largely passive. If anyone is the inheritor of Terence's Davos or Phormio in inventive trickery it is the Plesant.

And lyke ane man hir disagyse,
Unwomanlie, in sik ane wyse,
As gudget° for to gang! *camp-follower*

85

Fals mischant,° full of all mischeif,° *wretch; evil*
Dissaitfull traitour, commoun theif,
Of all thy kin curit not° the greif, *indifferent to*
For° fleschly, foull delyte. *Because of*
Quha sall into sik trumpers trust—
Quhais wickit wayis ar sa unjust,
And led with lewd, licentious lust
And beastlie appetyte?

86

Philotus:

O sex uncertaine, frayle and fals,
Dissimulate and dissaitfull als,
With honie lips to hald in hals,° *have power over*
Bot with ane wickit mynde;
Quhome will dois mair nor° reasoun mufe,°[49] *more than; (does) influence*
Mair lecherie nor honest lufe,
Mair harlotrie nor gude behufe—
Unconstant and unkynde!° *unnatural*

87

In quhome ane shaw,° bot na shame sinks,[50] *outward show*
That ane thing sayis and uther thinks,
Ane eye lukis up, ane uther winks,
With fair and feinyeit° face! *feigned*
Bot gossop, go quhill it is greine° *it is still fresh*
For to seik out quha hes hir seine;
Gif of hir moyen° wee get ane meine,° *circumstances; idea*
It war ane happie grace.° *a piece of good fortune*

[*Before they can hurry off to seek out Emilie*, *Philerno enters*.]

88

Philerno:

Gude sirs, is nane of yow can tell
In quhat streit dois Alberto dwell,
Or be quhat singe Ile knaw my sell[51]
Gude brethren, all about?
[*Aside*]

49. Plato's image in *The Republic* of the yoke of reason controlling the animal appetites is invoked in this speech.
50. Elliptical. '(Womankind) who sink through (preferring) an outward show of modesty to (genuine) shame.'
51. 'Or by what means/sign may I come to recognize (him) myself.'

For thocht I be his sone and heyre,° *heir*
I knaw him not a myte the mair,° *mite the more*
And to this town dois now repair,
  My father to find out.

[*The two old men think that Philerno is Emilie, in her male disguise, and rush to seize him*]

89

Alberto:
Yea, harlote, trowit thow for to skip?° *slip away*
Sen I have gottin of the ane grip,
Be Christ, I sall thy nurture nip[52]
  Richt scharply, or wee sched!° *before we part*
For God, nor I rax in ane raip,° *I'll be hung first*
And ever° thow fra my hand escaip, *If ever*
Quhill I have pullit the lyke ane paip,° *teat*
  Quhair nane sall be to red.° *rescue*

90

Philotus:
Rage not gude gosse,° bot hald your toung. *gossip/friend*
The las° bot bairnlie° is and young, *lass; childlike*
I wald be laith° to wit hir dung,° *unwilling; beaten*
  Suppose° scho hath offendit: *(Even) supposing*
Forgive hir this ane fault for mee,
And I sall souertie° for hir bee, *surety*
That instantly sho sall agree,
  That this slip sould be mendit.

[*Philerno, dimly understanding the situation, panders to their mistake*]

91

Philerno:
Father, I grant° my haill offence, *admit*
Thir° claithes I have tane till ga hence, *These*
And gif it please yow till dispence,
  With thir things that ar past:
Thir bygane faultes will ye forgive,
And efter, father, quhill° I live, *as long as*
Agane I sall yow never greive
  Quhill that my lyfe may last.

92

Schaw me the maner and the way,
And I your bidding sall obey,
And never sall your will gane say,° *go against*
  Bot be at your command:

52. ll. 707–8: 'By Christ, I shall take your education severely in hand.'

Alberto:
This fault heir frelie I forgive thee,
(Philotus is the man releives° thee, *(who) gets you off*
Or utherwayis I had mischeifit° thee!) *harmed*
And now give mee thy hand.

93

This is my ordinance and will:
Give thy consent Philotus till,
To marie him and to fulfill
That godlie blissit band:

Philerno:
Father, I hartlie am content
And heirto gives my full consent,
For it richt fair wald mee repent° *I'd quite fairly regret it*
Gif I sould yow gainstand.

94

Philotus:
Heir is my hand my darling dow° *dove*
To be ane faithfull spous to yow—
Now, be my saull, gossop, I trow
This is ane happie meiting!
This mater, gosse, is sa weill drest° *settled*
That all things ar cumde for the best,
Bot let us set amang the rest,
Ane day for all compleiting.

95

Alberto:
Ane moneth and na langer day,° *not a day longer*
For it requyres na grit delay,
Tak thair your wyfe with yow away,
And use hir as ye will:

Philotus:
Forsuith ye sall ga with me hame,
Quhair I sall keip yow saif fra schame.
Unto the day° (or than mee blame) *i.e. wedding day*
That scho° sall have nane ill.° *That woman; harm*

[*Exit all. Philotus takes Philerno to his house.*]

96

Plesant:
Quha ever saw in all thair lyfe,
Twa cappit cairlis° mak sik ane stryfe? *ill-humoured old fellows*
To tak a young man for his wyfe,
Yon cadgell° wald be glaid!° *wanton fellow; delighted*
The feind resave the, feckles frunt[53]—

53. 'The devil take you, you useless effigy!'

Put doun thy hand and graip° hir cunt— *grip*
The carle kennis not, he is sa blunt,° *slow-witted*
Gif scho be man or maid!

97

Auld guckis,° the mundie,° sho is a gillie!° *fool; lunatic; youth*
Scho is a colt-foill°, not a fillie,° *foal; filly*
Scho wants° a dow,° bot hes a pillie,° *lacks; vagina; penis*
That will play the ane passe!° *bring you to a pretty pass*
Put doun thy hand, vane° carle, and graip, *useless*
As thay had wont to cheis the paip,° *elect the pope (obsc.)*
For thow hes gotten ane jolie jaip,° *fine plaything*
In lykenes of ane lasse!

[Philotus speiks to his dochter Brisilla.]

98

Philotus:
Brisilla, dochter myne, give eir—
A mother I have brocht the heir,° *here to you*
To mee, a wyfe and darling deir—
I the command thairfoir:
Hir honour, serve, obey and luif,
Wirk ay the best for hir behuif,° *benefit*
To pleis hir sie thy pairt thow pruif
With wit and all devoir.° *duty*

[Philotus to his new bryde.]

99

Philotus:
Use hir even as your awin my dow,
Keip hir, for sho sall ly with yow
Quhill° I may lawfullie avow, *Until*
To lay yow be my syde:
Philerno:
I sall your dochter, husband sweit,
Na les nor my companyeoun treit,
And follow baith at bed and meit,° *i.e. bed and board*
Quhill that I be ane bryde.

[*Exit Philotus. Time is presumed to have passed.* Philerno to Brisilla.]

100

Philerno:
How dois the quheill of Fortoun go!
Quhat wickit weird° hes wrocht our wo *cruel fate*
Brisilla, youris and myne also
Unhappilie, I say?
Our fathers baith hes done agrie,

That I to youris—evin as ye sie—
And ye to myne, sall maryit be,
And all upon ane day.[54]

101

Hard is our hap° and luckles chance! *fortune*
Quha pities us, suppose wee pance...° *however we consider it*
Full oft this mater did I skance° *reflect upon*
Bot with my self, befoir:
I have bene threatnit and forflittin° *severely scolded*
Sa oft, that I am with it bittin,° *bitten/eaten up (by it)*
Invent a way or it be wittin,° *before it is discovered*
And remedie thairfoir.

102

Brisilla:
Maistres, allace for sik remeid!° *if only such a remedy existed*
That sik ane purpois° sould proceid— *intention/object*
I wald wisch rather to be deid
Nor in that maner matchit!° *Than make such a match*
Quhat aillit ye parentes to prepair
Your childrens deip continuall cair;
Your crewell handes quhy did ye spair
First, us to have dispatchit?[55]

103

Unnatural fathers! Now quhairfoir
Wald ye your dochters thus devoir° *prey upon*
For° your vane° fantasies, far moir *Out of; futile*
Nor° onie gude respeck?° *Than; worthy concern*
Is it not doittrie° hes yow drevin, *foolish behaviour*
Haiknayis[56] to seik for haist to heavin?
I trow that all the warld evin,
Sall at your guckrie geck.° *gawk at your foolishness*

104

Solace to seik, them selves to sla,° *slay*
Ane myre° to misse,° thay fall in ma,° *mire; avoid; more/deeper*
Thay get bot greif, quhen as thay ga *as they attempt*
To get thair greitest game!° *sport*
And wee young things tormentit to,
Thair daffing dois us swa undo,
Gif thay be wyse, thair doings, lo!
Will signifie the same.

54. This proposed marriage between Brisilla and Alberto is never mentioned again.
55. *ll. 815–6.* Brisilla wonders why they were not killed at birth.
56. 'Haiknayes' are ambling horses, suited for ladies. The inference is that the old men are making an obviously deluded choice.

105

Philerno:

It profeitis not for to compleine,
Let us forsie our selves betwene
How wee this perrell may preveine,° *take precautions against*
And saif us fra thair snairis;° *preserve us from their snares*
Gif that the goddes (as thay weill can!)
Wald mee transforme intill ane man,
Wee twa our selves sould marie than,
And saif us fra thair cairis!° *attentions*

106

Brisilla:

Mak yow a man! That is bot mowis!° *mere tomfoolery*
To think thairon your greif bot growis,
For that devyse, deuill haid it dowis,[57]
Sen it can never be:

Philerno:

Quhy not, gif that with faith we pray?
For oft the goddes as I hard say,
Hes done the lyke,° and yit thay may *the same*
Perchance till us agrie:

107

That Iphis[58] was a mayd we reid,
And swa did for his prayer speid,
For verie reuth,° the goddes indeid *pity*
Transformde hir in ane man;
Pigmaleon's[59] prayer purchast° lyfe *purchased*
Unto° his new eburneall° wyfe, *For; ivory-like*
(Quhais handis had carvit hir with ane knyfe,
With visage paill and wan.)

108

Quhy may not now, als weill as than,° *then*
The goddes convert me in ane man?
The lyke, gif that my prayer can,
I surelie will assay:
Maist secreit goddes celestiall,
Ye michtie muifers° greit and small, *movers*
And heavinlie powers, ane and all,
Maist humblie I yow pray:

57. 'As for that trick, leave that to the devil to do.'
58. Cretan daughter of Ligdos and Telethusa, Iphis was raised as a boy in order to save her life. On her engagement to Ianthe, she was transformed into a young man, through the intervention of Isis.
59. Pygmalion, King of Cyprus. Legend has it that, enraptured with the statue (possibly carved by himself) of Venus, he prayed to obtain a similarly lovely woman as his wife. Venus/Aphrodite caused the statue to come to life, so granting his request.

109

Luke doun from your impyre abone,° *realm above*
And, from your heich, triumphant trone,
Till us puir saullis° send succour sone *souls*
Of your maist speciall grace.
Behald how wee puir madynis murne,
For feir and luif how baith wee burne,
Thairfoir, intill ane man mee turne,
For till eschew° this cace. *avoid*

110

Behald, our parents hes opprest,
And by all dew° thair dochters drest° *due right; chastised*
With unmeit° matches to molest,° *unsuitable; harass*
Us sillie° saullis ye sie. *innocent*
Thairfoir, immortall goddes of grace,
Grant that our prayeris may tak place;
Convert my kynde,° this cairfull° cace *nature; anxious*
With solace to supplie.

111

Plesant:

Ane faith perfumit with fyne folie,° *foolishness*
And monie vane word alla-volie,° *at random*
Thy prayer is not half sa holie,
House-lurdane,° as it semis! *(You) household villain*
Bot all inventit for a wyle° *stratagem*
Thy bedfallow for to begyle,
The bonie lasse bot to defyle—
Na dowbilnes that demes!° *who suspects*

112

Brisilla:

Maistris quhat now? Me think ye dreme
(Or than to be in sowne° ye seime) *swoon*
Scho lyis als deid! quhat sall I deime
Of this unhappie chance?
Scho will not heir me for na cryis,
For plucking on, scho will not ryis,[60]
Sa larbair-lyke,° lo! as scho lyis, *exhausted*
As raveist° in a trance. *As (if) ravished*

113

Philerno:

O blisfull deitie divyne,
Maist happie convent,° court and tryne,° *company; retinue*
That dois your glorious eiris inclyne
Our prayeris to adheir;° *follow*
We rander thanks unto yow all,

60. I.e. 'Even if I pull at her (clothes) she will not get up.'

For herring us quhen that wee call,
And ridding us from bondage thrall°— *i.e. bonds of servitude*
As plainlie dois appeir.

114

I am ane man Brisilla, lo!
And with all necessaris thairto
May all that onie man may do—
I sall gar° yow considder! *have*
Now sen the goddis abone° hes brocht° *above; brought about*
This wonderous wark, and hes it wrocht,
And grantit all, evin as wee socht,
Let us be glaid° togidder. *rejoice*

115

Brisilla:
Now sen the gods hes succour sent
And done even as wee did invent,
My joy, I hartly am content,
To do as ye devyse.
Throw gods decreit,° my onlie choyse, *By godly decree*
In mutuall luif wee sall rejoyse,° *give great joy (to each other)*
Our furious fathers baith, suppose
Thay wald skip in the skyis![61]

[*Some time is presumed to have passed. Enter Philotus.*]

116

Philotus:
My dow,° suppois I did delay, *dove/sweetheart*
Now cum is our sweit nuptiall day—
Thairfoir mak haist swa that wee may
In tyme cum to the kirk:
Philerno:
Ga quhen ye list sir, I am readie.
(Thair is ane gus-heid,° for, be our ladie,° *goose; by our lady*
I was your sone, and ye my dadie,
This morning in the mirk!)° *dark*

[*They exit and reappear with the* Minister. *Flavius observes unseen.*]

117

Minister:
I dout not bot ye understand,
How God is Authour of this band,
And the actioun that wee have in hand,
He did himself out set:
To that effect, all men I meine[62]
Micht keip thair bodyes puir and cleine,

61. ll. 919–20: 'If our insane fathers were to get knowledge of this, they would both jump sky-high.'
62. Elliptical. 'For the end, I mean to say, that everyone.'

Fra fornication till absteine,
And children to beget.

118

Bot sen the mater cums athort° *about*
Ilk uther day, I will be schort,° *I'll keep it short*
And dois the parties baith exhort,
To charitie and luif.
Tak heir this woman for your wyfe,
Keip, luif and cherisch hir but° stryfe, *without*
All uther, als terme of your lyfe,[63]
Saif hir, ye sall remuif.

[*Minister addresses Philerno.*]

119

Tak for your spous Philotus than,
Obey and luif him as ye can,
Forsaik for him all uther man,
Quhill deith do yow dissever:
The Lord to sanctifie and blesse yow,
His grace and favour als° I wisch yow, *also*
Let not His luif and mercie miss yow,° *pass you by*
Bot be with yow for ever.

[*Exit all except Flavius.*]

120

Flavius: [64]
O mercie, God, how may this be?
Yon is indeid richt Emilie.
In forme of hir, a faith, I sie
Sum devill hes me desaifit!
I will in haist thairfoir gang hame,
Expell yon spreit for sin and schame,
And to tell me the awin richt name,
For Gods caus I will craif it.

[*Flavius is about to exit, when Emilie enters.*]

121

The Croce of God, our Saviour sweit,
To saif and sane[65] me fra that spreit,
That thow na hap° have for to meit, *chance*
With me in all thy lyfe!

63. 'All...remuif' i.e. 'Forsaking all others, for as long as you shall live.' Pauline doctrine and the Christian marriage service are evoked by the Minister.
64. Flavius, having viewed the wedding ceremony from afar, assumes Philerno to be the 'real' Emilie. Believing that he has been living with a demon or spirit, he proceeds to repudiate his former love.
65. To protect from an evil influence by ritual sign or act, particularly by making the sign of the cross.

In God's behalf I charge the heir:
That thow straik° in my hart na feir, *strike*
Bot pas thy way, and do na deir° *harm*
To neyther man nor wyfe.

122

First, I conjure the be Sanct Marie,
Be alrisch° king and queene of farie,° *elvish; faerie*
And be the Trinitie, to tarie° *stay*
Quhill° thow the treuth have taulde;[66] *Until*
Be Christ and His apostilles twell,° *twelve*
Be sanctis of hevin and hewis° of hell, *spectres*
Be auld Sanct Tastian[67] him sell,
Be Peter and be Paull.

123

Be Mathew, Mark, be Luik and Johne,
Be Leythe, Stix and Acherone,[68]
Be hellische furies everie one,
Quhair Pluto is the prince:[69]
That thow depart, and do na wonder,
Be lichtning, quhirle wind,° hayle nor thunder, *whirlwind*
That beast nor bodie get na blunder,° *distress*
Nor harme, quhen thow gais hence!

124

Throw power I charge the of the Paip,
Thow neyther girne, gowl, glowme, nor gaip,[70]
Lyke anker saidell,° lyke unsell aip,° *anchorite; evil-doing ape*
Lyke owle nor alrische elfe;
Lyke fyrie dragon full of feir,
Lyke warwolf,° lyon, bull nor beir, *werewolf*
Bot pas yow hence, as thow come heir,
In lykenes of thy selfe.

125

Emilie:
Gude-man, quhat meine° ye? Ocht bot gude!° *intend; No good, it seems to me*
Quha hes yow put in sik ane mude?
Befoir° I never understude, *From the start*
The forme of your conjuring.

Flavius:
I charge the yit as of befoir:° *the same as before*
Pas hence,° and troubill me no moir. *Go away from here*

66. ED. taulde] H; taull C.
67. Saint Augustine, 4th century Christian saint and influential theologian.
68. Lethe, Styx and Acheron are rivers of the underworld.
69. Greek god, ruler of the underworld.
70. 'You neither snarl, howl, scowl nor gape.'

Trowis thow to draw me ovir the scoir,°[71] *mark*
Fals feind, with thy alluring?° *enticement*

126

Emilie:
Gude-man, quhat misteris all thir mowis°— *what need for all these grimaces*
As ye war cumbred with the cowis?° *tormented by hobgoblins*
Ye ar, I think, lyke Johne of Lowis,[72]
Or ane out of his mynde!

Flavius:
In Gods behalfe I the beseiche,
Impesche° me not with word nor speiche! *Impede*
Ill spreit! To God I me beteiche,° *commit myself*
Fra° the and al thy kynd! *(To protect me) From*

127

Plesant:
Ha ha! Ha ha! Ha ha! Ha ha!
The feind resave° the lachters a!° *receive; all laughers*
Quhilk is the wysest of us twa,
Man, quhidder thow or I?
Flemit fuill,° hes thow not tint thy feill,[73] *Accursed fool*
That takis thy wyfe to be ane deill?
Thow is far vainest,° I wait weill, *by far the most foolish*
Speir at° the standers by. *Enquire of*

128

Flavius:
I charge the yit, as I have ellis,
Be halie relickis,° beidis and bellis, *holy relics*
Be ermeitis° that in desertis dwellis, *hermits*
Be lumitoris° and tarlochis:° *limiters (friars); low persons*
Be sweit Sanct Stevin, stanit to the deid,° *stoned to death*
And be Sanct Johne, his halie heid,[74]
Be Merling, Rymour, and be Beid,[75]
Be witchis and be warlochis,° *warlocks*

129

Be Sanct Maloy,[76] be Moyses rod,[77]
Be Mahomeit,° the Turkisch god, *Mahomet*

71. In conjurations chalk marks protected the innocent from evil powers.
72. King James V's jester.
73. 'tint thy feill.' Literally—'lost your intuitive logic.'
74. John the Baptist, beheaded on the order of Herod.
75. Merlin, Thomas the Rhymer and Bede were mythically associated with magic.
76. Probably Saint Malo, recognised as the first bishop of St Malo. He was a seventh century Welsh monk, who went to Brittany to work as a missionary.
77. Moses led the Israelites from oppression in Egypt, to freedom in the Promised Land. Dying of thirst in the desert, they were saved by God, who instructed Moses to strike a rock with his rod. Water flowed miraculously from the rock.

Be Julian and Sanct Elous nod,° *sign of command*
Be Bernard and be Bryde;[78]
Be Michaell that the Dragon dang,° *slew*
Be Gabriell and his auld sang,
Be Raphaell, in tyme of thrang,° *distress*
That is to be as gyde.[79]

130

Emilie:
My luif, I think it verie lyke
That ye war licht° or lunatyke, *light-headed*
Ye feir, ye fray,° ye fidge,° ye fyke,° *are alarmed; fidget; move restlessly*
As with a spreit possest!
Quhat is the mater that ye mene?
Quhat garris yow braid?° Quhair have ye bene? *makes you leap back*
Quhat aillis yow, joy? Quhair have ye sens
To rage with sik unrest?

131

Flavius:
Quhat have I sene, fals hound of hell?
I trowit, quhen I did with the mell,° *became intimate with you*
Thow was richt Emilie thy sell,
Not ane incarnate devill!
Bot I richt now, with my awin eine,
Richt Emilie have maryit seine!
Sa thow mon be ane spreit uncleine—
Lord saif me fra thy evill!

132

Be vertew of the Halie Ghaist
Depairt out of myne hous in haist,
And God, quhais power and micht is maist,
Conserve me fra thy cummer!° *power to distress*
Gang hence to hell or to the farie,
With me thow may na langer tarie;
For quhy? I sweir the be Sanct Marie,
Thou's be nane of my nummer.° *company*

[*Exeunt Flavius and Emilie. Enter Philerno and Philotus.*]

78. Julian was patron saint of travellers. 'St Elous'—Eligius, one of the most popular medieval saints, was a seventh century bishop, patron saint of metalworkers. Can be depicted leading Satan by the nose with a pair of tongs. Bernard of Clairvaux, a twelfth century monk and theologian, was the leading mystic of his day. St Bride proved his holiness by laughing aloud at the thought of the devil.
79. ll. 1029–32. Three archangels. St Michael is depicted as the slayer of Satan. Gabriel is primarily connected with the Annunciation; 'His auld sang' is the *Hail Mary*. Raphael was often viewed as the guide/protector of pilgrims and young people.

133

Philerno:

Gar usche° this hous for it grows lait; *Have cleared*
Husband, I have for to debait
With yow a lytill of estait,
Befoir wee go to bed:
Sen I am young and ye ar auld,
My curage° kene, and ye bot cauld, *vigour*
The ane mon to the uther fauld,° *yield*
A faith, befoir we sched.° *part*

134

Philotus:

We wil not for the maistrie stryve,
We mon grie° better and we thryve. *come to an agreement*

Philerno:

Na, be my saull, we'is wit belyve° *we'll know right away*
Quha gets the upper hand:
Indeid, thow sall beir mee a bevell,° *suffer a mighty blow from me*
For with my neives° I sall the navell!° *fists; pummel*
Auld custrone° carle, tak thair a revell,° *base-born; buffet*
Than do as I command!

135

Philotus:

I sie it cummis to cuffis the man,[80]
Ile end the play° that thow began; *game*
That victorie thow never wan
That sall be bocht sa deir!
[*Philerno successfully overpowers Philotus.*]
Ha mercie, mercie, Emilie—
Tak ye the maistrie all for me,
For I sall at your bidding be,
And slay me not, I sweir.

136

Plesant:

Wel clappit burd!° Quhan wil ye kisse? *Good stroke my girl*
Auld fuill, the feind resave the misse,° *make good the error*
Ye trowit to get ane burd of blisse,[81]
To have ane of thir maggies:° *these girls*
Quhat think ye now? How is the cace?
Now ye'ill all doit,° allace, allace! *act foolishly*
Now grace and honour on that face,
Quod Robein to the haggies.[82]

80. 'I see it's coming to the point where I shall have to cuff you.'
81. 'You thought to gain a blissful home-life' or 'You thought to win a blessed maiden'.
82. ll. 1087–8. Comic play on the bruised face of Philotus and the mottled appearance of the haggis skin leads into an early anticipation of Burns's address to the 'sonsie face' of the haggis. 'Robein' may be James VI's jester (Rob Stein) who could actually be playing the Plesant's part; see n. 72 and reference to other king's jester.

137

Philerno:

Than hecht° in haist thairfoir, that thow — *promise*
Sall readie° at my bidding° bow, — *readily; to my wishes*
Quhat ever I do, thow sall allow
 My fansie to fulfill:
Sa° gang I out, sa cum I in, — *Whether*
Sa gif I waist,° sa gif I win,° — *spend; earn*
Quhat ever I do, mak ye na din,° — *fuss*
 Bot let me wirk my will.

138

Thou may not speir° the caus and quhy, — *ask (after)*
Quhen that I list° not with yow ly: — *wish*
Quhat I the bid, and thow deny,
 Wee will not weill agrie:
Quhen that I pleis furth to repair° — *to go out*
Speir not the cumpanie, nor quhair—
Content° thy self, and mak na mair,° — *Contain; fuss*
 I man° thy maister be! — *must*

139

Philotus:

I am content quhen and how sone,° — *whenever and immediately*
All till obey that ye injone;° — *enjoin*
That ye command, it man be done—
 Thair is nane uther buit!° — *remedy*
[*Exit Philotus. Philerno addresses the Whore.*]

Philerno:

Quhat is your pryce, damesall fair,
Quhat tak ye for a nichts lair?° — *bedding down with a man*

Huir:

Ye sall a croun° upon me spair, — *crown (coin)*
 Bot quhom with sal I do it?

140

Philerno:

Ile get a man—have heir a croun—
Bot be weill strange° quhen ye ly doun, — *distant*
Mak nyce,° and gar the larbair lowne° — *Act coy; used-up old lecher*
 Beleve ye be a mayd:° — *virgin*

Huir:

The youngest las in all this citie,
Sall byde na mair requeist nor treitie,[83]
Ile cry as I war huirt, for pitie,
 Quhen I am with him laid.

83. 'Shall wait for/expect no more request or entreaty (than I shall).'

[*Exeunt. Enter from one side Alberto, with Stephano in attendance, and Emilie from the other.*]

141

Emilie:

Now sen my husband hes done sa,
But° caus for to put me him fra, — *Without*
I will unto my father ga,
Befoir his feit to fald:° — *At his feet to kneel*
[*She approaches Alberto.*]
Father, sa far I did offend,
That I may not my mis° amend, — *sin*
And am ouir pert° for to pretend — *forward*
Your dochter to be cald.

142

Alberto:

Lament not, let that mater be
Thy faltis ar buriet all with me.
Betwixt thy husband now, and thee,
Is onie new debait?° — *contention*

Emilie:

I knaw of nane, bot hee indeid,
Hes put mee fra him, quhat remeid,° — *i.e. without more ado*
And will na mair sik fosteris feid,° — *nourish such foundlings*
He sayis, of myne estait.° — *condition*

[*Enter Philotus*]

143

Alberto:

Quhat is the mater that ye meine,[84]
Against all ordour clair and cleine,
Schut hame° your wyfe that hes not bene, — *To expel from home*
Yit fyve dayes in your aucht!° — *possession*
Is this ane plesant, godlie lyfe
To be in barrate,° sturt° and stryfe? — *contention; conflict*
The feind wald faine man be your wyfe,
Can never sit in saucht.[85]

144

Philotus:

Knew ye the treuth, gude-man, I trow
Hir labour° ye sould not allow.° — *behaviour; praise*

84. 'What's your intention in this affair?'
85. ll. 1143–4: 'Devil a one would like to be your wife, my friend, for they would never be able to live in peace.' The first line, however, can also convey the sense, 'The devil would prefer you to have a man as your wife...'

Luke all my face! Behald my brow,
That is baith blak and bla!

Alberto:
It may weill be, I can not tell.
That scho durst° with that mater mell, *would dare to*
Let hir mak answer for hir sell,
To sie gif it be sa.

145

Dochter, gave I the this command,
That thow thy husband sould ganestand?° *oppose*
How durst thow, huir, him with thy hand
Put to the point of felling?° *knocking down/killing*

Emilie:
That war grit wrang, sir, gif sa bee,
Bot hee na husband is to mee,
Than how could wee twa disagree,
That never had na melling?° *intimate dealings*

146

Alberto:
Na melling, mistris? Wil ye than
Deny the mariage of that man
In face of halie kirk? Quha can
This open deid deny?

Emilie:
Let resoun, sir, with yow prevaill,
Condemne mee not first in the faill° *fault*
Befoir that ye have hard my taill—
The treuth syne may ye try.° *test*

147

Now this is all that I wald say:
That Flavius tuke mee away
About a moneth and a day,
Drest in a varlets weid,° *servant's clothes*
With quhome I have bene ever still.° *ever since*
Ane uther Emilie, ay and quhill,° *in the meantime*
Hee° saw yow give Philotus till,° *(Flavius); to Philotus*
And than, in verie deid,

148

Supponing mee ane devill of hell,
With crewell conjuratiounes fell° *hurtful*
Did mee out of his hous expell,
As with a bogill bazed!° *alarmed by a ghost*
As ane out of his mynde, or marrit,° *deranged*
He hes mee of his hous debarrit,
I can not tell quhat hes him skarrit° *terrified*
Or hes the man amazed.

149

Alberto:

This purpois, gosse, appeirs to me
Sa wonder nyce° and strange to be, *subtle*
That wee, to wit the veritie,
  For Flavius man° send. *must*
[*Stephano exits and returns with Flavius.*]
Sir, gif ye could declair us now
How lang this woman was with yow,
And all the maner quhen and how,
  Wee wald richt gladlie kend.

150

Flavius:

Sa far Alberto as I knaw,
I sall the suith unto yow schaw:° *reveal*
Quhen I your douchters bewtie saw,
  I offerit hir gude-will;
Accepting than the promise maid,
Cled lyke a boy, but mair abaid,° *without more ado*
Fra yow dissaitfullie° scho slaid° *deceitfully; slipped away*
  And come myne hous untill;

151

Quhair I hir keipit as my wyfe,
Tret,° luifit and chereist hir for lyfe, *Looked after*
Quhill efter-ward fell out ane stryfe
  Thir maters all amang;
For plainlie in the kirk I saw,
This man became your sone in law—
I did thairfoir perfytly knaw,
  My Emilie was wrang,° *false*

152

And that some spreit hir schaip had tane° *assumed her form*
(Sen Emilies thair was bot ane)
I thairfoir to that ghaist have gane,
  Conjuring hir my sell;
And fra my hous expellit hir to
This woman, seimis for to be scho,[86]
Sensyne° I had na mair ado *Since then*
  With that fals feind of hell.

153

Philotus:

Now Flavius, I wait richt weil,
Sen ane of them man be a deill,

86. ll. 1213–4: 'And also expelled from my house this woman that has her appearance.'

My maiglit° face maks mee to feill, *disfigured*
That myne man be the same.
For quhy,° richt° Emilie is youris, *Therefore; the right/real*
And that incarnate devill is ouris;
I gat—ye may sie be my clouris°— *lumps on my face*
A deill unto my dame!

[*Enter Philerno.*]

154

Philerno:
Heir I am cum to red° the stryfe,[87] *resolve*
For I am neyther deill nor wyfe,
Bot am ane young man, be my lyfe,
Your sone, sir, and your air°— *heir*
Quhome ye for Emilie haif tane,
And wald not, sirs, let mee allane,
Quhill ye saw quhat gait it is gane;[88]
I can tell yow na mair.

155

Philotus:
A man! Allace and harmisay!° *good grief*
That with my only dochter lay!
Syne dang° my sell! Quhat sall I say *struck down*
Of this unhappie chance?
Have I not maid a berrie block,° *bad bargain*
That hes for Jennie maryit Jock,
That mowit° my dochter for a mock?° *copulated with; laugh*
The devill be at the dance!

156

Allace, I am for ever schamit,
To be thus in my eild° defamit;° *old age; disgraced*
My dochter is not to be blamit,
For I had all the wyte.° *blame*
Auld men is twyse bairnis,° I persaif,° *are children twice; realize*
The wysest will in wowing° raif,° *wooing; lose (his) reason*
I, for my labour,° with the laif,° *efforts; rest*
Am drivin to this dispyte.° *scorned/scornful state*

157

Alberto:
Gude gosse, your wraith° to pacifie— *indignation*
Sen that thair may na better bee—
I am content, my sone that hee
Sall with your dochter marie.

87. The figure of youth enters to resolve the disputes of old age. This marks the opening of the resolution or comic 'catastrophe' in joy (as opposed to tragic pity).
88. 'Until you saw the way it went.'

Philerno:
I am content with hart and will,
This mariage, father, to fulfill.
Quhat neidis Philotus to think ill,
Or yit his weird to warie?° *curse his fate*

158

Flavius:
Be frolick,° Flavius, and faine° *merry; content*
To get thy Emilie againe.
To deme, my dow, was I not vaine,
That thow had bene a spreit![89]
Now sen I am fred° fra that feir, *set free*
And vaine illusioun did appeir,[90]
Welcum, my darling and my deir,
My sucker° and my sweit. *sugar*

159

Gude sirs, quhat is thair mair ado?
Ilk youth his lufe hes gotten, lo!
Let us thairfoir go quicklie to
And marie with our maitis;° *mates*
Let us foure lufers now rejoyse
Ilk ane° for to injoy his choyse, *Each one*
Ane meiter matche nor ane of those,
For tender young estaitis.[91]

160

Let us all foure now with ane sang,
With mirth and melodie amang,
Give gloir to God, that in this thrang,° *trouble*
Hes bene all our releif.
That hes fra thraldome set us frie,
And hes us placit in sik degrie,
Ilk ane, as hee wald wisch to be,
With glaidnes for his greif.

[Ane sang of the foure Lufearis.]

164

Were Jacob's sones° mair joyfull for to se *i.e. the Israelites*
The waltring waves° King Pharaois oist° cofound? *whirling waves; army*
Was Israel mair glaid in hart to be
Fred from all feir, befoir in bondage bound,

89. ll. 1259–60: 'Was I not crazy, my dove, to suppose you were an (evil) spirit?'
90. I.e. 'And illusion appeared to be delusion.'
91. ll. 1271–2: 'There can be no more suitable match than any one of those (just mentioned) for tender young lives.'

Quhen God the brocht fro the Egiptian ground?[92]
Was Mordocheus° merier nor wee, *Mordecai*
When Artaxerxes° alterit his decrie?[93] *Xerxes*

165

Was greiter glaidnes in the land of Greice,
Quhen Jason come from Colchos hame agane
And conqueist had the famous golden fleis,
With labour lang, with perrell° and with pane? *danger*
The Father Æzon was not half sa faine,
To sie his sone returning with sik gloir,°[94] *glory*
As wee, quhais myndis ar satisfyit, and moir.° *more*

166

Gif onie joy into this earth belaw,
Or warldlie plesour reput be° perfyte, *reputed (to) be*
Quhat greiter solace sall ye to mee shaw
Nor till° injoy your hartis all haill° delyte— *Than to; complete*
To have your lufe and lustie ladie quhyte,
In quhome ye may baith nicht and day rejoyse,
In quhome ye may your plesures all repose.

167

Let us thairfoir, sen evin as° we wald wisse,° *just as; wish*
Reciprocklie with leill° and mutuall lufe, *faithful*
As, fleitand° in the fludes of joy and blisse, *floating*
With solace sing, and sorrowes all remufe;
Let us the fructes° of present plesour prufe *fruits*
In recompence of all our former pane
And miserie, quhairin wee did remane.

168

Philotus [*to audience*]:
Bot now advert,° gude bretherin all about, *be warned*
That of my labour hes the succes seine:
Ye that hes hard° this haill discourse throw out,° *heard; throughout*
May knaw how far that I abusit have bene.
I grant indeid thair will na man me meine,° *pity*
For I my self am authour of my greif—
That by my calling° sould be caryit cleine,° *(own) invoking; clean away*
With youthlie toyis,° unto sa greit mischeif. *playthings*

92. ll. 1281–5: Pharaoh, having agreed to let the enslaved Israelites leave Egypt, changed his mind, and sent his armies to recapture them. The Red Sea miraculously parted to let the Israelites cross, but closed again over the pursuing soldiers.
93. ll. 1286–7: The Persian King Xerxes was persuaded by his beautiful (Jewish) Queen, Esther, to repeal a decree of murder on all Jews in Persia, including her own cousin, Mordecai.
94. ll. 1288–93: Jason, son of Aeson, was a Greek hero who successfully led the Argonauts on their expedition to capture the golden fleece from the king of Colchis.

169

Gif I had weyit° my gravitie and age, — *weighed*
Rememberit als my first and auncient sait,° — *position*
I had not sowmit° in sik unkyndlie° rage, — *plunged; unnatural*
For to disgrace mine honour and estait.
Quhat had I bocht bot to my self debait,° — *dissension*
Suppois the mater had cum than as I meinit?[95]
Nay, my repentance is not half sa lait,
As I had gotin the thing quhairfoir I greinit![96]

170

For thocht my folie did the Lord offend,
Yit my gude God hes wrocht all for the best,
And this rebuik hes thairfoir to me send,° — *sent*
All sik inordinate° doings to detest. — *disorderly*
Quhilk sweit rebuik I reckin with° the rest, — *add to*
From fatherlie affection to proceid,
That uthers with lyke passiouns possest,
May leirne, be my exampill, to tak heid.

171

Sen age thairfoir suld governit be with skill,
Let countenance accord with your gray hairis;
Ye auncients° all, let resoun rewll your will, — *old folks*
Subdew your sensis till eschew° thir snairis. — *avoid/escape*
Gif ye wald not incombred be with cairis,
Be maister ouer your awin affections haill.
For hailillie the praise is only thairs,
That may against sik passions prevaill.

172

The Messinger:

Gude sirs, now have ye hard and sene this ferse° — *farce*
(Unworthie of your audience I grant)
Unformallie set out in vulgar° verse, — *colloquial*
Of waillit out° words and leirnit leid° bot skant.° — *well chosen; matter; sparse*
The courteours that princes hallis do hant,° — *haunt*
I wait° will never for my rudenes° ruse° mee: — *know; uncouthness; praise*
Yit my gude-will for to supplie the want,
I hope sall of your courtesies excuse mee.

173

For passing weil I have imployit my panis,
Swa that ye can be with the same content:
For dew regaird gude acceptatiouns° gaines, — *audience reception*
And parties pleisit dois mak the tyme wel spent.
Gif God had greiter leirning to mee lent,

95. 'Even if the matter had then come about as I had intended?'
96. 'As it would have been had I achieved the thing I was hankering after.'

I suld have schawin the same with als gude will!
Wyte° ignorance that I did not invent *Blame*
Ane ferse, that micht your fantasies fulfill.

174

Last, sirs, now let us pray with ane accord,
For to preserve the persoun of our king:[97]
Accounting ay this gift as of the Lord,
Ane prudent prince above us for to ring.° *reign*
Than gloir° to God, and praysis let us sing: *glory*
The Father, Sone and Halie Gaist our gyde,
Of His mercies us to conduct° and bring *lead*
To hevin, for ay in plesoures to abyde.

[Finis.][98]

97. James VI.
98. Both editions indicate that Thomas Campion's 'What if a day or a month or a yeere' was sung after the play had been completed.

§ 21 Sir Thomas Urquhart (1611–60): *Ekskubalauron or The Jewel*

Sir Thomas Urquhart lived during the reign of Charles I and the Commonwealth. Legend has it that a burst of violent laughter occasioned by the news of Charles II's restoration finally consigned him to his grave. As he was a staunch Royalist and had a lively sense of humour, there may be more truth to this story than is usually supposed. Son of the elder Sir Thomas Urquhart of Cromartie and Christian, daughter of the fourth Lord Elphinstone, he enrolled at King's College, Aberdeen, at the age of 11, but left without a degree. An exciting life, involving European travel and domestic disputes, reached its most dramatic moment when he was imprisoned by Cromwell after the Battle of Worcester.

The Jewel, *from which the extract concerning the Admirable Crichton is taken, belongs to that period. Prior to the appearance of his major hero, Urquhart has contrived to turn himself, his family and the people of Scotland into the stars of his tale. He has also promised to Cromwell a Universal Language, so subtle in its grammatical categories that it will arm the Commonwealth with a much more precise vehicle for transmitting knowledge than that possessed by any other country or ruler. The price of this was to be the return of Sir Thomas to his estates. Cromwell did allow Urquhart some periods of freedom but these were probably occasioned by the practical problems of estate management, rather than any faith in the more extreme conclusions of the linguistic case.*

In almost all his writing, Urquhart joins linguistic virtuosity to imaginative exuberance. The effect is to produce a series of infectiously amusing but idiosyncratic texts. Apart from **The Jewel** *(1652), these range from his mathematical treatise,* **The Trissotetras** *(1645), through* **A Peculiar Promptuary of Time** *(1652) and the semi-biographical* **Logopandecteision** *(1653) with its extended account of the Universal Language, to his renowned translation of the first three books of Rabelais'* **Gargantua and Pantagruel** *(1653).*

EKSKUBALAURON or The Jewel[1]

[*After an Introductory Letter and a Genealogy, which praises Urquhart and his family,* The Jewel *opens with an advertisement for Sir Thomas's Universal Language. This is so subtle and thorough that 'it affordeth expressions both for copiousness, variety and conciseness, which no language else is able to reach unto.' The case for Scottish heroism is then argued. Long lists of names are produced and a wide range of excellencies covered, from the mercantile through the academic to the military. The tale of the Admirable Crichton is, in this context, exemplary. In his case, all the heroic excellencies are combined superlatively in the one individual.*]

To speak a little now of his compatriot Crichtoun,[2] I hope will not offend the ingenuous reader who may know, by what is already displayed, that it cannot be heterogeneal from° the proposed purpose to make report of that magnanimous act atchieved by him at the Duke of Mantua's[3] court to the honour, not only of his own, but to the eternal renown also of the whole Isle of Britain; the manner whereof was thus.

A certain Italian gentleman of a mighty, able, strong, nimble and vigorous body, by nature fierce, cruell, warlike and audacious, and in the gladiatory art° so superla-

heterogeneal from: *irrelevant to*; gladiatory art: *art of sporting combat*

tively expert and dextrous, that all the most skilful teachers of escrime° and fencing-masters of Italy (which in matter of choice professors in that faculty needed never as yet to yeild to any nation in the world) were by him beaten to their good behaviour and, by blows and thrusts given in, which they could not avoid, enforced to acknowledge him their over comer. Bethinking himself how, after so great a conquest of reputation, he might by such means be very suddenly enriched, he projected a course of exchanging the blunt to sharp and the foiles into tucks;° and in this resolution, providing a purse full of gold worth neer upon four hundred pounds English money, traveled alongst the most especial and considerable parts of Spaine, France, the Low Countryes, Germany, Pole, Hungary, Greece, Italy and other places, where ever there was greatest probability of encountring with the eagerest and most atrocious° duellists; and immediately after his arrival to any city or town that gave apparent likelihood of some one or other champion that would enter the lists[4] and cope° with him, he boldly challenged them with sound of trumpet in the chief marketplace, to adventure an equal sum of money against that of his, to be disputed at the sword's point who should have both. There failed not several brave men, almost of all nations, who accepting of his cartels,° were not afraid to hazard both their person and coine against him; but, till he midled° with this Crichtoun, so maine° was the ascendent° he had above all his antagonists, and so unlucky the fate of such as offered to scuffle with° him, that all his opposing combatants of what state or dominion soever they were, who had not lost both their life and gold, were glad for the preservation of their person (though sometimes with a great expence of blood), to leave both their reputation and mony behind them.

At last, returning homewards to his own country, loaded with honor and wealth (or rather the spoile of the reputation of those forraigners whom the Italians call *Tramontani*)[5] he, by the way, after his accustomed manner of abording° other places, repaired to the city of Mantua, where the Duke, according to the courtesie usually bestowed on him by other princes, vouchsafed him a protection and savegard for his person. He, as formerly he was wont to do, by beat of drum, sound of trumpet and several printed papers disclosing his designe, battered° on all the chief gates, posts and pillars of the town, gave all men to understand that his purpose was to challenge at the single rapier any whosever of that city or country, that durst be so bold as to fight with him, provided he would deposite a bag of five hundred Spanish pistols° over against another of the same value, which himself should lay down; upon this condition, that the enjoyment of both should be the conqueror's due.

His challenge was not long unanswered, for it happened at the same time that three of the most notable cutters° in the world—and so highly cryed up° for valour that all the bravos° of the land were content to give way to their domineering, how insolent soever they should prove, because of their former constantly-obtained victories in the field—were all three together at the court of Mantua; who, hearing of such a harvest of five hundred pistols to be reaped, as they expected very soon and with ease, had almost contested amongst themselves for the priority of the first encounterer, but that one of my lord duke's courtiers moved them to cast lots for who should be first, second and third, in case none of the former two should prove victorious.

escrime: *the art of fencing especially with sabre or sword*; tucks: *rapiers*; atrocious: *fierce*; cope: *contend*; cartels: *written challenges*; midled: *crossed swords*; maine...ascendent: *great...superiority (astron.)*; scuffle with: *challenge*; abording: *aproaching*; battered: *pasted up*; pistols: *coins*; cutters: *swordsmen*; cryed up: *vaunted*; bravos: *young blades*

Without more adoe, he whose chance it was to answer the cartel with the first defiance, presented himself within the barriers° or place appointed for the fight, where—his adversary attending him—as soon as the trumpet sounded a charge, they jointly fel to work; and, because I am not now to amplifie the particulars of a combat, although the dispute was very hot for a while, yet, whose fortune it was to be the first of the three in the field had the disaster to be the first of the three that was foyled;[6] for at last, with a thrust in the throat he was killed dead upon the ground. This nevertheless not a whit dismayed the other two, for the nixt day he that was second in the roll° gave his appearance after the same manner as the first had done, but with no better success, for he likewise was laid flat dead upon the place by means of a thrust he received in the heart. The last of the three, finding that he was as sure of being engaged in the fight as if he had been the first in order, pluckt up his heart, knit his spirits together and, on the day after the death of the second, most couragiously entering the lists, demeaned himself° for a while with great activity and skill; but at last, his luck being the same with those that preceded him, by a thrust in the belly he, within four and twenty hours after, gave up the ghost.

These, you may imagine, were lamentable spectacles to the Duke and citie of Mantua who, casting down their faces for shame, knew not what course to take for reparation of their honour. The conquering duellist, proud of a victory so highly tending to both his honour and profit, for the space of a whole fortnight or two weeks together, marched daily along the streets of Mantua, without any opposition or controulment, like another Romulus or Marcellus in triumph;[7] which, the never-too-much-to-be-admired Crichtoun perceiving, to wipe off the imputation of cowardise lying upon the court of Mantua to which he had but even then arrived (although formerly he had been a domestick thereof)° he could neither eat nor drink till he had first sent a challenge to the conqueror, appelling° him to repair with his best sword in his hand by nine of the clock in the morning of the next day, in presence of the whole court and in the same place where he had killed the other three, to fight with him upon this quarrel: that, in the court of Mantua, there were as valiant men as he; and, for his better encouragement to the desired undertaking, he assured him that to the aforesaid five hundred pistols he would adjoyn a thousand more, wishing him to do the like, that the victor, upon the point of his sword might carry away the richer booty.

The challenge with all its conditions is no sooner accepted of, the time and place mutually condescended upon° kept accordingly and the fifteen hundred pistols *hinc inde*° deposited, but—of the two rapiers of equal weight, length and goodness, each taking one in presence of the duke, dutchess, with all the noblemen, ladies, magnificos° and all the choicest of both men, women and maids of that citie, as soon as the signal for the duel was given by the shot of a great piece of ordnance° of threescore and four pound ball—the two combatants, with a lion-like animosity, made their approach to one another, and, being within distance, the valiant Crichtoun, to make his adversary spend his fury the sooner, betook himself to the defensive part; wherein for a long time he shewed such excellent dexterity in warding the other's blow, slighting his falsifyings, in breaking measure[8] and often, by the agility of his body, avoiding his thrusts, that he seemed but to play whilst the other was in earnest.

barriers: *lists*; roll: *list;* demeaned himself: *conducted himself*; a domestick thereof: *familiar with it*; appelling: *challenging*; condescended upon: *agreed upon*; hinc inde: *there and then*; magnificos: *exalted persons*; ordnance: *artillery*

The sweetness of Crichtouns's countenance in the hotest of the assault, like a glance of lightning on the hearts of the spectators, brought all the Italian ladies on a sudden to be enamoured of him; whilst the sternness of the other's aspect (he looking like an enraged bear) would have struck terrour into wolves and affrighted an English mastiff. Though they were both in their linens,° to wit, shirts and drawers, without any other apparel, and in all outward conveniencies equally adjusted, the Italian, with redoubling his stroaks, foamed at the mouth with a cholerick° heart and fetched a pantling° breath. The Scot, in sustaining his charge, kept himself in a pleasant temper without passion and made void his designes. He alters his wards from tierce to quart; he primes and seconds it,[9] now high now lowe, and casts his body like another Prothee[10] into all the shapes he can to spie an open on his adversary and lay hold of an advantage, but all in vain; for the invincible Crichtoun, whom no cunning was able to surprise, contrepostures° his respective wards and, with an incredible nimbleness of both hand and foot, evades his intent and frustrates the invasion.

Now is it that the never before conquered Italian, finding himself a little faint, enters into a consideration that he may be overmatched; whereupon, a sad apprehension of danger seizing upon all his spirits, he would gladly have his life bestowed on him as a gift, but that, having never been accustomed to yeeld, he knows not how to beg it. Matchless Crichtoun, seeing it now high time to put a gallant catastrophe° to that so long dubious combat, animated with a divinely inspired fervencie° to fulfil the expectation of the ladies and crown the duke's illustrious hopes, changeth his garb,° falls to act another part, and from defender turns assailant. Never did art so grace nature, nor nature second the precepts of art with so much liveliness and such observancie of time, as when, after he had struck fire out of the steel of his enemie's sword and gained the *feeble* thereof with the *fort*[11] of his own; by angles of the strongest position, he did, by geometrical flourishes of straight and oblique lines, so practically execute the speculative part,[12] that, as if there had been remoras° and secret charms in the variety of his motion, the fierceness of his foe was in a trice transqualified° into the numness° of a pageant.

Then was it, that to vindicate the reputation of the duke's family and expiate the blood of the three vanquished gentlemen, he° alonged a stoccade *de pied ferme*,[13] then recoyling, he advanced another thrust and lodged it home; after which, retiring again, his right foot did beat the cadence of the blow that pierced the belly of this Italian, whose heart and throat being hit with the two former stroaks—these three franch° bouts given in upon the back of the other; besides that, if lines were imagined drawn from the hand that livered° them to the places which were marked by them, they would represent a perfect isosceles triangle, with a perpendicular from the top angle cutting the basis in the middle.[14] They likewise gave us to understand, that by them he was to be made a sacrifice of atonement for the slaughter of the three aforesaid gentlemen, who were wounded in the very same parts of their bodies by other such three venees° as these, each whereof being mortal; and his° vital spirits exhaling as his blood gushed out, all he spoke was this, that seeing he could not execute, his comfort in dying was that he could not dye by the hand of a braver man; after the uttering of which words, he expiring with the

linens: *underclothes*; cholerick: *angry*; pantling: *panting*; contrepostures: *counters*; gallant catastrophe: *noble outcome*; fervencie: *ardour*; garb: *style*; remoras: *hindrances*; transqualified: *changed (from one trait into another)*; numness: *frozen image*; he: *i.e. Crichtoun*; franch: *open*; livered: *delivered*; venees: *thrusts*; his: *i.e. the Italian challenger* shril clareens° of trumpets, bouncing thunder of artillery, bethwacked beating of drums, universal clapping of hands and loud acclamations of joy for so glorious a victory, the aire above them was so rarified by the extremity of the noise and the vehement sound, dispelling the thickest and most condensed parts thereof, that, as Plutarch speakes of the Grecians, when they raised their shouts of allegress° up to the very heavens at the hearing of the gracious proclamations of Paulus Æmilius in favour of their liberty,[15] the very sparrows and other flying fowls were said to fall to the ground for want of aire enough to uphold them in their flight.

When this sudden rapture was over and all husht into its former tranquility, the noble gallantry and generosity beyond expression of the inimitable Crichtoun did transport them all againe into a new extasie of ravishment, when they saw him like an angel in the shape of a man, or as another Mars with the conquered enemie's sword in one hand and the fifteen hundred pistols he had gained in the other, present the sword to the duke as his due and the gold to his high treasurer, to be disponed° equally to the three widowes of the three unfortunate gentlemen lately slaine, reserving only to himself the inward satisfaction he conceived for having so opportunely discharged his duty to the House of Mantua.

The reader perhaps will think this wonderful and so would I too, were it not that I know, as Sir Philip Sydney sayes, that a wonder is no wonder in a wonderful subject,[16] and consequently not in him who, for his learning, judgement, valour, eloquence, beauty and good-fellowship, was the perfectest result of the joynt labour of the perfect number of those six deities, Pallas, Apollo, Mars, Mercury, Venus and Bacchus, that hath been seen since the dayes of Alcibiades; [17] for he was reported to have been inriched with a memory so prodigious that any sermon, speech, harangue or other manner of discourse of an hour's continuance, he was able to recite without hesitation, after the same manner of gesture and pronuntiation in all points wherewith it was delivered at first; and of so stupendious a judgement and conception, that almost naturally he understood quiddities° of philosophy; and as for the abstrusest and most researched mysteries of other disciplines, arts and faculties, the intentional species[18] of them were as readily obvious to the interiour view and perspicacity of his mind as those of the common visible colours to the external sight of him that will open his eyes to look upon them; of which accomplishment and encyclopedia of knowledge, he gave on a time so marvelous a testimony at Paris, that the words of *Admirabilis Scotus*, the Wonderful Scot,[19] in all the several tongues and idiomes of Europ were, for a great while together, by the most of the echos resounded to the peircing of the very clouds.

To so great a hight and vast extent of praise did the never-too-much-to-be-extolled reputation of the seraphick° wit of that eximious° man attaine, for his commanding to be affixed programs on all the gates of the schooles, halls and colledges of that famous university, as also on all the chief pillars and posts standing before the houses of the most renowned men for literature, resident within the precinct of the walls and suburbs of that most populous and magnificent city, inviting them all, or any whoever else versed in any kinde of scholastick faculty, to repaire at nine of the clock in the morning of such a day, moneth and yeer, as by computation came to be just six weeks after the date of the affixes,° to the common schoole of the Colledge of Navarre,[20] where (at the prefixed time) he should, God willing, be ready to answer to what should be propounded to him concerning any

clareens: *blasts*; allegress: *joy*; disponed: *distributed*; quiddities: *distinctions*; seraphick: *angelic/ecstatic*; eximious: *eminent*; affixes: *public notices*

science, liberal art, discipline or faculty—practical or theoretick—not excluding the theological nor jurisprudential habits, though grounded but° upon the testimonies of God and man, and in any of these twelve languages: Hebrew, Syriack, Arabick, Greek, Latin, Spanish, French, Italian, English, Dutch, Flemish and Sclavonian, in either verse or prose, at the discretion of the the disputant. Which high enterprise and hardy undertaking, by way of challenge to the learnedst men in the world, damped° the wits of many able scholars to consider whether it was the attempt of a fanatick° spirit or lofty designe of a well-poised judgment.

Yet, after a few dayes enquiry concerning him, when information was got of his incomparable endowments, all the choicest and most profound philosophers, mathematicians, naturalists, mediciners, alchymists, apothecaries, surgeons, doctors of both civil and canon law, and divines both for controversies and positive doctrine,[21] together with the primest grammarians, rhetoricians, logicians and others—professors of other arts and disciplines at Paris—plyed their studys in their private cels for the space of a moneth exceeding hard, and with huge paines and labor set all their braines awork how to contrive the knurriest° arguments and most difficult questions could be devised, thereby to puzzle him in the resolving of them, meander° him in his answers, put him out of his medium and drive him to a nonplus; nor did they forget to premonish° the ablest there of forraign nations not to be unprepared to dispute with him in their own maternal dialects, and that sometimes metrically, sometimes otherwayes, *pro libitu.*°

All this while the Admirable Scot (for so from thence forth he was called) minding more his hawking, hunting, tilting, vaulting, riding of well-managed° horses, tossing of the pike, handling of the musket, flourishing of colours, dancing, fencing, swimming, jumping, throwing of the bar; playing at the tennis, baloon° or long catch and sometimes at the house games of dice, cards, playing at the chess, billiards, trou-madam[22] and other such like chamber-sports; singing, playing on the lute and other musical instruments; masking, balling, reveling and—which did most of all divert, or rather distract him from his speculations and serious employments, being more addicted to and plying closer the courting of handsome ladyes and a jovial cup in the company of bacchanalian blades,° then° the forecasting how to avoid, shun and escape the snares, girns° and nets of the hard, obscure and hidden arguments, ridles and demands to be made, framed and woven by the professors, doctors and others of that thrice-renowned university[23]—there arose upon him an aspersion of too great proness to such like debordings[24] and youthful emancipations, which occasioned one less acquainted with himself then his reputation to subjoyn,° some two weeks before the great day appointed, to that program of his, which was fixed on the Sorbone-gate, these words: If you would meet with this monster of perfection, to make search for him either in the taverne or bawdy-house is the readyest way to finde him.

By reason of which expression (though truly as I think, both scandalous and false) the eminent sparks of the university, imagining that those papers of provocation had been set up to nother° end but to scoff and delude them in making them waste their spirits upon quirks and quiddities more then was fitting, did resent a little of°

grounded but: *founded solely*; damped: *confounded*; fanatick: *fanatical*; knurriest: *most knotty*; meander: *bewilder*; premonish: *forewarn*; pro libitu: *at one's pleasure*; well-managed: *well-trained*; baloon: *game played with large inflated ball of strong leather*; bacchanalian blades: *roistering young fellows*; then: *than*; girns: *traps*; subjoyn: *to add (to end of statement)*; nother: *no other*; resent...of: *regret*

their former toyle and slack their studyes, becoming almost regardless thereof, till the several peals of bells ringing an hour or two before the time assigned, gave warning that the party was not to flee the barriers nor decline the hardship of academical assaults—but on the contrary, so confident in his former resolution, that he would not shrink to sustaine the shock of all their disceptations.°

This sudden alarm so awaked them out of their last fortnight's lethargy, that, calling to minde the best way they might, the fruits of the foregoing moneth's labour, they hyed° to the forenamed schoole with all diligence; where, after all of them had, according to their several degrees and qualities,° seated themselves, and that by reason of the noise occasioned through the great confluence of people (which so strange a novelty brought thither out of curiosity) an universal silence was commanded. The Orator° of the university, in most fluent Latine addressing his speech to Crichtoun, extolled him for his literature° and other good parts, and for that confident opinion he had of his own sufficiency in thinking himself able to justle° in matters of learning with the whole University of Paris.

Crichtoun, answering him in no less eloquent terms of Latine, after he had most heartily thanked him for his elogies° so undeservedly bestowed, and darted some high encomions upon° the university and the professors therein, he very ingenuously protested that he did not emit his programs out of any ambition to be esteemed able to enter in competition with the university, but meerly to be honoured with the favour of a publick conference with the learned men thereof. In complements after this manner *ultro citroque habitis*,° tossed to and again, retorted, contrerisposted,° backreverted° and now and then graced with a quip or a clinch° for the better relish of the ear, being unwilling in this kind of straining curtesie to yeeld to other, they spent a full half hour and more; for he, being the centre to which the innumerable diameters of the discourses of that circulary convention did tend, although none was to answer but he, any of them all, according to the order of their prescribed series, were permitted to reply or comence new motions on any subject, in what language soever and howsoever expressed.

To all which, he being bound to tender himself a respondent in matter and form suitable to the impugners propounding,° he did first so transcendently acquit himself of that circumstantial° kinde of oratory that, by well-couched periods° and neatly running syllables in all the twelve languages, both in verse and prose, he expressed to the life his courtship and civility; and afterwards, when the Rector° of the university, unwilling to have any more time bestowed on superficial rhetorick,[25] or to have that wasted on the fondness of quaint phrases which might be better employed in a reciprocacy of discussing scientifically the nature of substantial things, gave direction to the professors to fall on, each according to the dignity of precedency of his Faculty; and that, conform to the order given, some metaphysical notions were set abroach,° then mathematical, and of those arithmetical, geometrical, astronomical, musical, optical, cosmographical, trigonometrical, statical° and so forth, through all the other branches of the prime and mother sciences thereof.

disceptations: *disputations*; hyed: *hastened*; qualities: *social positions*; Orator: *official spokesman*; literature: *humane learning*; justle: *contend*; elogies: *eulogies*; darted...encomions upon: *directed ...commendations to*; ultro citroque habitis: *bandied back and forth*; contrerisposted: *replied sharply*; backreverted: *used a reply to demolish its propagator*; clinch: *piece of word play*; impugners propounding: *challengers postulating*; circumstantial: *consequential*; well-couched periods: *well-turned sentences*; Rector: *elected head of medieval university*; set abroach: *allowed to flow*; statical: *pertaining to weighing*

The next bout was through all natural philosophy according to Aristotle's method from the acroamaticks,[26] going along the speculation of the nature of the heavens and that of the generation and corruption of sublunary° things, even to the consideration of the soul and its faculties. In sequel hereof, they had a hint at chymical extractions and spoke of the principles of corporeal and mixed bodies, according to the precepts of that art. After this, they disputed of medicine in all its therapeutick, pharmacopeutick and chirurgical° parts; and not leaving natural magick untouched, they had exquisite disceptations concerning the secrets thereof. From thence they proceeded to moral philosophy, where—debating of the true enumeration of all vertues and vices—they had most learned ratiocinations° about the chief good of the life of man; and (seeing the oecumenicks° and politicks are parts of that philosophy) they argued learnedly of all the several sorts of governments with their defects and advantages; whereupon, perpending° that, without an established law, all the duties of ruling and subjection to the utter ruine of humane society would be as often violated as the irregularity of passion, seconded with power, should give way thereto.

The Sorbonist canonical and civilian doctors most judiciously argued with him about the most prudential° maximes, sentences, ordinances, acts and statutes for ordering all manner of persons in their consciences, bodyes, fortunes and reputations; nor was there an end put to those literate exercitations till the grammarians, rethoricians, poets and logicians had assailed him with all the subtleties and nicest *quodlibets*° their respective habits° could afford. Now, when to the admiration of all that were there, the incomparable Crichtoun had, in all these faculties above, written; and in any of the twelve languages wherein he was spoke to, whether in verse or prose, held tack to° all the disputants who were accounted the ablest scholars upon the earth in each their own profession; and publickly evidenced such an universality of knowledge and accurate promptness in resolving of doubts, distinguishing of obscurities, expressing the members of a distinction in adequate terms of art, explaining those compendious tearms° with words of a more easie apprehension to the prostrating of the sublimest mysteries to any vulgar capacity; and with all excogitable° variety of learning, to his own everlasting fame, entertained after that kinde the nimble witted Parisians from nine a clock in the morning till six at night.

The Rector, now finding it high time to give some relaxation to these worthy spirits which, during such a long space, had been so intensively bent upon the abstrusest speculations, rose up, and saluting the divine Crichtoun, after he had made an elegant panegyrick or encomiastick° speech of half an houre's continuance, tending to nothing else but the extolling of him for the rare and most singular gifts wherewith God and nature had endowed him, he descended from his chaire and, attended by three or four of the most especial professors, presented him with a diamond ring and a purse full of gold, wishing him to accept thereof, if not as a recompense proportionable to his merit, yet as a badge of love and testimony of the universitie's favour towards him; at the tender of which ceremony there was so great a plaudite in the schoole, such a humming and clapping of hands, that all the

sublunary: *terrestrial*; pharmacopeutick and chirurgical: *chemical and surgical*; ratiocinations: *conclusions arrived at by reasoning*; oecumenicks: *considerations concerning the universal church*; perpending: *considering*; prudential: *judicious/judicial*; quodlibets: *scholastic debates*; habits: *faculties/schools of thought*; held tack to: *proved equal to (nautical)*; compendious tearms: *succinct, precise phrases*; excogitable: *thoughtfully developed*; encomiastick: *laudatory*

concavities of the colledges there about did resound with the eccho of the noise thereof.

Notwithstanding the great honour thus purchased by him for his literatory accomplishments, and that many excellent spirits to obtaine the like would be content to postpose° all other employments to the enjoyment of their studyes, he nevertheless the very next day, to refresh his braines as he said for the toile of the former day's work, went to the Louvre in a buff suit,° more like a favorite of Mars then one of the Muses' minions; where, in presence of some princes of the court and great ladies that came to behold his gallantry, he carryed away the ring fifteen times on end and broke as many lances on the Saracen.[27]

When for a quarter of a yeer together he, after this manner, had disported himself what° martially, what° scholastically, with the best qualified men in any Faculty so ever, that so large a city, which is called the world's abridgement, was able to afford; and now and then solaced these his more serious recreations (for all was but sport to him) with the alluring imbellishments of the tendrer sexe, whose *inamorato*° that he might be was their ambition, he on a sudden took resolution to leave the Court of France and return to Italy, where he had been bred for many yeers together; which designe he prosecuting within the space of a moneth without troubling himself with long journeys, he arrived at the Court of Mantua, where immediately after his abord,° as hath been told already, he fought the memorable combat whose description is above related.

Here was it that the learned and valiant Crichtoun was pleased to cast anchor and fix his abode; nor could he almost otherwayes do without disobliging the duke and the prince his eldest son, by either whereof he was so dearly beloved that none of them would permit him by any means to leave their court, whereof he was the only *privado*,° the object of all men's love and subject of their discourse; the example of the great ones and wonder of the meaner people; the paramour of the female sexe and paragon of his own: in the glory of which high estimation, having resided at that court above two whole yeers, the reputation of gentlemen there was hardly otherwayes valued but by the measure of his acquaintance; nor were the young unmaryed ladies of all the most eminent places thereabouts any thing respected of one another, that had not either a lock of his haire or copy of verses of his composing.

Nevertheless, it happening on a Shrove Tuesday at night, at which time it is in Italy very customary for men of great sobriety, modesty and civil behaviour all the rest of the yeer, to give themselves over on that day of carnavale, as they call it, to all manner of riot, drunkenness and incontinency (which that they may do with the least imputation they can to their credit, they go maskt and mum'd with vizards° on their faces and in the disguise of a Zanni or Pantaloon[28] to ventilate their fopperies,° and sometimes intolerable enormities, without suspicion of being known) that this ever renowned Crichtoun who, in the afternoon of that day, at the desire of my lord duke, the whole court striving which should exceed other in foolery and devising of the best sports to excite laughter (neither my lord, the dutchess nor prince being exempted from acting their parts as well as they could) upon a theater, set up for the purpose, begun to prank it a la Venetiana,[29] with such a flourish of mimick and ethopoetick° gestures, that all the courtiers of both

postpose: *place afterwards*; buff suit: *military coat made of buff leather*; what...what: *both...and*; inamorato: *beloved*; abord: *landing*; privado: *confidant*; mum'd with vizards: *acted in dumb show with masks*; ventilate their fopperies: *give vent to their folly*; ethopoetick: *representing character or manners*

sexes—even those that, a little before that, were fondest of their own conceits—at the sight of his so inimitable a garb,° from ravishing actors that they were before, turned then ravished spectators.

O, with how great liveliness did he represent the conditions of all manner of men! How naturally did he set before the eyes of the beholders the rogueries of all professions, from the overweening monarch to the peevish swaine, through all the intermediate degrees of the superficial courtior or proud warrior, dissembled churchman, doting old man, cozening° lawyer, lying traveler, covetous merchant, rude° seaman, pedantick scolar, the amourous shepheard, envious artisan, vainglorious master and tricky servant!

He did, with such variety, display the several humours of all these sorts of people[30] and with a so bewitching energy, that he seemed to be the original, they the counterfeit, and they the resemblance whereof he was the prototype. He had all the jeers, squibs,° flouts,° buls,° quips, taunts, whims, jests, clinches, gybes, mokes,° jerks,° with all the several kinds of equivocations and other sophistical captions,° that could properly be adapted to the person, by whose representation he intended to inveagle the company into a fit of mirth; and would keep in that miscelany discourse of his, which was all for the splene and nothing for the gall, such a climacterical and mercurially digested method,[31] that when the fancy of the hearers was tickled with any rare conceit, and that the jovial blood was moved, he held it going with another new device upon the back of the first, and another, yet another and another againe, succeeding one another for the promoval° of what is a stirring into a higher agitation; till in the closure of the luxuriant° period, the decumanal° wave of the oddest whimzy of all, enforced the charmed spirits of the auditory, for affording room to its apprehension, suddenly to burst forth into a laughter, which commonly lasted just so long as he had leasure to withdraw behind the skreen, shift off with the help of a page the suite he had on, apparel himself with another and return to the stage to act afresh; for by that time their transported, disparpled° and sublimated° fancies—by the wonderfully operating engines[32] of his solacious° inventions—had from the hight to which the inward scrues, wheeles and pullies of his wit had elevated them, descended by degrees into their wonted stations, he was ready for the personating of another carriage; whereof to the number of fourteen several kinds (during the five hours' space that at the duke's desire, the sollicitation of the court and his own recreation, he was pleased to histrionize° it) he shewed himself so natural a representative, that any would have thought he had been so many several° actors, differing in all things else save the only stature of the body; with this advantage above the most of other actors, whose tongue with its oral implements is the onely instrument of their mind's disclosing, that, besides his mouth with its appurtenances, he lodged almost a several oratour in every member of his body—his head, his eyes, his shoulders, armes, hands, fingers, thighs, legs, feet and breast, being able to decipher any passion whose character he purposed to give.

First, he did present himself with a crown on his head, a scepter in his hand, being clothed in a purple robe furred with ermyne; after that with a miter on his head, a crosier in his hand and accoutred with a pair of lawn-sleeves;° and thereafter with a

garb: *stylishness of appearance*; cozening: *deceitful*; rude: *rough*; squibs: *sarcastic comments*; flouts: *scoffing remarks*; buls: *falsehoods*; mokes: *mockeries*; jerks: *sallies*; captions: *quibbles*; promoval: *furthering*; luxuriant: *prolific*; decumanal: *immense*; disparpled: *scattered*; sublimated: *elevated*; solacious: *entertaining*; histrionize: *enact*; several: *different*; lawn-sleeves: *sleeves of lawn, typical of a bishop's dress*

helmet on his head (the visiere up), a commanding-stick° in his hand and arayed in a buff suit with a scarf about his middle. Then in a rich apparel after the newest fashion, did he shew himself like another Sejanus with a periwig daubed with Cypres powder.[33] In sequel of that, he came out with a three corner'd cap on his head, some parchments in his hand and writings hanging at his girdle like Chancery bills;° and next to that, with a furred gown about him, an ingot of gold in his hand and a bag full of money by his side. After all this he appeares againe clad in a country-jacket with a prong in his hand and a Monmouth-like cap[34] on his head. Then, very shortly after, with a palmer's° coat upon him, a bourdon° in his hand and some few cockle-shels stuck to his hat he look't as if he had come in pilgrimage from Saint Michael.[35]

Immediately after that, he domineers it in a bare, unlined gowne with a pair of whips in the one hand and Corderius° in the other; and in suite thereof° he honderspondered it° with a pair of pannier-like breeches, a Mountera cap° on his head and a knife in a wooden sheath dagger-ways by his side. About the latter end he comes forth again with a square in one hand, a rule in the other and a leather apron before him; then, very quickly after, with a scrip° by his side, a sheep-hook in his hand and a basket of flowers to make nosegayes for his mistris. Now drawing to a closure, he rants it first *in cuerpo*° and vapouring it° with gingling spurrs and his armes *a kenbol*° like a Don Diego he strouts it° and, by the loftiness of his gate,° plaies the Capitan Spavento.[36] Then in the very twinkling of an eye, you would have seen him againe issue forth with a cloak upon his arm in a livery garment, thereby representing the serving-man; and lastly, at one time amongst those other, he came out with a long gray beard and bucked ruff,[37] crouching on a staff tip't with the head of a barber's cithern,° and his gloves hanging by a button at his girdle.

Those fifteen several personages he did represent with such excellency of garb and exquisiteness of language, that condignely to perpend° the subtlety of the invention, the method of the disposition, the neatness of the elocution, the gracefulness of the action and wonderful variety in the so dextrous performance of all, you would have taken it for a comedy of five acts, consisting of three scenes each composed by the best poet in the world and acted by fifteen of the best players that ever lived—as was most evidently made apparent to all the spectators in the fifth and last hour of his action which, according to our western account, was about six a clock at night and, by the calculation of that country, half an hour past three and twenty at that time of the yeer; for, purposing to leave of with the setting of the sun, with an endeavour nevertheless to make his conclusion the master-piece of the work, he, to that effect, summoning all his spirits together (which never failed to be ready at the cal of so worthy a commander) did, by their assistance, so conglomerate, shuffle, mix and interlace the gestures, inclinations, actions and very tones of the speech of those fifteen several sorts of men (whose carriages° he did personate into an inestimable *ollapodrida*° of immaterial morsels of divers kinds, sutable to the very ambrosian relish of the Heliconian nymphs)° that in the peripetia° of this

commanding-stick: *staff of authority*; Chancery bills: *the documents from High Court or Treasury*; palmer's: *pilgrim's*; bourdon: *pilgrim's staff*; Corderius: *a popular Latin grammar*; in suite thereof: *following upon that*; honderspondered it: *acted like a German mercenary*; Mountera cap: *Spanish hunter's cap*; scrip: *satchel*; in cuerpo: *in his shirt*; vapouring it: *swaggering*; a kenbol: *akimbo*; strouts it: *struts about*; gate: *gait*; cithern: *guitar-like instrument, often with grotesquely carved head, commonly kept in barbers' shops for customers' use*; condignely to perpend: *adequately to consider*; carriages: *characteristics*; ollapodrida: *hotchpotch*; Heliconian nymphs: *the nine muses*; peripetia: *abrupt turn of events (esp. in drama)*

drammatical exercitation, by the inchanted transportation of the eyes and eares of its spectabundal° auditorie, one would have sworne that they all had looked with multiplying glasses,° and that, like that angel in the Scripture whose voice was said to be like the voice of a multitude,[38] they heard—in him alone—the promiscuous° speech of fifteen several actors; by the various ravishments of the excellencies whereof, in the frolickness of a jocound straine beyond expectation, the logofascinated° spirits of the beholding hearers and auricularie spectators were so on a sudden seazed upon in their risible faculties of the soul, and all their vital motions so universally affected in this extremitie of agitation, that—to avoid the inevitable charmes of his intoxicating ejaculations and the accumulative influences of so powerfull a transportation—one of my lady dutchess' chief maids of honour, by the vehemencie of the shock of those incomprehensible raptures, burst forth into a laughter, to the rupture of a veine in her body.

And another young lady—by the irresistible violence of the pleasure, unawares infused where the tender receptibilitie of her too too tickled fancie was least able to hold out—so unprovidedly was surprised, that with no less impetuositie of ridibundal° passion than as hath been told, occasioned a fracture in the other young ladie's modestie. She not being able longer to support the well-beloved burthen of so excessive delight and intransing joys of such mercurial exhilarations, through the ineffable extasie of an overmastered apprehension, fell back into a swown without the appearance of any other life into her, then what by the most refined wits of theological speculators is conceived to be exerced by the purest parts of the separated entelechies° of blessed saints in their sublimest conversations with the celestial hierarchies. This accident procured the incoming of an apothecarie with restoratives as the other did that of a surgeon with consolidative medicaments.[39]

The Admirable Crichtoun (now perceiving that it was drawing somewhat late and that our occidental rays of Phoebus were, upon their turning, oriental to the other hemisphere of the terrestrial globe—being withall jealous that the uninterrupted operation of the exuberant diversitie of his jovialissime° entertainment, by a continuate° winding up of the humours there present, to a higher, yet higher and still higher pitch above the supremest Lydian note of the harmonie of voluptuousness, should in such a case through the too intensive stretching of the already-super-elated strings of their imagination, with a transendencie overreaching Ela and beyond the well-concerted *gam*[40] of rational equanimitie, involve the remainder of that illustrious companie into the sweet labyrinth and mellifluent aufractuosities° of a lacinious° delectation, productive of the same inconveniences which befel the two afore-named ladies—whose delicacie of constitution, though sooner overcome—did not argue but that the same extranean causes from him proceeding, of their pathetick alteration° might by a longer insisting in an efficacious agencie and unremitted working of all the consecutively imprinted degrees that the capacity of the patient is able to containe, prevaile at last and have the same predominancie over the dispositions of the strongest complexioned males of that splendid society) did,[41] in his own ordinary wearing apparel, with the countenance of a prince, and garb befitting the person of a so well bred gentleman and cavalier,

spectabundal: *eager to see*; multiplying glasses: *kaleidoscopes*; promiscuous: *various kinds combined without order*; logofascinated: *fascinated by words*; ridibundal: *inclined to laughter*; entelechies: *souls*; jovialissime: *most good-humoured*; continuate: *long-continued*; aufractuosities: *skilfully broken up language of rhetoric*; lacinious: *prolix*; pathetick alteration: *emotion-stirred change of condition*

κατ' ἐξοχήν° full of majesty and repleat with all excogitable civilitie, to the amazement of all that beheld his heroick gesture, present himself to epilogate° this, his almost extemporanean comedie—though of five hours continuance without intermission—and *that* with a peroration so neatly uttreed, so distinctly pronounced, and in such elegancie of selected terms expressed by a diction so periodically contexed with isocoly of members,[42] that the matter thereof, tending in all humility to beseech the highnesses of the duke, prince and dutchess, together with the remanent° lords, ladies, knights, gentlemen and others of both sexes of that honorable convention, to vouchsafe him the favour to excuse his that-afternoon's-escaped extravagancies, and to lay the blame of the indigested irregularity of his wit's excursions and the abortive issues of his disordered brain upon the customarily-dispensed-with priviledges in those Cisalpinal° regions, to authorize such like impertinences at carnavalian festivals; and that although, according to the most commonly received opinion in that country (after the nature of Loadhim, a game at cards where he that wins loseth, he who at that season of the year playeth the fool most egregiously is reputed the wisest man) he, nevertheless, not being ambitious of the fame of enjoying good qualities by vertue of the antiphrasis° of the fruition of bad ones, did meerly undergo that emancipatorie task of a so profuse liberty, and to no other end embraced the practising of such roaming and exorbitant diversions but to give an evident, or rather infallible, demonstration of his eternally bound duty to the House of Mantua, and an inviolable testimony of his never-to-be-altered designe, in prosecuting all the occasions possible to be laid hold on, that can in any manner of way prove conducible to the advancement of, and contributing to, the readiest means for improving those advantages, that may best promove° the faculties of making all his choice endeavours and utmost abilities at all times effectual to the long wished for furtherance of his most cordial and endeared service to the serenissime° highnesses of my lord duke, prince and dutchess; and of consecrating with all addicted obsequiousness and submissive devotion, his everlasting obedience to the illustrious shrine of their joynt commands. Then, incontinently° addressing himself to the lords, ladies and others of that rotonda° (which, for his daigning to be its inmate, though but for that day, might be accounted in nothing inferiour to the great colisee of Rome or amphitheater at Neems)° with a stately carriage and port, suitable to so prime a gallant, he did cast a look on all the corners thereof, so bewitchingly amiable and magnetically efficacious as if in his eys had bin a muster of ten thousand cupids, eagerly striving who should most deeply pierce the hearts of the spectators with their golden darts.

And truly so it fell out, that there not being so much as one arrow shot in vain, all of them did love him, though not after the same manner nor for the same end; for, as the manna of the Arabian desarts is said to have had in the mouths of the Egyptian Israelites the very same tast of the meat they loved best,[43] so the princes that were there did mainly cherish him for his magnanimity and knowledge; his courtliness and sweet behaviour being that for which chiefly the noblemen did most respect him. For his pregnancie of wit and chivalrie in vindicating the honour of ladies, he was honoured by the knights; and the esquires and other gentlemen courted him for his affability and good fellowship. The rich did favour him for his

κατ' ἐξοχήν: *par excellence*; epilogate: *speak the epilogue*; remanent: *remaining*; Cisalpinal: *on the south side of the Alps*; antiphrasis: *words used in sense opposite to their usual meaning*; promove: *progress*; serenissime: *most serene*; incontinently: *immediately*; rotonda: *circle/gathering*; Neems: *Nîmes*

judgement and ingeniosity, and for his liberality and munificence he was blessed by the poor. The old men affected° him for his constancie and wisdome, and the young for his mirth and gallantry. The scholars were enamoured of him for his learning and eloquence and the souldiers for his integrity and valour. The merchants for his upright dealing and honesty praised and extolled him, and the artificers for his goodness and benignity. The chastest lady of that place would have hugged and imbraced him for his discretion and ingenuity, whilst for his beauty and comeliness of person he was, at least in the fervency of their desires, the paramour of the less continent; he was dearly beloved of the fair women because he was handsom, and of the fairest more dearly becaus he was handsomer. In a word, the affections of the beholders, like so many several diameters drawn from the circumference of their various intents, did all concenter in the point of his perfection.

After a so considerable insinuation and gaining of so much ground upon the hearts of the auditory, though in shorter space then the time of a flash of lightning, he went on as before in the same thred of the conclusive part of his discourse, with a resolution not to cut it till the over-abounding passions of the company, their exorbitant motions and discomposed gestures, through excess of joy and mirth, should be all of them quieted, calmed and pacified and every man, woman and maid there, according to their humour, reseated° in the same integrity° they were at first; which when, by the articulatest elocution of the most significant words expressive of the choisest things that fancie could suggest, and, conforme to the matter's variety, elevating or depressing, flat or sharply accinating° it, with that proportion of tone that was most consonant with the purpose he had attained unto, and by his verbal harmony and melodious utterance setled all their distempered pleasures and brought their disorderly raised spirits into their former capsuls; he with a tongue tip't with silver, after the various diapasons° of all his other expressions and, making of a leg for the spruceness of its courtsie of greater decorement° to him then cloth of gold and purple, farewel'd the companie with a complement of one period so exquisitely delivered and so well attended by the gracefulness of his hand and foot with the quaint miniardise° of the rest of his body in the performance of such ceremonies as are usual at a court-like departing, that from the theater he had gone into a lobbie—from thence along three spacious chambers, whence descending a backstaire, he past through a low gallerie which led him to the outer gate, where a coach with six horses did attend him—before that magnificent convention of both sexes (to whom that room, wherein they all were, seemed in his absence to be as a body without a soul) had the full leisure to recollect their spirits which, by the neatness of his so curious a close,° were *quoquoversedly*° scattered with admiration, to advise on the best expediency how to dispose of themselves for the future of that licentious night.

During which time of their being thus in a maze, a proper young lady (if ever there was any in the world) whose dispersed spirits, by her wonderful delight in his accomplishments, were by the power of Cupid with the assistance of his mother,° instantly gathered and replaced, did (upon his retiring) without taking notice of the intent of any other, rise up out of her boxe, issue forth at a posterne door° into some secret transes,° from whence—going down a few steps that brought her to a

affected: *were drawn to*; reseated: *replaced*; integrity: *dignity*; accinating: *accenting*; diapasons: *melodies*; decorement: *embellishment*; miniardise: *delicacy of behaviour*; so curious a close: *so ingenious a conclusion*; quoquoversedly: *in every direction*; mother: *i.e. Venus*; posterne door: *private door*; transes: *passages*

parlour—she went through a large hall, by the wicket° of one end whereof, as she entered on the street, she encountered with Crichtoun who was but even then come to the aforesaid coach, which was hers; unto which sans° ceremony (waving° the frivolous windings of dilatory circumstances) they both stepped up together without any other in their company save a waiting gentlewoman that sate in the furthest side of the coach, a page that lifted up the boot thereof and walked by it, and one lacky that ran before with a kindled torch in his hand—all domestick servants of hers, as were the coach-man and postillion who, driving apace and having but a half mile to go, did with all the expedition required, set down my lady with her beloved mate at the great gate of her own palace; through the wicket whereof, because she would not stay till the whole were made wide open, they entred both; and injunction being given that forthwith, after the setting up of the coach and horses, the gate should be made fast and none (more then was already) permitted to come within her court that night, they joyntly went along a private passage, which led them to a lanterne scalier,° whose each step was twelve foot long. Thence, mounting up a paire of staires, they past through and traversed above nine several° rooms on a floor before they reached her bedchamber; which, in the interim of the progress of their transitory walk,° was with such mutual cordialness so unanimously aimed at, that never did the passengers of a ship in a tedious voyage long for a favourable winde with greater uniformity of desire then the blessed hearts of that amorous and amiable couple were—without the meanest variety of a wish—in every jot united.

Nevertheless, at last they entred in it, or rather in an Alcoranal paradise,[44] where nothing tending to the pleasure of all the senses was wanting. The weather being a little chil and coldish, they on a blew velvet couch sate by one another towards a charcoale fire burning in a silver brasero,° whilst in the next room adjacent thereto, a pretty little round table of cedar-wood was a covering for the supping of them two together. The cates° prepared for them and, a week before that time bespoke, were of the choisest dainties and most delicious junkets,° that all the territories of Italy were able to afford—and that deservedly—for all the Romane Empire could not produce a completer paire to taste them.

In beauty she was supream, in pedigree equal with the best; in spirit not inferiour to any, and in matter of affection a great admirer of Crichtoun, which was none of her least perfections. She many times used to repaire to my lady dutchesse's court, where now and then the prince would cast himself, as *à l'improviste,*° into her way, to catch hold the more conveniently of someone or other opportunity for receiving her employments; with the favour whereof, he very often protested if she would vouchsafe to honour him, and be pleased to gratifie his best endeavours with her only gracious acceptance of them, none breathing should be able to discharge that duty with more zeal to her service nor reap more inward satisfaction in the performance of it; for that his obedience could not be crowned with greater glory then by that of a permanently fixed attendance upon her commandments.

His highness' complements (whereof to this noble lady he was at all times very liberal) remained never longer unexchanged then after they were delivered and that in a coine so pretious[45] for language, matter, phrase and elocution, that he was still assured of his being repayed with interest; by means of which odds of her retali-

wicket: *gateway*; sans: *without*; waving: *waiving*; lanterne scalier: *winding staircase*; several: *different*; transitory walk: *walking across*; brasero: *brasier*; cates: *provisions*; junkets: *confections*; à l'improviste: *without warning*

ation, she, though unknown to her self, conquered his affections and he thenceforth became her *inamorato.*° But with so close and secret a minde did he harbour in his heart that new love and nourish the fire thereof in his veins, that remotely skonsing it from° the knowledge of all men, he did not so much as acquaint therewith his most intimate friend Crichtoun; who, by that the sun had deprest our western horizon by one half of the quadrant of his orb, did, after supper with his sweet lady, whom he had by the hand, return againe to the bedchamber wherein formerly they were.

And there, without losing of time, which by unnecessary puntilios° of strained civility and affected formalities of officious respect, is very frequently but too much lavished away and heedlessly regarded by the young Adonises and faint-hearted initiants in the exercises of the Cytheraean Academy,[46] they barred all the ceremonies of Pindarising their discourse[47] and sprucifying° it in *à la mode* salutations; their mutual carriage shewing it self as it were in a meane° betwixt the conjugal of man and wife, and fraternal conversation of brother and sister, in the reciprocacy of their love transcending both, in the purity of their thoughts equal to this, and in fruition of pleasure nothing inferior to the other; for when, after the waiting damsel had, by putting her beautiful mistris into her nocturnal dress, quite impoverished the ornaments of her that daye's wear in robbing them of the inestimably rich treasure which they inclosed, and then performed the same office to the lord of her ladie's affections by laying aside the impestring° bulk of his journal abiliaments,° and fitting him in the singlest manner possible with the most genuine habit *a la Cypriana*,[48] that Cupid could devise; she, as it became an obsequious servant and maid, observant of her mistrisse's directions, bidding them good night with the inarticulate voyce of an humble curtesie, locked the doors of the room behind her and shut them both in to the reverence of one another, him to her discretion, her to his mercy and both the passion of each other. Who then, finding themselves not only together but alone with other, were in an instant transported both of them with an equal kinde of rapture; for as he looked on her and saw the splendor of the beams of her bright eyes and with what refulgency her alabaster-like skin did shine through the thin cawle° of her Idalian° garments, her appearance was like the antartick oriency° of a western aurore° or acronick° rising of the most radiant constellation of the firmament; and whilst she viewed him and perceived the portliness of his garb,° comeliness of his face, sweetness of his countenance, and majesty in his very chevelure,° with the goodliness of his frame, proportion of his limbs and symmetry in all the parts and joints of his body which, through the cobweb slenderness of his Cyllenian° vestments, were represented almost in the *puris naturalibus*;[49] his resemblance was like that of Aeneas to Dido, when she said that he was in face and shoulders like a god;[50] or rather to her he seemed as to the female deities did Ganimed when, after being carryed up to heaven, he was brought into the presence of Jupiter.[51]

Thus for a while their eloquence was mute and all they spoke was but with the eye and hand, yet so persuasively, by vertue of the intermutual unlimitedness of

inamorato: *passionate admirer*; remotely skonsing it from: *concealing it well out of reach of*; puntilios: *petty formalities*; sprucifying: *smartening*; meane: *a middle point*; impestring: *encumbering*; journal abiliaments: *day clothes*; cawle: *mesh*; Idalian: *Idalion was a city in Cyprus, sacred to Venus*; oriency: *lustre*; aurore: *dawn*; acronick: *at sunset*; portliness of his garb: *stateliness of his appearance*; chevelure: *head of hair*; Cyllenian: *pertaining to Mercury/Cylleneius, or Mount Cyllene, area of his birth*

their visotactil° sensation, that each part and portion of the persons of either was obvious to the sight and touch of the persons of both. The visuriency° of either, by ushering the tacturiency° of both, made the attrectation° of both consequent to the inspection of either. Here was it that passion was active and action passive, they both being overcome by other and each the conquerour. To speak of her hirquitalliency° at the elevation of the pole of his microcosme or of his luxuriousness° to erect a gnomon on her horizontal dyal,[52] will perhaps be held by some to be expressions full of obscoeness and offensive to the purity of chaste ears; yet seeing she was to be his wife and that she could not be such without consummation of marriage—which signifieth the same thing in effect—it may be thought, as *definitiones logicae verificantur in rebus*,[53] if the exerced act° be lawful, that the diction which suppones° it can be of no great transgression, unless you would call it a solaecisme,° or that vice in grammar which imports the copulating of the masculine with the feminine gender.

But as the misery of the life of man is such that bitterness for the most part is subsequent to pleasure and joy, the prognostick of grief to come, so the Admirable Crichtoun—or to resume my discourse where I broke off—I say it hapened on a Shrove Tuesday at night, that the ever-renowned Crichtoun was warned by a great noise in the streets to be ready for the acting of another part; for the prince who, till that time, from the first houre of the night inclusively for the space of four hours, together with all his attendants, had done nothing else but rant it, roar and roam from one taverne to another with hautbois,° flutes and trumpets, drinking healths, breaking glasses, tossing pots, whitling° themselves with Septembral juyce,° tumbling in the kennel° and acting all the devisable feats of madness, at least so many as in their irregular judgements did seem might contrevalue all the penance they should be able to do for them the whole Lent thereafter; being ambitious to have a kiss of his mistris' hand (for so, in that too frolick humour of his, he was pleased to call this young lady) before he should go to bed, with nine gentlemen at his back and four pages carrying waxe tapers before him, come to the place where Crichtoun and the foresaid lady were—though the prince knew nothing of Crichtoun's being there—and knocks at the outer gate thereof.

No answer is made at first, for the whole house was in a profound silence and all of them in the possession of Morphee° save that blessed pair of pigeon-like lovers in whom Cupid, for the discharge of Hymenaean° rites, had inspired a joynt determination to turne that whole night's rest to motion. But the fates being pleased otherways to dispose of things then° as they proposed them, the clapper° is up again and they rap with a flap° till a threefold clap made the sound to rebound. With this the porter awakes, looks out at a lattice window of his lodge and, seeing them all with masks and vizards on their faces, asked them what their desire was or what it might be that moved them to come so late in such a disguise. The prince himself answered that they were gentlemen desirous only to salute° my lady, which courtesie when obtained, they should forthwith be gone.

visotactil: *involving both sight and touch*; visuriency...tacturiency: *desire of seeing...touching*; attrectation: *touching with hands*; hirquitalliency: *strongly voiced delight*; luxuriousness: *voluptuous pleasure*; exerced act: *technical or logical term, for an act performed*; suppones: *supports*; solaecisme: *solecism/violation of grammar or etiquette*; hautbois: *wooden double-reeded instruments of high pitch*; whitling: *intoxicating*; Septembral juyce: *wine*; kennel: *gutter*; Morphee: *Morpheus, Greek god of dreams, son of Sleep*; Hymenaean: *pertaining to Hymen, Greek god of marriage*; then: *than*; clapper: *knocker*; flap: *slap*; salute: *pay their respects to*

The porter advertiseth° the page and tells him all, who doing the same to the waiting gentlewoman, she, to receive orders from her mistris, opens the chamber doore, enters in, relates the story and demands direction from my lady, who immediately bids her call the page to her. She does it; he comes, and enquiring what the will of her *signoria*° was with him, she enjoynes him to go down and beseech those gentlemen to be pleased to have her excused for that night, because she was abed and not so well as she could wish to bear them company; yet, if they conceived any fault in her, she should strive to make them amends for it some other time.

The page accordingly acquits himself of what is recommended to him for, after he had caused open the wicket of the gate and faced the street, he first saluted them with that court-like dexterity which did bespeak him a well-educated boy and of good parentage, then told them that he was commanded by his lady mistris to intreat them—seeing she knew not what they were and that their wearing of vizards did in civility debar her from enquiring after their names—to take in good part her remitting of that their visit to another time, by reason of her present indisposure and great need of rest; which if they should have any pretext to except against, she would heartily make atonement for it and give them satisfaction at any other time.

The prince's answer was that he thought not but that he should have been admitted with less ceremony, and that though the time of the night and his lady mistris her being in a posture of rest might seem to plead somewhat for the non-disturbance of her desired solitariness, that nevertheless the uncontrolled priviledges of the season exempting them from all prescribed—and at all other times observed—boundaries, might in the carnavale-eeve° and supremest night of its law-transcendent jollities, by the custome of the whole country, very well apologize for that trespass. Which words being spoken he, without giving the page leisure to reply, pretending it was cold in the streets, rusht in at the open wicket even into the court with all his gentlemen and torch-bearers, each one whereof was no less cup-shotten° then himself.

The page, astonished at such unexpected rudeness, said with an audible voice, 'What do you mean, gentlemen? Do you intend to break in by violence, and at such an undue time enforce my lady to grant you admittance? Look, I pray you, to your own reputations; and if regardless of any thing else, consider what imputation and stain of credit wil lye upon you, thus to commit an enormous° action because of some colour° of justifying it by immunities of set times,[54] grounded upon no reason but meer toleration, without any other warrant then a feeble inveterate prescription.° Therefore, let me beseech you gentlemen, if you love your selves and the continuation of your good names, or tender any kind of respect to the honor of ladys, that you would be pleased, of your own accords, to chuse rather to return from whence you came or go whither elsewhere you will, then to imagin any rational man wil think that your masks and vizards can be sufficient covers wherewith to hide and palliate the deformedness of this obtrusive incivility.'

One of the prince's gentlemen, whose braines the fumes of Greek and Italian wines had a little intoxicated, laying hold only upon the last word (all the rest having escaped both his imagination and memory like an empty sound which makes no impression) and most eagerly grasping at it like a snarling curr that in his

advertiseth: *notifies*; signoria: *ladyship*; carnaval-eeve: *the action takes place during carnival—the season of revelry preceding Lent—used precisely here for the night of Shrove Tuesday*; cup-shotten: *drunk*; enormous: *shocking/monstrous*; colour: *pretence/excuse*; inveterate prescription: *long-standing claim*

gnarring° snatcheth at the taile, ecchoes it: 'Incivility?' Then, coming up closer to him and saying, 'How now Jackanapes! Whom do you twit with incivility?' he gave him such a sound thwhack over the left shoulder with his sword, scabard and all, that the noise thereof reached to all the corners of my Ladye's bedchamber; at which the generous° page who, besides his breeding otherwayes, was the son of a nobleman, being a little commoved° and vexed at an affront so undeservedly received and barbarously given, told the esquire who had wronged him, that if he had but had one drop of any good blood within him, he never would have offered to strike a gentleman that wanted° a weapon wherewith to defend himself; and that, although he was but of fourteen yeers of age and for strength but as a springal° or stripling in regard of him, he should nevertheless (would any of those other nine gentlemen, as he called them, be pleased to favour him but with the lend of a sword) take upon him even then and on that place, to humble his cockescomb,° pull his crest a little lower down and make him faine, for the safety of his life, to acknowledge that he is but a base and unworthy man.

Whilst the gentleman was about to have shapen him an answer, the prince being very much taken with the discretion, wit, garb and courage of the boy, commanded the other to silence; and forthwith taking the speech in hand himself, commended him very much for his loyalty to his mistris and, for his better ingratiating in the page's favour, presented him with a rich saphir to shew him but the way to my ladye's chamber, where he vowed that, as he was a gentleman, he would make no longer stay then barely might afford him the time to kiss her hands and take his leave. The sweet boy, being more incensed at the manner of that offer of the prince, whom he knew not, then at the discourtesie he had sustained by his aforesaid gentleman, plainly assured him that he might very well put up his saphir into his pocket againe, for that all the gifts in the world should never be able to gaine that of him which had not ground enough in reason for persuading the grant thereof without them.

After that the prince and Pomponacio, for so they called the page, had thus for a long time together debated to and againe° the reasons for and against the intended visit, with so little success on either side that the more artifice was used in the rhetorick, the less effect it had in the persuasion; the prince, unwilling to miss of his mark, and not having in all the quivers of his reason one shaft wherewith to hit it, resolved to interpose some authority with his argumentations and, where the foxe's skin could not serve, to make use of the lyon's. To the prosecuting of which intent, he with his vinomadefied° retinue resolved to press in upon the page and maugre° his will, to get up staires and take their fortune in the quest of the chamber they aimed at; for albeit the stradling as wide as he could of pretty Pomponacio at the door whereat they made account to force their passage, did for a while retard their designe because of their chariness to struggle with so hopeful° a youth and tender imp of so great expectation; yet at last, being loath to faile of their end, by how indirect meanes soever they might attaine thereto, they were in the very action of crowning their violence with prevalency,° when the admirable and ever-renowned Crichtoun who, at the prince's first manning of the court, taking the alarm, step'd from the shrine of Venus to the oracle of Pallas Armata;[55] and by the

gnarring: *growling*; generous: *noble-minded*; commoved: *disturbed*; wanted: *lacked*; springal: *youth*; his cockescomb: *i.e. the Prince's gentleman's coxcomb/pride*; to and againe: *back and forth*; vinomadefied: *maddened with wine*; maugre: *despite*; hopeful: *promising*; prevalency: *greater power*

help of the waiting gentlewoman having apparelled himself with a paludamental vesture° after the antick° fashion of the illustrious Romans, both for that he minded not to make himself then known, that to walk then in such like disguise was the anniversary custome of all that country, and that all (both gentlemen and others standing in that court) were in their mascaradal° garments, with his sword in his hand like a messenger from the gods, came down to relieve the page from the poste whereat he stood sentry; and when, as the light of the minor planets appeares not before the glorious rayes of Titan, he had obscured the irradiancy of Pomponacio with his more effulgent presence and that—under pretext of turning him to the page to desire him to stand behind him, as he did—he had exposed the full view of his left side, so far as the light of torches could make it perceivable to the lookers on, who (being all *in cuerpo*,° carying swords in their hands in stead of cloaks about them) imagined really, by the badge or cognizance they saw neer his heart, that he was one of my ladie's chief domestick servants.

He addressed his discourse to the prince and the nine gentlemen that were with him; neither of all whereof, as they were accoutred,° was he able (either by the light of the tapers or that of the moon, which was then but in the first week of its waxing, it being the Tuesday next to the first new moon that followed the Purification Day)° to discern in any manner of way, what they were. And for that he perceived by their unstedfast postures, that the influence of the grape had made them subjects to Bacchus, and that their extranean-like° demeanour towards him, not without some amazement, did manifest his certainty of their not knowing him; he therefore, with another kind of intonation—that his speech might not bewray° him—then° that which waited upon his usual note of utterance, made a pithy panegyrick in praise of those that endeavoured by their good fellowship and bacchanalian compagnionry to cheer up their hearts with precious liquour and renew the Golden Age; whence, descending to a more particular application, he very much applauded the ten gentlemen for their being pleased, out of their devotion to the Lyaean god° (who had with great respect been bred and elevated amongst the nymphs) not to forget amidst the most sacred plying of their symposiasms° that duty to ladyes, which was incumbent on them to be performed in the discharge of a visite.

Then, wheeling neatly about to fetch another careere,° he discreetly represented to them all the necessary circumstances at such a visit observable, and how the infringing of the meanest title or particle of any one thereof, would quite disconcert the mutual harmony it should produce and bring an unspeakable disparagement to the credits and honors of all guilty of the like delinquency. In amplifying hereof and working upon their passions, he let go so many secret springs and inward resorts of eloquence, that being all persuaded of the unseasonableness of the time and unreasonableness of the suit, none of them for a thousand ducats that night would have adventured to make any further progress in that after which, a little before, they had been so eager—so profound was the character of reverence toward that lady, which he so insinuatingly had imprinted into the hearts of them all. Wherefore they, purposing to insist no longer upon the visitatory design, did cast their minds on a sudden upon another far more hairbrained consideration—when

paludamental vesture: *garment similar to the military cloak worn by Roman generals*; antick: *ancient*; mascaradal: *intended to disguise, used in masques etc*; in cuerpo: *in a state of undress*; accoutred: *arrayed*; Purification Day: *i.e. Candlemas (2 February)*; extranean-like: *alien/unfamiliar*; bewray: *expose*; then: *than*; Lyaean god: *i.e. Bacchus, popularly the god of wine*; symposiasms: *convivial gatherings*; careere: *charge*

the prince to one of his chief gentlemen said: 'We wil do this good fellow no wrong. Yet, before we go hence, let us try what courage is in him, that after we have made him flee for it, we may tomorrow make one excuse for all to the lady, whom he serveth. Do not you see,' sayes he, 'how he dandleth the sword in his hand as if he were about to braveer° us and how he is decked and trimm'd up in his cloaths like another Hector of Troy? But I doubt if he be so martial. He speaks too well to be valiant. He is certainly more Mercurial then military. Therefore, let us make him turn his back, that we may spie if, as another Mercury, he hath any wings on his heels.'[56]

This foolish chat no sooner was blattered out° to the ears of three of his gentlemen that were nearest to him, but the sudden drawing of their swords, though but in jest, made the other six (who heard not the prince) as if they had bin mad to adventure the rashness (wherewith the spirit of wine had inspired them) against the prudensequal and invincible fortitude[57] of the matchless Crichtoun; who, not being accustomed to turn his back to those that had any project against his brest, most manfully sustained their encounter; which, although furious at first, appearing nevertheless unto him because of the odds of ten to one not to have been in earnest, he for twenty several bouts did but ward their blows and pary with the fort° of his sword till, by plying the defensive part too long, he had received one thrust in the thigh and another in the arme; the trickling of his blood from the wounds whereof prompted his heroick spirit as at a desperate stake to have at all or none, to make his tith outvy their stock[58] and set upon them all. In which resolution, when from the door whereat he stood he had lanched forth three paces in the court,° having lovely Pomponacio behind him to give him warning in case of surprisal in the reer, and all his ten adversaries in a front before him, who—making up above a quadrant° of that periphery° whereof his body was the center—were about, from the exterior points of all their right shoulder-blades alongst the additional line of their armes and tucks,° to lodge home in him so many truculent semi-diameters, he, retrograding° their intention and beginning his agency where they would have made him a patient,[59] in as short space as the most diagrammatically-skilled hand could have been able to describe lines representative of the distance 'twixt the earth and the several *kardagas* or horary expeditions of the sun's diurnal motion[60] from his aequinoxial horizontality to the top of his meridian hight, which, with the help of a ruler, by six draughts of a pen is quickly delineated, livered out° six several thrusts against them. By vertue whereof, he made such speedy work upon the respective segments of that debauch'd circumference through the red ink marks which his streight-drawn stroaks imprinted, that being alonged° from the center-point of his own courage, and with a thunderbolt-like swiftness of hand radiated upon their bodies, he discussed° a whole quadrant of those ten, whereof four and twenty make the circle and, laying six of the most inraged of them on their backs, left in the other four but a sextant of the aforesaid ring[61] to avenge the death of their dismal associates.

Of which quaternity,° the prince, being the most concerned in the effects of this disaster as being the only cause thereof, though his intentions levelled at another issue, and like to burst with shame to see himself loadned on all sides with so much

braveer: *act the bravo towards*; blattered out: *babbled*; fort: *upper blade*; court: *court-yard*; quadrant...periphery: *i.e. quarter of that circumference*; tucks: *rapiers*; retrograding: *reversing*; livered out: *handed out*; alonged: *placed at a distance from*; discussed: *dispatched*; quaternity: *group of four*

dishonour by the incomparable valour of one single man, did set forward at the sword's point to essay° if in his person so much lost credit might be recovered; and to that purpose comming within distance, was upon the advancing of a thurst in quart,[62] when the most agil Crichtoun, pareing° it in the same ward,° smoothly glided along the prince's sword and being master of its feeble, was upon the very instant of making his highness very low and laying his honor in the dust, when one of the three courtiers whom fortune had favoured not to fall by the hand of Crichtoun, cryed aloud, 'Hold, hold! Kill not the prince!'

At which words, the courteous Crichtoun recoyling and putting himself out of distance, the prince pulled off his vizard and, throwing it away, shew his face so fully that the noble-hearted Crichtoun, being sensible of his mistake and sory so many of the prince's servants should have enforced him, in his own defence, to become the actor of their destruction, made unto the prince a very low obeisance; and setting his left knee to the ground as if he had been to receive the honour of knighthood, with his right hand presented him the hilts of his own conquering sword with the point thereof towards his own brest, wishing his highness to excuse his not knowing him in that disguise and to be pleased to pardon what unluckily had ensued upon the necessity of his defending himself, which at such an exigent° might have befaln to any other that were not minded to abandon their lives to the indiscretion of others.

The prince, in the throne of whose judgement the rebellious vapours of the tun° had installed Nemesis° and caused the irascible faculty shake off the soveraignty of reason, being without himself° and unable to restraine the impetuosity of the will's first motion, runs Crichtoun through the heart with his own sword and kils him. In the interim of which lamentable accident, the sweet and beautiful lady (who by this time had slipped her self into a cloth-of-gold petticoat, in the anterior fente° whereof was an asteristick ouch,° wherein were inchased fifteen several diamonds representative of the constellation of the primest stars in the signe of Virgo, had enriched a tissue° gown and wastcoat of brocado° with the precious treasure of her ivory body, and put the foot-stals° of those marble pillars which did support her microcosme[63] into a paire of incarnation° velvet slippers, embroydered with purle)° being descended to the lower door which jetted out to the courtwards where Pomponacio was standing, with the curled tresses of her discheveled haire dangling over her shoulders, by the love-knots of whose naturally guilded filaments were made fast the hearts of many gallant sparks, who from their liberty of ranging after other beauties were more forcibly curbed by those capillary fetters than by so many chaines of iron; and in the daedalian° windings of the crisped pleats whereof, did lye in ambush a whole brigade of Paphian archers° to bring the loftiest martialists to stoop to the shrine of Cupid; and, Arachne-like,[64] now careering,° now caracoling° it alongest the polygonal plainness of its twisted threds, seaze on the affections of all whose looks should be involved in her locks; and, with a presentation exposing to the beholders all the perfections that ever yet were by the Graces conferred on the female sexe, all the excellencies of Juno, Venus and Minerva[65]—

essay: *test*; pareing: *parrying*; ward: *the part of the hilt which protects the hand*; exigent: *emergency*; tun: *vat*; Nemesis: *Greek goddess of retribution*; without himself: *beside himself*; anterior fente: *front slash/vent*; asteristick ouch: *starry brooch*; tissue: *woven material of gauzy nature*; brocado: *corr. to Italian 'broccato', cloth of gold and silver with richly raised pattern*; foot-stals: *pedestals*; incarnation: *flesh colour*; purle: *pearl*; daedalian: *maze-like*; Paphian archers: *i.e. archers of Venus*; careering: *charging*; caracoling: *wheeling*

the other feminean deities and semi-goddesses of former ages seeming to be of new revived and within her compiled as the compactedst abbridgement of all their best endowments—stepped a pace or two into the court with all the celerity that the intermixed passions of love and indignation was able to prompt her to.

During which time, which certainly was very short because—to the motions of her angelically composed body, the quantity attending the matter of its constitution was no more obstructive then were the various exquisite qualities flowing from the form thereof, wherein there was no blemish—the eyes of the prince's thoughts and those were with him (for the influences of Cupid are like the actions of generation which are said to be *in instanti*°) pryed into, spyed and surveyed from the top of that sublimely framed head, which culminated her accomplishments, down along the wonderful symmetry of her divinely proportioned countenance; from the glorious light of whose two luminaries Apollo might have borrowed rayes to court his Daphne and Diana her Endymion;[66] even to the rubies of those lips, where two Cupids still were kissing one another for joy of being so neer the enjoyment of her two rows of pearles inclosed within them; and from thence through the most graceful objects of all her intermediate parts to the heaven-like polished prominences of her mellifluent and heroinal breast whose porphyr streaks,° like arches of the ecliptick° and colures,° or azimuth and almicantar circles intersecting other,[67] expansed in pretty veinlets through whose sweet conduits run the delicious streams of nectar, wherewith were cherished the pretty sucklings of the Cyprian goddesse,° smiled on one another to see their courses regulated by the two niple-poles above them elevated in each their own hemisphere; whose magnetick vertue (by attracting hearts and sympathy in their refocillation)° had a more impowering ascendent over poetick lovers for furnishing their braines with choise of fancy, then ever had the two tops of Parnassus hill, when animated or assisted by all the wits of the Pierian Muses.[68] Then, from the snow-white galaxy betwixt those gemel-monts° whose milken paths, like to the plaines of Thessaly,° do by reflexion calefie° to that protuberant and convexe ivory whose meditullian node,[69] compared with that other where the ecliptick cuts the aequinoxial, did far surpass it in that property whereby the night is brought in competition with the day; whence, having past the line and seeming to depress the former pole to elevate another, the inward prospect of their minde discovered a new America, or land unknown, in whose subterranean and intestine cels were secret mines of greater worth then those of either Tibar or Peru;[70] for that, beside the working in them could not but give delight unto the mineralist, their metal was so reciptible for impression and to the mint so plyable, that alchymists[71] profoundly versed in chymical extractions, and such as knew how to imbue it with syndon° and crown the magisterum° with the elixir,° instead of treasures merchants bring from the Indias, would have educed little worlds more worth then gold or silver.

All this from their imagination being convoyed into the penitissim° corners of their souls in that short space which I have already told, she, rending her garments and tearing her haire like one of the Graces possest with a Fury, spoke thus: 'O villains! What have you done? You vipers of men, that have thus basely slaine the

in instanti: *quickly done*; porphyr streaks: *i.e. crimson veins*; ecliptick: *great circle of the celestial sphere*; colures: *the two great circles which intersect at right angles at the poles*; Cyprian goddesse: *Venus*; refocillation: *revival*; gemel-mounts: *twin-mounts*; Thessaly: *a region in northern Greece*; calefie: *heat*; syndon: *thin linen fabric*; magisterum: *philosopher's stone*; elixir: *preparation intended to change base metals into gold*; penetissim: *innermost*

valiant Crichtoun, the sword of his own sexe and buckler° of ours; the glory of this age and restorer of the lost honor of the Court of Mantua. O Crichtoun, Crichtoun!'

At which last words the prince, hearing them uttered by the lady in the world he loved best and of the man in the world he most affected, was suddenly seazed upon by such extremity of sorrow for the unhappiness of that lamentable mischance, that not being able to sustaine the rayes of that beauty whose percing aspect made him conscious of his guilt, he fell flat upon his face like to a dead man. But knowing *omne simile*° not to be *idem*,° he quickly arose and (to make his body be what it appeared) fixed the hilt of the sword, wherewith he had killed Crichtoun, fast betwixt two stones at the foot of a marble statue standing in the court—after the fashion of those staves with iron pikes at both ends commonly called Swedish feathers, when stuck into the ground to fence musketeers from the charge of horse. Then, having recoyled a little from it, was fetching a race° to run his brest, which for that purpose he had made open, upon the point thereof, as did Cato Uticensis[72] after his lost hopes of the recovery of the Commonwealth of Rome; and assuredly, according to that his intent, had made a speedy end of himself but that his three gentlemen, one by stopping him in course, another by laying hold on him by the middle and the third by taking away the sword, hindred the desperate project of that autochthony.[73]

The prince being carryed away in that mad, frantick and distracted humour, befitting a bedlam° better then a *serralio*,° into his own palace, where all manner of edge-tools were kept from him all that sad night, for fear of executing his former designe of self-murther. As soon as to his father, my lord duke, on the next morning by seven a clock (which, by the usual computation of that country, came at that season of the yeer to be neer upon fourteen hours or fourteen a clock) the story of the former night's tragedy was related, and that he had solemnly vowed he should either have his son hanged, or his head struck off for the committing of a so ingrate, enormous and detestable crime, one of his courtiers told him that by all appearance his son would save his highness' justice a labour and give it nothing to do, for that he was like to hang himself or—after some other manner of way—to turn his own Atropos.[74]

The whole court wore mourning for him full three quarters of a yeer together. His funeral was very stately and on his hearse were stuck more epitaphs, elegies, threnodies° and epicediums° then, if digested° into one book, would have outbulkt all Homer's works; some of them being couched in such exquisite and fine Latin, that you would have thought great Virgil and Baptista Mantuanus[75] for the love of their mother-city had quit the Elysian fields° to grace his obsequies;° and other of them, besides what was done in other languages, composed in so neat Italian and so purely fancied, as if Ariosto, Dante, Petrark and Bembo[76] had been purposely resuscitated to stretch even to the utmost their poetick vein to the honour of this brave man, whose picture (till this hour) is to be seen in the bedchambers or galleries of the most of the great men of that nation—representing him on horseback with a lance in one hand and a book in the other. And most of the young ladies likewise, that were any thing handsome, in a memorial of his worth had his effigies in a little

buckler: *shield*; omne simile...idem: *similar in all respects...the same*; fetching a race: *gathering himself*; bedlam: *hospital for lunatics*; serralio: *harem, here presumably a dwelling reserved for women*; threnodies: *dirges*; epicediums: *funeral odes*; digested: *compressed*; Elysian fields: *abode of the virtuous dead (Greek legend)*; obsequies: *funeral ceremonies*

oval tablet° of gold hanging 'twixt their breasts, and held for many yeers together that metamazion° or intermammillary ornament an as necessary outward pendicle° for the better setting forth of their accoutrements, as either fan, watch or stomacher.

My lord duke, upon the young lady that was Crichtoun's mistris and future wife (although she had good rents and revenues of her own by inheritance) was pleased to conferr a pension of five hundred ducats a yeer. The prince also bestowed as much on her during all the days of his life, which was but short, for he did not long enjoy himself after the cross fate of so miserable an accident. The sweet lady, like a turtle bewailing the loss of her mate, spent all the rest of her time in a continual solitariness and resolved, as none before Crichtoun had the possession of her body, that no man breathing should enjoy it after his decease.

The verity of this story I have here related concerning this incomparable Crichtoun may be certified by above two thousand men yet living, who have known him; and truly of his acquaintance there had been a far great number, but that before he was full thirty two yeers of age he was killed, as you have heard. And here I put an end to the Admirable Scot.

tablet: *locket*: metamazion: *object worn between the breasts*; pendicle: *pendant*

NOTES

1. ED. COPY TEXT: London, 1652. EKSKUBALAURON is one of Urquhart's classical coinages. It joins the Greek for 'out of dung' with the Latin for 'gold'. He explains this in a final section, following the Errata. The English rendering—'Jewel'—stems from the fable of the cock and the jewel. (See § 4.)
2. The original 'Admirable Crichton' was James Crichton (1560–82). His genius and courage are well attested.
3. Guglielmo Gonzaga (1550–87), Duke of Mantua and a leading patron of the arts.
4. The 'lists' refer to any area marked off for fencing. Later, Urquhart provides his own gloss, 'within the barriers or place appointed for the fight'.
5. '*Tramontani.*' Literally—'from across the mountains.' That is, from North Europe.
6. 'foyled.' Here in its literal sense, 'being struck by a fencing sword.'
7. 'in triumph.' In triumphant procession, imitating the return of victorious Roman generals. Livy describes the triumph of Romulus, legendary founder of Rome, over the Cainini; Marcellus, a Roman consul, conquered Viridimarus.
8. 'slighting his falsifyings in breaking measure.' Parrying the feints he makes with his rapier, by changing his own parrying rhythms.
9. 'from tierce to quart; he primes and seconds it.' Within the eight types of parrying available, Crichton may, for example, change from third and fourth to first and second.
10. 'like another Prothee.' In classical legend, Proteus (Neptune's herdsman) could change his form at will.
11. The '*feeble*' is the part of the blade from middle to point; the '*fort*' stretches from upper to middle.
12. 'the speculative part.' In modern terms, he would have got points for 'style' as well as effectiveness.
13. 'he alonged a stoccade *de pied ferme*.' He lunged but kept his feet firmly on the ground.
14. 'perfect isosceles triangle...middle.' Geometry was one of the four sciences in the educational curriculum. The imagery marks out his text book style.
15. ED. Titus Flaminius is substituted for Paulus Aemilius in the Errata provided by Urquhart. The story of the birds and Titus is told by Plutarch in *Flaminius* 10.
16. Philip Sidney, *Arcadia*, II, 7. 2.
17. Alcibiades (c.450–404 B.C.). An Athenian leader and disciple of Socrates.
18. 'the intentional species'. As in fencing, Crichton is a master of practice and theory, so in all other arts and sciences he understands the unique methods and ends which distinguish one discipline from another.
19. '*Admirabilis Scotus*, the Wonderful Scot.' Crichton's nickname was well known in his own time. Later, it would be used by James Barrie for his heroic butler in *The Admirable Crichton*.

20. The College of Navarre, founded in 1304, was a leading medieval institution, especially famed for its theological faculty.
21. 'controversies and positive doctrine'. The professors were famed for their new ideas and their power to sustain them in debate.
22.'trou-madam.' A game similar to bagatelle.
23. Navarre was a college within the University of Paris.
24. 'an aspersion of toq great proness to such like debordings'. Rumour suggests that Crichton is too much given to riotous behaviour.
25. 'superficial rhetorick'. The debate moves upwards through the educational curriculum established by Aristotle and Boethius. So far, the verbal skills of the lower 'trivium' have been the focus. The Rector wishes to move on to the higher branches of study.
26. 'acroamaticks'. The more esoteric branches of philosophy. The debate had moved to the 'quadrivium' or natural sciences—arithmetic, geometry, music and astronomy. Now metaphysical questions introduce the highest, theological area of disputation.
27. 'broke as many lances on the Saracen.' A Turk's head, used for jousting practice.
28. 'in the disguise of a Zanni or Pantaloon.' Clown and old man characters in the early *commedia dell'arte* dramatic tradition.
29. 'a la Venetiana.' In the elaborate, stylized manner of the Venetian school of acting.
30. 'the several [i.e. different] humours of all these sorts of people'. The four humours (i.e. melancholic, choleric, sanguine, phlegmatic) were held to determine character traits. This led to the 'comic humour' or character defined dramatically by one ruling trait—e.g. avarice, hypocrisy.
31. 'the splene...the gall...such a climacterical and mercurially digested method'. Comic rather than tragic; for the merry 'humour' rather than the bitter one. Crichton has the ability to highlight critical moments; he understands the quicksilver changes needed to move from one role to another.
32. 'engines.' An example of Urquhart using a word with many senses, all potentially relevant. 'Talents', 'skills', 'props' and 'plans' are all, enrichingly, possible.
33. *Sejanus* (1603) was a tragedy written by Ben Jonson. 'Cypres powder' was used to treat the more elaborate types of wig.
34. 'a Monmouth-like cap.' Round caps, especially favoured by soldiers and sailors.
35. 'in pilgrimage from Saint Michael.' An island abbey in Normandy.
36. 'Capitan Spavento.' A braggart captain in Andreini's *Le Bravure del Capitano Spavento* (1607). In Italian his name means 'I terrify'.
37. 'bucked ruff'. One that has been boiled in a dye, beaten and rinsed in clean water.
38. 'that angel...voice of a multitude'. Gabriel as described in Daniel 10.6.
39. 'This accident...with consolidative medicaments.' To cure the lady who has been so excited that she has suffered from diarrhoea.
40. 'supremest Lydian note...overreaching Ela and beyond the...*gam*'. The Lydian mode in music was soft and effeminate and derived its name from the region of Lydia in Asia Minor. 'Ela' (upper E in the seventh hexachord) was the highest note in the gamut, according to the 11th century system of Guido d'Arezzo.
41. A good example of how long Urquhart's parenthetic explanations may be. The subject of 'did' is 'The Admirable Crichtoun' at the start of the paragraph.
42. 'so periodically contexed with isocoly of members'. The length of the discourse is skilfully broken up by well balanced phraseology.
43. 'manna...the meat they loved best' Exodus 16.10–35.
44. 'an Alcoranal paradise'. The account of the sensual pleasures awaiting the true believer in the Muslim scriptures of the Koran.
45. 'in a coine so pretious'. The 'coining' of words.
46. 'young Adonises...the Cytheraean Academy'. Adonis was a handsome youth, loved by Venus, to whom the island of Cytherea was sacred.
47. 'Pindarising their discourse'. They talked in a lofty style, imitative of that used by the Greek lyric poet Pindar (5th century B.C.).
48. 'habit *a la Cypriana*,' Cyprus was the supposed birthplace of Venus. The sense here is 'clothes suited to night-time and lovemaking.'
49. 'almost in the *puris naturalibus*'. 'Almost in their natural purity'—i.e. almost as if naked.
50. 'Aeneas to Dido...like a god.' Virgil, *Aeneid* I. 588–9: 'restitit Aeneas claraque in luce refulsit/os umerosque deo similis.'
51. 'Ganimed...into the presence of Jupiter'. Ganymede was a youth carried off by an eagle to become Jupiter's cupbearer. *Aeneid* I. 28, 'rapti Ganymedi honores'; and Ovid, *Metamorphoses* X. 155–61.
52. 'to erect a gnomon on her horizontal dyal.' The sundial image of 'rod' and 'dial' is used to convey the stimulation of the lady's clitoris.

53. '*definitiones logicae verificantur in rebus*': 'Logical definitions are verified by objects.'
54. 'justifying it by immunities of set times'. The page opposes the prince's argument that carnival days 'exempt' people from 'all prescribed boundaries of time'.
55. 'Pallas Armata'. The armed Pallas is one of the aspects of the goddess Athena, patroness of war.
56. 'as another Mercury, he hath any wings on his heels'. The winged heels of Mercury signified his speed as messenger of the gods.
57. 'the rashness...the prudensequal and invincible fortitude.' The Epic/Romantic virtues of courage and wisdom are here attributed to Crichton. Unlike his rash opponents he shows 'the invincible courage deriving from prudence'. Cf. § 1 and the depiction of Bruce.
58. 'to make his tith outvy their stock.' Swordsmanship and usury are wittily combined. 'Tith' (tenth) and 'stock' (capital) are both types of sword and moneylending terms.
59. 'beginning his agency...made him a patient.' Wordplay. His opponents seek to turn Crichton from 'agency' to being 'a patient' in two senses—(i) from action to hospitalization; (ii) from being the initiator of action to becoming their passive victim.
60. 'several *kardagas*...sun's diurnal motion'. Astronomical term meaning a 15° sector of the earth's 360° and, therefore, one hour out of twenty four.
61. 'whole quadrant of those ten...a sextant of the aforesaid ring.' Geometrical imagery continues to be applied to fencing. Two other quadruvial disciplines—arithmetic and astronomy—are also involved in this calculation. By killing six out of ten, within a supposed circumference of twenty four, he cuts down 6 (a quarter) and leaves 4 (a sixth). A 'quadrant' thus becomes a 'sextant. '
62. 'thurst into quart.' The metathesis 'thurst' for 'thrust' is one of the few Scotticisms in the text. For 'quart' see n. 9.
63. 'microcosme'. As mankind was made in God's image, the human body was held to mirror in small (microcosmically) the larger harmony (macrocosm) of His world.
64. 'Arachne-like'. Arachne was a Lydian woman so skilled at spinning that the goddess Athena became jealous, murdered her and then turned her into a spider. Ovid, *Metamorphoses* VI.
65. 'all the excellencies of Juno, Venus and Minerva'. The three goddesses whose beauty was judged by Paris.
66. 'Apollo...Daphne...Diana her Endymion'. The loves of sun-god and moon-goddess for mortals are used to strengthen the idea that the lady's appearance is almost godlike.
67. 'azimuth and almicantar circles intersecting other'. Arabic astronomical terms referring to longitude and latitude respectively.
68. 'the Pierian muses'. Pieria in northern Thessaly was the reputed home of the Muses.
69. 'meditullian node': 'pertaining to the middle of the earth'. Astronomical reference to one of the two points at which the orbit of a planet intersects the ecliptic, or in which two great circles of the sphere intersect one another.
70. 'Tibar or Peru.' While Peru is a known site for mining, Tibar is a problem. The home of the Tibareni in Asia Minor is referred to by Xenophon but does not fit this context.
71. 'alchymists...' Unusually, in British literature, alchemy's mysterious skills are positively viewed as a means of imitating, microcosmically, divine knowledge and skill. The finest alchemists would best handle the small worlds of the lady's body.
72. 'as did Cato Uticensis'. He commited suicide in 46 B.C. after the defeat of Pompey's forces (Plutarch, *Cato Minor* 67–70).
73. 'that autochthony': 'That son of the soil'. The phrase is deliberately reductive. When the murderer-prince is about to return himself to dust and ashes, the worldly nature of even God's chosen rulers is emphasized.
74. 'to turn his own Atropos'. To kill himself—Atropos being one of the three fates who wove and cut the threads of human life.
75. 'Baptista Mantuanus' (1448–1516): General of the Carmelite Order, whose Latin lyrics were popular in the Renaissance.
76. 'Ariosto, Dante, Petrark (Petrarch) and Bembo.' The acknowledged masters of Italian literature.

§ 22: James VI (1566–1625): *Ane Schort Treatise Conteining Some Reulis and Cautelis to be Observit and Eschewit in Scottis Poesie*

James's swift positioning of himself at the head of a courtly Renaissance under his own patronage was, no doubt, in part inspired by his friend Esmé Stuart's enthusiasm for the French Pléiade. It is equally likely that this most self-conscious of kings had learned of the role played by pernicious poetic propaganda in hastening the downfall of his mother, Mary, Queen of Scots. In the **Reulis,** *James not only voices a rallying call aimed at bringing Scottish culture into the vanguard of European humanism—he also determines the conditions on which membership of his cultural (Castalian) band will be gained. Political topics should not be handled in the vernacular but in Latin; divine themes and personal eulogies are encouraged; the 'game' of Flyting is recommended for the poetics of vituperation. In James's own case, these 'cautelis' worked extremely well. Soon, as Apollo-David-Maecenas, he was divine poet-king and patron. Meanwhile, his precocity in assuming to teach and practise poetics while still in his teens was safeguarded by the modesty topos under which his works were published.* **The Essayes of a Prentise** *(an apprentice)* **in the Divine Art of Poesie,** *which contained the* **Reulis**, *appeared in 1584, at the very beginning of his personal reign.*

Historically, James has been undervalued. Concentration on the English period of his reign, with the 'wisest fool in Christendom' tag attached to his shambling figure, leads to his pragmatic skills as diplomat and peace-provider being overlooked. Whether those who idolize the dynamic figure of Elizabeth Tudor would have preferred to live through the martial melodrama of her reign in the south or the carefully preserved peace which James crafted for war-torn Scotland is another matter. Certainly, James brought relative security to both countries over a period of forty years. That this was not a simple achievement is eloquently illustrated by the bloody histories of both nations before and after his reign.

The **Reulis** *should be read along with* **Basilicon Doron**, *a treatise on government, composed by James for his elder son, Henry. It develops his aesthetic and political views on the literary game at court. As a creative writer, he is at his best in his prose essays. There, his analytic and logical mind can express itself directly, while his tendency to expansiveness is controlled by the brevity of the form. In that mode, he ranges widely—from satanic powers to tobacco. Nonetheless, his verse is not so poor nor so odd as a surface perusal might suggest. His studiously balanced, but intensely personal poems to Anne of Denmark may warrant their title of* **Amatoria** *more honestly than many a conventional sequence, full of the excessive praise the king critically shuns. James also experiments with concrete verse, as advocated by Puttenham. Of his longer poems, the eulogy on the death of Esmé Stuart,* **Ane Metaphoricall Invention of a Tragedie called Phoenix** *is worthy of study, as is his celebration of Don John of Austria* in **Lepanto.** *The king's powerful support of the Scottish translation movement is reflected in his own lyrical echoing of Saint Gelais and Desportes as well as his narrative rendering of the third book in the first day of Du Bartas'* **La Seconde Sepmaine.** *As King of Britain, he records that cares of state ended his career as a poet. His alliance with Drummond (§ 19) and Alexander (§ 23) in versifying the* **Psalms** *proved the only major exception to this rule.*

Ane Schort Treatise Conteining Some Reulis and Cautelis to be Observit and Eschewit in Scottis Poesie[1]

A Quadrain° of Alexandrin Verse, declaring to quhome the authour hes directit his labour:

To ignorants obdurde, quhair wilfull errour lyis,
Nor yit to curious folks, quhilkis carping° dois deject thee,
Nor yit to learned men, quha thinks thame onelie° wyis,
But to the docile bairns of knawledge I direct thee.

THE PREFACE TO THE READER

The cause why (docile reader) I have not dedicat this short treatise to any particular personis (as commounly workis usis to be) is that I esteme all thais quha hes already some beginning of knawledge, with ane earnest desyre to atteyne to farther, alyke meit° for the reading of this worke, or any uther, quhilk may help thame to the atteining to thair foirsaid desyre.[2] Bot, as to this work, quhilk is intitulit° *The Reulis and Cautelis° to be observit and eschewit° in Scottis Poesie*, ye may marvell paraventure, quhairfore I sould have writtin in that mater,° sen sa mony learnit men, baith of auld and of late,° hes already written thairof in dyvers and sindrie° languages.[3] I answer that, nochtwithstanding, I have lykewayis° writtin of it, for twa caussis. The ane is, as for them that wrait of auld, lyke as the tyme is changeit sensyne,° sa is the ordour° of poesie changeit. For then they observit not flowing,° nor eschewit not ryming in termes,° besydes° sindrie uther thingis, quhilk now we observe and eschew and dois weil in sa doing, because that now, quhen the warld is waxit auld, we have all their opinionis in writ, quhilk were learned before our tyme, besydes our awin ingynis,° quhair as they then did it onelie be thair awin ingynis but help of any uther.

Thairfore, quhat I speik of poesie now, I speik of it as being come to mannis age° and perfectioun, quhair as then it was bot in the infancie and chyldheid. The uther cause is that, as for thame that hes written of late, there hes never ane of thame written in our language. For albeit sindrie hes written of it in English, quhilk is lykest to our language, yit we differ from thame in sindrie reulis of poesie,[4] as ye will find be experience. I have lykewayis omittit dyvers figures,° quhilkis are necessare to be usit in verse, for twa causis. The ane is because they are usit in all languages and thairfore are spokin of be Du Bellay[5] and sindrie utheris, quha hes written in this airt.° Quhairfore, gif I wrait of thame also, it sould seme that I did bot repete that quhilk thay have written and yit not sa weil as thay have done already.

The uther cause is that they are figures of rhetorique and dialectique,° quhilkis airtis I professe° nocht and thairfor will apply to my selfe the counsale, quhilk Apelles° gave to the shoomaker, quhen he said to him, seing him find falt with the

Quadrain: *quatrain*; quhilkis carping: *whose cavilling*; thame onelie: *themselves alone*; alyke meit: *equally fitted for*; intitulit: *entitled*; Cautelis: *Warnings*; eschewit: *avoided*; mater: *subject*; of auld and of late: *of ancient and of recent times*; sindrie: *various*; lykewayis: *likewise*; sensyne: *since then*; ordour: *manner*; flowing: *musical rhythm (see Ch. 2)*; ryming in termes: (*see Ch. 1. para 5)*; besydes: *in addition to*; ingynis: *inventive minds*; mannis age: *maturity*; figures: *i.e. figures of speech*; airt: *branch of knowledge/skill*; dialectique: *art of argument*; professe (nocht): *am not qualified (in)*; Apelles: *Greek artist of 4th century* B.C.

shankis° of the image of Venus, efter that he had found falt with the pantoun,° '*Ne sutor ultra crepidam.*'°[6]

I will also wish yow (docile readar) that,° or ye cummer yow° with reiding thir reulis, ye may find in your self sic a beginning of nature,°[7] as ye may put in practise in your verse many of thir foirsaidis preceptis or ever ye sie them as they are heir set doun. For gif nature be nocht the cheif worker in this airt, reulis wilbe bot a band° to nature and will mak yow within short space weary of the haill airt; quhair as, gif nature be cheif and bent[8] to it, reulis will be ane help and staff to nature. I will end heir, lest my preface be langer nor my purpose and haill mater following; wishing yow, docile reidar, als gude succes and great proffeit by reiding this short treatise as I tuke earnist and willing panis to blok° it, as ye sie, for your cause. Fare weill.

I have insert in the hinder end of this treatise, maist kyndis of versis quhilks are not cuttit or brokin° bot alyke many feit° in everie lyne of the verse and how they are commounly namit, with my opinioun for what subjectis ilk kynde of thir verse is meitest° to be usit.°

To knaw the quantitie of your lang or short fete in they lynes, quhilk I have put° in the reule, quhilk teachis yow to knaw what is flowing, I have markit the lang fute with this mark, –, and abone° the heid of the short fute, I have put this mark, υ.

SONNET OF THE AUTHOUR TO THE READER

Sen for your saik I wryte upon your airt,
Apollo, Pan and ye, O Musis nyne,
And thou, O Mercure, for to help thy pairt
I do implore, sen thou, be thy ingyne,
Nixt efter Pan had found the quhissill,° syne°[9]
Thou did perfyte that quhilk he bot espyit:°
And efter that made Argus for to tyne°
(Quha kepit Io) all his windois° by it.[10]
Concurre ye gods, it can not be denyit,
Sen in your airt of poësie I wryte.
Auld birds to learne by teiching it is tryit:
Sic docens discam,° gif ye help to dyte.
Then reidar, sie of nature thou have pairt,
Syne laikis thou nocht bot heir to reid the airt.[11]

SONNET DECIFRING° THE PERFYTE POETE

Ane rype ingyne, ane quick and walkned° witt,
With sommair° reasons, suddenlie° applyit,
For every purpose using reasons fitt,
With skilfulnes, where learning may be spyit,
With pithie wordis, for to expres yow° by it,
His full intention in his proper leid,°

shankis: *legs*; pantoun: *slipper*; 'Ne sutor ultra crepidam': *let the cobbler stick to his last*; or...yow: *before you trouble yourself*; nature: *natural ability*; band: *constriction*; blok: *shape/plan*; cuttit/brokin: *rhythmically irregular*; feit: *syllable (See Ch. 1. para 4)*; meitest...usit: *metrically most relevant*; put: *cited*; abone: *above*; quhissill: *pipe*; syne: *then*; espyit: *glimpsed*; tyne: *lose*; windois: *eyes (poetical)*; Sic docens discam: *thus, by teaching I shall learn*; Decifring: *Delineating*; walkned: *alert*; sommair: *concise*; suddenlie: *promptly*; yow: *oneself*; proper leid: *own tongue*

The puritie quhairof weill hes he tryit,
With memorie to keip quhat he dois reid,
With skilfulnes and figuris, quhilks proceid
From rhetorique, with everlasting fame,
With uthers woundring, preassing° with all speid
For to atteine to merite sic a name:
All thir into the perfyte poëte be.
Goddis, grant I may obteine the laurell trie.°[12]

CHAPTER I

First, ye sall keip just cullouris,° quhairof the cautelis are thir.°

That ye ryme nocht twyse in ane syllabe. As, for exemple, that ye make not 'prove' and 'reprove' ryme together nor 'hove',° for hoving on hors bak and 'behove'.°[13]

That ye ryme ay to the hinmest° lang syllabe (with accent) in the lyne, suppose° it be not the hinmest syllabe in the lyne, as 'bakbyte yow' and 'out flyte'° yow. It rymes in 'byte' and 'flyte' because of the lenth of the syllabe and accent being there and not in 'yow,' howbeit it be the hinmest syllabe of ather° of the lynis. Or 'question' and 'digestion'—it rymes in 'ques' and 'ges' albeit they be bot the antepenult syallabis and uther twa behind ilkane of thame.

Ye aucht alwayis to note that, as in thir foirsaidis° or the lyke wordis, it rymes in the hinmest lang syllabe in the lyne althoucht there be uther short syllabis behind it. Sa is the hinmest syllabe the hinmest fute, suppose there be uther short syllabis behind it, quhilkis are eatin up in the pronounceing and na wayis comptit as fete.

Ye man be war lykewayis (except necessitie compell yow) with ryming in termis, quhilk is to say that your first or hinmest word in the lyne exceid not twa or thre syllabis at the maist, using thrie als seindill° as ye can. The cause quhairfore ye sall not place a lang word first in the lyne is that all lang words hes ane syllabe in them sa verie lang as the lenth thairof eatis up in the pronouncing evin the uther syllabes, quhilks are placit lang in the same word, and thairfore spillis° the flowing of that lyne. As, for exemple, in this word—'Arabia'—the secound syllabe (ra) is sa lang that it eatis up in the pronouncing [a] quhilk is the hinmest syllabe of the same word. Quhilk [a], althocht it be in a lang place, yit it kythis° not° sa because of the great lenth of the preceding syllabe (ra). As to the cause quhy ye sall not put a lang word hinmest in the lyne, it is because that the lenth of the secound syllabe (ra) eating up the lenth of the uther lang syllabe [a], makis it serve bot° as a tayle° to it, together with the short syllabe preceding. And because this tayle nather servis for cullour nor fute, as I spak before, it man° be thairfore repetit in the next lyne ryming unto it, as it is set doune in the first, quhilk makis that ye will scarcely get many wordis to ryme unto it. Yea, nane at all will ye finde to ryme to sindrie uther lang wordis. Thairfore, cheifly be warre of inserting sic lang wordis hinmest in the lyne, for the cause quhilk I last allegit.° Besydes that nather first nor last in the lyne, it keipis na flowing. The reulis and cautelis quhairof are thir, as followis.

preassing: *striving*; laurell trie: *i.e. laurel wreath*; just cullouris: *exact metres/ rhythms*; thir: *these*; hove: *remain stationary (on horseback)*; behove: *necessary*; hinmest: *final/last*; suppose: *even supposing*; out flyte: *defeat in a poetic backbiting contest*; ather: *either*; foresaidis: *those noted before*; seindill: *seldom*; spillis: *mars*; kythis: *appears*; bot…tayle: *i.e. without metrical value*; man: *must*; allegit: *stated*

CHAPTER II

First, ye man understand that all syllabis are devydit in thrie kindes: that is, some are schort, some lang and some indifferent. Be 'indifferent', I meane that quhilk are ather lang or short, according as ye place thame.[14]

The forme of placeing syllabes in verse is this. That your first syllabe in the lyne be short, the second lang, the thrid short, the fourt lang, the fyft short, the sixt lang and sa furth to the end of the lyne. Alwayis tak heid that the nomber of your fete in every lyne be evin and nocht odde: as four, six, aucht or ten: and nocht thrie, fyve, sevin or nyne, except it be in broken verse, quhilkis are out of reul and daylie inventit be dyvers poetis. But gif ye wald ask me the reulis, quhairby to knaw every ane of thir thre foirsaidis kyndis of syllabes, I answer, 'Your eare man be the onely judge and discerner thairof.' And to prove this, I remit to the judgement of the same, quhilk of thir twa lynis following flowis best:

v – v – v – v – v –
Into the sea then Lucifer upsprang.
v – v – v – v – v –
In the sea then Lucifer to upsprang.

I doubt not bot your eare makkis yow easilie to persave° that the first lyne flowis weil and the uther nathing at all. The reasoun is because the first lyne keipis the reule abone written—to wit, the first fute short, the secound lang and sa furth, as I shewe before; quhair as the uther is direct contrair to the same. Bot specially tak heid, quhen your lyne is of fourtene, that your sectioun°[15] in aucht° be a lang monosyllabe, or ellis the hinmest syllabe of a word alwais being lang, as I said before. The cause quhy it man be ane of thir twa is for the musique because that quhen your lyne is ather of fourtene or twelf fete, it wilbe drawin sa lang in the singing as ye man rest in the middes of it, quhilk is the sectioun. Sa as,° gif your sectioun be nocht ather a monosyllabe or ellis the hinmest syllabe of a word, as I said before, bot the first syllabe of a polysyllabe, the musique, sall make yow sa to rest in the middes of that word, as it sall cut the ane half of the word fra the uther and sall mak it seme twa different wordis, that is bot ane. This aucht onely to be observit in thir foirsaid lang lynis: for the shortnes of all shorter lynis, then thir befor mentionat, is the cause that the musique makis na rest in the middes of thame and thairfore thir observationins servis nocht for thame.[16] Onely tak heid, that the sectioun in thame kythe° something langer nor any uther feit in that lyne, except the secound and the last as I have said before.

Ye man tak heid lykewayis that your langest lynis exceid nocht fourtene fete and that your shortest be nocht within foure.

Remember also to mak a sectioun in the middes of every lyne, quhether the lyne be lang or short. Be sectioun I meane, that gif your lyne be of fourtene fete, your aucht fute man not only be langer then the sevint or uther short fete, bot also langer nor any uther lang fete in the same lyne, except the secound and the hinmest. Or gif your lyne be of twelf fete, your sectioun to be in the sext. Or gif of ten, your sectioun to be in the sext also.

The cause quhy it is not in fyve is because fyve is odde and everie odde fute is short. Or gif your lyne be of aucht fete, your sectioun to be in the fourt. Gif of sex,° in the fourt also. Gif of four, your sectioun to be in twa.

persave: *perceive*; section: *caesural break*; aucht: *eight*; Sa as: *Therefore*; kythe: *signify*; sex: *six*

Ye aucht lykewise to be war with° oft composing your haill lynis of monosyllabis onely (albeit our language have sa many, as we can nocht weill eschewe it), because the maist pairt of thame are indifferent, and may be in short or lang place, as ye like.

Some wordis of divers syllabis are lykewayis indifferent,° as

Thairfore, restore.
I thairfore, then.

In the first, 'thairfore' (thair) is short and (fore) is lang. In the uther, (thair) is lang and (fore) is short, and yit baith flowis alike weill. Bot thir indifferent wordis, composit of dyvers syllabes, are rare, suppose° in monosyllabes, commoun. The cause then, quhy ane haill lyne aucht nocht to be composit of monosyllabes only, is, that they being for the maist pairt indifferent, nather the secound, hinmest, nor sectioun, will be langer nor the other lang fete in the same lyne. Thairfore, ye man place a word composit of dyvers syllabes, and not indifferent, ather in the secound, hinmest or sectioun, or in all thrie.

Ye man also tak heid that, quhen thare fallis any short syllabis efter the last lang syllabe in the lyne, that ye repeit thame in the lyne quhilk rymis to the uther, evin as ye set them down in the first lyne: as, for exempill, ye man not say

Then feir nocht
Nor heir ocht.

Bot

Then feir nocht
Nor heir nocht; [17]

Repeting the same 'nocht' in baith the lynis because this syllabe 'nocht,' nather serving for cullour nor fute is bot a tayle to the lang fute preceding and thairfore is repetit lykewayis in the nixt lyne quhilk rymes unto it, even as it [wes] set doun° in the first.

There is also a kynde° of indifferent wordis, asweill as of syllabis, albeit few in nomber, the nature quhairof is that gif ye place them in the begynning of a lyne, they are shorter be a fute nor they are gif ye place thame hinmest in the lyne, as

Sen patience I man have, perforce,
I live in hope with patience.

Ye se there are but aucht fete in ather of baith thir lynis above written. The cause quhairof is that 'patience' in the first lyne, in respect it is in the beginning thairof, is bot of twa fete and, in the last lyne, of thrie, in respect it is the hinmest word of that lyne. To knaw and discerne° thir kynde of wordis from utheris, youre eare man be the onely judge, as of all the uther parts of flowing, the verie tuichestane° quhairof is musique.[18]

I have teachit yow now shortly° the reulis of ryming, fete and flowing. There

be war with: *be wary of*; indifferent: *either short or long*; suppose: *albeit*; [wes] set doun: *was placed*; kynde: *type/group*; discerne: *distinguish*; tuichestane: *touchstone*; shortly: *briefly/economically*

restis° yet to teache yow the wordis, sentences and phrasis necessair for a poet to use in his verse, quhilk I have set doun in reulis, as efter followis.

CHAPTER III

First, that in quhatsumever ye put in verse, ye put in na wordis ather *metri causa*° or yit for filling furth the nomber of the fete bot that they be all sa necessare as ye sould be constrainit to use thame in cace° ye wer speiking the same purpose in prose. And thairfore that your wordis appeare to have cum out willingly and by nature and not to have been thrawin out constrainedly be compulsioun.

That ye eschew to insert in your verse a lang rable° of mennis names or names of tounis or sik uther names, because it is hard to mak many lang names all placit together to flow weill. Thairfore, quhen that fallis out in your purpose, ye sall ather put bot twa or thrie of thame in everie lyne, mixing uther wordis amang thame or ellis specifie bot twa or thrie of thame as all, saying 'With the laif° of that race' or 'With the rest in thay pairtis'° or sic uther lyke wordis: as, for exemple,

Out through his cairt, quhair Eo[l]us was eik°
With other thre, quhilk Phaëton had drawin.[19]

Ye sie there is bot ane name there specifeit,° to serve for uther thrie of that sorte.

Ye man also take heid to frame your wordis and sentencis° according to the mater: as in flyting° and invectives, your wordis to be cuttit short and hurland over heuch.°[20] For thais quhilkis are cuttit short, I meane be sic wordis as thir,

Iis neir cair

for 'I sall never cair,' gif your subject were of love or tragedies because in thame your words man be drawin lang, quhilkis in flyting man be short.

Ye man lykewayis tak heid, that ye waill° your wordis according to the purpose: as in ane heich and learnit purpose to use heich, pithie and learnit wordis.

Gif your purpose be of love: to use commoun° language with some passionate wordis.

Gif your purpose be of tragicall materis: to use lamentable° wordis, with some heich, as ravisht° in admiratioun.

Gif your purpose be of landwart effairis:° to use corruptit and uplandis° wordis.

And finally, quhatsumever be your subject, to use *vocabula artis*,°[21] quhairby ye may the mair vivelie° represent that persoun quhais pairt ye paint out.°

This is likewayis neidfull to be usit in sentences, alsweill as in wordis: as, gif your subject be heich and learnit, to use learnit and infallible° reasonis, provin be necessities.[22]

Gif your subject be of love: to use wilfull° reasonis, proceeding rather from passioun nor reasoun.

restis: *remains*; metri causa: *for the sake of metre alone*; in cace: *just as if*; rable: *lengthy, incoherently constructed list of words*; laif: *remainder*; thay pairtis: *those districts*; eik: *also*; specefeit: *specified*; sentencis: *topics*; flyting: *literary backbiting*; hurland over heuch: *rushing to leap off a crag*; waill: *choose*; commoun: *ordinary/everyday*; lamentable: *evoking pity*; as ravisht: *as if transported*; landwart effairis: *rural matters*; uplandis: *countrified*; vocabula artis: *poetic diction*; vivelie: *vividly*; paint out: *depict*; infallible: *certain*; wilfull: *headstrong*

Gif your subject be of landwart effaris; to use sklender° reasonis mixt with grosse ignorance, nather keiping forme nor ordour. And sa furth, ever framing your reasonis according to the qualitie of your subject.

Let all your verse be literall,°[23] sa far as may be, quhatsumever kynde they be of, bot speciallie tumbling[24] verse for flyting. By 'literall', I meane that the maist pairt of your lyne sall rynne upon a° letter, as this tumbling lyne rynnis upon 'f'.

Fetching fude for to feid it fast furth of the farie.[25]

Ye man observe that thir tumbling verse flowis not on that fassoun° as utheris dois. For all utheris keipis the reule quhilk I gave before; to wit, the first fute short, the secound lang and sa furth. Quhair as thir has twa short and ane lang throuch all the lyne, quhen they keip ordour,° albeit the maist pairt of thame be out of ordour and keipis na kynde nor reule of flowing and for that cause are callit tumbling verse; except the short lynis of aucht in the hinder end of the verse, the quhilk flowis as uther verses dois as ye will find in the hinder end of this buke, quhair I give exemple of sindrie kyndis of versis.

CHAPTER IV

Mark also thrie speciall ornamentis to verse, quhilkis are: comparisons, epithetis and proverbis.

As for comparisons, take heid that they be sa proper for the subject that nather they be over bas,° gif your subject be heich, for then sould your subject disgrace your comparisoun; nather your comparisoun be heich quhen your subject is basse, for then sall your comparisoun disgrace your subject. Bot let sic a mutuall correspondence and similitude be betwixt them, as it may appeare to be a meit° comparisoun for sic a subject and sa sall they ilkane° decore uther.°

As for epithetis, it is to descryve brieflie, *en passant*,° the naturall° of everie thing ye speik of, be adding the proper adjective unto it,[26] quhairof there are two fassons. The ane is to descryve it be making a corruptit worde, composit of twa dyvers simple wordis, as

'Apollo gyde-sunne.'[27]

The uther fasson is, be circumlocution, as

'Apollo, reular of the sunne.'

I esteme this last fassoun best because it expressis the authouris meaning als weill as the uther and yit makis na corruptit wordis, as the uther dois.

As for the proverbis, they man be proper for the subject to beautifie it, chosen in the same forme as the comparisoun.

sklender: *slight (lacking in rigour)*; literall: *alliterative (Fr. vers lettrisé)*; a: *one*; fassoun: *manner/fashion*; keip ordour: *keep a regular rhythm*; over bas: *too low*; meit: *fitting*; ilkane...uther: *embellish/relate decorously (to) the other*; en passant: *in passing*; naturall: *the (precise) nature*

CHAPTER V

It is also meit for the better decoratioun of the verse to use sumtyme the figure of repetitioun, as:

Quhylis joy rang,
Quhylis noy° rang. etc.

Ye sie this word 'quhylis' is repetit heir. This forme of repetitioun, sometyme usit, decoris the verse very mekle. Yea, quhen it cummis to purpose, it will be cumly° to repete sic a word aucht or nyne tymes in a verse.

CHAPTER VI

Ye man also be warre with° composing ony thing in the same maner as hes bene ower oft usit of before. As, in speciall, gif ye speik of love, be warre ye descryve your Loves makdome° or her fairnes.[28] And siclyke° that ye descryve not the morning, and rysing of the sunne in the preface of your verse, for thir thingis are sa oft and dyverslie writtin upon be poetis already, that gif ye do the lyke, it will appeare ye bot imitate and that it cummis not of your awin inventioun,[29] quhilk is ane of the cheif properteis of ane poete. Thairfore, gif your subject be to prayse your love, ye sall rather prayse hir uther qualiteis nor her fairnes nor hir shaip; or ellis ye sall speik some lytill thing of it and syne say that your wittis are sa smal and your utterance so barren, that ye can not discryve any part of hir worthelie; remitting alwayis to the reider to judge of hir in respect sho matches, or rather excellis, Venus or any woman quhome to it sall please yow to compaire her. Bot gif your subject be sic as ye man speik some thing of the morning or sunne rysing, tak heid that quhat name ye give to the sunne, the mone or uther starris, the ane tyme, gif ye happin to wryte thairof another tyme, to change thair names. As, gif ye call the sunne, Titan, at a time, to call him Phebus or Apollo the uther tyme and siclyke the mone and uther planettis.

CHAPTER VII

Bot sen invention is ane of the cheif vertewis in a poete, it is best that ye invent your awin subject your self and not to compose of sene subjectis.° Especially, translating any thing out of uther language, quhilk doing, ye not onely assay° not your awin ingyne° of inventioun, bot be the same meanes ye are bound as to a staik to follow that buikis phrasis, quhilk ye translate.[30]

Ye man also be war of wryting anything of materis of commoun weill°[31] or uther sic grave sene subjectis (except metaphorically; of manifest treuth opinly knawin; yit nochtwithstanding using it very seindil)° because nocht onely ye essay nocht your awin inventioun, as I spak before, bot lykewayis they are to grave materis for a poet to mell in;° bot, because ye can not have the inventioun except it come of nature,° I

Quhylis noy: *Sometimes misery*; cumly: *charming/pleasing*; be warre with: *be wary of*; makdome: *shapeliness*; siclyke: *similarly*; sene subjectis: *written authorities*; assay: *test*; ingyne: *ingenuity*; commoun weill: *public good*; seindil: *seldom*; mell in: *concern(himself) with*; nature: *n. as natural ability*

remit it thairunto as the cheif cause, not onely of inventioun, bot also of all the uther pairtis of poesie. For airt is onely bot ane help and a remembraunce to nature,° as I shewe yow in the preface.

CHAPTER VIII
(Tuiching the kyndis of versis, mentionat in the Preface)

First, there is ryme quhilk servis onely for lang historeis, and yit are nocht verse. As for exemple,

> In Maii when that the blissefull Phoebus bricht,
> The lamp of joy, the heavens gemme of licht,
> The goldin cairt and the etheriall king,
> With purpour° face in orient dois spring,
> Maist angel-lyke ascending in his sphere;
> And birds, with all thair heavenlie voces clere
> Dois mak a sweit and heavinly harmony,
> And fragrant flours dois spring up lustely:°
> Into this season, sweitest of delyte,
> To walk I had a lusty appetyte.[32]

And sa furth.

For the description of heroique actis, martiall and knichtly faittis° of armes, use this kynde of verse following, callit heroicall, as:

> Meik mundane mirrour, myrrie and modest,
> Blyth, kynde and courtes,° comelie, clene° and chest,°
> To all exemple for thy honestie:
> As richest rose, or rubie, by the rest
> With gracis grave and gesture maist digest,°
> Ay to thy honnour alwayis having eye;
> Were fassons fliemde,° they micht be found in the:
> Of blissings all, be blyth, thow hes the best;
> With everie berne° belovit for to be.[33]

For any heich and grave subjectis, specially drawin out of learnit authouris, use this kynde of verse following, callit ballat royal, as:

> That nicht he ceist, and went to bed, bot greind°
> Yit fast° for day, and thocht the nicht to lang.
> At last Diana doun her head recleind
> Into the sea. Then Lucifer upsprang,
> Auroras post,° whome sho did send amang
> The jeittie cludds,° for to foretell ane hour,
> Before sho stay her tears, quhilk Ovide sang
> Fell for her love, quhilk turnit in a flour.[34]

nature: n. *as shadow of higher truths*; purpour: *crimson*; lustely: *pleasantly*; faittis: *feats*; courtes: *courteous*; clene: *pure*; chest: *chaste*; digest: *composed*; fliemde: *banished*; berne: *being*; greind: *longed*; fast: *fervently*; post: *messenger*; jeittie cludds: *jet black clouds*

For tragicall materis, complaintis or testamentis, use this kynde of verse following, callit Troilus verse, as:

To thee, Echo, and thow to me agane,
In the desert,° amangs the wods and wells,°
Quhair destinie hes bound the to remane
But company, within the firths and fells;
Let us complein, with wofull youtts° and yells,
A shaft, a shotter,° that our harts hes slane:
To thee, Echo, and thow to me agane.[35]

For flyting or invectives, use this kynde of verse following, callit rouncefallis[36] or tumbling verse:

In the hinder end of harvest, upon Alhallow ene,°
Quhen our gude nichtbors rydis (now gif I reid richt),
Some bucklit on a benwod,° and some on a bene,°
Ay trottand into troupes fra the twylicht:
Some sadland° a sho° ape, all grathand° into grene:
Some hotcheand° on a hemp stalk, hovand° on a heicht:°
The king of fary with the court of the elf quene,
With many elrage° incubus rydand that nicht:
    There ane elf on ane ape ane unsell° begat,
    Besyde a pot baith auld and worne:
    This bratshard° in ane bus° was borne:
    They fand a monster, on the morne,
        War facit nor a cat.[37]

For compendious praysing of any bukes or the authouris thairof or ony argumentis of uther historeis, quhair sindrie sentences and change of purposis are requyrit, use sonet verse of fourtene lynis and ten fete in every lyne. The exemple quhairof I neide nocht to shaw yow, in respect I have set doun twa in the beginning of this treatise.[38]

In materis of love, use this kynde of verse, quhilk we call commoun verse, as:

Quhais answer made thame nocht sa glaid
That they sould thus the victors be,
As even the answer quhilk I haid
Did greatly joy and confort me:
Quhen lo, this spak Apollo myne,
All that thou seikis, it sall be thyne.[39]

Lyke verse of ten fete, as this foirsaid is of aucht, ye may use lykewayis in love materis: as also all kyndis of cuttit and brokin verse, quhairof new formes are daylie inventit according to the poëtes plesour, as:

desert: *wilderness*; wods and wells: *woods and springs*; youtts: *howls*; shottter: *archer*; Alhallow ene: *Hallowe'en*; benwod: *stalk of ragwort*; bene: *bean plant*; sadland: *saddling*; sho: *she*; grathand: *arrayed*; hotcheand: *bobbing*; hovand: *hovering*; heicht: *hill top*; elrage: *weird/elvish*; unsell: *misdeed*; bratshard: *little brat*; bus: *bush*

Quha wald have tyrde to heir that tone,
Quhilk birds corroborat ay abone
    Throuch schouting of the larkis!
They sprang sa heich into the skyes,
Quhill Cupide walknis with the cryis
    Of Naturis chapell clarkis.
Then, leaving all the heavins above,
    He lichted on the eard.
Lo! how that lytill god of love
    Before me then appeard,
        So myld-lyke,
        And chyld-lyke,
        With bow thre quarters skant°
        So moylie°
        And coylie,
        He lukit lyke a sant.[40]

And sa furth.

This one kynd of brokin verse abone writtin man of necessitie, in thir last short fete, as 'so moylie and coylie,' have bot twa fete and a tayle to ilkane of thame, as ye sie, to gar the cullour and ryme be in the penult syllabe.

Any of thir foirsaidis kyndes of ballatis of haill verse, and not cuttit or brokin[41] as this last is, gif ye lyk to put ane overword° to ony of thame, as making the last lyne of the first to be the last lyne of everie uther verse in that ballat, will set weill for love materis.

Bot besydis thir kyndes of brokin or cuttit verse, quhilks ar inventit daylie be poetis, as I shewe before, there are sindrie kyndes of haill verse, with all thair lynis alyke lang, quhilk I have heir omittit and tane bot onelie thir few kyndes abone specifeit as the best, quhilk may be applyit to ony kynde of subject, bot rather to thir quhairof I have spokin before.

skant: *stretched*; moylie: *demurely*; overword: *refrain*

NOTES

1. ED. COPY TEXT: *The Essayes of A Prentise in the Divine Art of Poesie* (Edinburgh, Vautroullier, 1584/85). The full title is 'Ane Schort Treatise, conteining some reulis and cautelis to be observit and eschewit in Scottis Poesie'.
2. Like Gascoigne's *Certayne Notes of Instruction* (1575), James's treatise is directed at those who wish to learn the art of poetry.
3. He was, after all, only seventeen. His major sources are Du Bellay, *Deffense et Illustration de la Langue Françoise* (1549) and Gascoigne (see n. 2). Other non-Scottish influences include Trissino's *La Poetica* (Vicenza, 1529), Vida's *Ars Poetica* (London, 1536) and Ronsard's *Abrégé de l'Art Poétique François* (1565). His tutor Buchanan's *De Prosodia* equally may have suggested to his royal pupil the idea of producing a reply in kind. Classical treatises—especially Horace's *Ars Poetica*—also make their voice heard, despite the rigorously vernacular focus of the king's argument.
4. While arguing that Scottish writing differs from English and the Scots tongue from Inglis, James consistently sees them as stemming from the same root. This image for linguistic interrelationship is also used by his major source, Du Bellay (see *Deffense*, Bk. 2. Ch. xi). Cf. 'Sonnet Decifring The Perfyte Poete', ll. 5–7.
5. The French bias within the *Reulis* reflects the young king's special interest in the Pléiade. This was fostered by his cousin Esmé Stuart, Sieur d'Aubigné.
6. The source of this proverb—which is misquoted—is Pliny's *Natural History* XXV. x.

7. Consistently, James warns those who have no natural ability that rules on their own are not enough to make a poet.
8. Heraldic: two sections of a shield, totalling two-thirds of the space.
9. Pan's pipes: James conflates different traditions here. Usually, the invention of the pan-pipe was attributed to Pan, but Homer grants the credit to Mercury. Crucially, however, the Castalians associated the sonnet and most lyrical forms with singing. The earlier emphasis on 'flowing' has anticipated this. The argument becomes explicit in Chapter 2. See n. 16.
10. Argus, in Greek myth, had a hundred eyes. Juno set him to watch over the priestess Io, with whom Jupiter had become infatuated.
11. The general sense is—'Then, reader, supposing you do have some natural ability, then all you need is to read, here, about the mechanics of the art.'
12. In his *Basilicon Doron*, James teaches similar lessons to Henry, Prince of Wales. The interlacing rhyme-scheme used by the king was one of the distinctive signs of the Scottish sonnet. It had been practised by Montgomerie before Spenser introduced it to England. (See Introduction p. xxviii).
13. Cf. Du Bellay, *Deffense*, Bk 2. Ch vii.
14. Cf. Gascoigne, *Notes*, 4.
15. James uses a French coinage—'sectioun', where Gascoigne employs 'ceasure'. The King's critical vocabulary is also in this sense distinctive.
16. James's earlier discussions of rhythm ('flowing') lead up to this explicit statement that he is primarily thinking of these stanzas being sung. James encouraged music through the Chapel Royal and through active patronage of musicians at court.
17. James frequently takes his poetic examples from the work of his senior poet, Alexander Montgomerie. In this case he cites *The Cherrie and Slae*, 27. 11; Wald II.
18. Ronsard makes a similar claim in *L'Abrégé*. James's poet laureate, Alexander Montgomerie, when translating Ronsard's sonnets (see § 18), was aware that they were intended to be sung.
19. These lines come from the king's own poem, 'Admonitioun to the Maister Poete', ll. 85–6.
20. 'Hurland ouer heuch' means 'Rushing over a steep cliff'. It is used by Montgomerie to represent thoughtless haste in *The Cherrie and the Slae*. See also Du Bellay's description of uneven rhythms as 'tumbant en icelle' (falling over themselves) in *Deffense*, 2.vii.
21. '*Vocabula artis*.' This is a larger claim than Gascoigne's for 'apt vocables'. James's claim for the artifice of all poetic diction echoes the classical view of art, overtly opposed by Wordsworth in his Preface to the *Lyrical Ballads*.
22. The classical law of decorum, very fully argued by Horace, is a central tenet of all rhetorical treatises. By including 'sentences' (topics) in his definition, James already moves to a broader definition (comprehending modes of argument as well as diction) than that to be found in Gascoigne or Puttenham.
23. 'Literall'. Once more, James derives a new critical term from French practice—'lettrisé'. Gascoigne in *Certayne Notes of Instruction* (1575), had been less enthusiastic about alliteration in both Section 1 ('For it is not inough...to thunder in Rym Ram Ruff') and in Section 8 ('they do so hunte a letter to death...') James again consciously opposes English practice to argue a differentiated case for Scots. Here, its harsher consonantal sounds are held to make it a more powerful vehicle for alliteration than English.
24. 'Tumbling verse.' Again from Du Bellay ('vers tombant') and see n. 20.
25. 'Polwart and Montgomerie's Flyting' l. 476. This exchange of poetic insults was performed before the king. It may well have been a contest for the position of laureate.
26. Classical influence, mainly from Horace, underlies James's vernacular French and English sources in this section especially. The 'appropriate epithet' is an example of decorous practice. But cf. Ronsard, *Préface sur La Franciade* (1572) ed. Blanchemain iii.18.
27. James had translated poems by Du Bartas, who was especially fond of compound words.
28. Cf. Gascoigne, *Notes*, Section 1. James found romantic writing very difficult, often substituting rational arguments for praise, even in his love sequence, the *Amatoria*. See § 18.
29. James follows Ronsard especially in arguing for poetic ingenuity. Invention is the term used in classical and neoclassical criticism to counterpoise the reliance on imitation and authority.
30. Du Bellay makes the same case in the epistle preceding the first edition of *L'Olive* (1549) but the original source is Horace, as Douglas notes in the Prologe to *Eneados*, Book 1. ll. 399–402: 'And to the sammyn purpos we may apply/Horatius in hys Art of Poetry: "Press nocht," says he, "thou to traste interpreter,/Word eftir word to translait thi mater."'
31. James's mother, Mary, having suffered from particularly scurrilous versifying, her son uses his power as patron to warn Castalian poets away from political topics.
32. 'In Maii when that the blissefull Phoebus bricht.' A conventional opening; the language with English 'when' and Scots 'bricht' suggests that this is another Castalian quotation.
33. 'Meik mundane mirrour, myrrie and modest' is an example of the alliterative style favoured by James

in the treatise. Cf. Montgomerie in praise of Lady Margaret Montgomerie, 'The mundane mirrour of maikles margareit.'

34. 'Ballat royal'. Another example of James's attempt to distinguish Scottish Renaissance practice from English. This eight line stanza with interlinking rhyme-scheme had long been favoured in Scotland. It stems from French *chant royal*. The stanza is from the king's 'Admonitioun to the Maister Poete', ll. 73–80.

35. 'Troilus verse'. The seven line stanza of Chaucer's *Troilus and Criseyde* is rhyme royal in the English tradition and 'rythme royall' in Gascoigne's *Notes*. The cited stanza opens Montgomerie's lyric, 'Echo'.

36. Rouncevallis. A reference to the battle of Roncevaux, a key event in Charlemagne Romances (e.g. *La Chanson de Roland*). As James uses the anglicized form of the name, he is almost certainly referring to the north British versions in the uneven, alliterative stanza, as exemplified in *Rauf Coilyear* (§ 3).

37. From the second stanza of Montgomerie's third invective in *Polwart and Montgomeries Flyting*.

38. A broad thematic range is proposed for the Scottish sonnet, in a definition which, notably, excludes love. James's call for sonnets in praise of poets had clearly been transferred in advance to the Castalian band, five of whom provided introductory sonnets for *The Essayes of a Prentise*.

39. 'commoun verse'. Gascoigne calls this stanza, the 'Ballade', *Notes*, Section 14. The cited stanza concludes Montgomerie's 'Before the Greeks durst enterpryse.'

40. Montgomerie, *Cherrie and Slae*, st. 8. (See § 16)

41. 'haill...not cuttit or brokin'. This is simply a distinction between stanzas all of whose lines are syllabically equal and those which alternate shorter with longer lines.

§ 23: Sir William Alexander (1567–1640): *Anacrisis*

William Alexander, son of the fourth laird of Menstrie, was taught by Thomas Buchanan, brother of James's tutor. He attended Glasgow University and went on the 'Grand Tour of Europe' to round off his education. In these earlier days, his closest literary companion was **Alexander Hume**, *author of* **Of the Day Estivall** *and, at that time, minister at Menstrie. Alexander composed most of his lyrical sequence,* **Aurora** *(§ 18), during the Castalian period, but the work was not published until after the Union of the Crowns, in 1604.The early years of James's London reign saw the earl's career reach its zenith. After service as tutor to Henry, Prince of Wales, he was knighted in 1609 and given a charter to explore and colonise Nova Scotia in 1623. Three years later, he became Secretary of State for Scotland, a post he held until his death in 1640. The Nova Scotia scheme had, however, caused bankruptcies. Moreover, Alexander's strict Protestantism and Royalism made him an unpopular secretary; other people were distanced by his ambitious and haughty temperament, At his funeral, a mob tried to overturn his coffin in an effort to draw public attention to the losses they had incurred becuase of him. Ironically, there was no point to this unseemly display, as the proud Earl of Stirling had also been reduced to bankruptcy.*

*In literary terms, Alexander was recognized along with Ayton as the senior Scottish poet at the London court, numbering Drayton and Jonson among his admirers. He is also, by far, the most prolific of early Scots writers. While his lyrics combine concision and apt imagery with depth of thought, he viewed himself as a serious Protestant poet and, to that end, moved into the realms of epic and verse tragedy. His Senecan dramas, which include the four Monarchicke Tragedies—***Darius, Croesus, The Alexandrian Tragedy** *and* **Julius Caesar***—are far less dramatic than his own life and were probably not designed for performance. Most disappointing of all are his attempts to provide Scotland with a religious Epic. By the time he composed* **Jonathan** *and* **Doomesday** *Alexander had decided to avoid imagery wherever possible. The resulting abstract verse, combined with a lack of narrative control and a passion for lengthy moralising make these works a disappointing reading experience.*

Anacrisis, *however, demonstrates just how widely read and critically astute the Scottish literati were at this time. Its major value as a later Protestant and humanist contribution to Scottish rhetorical criticism lies in its broad European perspective. Alexander's specific warnings against critical parochialism precede evidence of the variety of texts (classical and vernacular) he has read, and the variety of critical techniques he employs in accommodating himself to their diversity in uniqueness.*

Anacrisis or A Censure[1] of Some Poets Ancient and Modern.

After a great travel° both of body and of mind which, since not voluntary but imposed upon me, was the more painful by retiring for a time where I was born of late,[2] gladly embracing this rarely offered opportunity to refresh my self, and being curious° (as the most dainty° kind of pleasure for such as are capable of° their delicacies) to recreate my self with the muses—I may justly say recreate, since they create new spirits which (shaking off gross affections, diving into the depths, reaching the heights and contemplating both) are transported with these things, which are only worthy to entertain so noble a thing as the mind of man—I began to renew

travel: *labour*; curious: *anxious/desirous*; dainty: *choice*; capable of: *able to appreciate*

my acquaintance there, having of a long time been a stranger with them, so that at the first I could not begin to practise as one of their ordinary train,° but only to court with° these whose credit might procure my access.[3] I conversed with some of the modern as well as with the ancients, kindling my fire at those fires which do still burn out of the ashes of ancient authors, to whom I find them no way inferior, though like affectioned° patriots, by writing in the vulgar° tongues, seeking to grace their own country.[4] I have pitied the ignorance of some who might be admitted for versifiers and poets, that would extol as an excellent piece of poesy that which, wanting life, had nothing but language, masking ignorance with *Greek* and *Latin*, whose treasure long feeding upon, they had by time digested, and converted to their own use, though venting it but in excrements.

Language is but the apparel of poesy, which may give beauty, but not strength:[5] and when I censure° any poet, I first dissolve° the general contexture° of his work in several pieces, to see what sinews it hath, and to mark what will remain behind, when that external gorgeousness—consisting in the choice or placing of words, as if it would bribe the ear to corrupt the judgment—is first removed, or at least only marshalled in its own degree. I value language as a conduit, the variety thereof to several shapes, and adorned truth or witty inventions, that which it should deliver. I compare a poem to a garden, the disposing of the parts of the one to the several walks of the other: the decorum kept in descriptions, and representing of persons, to the proportions and distances to be observed in such things as are planted therein, and the variety of invention to the diversity of flowers thereof; whereof three sorts do chiefly please me: a grave sentence,° by which the judgment may be bettered; a witty conceit,° which doth harmoniously delight the spirits; and a generous rapture° expressing magnanimity, whereby the mind may be inflamed for great things.[6] All the rest, for the most part, is but a naked narration or gross staff to uphold the general frame; yet the more apt, if well contrived and eloquently delivered, to angle° vulgar readers, who perchance can scarce conceive the other.

I condemn their opinions, who, as they would include all perfection in one, do prefer someone with whom they sympathize, or whom they have most practised, to all others. There is none singular° in all, and yet all are singular in some things. There is none so excellent that is not excelled in some pieces by some others, and every one hath his own particular grace; none being positively but only comparatively to be praised, and that for parts, not in the whole; men's works, like themselves, not being all of one quality, nor ever alike.

I like the phrase, stile, method and discreet carriage° of Virgil; the vigour and variety of invention in Ovid; the deep judgement and grave sentences of Horace and Juvenal; the heroical conceptions, showing an innate generosity, in Statius Papinianus and Lucan;[7] and I cannot wonder enough at that man (deservedly renowned and admirably learned) who with a passionate kind of partiality (the more strange that it is against dead men, who have exceeded envy, having their just value set upon them by sundry ages) would advisedly vilify Lucan in so extreme a measure, saying, *Videtur potius latrare quam canere*,[8] whom Statius Papinianus and Martial—his superiours in poesy—both celebrating his birth by eternal testimonies, have magnified so much:

train: *followers*; court with: *try to win favour with*; affectioned: *biassed*; vulgar: *vernacular*; censure: *evaluate*; dissolve: *break up*; contexture: *structure composed of many elements*; sentence: *theme*; conceit: *fanciful turn of thought*; generous rapture: *benevolent ecstasy*; angle: *lure*; singular: *unique*; carriage: *manner of conveying*

Hæc est illa dies, quæ magni conscia partus
Lucanum populis et tibi, Polla, dedit.

And thereafter,

Vatis Apollinei magno memorabilis ortu
Lux redit, Aonidum turba favete sacris.
Hæc meruit, cum te terris, Lucane, dedisset,
Mixtus Castaliæ Bœtis ut esset aquae.[9]

Julius Scaliger doth aggravate° much any hyperbole, wherein he hath seemed to exceed, and hath not remarked° (at least will not remember) the unmatchable height of his ravishing conceits to provoke magnanimity. If he had as narrowly sifted Virgil, whom he will needs justify as without any blemish, without reposing° as by an implicite faith upon his sufficiency,° he would have found an error in him more gross than any that is in Lucan;[10] as this – where the praise° of an epick poem is to feign° a person exceeding nature (not such as all ordinarly be, but with all the perfections whereof a man can be capable) every deficiency in that imaginary man being really the author's own, whose unlimited invention, for lack of judgment, could reach to no greater height: he° (seeking to extol the valour of Æneas, which only could be done by the valour of some valorous enemy whom he had vanquished) doth so extreamly extenuate the courage of Turnus at his death, leaving him no time to recover it, that where out of a poetick liberty he should have afforded more than was ordinary, wanting nothing but fortune, and at least inferiour to none but to him whom he would grace with his ruin, he doth make him die like a dastard, casting thereby down all the glory intended for Æneas, overcoming but a coward; and in a more abject manner than the lowest minded man could have descended to conceive, burdening the gods with his cowardice, whose mind, in whatsoever state his body was, should have continued free, not basely begging his life.

Ille humilis supplexque oculos dextramque precantem
Protendens, equidem merui, nec deprecor, inquit.
Utere sorte tua; miseri te si qua parentis
Tangere cura potest, oro (fuit et tibi talis
Anchises genitor) Dauni miserere senectae
Et me, seu corpus spoliatum lumine mavis,
Redde meis: Vicisti, tua est Lavinia conjux.[11]

Thus would he unworthily ransom his life with loss of his honour and of his lady.

And I never read that part of Virgil but I remember the speech of Paulus Æmilius, when Perseus, King of Macedon, came with tears a suiter to him, that he might not be led in triumph: 'Fy upon you, beast', said he, 'you beg that which you ought to give unto your self, and hath disgraced my victory, who now, after all my travels, can have no credit, having only overcome such a base coward as was not worthy to have been contended with.'[12] If I have been too bold in censuring Julius Scaliger, let me be excused by his example in censuring all his betters; and it is only to give Lucan his due, not to derogate from him.

aggravate: *exaggerate*; remarked: *noted*; reposing: *relying*; sufficiency: *competence*; praise: *merit*; feign: *conjure up*; he: *i.e. Virgil*

There is no man doth satisfy me more than that notable Italian, Torquato Tasso, in whom I find no blemish but that he doth make Solyman, by whose overthrow he would grace Rinaldo, to die fearfully, belying the part that he would have personated° during his life,[13] as if he would choose rather to err in imitating others, than to prove singular by himself. Speron Speron, thinking his exquisite work of Godfred[14] to be too full of rich conceits, and more dainty than did become the gravity of such a work, said, that it was a heroick poem written in madrigals; and yet, when he wrote a *Week of the Creation*, in emulation of Du Bartas, it did no way approach to the perfections of the other;[15] which doth confirm me in my first opinion, that every author hath his own genius, directing him by a secret inspiration to that wherein he may most excell, and, as I said, excelling in some things, and none in all.

Many would bound the boundless liberty of a poet, binding him only to the birth of his own brains, affirming that there can be no perfection but in a fiction; not considering that the ancients, upon whose example they ground their opinion, did give faith unto those fables, whereby they would abuse our credulity, not only as to true history but as to true divinity, since containing the greatness of their gods and grounds of their religion, which they in their own kind did strive superstitiously° to extol; so that hereby they would either make our religion (or our affection thereunto)° inferior unto theirs, and imaginary matters to be more celebrated than true deeds, whose envied price, affectionately looked upon, must beget a generous emulation in any virtuous reader's mind.

The treasures of poesie cannot be better bestowed than upon the apparelling of truth, and truth cannot be better apparelled to please young lovers than with the excellencies of poesy. I would allow that an epick poem[16] should consist altogether of a fiction, that the poet, soaring above the course of nature, making the beauty of virtue to invite and the horrour of vice to affright the beholders, may liberally furnish his imaginary man with all the qualities requisite for the accomplishing of a perfect creature, having power to dispose of all things at his own pleasure.

But it is more agreeable with the gravity of a tragedy that it be grounded upon a true history, where the greatness of a known person, urging regard, doth work the more powerfully upon the affections. As for the satyrist and the epigrammatist, they may mix both the two, who (shadowing truth with fables, and discovering true persons with feigned names) may, by alluding to antiquity, tax the modern times. I have heard some, with a pretended theological austerity, condemn the reading of fictions as only breathing a contagious dissoluteness to impoison the spirits, where such works must be acknowledged as the chief springs of learning, both for profit and pleasure, showing things as they should be, where histories represent them as they are, many times making vice to prosper and virtue to prove miserable. I like not the *Alexander* of Curtius so well as the *Cyrus* of Xenophon, who made it first appear unto the world with what grace and spirit a poem might be delivered in prose.[17]

The *Æthiopian History* of Heliodorus[18] (though far inferiour to that for the weight and state of the matter, as fitted to instruct greatness) yet above it for the delicacy of the invention and variety of accidents, strange yet possible, leading the curious reader by a baited° appetite, with a methodical intricateness, through a labyrinth of labours, entertaining his expectation till he come unto the end, which

personated: *impersonated/played*; superstitiously: *illogically*; affection thereunto: *emotional bias towards*; baited: *enticed/tempted*

he must seek that he may understand the beginning: a work whereof the author (though he had loss thereby, being a bishop) needed not to be ashamed, his chief person doing nothing that was not worthy to be imitated. But I confess that the *Arcadia* of S(ir) P(hilip) Sidney – either being considered in the whole or in several lineaments—is the most excellent work that, in my judgment, hath been written in any language that I understand,[19] affording many exquisite types of perfection for both the sexes; leaving the gifts of nature, whose value doth depend upon the beholders, wanting no virtue whereof a humane mind could be capable. As, for men: magnanimity, carriage, courtesy, valour, judgment, discretion; and, in women: modesty, shamefastness,° constancy, continency,° still accompanied with a tender sense of honour. And his chief persons being eminent for some singular virtue, and yet all virtues being united in every one of them, men equally excelling both for martial exercise and for courtly recreations, showing the author, as he was indeed, alike well versed both in learning and arms. It was a great loss to posterity that his untimely death did prevent the accomplishing of that excellent work.

Long since, being young, I adventured a piece with him (beginning at the very half sentence where he left with the combat between Zelmane and Anaxius, and continuing till the ladies were returned to their father, intending further, if I had not been otherways diverted)° meerly out of my love to the author's memory, which I celebrated under the name of Phil(i)sides; intending to have altered all that followed after my addition, having conformed my self only to that which went before. And though, being there but an imitator, I could not really give the principall it self, but only as it were the pourtrait, and that done by too gross a pencil, *Non cuiuis homini contingit adire* Corinthum,[20] it were enough to be excellent by being second to Sidney, since who ever could be that, behoved to be before° others.

This kind of invention in prose hath been attempted by sundry in the vulgar languages, as (leaving as not worthy to be named here those ridiculous works composed of impossibilities, and considering the best) Sanazarius's *Arcadia* in Italian, *Diana de Montemajor* in Spanish, *Astrea* in French,[21] whose authors being all of excellent wits, in a bucolick strain,° disguising such passions of love as they suffered or devised under the persons of shepherds, were bound by the decorum of that which they profess'd, to keep so low a course, that though their spirits could have reach'd to more generous conceptions,° yet they could not have delivered them in pastorals, which are only capable of affections° fit for their quality; where S.P. Sidney, as in an epick poem, did express such things as both in war and in peace were fit to be practised by princes. The most lofty of the other is the Marquis d'Urfee in his *Astrea*, and the choise pieces there, representing any of the better sorts, do seem borrowed from ancient histories or else narrations that hapned in modern times – rather true discourses showing persons such as they were indeed, though with other names, than (for the framing of them for perfection) they should have been devised° to be.

I have lately seen my country-man Barclay's *Argenis*, printed at Rome,[22] though the last in this kind, yet no way inferior to the first; he doth only meddle° with matters of state, war and love, all chief persons being princes, which in my judgment he doth discharge with a great dexterity; and where he doth represent some things which either are passages of this time or, at least – as having a great confor-

shamefastness: *modesty*; continency: *temperance*; diverted; *deflected*; behoved to be before: *must necessarily be above*; bucolick strain: *pastoral vein*; generous conceptions: *noble concepts*; affections: *emotions*; devised: *constructed/conceived*; meddle: *concern himself*

mity therewith—may be easily apply'd to the same. He doth it so finely, as if he found such purposes in his way, and went not astray with a search too curiously elaborated. And if any part of his work distaste the reader, it will be the extreme affecting of policy,° by clogging his muse with too long and serious discourses, which (though they be full of wit and judgment) will seem tedious to some. But his work, whether judged of in the whole, or parted in pieces, will be found to be a body strong in substance and full of sinews in every member.

affecting of policy: *affectation of wisdom*

NOTES

1. ED. Copy Text: *Works of William Drummond of Hawthornden*, 1711. 'Anacrisis' (Gk.) and 'Censure' both mean 'judgement' or 'evaluation'. The English word did not necessarily have negative connotations at that time. It is usually dated in the late 1630s. The opening paragraph and the later phrase – 'Long since, being young' – certainly suggest the views of an older man, looking back.
2. I.e. 'was made more painful (because I) had recently returned to my birthplace.' Alexander was born in Menstrie Castle, near Stirling. Affairs of state kept him away from home for long periods of time.
3. Alexander's style is influenced by his classical studies. A plethora of subordinate, co-ordinate and parallel clauses bring to an end the sentence which opened the essay.
4. Alexander is here concerned with readers who praise writers uncritically, on the grounds of 'what' they say, rather than assessing 'how well' they say it.
5. The series of images used for language in this paragraph – clothes, conduit, flowers – invite an assessment of its effectiveness persuasively and attractiveness aesthetically.
6. The causal end of the 'literary' branch of knowledge is usually defined in this way by Aristotelians. Poetry's function was to make men better, and hence happier, by examples of good and evil taken from historical sources. Cf. Dante, *Epistle to Can Grande*. 15.
7. Alexander exemplifies his principles of comparative criticism by following his assessments of Vergil and Ovid with a linking of the urbane Horace (65–8 BC) and scurrilous Juvenal (fl. second century BC) around one agreed point of contact. He may well grant innate generosity to Statius (AD 45–c.96) and Lucan (AD 39–65) simply because they belong to the Christian era and so translate the new spirit of 'mercy' and 'gentilesse' introduced by Christ.
8. Alexander recalls the line inaccurately but retains the sense. '*Interdum mihi latrare non canere videtur*': 'Sometimes he seems to me to bark rather than sing', Scaliger *Poetics* VI. 6. Julius Scaliger (1484–1540) was highly regarded by Renaissance critics – Henry Peacham called him 'the prince of learning'.
9. Martial (c.AD 40–103/4) wrote more than 1,500 epigrams. The first quotation (VII. 21) celebrates the day, made illustrious by his birth; the second (VII. 22) names him a poet of Apollo and the Castalian springs.
10. This is an example of the all-praise or all-vilification school of criticism opposed by Alexander in his argument for critical nicety and balanced judgments (see n. 4).
11. Virgil, *Aeneid*, XII. 930–37. Turnus, who has wooed and threatened Aeneas' wife when the hero was on his journey, piteously pleads for mercy rather than showing the courage expected from a nobleman.
12. The speech is in Plutarch's life of Aemilius Paulus.
13. Torquato Tasso (1544–95), *Gerusalemme Liberata*, XX. 104–107. This is, indeed, a 'slight blemish', as it is confined to stanza 104. Solyman recovers quickly from this instinctive lapse and dies a dignified death three stanzas later. Alexander's high opinion of Tasso, at a time when he was held to be mad, may be influenced by their closeness critically, poetically and spiritually.
14. Godfrey of Boulogne is the hero of Tasso's epic.
15. Sperone Speroni (1500–88) was a scholar and writer, who met Tasso in Padua. A strict Aristotelian, Speroni's views on Tasso were given credence because the poet discussed his work (especially composition of the *Gerusalemme Liberata*) with him. Tasso's *Sette Giornate del mondo creato* is an original poem modelled on, but not directly imitating, Du Bartas' *La Sepmaine*.
16. Alexander demonstrates that each mode sets up different critical criteria. To these, the critic must adapt. He illustrates his own method and draws his 'Evaluation' to a close by moving from epic through tragedy, history and pastoral to epigram and satire, accommodating to the terms of each in turn.
17. Prose is included in the definition of 'poesie'. Quintus Curtius was a Roman historian of the first century AD, who wrote a ten volume history of Alexander. Xenophon (c.428–c.354 BC) was an

Athenian historian whose history of Cyrus the Younger (*Anabasis*) was based on personal experience of the expedition it describes.
18. Little is known of Heliodorus, author of the *Aethaeopica*, except that he was born in Sicily. He probably belonged to the third or fourth century AD and has been identified with a Bishop Heliodorus of Thessaly, who lived at that time.
19. The *Arcadia* of S(ir) P(hilip) Sidney is the outstanding example of English pastoral romance. Alexander provided the bridging passage in Book 3, needed to link the Old Arcadia text to the revised version. He adapted the material in such a way that Sidney's own death is lamented as a character (Philisides) in his own book.
20. '*Non cuiuis homini contingit adire Corinthum*,' 'Not everybody is fated to go to Corinth.' Horace, *Epistles*, I.17.36.
21. Alexander places Sidney's *Arcadia* in its European context. *Italy*: Sannazaro (1456–1530) is the author of *Arcadia*. This pastoral has twelve prose and twelve verse sections. It appeared in 1504. *Iberia*: The first pastoral novel in prose – *Los siete libros de la Diana* – was composed by the Portuguese author, Jorge de Montemayor (1520?-61). *France*: The first book of *L'Astrée* by Honoré d'Urfé (1568–1625) appeared in 1610.
22. John Barclay (1582–1621). The *Argenis* (1621), a Latin satire, was translated into English, French and Italian.

§ 24: Appendix
The Legacy of the Seventeenth Century
[Latin, Scots, English and Gaelic]

[As discussed in the Introductions, the Anthology is devoted to imaginative writing in Scots and English. An Appendix of this sort was deemed necessary to remind readers that the Scottish literary heritage is not limited to these languages or to the courtly register. The presentation (in this section alone) of Latin, Gaelic and Ballad is intended to show that these other rich traditions had not died off in the face of increasing anglicization. Along with written Scots, they still existed for the eighteenth century to employ in all the linguistic variety they offered. To that end, texts which were composed in the seventeenth century or remained popular in that century, form the basis for choice.]

English Prose *opens this grouping with a regrettably brief extract from George MacKenzie. The move towards prose would be of prime importance in the eighteenth century. As MacKenzie's* **Aretina (§ A)** *and Urquhart's* **Jewel (§ 21)** *eloquently illustrate, Scotland had writers who were skilfully adapting to its challenges before the days of Hogg and Scott.*

Latin, *as the language of scholarship, offered a powerful alternative to vernacular expression in Scotland from before Barbour until the eighteenth century. The choice, therefore, while biassed towards the seventeenth century, includes one excerpt from the earlier writings of George Buchanan, the finest Scottish writer in this area. §* **BI: Somnium** *(The Dream) not only reflects this quality, it reminds us that Latin poets imitated Scots writers (in this case Dunbar). Most pertinently, however, the power of the printing presses had made this 'Poeta sui saeculi facile princeps' ('Easily the first poet of his generation') more widely known in the succeeding century than in his own. The rest of the selection is drawn from the major seventeenth century anthology of Latin verse. The* **Delitiae Poetarum Scotorum (1637)**, *with its wide range of topics, demonstrates that Latin verse was not restricted to the high style and the serious vein. Beside Thomas Craig's panegyric of farewell to King James (§* **BII**) *and Ayton's dramatic evocation of the Gunpowder Plot* **(§ BIII),** *Dr Arthur Johnston's mock Georgic (§* **BIV**) *and satiric portrait of 'Nosey'* **(§ BV)** *prove that the Scottish genius for reductive and parodic representation is as strong in Latin as in Scots.*

Scots and English *voices are focussed within* **Watson's Choice Collection of Verse in Scots and English (1706).** *These selections, like the Latin, take account of continued transmission, as well as later seventeenth century practice. For the Scots voice in particular, this permits inclusion of modes which originated earlier, but have endured until Watson's time. These include developments on the macaronic tradition (§* **DI),** *Flyting* **(§ DII)**, *the medieval brawl poem* **(§ DIII)** *and the dramatic monologue* **(§ DIV).** *Other stanza-forms remain popular but are adapted to later practice. Standart Habbie and the Heliconean stanza of Montgomerie's* **The Cherrie and the Slae** *fall into this class. The English voice of the later seventeenth century, as represented in that anthology, shows the degree to which the witty, 'strong lines' of Ayton had taken over from the more expansive and complex mannerism of Drummond. Ayton's own colloquial account of a courtier's imminent downfall* **(§ DV)** *and the later, anonymous, 'Election' (§* **DVII)** *represent this trend, while 'Inconstancy Reproved'* **(§ DVI)**, *moves us forward to Burns. The Ayrshire poet was so impressed by 'the simplicity of its sentiments', that he '(gave) them a Scots dress' in 'I do confess thou art sae fair'. It is this continuity which the four versions of 'Auld Lang Syne'* **(§ FI-IV),** *which conclude the Anthology, seek to demonstrate.*

The Ballad and Gaelic Literature *within the early period have been well served by editors and critics. Such interest and care are, qualitatively, well deserved. Only the designated remit of this Anthology has so far kept them outside the boundaries of selection. When the Union of the Parliaments of England and Scotland evoked a spirit of betrayed nationalism north of the Tweed, most of the earlier jealousies separating these traditions from courtly verse in Scots and English were forgotten. While the Ballad (represented by two examples stemming from seventeenth century history—*§ **CI-II***) had always enjoyed a high standing in Lowland culture, the makars had tended to 'flyte' against, rather than welcome the rival Highland tradition. (See* **Critical Introduction.***) In the seventeenth century, two major movements affected Gaelic composition. In the Highlands in the sixteenth century, Gaelic, Latin and Scots were all used as written languages. In 1609, the Statutes of Iona ordered the more resolutely Gaelic areas to follow suit. 'Everie gentilman or yeaman' in the Western Isles was to send his children to Lowland schools, there to learn 'sufficientlie to speik, reid, and wryte Inglische'. Secondly,*[1] *by the end of the seventeenth century, the classical period of Gaelic literature, which had endured from the twelfth century onwards, was reaching its end, although the last of the learned bards, Domhnall MacMhuirich, did not die until 1722. The court of the MacLeod of Dunvegan presents a convenient microcosm of the changing situation and the two, contrasted laments chosen* (**§ E I-II***) were both composed by poets at that court. The classical 'bard' in residence was the Irishman, Toirdhealbhach Ó Muirgheasáin. But his syllabic verse, chanted in free rhythm and deriving principally from written sources, was rivalled by the growing influence of popular diction and versification. Among this class of poets ('filidh') Màiri nighean Alasdair Ruaidh (Mary MacLeod) rivalled the finest. Her modes are, characteristically, eulogy and elegy; her language is the vernacular and she uses stressed metres within variable stanza forms. Ruaidhri Mac Mhuirich (Roderick Morison), whose period of fame mainly coincides with Mary's exile, differs from her in employing symmetrical stanzas. Morison, better known as the Blind Harper, was, first and foremost, a musician. William Matheson calls him 'the only example in Gaelic Scotland of the minstrel, skilled in the arts of poetry and music and singing his own songs to his own accompaniment'. He would not himself have claimed 'filidh' status. His songs ('amhran' or 'òran') usually conform to the four phrase structure illustrated in* **§ EII**.

See **Sectional Introductions** *for Montgomerie,* **§ 16**; *Thomas Maitland,* **§ 13**; *Ayton,* **§ 19**; *Drummond,* **§ 19**.

See **Notes** *for George MacKenzie; George Buchanan; Thomas Craig; Arthur Johnston; Patrick Hume of Polwarth; William Hamilton of Gilbertfield; Mary MacLeod and Roderick Morison.*

1. The argument for the three traditions of 'bard', 'filidh' and 'minstrel' co-existing at Dunvegan relies on William Matheson's account in An *Clarsair Dall*, Scottish Gaelic Texts Society, XII, 149–52.

§ 24A: *Prose Romance*

George MacKenzie (1636–1697)[2]

Aretina (1660)[3]

Book III

[This portion of the Romance deals allegorically with the historical period from the execution of Charles I until the Restoration. In this episode, Theopemptus (Charles II) has returned to rule the country.]

In this senate, Theopemptus is called home; not limited by conditions as some desired (for how could subjects give law to a king, and possibly these conditions would have been, by the next, ensuing senate, declared treason, and the treaters declared traitors) but absolutely; each endeavouring who should strengthen his prerogative most.

At his Proclamation, the people kindled innumerable bonfires, as if by them they intended to purge the air of these nations, which had been polluted with blasphemy against the gods and rebellion against the king formerly; or else, as if they intended to bury in these graves and burn to ashes those cares, wherewith they had been formerly afflicted. Their flames mounted so high, that one might have thought that they intended to carry news of those solemnities to heaven, and the smoke covered the towns pend-ways,° lest heaven should have discerned the extravagancies whereof the inhabitants were guilty; for gravity was banished as an enemy to their duty, and madnesse was judged true loyalty; the trumpets were ecchoed by the vociferations of the people, and those vociferations seemed to obey the summons of the trumpets; the bells likewise kept a part with the singing multitude, so that both bells and people did sing and dance all at once; and the air no sooner received these news, but it dispersed them to all the corners of the city and ears of the citizens, it being no crime to be in this a talebearer; and the bullets did flee out of the cannons, as if they intended to meet them half way. Wine was sent in abundance to the earth, that it might drink his majesties health also, and the glasses capreoled° in the air for joy to hear his name. Some danced through the fire, knowing that the wine had so madefied them, that they needed not fear burning; and others had bonfires kindled in their faces by the wine which they had drunk.

pend-ways: *like a vault*; capreoled: *capered*

2. Sir George MacKenzie was born in Dundee and studied at the Universities of St Andrews, Aberdeen and Bourges. His legal career culminated with his appointment as Lord Advocate. That he wrote this Romance and a number of Moral Essays may help to lead a mitigating case in his own defence against the prosecution view of 'Bluidy MacKenzie', led by Walter Scott via Davie Deans and 'Wandering Willie's Tale'.

3. ED. COPY TEXT: *Aretina* (1st. ed., 1660).

§ 24B: *The Neo-Latin Poets*

I

George Buchanan (1506–1582)[4]

Somnium[5]

[Dream Vision]

[Based on: William Dunbar (c.1460–c.1520): 'How Dunbar was desyrd to be ane Frere']

Mane sub auroram nitidae vicinia lucis
Pallida venturo cum facit astra die,
Arctior irriguos somnus complectitur artus,
Demulcens placido languida membra sinu,
Cum mihi Franciscus, nodosa cannabe cinctus,
Astitit ante torum, stigmata nota gerens.[6]
In manibus sacra vestis erat, cum fune galerus,
Palla, fenestratus calceus,[7] hasta, liber;
Et mihi subridens, 'Hanc protinus indue' dixit,
'Et mea dehinc mundi transfuga castra subi.[8]
Linque voluptates cum sollicitudine blandas,
Vanaque continui gaudia plena metus.
Me duce, spes fragiles et inanes despice curas,
Et superum recto tramite limen adi.'[9]

[Early in the morning at dawn when the approach of bright daylight makes the stars pale, on the point of daybreak, a deeper sleep swamped my limbs, caressing my languid body in its peaceful bosom, when Francis stood before my bed, wearing a knotted rope around his waist and bearing his well-known stigmata. There was a religious habit in his hands, a hood with a rope, a mantle, the holed shoe, a staff and

4. Educated at the Universities of Paris and St Andrews, George Buchanan became Professor of Latin at Bordeaux and of Philosophy at Coimbra. In 1566, he became Principal of St Leonards College, St Andrews. As tutor to James VI, he transferred to the young king his own enthusiasms for Latin and Protestantism. Almost all of his works are in Latin. He was, in his own day, held by many to be the finest poet and most profound philosopher in Europe.

5. ED. § 24B COPY TEXT I: *Opera Omnia*, Leiden, 1725. Buchanan's dream is loosely based on William Dunbar's poem, 'How Dunbar was desyrd to be ane Frere', which has been printed below the translation. A good discussion of the interrelation between the two texts is to be found in Philip J. Ford and W.S. Watt's *George Buchanan: Prince of Poets* (Aberdeen, 1982). The translation for the *Somnium* has also been taken from that text.

6. ll. 5–6. St Francis of Assisi (1182–1226). He is usually shown with a three-knotted cord round his waist; the knots signify the vows of poverty, chastity and obedience. He bears the wounds of Christ, because, in 1424, when the saint had gone to live on Mt. Verna, Christ appeared to him as a seraph, emanating light, which imprinted the stigmata on his body.

7. The holes in his shoes show where the light, impressing the stigmata, has burned through his clothing.

8. ll. 9–10. The call to leave the world and follow him echoes the words of Christ to his disciples in Mark 10. 29–30.

9. ll. 1–14. Buchanan expands Dunbar's first stanza to fourteen lines, following the rhetorical device of copiousness, referred to by Gavin Douglas, when explaining possible translation techniques (§ 15: 123–4)—'to mak my sayng... sum tyme Mair compendyus.'

a book. Smiling at me, he said: 'Put this on straightaway, come over from here to my camp, deserting the world. Leave behind pleasant delight along with anxiety and empty joys, which are full of constant fear. Under my leadership, despise fragile hopes and empty worries, and approach the gateway of the gods on the straight and narrow path.']
[**Dunbar St. 1**: *This nycht befoir the dawing cleir/Me thocht Sanct Francis did to me appeir/With ane religious abbeit in his hand,/And said, 'In this go cleith the my servand: /Refuss the warld, for thow mon be a freir.'*]

Obstupui subita defixus imagine, donec
Vix dedit hos tandem lingua coacta sonos.
'Pace' inquam, 'vestri liceat depromere verum
Ordinis; haud humeris convenit ista meis.
Qui feret hanc vestem, fiat servire paratus:
At mihi libertas illa paterna placet.
Qui feret hanc, ponat perfricta fronte ruborem:
At non ingenuus nos sinit ista pudor.
Qui feret hanc, fallat, palpet, pro tempore fingat:
At me simplicitas nudaque vita iuvat.[10]
Nec me Phthiriasis, nec rancida cantio terret,
Inque diem ignavae vivere more ferae:
Ostia nec circum magno mugire boatu,
Si tamen his nugis aetheris aula patet.

[I was amazed and astonished by the sudden apparition, until at last I forced my tongue to give forth these sounds: 'By your leave, allow me to bring out the truth about your order. This garment does not suit my shoulders. Whoever wears this, let him be prepared to be a slave; but I like my ancestral freedom. Whoever wears this, let him put on a bold face and cast off modesty; but a noble sense of shame does not allow me to do that. Whoever wears this, let him deceive, flatter, and feign to suit circumstances; but I like simplicity and a life unadorned. I am neither alarmed by the prospect of being lousy, nor the nauseous chanting, and living for the day like an ignoble beast, or groaning in a loud bellow outside doorways, but only if the heavenly courts lie open by such nonsense.]
[**Dunbar St. 2**: *With him and with his abbeit bayth I skarrit/Lyk to ane man that with ane gaist wes marrit; /Me thocht on bed he layid it me abone,/Bot on the flure delyverly and sone, I lap thairfra,/ and nevir wad cum nar it.* **St. 3**: *Quoth he, 'Quhy skarris thow with this holy weid?/Cleith the thairin, for weir it thow most neid; /Thow that hes lang done Venus lawis teiche/Sal now be freir and in this abbeit preiche/Delay it nocht, it mon be done bot dreid.* **St. 4**: *My brethir oft hes maid the supplicationis/Be epistillis, sermonis and relationis,/To take the abyte, but thow did postpone; /But ony proces cum on thairfoir annone,/All sircumstance put by and excusationis.'* **St. 5**: *Quod I, 'Sanct Francis, loving be the till,/And thankit mot thow be of thy gude will/ To me, that of thy clayis ar so kynd; /Bot thame to weir it nevir come in my mynd: /Sweit confessour, thow tak it nocht in ill.* **St. 6**: *In haly legendis haif I hard allevin/Ma sanctis of bischoppis nor freiris, be sic sevin;*

10. ll. 17-24. Buchanan extends Dunbar's attack on the friars; he also uses anaphora (ll. 19,21,23) to highlight stylistically his opposition to that group. Unlike the makar, Buchanan was a Protestant. The greater intensity of this section and the added detail of l. 24 ('I like simplicity and a life unadorned') confirm this.

/Off full few freiris that hes bene sanctis I reid; /Quhairfoir ga bring to me ane bischopis weid/Gife evir thow wald my sawle gaid into hevin.]

'Pervia sed raris sunt coeli regna cucullis,
Vix Monachis illic creditur esse locus.
Mentior, aut peragra saxo fundata vetusto
Delubra, et titulos per simulacra lege
Multus honoratis fulgebit episcopus aris,
Rara cucullato sternitur ara gregi
Atque inter Monachos erit haec rarissima vestis
Induat hanc, si quis gaudeat esse miser.
Quod si tanta meae tangit te cura salutis,
Vis mihi, vis animae consuluisse meae?
Quilibet hac alius mendicet veste superbus;
At mihi da mitram, purpureamque togam.'

['But the kingdom of heaven is accessible to few cowls, and there is thought to be scarcely any place for friars. Either I am lying, or if you wander through churches built with ancient stone, and read the inscriptions on the statues, many a bishop will shine out among the honoured monuments, but rare is the monument set up for the hooded flock. And this habit will be very rare among the friars. Let anyone who delights in being wretched wear this. But if you are affected with so much solicitude for my salvation, do you want to look after me and my soul? Let anyone else proudly beg in this habit; but give me a bishop's mitre and purple cassock.']
[**Dunbar St. 7:** '*Gif evir my fortoun wes to be a freir/The dait thairof is past ful mony a yeir; /For into every lustie toun and place/Off all Yngland, frome Berwick to Kalice,/I haif in to thy habeit maid gud cheir.* **St. 8:** *In freiris weid full fairly haif I fleichit; /In it haif I in pulpet gon and preichit/In Derntoun kirk and eik in Canterberry; /In it I past at Dover our the ferry/Throw Piccardy, and thair the peple teichit.* **St. 9:** *Als lang as I did beir the freiris style/In me, God wait, wes mony wrink and wyle; /In me wes falset with eviry wicht to flatter/Quhilk mycht be flemit with na haly watter—/I wes ay reddy all men to begyle.*' **St. 10:** *This freir that did Sanct Francis thair appeir/Ane feind he wes in liknes of ane freir; /He vaneist away with stynk and fyrie smowk; /With him me thocht all the hous end he towk,/And I awoik as wy that wes in weir.*]

Delitiae Poetarum Scotorum Huius Aevi Illustrium

[This anthology represents the culminating point of the history of Latin poetry in Scotland. In its two massive volumes resides most of the serious historical and political verse commenting on the crucial period surrounding the Union of the Crowns. This is no accident. Although James as patron of the Castalian band had encouraged wide use of the vernacular, one topical area was excluded. Only the learned should discuss 'affairs of state' and they should do so in Latin. It follows that those who wish to evaluate the patriotic and political line within Scottish verse must first seek here. Everything from verse chronicle through political and legal analysis to direct satire is available. Latin may also, however, be used for witty and even scurrilous topics, as the latter part of the selection **(IV–V)** *demonstrates.]*

II

Thomas Craig (1538–1608)[11]

Jacobo Magnae Britanniae, Franciae et Hiberniae Regi Valedicens.

[Bidding farewell to James, King of Britain, France and Ireland][12]

Dulcis amor populi, patriae lux unica, regum
Optime, post oculis nuncquam àdeunde meis.
Vive, vale! te cingat honos, te gloria obumbret,
Dum Pylii vincas saecula lenta senis.
Vivat et illa tuae coniunx[13] pars altera vitae,
Et tua felici taedia prole levet;
Et veri exemplum semper maneatis amoris,
Parque Dionaeo[14] nobile conjugio.

[Sweet darling of the people, sole light of the fatherland, best of kings, never again shall I set my eyes on you. Live on, flourish! May honour encircle you; may your glory protect you until you surpass the long ages of old Nestor. And long live your wife, the other half of your life, and may she relieve your weariness with happy offspring; and may you both remain an example of true love—equal in its nobility to the marriage of Dione.]

Quiq(ue), modo in patriam surgit non degener hastam
Henricus[15] solo nunc genitore minor
Quique refert patrem tam certo Carolus ore,
Carolus aetatis gloria rara suae:
Vivat uterque precor, dum famam terminet astris
Et meritis superet Solis utramque domum.
Quaeque refert matrem formae superantis honore
Sorte thori matri par sit Elisa suae.

[And also Henry who now, no less worthy, aspires to the ancestral spear—second now only to his father; and Charles, who recalls his father with his authoritative voice; Charles, the rare glory of his age. I pray that both may live until their fame reaches to the stars and until they surpass with their merits both houses of the Sun. And may Elizabeth, who calls to mind her mother in the surpassing glory of her beauty, be equal to her mother in the glory of her marriage.]

11. Thomas Craig became an advocate in 1563 and was later appointed Sheriff of Edinburgh. He wrote an influential textbook on feudal law and was one of James's major advisers on the problems posed by the Union. His *De Unione Regnorum Britanniae Tractatus* appeared in 1605.
12. ED. § 24B COPY TEXT II-V: *Delitiae Poetarum Scotorum Huius Aevi Illustrium*, 2 vols, edited by Arthur Johnston (Amsterdam, 1637) Craig I, 266; Ayton I, 65; Johnston I, 564, I, 554. For many of the notes in this section, the editors are indebted to John and Winifred MacQueen.
13. James's wife, Anne of Denmark (1574–1619).
14. The name Dione is used for Venus, whose marriage to Anchises produced Aeneas, ancestor of the Caesars, rulers of Rome.
15. Henry (l. 10)...Charles (l. 11)...Elizabeth (l. 16) are James's children—Henry, Prince of Wales (1594–1612), the future Charles I (1600–49) and Elizabeth (1596–1662): 'Winter Queen' of Bohemia, 1619–20.

Gratulor ipse mihi me hoc demum tempore natum,
Quo potui numeris te cecinisse meis
Et mihi adhuc vitae tempus quodcunque peractum est
Ingenium genio serviet omne tuo
Ast ego per dubios vitaeque viaeque labores
Iam repeto patrii tristia tecta soli.
Triste solum sine Sole, suo sine Principe cernam,
Nunc verum a Graeco nomine nomen habes,[16]
Aeternum Domini vultu cariturus amoeno,
Hoc peperit vitae sors mihi dura meae.

[I congratulate myself that I was born precisely at this time in which I have been able to sing your praises in my poems, and, however long I live, all my talents will be at the service of your spirit. But through the hardships of my life and journey, I now seek the sad dwellings of my native land. I shall see that sad soil, deprived of its Sun, without its Prince. Now [Scotland,] the name you have is derived indeed from the Greek word, for you will be forever deprived of the lovely face of your Lord. This is what the harsh condition of my life has brought about for me.]

Hic itaque et steriles Musas et carmina pono,
Carmina post calamo non repetenda meo.
Vive, vale! interea et magni per moenia mundi
Fortuna, virtus te, famulante, vehat.
Vive, vale! et nuncquam meritorum fama senescat.
Ah, oculis posthac nuncquam adeunde meis!

[So here I lay aside my barren Muses and songs; songs which I must never again set down with my pen. Live on, flourish, and meanwhile may your virtue, aided by good fortune, carry you beyond the walls of the great universe. Live on, flourish, and may the fame of your good deeds never grow old. Alas, never shall I set eyes on you again!]

III

Sir Robert Ayton (1569–1638)[17]

De proditione pulverea, quae incidit in diem Martes[18]

[Of the Gunpowder Treason which happened on the Day of Mars]

Heu Marti sacrata dies—quam paene fuisti
Sacra Jovi inferno[19] et caecis devota tenebris!
Sanguineo torrente suis te inscribere fastis
Cerberus[20] et Stygiae properabat cura catervae,

16. The name 'Scotia' (Scotland) is ingeniously derived from the Greek word 'skótos', meaning 'darkness'.
17. For Ayton's biography see § 19 Introduction; his vernacular verse is illustrated in § 18 and § 19.
18. 'The day of Mars': i.e. Tuesday 5th November, 1605, when Catholic conspirators attempted unsuccessfully to blow up King James in parliament.
19. Jupiter of the underworld: i.e. Pluto.
20. ll. 3–4. Cerberus was the dog of Hell.

Sed Superi vetuere nefas. Tu primus, Apollo,[21]
Infandas scelerum fraudes, deposta latebris
Sulphura, et ardenti glomeranda incendia ligno
Sensisti, et roseos potius tenebrescere vultus
Passus es insoliti marcentes tabe laboris
Quam si magna suo viduata Britannia Phoebo[22]
In tenebras totum traxisset funditus orbem.

[Alas, day sacred to Mars, how narrowly you missed becoming sacred to Jupiter of the Underworld and devoted to the shades of darkness. Cerberus and the attentions of the Stygian throng were anxious to inscribe you in their calendar with a torrent of blood. You, Apollo, were the first to be aware of the unspeakable treachery of their crimes; of the brimstone laid down in hidden places, and the fires to be set rolling with burning wood; and you suffered your rosy countenance to shrivel up and be blackened with the decline caused by your unaccustomed labour, rather than that Great Britain, bereft of its Sun's light, should have dragged the whole world into its total darkness.]

Nec tibi cura minor, nocturna Diana, Dianae
Saxonidis fuerat,[23] te caeca silentia noctis
Quae sceleri indictam praecessit proxima lucem,
Destituisse ferunt flamma ductrice, et opaci
Pensa ministerii facibus mandasse cruentis,
Quae totum per inane vagae flammante ruboris,
Prodigio eriperent Arctoam protenus Annam
Caede cruore rogis. Sed quo portenta[24] Deorum
Consiliis inscripta polo, si caeca futuri
Mens hominum nescit superos audire vocantes
Si visis tam parca fides? Scelerata nocentum
Perfidia admissas fraudi laxabat habenas,

[Nor did you, Diana of the night, neglect the Saxon Diana. They say that the blind silence of the night, which immediately preceded the day marked out for the crime, was deprived of your guiding flame, and that you handed over the duties of your shady office to blood-stained torches, which were to carry off immediately the northern Anna in slaughter, bloodshed and funeral pyres, as the flaming portent of redness wandered through the whole void. But to what purpose are portents inscribed in the heavens by the counsels of the gods, if the minds of men—blind to the future—do not know how to listen to the voices of the gods above, if there is so little faith in things seen? The wicked perfidy of evil-doers relaxed restraint and gave free reign to treachery...]

21. The unaccustomed labour refers to the sun l. 5 staying on guard from May, when the barrels of gunpowder were first put in place, until November—well after its usual decline into the summer solstice.
22. James, who was frequently referred to as Phoebus Apollo in courtly verse. Thus, one sun rescues another.
23. ll. 12–13. Diana of the night is the moon; Diana of the Saxons is Anne of Denmark. She is also the 'northern Anna' of l. 18.
24. The portents are the behaviour of the sun and the moon mentioned above.

Et coeptum peragebat opus, cum Martis[25] ab alto
Cura vigil propius, terras despexit inerteis;
Henricique memor,[26] cuius victricibus armis
Deberi Imperium mundi fatale sciebat,
Non tulit ulterius, sed dedignatus amores
Deliciasque suas in aperta pericula ferri,
Luce sibi sacra roseis ubi vecta quadrigis
Venit agens Aurora diem,[27] molimina cuncta
Criminis infandi dedit innotescere mundo.

[...and was bringing to fruition the work that was begun when Mars, with watchful care, took a closer look at slothful earth, and—mindful of Henry, to whose victorious arms, as he knew, his fated rule over the world was indebted—he did not endure any longer, but (deeming it unworthy that his loved ones, his darlings should be endangered openly) when Aurora came riding on her chariot bringing day, rosy with the light sacred to her, he caused all the machinations of the unspeakable crime to be blazoned to the world.]

I nunc et superos infami fraude lacesse
Cerbere, et his meritis inde sperare salutem.

[Go now, Cerberus and assail the gods above with your infamous crime and, by these deeds, hope for salvation from there.]

IV

Arthur Johnston (1577–1641)[28]

'Ad Robertum Baronum'[29]

Adspice, Gadiacis[30] quod misi tristis ab undis
Baroni, plenum rusticitatis opus.
Urbe[31] procul, parvus, nec fat foecundus agellus
Est mihi, saxosis asper ubique iugis.
Hic ego, qui Musis olim Phoeboque litavi,
Devotus Cereri praedia bobus aro.[32]
Curvus humum spectans, interdum pone iuvencos

25. Mars, as presiding deity of Tuesday, the day when the plot was due to come to fruition.
26. Prince Henry had already made a name for himself in the martial arts.
27. Aurora, goddess of the dawn.
28. Born near Inverurie, Arthur Johnston was educated at the University of Aberdeen. He travelled widely, mainly in Sudan, returning to Scotland in 1622. He was physician to both James VI and Charles I. His Latin verse begins under the influence of Ovid and the commentating tradition, but latterly becomes more personal and witty.
29. Robert Baron (1593–1639) was an Episcopalian churchman and one of the 'Aberdeen Doctors', Professor of Divinity at Marischal College.
30. The Gadie is a tributary of the Urie, which flows into the Aberdeenshire River Don.
31. I.e. Aberdeen.
32. ll. 5–6: 'made offerings...Phoebus...Ceres.' As poet, scholar and physician, he had been a devotee of Phoebus, god of light, learning and health, but as a farmer, he now follows Ceres, the goddess of agriculture.

Sector, et impresso vomere findo solum.
Interdum stimulo, nec rarò vocibus utor
Et stupidum numeros discere cogo pecus.

[Look, Baron, upon the work I have sent you in sadness from the waters of the Gadie Burn, a work full of rusticity. I have a small piece of land far from the city, not very fertile and everywhere rough with stony ridges. Here I, who once made offerings to the Muses and to Phoebus, am now devoted to Ceres and plough the land with oxen. Bent over, with my eyes directed at the earth, I follow behind the oxen and cleave the ground with the pressure of the plough. Sometimes, I use a goad—quite often I employ my voice and I force the stupid thing to learn verse.]

Nunc subigo rastris, nunc terram crate fatigo,
Horrida nunc duro tesqua bidente domo.
Hîc manus exossat lapidosa novalia lymphis
Hîc rigat inductis, hîc scrobe siccat humum.
Saepè flagellatae lassant mihi brachia fruges,
Ambo fatigantur saepè ligone pedes.
Ipse lutum nudus furcâ versare tricorni
Cogor, et immundo spargere rura fimo.
Vere novo videas mandantem semina sulcis;
Arva sub Arcturi sidere[33] falce meto.

[At times I work the soil with the drag-hoe, at times I weary it with the harrow, at times I tame the rough, rude land with the hard, two-pronged hoe. Here, my hand takes the stones from land ploughed for the first time; here, by introducing spring water, it irrigates the land; here, by means of a shallow pit, it dries the ground. Often, threshing the crops tires out my arms; often both my feet are wearied with wielding the mattock. I, myself, stripped of my clothing, am forced to turn over heavy, damp ground with a three-pronged fork and to strew the countryside with foul dung. In early spring you could see me consigning the seeds to the furrows. Beneath Arcturus' star, I reap the fields with my scythe.]

Pars messis torrenda focis, frangendaque saxo est,
Pars mihi flumineis mersa domatur aquis.[34]
Aestibus in mediis, hyemis memor, ignibus apta
Pabula suffossa quaerere cogor humo.
Viscera dum rimor terrae, propè conspicor umbras,
Ignotum nec me Manibus esse reor.
Ingeminant curae, ceu tempestate coortâ
Cum prior urgetur fluctibus unda novis.
Vix intempestata clauduntur lumina nocte,
Excitor ut cecinit nuncia lucis avis.

[Part of the harvest has to be scorched by the hearth and ground down with a stone; part of it I subdue by immersing it in water from the river. In midsummer, mindful of

33. 'Beneath Arcturus' star,' i.e. in late summer or early autumn, when that star is high in the western evening sky.
34. ll. 21–2 describe the treatment of flax.

winter, I have to dig up from the ground and collect turf suitable for fires in winter. While I turn over the bowels of the earth, I almost catch sight of ghosts and think I am not unknown to the souls of the dead. My cares are redoubled, just as when a storm has arisen, the first wave is hard pressed by the waves following it. Scarcely have I closed my eyes at dead of night, when I am aroused by the bird that announces dawn.]

Pellibus hirsutis humeros involvo, pedesque:
Rapa famem pellit, fluminis unda sitim.
Mille modis pereo; nil infaelicius uno
Me miserabilius nil gravis Orcus[35] habet.
Me mea nunc genitrix, et quae dedit ubera nutrix,
Horreret, vultu terreor ipse meo.
Non ego sum quod eram, foedantur pulvere cani,
Ora situ turpi, crura pedesque luto.
Obstipum caput est, et adunco suetus aratro
Semper humi figo lumina, more bovis.

[I wrap my shoulders and feet in shaggy skins; a turnip drives away my hunger; river-water my thirst. In a thousand ways, I am dying; harsh Orcus contains nothing unhappier, more miserable than me alone. I am even terrified of my own face. I am not the man I used to be. My white hair is becoming polluted with dust, my lips with disgusting filth; my legs and feet with muck. My head is bowed down and, now that I have become accustomed to the plough, my eyes are fixed to the ground like an ox.]

V

'De naso Nasonis cuiusdam nasutissimi'

[On the nose of a certain Nosey with the largest of all noses]

Conditur hoc tumulo nasorum maximus, orbem
Flere decet; nil non hoc pereunte perit.
Hic poterat vel more tubae fera bella ciere,
Scindere vel patriam vomeris instar humum.
Non alium fornax optasset Lemnia follem;[36]
Nec magis incudi malleus aptus erat.
Hoc exentlari poterat siphone carina;
Hoc poterat clavo per vada caeca regi.
Haec Libycas in bella feras armare proboscis,
Haec poterant Pharios rostra decere boves.
Non hoc Alciden, caeli qui sustinet axem,
Non hoc Atlantem dedecuisset onus.[37]

[In this grave the largest of noses is laid to rest; the world should weep. Everything perishes if it perishes. Like a trumpet it could call up savage wars or cut through its

35. Orcus is a god of the Underworld.
36. Vulcan was the blacksmith of the gods.
37. ll. 11–12. Hercules, strongest of mortals, once briefly relieved the Titan, Atlas, from his task of supporting the heavens.

native land like a ploughshare. Vulcan could not have wished for a better pair of bellows for his furnace, nor was any great mallet forged more fittingly. Water could be emptied from a boat with it as the pump; with it as a tiller, a vessel could be steered through hidden shallows. Snouts such as this could arm with trunks the elephants of Libya, destined for battle, or could do very well for the cattle of Egypt. As a burden, it would not have disgraced Hercules who holds up the axis of heaven, nor would it have disgraced Atlas.]

Vasta minus Rodii gesserunt rostra colossi,[38]
Vel moles si quae maior in urbe fuit.
Pes tripodi, radius caeli mensoribus aptus;
Pastori poterat nasus hic esse pedum.
Pistillo hoc poterat salsamentarius uti;
Spongia, quae mensas tergere posset, erat.
Nasus hic admotas potuit succendere taedas,
Eminus exstinctas vidi animare faces.
Arcuit hic Solis radios, et praebuit umbram,
Hoc dominus pluvio tutus ab imbre fuit.
Victa mero quoties tradebat lumina somno,
Huic pulvinari colla ferenda dedit.

[Of lesser magnitude are the noses on the great statues of Rhodes, or on any larger structure that was in the city. This nose could have been a foot suitable for a tripod, a rod for those surveying the sky, a shepherd's crook. A salt-fish merchant could have used it as a pestle; it was a sponge that could have wiped tables clean. This nose could have ignited torches, that had been applied to it. I have even seen it revive, from a distance, torches that had gone out. It kept off the rays of the sun and provided shade. With it, its master was safe from a shower of rain. Whenever he surrendered to sleep eyes that were overcome by undiluted wine, to this nose he entrusted the support of his neck.]

Rostra quod esse solent aeratis puppibus, illi,
Quod suo sunt cochleae cornua, nasus erat.
Hoc iter in tenebris sibi praetentabat eunti,
Hoc duce securam carpsit ubique viam.
Hoc prohibene nefas, irritamenta malorum,
Nullius admisit basia, nulla dedit.
Hic ubi rore madens spirabat, pacula nemo,
Audebat positas tangere nemo dapes.
Buccina Tritonis[39] quae convocat aequora talis,
Talis et Alcidae clava trinodis erat.

[That nose was for him what beaks usually are for ships of bronze; what its shell is for a snail. This snout searched out beforehand the way for him as he travelled in darkness. With it as his guide he took the safe way everywhere. With this nose standing in the way of wickedness, he received kisses, that are the enticement to misdeeds, from nobody, nor gave any. When this nose, dripping with moisture, exhaled, no one dared to touch the cups, no one dared to touch the feast set out before them. It

38. The Colossus of Rhodes, one of the Seven Wonders of the World.
39. Triton was the merman of Greek mythology.

was like the trumpet of Triton that calls up the seas, like the three-knotted club of Hercules.]

Hic geminam poterat nasus praebere cloacam,
Romulidûm populo quae satis ampla foret.
Hunc aversari tenerae suevere puellae,
Hellespontiaci ceu rubra membra Dei.[40]
Mollior hic plumâ fuit, et rubicundior ostro,
Floridior prato, splendidiorque vitro.
Nubibus humidior bibulis et olentior hirco,
Mobilior caudâ, blande catelle tuâ
Non tot vere novo turgent in palmite gemmae,
Rorida tot guttas vix, reor, iris habet.
Nemo tot exeso latebras in pumice, cellas
Nemo tot Hyblaeo vidit inesse favo.
Celtiber[41] haec poterat coluisse cuniculus antra,
Hic poterat caecos figere talpa lares.
Nil naso, nil par Nasoni protulit orbis,
Omnia nasus erat, Naso sed ipse—nihil!

[This nose could have been employed as a double sewer, ample enough for the people of Rome. Young girls would turn away in horror from it, as from the red members of the god of the Hellespont. It was softer than a feather and redder than purple dye; more flourishing than a meadow, more shining than glass; damper than clouds heavy with rain; smellier than a he-goat; more mobile than your tail, fawning puppy. Not so many buds swell on the vine branch in the early spring. The dewy rainbow has not, I think, quite as many drops. Nobody has ever seen so many holes in wasted pumice stone nor beheld so many cells in Hyblaean honey. A Celtiberian rabbit could have made its home in these cavities. Here, a mole could have set up its hidden dwelling place. The world has produced nothing to equal the nose, nothing equal to Nosey. The nose was everything but Nosey himself was nothing!]

§ 24C: *The Seventeenth Century Ballad*[42]

I

'Lord Maxwell's Last Goodnight'[43]

[*A longstanding feud existed between the Maxwell and Johnstone families. The immediate context of the ballad concerns a meeting on 6th April, 1608, which culminated in John,*

40. The god of Hellespont is Priapus, god of fertility, who was originally worshipped at Lampsacus on the Hellespont (Dardanelles). The 'red members' refer to his huge penis, as represented in statues or paintings of him.

41. Celtiberian: i.e. Spanish.

42. Both ballad texts are based on seventeenth century events and so fall into the chronological remit of this section.

43. ED. COPY TEXT: Glenriddell MSS, XI, 18. (Child 195B). The ballad was first published in the *Minstrelsy of the Scottish Border*, from a copy in Glenriddell's MS (G), with some slight variations from tradition. Variations in the *Minstrelsy* (BM) are, therefore, editorial and only noted when they are of critical interest. Lord Byron states that the evening farewell at the beginning of *Childe Harold's Pilgrimage* was suggested by this ballad.

9th Lord Maxwell, shooting Sir James Johnstone in the back. Maxwell fled the country, returning in 1613, when he was betrayed and executed. The ballad allows us to 'hear' his farewell to family and supporters.]

1
'Adiew, madam,[44] my mother dear,
But and° my sisters two! — *Also/As well as*
Adiew, fair Robert of Oarchyardtoan![45]
For thee, my heart is woe.[46]

2
'Adiew, the lilly and the rose,
The primrose, sweet to see!
Adiew, my lady and only joy!
For I manna° stay with thee. — *must not*

3
'Tho I have killed the laird Johnston,
What care I for his feed?° — *enmity*
My noble mind d[o]is still incline;° — *is still disposed to think*
He was my father's dead.[47]

4
'Both night and day I laboured oft
Of him revenged to be;
And now I've got what I long sought;
But I manna stay with thee.

5
'Adiew, Drumlanrig! false was ay,
And Cloesburn! in a band,° — *bond of alliance*
Where the laird of Lagg, fra my father fled,[48]
When the Johnston struck off his hand.

6
'They were three brethren in a band—
Joy may they never see!

44. Maxwell's loving relations with his wife, the daughter of the first Marquis of Hamilton, assumed here (and throughout) are fictive. He instituted divorce proceedings against her and she died before 1608 with these still pending.
45. The name suggests Maxwell's cousin, Sir Robert Maxwell of Orchardton; the close domestic context suggests his brother—also Robert—who later inherited the Maxwell estates.
46. ED. woe] G; wae BM. Scott, in the *Border Minstrelsy*, regularly strengthens the Scots of the MS version to increase the archaic effect—cf. BM. 'feid' (3.2); 'faither' (3.4); 'tuik aff' (13.1); 'didna spair' (16.1); 'gude' (16.2) etc.
47. '(That) he was the death of my father.' This may well have been the case. Maxwell's father fell from his horse and died in suspicious circumstances after an encounter with the Johnstones in 1593. The belief that his enemy cut off his hand, outstretched for aid, is again referred to in 5.4.
48. 5.1–3. It was believed that these three attendants on Maxwell's father—Douglas of Drumlanrig, Kirkpatrick of Closeburn, and Grierson of Lagg—were involved in a conspiracy to abandon him and facilitate his murder.

But now I've got what I long sought,
    And I maunna stay with thee.

7

'Adiew, Dumfries, my proper° place, *own/native*
    But and° Carlaverock fair, *Also*
Adiew, the castle of the Thrieve,[49]
    And all my buildings there!

8

'Adiew, Lochmaben's[50] gate so fair,
    The Langholm-shank,[51] where birks they be! *birches*
Adiew, my ladye and only joy!
    And, trust me, I maunna stay with thee.

9

'Adiew, fair Eskdale,° up and down, *valley of River Esk*
    Where my poor friends do dwell!
The bangisters° will ding° them down, *ruffians/outlaws; strike*
    And will them sore compel.

10

'But I'll revenge that feed° mysell *feud*
    When I come ou'r the sea;
Adieu, my ladye, and only joy!
    For I maunna stay with thee.'

11

'Lord of the land, will you go then
    Unto my father's place,
And walk into the gardens green,
    And I will you embrace.

12

'Ten thousand times I'll kiss your face,
    And sport and make you merry!'
'I thank thee, my lady, for thy kindness,
    But, trust me, I maunna stay with thee.'

13

Then he took off a great gold ring,
    Where at hang signets[52] three;

49. 7.1–3. The Maxwells owned Caerlaverock Castle and Thrieve Castle as well as a large house in Dumfries, the major town of Galloway. 8.1–2 continue this list of the properties he is leaving with reference to his estates in Lochmaben and Langholm.
50. Lochmaben Castle, near Lockerbie, was built in the thirteenth century. Mary Queen of Scots came there with Darnley.
51. Langholm is a Scottish border town. A 'shank' is the projecting point of the hill, where it joins the flat ground.
52. 'signets': Ornaments, usually seals, attached to earrings or, in this instance, a finger ring. Cf. *Bonny John Seton*, st. 13, 'His fingers they were sae sair swelld/ The rings would not come off; / They cutted the grips out o' his ears,/ Took out the gowd signots.'

'Hae!° take thee that, my ain dear thing, *Here*
And still hae mind of me.

14
'But if thow marry another lord,
Ere I come ou'r the sea-
Adiew, my lady and only joy!
For I maunna stay with thee.'

15
The wind was fair, the ship was clear,
That good lord went away;
And most part of his friends were there,
To give him a fair convay.° *fine send-off*

16
They drank thair wine, they did not spare,
Even in that good lord's sight—
Now he is o'er the floods so gray,
And Lord Maxwell has ta'en his good-night.

II

'The Baron of Braikly'[53]

[The story of this ballad conflates (at least) two episodes in the running feud between the Gordon family and the Farquharsons of Inverey; the first of these took place in 1592 and the second in 1666. The latter provides the principal focus for the poem.]

O Inverey came down Dee side, whistling and playing;[54]
He's landed at Braikly's yates,° at the day dawing.° *gates; dawning*

Says, 'Baron of Braikly, are ye within?
There's sharp swords at the yate will gar° your blood spin.'° *make; gush out*

The lady raise up, to the window she went;
She heard her kye° lowing oer hill and oer bent.° *cattle; moor*

'O rise up, John,' she says, 'turn back your kye;
They're oer the hills rinning, they're skipping away.'

'Come to your bed, Peggie,[55] and let the kye rin,
For were I to gang out, I would never get in.'

53. ED. COPY TEXT: *Jamieson's Popular Ballads*, 1806. (Child 203Cb). This was the first printing of the ballad. It is also a good example of the ever-changing state of aurally-derived material—being Jamieson's collation of Walter Scott's version and Mrs Brown's, both taken down from recitation. Brackley is in the north-east of Scotland, close to Ballater.
54. The late seventeenth century Inverey was a freebooter. He was also generally believed to be a wizard.
55. 'Peggie' is Margaret Burnet, daughter of Sir Thomas Burnet of Leys. She married John Gordon against her parents' wishes. There is no evidence to support or deny her treachery as suggested at the end of the ballad. After her husband's death, she married a doctor.

Then she's cry'd on her women, they quickly came ben;° *inside*
'Take up your rocks,° lassies, and fight a' like men. *distaffs*

'Though I'm but a woman, to head° you I'll try, *lead*
Nor let these vile Highland-men steal a' our kye.'

Then up gat the baron, and cried for his graith;° *equipment*
Says, 'Lady, I'll gang, tho to leave you I'm laith° *unwilling*

'Come, kiss me, my Peggie, nor think I'm to blame;
For I may well gang out, but I'll never win in.'°[56] *(re)gain entry*

When the Baron of Braikly rade through the close° *courtyard*
A gallanter baron neer° mounted a horse. *never*

Tho' there came wi Inverey thirty and three,
There was nane wi bonny Braikly but his brother and he[57]

Twa gallanter Gordons did never sword draw;
But against four and thirty, wae's° me, what was twa? *woe is*

Wi swords and wi daggers they did him surround,
And they've pierc'd bonny Braikly wi mony a wound.

Frae the head of the Dee to the banks of the Spey,[58]
The Gordons may mourn him and bann° Inverey. *curse*

'O cam ye by Braikly, and was ye in there?
Or saw ye his Peggy dear, riving° her hair?' *tearing*

'O I came by Braikly, and I was in there,
But I saw not his Peggy dear riving her hair.'[59]

'O fye on ye, lady! how could ye do sae?
You opend your yate to the faus° Inverey.' *false*

She eat wi him, drank wi him, welcomd him in;
She welcomd the villain that slew her baron.

She kept him till morning, syne bad him be gane,° *then told him to go*
And show d him the road that° he woud na be tane.° *on which; caught*

'Thro Birss and Aboyne,' she says, 'lyin in a tour,
Oer the hills o' Glentanor, you'll skip in an hour.'[60]

56. ED. Some versions add an additional detail at this point. 'I ay was for peace, tho' I never fear'd weir.' This was truer of the older Brackley. The younger Baron treated Inverey's people quite harshly. It is possible that, as in Barbour's *Bruce*, family characteristics are being eclectically represented in order to maximize pathos.
57. In the edition to be found in *Scarce Ancient Ballads*, 1822 (Child 203A), an uncle and cousin join his brother, William.
58. The Spey and the Dee are rivers in north-east Scotland.
59. The treachery of his wife is more directly related in some versions, where Peggy is recorded as 'a-making good cheer'.
60. ll. 39–40. She directs him on a straight route ('lyin in a tour') through the neighbouring villages of Birse and Aboyne, south west into Glen Tanar.

There is grief in the kitchen and mirth in the ha;[61]
But the Baron of Braikly is dead and awa.

§ 24D: *James Watson's Choice Collection of Comic and Serious Scots Poems*[62]

[This Anthology was produced shortly after the Darien scheme failure—blamed by Scots on the English—had been revealed. As the full extent of the national economic disaster became known, Burns's 'parcel of rogues in a nation' prepared to recoup their personal losses by 'selling' Scotland into parliamentary Union. In 1706, with Edinburgh practically in a state of mob rule, James Watson published the first of his three volumes. That nationalist motivations lay behind the venture is guaranteed by Watson's known royalist sympathies. In gathering together Scottish vernacular verse in Scots and English, drawn mainly from the sixteenth and seventeenth centuries, he reminded his countrymen of their national heritage. That the second and third volumes (1709; 1711) are less carefully collected and may even contain work by one or two English writers results from the haphazard method used to build upon Volume I. On the day when that book appeared, an advertisement was placed in The Edinburgh Courant *appealing for any readers who had similar poems in their posession to contact the printers at once. See Harriet Harvey Wood's Introduction to Volume II of the Scottish Text Society edition (1991) for a full account.]*

The Macaronic Voice

I

William Drummond (1585–1649)

Polemo-Middinia inter Vitarvam et Nebernam[63]

[The midden war between the Scotstarvit and Newbarns]

(ll. 1–22: A mock-heroic description of the east-neuk of Fife has set the scene for battle between the Scot and Cunningham families.)

61. The 'upstairs'/'downstairs' contrast increases the pathos. The Baron is loved by his servants (kitchen) but betrayed by his wife and fellow nobles (hall).
62. ED. § 24D COPY TEXT I-VII: *A Choice Collection of Comic and Serious Scots Poems both Ancient and Modern* (Printed by James Watson, Edinburgh 1706, 1709, 1711). Volume and page references in Watson are as follows: I: *Polemo Middinia* I, 129; II: 'Scots', Flyting III, 1; II, 54; III: *Christis Kirk* I, 1; IV: 'Bonny Heck' I, 68; V: 'Returning Late' II, 116; VI: 'Inconstancy Reproved' III, 91; VII: 'Election' III, 71. This text is not always the most authoritative, but it has been adopted because of the historical context set out at the head of this section. The translation of the *Polemo Middinia* relies heavily on that provided by Allan H. Maclaine and Kenneth H. Rogers in the former's *The Christis Kirk Tradition* (Glasgow, 1996). The editors are grateful to John and Winifred MacQueen for markedly improving their own translations of II-VII.
63. This is one of Drummond's later works; usually dated c.1645. It derives from the medieval brawl poem and belongs to the same tradition as *Christis Kirk on the Green*. 'Vitarvam et Nebarnam': The rural convention of identifying families—here, the Scots of Scotstarvit; the Cunninghams of Newbarns— by the names of their properties still exists in Scotland. See ll. 24–5, where the lady lairds are similarly described.

Namque in[64] principio Storiam tellabimus omnem
Muckreilium[65] ingentem turbam Vitarva per agros
Nebernae marchare fecit, et dixit ad illos,
'Ite hodie armati grippis, dryvate caballos
Nebernae per crofta, atque ipsas ante fenestras.
Quod si forte ipsa Neberna venerit extra,
Warrantabo omnes, et vos bene defendebo.'

[And now in the beginning—we will tell the whole story—the lady of Scotstarvit formed a large disorderly mob of muckrakers to march across the fields of Newbarns, and she said to them, 'Advance to-day, armed with forks; drive the horses off through the farm and fields of Newbarns and even past its windows; but should the lady of Newbarns herself come outside, I warrant you all and will protect you well.']

Hic aderant Geordy Akinhedius et little Johnus,
Et Jamy Richaeus, et stout Michel Hendersonus,
Qui jolly tryppas ante alios dansare solebat,
Et bobbare bene et lassas kissas bonaeas;
Duncan Olyphantus, valde stalvartus, et eius
Filius eldestus jolyboyus, atque Oldmoudus,[66]
Qui Pleugham longo Gaddo dryvare solebat;
Et Rob Gib wantonus homo, atque Oliver Hutchin
Et ploucky-fac'd Waty Strang, atque in kneed Alsinder Atken
Et Wily Dick heavy-arstus homo, pierrimus omnium,
Qui tulit in pileo magnum rubrumque favorem,[67]
Valde lethus pugnare, sed hunc Corngrevius heros[68]
Noutheadum vocavit, atque illum forcit ad arma.

[Geordie Aitkenhead and Little John and Jamie Richie were there and stout Michael Henderson, who was given to performing merry capers when dancing in public; Duncan Oliphant, so stalwart, and his eldest son, a pretty boy, and Oldmouth as well, who was given to driving the plough with a long stick, and that wanton fellow, Rob Gib, and also Oliver Hutchin and spotty-faced Wattie Strang, and knock-kneed Alexander Atkin; and heavy-arsed Willie Dick—laziest of them all—who wore a big red favour in his cloth skull-cap—he was very reluctant to fight; the hero-reeve, however, called him blockhead and forced him into the conflict.]

[*In the remainder of the poem (ll. 43–166) the opposition is described; battle joined, and, in the end, the women of Newbarns defeat Scotstarvit's cowardly masculine force.*]

64. ED. in] B; à Watson.
65. This is a Latin form of a Scots contraction. Strictly 'muck-rakes', it is here transferred to those who use them.
66. 'Oldmoudus' is a Latin form of Scots 'auld-mou'd'. Literally, this means old-mouthed but may have the applied sense of 'wise in speech'.
67. This line is omitted in some texts, including NLS Adv MS 19.3.4 and Aldis (1684). It is needed to maintain the rhyme-scheme.
68. 'Corngrevius heros'—'the corn-grieve hero'. The corn-grieve held a position similar to that of the Reeve in Chaucer's *Canterbury Tales*. He was general foreman of a farm or manor, responsible to his lord or lady for overseeing work and presenting the accounts.

The 'Scots' Voice

IIa

Flying

'The Flyting betwixt Polwart and Montgomery'[69]

Montgomerie:

False stridand° and stickdirt° I's gar thee stink,	*strident; piece of dirt*
How durst thou mint° with thy master to mell,°	*venture; compete*
One sik as thy self, little pratling pick,°	*insignificant thing*
Could thou not ware° ink, thy trattling° to tell	*expend; chattering*
(Hoie! hursone of hell) amang the fiends fell?°	*cruel*
To drink of that well that poison'd thy pen,	
Where devils in their den do yammer° and yell,	*lament/cry in pain*
Here I thee expell from all Christen men!	

Polwarth:

Bleird babling bystour-bard obey,[70]	
Learn skybald° knave to know thy sell,°	*rascally; yourself*
Vile vagabond, or I invey,°	*before I inveigh*
Custroun° with cuffs° thee to compell,	*Base fellow; blows*
Yet, tratling tru[i]ker,° truth to tell.	*glib trickster*
Stoup thou not at the second charge,[71]	
Mischievous mishant,° we shall mell°	*Evil miscreant; spar verbally*
With laidly° language loud and large:°	*loathsome; unrestrained*

IIb

Thomas Maitland's Satyr upon Sir Niel Laing[72]

Canker'd,° cursed creature, crabbed, corbit kittle,°	*Malignant; curved whelp*
Buntin-ars'd,° beugle-back'd,° bodied like a beetle;	*Plump-arsed; crook-backed*
Sarie° shitten, shell-padock,° ill shapen shit,	*Grievously; tortoise*
Kid-bearded gennet, all alike great:[73]	

69. Patrick Hume of Polwarth (d.1609) was a Gentleman of the bedchamber and, later, Warden of the Marshes under James VI. This Flyting probably took place in the early 1580s but the broader tradition of vituperative virtuosity in verse remained powerful throughout the seventeenth century. The 'flyting' mode usually involves two poets indulging in scurrilous name-calling so as to display their verbal skills. This poem and its best known predecessor (the Flyting between William Dunbar and Walter Kennedy) should be thought of as a poetic competition undertaken to entertain the court and not as evidence of a personal feud. The chosen extract contains the last stanza of Montgomerie's first reply, followed by the first stanza of Polwarth's rejoinder.

70. 'Bleary-eyed, babbling braggart of a bard, obey.'

71. The metaphor is from jousting. If Montgomerie does not concede at the end of this, Polwarth's second invective, their battle of words must continue.

72. For Thomas Maitland, see § 13. The full title adds the following description of Laing: 'who was a priest and one of the Pope's knights about the time of the Reformation.'

73. The jibe is at his lack of masculinity. His beard lacks growth, resembling that on a female donkey; cf. Chaucer's Pardoner as described in the 'General Prologue' to *The Canterbury Tales*.

Fiddle-douped, flindrikin, fart of a man,
Wa worth the, wanwordie, wanshapen wran![74]

III

Anonymous

Christ's Kirk on the Green[75]

[*The medieval brawl poem is characterized by a narrator, who observes a festive scene and comments wittily on the people who attend it. At the centre of the structure, there is usually a physical brawl. In some later developments of the form (such as* Burns's Holy Fair) *this may become a battle of words. The tone usually lies between light satire and simple celebration. A ten line stanza, made up of two ballad quatrains plus a shorter two-line wheel, is the norm. This is mirrored in the Bannatyne and Maitland versions of* Christ's Kirk. *The Laing MS version is the only earlier text to anticipate the simplified, single line tag reproduced in Watson. This tradition continued throughout the sixteenth and seventeenth centuries—e.g.* The Blythsome Wedding.]

1

Was ne'er in Scotland heard nor seen
Such dancing and deray;° — *disorder*
Neither at Faulkland on the green,
Nor Peebles at the play,[76]
As was of wooers as I ween° — *believe*
At Christ's Kirk on a day:
For there came Katie,[77] washen clean
With her new gown of gray,
Full gay that day.

2

To dance these damosels° them dight,° — *young women; set themselves*
These lasses light of laits,° — *skittish in manners*
Their gloves were of the raffal° right, — *doeskin*
Their shoes were of the straits;°[78] — *of Morocco leather*
Their kirtles° were of Lincoln-light,[79] — *frocks*
Well prest with many plaits;
They were so nice° when men them neigh'd° — *coy; approached*

74. ll. 5–6: 'Fart of a man with your scraggy posterior and empty head, woe upon you, unworthy, mis-shapen hedge-sparrow!' 'Wran' was used to signify anything small and malicious.

75. ED. St. 1: Compare Watson's text with the earlier, Bannatyne MS—(B) version, editorially inserted into David Lindsay's *Satyre* (§ 12) at l. 416. Maitland (M) has another good, early text. For the tradition stemming from the medieval brawl poem, see *The Christis Kirk Tradition*, edited by Allan H. Maclaine (Glasgow, 1996) pp. v-xiv.

76. ll. 3–4. The oldest surviving specimen of the medieval brawl poem is *Peblis to the Play*, c.1450. The second reference is thought to be to another poem celebrating festivities on the green at Falkland.

77. 'Katie' and cf. B. 'kitteis'; M. 'our kittie'. The earlier forms suggest loose morals, being associated with 'kittock', a woman of easy morals; cf. 2.2. 'Gillie', 3.2, has the same sense.

78. Alternatively, 'of the straits' may simply mean 'tight-fitting'.

79. 'Lincoln-light' here means Lincoln green, although the 'lynkome licht' of earlier texts may simply have meant 'made of light linen cloth'.

They squell'd° like any gaits,° — *squealed; goats*
Full loud that day.

3

Of all these maidens mild as mead,[80]
Was none so gimp° as Gillie, — *dainty*
As any rose her rude° was red, — *complexion*
Her lire° was like the lillie, — *cheek*
But yellow, yellow was her head,
And she of love so silly,
Though° all her kin had sworn her dead — *Even if*
She would have none but Willie
Alone that day.

4

She scorn'd Jack, and scripped at° him, — *scoffed*
And murgeon'd° him with mocks;° — *derided; grimaces*
He would have lov'd her, she would not let him
For all his yellow locks.
He cherisht her, she bade go chat him° — *hang himself*
She counted° him not two clocks:° — *valued (at); beetles*
So shamefully his short jack[81] set him,
His legs were like two rocks,° — *distaffs (i.e. thin)*
Or rungs° that day. — *sticks*

5

Tom Lutter[82] was their minstrel meet° — *well-qualified*
Good Lord, how he could lance;° — *leap*
He play'd so shril, and sang so sweet
While° Tousie took a trance:° — *Until; fainted away*
Old light foots°[83] there he could foreleet,° — *dances; had abandoned*
And counterfitted° France, — *imitated (music of)*
He held him like a man discreet,
And up the Morice Dance
He took that day.[84]

6

Then Stephen came stepping in with stends,° — *firm bouncing steps*
No rink° might him arrest,° — *strong fellow; stop*

80. Mead is a drink made from honey and water, fermented. It was very popular in the medieval period especially.
81. Short jackets in morality dramas used to be a sign of moral decadence. By this time, the emphasis is only on his ridiculous appearance.
82. Harriet Harvey Wood in the Scottish Text Society edition persuasively suggests that the original B. form of this name—'Thome Lular'—meant 'Tom the Bagpiper' (Ger. 'lüller', B. 'Thome Lular'). Certainly names in this mode often suggest occupations in the manner of Chaucer in *The Canterbury Tales*.
83. ED. Old light foots] eds.; 'Old Lightfoot' (Watson) makes little sense. It draws from Bannatyne's 'Auld lychtfute', rather than Maitland's 'auld lycht futtis'.
84. ll. 6–9. They imitate the latest French dances but also participate in the folk dances (morris dancing), which derive from the ancient fertility rituals. ll. 8–9: 'And he struck up the music for the Morris dancing, that day.'

Splayfoot[85] did bob° with many bends,° — *hop; ribbons*
 For Masie he made request,
He lap while he lay on his lends,° — *until he fell (lay on loins)*
 And rising was so preast,° — *beset*
While he did hoast° at both the ends — *cough/expel wind*
 For honour of the feast,
 And danc'd that day.[86]

7

Then Robin Roy began to revel,[87]
 And Tousie to him drugged:° — *drew forcibly*
'Let be!' quoth Jack, and call'd him, 'Jevel!'° — *Ruffian*
 And by the tail him tugged,[88]
Then Kensie[89] clicked to a kevel,° — *seized a hammer*
 God wots as they two lugged;° — *set upon each other*
They parted there upon a nevel° — *heavy punch*
 Men say that hair was rugged° — *tugged*
 Between them twa.

8[90]

With that a friend of his cry'd, 'Fy!'
 And forth an arrow drew:
He forged° it so fiercefully,° — *drew; violently*
 The bow in flinders° flew, — *splinters*
Such was the grace of God, trow I
 For had the tree been true;[91]
Men said, who knew his archery,
 That he had slain anew,
 Belyve° that day. — *Quickly*

9

A yap° young man that stood him neist,° — *bold; next to*
 Soon bent his bow in ire,
And etled the bairn° in at the breast, — *aimed at the fighting man*
 The bolt° flew ov'r the bire:° — *arrow; byre*

85. This is a translation of 'Platfute' (B; M), the name of an energetic Scottish dance, referred to by Lindsay in the *Testament of the Papyngo*, 'To play Platfute and quhissill Fute befoir', l. 88. The Watson reading misinterprets this, turning it into a description of Stephen's clumsy, splayfooted manner of dancing.
86. cf § 10.ii, Dunbar, 'Ane Dance in the Quenis Chalmer'.
87. The physical brawl starts at this point. The idea of wrestling was an image of disorder in the Miracle Cycles, being intended as a physical parody of the man's proper, spiritual wrestling with his sins. The figure 'Robin Roy' (King Robin) derives from folk ritual and the mock-king figure, played by Robin Hood.
88. ED. tugged] eds.; rugged W. The Watson printer may have anticipated 'rugged' four lines later and so loses both the alliteration and the readings ('tuggit'; 'tugged') of all the earlier manuscripts.
89. ED. Then Kensie] W; The kensy B. The latter means 'the lout' and refers to Robin. This has been misunderstood and Watson introduces another character, 'Kensie', into the struggle.
90. ED. Watson and the later broadside versions omit the eighth stanza in B. and in Maitland. In B. the omitted stanza begins, 'Ane bent a bow, sic sturt cowd steir him…'
91. The idea of God's grace in the previous line is strengthened by the 'true' tree reference. This refers to the belief that the tree of knowledge in Eden supplied the wood for Christ's cross at the crucifixion.

And cry'd, 'Fy, he hath slain a priest,
  A mile beyond the mire!'
Both bow and bagg° from him he kiest,° *quiver; cast away*
  And fled as fast as fire
    From flint that day.

[*In sts. 10–21 the brawl intensifies.*]

22[92]

By this Tom Tailor was in his gear,
  When he heard the common° bell, *communal*
He said, he should make all a stear° *commotion*
  When he came there himsell,
He went to fight with such a fear
  While° to the ground he fell, *Until*
Out came a wife, hit him on the ear[93]
  With a great knocking mell,° *heavy hammer*
    Fell'd him that day.

23

The bridegroom brought a pint of ale,
  And bade the piper drink it,
'Drink it,' quoth he, 'and it so stale?
  Ashrew me if I think it.'° *(even) contemplate it*
The bride her maidens stood near by,
  And said it was not blinked,° *had not become sour*
And Bartagesie the bride so gay,
  Upon him fast she winked,
    Full soon that day.

24

When all was done, Dick with an ax
  Came forth to fell a fother,° *to strike down many*
Quoth he, 'Where are you, whoreson smaiks,° *wretches*
  Right now that hurt my brother?'
His wife bade him go home Gib Glaiks,[94]
  And so did Meg his mother;
He turn'd and gave them both their paiks,° *a thrashing*
  For he durst ding° no other *dared to strike*
    But them that day.[95]

92. ED. Sts. 22 and 23 do not appear in B or M. They do appear in Laing and most of the later broadside versions.
93. ED. 22.7] eds; Out came a wife hitt him on the eare MS Lansdowne 740. Watson's reading, 'A wife that hit him on the ear' makes little sense.
94. 'Gib Glaiks' has the general sense of 'foolish fellow'. It is capitalized in Watson because it also suggests a nickname, 'Gilbert the Glaikit'. ED. gub glaikis] B; gud glaikis M, Laing.
95. *The Blythsome Wedding* continues the tradition of the 'brawl' poem into the late seventeenth century. In the eighteenth century there are many imitators, including Robert Fergusson in *Hallow-Fair* and *Leith Races*; Robert Burns in *The Holy Fair*.

IV

(?) William Hamilton of Gilbertfield (1665?–1751)[96]

'The Last Dying Words of Bonny Heck, A Famous Grey-Hound in the Shire of Fife'

1

'Alas, alas,' quo' bonny Heck,
'On former days, when I reflect!
I was a dog much in respect
For doughty deed:
But now I must hing by the neck
Without remeed.° *remedy*

2

'O fy, sirs, for black burning shame,
Ye'll bring a blunder on your name![97]
Pray tell me, wherein I'm to blame?
Is't in effect
Because I'm criple, auld and lame?'
Quo' bony Heck.

3

'What great feats I have done my sell° *myself*
Within clink° of Kilrenny[98] bell, *the clinking sound*
When I was souple, young and fell° *savage/fierce*
But° fear or dread: *Without*
Jhon Ness and Paterson can tell,[99]
Whose hearts may bleid.

4

'They'll witnes that I was the vier° *prize specimen*
Of all the dogs within the shire;
I'd run all day and never tyre;
But now my neck
It must be stretched for my hyre.'° *recompense*
Quo' bonny Heck.

5

'How nimbly could I turn the hair,° *hare*
Then serve my self—that was right fair!

96. William Hamilton of Gilbertfield (1665?-1751) was influenced by Ramsay's example. He also wrote the translation cum redaction of Blind Hary's *Wallace*, which proved so popular with Burns and others in the eighteenth century.

ED. Watson's version is thought to be the earliest printing of the text. That text has been been compared with NLS S.302.b.2(47). Readings from that text are noted as S(47).

97. Literally: 'You'll bring a (mark of) trouble on your name.' I.e. 'You'll bring your name into disrepute.'

98. Formerly a Royal Burgh in Fife; now amalgamated with Anstruther,

99. Harriet Harvey Wood correctly notes that 'Heck lives in the imagination as a dog, not a pseudo human being.' Nonetheless, the references to these men, to hanging (sts. 1; 4; 8) and Heck's thieving activities (st. 10) keep the latter possibility intriguingly open. See also 14.2.

For still it was my constant care
The van° to lead. *vanguard*
Now, what could sery° Heck do mair, *poor old*
Syne kill her dead?

6
'At the King's-muir and Kelly-law,[100]
Where good, stout hairs gang fast awa,
So cliverly I did it claw,
With pith° and speed, *vigour*
I bure the bell before them a[101]
As clear's a beid.[102]

7
'I ran alike on a' kind° grounds; *all sorts of*
Yea, in the midst of Ardry whines,° *the whins of Airdrie*
I grip't the mackings° be the bunns° *hares; (their) rears*
Or be the neck,
Where nathing could slay them but guns,
Save bonny Heck.

8
'I wily, witty was, and gash,° *smart*
With my auld, felni, packy pash,° *old cunning crafty head/brain*
Nae man might anes° buy me for cash; *once*
In some respect,
Are they not then confounded rash,
That hangs poor Heck?

9
'I was a bardy tyk° and bauld;° *forward cur/tyke; bold*
Tho' my beard's gray, I'm not so auld.
Can any man to me unfald° *unfold/explain*
What is the feid,° *(cause of) enmity*
To stane° me ere I be well cauld?° *stone; fully cold*
A cruel deed!

10
'Now, honesty was ay my drift,° *driving force*
An innocent and harmless shift,° *strategy*
A kaill-pot°-lid gently to lift, *soup-pot*
Or amry-sneck.° *cupboard latch*
Shame fa° the chasts° dare call that thift!' *fall upon; castigators*
Quo' bonny Heck.

100. King's Muir is an open area in East Fife; Kellie Law is a hill to the north of Anstruther.
101. ED. a] S (47). Watson omits but the word is needed both syllabically and for the rhyme.
102. 6.5–6: 'I stood out above all others [carried off the prize] as clearly [translucently] as a rosary bead.'

11

'So well's I cou'd play *Hocus Pocus*,[103]
And of the servants mack *Jodocus*,° *sport*
And this I did in every *Locus*° *place*
Throw their neglect.
And was not this a merry Jocus?'
Quo' bonny Heck.

12

'But now, good sirs, this day is lost,
The best dog in the east-nook° coast:[104] *corner*
For never ane durst brag nor boast
Me, for their neck.
But now I must yeild up the ghost,'
Quo' bonny Heck.

13

'And put a period to my talking,
For I'm unto my exit making:
Sir, ye may a' gae to the hawking,
And there reflect,
Ye'l ne'er get sick a dog for makin° *coursing the hare*
As bonny Heck.

14

'But if my puppies ance were ready,
Which I gat on a bony lady:
They'l be baith cliver, keen and beddy,° *eager to catch the prey*
And ne'er neglect,
To clink it° like their ancient deddy,° *sing out; daddy*
The famous Heck.[105]

103. 'play *Hocus Pocus*' means 'play tricks in order to deceive', as magicians did, when chanting such meaningless words to draw attention away from what they were doing.
104. The East Neuk remains the name for this coastal district in Fife.
105. Ramsay, Fergusson and Burns continue the seventeenth century's enthusiasm for the dramatic monologue, for talking animals and for this verse form.

The 'English' Voice

V

Sir Robert Ayton

'On Returning Late at Night from Court'[106]

The other night, from court returning late,
Tir'd with attendance, out of love with state,° *statecraft*
I met a boy, who ask'd if he should go
Along, to light me home? I answer'd, 'No.'
Yet he did urge the darkness of the night,
The foulness of the way, requir'd a light.
'It's true, good boy,' quoth I. 'Yet thou may'st be
More useful to some other, than to me.
I cannot miss my way; but they that take
The way from whence I come, had need to make
A light their guide; for I dare boldly say,
It's ten to one but they shall lose the way.'

VI

Anonymous

'Inconstancy Reproved'[107]

I do confess thou'rt smooth and fair,
And I might have gone near to love thee,
Had I not found, the slightest prayer
That lips could speak, had power to move thee;
But I can let thee now alone,
As worthy to be lov'd by none

I do confess thou'rt sweet, yet find
Thee such an unthrift° of thy sweets, *spendthrift*
Thy favours are but like the wind,
That kisseth everything it meets;
And since thou canst love more than one,
Thou'rt worthy to be lov'd by none.

The morning rose that untouch'd stands,
Arm'd with her briars, how sweetly smells,
But plukt, and strain'd through ruder hands,

106. Also known as 'Upon Mr Thomas Murray's fall'. British Library MS Add. 10308. The title is added in Sir John Ayton's hand. The precise incident is unknown but the man in question is, almost certainly, Thomas Murray (1564–1623), the son of Murray of Woodend. He led an honourable life at court but fell out of favour in 1621, when opposing James's plans for Charles to marry into the Spanish royal family. The idea of an honourable man finding court unbearable would strengthen the satire.
107. This poem is sometimes attributed to Ayton but is, more probably, by a later poet imitating Ayton's manner. Burns adapted it.

Her sweets no longer with her dwells,
But scent and beauty both are gone,
And leaves fall from it one by one.

Such fate e're long will thee betide,
When thou hast handled been a while,
Like fair flowers to be thrown aside,
And you shall sigh when I shall smile,
To see thy love to everyone
Hath brought thee to be lov'd be none.

VII

Anonymous

'The Election'

Some loves[108] a woman for her wit,
Some beauty does admire,
Some loves a handsome leg or foot,
Some upwards does aspire;
Some loves a mistress nice and coy,
Some freedom does approve;
Some like their persons to enjoy,
Some for platonick love.
Some loves a widow, some a maid,
Some loves the old, some young;
Some love until they be betray'd,
Some till they be undone:
Some love for money, some for worth,
Some love the proud and high;
Some love for fancy, some for birth,
Some love and knows[109] not why.
Some love the little, plump and fat,
Some love the long and small:
Some loves for kindness—and 'tis that,
Moves me beyond them all.

108. The Scots form, 'Some loves' shows that this is not one of the (very few) poems by English writers to gain entry into the latter parts of Watson's Anthology. It is a late seventeenth century example of the simple, witty line in courtly verse.
109. The English form ('love') and Scots form ('knows') are presented as alternatives in the same line.

§ 24E: *The Gaelic Voice*

Màiri nighean Alasdair Ruaidh

(Mary Macleod, ?1615–?1705)[110]

I

'Luinneag Mhic Leòid'[111]

(MacLeod's Lilt)

1

Is mi am shuidhe air an tulaich fo mhulad 's fo imcheist,
Is mi ag coimhead air Ile,[112] is ann de m' iongnadh 's an ám so;
Bha mi uair nach do shaoil mi, gus an do chaochail air m'aimsir,
Gun tiginn an taobh so dh'amharc Dhiùraidh á Sgarbaidh.[113]

I hurabh o i hoiriunn o,
i hurabh o i hoiriunn o,
I hurabh o i hogaidh ho ro,
hi ri ri rithibh ho i ag o.

[Sitting here on the knoll, forlorn and unquiet, I gaze upon Islay and marvel the while; there was a time I never thought—till my circumstances changed—that I should come hither to view Jura from Scarba.
I hurabh o...]

110. ED. COPY TEXT: *Bàrdachd Ghàidhlig* (BGh). The text, translation and notes are heavily reliant on J. Carmichael Watson's edition for the Scottish Gaelic Texts Society, Volume IX (1965). The editors are grateful to William Gillies for advice on both Gaelic selections.

Mary Macleod was nurse to five of the MacLeods at Dunvegan. When she began composing verse, her activities were viewed with suspicion. For a woman to vie with male bards, however humbly, was viewed by many as overstepping the bounds of propriety and may indeed have caused her exile from Dunvegan to Mull. If so, the punishment was ineffective, as she composed more regularly after her expulsion than before it. It may be that her praise of Sir Norman of Bernera, the hero of *Luinneag Mhic Leòid*, contributed to the chief's anger. Alexander Nicolson places her exile in the time of Roderick, the seventeenth chief—that is, after 1693 (when Roderick became chief). Her return would be delayed until after his death in 1699. Doubts about her nature and status must have continued even after this reconciliation, for she was buried face down, in the manner thought appropriate for witches.

111. 'Luinneag' means a 'lilt'; that is—an informal and 'feminine' tune. When defending herself for entering the male realms of the bard, Mary noted that she only composed lilts of this sort. 'Mhic Leoid', i.e. Macleod of Dunvegan. The hero of the poem is, in fact, not the MacLeod of Dunvegan but Norman of Bernera. The title may refer to the tune.

112. ll. 2–4: Islay (l. 2), Jura and Scarba (l. 4) are islands in the Southern Hebrides. Part of Mary's exile was spent in Scarba.

113. ED. á Sgarbaidh] BGh. This means that she viewed Jura 'from Scarba'. The 'a Sgarbaidh' of the Eigg Collection makes no sense but the *Sar-Obair nam Bard Gaelach* reading of 'a's Sgarbaidh'—she viewed 'from (Jura) and Scarba' is a genuine alternative. The BGh reading is retained because Scarba was at that time (on the evidence of Pont's maps) inhabited and it is thought that Mary did spend part of her exile on that island. Carmichael Watson's edition has eight-line stanzas. We have preferred the quatrain form which shows the four stress pattern more clearly. The second and third stressed words rhyme within each line and the final stress rhymes throughout the quatrain. Also, in this song, the last line of each quatrain is repeated as the first of the next. This linking technique ('concatenatio') is shared by Scottish and Northern English Medieval Romances.

2

Gun tiginn an taobh so dh'amharc Dhiùraidh á Sgarbaidh!
Beir mo shoraidh do'n dùthaich[114] tha fo dhubhar nan garbhbheann,
Gu Sir Tormod ùr allail fhuair ceannas air armailt,[115]
Is gun cainte anns gach fearann gum b'airidh fear t'ainm air.

[To come hither and view Jura from Scarba! Carry my greetings to the land which lies shadowed by the rugged peaks, to the young, renowned Sir Norman, who has won headship over an armed host—for it is said in every land, that one of his name would be worthy thereof.]

3

Gun cainte anns gach fearann gum b'airidh fear t'ainm air,
Fear do chéille is do ghliocais, do mhisnich 's do mheanmain,
Do chruadail 's do ghaisge, do dhreach is do dhealbha,
Agus t'fholachd is t'uaisle cha bu shuarach ri leanmhainn.

[In every land, they say that one of thy name would be worthy thereof, one of thy prudence and thy wisdom; thy courage and thy spirit, one of thy hardihood and valour, of thy mien and of thy mould; and thy lineage and thy nobility were no trifle to trace.]

4

Agus t' fholachd is t'uaisle cha bu shuarach ri leanmhainn;
D'fhuil dìrich rìgh Lochlainn b'e sud toiseach do sheanchais.
Tha do chàirdeas so-iarraidh ris gach Iarla tha an Albainn,
Is ri h-uaislean na h-Eireann: cha bhreug ach sgeul dearbhta e.

[Thy lineage and thy nobility were no trifle to trace; from the blood of Lochlann's kings[116] thine ancestry arises, unbroken; thy kinship with every earl in Scotland and with the nobles of Ireland is not far to seek out; this is no lie but a proven tale.]

5

Is ri h-uaislean na h-Eireann: cha bhreug ach sgeul dearbhta e.
A Mhic an fhir chliùitich, bha gu fiùghantach ainmeil;
Thug barrachd an gliocas air gach Ridir bha an Albainn
Ann an cogadh 's an sìothshaimh, is ann an dìoladh an airgid.

[And this is no lie but a tale well-proven, thou son of the renowned sire, who was open-handed and far-famed; who, in wisdom, excelled every one of Scotland's knights, in war and in peace and in the bestowal of silver.]

6

Ann an cogadh 's an sìothshaimh, is ann an dìoladh an airgid.
Is beag an t-iongnadh do mhac-sa bhith gu beachdail mór meanmnach,

114. do'n dùthaich: Harris.

115. On behalf of Roderick of Talisker, Norman of Bernera had led a force in response to a proclamation issued by Charles II on his arrival in Scotland.

116. The Norse descent of the Macleods is discussed by Mary at greater length in 'Cumha do Mhac Leoid'.

Bhith gu fiùghant' fial farsaing o'n a ghlac sibh mar shealbh e:
Clann Ruairidh nam bratach, is e mo chreach-sa na dh'fhalbh dhiubh!

[In war and in peace and in the bestowal of silver; no marvel that his son should be prudent, great and spirited, should be liberal and free-handed, since ye have received that character as an inheritance, the sons of Roderick of war-banners—my sorrow, that so many of them are dead and gone!]

7

Clann Ruairidh nam bratach, is e mo chreach-sa na dh'fhalbh dhiubh;
Ach an aon fhear a dh'fuirich nìor chluinneam sgeul marbh ort;
Ach, eudail de fhearaibh, ge do ghabh mi uat tearbadh
Fhir a' chuirp as glan cumadh, gun uireasbhuidh dealbha.

[The sons of Roderick—so many of them are dead and gone; but thou, the one who remains, may I never hear news of thy death—thou treasure among men, though I am sundered from thee, thou whose form is so fair, without flaw of fashioning.]

8

Fhir a' chuirp as glan cumadh, gun uireasbhuidh dealbha;
Cridhe farsaing fial fearail, is maith thig geal agus dearg ort.
Sùil ghorm as glan sealladh mar dhearcaig na talmhainn,
Làmh ri gruaidh ruitich mar mhucaig na fearradhris.

[Thou of form so fair, without flaw of fashioning, thou of the manly and generous heart, well do red and white become thee; thy clear-seeing eye, blue as the blaeberry, set by thy cheek, ruddy as the berry of the dog-rose.]

9

Làmh ri gruaidh ruitich mar mhucaig na fearradhris.
Fo thagha na gruaige cùl dualach nan camlùb.
Gheibhte sud ann ad fhàrdaich an càradh air ealchainn,
Miosair is adharc is rogha gach armachd.[117]

[Thy cheek is as ruddy as the berry of the dog-rose, and under the choicest head of hair thy curling locks entwine. In thy dwelling would be found, ranged upon the weapon-rack, powder-horn and shot-horn and the pick of every armoury.]

10

Miosair is adharc is rogha gach armachd,
Agus lanntainean tana o'n ceannaibh gu'm barrdhéis.
Gheibhte sud air gach slios dhiubh isneach is cairbinn,
Agus iubhair chruaidh fhallain le an taifeidean cainbe.

[Powder-horn and shot-horn and the pick of every armoury, and sword-blades slender-tapering from hilt to tip would be found; on each side of them rifle and carabine and bows tough and sound with their bowstrings of hemp.]

117. st. 9.4–st. 10.1. Firearms are given primacy over sword (10.1) and bow (10.4).

11

Agus iubhair chruaidh fhallain le an taifeidean cainbe,
Is cuilbheirean caola[118] air an daoiread gun ceannaichte iad;
Glac nan ceann lìomhta air chur sìos ann am balgaibh
O iteach an fhìreoin is o shìoda na Gailbhinn.

[And bows tough and sound with their bowstrings of hemp, and narrow culverins would be bought though they be dear; a handful of polished arrows thrust down into quivers, fledged from the plumage of the eagle and the silk of Galway.]

12

O iteach an fhìreoin is o shìoda na Gailbhinn.
Tha mo chion air a' churaidh. Mac Mhuire chur sealbh air.
Is e bu mhiannach le m' leanabh bhith am beannaibh na sealga,
Gabhail aighir na frìthe is a' dìreadh nan garbhghlac.

[Fledged from the plumage of the eagle and the silk of Galway; the hero hath my love—may Mary's son prosper him! It would be my dear one's pleasure to be a-hunting in the peaks, taking joy of the forest and climbing up the rough dells.]

13

Gabhail aighir na frìthe is a' dìreadh nan garbhghlac.
A' leigeil nan cuilean is a' furan nan seanchon;
Is e bu deireadh do'n fhuran ud fuil thoirt air chalgaibh
O luchd nan céir geala is nam falluingean dearga.[119]

[Taking joy of the forest and climbing up the rough dells, letting slip the young hounds and inciting the old ones; of that incitement, it would come that blood would flow on the bristles of the folk with wax white rumps and russet mantles.]

14

O luchd nan céir geala is nam falluingean dearga.
Le do chomhlan dhaoine uaisle rachadh cruaidh air an armaibh;
Luchd aithneachadh latha is a chaitheadh an fhairge
Is a b'urrainn g'a seòladh gu seòlaid an tarruinte i.

[Blood on the folk with wax white rumps and russet-mantles, at the hands of thy company of nobles that bear hardly on their weapons; men that well would read the day, and speed over the ocean, and fit to sail the vessel to the haven wherein she would be beached.]

118. 'cuilbheirean caola' (narrow culverins). The adjective places the weapon as the early form of the musket rather than the cannon.
119. I.e. deer.

II

Ruaidhri Mac Mhuirich (Roderick Morison ?1656–?1714)[120]

'Féill nan Crann'[121]

('Harp-key Fair')

1

A rìgh, gur cruaidh mo sgeul,
  mo chràdh geur, mo chreach, mo chall,
o laigh air m'inntinn sac
  's a laigh air m'acfhainn mall;
on dh'imich uam an crann,
  's nach fhaigh mi shamhla 's tìr,
gur adhbhar mulaid leam
  mo chrann a bhith d'am dhìth.

[Ah me! my tale is distressing, it is for me a sharp pain, a calamity, a loss—since a load settled on my mind and a slackness on my gear; since my harp-key parted from me, and I cannot get one like in the country round, I reckon it a cause of grief that I am without my harp-key.]

2

Chan fhasa leam na 'm bàs
  a bhith fo thàir nam ban;
chan fhaod mi dhol 'nan dàil
  on dh'fhàilnich air mo ghean;
's e their iad, "Ciod am feum
  a dh'fheudas a bhith ann?
Chaidh ionnstramaid o ghleus
  on chaill e fhéin a chrann."

[I find it no easier than death to suffer the scorn of women; I may not go near them since my ability to please has failed me. "Of what use can he be?" is what they say. "His instrument has gone out of tune since he lost his harp-key."]

3

Gur fanaideach an gàire
  dhèanadh àd fa leth
'n uair chì iad fear gun chrann
  'na shuidhe thall 'san t-sreath;[122]

120. ED. The text, translation and notes are heavily reliant on William Matheson's edition for the Scottish Gaelic Texts Society, Volume XII (1970). Most of the notes also rely on this text. Morison was better known as 'An Clàrsair Dall', the blind harper. He lived in the household of the Macleod of Dunvegan in Queen Anne's time. He is the only known example in Gaelic Scotland of a minstrel, singing his own songs to his own accompaniment.

121. The idea for the poem is thought to have arisen when Morison dropped the key of his harp on the kitchen fire. In the ensuing conversation a maid explained the situation in a way which reminded the harper of the extended meaning of the word.

122. 'san t-sreath'. The idea of a rank or row evokes the drinking habits of the Lords of the Isles who were called to table in hierarchical order.

ma tharlas mi 'nan caraibh,
's ann theannas iad ri cainnt,
is their gach té le fanaid,
"Am faic thu 'm fear gun chrann!"

[Mocking is their laugh, every one of them, when they see a man with no harp-key sitting yonder with others in the convivial rank order. If I happen among them, they only begin to chatter and each one says mockingly, "See the man with no harp-key!"]

4

An caidreabh nam ban òg
d'am dheòin cha téid mi ann;
chan èalaidh mi d'an còir
o nach éisdear leò mo chainnt;
ma theannas mi ri comhradh,
's ann bheir iad dhomh-s' an cùl,
is their iad le fum-fam,
"Am fear a chaill a chrann 'san smùr!"

[Into the company of young women I shall not willingly go. I shall not creep close to them since they will not listen to what I say. If I begin to talk, they will only turn their backs on me, and say with a fim-fam, "That man! He lost his harp-key in the peat-dust."]

5

Thuirt Baintighearna Mhic Leòid,[123]
"Cha chreach gun tòir rug ort
(ma tha do chrann ad dhìth,
chan iongn' thu bhith fo sproc);
ach air nàile dhèanainn uircheas,
on dh'éirich dhuit an call,
's nam faight' a shamhl' air féill,
gun ceannaichinn féin duit crann.

[MacLeod's lady said, "It is not a calamity beyond retrieval that has befallen you. (If you are without your harp-key, it is no wonder that you are cast down.) But, by my troth, I would willingly show you kindness, since you chanced to lose it; and, if another like it could be got at a fair, I would buy you a harp-key.]

6

"Tha agam-sa riut iochd,
ged nach bithinn aig Mac Leòid,
gu t'fhiosrachadh roimh chàch
le mo làmh a chur am phòc;
gun gleidhinn-sa dhuit crann,
is gum pàigheadh le òr dearg,

123. The reference is to MacLeod's wife, who took up the maid's suggestive use of the harp-key, when the bard dropped it. The song may have been set to the famous tune known as *Craobh nan Teud*.

's cha bhi do chrann ad dhìth,
ged a chosd e mìle marg."

["Even though I were not married to MacLeod, my sympathy for you is such that I would succour you before all others, by putting my hand in my pocket. I would secure a harp-key for you, and pay with red gold; and you will not be without a harp-key though it should cost a thousand merks."]

7

"Beannachd dhuibh-s' is buaidh,
on 's sibh thuigeadh uam mar tha,
ag amharc air mo thruaigh',
on tha mi cruaidh an càs.
Air eagal mi dhol bàs,
cuiribh sgioba 's bàt air tuinn
a bheir a Barraidh crann,
ar neo geall a bhith d'a chionn."[124]

["Blessing and success be yours, since you, and you alone, looking on my plight, were the one to grasp how matters stand, and indeed I am sore beset. For fear that I may die, order a boat and crew to sea to bring a harp-key from Barra, or else let a forfeit be given up in its behalf."]

8

"Tha agam-sa ri t'fheum
nach leig éislean anns an tòir—
bàta gnìomhach gleusd'
agus sgioba treun do-leòn:
théid nighean Mhic Leòid[125]
is Nic Neacail mhór na suinn,
is nighean a Ghoill Ghlais[126]
chur a mharsantachd a' chroinn.

["To meet your need, I have what ensures that the quest will not flag—a fully rigged boat, fit for service, and a valiant, tireless crew: MacLeod's daughter and the big Nicolson wench, the warriors, and the daughter of Glass the Low Country man, will be sent to make offers for the harp-key.]

9

"Bidh Nic Fhionghain air an stiùir
is nigh'n Uisdein anns a' bheirt,
Nic Fhearghuis anns an sgòid
is an stagh aig Seònaid Bhreac;

124. St. 7.5–8. The reference to Barra is witty. A feud existed between the MacLeods and MacNeil of Barra. No welcome would have been forthcoming. The wager appears to be a forfeit, should the expedition return empty-handed.

125. St. 8.5–10.8. A daughter of MacLeod (possibly from his unrecorded first marriage) is the first-named of those who will seek out the merchant booths for a replacement 'harp-key'. The others are maids serving in MacLeod's household.

126. The daughter of James Glass, 'violer' and fiddler in the household.

nigh'n Anndra Chaoil 'na draip,
    is i 'n taice ris an aoir,[127]
's i trusadh leatha suas
    mar bu luime luaithe ghaoth.

["The Mackinnon wench will be at the helm and Hugh's daughter in the shrouds, the Ferguson wench at the sheet and pock-marked Janet in charge of the stay. Lanky Andrew's daughter will be hard-pressed as she strains at the bolt-rope, gathering it in as the wind blows steadier and harder.]

10
"Nic Mhaol-mhoire air thùs siùil,
    's i a' déanamh iùil gu grinn,
nigh'n Domhnaill Ruaidh 'san truis
    's Seònaid Fhriseal anns an taoim;
Nic an Fhleisdeir gu trom tinn,
    's i cur os a cinn a luchd;[128]
is bidh 'n allsa ealamh réidh
    aig nigh'n Thormoid Léith nam muc."

["The MacInnes wench will be for'ard of the mainsail, setting a course skilfully, Red Donald's daughter among the reef-ropes, and Janet Fraser dipping in the bilge; the Fletcher wench will be overcome and sick, discharging her cargo, and the quick, even down-haul of the sail will be left to the daughter of Grey Norman, the swineherd."]

11
Dh'fhalbh am bàta bhuainn
    is air chuan cha d' rinn i dàil
gus an deachaidh i air tìr
    ann an Cìosamal[129] Mhic Nèill.
An uair ghabh na seòid mu thàmh
    is a chaisg iad pàirt de'n sgìos,
chaidh fios an tuath 's an deas
    dh'fheuch 'n robh crann r'a reic as tìr.

[The boat left us, and did not tarry at sea till it touched land at Kishmul, the seat of MacNeil. After the dauntless band had rested themselves and overcome their weariness in part, word was sent north and south to see if there was a harp-key for sale in the country.]

12
An sin 'n uair sgaoil an sgeul
    feadh tìr Mhic Neill air fad,
chruinnich iad gun dàil
    eadar làidir agus lag;

127. 'an aoir' is the bolt-rope sewn round the edge of the sail.
128. St. 10.5–6. The reference is to sea-sickness.
129. Cìosamal: Kishmul Castle, situated on a rock in Castlebay harbour and the seat of the MacNeils of Barra.

gach té is fear gun stad,
's gum bu bhras a chaidh iad ann,
's mnài òga 'm feum nam bréid,
's iad 'nan ruith gu féill nan crann.

[When the news now spread through all Macneil's country, they gathered without delay, both strong and weak. Every woman and man, without pause for rest, eagerly arrived on the scene; and there were young married women who lost their kerchiefs running to the Harp-key Fair.]

13
Sin 'n uair ghlac a' bhreisleach
Nic an Fhleisdeir anns a' bhùth;[130]
chaidil i 'n déidh chàich,
's b'adhbhar gàire i 'n uair dhùisg;
an uair dh'fhosgail i dà shùil
is a ghlac i lùths na clì:
"Rinn luchd na foille fàth orm—
's ann gun fhios a dh'fhàg iad mì."

[And now it was that panic seized the Fletcher wench in the booth; she had slept after the rest, and raised a laugh when she awoke. When she opened her two eyes and summoned up strength in her body: "The deceivers have taken advantage of me,' (she said) 'they have crept away from me by stealth."]

14
An uair dh'fhosgail i dà shùil
gun do ghlac i lùths nan eang,
is ràinig i an fhéill
's iad a' réiteachadh mu'n chrann;
'n uair tharlaidh i 'nan car
ghlac i gad nan crann 'na dorn,
is thàr i leis gun fhios
far 'n robh nighean mhór Mhic Leòid.

[When she opened her two eyes she summoned up strength in her legs and reached the fair as they were coming to terms about the harp-key. When she got in among them she caught the string of keys in her fist and stole away unnoticed with it to MacLeod's big daughter.]

15
Thuirt nighean Mhic Leòid
gum bu[131] leòr siod mur bu ghann;
thuirt Meig nigh'n Domhnaill Ruaidh
gum bu truagh e bhith gun cheann;
bha Nic Mhaol-mhoire 'g ràitinn
gum bu stàilinn bha 'sa' chrann,

130. Sts. 13–15. Most of the girls mentioned in these three stanzas are those in sts. 8–10.
131. Note the use of anaphora in this final stanza.

's nam faigheadh e 'na ruagairean
gum biodh e shuas air ball.

[Said MacLeod's daughter, that it would suffice if it was not too small; said Red Donald's daughter Meg that it was a pity it was without a head. The Macinnes wench kept saying that the harp-key was of steel, and that, if it got in her shift, it would be up at once.]

§ 24F: *'For the Sake of Auld Lang Syne'*

[Robert Burns' words are sung to invoke the memory of friendship at the end of celebrations and festivities throughout the world. But the sentiment they express appears much earlier in the Bannatyne MS of 1568, as a refrain ('And auld kyndnes is quyt foryett') to the song 'This warld is all bot fenyeir fair' (II, 204). An early broadside, with the chorus—'On old long syne,/On old long syne, my jo/On old long syne/That thou canst never once reflect/On old long syne'—is cited by Henley and Henderson in the centenary edition of Burns's works, III, 408. It seemed fitting, therefore, to conclude by citing three other, earlier openings to the folk song, as a means of leading in to the Ayrshire poet's famous version for Johnson's Scots Musical Museum.]

I

Anonymous (Late Seventeenth Century)

'An Excellent and Proper New Ballad'[132]

Should old acquaintance be forgot,
And never thought upon,
The flames of love extinguished
And fully past and gone?
Is thy sweet heart now grown so cold
In that loving breast of thine,
That thou canst never once reflect
On Old-long-syne?

II

Anonymous (Late Seventeenth Century)[133]

'Old-long-syne'

Should old acquaintance be forgot
And never thought upon,
The flames of love extinguished,
And freely past and gone?

132. ED. § 24F COPY TEXT I: National Library of Scotland Ry.IIIa.10(70).
133. ED. § 24F COPY TEXT II: Watson's *Choice Collection* III, 71 (1711). Sometimes attributed to Francis Sempill of Beltrees (1616–82).

Is thy kind heart now grown so cold
In that loving breast of thine,
That thou canst never once reflect
On Old-long-syne?

III

Allan Ramsay (1684–1758)[134]

'The Kind Reception'

(To the tune of Auld Lang Syne)

Should auld acquaintance be forgot,
Tho they return with scars?
These are the noble Heroe's lot,
Obtain'd in glorious wars;
Welcome my Varo[135] to my breast,
Thy arms about me twine,
And make me once again as blest.
As I was lang syne.

IV

Robert Burns (1759–96)[136]

Should auld acquaintance be forgot
And never brought to mind?
Should auld acquaintance be forgot,
And auld lang syne!

Chorus
For auld lang syne, my jo,° *love*
For auld lang syne,
We'll tak a cup[137] o' kindness yet
For auld lang syne.

And surely ye'll be your pint stowp!
And surely I'll be mine!
Ane we'll tak a cup o' kindness yet
For auld lang syne.

134. ED. § 24F COPY TEXT III: Ramsay, *Poems*, 1721. The fact that Ramsay opens with a Horatian reference and a heroic setting warns critics against the easy assumption that the eighteenth century revival always moved towards simpler forms and folk influences.
135. Varus was a literary friend to the Roman writer, Horace. Ramsay's version is the most overtly literary and learned of the three. He also opens on a heroic and martial rather than domestic and loving note.
136. ED. § 24F COPY TEXT IV: Burns, *Johnson's Scots Musical Museum* 1796.
137. Burns notes, 'Some sing "Kiss", in place of "Cup".' This suggests he is recording current practice and variants in his capacity as a folk-song collector.

Bibliography

1. GENERAL CRITICISM

1a. Scottish Literature

i. R.D.S. Jack, ed. *The History of Scottish Literature. I: Origins to 1660* (Aberdeen, 1988).
ii. Andrew Hook, ed. *The History of Scottish Literature. II: 1660-1800* (Aberdeen, 1988).
iii. Helena Mennie Shire, *Song, Dance and Poetry at the Court of Scotland under King James VI* (Cambridge, 1969).

1b. Comparative Literature

i. R.D.S.Jack, *The Italian Influence on Scottish Literature* (Edinburgh, 1972).
ii. and Kevin McGinley, eds. *Of Lion and of Unicorn: Essays on Anglo-Scottish Literary Relations in Honour of Professor John MacQueen* (Edinburgh, 1993).
iii. Gregory Kratzmann, *Anglo-Scottish Literary Relations* (Cambridge, 1980).
iv. Janet M. Smith, *The French Background of Middle Scots Literature* (Edinburgh, 1934).

1c. Cultural Contexts

i. *Fine Art:*
Duncan MacMillan, *Scottish Art 1460-1990* (Edinburgh, 1992).
ii. *History:*
Ian B. Cowan, *Renaissance and Reformation in Scotland* (Edinburgh, 1982)
Michael Lynch, *Scotland: A New History* (Edinburgh, 1992).
Julian Goodare and Michael Lynch, eds. *The Reign of James VI* (East Linton, 2000)
Jenny Wormald, *Court, Kirk, Community: Scotland 1470-1625* (Edinburgh, 1981).
iii. *Language:*
Charles Jones, ed. *The Edinburgh History of the Scots Language* (Edinburgh, 1997).
J. Derrick McClure, *Why Scots Matters* (Edinburgh, 1988). Introductory.
iv. *Music:*
Kenneth Elliott, *Musica Scotica II: Sixteenth-century Scots songs for voice and lute* (Glasgow, 1996).
John Purser, *Scotland's Music* (Edinburgh, 1992).
Theo van Heijnsbergen, 'The Scottish Chapel Royal as Cultural Intermediary between Town and Court' in *Centres of Learning*, eds. J.W Drijvers and A.A. MacDonald (Leiden, 1995) 299-313.
v. *General:*
James Kirk ed. *Humanism and Reform in Europe, England and Scotland* (London, 1991).
John MacQueen ed. *Humanism in Renaissance Scotland* (Edinburgh, 1989).
A.A. MacDonald et. al. eds. *The Renaissance in Scotland* (Leiden, 1994).

2. CRITICISM 1988-

[This section offers a personal and, necessarily, eclectic selection. Scottish Literary Criticism is confined to major books, chapters and articles published after 1988. For earlier work, the chapter references in Jack (1a.i) and Hook (1a.ii) are cited. These contain the relevant bibliographies. Among periodicals, *Studies in Scottish Literature–SSL*–and *The Scottish Literary Journal–SLJ*–are the most obvious (topically dedicated) sources for articles on early Scottish Literature.]*

* The *Critical Idiom* series edited by John Jump for Methuen will provide brief introductions to most of the major modes covered in this Anthology.

Essay Collections

J. Derrick McClure and Michael R.G. Spiller, eds. *Brycht Lanternis* (Aberdeen, 1989).
G. Ross Roy, ed. *Studies in Scottish Literature*, 26 (1991).

§ 1 John Barbour

[1a.i: Chapter 1: M.P. McDiarmid, pp. 27-38.]
Diane Abbott, 'Nationalism in Barbour's Bruce', *Parergon* 12 (1994) 89-107.
R. James Goldstein, *The Matter of Scotland: Historical Narrative in Medieval Scotland* (Nebraska, 1993).

§ 2 James I

[1a.i: Chapter 3: John MacQueen, pp. 55-72.]
Michael Brown, *James I* (Edinburgh, 1994). Historical.
Sally Mapstone, 'Kingship and the Kingis Quair' in *The Long Fifteenth Century*, ed. Helen Cooper and Sally Mapstone (Oxford, 1997).
A.C. Spearing, 'Prison, Writing, Absence: Representing the Subject in the English poems of Charles d'Orléans', *Modern Language Quarterly*, 53 (1992) 83-99.

§ 3 *Rauf Coilyear*

[1a.i: Chapter 2: Felicity Riddy, pp. 39-54.]
S.H.A. Shepherd, ' "Of thy glitterand gyde have I na gie": *The Taill of Rauf Coilyear*', *Archiv* 228 (1991) 135-50.

§ 4, 5, 14 Robert Henryson

[1a.i: Chapter 4: MacQueen, pp. 55-72.]
Gerald Baird, *The Poems of Robert Henryson* (Scotnotes, 1996). Introductory.
Phillipa M. Bright, 'Medieval Concepts of the Figure and Henryson's Figurative technique in the Fables', *SSL* 25 (1990) 134-53.
Rosemary Greentree, *Reader, Teller and Teacher: the Narrator of Robert Henryson's Morall Fabillis* (Frankfurt am Main, 1993).
Robert L. Kindrick, *Henryson and the Medieval Arts of Rhetoric* (New York, 1993).
Jill Mann, 'The Planetary Gods in Chaucer and Henryson' in *Chaucer Traditions: Essays in Honour of Derek Brewer* (Cambridge, 1990) 91-106.
Stephen McKenna, *Henryson's Tragic Vision* (Frankfurt am Main, 1994).
E. Wheatley, 'Scholastic Commentary and Robert Henryson's Moral Fables', *Studies in Philology* 91 (1994) 70-99.

§ 6, 7, 10 William Dunbar

[1a.i: Chapter 5: Priscilla Bawcutt, pp. 73—90.]
Priscilla Bawcutt, *William Dunbar* (Oxford, 1992).
Lois Ebin, *Illuminator, Makar, Vates: Visions of Poetry in the Fifteenth Century* (Nebraska, 1988).
Louise Fradenburg, *City, Marriage, Tournament: Arts of Rule in Late Medieval Scotland* (Madison, Wis., 1991).
R.D.S. Jack, *The Poems of William Dunbar* (Scotnotes, 1997). Introductory.
Joanne S. Normann, 'A Postmodern Look at a Medieval Poet: the case of William Dunbar', *SSL* 26 (1991) 343-53.

§ 8 *The Freiris of Berwik*

[1a.i: Chapter 7: Gregory Kratzmann, pp. 105-124.]

§ 9 Gavin Douglas
[1a.i: Chapter 5: Bawcutt, pp. 73-90.]
Douglas Gray, 'Some Chaucerean Themes in Scottish Writers' in *Chaucer Traditions*, op. cit., pp. 81-90.
Ruth Morse, 'Gavin Douglas: "Off Eloquence the flow and balmy strand" ' in *Chaucer Traditions*, op. cit., pp. 107-21.

§ 11 Marian and Reformation Lyric
[1a.i: Chapters 6 and 7: Alasdair A. MacDonald, pp. 91-104; Kratzmann, pp. 105-124.]
Theo van Heijnsbergen, 'Love in the lyrics of Alexander Scott', *Studies in Scottish Literature* 26 (1991) 366-79

§ 12 David Lindsay
[1a.i: Chapter 12: Sarah Carpenter, pp. 199-212.]
Carol Edington, *Court and Culture in Renaissance Scotland: Sir David Lindsay of the Mount* (Amherst, Mass., 1994).
R.J. Lyall, Introduction to *Sir David Lindsay of the Mount: Ane Satyre of the Thrie Estaitis* (Edinburgh, 1989).
Greg Walker, 'Sir David Lindsay's *Ane Satire of the Thrie Estaitis* and the Politics of the Reformation', *SLJ* 11 (1989) 5-17.
Janet Hadley Williams, 'David Lyndsay and the making of James V', in *Stewart Style 1513-42: Essays on the Court of James V*, ed. Janet Hadley Williams (East Linton, 1996) 201-26.

§ 13 Thomas Maitland and Early Prose
[1a.i: Chapter 10: R.J. Lyall, pp. 163-82.]

§ 16 Alexander Montgomerie
[1a.i: Chapter 8: R.D.S. Jack, pp. 125-40.]
Scottish Literary Journal—Alexander Montgomerie Special Number 26. 2 (1999).
R.J. Lyall, 'Montgomerie and Marot. A sixteenth century translator at work', *Etudes Ecossaises* 2 (1993) 79-94.

§ 17 John Stewart of Baldynneis
[1a.i: Chapter 8: Jack, pp. 125-40.]
Sarah M. Dunnigan, 'Poetic Objects of Desire: Rhetorical culture and seductive arts in the poetry of John Stewart of Baldynneis', *Scottish Literary Journal* 26. 1 (1999) 7-28.

§ 18 Sonnet
[1a.i: Chapter 8: Jack, pp. 125-40.]
Sarah M. Dunnigan, 'Rewriting the Renaissance Language of Love and Desire: The "bodily burdein" in the Poetry of Mary, Queen of Scots', *Gramma* 4 (1996) 181-95.
Morna Fleming, 'And so her Voice and Shape Alike were new', *Scottish Literary Journal Montgomerie Special Number* 26. 2 (1999) 79-5.
Michael Spiller, *The Development of the Sonnet: An Introduction* (London, 1992).

§ 19 Pastoral
[1ai: Chapter 9: Michael Spiller, pp. 141-62.]

§ 20 *Philotus*
[1a.i: Chapter 12: Carpenter, pp. 199-212.]

§ 21 Thomas Urquhart
[1a.i: Chapter 11: Reid, pp. 183-198.]

§ 22 James VI
[1a.i: Chapter 8: Jack, pp. 125-40.]
David Bergeron, *Royal Family, Royal Lovers* (Missouri, 1991). Historical.
Richard M. Clewett, 'James VI of Scotland and his Literary Circle', *Aevum* 47 (1998-9) 445-6.
Jonathan Goldberg, *James I and the Politics of Literature* (Stanford, 1989).
J. Derrick McClure, '"O Phoenix Ecossais": James VI as Poet' in *A Day Estivall*, eds. A. Gardner Medwin and J. Hadley Williams (Aberdeen, 1990) 96-111.

§ 23 William Alexander
[1a.i: Chapter 9: Spiller, pp. 141-62.]

§ 24 Appendix

English and Scots:
[1a.i: Chapter 9, Spiller, pp. 141-62.]
[1a.ii: Chapters 1-5, pp. 11-99. Hugh Ouston, pp. 11-32; Iain G. Brown, pp. 33-50; Douglas Duncan, pp. 51-64; Alexander Kinghorn and Alexander Law, pp. 65-80; Mary Jane Scott, pp. 81-100.]
R.D.S. Jack, 'Burns and Rhetoric' in *Love and Liberty*, ed. Kenneth Simpson (Edinburgh, 1997) 111-8.
Allan H. MacLaine, Introduction to *The Christis Kirk Tradition* (Glasgow, 1996).
Murray Pittock, *The Invention of Scotland: the Stuart Myth and the Scottish Identity* (London, 1991).
——— *New Jacobite songs of the Forty-five*, Studies on Voltaire and the Eighteenth Century No. 267 (1989).

Latin:
[1a.i: Chapters 13 and 14: James MacQueen, pp. 213-26; John and Winifred MacQueen, pp. 227-44.]

Gaelic:
[1a.i: Chapter 15: W. Gillies, pp. 245-62.]

Ballad:
[1a.i: Chapter 16, Hamish Henderson, pp. 263-84.]
Emily Lyle, ed. Introduction to *The Scottish Ballad* (Edinburgh, 1994).

Index of First Lines

(Prose Texts are listed in italics under short title.)

Index of Authors